ESSENTIALS OF ECONOMICS
SECOND EDITION

1   1, 2, 3, 4, 12, 13, 14

2   15, 16, 17, 18

ESSENTIALS OF
ECONOMICS

JAMES D. GWARTNEY
Florida State University

RICHARD STROUP
Montana State University

J. R. CLARK
Fairleigh Dickinson University

A «Holderbank» Group Company

THOMAS R. MINNICK
MANAGER, HUMAN RESOURCES

INDEPENDENT CEMENT CORPORATION
187 Wolf Road
Post Office Box 12-310
Albany, New York 12212

(518) 459-3211

SECOND EDITION

ACADEMIC PRESS, INC.
(Harcourt Brace Jovanovich, Publishers)
Orlando   San Diego   San Francisco   New York   London
Toronto   Montreal   Sydney   Tokyo   São Paulo

Academic Press, Inc.
Orlando, Florida 32887

United Kingdom Edition published by Academic Press, Inc. (London) Ltd.
24/28 Oval Road, London NW1 7DX

ISBN: 0-12-311035-1
Library of Congress Catalog Card Number: 84-70637

PRINTED IN THE UNITED STATES OF AMERICA

TO CHERI, ROB, AND JERRY
(1973–1982)

CONTENTS

PREFACE

The second edition of *Essentials of Economics* is designed specifically for a one-term course in economics. For some students, this course will be their only exposure to economics in an entire college career. Others will take the one-term course as the foundation for more advanced study. The challenge for a text intended for a course such as this is to meet the needs of both of these groups of students. We feel that *Essentials of Economics* does just that.

Numerous features make this edition of *Essentials of Economics* accessible to majors and nonmajors, alike. Two are of particular importance. First, the text is analytical rather than descriptive in nature. It attempts to teach students the economic way of thinking rather than merely acquaint them with a large collection of fact and fiction about economics. The text is not a random walk through economics but a very specific guided tour that teaches students to view human interaction through the eyes of the economist. It stresses economics as a method of inquiry and a tool to greater understanding of the how and why human beings make choices at both the individual and societal levels. *Essentials of Economics* stresses that human decision makers respond to incentives, and it carefully traces out the analytical process that guides individuals in their choices.

Second, *Essentials of Economics* is one of a very few texts that teaches students the basic of *political economy* and uses this knowledge to explain the choice process in the public sector. If economists have learned anything of significance in the 1970s and 1980s, it has been that the choice process of the entire society has significantly different characteristics than individual choice. This text not only traces out the micro foundations of macroeconomic theory but also provides students with an excellent exposure to contemporary public-choice theory. The strength of using this approach in a survey course is that it provides sufficient material to accurately explain and predict current economic events without having to ask students to accept sets of assumptions that appear to cloud the relevance of the theory being presented.

Several theoretical and content features also distinguish the second edition of *Essentials of Economics*. First, since microeconomic reasoning is a fundamental component of macroeconomic analysis and the importance of incentives is the central principle of economics, we have chosen to highlight the importance of the microincentive structure as the foundation of macroeconomic markets. Microincentives influence such macrofactors as the rate of unemployment, the level of savings and investment, and aggregate output.

Second, we have incorporated a supply-constrained model into the standard Keynesian analysis in this edition. In doing so, we have identified the determinants of supply, as well as the impact of public policy on those determinants. We have also looked closely at such things as how tax policy can affect the aggregate supply constraint of the economy. In addition, there are significant changes in the money and banking chapter to reflect the impact of the Deregulation and Monetary Control Act.

Third, we have also placed much more emphasis on the role of expectations in macroeconomics. A more up-to-date presentation of both adaptive and rational expectations theory is included in this edition of *Essentials of Economics*. We have also taken a closer look at how the application of expectations theory might impact on the effectiveness of public-sector policymaking.

Finally, we have strengthened the micro chapters a great deal. For example, we have improved our coverage of the linkage between production theory and the cost curves faced by the firm. Two chapters are devoted to market structure. In these chapters, we have compared and contrasted perfect competition and monopoly and then examined the hybrid cases of monopolistic competition and oligopoly. Finally, we have placed more emphasis on the role of regulation and deregulation by affording this material its own complete chapter.

DISTINGUISHING PEDAGOGICAL FEATURES OF OUR PRESENTATION

We have employed several features of organization and design in order to make the presentation of material more interesting to students.

• **Myths of Economics.** In a series of boxed articles, several commonly held fallacies of economic reasoning are dispelled. Following a statement of each myth is a concise explanation of why it is incorrect. Each myth falls in a chapter that contains closely related material.

• **Perspectives of Economics.** These features provide additional detail on a specific topic or issue. They permit us to provide additional breadth on a topic or focus on the application of an economic principle without disrupting the normal flow of the text.

• **Outstanding Economists.** Designed to foster the student's lasting interest in economics, these articles present brief profiles of several economists who either have made major contributions to the field or are currently influencing economic thought. This series serves to enhance the student's appreciation of economic history and highlight the contributions of many prominent present-day economists.

- **Key Terms.** The terminology of economics is often confusing to introductory students. To help remedy this, key terms are introduced in the text in boldface type; simultaneously, each term is defined in the margin opposite the first reference to the term.

- **Chapter Learning Objectives.** A statement of learning objectives, composed of the major concepts discussed, follows the text of each chapter. Students are encouraged to study the learning objectives before and after reading each chapter.

- **Discussion Questions.** Intended to test the student's grasp of the economic way of thinking, a set of discussion questions concludes each chapter. These questions, and the discussions they provoke, provide students with the opportunity for self-testing and the review of important material.

SUPPLEMENTARY MATERIALS

This textbook is also accompanied by a *Study Guide*. More than just a guide, it contains numerous true-false, multiple choice, and discussion questions of various levels of difficulty. This edition of the *Study Guide* includes a greater number of difficult questions than earlier versions, giving students increased opportunities to test and improve their analytical skills. Also included are problems and projects, as well as discussion questions. Most chapters contain a short article designed to supplement the classroom teaching of important concepts. These readings often present contrasting points of view. Discussion questions follow each article, challenging the students to demonstrate their understanding of the material and distinguish a sound argument from economic nonsense. This process emphasizes the development of the economic way of thinking.

An *Instructor's Manual and Test Bank* are also available. Divided into three sections, this supplement provides (a) suggested teaching tips and information on data sources, (b) a comprehensive test bank containing more than 1000 multiple-choice questions, and (c) a detailed outline of each chapter in lecture note form.

ACKNOWLEDGMENTS

This volume is, of course, built upon earlier and more comprehensive work by James D. Gwartney and Richard Stroup, with significant assistance by Woody Studenmund. The vision, insight, and scholarship of these individuals made this work possible. Professor Gwartney's ability to reduce complex ideas, especially in the areas of public choice and public finance, to a level at which their implications can be understood by introductory students will be a key to the success of this text. Rick Stroup's command of resource economics and the interesting role of externalities in this area of study also represents a major contribution. Woody Studenmund contributed substantially to the international sections and made improvements to the micro core material. Woody also made major contributions to testing materials, readings, and the problems and projects sections of the accompanying *Study Guide*. His command of pedagogy and effective teaching methods was especially helpful.

The book also benefited from professional conversations with Robert Greenfield (Fairleigh Dickinson University), Charles Goetz (University of Virginia), and Todd Idson (Fairleigh Dickinson University). The support and encouragement of Campbell McConnell, Bert Bowden, Richard Leftwich, and Otto Eckstein should also be acknowledged. The assistance of Lenn Holland, Frank Soley and Sue Miller of Academic Press made it possible to produce the book on time. Their help is deeply appreciated.

J. R. CLARK   JUNE 1984

PART ONE

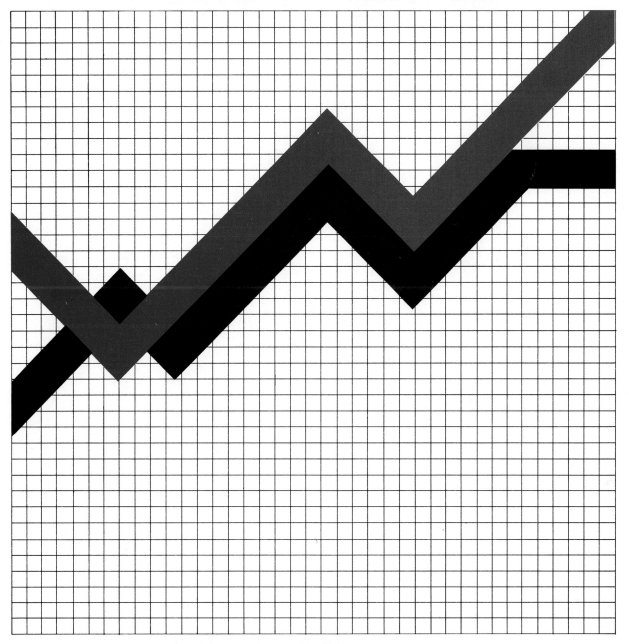

THE ECONOMIC WAY OF
THINKING—AN INTRODUCTION

THE ECONOMIC APPROACH

The ideas of economists and political philosophers, both when they are right and when they are wrong, are more powerful than is commonly understood. Indeed, the world is ruled by little else. Practical men, who believe themselves to be quite exempt from any intellectual influences, are usually slaves of some defunct economist.[1]
John Maynard Keynes

As Professor Keynes's own example has since proved, ideas have consequences and influence events in the real world. In turn, ideas are influenced by real-world experience. Economic ideas are no exception. The events and patterns of the last 15 years—soaring inflation, rising unemployment, and a decline in the after-tax income of many Americans—have exerted a dramatic impact upon the economics profession. They have also generated additional interest in the subject matter of economics. People are seeking to comprehend more fully the continually unfolding economic events.

We believe that this book will help you understand the recent economic turmoil—the ideas that undergirded it, the policies that contributed to it, and the possible directions that can now be taken to escape its grasp. This is not to imply that economists have the answer to the problems of a troubled world. Economics is not an answer but, rather, a way of thinking. In fact, economics is more likely to provide an appreciation of the limitations of "grand design" proposals than it is to offer utopian solutions. Nonetheless, we believe that "economic thinking" is a powerful tool capable of illuminating a broad range of real-world events. Our goal is to communicate the basics of economics and to illustrate their power.

WHAT IS ECONOMICS ABOUT?

Economics is about people and the choices they make. The unit of analysis in economics is the individual. Of course, individuals group together to form collective organizations such as corporations, labor unions, and governments. However, the choices of individuals still underlie and direct these organizations.

---

[1]John Maynard Keynes (1883–1946) was an English economist whose writings during the 1920s and 1930s exerted an enormous impact on both economic theory and policy. Keynes established the terminology and the economic framework that are still widely used today when economists study problems of unemployment and inflation.

EXHIBIT 1   A general listing of desired economic goods and limited resources

Economic Goods	Limited Resources
Food (bread, milk, meat, eggs, vegetables, coffee, etc.)	Land (various degrees of fertility)
Clothing (shirts, pants, blouses, shoes, socks, coats, sweaters, etc.)	Natural resources (rivers, trees, minerals, oceans, etc.)
Household goods (tables, chairs, rugs, beds, dressers, television sets, etc.)	Machines and other man-made physical resources
Space exploration	Nonhuman animal resources (cattle, horses, buffalo, etc.)
Education	Technology (physical and scientific "recipes" of history)
National defense	Human resources (the knowledge, skill, and talent of individual human beings)
Recreation	
Time	
Entertainment	
Clean air	
Pleasant environment (trees, lakes, rivers, open spaces, etc.)	
Pleasant working conditions	
More productive resources	
Leisure	

Our history is a record of our struggle to transform available, but limited, resources into things that we would like to have—economic goods.

Thus, even when we study collective organizations, we will focus on the ways in which their operation is affected by the choices of individuals.

Economic theory is developed from fundamental postulates about how individual human beings behave, struggle with the problem of scarcity, and respond to change. The reality of life on our planet is that productive resources—resources used to produce goods—are limited. Therefore, goods and services are also limited. In contrast, the desires of human beings are virtually unlimited. These facts confront us with the two basic ingredients of an economic topic—scarcity and choice. **Scarcity** is the term used by economists to indicate that man's desire for a "thing" exceeds the amount of it that is freely available from Nature. Nature has always dealt grudgingly with man; the Garden of Eden has continually eluded man's grasp.

A good that is scarce is an **economic good.** The first column of Exhibit 1 contains a partial listing of scarce or economic goods. The list includes food, clothing, and many of the items that all of us commonly recognize as material goods. But it also includes some items that may surprise you. Is leisure a good? Would you like to have more leisure time than is currently available to you? Most of us would. Therefore, leisure is a scarce good. What about clean air? A few years ago many economics texts classified clean air as a free good, made available by nature in such abundant supply that everybody could have all of it they wanted. This is no longer true. Our utilization of air for the purpose of waste disposal has created a scarcity of clean air. Many of the residents of Los Angeles, New York, Chicago, and other large cities would like to have more clean air.

Few of us usually think of such environmental conditions as economic goods. However, if you are someone who would like more open spaces, green areas, or dogwood trees, you will recognize that these things are scarce. They, too, are economic goods.

Scarcity: Fundamental concept of economics which indicates that less of a good is freely available than consumers would like.

Economic Good: A good that is scarce. The desire for economic goods exceeds the amount that is freely available from Nature.

Time is also an economic good. Most of us would like to have more time to watch TV, take a walk in the woods, do our schoolwork, or sleep; but we each have only 24 hours in a day. The scarcity of time imposes a definite limitation on our ability to do many of the things we would like to do.

Since scarcity of productive resources, time, and income limit the alternatives available to us, we must make choices. **Choice** is the act of selecting among restricted alternatives. A great deal of economics is about how people choose when the alternatives open to them are restricted. The choices of the family shopper are restricted by the household budget. The choices of the business decision-maker are restricted by competition from other firms, the cost of productive resources, and technology. The spending choices of the political decision-maker are restricted by the taxable income of the citizenry and voter opposition to taxes.

The selection of one alternative generally necessitates the foregoing of others. If you choose to spend $10 going to a football game, you will have $10 less to spend on other things. Similarly, if you choose to spend an evening watching a movie, you must forego spending the evening playing Ping-Pong (or participating in some other activity). You cannot eat your cake and have it, too.

Each day, we all make hundreds of economic choices, although we are not normally aware of doing so. The choices of when to get up in the morning, what to eat for breakfast, how to travel to work, what television program to watch—all of these decisions are economic. They are economic because they involve the utilization of scarce resources (for example, time and income). We all are constantly involved in making choices that relate to economics.

Our Losing Struggle with Scarcity

Scarcity restricts us. How can we overcome it? **Resources,** including our own skills, can be used to produce economic goods. Human effort and ingenuity can be combined with machines, land, natural resources, and other productive factors (see the second column of Exhibit 1) to increase the availability of economic goods. These are our "tools" in our struggle with scarcity. It is important to note that most economic goods are not like manna from heaven. Human energy is nearly always an ingredient in the production of economic goods.

The lessons of history confirm that our desire for economic goods far outstrips our resources to produce them. Are we destined to lead hopeless lives of misery and drudgery because we are involved in a losing battle with scarcity? Some might answer this question in the affirmative, pointing out that a substantial proportion of the world's population go to bed hungry each night. The annual income of a typical worker in such countries as Pakistan and India is less than $200. And the population in these and other areas is increasing almost as rapidly as their output of material goods.

Yet the grip of scarcity has been loosened in most of North America, Western Europe, Japan, and the Soviet Union. Most Americans, Japanese, and Europeans have an adequate calorie intake and sufficient housing and clothing. Many own luxuries such as automatic dishwashers, home video games, and electric carving knives. Over the last century, the average number of hours worked per week has fallen from 60 to about 40 in most Western nations. From a material viewpoint, life is certainly more pleasant for those people than it was for their forefathers 250 years ago. However, despite this progress, scarcity is still a fact of life, even in relatively affluent countries. Most of us have substantially fewer goods and resources and less time than we would like to have.

Choice: **The act of selecting among alternatives.**

Resource: **An input used to produce economic goods. Land, labor skills, natural resources, and capital are examples.**

Scarcity and Poverty Are Not the Same Thing

It should be noted that scarcity and poverty are not the same thing. Poverty implies some basic level of need, either in absolute or relative terms. Absence of poverty means that the basic level has been attained. In contrast, the absence of scarcity means that we have not merely attained some basic level but have acquired as much of all goods as we desire. Poverty is at least partially subjective, but there is an objective test to determine whether a good is scarce. If people are willing to pay—give up something—for a good, that good is scarce. Although the battle against poverty may ultimately be won, the outcome of the battle against scarcity is already painfully obvious. Our productive capabilities and material desires are such that goods and services will always be scarce.

THE ECONOMIC WAY OF THINKING

It [economics] is a method rather than a doctrine, an apparatus of the mind, a technique of thinking which helps its possessor to draw correct conclusions. [J. M. Keynes]

Reflecting on a television appearance with the economist Paul Samuelson and other social scientists (noneconomists), Milton Friedman stated that he was amazed to find that economists, although differing in their ideological viewpoints, usually find themselves to be allies in discussions with other social scientists.[2] One does not have to spend much time around economists to recognize that there is "an economic way of thinking." Admittedly, economists, like others, differ widely in their ideological views. A news commentator once remarked that "any half-dozen economists will normally come up with about six different policy prescriptions." Yet in spite of their philosophical differences, there is a common ground to the approach of economists.

Economic Theory: A set of definitions, postulates, and principles assembled in a manner that makes clear the "cause and effect" relationships of economic data.

That common ground is **economic theory,** developed from basic postulates of human behavior. Theory has a reputation for being abstract and difficult, but this need not be the case. Economic theory, somewhat like a road map or a guidebook, establishes reference points, indicating what to look for and what can be considered significant in economic issues. It helps us understand the interrelationships among complex and often seemingly unrelated events in the real world. A better understanding of cause and effect relationships will enhance our ability to predict accurately the probable and possible consequences of alternative policy choices. Economics has sometimes been called the "science of common sense." This is as it should be. After all, common sense is nothing more than a set of beliefs based on sound theories that have been tested over a long period of time and found to be accurate.

Seven Guideposts to Economic Thinking

The economic way of thinking involves the incorporation of certain guidelines—some would say the building blocks of basic economic theory—into one's thought process. Once these guidelines are incorporated, we believe that economics can be a relatively easy subject to master.

Students who have difficulty with economics almost always do so because they fail to develop the economic way of thinking. Their thought process is not

---

[2]The philosophical views of Professor Friedman and Professor Samuelson differ considerably. They are often on opposite sides of economic policy issues.

consistently directed by a few simple economic concepts or guideposts. Students who do well in economics learn to utilize these basic concepts and allow their thought process to be governed by them. We will outline and discuss seven principles that are fundamental characteristics of economic thinking and essential to the understanding of the economic approach.

1. Scarce Goods Have a Cost—There Are No Free Lunches. The benefits of scarce goods can be obtained only if someone is willing to exert personal effort or give up something. Using the terms of economics, scarce goods cost someone something. The cost of many scarce goods is obvious. A new car costs $9000. The purchaser must give up $9000 of purchasing power over other goods in order to own the car. Similarly, the cost to the purchaser of a delightful meal, new clothes, or a Las Vegas weekend is obvious. But what about a good such as public elementary education? Even though the education is usually free to students, it is not free to the community. Buildings, books, and teachers' salaries must be paid for from tax revenues. The taxpayer incurs the cost. If these scarce resources were not used to produce elementary education, they could be used to produce more recreation, entertainment, housing, and other goods. Providing for public education means that some of these other scarce goods must be foregone. Similarly, provision of free medical service, recreation areas, tennis courts, and parking lots involves the use of scarce resources. Again, something must be given up if we are to produce these goods. Taxpayers usually bear the cost of "free" medical services and tennis courts. Consumers often bear the cost of "free" parking lots in the form of higher prices in areas where this service is provided. By now the central point should be obvious. Economic thinking recognizes that the provision of a scarce good, any scarce good, involves a cost. We must give up other things if we are to have more of a scarce good. Economic goods are not free.

2. Decision-Makers Choose Purposefully. Therefore, They Will Economize. Since resources are scarce, it is all the more important that decisions be made in a purposeful manner. Decision-makers do not deliberately make choices in a manner that wastes and squanders valuable resources. Recognizing the restrictions imposed by their limited resources (income, time, talent, etc.), they seek to choose wisely; they try to select the options that best advance their own personal objectives. In turn, the objectives or preferences of individuals are revealed by the choices they make.

Economizing behavior results directly from purposeful decision-making. Economizing individuals will seek to accomplish an objective at the least possible cost. When choosing among things that yield equal benefit, an economizer will select the cheapest option. For example, if a hamburger, a fish dinner, and a New York sirloin steak are expected to yield identical benefits, economizing behavior implies that the cheapest of the three alternatives, probably the hamburger, will be chosen. Correspondingly, when choosing among alternatives of equal cost, economizing decision-makers will select the option that yields the greatest benefit (that is, utility or satisfaction). Purposeful decision-makers will not deliberately pay more for something than is necessary.

Purposeful choosing implies that decision-makers have some knowledge on which to base their evaluation of potential alternatives. Economists refer to this evaluation as utility. **Utility** is the subjective benefit or satisfaction that an individual expects from the choice of a specific alternative.

Economizing Behavior: Choosing with the objective of gaining a specific benefit at the least possible cost. A corollary of economizing behavior implies that when choosing among items of equal cost, individuals will choose the option that yields the greatest benefit.

Utility: The benefit or satisfaction expected from a choice or course of action.

3. Incentives Matter—Human Choice Is Influenced in a Predictable Way by Changes in Economic Incentives. This guidepost to clear economic thinking might be called the basic postulate of all economics. As the personal benefits from choosing an option increase, other things constant, a person will be more likely to choose that option. In contrast, as the costs associated with the choice of an item increase, the person will be less likely to choose that option. Applying this basic economic postulate to a group of individuals suggests that as an option is made more attractive, more people will choose it. In contrast, as the cost of a selection to the members of a group increases, fewer of them will make this selection.

This basic economic concept provides a powerful tool with which to analyze various types of human behavior. According to this postulate, what would happen to the birthrate if the U.S. government (a) removed the income tax deduction for dependents, (b) imposed a $1500 "birth tax" on parents, and (c) made birth-control pills available, free of charge, to all? The birthrate would fall—that's what. What would happen if the government imposed a $5000 tax on smokestacks, required automobile owners to pay a substantial license fee that was directly related to the exhaust level of the car, and gave a 10 percent tax reduction to all corporations that did not utilize the air for waste disposal purposes? Answer: There would be a decline in air pollution. In both of these hypothetical examples, the policy would increase the cost and/or reduce the benefits of a specific activity. Economics suggests that the level of the activities would be reduced in both cases because of the "predictable" impact that changes in personal benefits and costs have on human actions.

Our analysis suggests that an instructor could influence the degree of cheating on an examination simply by changing the student payoffs. There would be little cheating on a closely monitored, individualized, essay examination. Why? Because it would be difficult (that is, costly) to cheat on such an exam. Suppose, however, that an instructor gave an objective "take-home" exam, basing the students' course grades entirely on the results. Many students would cheat because the benefits of doing so would be great and the risk (cost) minimal. The economic way of thinking never loses sight of the fact that changes in incentives exert a powerful and predictable influence on human decisions.

4. Economic Thinking Is Marginal Thinking. Fundamental to economic reasoning and economizing behavior are the effects stemming from decisions to change the status quo. Economists refer to such decisions as **marginal.** Marginal choices always involve the effects of net additions or subtractions *from the current conditions.* In fact, the word "additional" is often used as a substitute for marginal. For example, we might ask, "What is the marginal (or additional) cost of producing one more automobile?" Or, "What is the marginal (or additional) benefit derived from one more glass of water?"

Marginal decisions need not always involve small changes. For example, the decision to build a new plant is a marginal decision. It is marginal because it involves a change at the border. *Given the current situation,* what marginal benefits (additional sales revenues, for example) can be expected from the plant, and what will be the marginal cost of constructing the facility?

It is important to distinguish between "average" and "marginal." Even though a manufacturer's current average cost of producing automobiles may be $10,000, for example, the marginal cost of producing an additional automobile

Marginal: Term used to describe the effects of a change, given the current situation. For example, the marginal cost is the cost of producing an additional unit of a product, given the producer's current facility and production rate.

(or an additional 1000 automobiles) might be much lower, say, $5000. Costs associated with research, testing, design, molds, heavy equipment, and similar factors of production must be incurred whether the manufacturer is going to produce 1000 units, 10,000 units, or 100,000 units. Such costs will clearly contribute to the average cost of an automobile. However, given that it is necessary to undertake these activities in order to produce the manufacturer's current output level, they may *add little* to the cost of producing *additional* units. Thus, the manufacturer's marginal cost may be substantially less than the average cost. When determining whether to *expand* or *reduce* the production of a good, the choice should be based on marginal costs, not the current average cost.

We often confront decisions involving a possible change, *given the current situation.* The marginal benefits and marginal costs associated with the choice will determine the wisdom of our decisions. Thus, what happens at the margin is an important part of economic analysis.

5. Information, Like Other Resources, Is Scarce. Therefore, Even Purposeful Decision-Makers Will Not Have Perfect Knowledge about the Future When They Make Choices. Rational decision-makers recognize that it is costly to obtain information and make complex calculations. Although additional information and techniques that improve one's decision-making capabilities are valuable, often the potential benefit is less than its expected cost. Therefore, sensible consumers will conserve on these limited resources, just as they conserve on other scarce resources.

6. Remember the Secondary Effects—Economic Actions Often Generate Secondary Effects in Addition to Their Immediate Effects. Frédéric Bastiat, a nineteenth-century French economist, stated that the difference between a good and a bad economist is that the bad economist considers only the immediate, visible effects, whereas the good economist is also aware of the **secondary effects,** effects that are indirectly related to the initial policy and whose influence is often seen or felt only with the passage of time.

Secondary Effects: Economic consequences of an initial economic change, even though they are not immediately identifiable. Secondary effects will be felt only with the passage of time.

Secondary effects are important in areas outside of economics. The immediate effect of an aspirin is a bitter taste in one's mouth. The indirect effect, which is not immediately observable, is relief from a headache. The immediate effect of drinking six quarts of beer might be a warm, jolly feeling. The indirect effect, for many, would be a pounding headache the next morning. In economics, too, the secondary effects of an action may be quite different from the initial impact. According to the economic way of thinking, the significant questions are: In addition to the initial result of this policy, what other factors will change or have changed? How will future actions be influenced by the changes in economic incentives that have resulted from policy A?

An economic system is much like an ecological system. An ecological action sometimes generates indirect and perhaps unintended secondary effects. For example, the heavy use of DDT on a field in order to kill a specific population of insects may have an undesirable effect on other creatures. Economic actions can generate similar results. For example, price controls on natural gas have the desired effect of reducing heating expenditures for some consumers, but they also reduce the incentive of producers to bring more natural gas to the market. Other consumers will therefore be forced to rely more heavily on more expensive energy sources, pushing the prices of these energy sources upward. Thus, the controls also generate an unintended result: an increase in the energy costs of some consumers. Straight economic thinking demands that we recognize the secondary effects, which will often be observed only with the passage of time.

7. The Test of a Theory Is Its Ability to Predict. Economic Thinking Is **Scientific Thinking.**   The proof of the pudding is in the eating. The usefulness of an economic theory is revealed by its ability to predict the future consequences of economic action. Economists develop economic theory from the analysis of how incentives will affect decision-makers. The theory is then tested against the events of the real world. Through testing, we either confirm the theory or recognize the need for amending or rejecting it. If the events of the real world are consistent with a theory, we say that it has predictive value. In contrast, theories that are inconsistent with real-world data must be rejected.

If it is impossible to test the theoretical relationships of a discipline, the discipline does not qualify as a science. Since economics deals with human beings, who can think and respond in a variety of ways, can economic theories really be tested? The answer to this question is yes, if, *on average,* human beings will respond in a predictable way to a change in economic conditions. The economist believes that this is the case. Note that this does not necessarily imply that *all* individuals will respond in a specified manner. Economics usually does not seek to predict the behavior of a specific individual; it focuses, rather, on the general behavior of a large number of individuals.

How can one test economic theory when, for the most part, controlled experiments are not feasible? Although this does impose limitations, economics is no different from astronomy in this respect. Astronomers also must deal with the world as it is. They cannot change the course of the stars or planets to see what impact the changes would have on the gravitational pull of the earth.

MYTHS OF ECONOMICS

"Economic analysis assumes that people act only out of selfish motives. It rejects the humanitarian side of humankind."

Probably because economics focuses on the efforts of individuals to satisfy material desires, many casual observers of the subject argue that its relevance hinges on the selfish nature of humankind. Some have even charged that economists, and the study of economics, encourage people to be materialistic rather than humanitarian.

This point of view stems from a fundamental misunderstanding of personal decision-making. Obviously, people act for a variety of reasons, some selfish and some humanitarian. The economist merely assumes that actions will be influenced by costs and benefits, as viewed by the decision-maker. As an activity becomes more costly, it is less likely that a decision-maker will choose it. As the activity becomes more attractive, it is more likely that it will be chosen.

The choices of both the humanitarian and the egocentric individual will be influenced by changes in personal costs and benefits. For example, both will be more likely to try to save the life of a small child in a three-foot swimming pool than in the rapid currents approaching Niagara Falls. Both will be more likely to give a needy person their hand-me-downs rather than their best clothes. Why? Because in both cases, the latter alternative is more costly than the former.

Observation would suggest that the right to control one's destiny is an "economic" good for most persons. Most of us would prefer to make our own choices rather than have someone else decide for us. But is this always greedy and selfish? If so, why do people often make choices in a way that is charitable toward others? After all, many persons freely choose to give a portion of their wealth to the sick, the needy, the less fortunate, religious organizations, and charitable institutions. Economics does not imply that these choices are irrational. It does imply that if you make it more (less) costly to act charitably, fewer (more) persons will do so.

Economics deals with people as they are—not as we would like to remake them. Should people act more charitably? Perhaps so. But this is not the subject matter of economics.

So it is with economists. They cannot arbitrarily institute changes in the price of cars or unskilled labor services just to observe the effect on quantity purchased or level of employment. However, this does not mean that economic theory cannot be tested. Economic conditions (for example, prices, production costs, technology, transportation cost, etc.), like the location of the planets, do change from time to time. As actual conditions change, economic theory can be tested by analyzing its consistency with the real world. The real world is the laboratory of the economist, just as the universe is the laboratory of the astronomer.

In some cases, observations of the real world may be consistent with two (or more) economic theories. Given the current state of our knowledge, we will sometimes be unable to distinguish between competitive theories. Much of the work of economists remains to be done, but in many areas substantial empirical work has been completed. Throughout this book we will refer to this evidence in an effort to provide information with which we can judge the validity of various economic theories. We must not lose sight of the scientific method of thinking, because it is a requisite for sound economic thinking.

POSITIVE AND NORMATIVE ECONOMICS

Positive Economics: The scientific study of "what is" among economic relationships.

Economics as a social science is concerned with predicting or determining the impact of changes in economic variables on the actions of human beings. Scientific economics, commonly referred to as **positive economics,** attempts to determine "what is." Positive economic statements postulate a relationship that is potentially verifiable. For example: "If the price of butter were higher, people would buy less." "As the money supply increases, the price level will go up." We can statistically investigate (and estimate) the relationship between butter prices and sales, or the supply of money and the general price level. We can analyze the facts to determine the correctness of a statement about positive economics.

Normative Economics: Judgments about "what ought to be" in economic matters. Normative economic views cannot be proved false because they are based on value judgments.

Because it utilizes ethical judgments as well as knowledge of positive economics, **normative economics** involves the advocacy of specific policy alternatives. Normative economic statements are about "what ought to be," given the philosophical views of the advocate. Value judgments may be the source of disagreement about normative economic matters. Two persons may differ on a policy matter because one is a socialist and the other a libertarian, one a liberal and the other a conservative, or one a traditionalist and the other a radical. They may agree as to the expected outcome of altering an economic variable (that is, the positive economics of an issue) but disagree as to whether that outcome is "good" or "bad."

In contrast with positive economic statements, normative economic statements cannot be tested and proved false (or confirmed to be correct). The government *should* increase defense expenditures. Business firms *should not* maximize profits. Unions *should not* increase wages more rapidly than the cost of living. These normative statements cannot be scientifically tested, since their validity rests on value judgments.

Positive economics does not tell us which policy is best. The purpose of positive economics is to increase our knowledge of all policy alternatives, thereby eliminating a potential source of disagreement about policy matters. The knowledge that we gain from positive economics also serves to reduce a potential source of disappointment with policy. Those who do not understand how the economy operates may advocate policies that are actually inconsistent with their philosophical views. Sometimes what one thinks will happen if a policy is instituted may be a very unlikely result in the real world.

Our normative economic views can sometimes influence our attitude toward positive economic analysis. When we agree with the objectives of a policy, it is easy to overlook its potential liabilities. However, desired objectives are not the same as workable solutions. The effects of policy alternatives often differ dramatically from the objectives of their proponents. Sound positive economics will help each of us evaluate more accurately whether or not a policy alternative will, in fact, accomplish the desired objective.

The task of the professional economist is to expand our knowledge of how the real world operates. If we do not fully understand the implications, including the secondary effects, of alternative policies, we will not be able to choose intelligently among them. It is not always easy to isolate the impact of a change in an economic variable or policy. Let us consider some of the potential pitfalls that retard the growth of economic knowledge.

Violation of the Ceteris Paribus Condition

Economists often preface their statements with the words *ceteris paribus,* meaning "other things constant." "Other things constant, an increase in the price of housing will cause buyers to reduce their purchases." Unfortunately for the economic researcher, we live in a dynamic world. Other things seldom remain constant. For example, as the price of housing rises, the income of consumers may simultaneously be increasing. Both of these factors, higher housing prices and an expansion in consumer income, will have an impact on housing purchases. In fact, we would generally expect them to exert opposite effects—higher prices retarding housing purchases but the rise in consumer income stimulating the demand for housing. Thus, the task of sorting out the specific effects of interrelated variables becomes more complex when several changes take place at the same time.

Economic theory acts as a guide, suggesting the probable linkage among economic variables. However, the relationships suggested by economic theory must be tested as to their consistency with events in the real world.

Statistical procedures can often be utilized to help economists identify correctly and measure more accurately relationships among economic variables. In fact, the major portion of the day-to-day work of many professional economists consists of statistical research designed to improve our knowledge of positive economics. Without accurate knowledge of positive economics, policymakers will be unable to establish a consistent link between their programs and economic goals.

Association Is Not Causation

In economics, causation is usually very important. The incorrect identification of causation is a potential source of error. Statistical association does not establish causation. Perhaps an extreme example will illustrate the point. Suppose that each November a medicine man performs a voodoo dance to arouse the cold-weather gods of winter and that soon after he performs his dance, the weather in fact begins to turn cold. The medicine man's dance is *associated* with the arrival of winter, but does it *cause* the arrival of winter? Most of us would answer in the negative, even though the two are linked statistically.

Unfortunately, cause and effect relationships in economics are not always self-evident. For example, it is sometimes difficult to determine whether a rise in income has caused consumption to increase or, conversely, whether an increase in consumption has caused income to rise. Similarly, economists sometimes argue whether rising money wages are a cause or an effect of inflation. Economic theory, if rooted to the basic postulates, can often help to determine the source of causation, but sometimes competitive theories may suggest alternative directions of causation. Thus, we must guard against drawing unwarranted conclusions when the direction of causation is unclear.

The Fallacy Of Composition

Fallacy of Composition:
Erroneous view that what is true for the individual (or the part) will also be true for the group (or the whole).

What is true for the individual (or subcomponent) may not be true for the group (or the whole). If you stand up for an exciting play during a football game, you will be able to see better. But what happens if everybody stands up at the same time? What benefits the individual does not benefit the group as a whole. When everybody stands up, the view of individual spectators fails to improve; in fact, it probably becomes even worse.

Persons who argue that what is true for the part is also true for the whole may err because of the **fallacy of composition.** Consider an example from economics. If you have an extra $10,000 in your bank account, you will be better off. But what if everyone suddenly has an additional $10,000? This increase in the supply of money will result in higher prices, as persons with more money bid against each other for the existing supply of goods. Without an increase in the availability (or production) of scarce economic goods, the additional money will not make everyone better off. What is true for the individual is misleading and fallacious when applied to the entire economy.

Microeconomics: The branch of economics that focuses on how human behavior affects the conduct of affairs within narrowly defined units, such as individual household or business firms.

Potential error associated with the fallacy of composition highlights the importance of considering both a micro- and a macroview in the study of economics. Since individual human decision-makers are the moving force behind all economic action, the foundations of economics are clearly rooted in a microview. Analysis that focuses on a single consumer, producer, product, or productive resource is referred to as **microeconomics.** As Professor Abba Lerner puts it, "Microeconomics consists of looking at the economy through a microscope, as it were, to see how the millions of cells in the body economic—the individuals or households as consumers, and the individuals or firms as producers—play their part in the working of the whole organism."[3]

Macroeconomics: The branch of economics that focuses on how human behavior affects outcomes in highly aggregated markets, such as the markets for labor or consumer products.

However, as we have seen, what is true for a small unit may not be true in the aggregate. **Macroeconomics** focuses on how the aggregation of individual microunits affects our analysis. Macroeconomics, like microeconomics, is concerned with incentives, prices, and output. But in macroeconomics the markets are highly aggregated. In our study of macroeconomics, the 80 million households in this country will be lumped together when we consider the importance of consumption spending, saving, and employment. Similarly, the nation's 15 million firms will be lumped together into something we call

---

[3]Abba P. Lerner, "Microeconomy Theory," in *Perspectives in Economics,* ed. A. A. Brown, E. Neuberger, and M. Palmatier (New York: McGraw-Hill, 1968), p. 29.

"the business sector." In short, macroeconomics examines the forest rather than the individual trees. As we move the microcomponents to a macroview of the whole, it is important that we bear in mind the potential pitfalls of the fallacy of composition.

WHAT DO ECONOMISTS DO?

The primary functions of economists are to teach, conduct research, and formulate policies. Approximately one-half of all professional economists are affiliated with an academic institution. Many of these academicians are involved in both teaching and scientific research.

The job of the research economist is to increase our understanding of economic matters. The tools of statistics and mathematics help the researcher to carry out this task. Government agencies and private business firms generate a vast array of economic statistics on such matters as income, employment, prices, and expenditure patterns. A two-way street exists between statistical data and economic theory. Statistics can be utilized to test the consistency of economic theory and measure the responsiveness of economic variables to changes in policy. At the same time, economic theory helps to explain *which* economic variables are likely to be related and *why* they are linked. Statistics do not tell their own story. We must utilize economic theory to interpret properly and understand more fully the actual statistical relationships among economic variables.

Economics is a social science. The fields of political science, sociology, psychology, and economics often overlap. Because of the abundance of economic data and the ample opportunity for scientific research in the real world, economics has sometimes been called the "queen of the social sciences." Reflecting the scientific nature of economics, the Swedish Academy of Science in 1969 instituted the Nobel Prize in economics. The men and women of genius in economics now take their place alongside those in physics, chemistry, physiology and medicine, and literature.

A knowledge of economics is essential for wise policy-making. Policy-makers who do not understand the consequences of their actions will be unlikely to reach their goals. Their actions may even be in conflict with their targeted objectives. Recognizing the link between economic analysis and policy, Congress in 1946 established the Council of Economic Advisers. The purpose of the council is to provide the president with analyses of and recommendations on the economic activities of the federal government, particularly the attainment of maximum employment. The chairmanship of the Council of Economic Advisers is a cabinet-level position.

Final Word

The primary purpose of this book is to encourage you to develop the economic way of thinking so that you can differentiate sound reasoning from economic nonsense. Once you have developed the economic way of thinking, economics will be relatively easy. And utilizing the economic way of thinking can be fun. Moreover, it will help you to become a better citizen. It will give you a different and fascinating perspective about what motivates people, why they act the way they do, and why their actions sometimes are in conflict with the best interest of the community or nation. It will also give you some valuable insight into

Economic principles are as old as recorded history. However, in comparison with other disciplines, the study of economics as a science is a recent development. English, French, and German scholars wrote essays and pamphlets on the subject during the first half of the eighteenth century, but the foundation of economics as a systematic area of study was not laid until 1776, when Adam Smith published his monumental work, *An Inquiry into the Nature and Causes of the Wealth of Nations*.

One can build a strong case that *The Wealth of Nations* was the most influential book that had been written since the Bible. The political and intellectual leaders of Smith's time thought that national wealth consisted of money held in the form of gold and silver. Thus, governments established all sorts of constraints on the freedom of individual economic activity. Political institutions encouraged citizens to sell their produce abroad in exchange for gold and silver. Simultaneously, people were discouraged, and in some cases restrained, from purchasing foreign-made goods. In addition, governmental infringements on the economic freedom of individuals promoted monopolies, protected guild associations from potential competitors, and in general discouraged production and limited exchange. Economic action motivated by private gain was generally thought to be antisocial.

Smith's book was nothing less than a revolutionary attack on the existing orthodoxy. He declared that the wealth of a nation did not lie with gold and silver but rather was determined by the goods and services available to the people, regardless of whether the products were produced at home or abroad. Smith had no confidence in appeals to altruism or attempts to upgrade the moral behavior of humankind. He believed that the public interest was best served by governments which established an environment that encouraged the free exchange of goods and services.

The harmony of individual self-interest, voluntary exchange, and economic progress was the central theme of *The Wealth of Nations*. Smith believed that individual self-interest would be harnessed and directed by the "invisible hand" of competitive market prices if kings and politicians would remove legal restrictions that retarded productive activity and exchange. Smith perceived individual self-interest not as a curse but as a powerful vehicle for economic progress. If left to pursue their own interests, individuals would apply their talents to the activities they performed best. For example, skilled hunters would employ their talents in the provision of game and exchange their product for other goods. Similarly, skilled tradesmen would specialize in their craft and trade the fruits of their labor for other requirements of life. Smith believed that if freed from government regulation, buyers and sellers would find it in their own interest to work, produce, and exchange goods and services in a manner that promoted the public interest. Production and the wealth of a nation would be increased in the process.

As Keynes noted 160 years later, the world is ruled by ideas. Even though Smith's thinking conflicted with the social environment of his time, his idea that self-interest, economic freedom, and national wealth were all in harmony eventually turned the world upside down. The English historian Henry Thomas Buckle declared that *The Wealth of Nations* represented "the most valuable contribution ever made by a single man towards establishing the principles on which government should be based." It has been said that with this single book Smith laid down the principles by which the next several generations would be governed. Smith's idea greatly influenced those who mapped out the structure of government in the United States. By the end of the eighteenth century, institutional reform had lifted the hand of government from several areas of economic activity in England and throughout Europe. Today the nineteenth century is sometimes referred to as the "era of economic freedom." Adam Smith, more than any other individual, deserves the credit for establishing the intellectual climate that eventually led to the economic freedom, industrialization, and prosperity of the Western world during the nineteenth century.

By the time of Smith's death in 1790, five editions of *The Wealth of Nations* had been published, and it had been translated into several foreign languages. The study of the relationship between production, exchange, and wealth began to occupy the time of an increasing number of intellectuals. Economics was soon to become a new and widely accepted field of study in major universities throughout the world.

how people's actions can be rechanneled for the benefit of the community at large.

Economics is a relatively young science. Current-day economists owe an enormous debt to their predecessors. The Outstanding Economist feature analyzes the contribution of Adam Smith, the father of economics.

CHAPTER LEARNING OBJECTIVES

1 Scarcity and choice are the two essential ingredients of an economic topic. Goods are scarce because desire for them far outstrips their availability from Nature. Since scarcity prevents us from having as much of everything as we would like, we must choose from among the alternatives available to us. Any choice involving the use of scarce resources requires an economic decision.

2 Scarcity and poverty are not the same thing. Absence of poverty implies that some basic level of need has been met. Absence of scarcity would mean that all of our desires for goods have been met. We may someday be able to eliminate poverty, but scarcity will always be with us.

3 Economics is a method of approach, a way of thinking. The economic way of thinking emphasizes the following:

(a) Among economic goods, there are no free lunches. Someone must give something up if we are to have more scarce goods.

(b) Individuals make decisions purposefully, always seeking to choose the option they expect to be most consistent with their personal goals. Purposeful decision-making leads to economizing behavior.

(c) Incentives matter. People will be more likely to choose an option as the benefits expected from that option increase. In contrast, higher costs will make an alternative less attractive, reducing the likelihood that it will be chosen.

(d) Marginal costs and marginal benefits (utility) are fundamental to economizing behavior. Economic reasoning focuses on the impact of marginal changes.

(e) Since information is scarce, uncertainty will be present when decisions are made.

(f) In addition to their initial impact, economic events often alter personal incentives in a manner that leads to important secondary effects that may be felt only with the passage of time.

(g) The test of an economic theory is its ability to predict and to explain events of the real world.

4 Economic science is positive. It attempts to explain the actual consequences of economic actions and alternative policies. Positive economics alone does not state that one policy is superior to another. Normative economics is advocative; using value judgments, it makes suggestions about "what ought to be."

5 Testing economic theory is not an easy task. When several economic variables change simultaneously, it is often difficult to determine the relative importance of each. The direction of economic causation is sometimes difficult to ascertain. Economists consult economic theory as a guide and use statistical techniques as tools in attempting to improve our knowledge of positive economics.

6 Microeconomics focuses on narrowly defined units, such as individual consumers or business firms. Macroeconomics is concerned with highly aggregated units, such as the markets for labor or goods and services. When shifting focus from micro- to macrounits, one must be careful not to commit the fallacy of composition. Both micro- and macroeconomics utilize the same postulates and tools. The level of aggregation is the distinction between the two.

7 The origin of economics as a systematic method of analysis dates back to the publication of *The Wealth of Nations* by Adam Smith in 1776. Even though legal restraints on

economic activity abounded at the time, Smith argued that production and wealth would increase if individuals were left free to work, produce, and exchange goods and services. Smith believed that individuals pursuing their own interests would be led by the "invisible hand" of market incentives (prices) to employ their productive talents in a manner "most advantageous to the society." Smith's central message is that when markets are free—when there are no legal restraints limiting the entry of producer-sellers—individual self-interest and the public interest are brought into harmony.

THE ECONOMIC WAY OF THINKING—DISCUSSION QUESTIONS

1 Indicate how each of the following changes would influence the incentive of a decision-maker to undertake the action described.

(a) A reduction in the temperature from 80° to 50° on one's decision to go swimming

(b) A change in the meeting time of the introductory economics course from 11:00 A.M. to 7:30 A.M. on one's decision to attend the lectures

(c) A reduction in the number of exam questions that relate to the text on the student's decision to read the text

(d) An increase in the price of beef on one's decision to have steak every night this week

(e) An increase in the rental price of apartments on one's decision to build additional housing units

2 What does it mean to economize? Do you attempt to economize? Why or why not?

3 Write a couple of paragraphs, explaining in your own words the meaning and essential ingredients of the economic way of thinking.

4 What's Wrong with This Economic Experiment?

A researcher hypothesizes that the medical attention received by U.S. citizens is inadequate because many people cannot afford medical care. The researcher interviews 100 randomly selected individuals and asks them, "Would you use physician services or hospital and nursing-home medical facilities more if they were not so expensive?" Ninety-six of the 100 answer in the affirmative. The researcher concludes that there is a critical need to allocate more resources to the provision of free medical care for all citizens.

5 "Reasonable rental housing could be brought within the economic means of all if the government would prevent landlords from charging more than $200 per month rent for a quality three-bedroom house." Use the economic way of thinking to evaluate this view.

6 SENATOR DOGOODER: I favor an increase in the minimum wage because it would help the unskilled worker.

SENATOR DONOTHING: I oppose an increase in the minimum wage because it would cause the unemployment rate among the young and unskilled to rise.

Is the disagreement between Senator Dogooder and Senator Donothing positive or normative? Explain.

The goods people sell usually are made by processes using a high proportion of the skills they are gifted in, whereas the goods people buy usually are made by processes they are comparatively ungifted in.[1]
Robert A. Mundell

2

SOME TOOLS OF THE ECONOMIST

In the last chapter you were introduced to the economic approach. In this chapter, we discuss a few important tools that will help you to develop the economic way of thinking.

What Shall We Give Up?

Scarcity calls the tune in economics. We cannot have as much of everything as we would like. Most of us would like to have more time for leisure, recreation, vacations, hobbies, education, and skill development. We would also like to have more wealth, a larger savings account, and more consumption goods. However, all of these things either are scarce or require the use of scarce resources. They are in conflict with one another. How can I have more leisure time and simultaneously accumulate more wealth? How can I increase my current consumption and simultaneously increase my savings account? The answer is, I can't. The choice of one requires me to give up something of the other.

OPPORTUNITY COST IS THE HIGHEST VALUED OPPORTUNITY LOST

An unpleasant fact of economics is that the choice to do one thing is, at the same time, a choice *not* to do something else. Your choice to spend time reading this book is a choice *not* to play tennis, go out on a date, listen to a math lecture, or attend a party. These things must be given up because of your decision to read. The highest valued alternative that must be sacrificed because one chooses an option is the **opportunity cost** of the choice.

Opportunity Cost: **The highest valued benefit that must be sacrificed (foregone) as the result of choosing an alternative.**

Note that the cost of an event is *not* the drudgery and undesirable aspects

[1]Robert A. Mundell, *Man and Economics: The Science of Choice* (New York: McGraw-Hill, 1968), p. 19.

that may be associated with the event. The distinction between (a) the undesirable attributes of an option and (b) the highest valued opportunity foregone in order to realize the option is a fundamental distinction because only the latter is considered a cost by the economist.[2]

Cost is subjective; it exists in the mind of the decision-maker. It is based on expectation—the expectation of how one would evaluate the alternative given up. Cost can never be directly measured by someone other than the decision-maker because only the decision-maker can place a value on what is foregone.[3]

Cost, however, often has a monetary component that enables us to approximate its value. For example, the cost of attending a movie is equal to the highest valued opportunity that is given up because of (a) the time necessary to attend and (b) the purchasing power (that is, money) necessary to obtain a ticket. The monetary component is, of course, objective and can be measured. When there is good reason to expect that nonmonetary considerations are relatively unimportant, the monetary component will approximate the total cost of an option.

Opportunity Cost and the Real World

Is real-world decision-making influenced by opportunity cost? Remember, the basic economic postulate states that the likelihood that an option will be chosen varies inversely with its cost to the decision-maker. So economic theory does imply that differences (or changes) in opportunity cost will influence how decisions are made.

Let us consider several examples that demonstrate the real-world application of the opportunity cost concept. Poor people are more likely to travel long distances by bus, whereas the wealthy are more likely to travel by airplane. Why? A simple answer would be that the bus is cheaper; therefore, the poor will be more likely to purchase the cheaper good. But is the bus cheaper for a relatively well-off individual whose opportunity cost of travel time is high? Suppose that a round-trip airline ticket from Kansas City to Denver costs $150, whereas a bus ticket costs only $110. However, the bus requires ten hours of travel time, and the airplane only two hours. Which would be cheaper? It depends on one's opportunity cost of time. If one's opportunity cost is evaluated at less than $5 per hour, the bus is cheaper, but if one's time is valued at more than $5 per hour, the airplane is clearly the cheaper option. Since the opportunity cost of the travel time will usually be greater for the wealthy than for the poor, the airplane is more likely to be cheaper for high-income recipients.

The concept of opportunity cost helps us to understand labor allocation and wage differences. Workers whose skills make them valuable elsewhere must be paid wages sufficient to compensate them for the foregoing of their highest valued employment alternatives. Thus, a filling station owner is unlikely to hire a physician as an attendant because the physician would have to be paid a wage at least equal to his or her opportunity cost—perhaps $100 per hour or more for delivering babies or removing infected tonsils. Similarly, it would be necessary for an employer to pay a skilled carpenter a higher wage than an unskilled

---

[2]For an excellent in-depth discussion of this subject, see A. A. Alchian, "Cost," in *International Encyclopedia of the Social Sciences* (New York: Macmillan, 1969), 3: 404–415.

[3]See James M. Buchanan, *Cost and Choice* (Chicago: Markham, 1969), for an analysis of the relationship between cost and choice.

worker because of the carpenter's opportunity cost; the wage opportunities foregone with another employer would be greater for the more skilled worker. Skills and abilities, inasmuch as they make one more valuable to alternative employers, will also increase one's earnings capability.

Elderly retirees watch considerably more television than high-income lawyers, accountants, and other professionals. Why? Is it because the elderly can better afford the money cost of a TV? Clearly, this is not the case. This phenomenon is straightforward when one considers the differences in the opportunity cost of time between the retirees and the professionals. In terms of earnings foregone, watching television costs the professional a lot more than it costs the elderly. The professional watches less TV because it is an expensive good in terms of time.

Why do students watch less television and spend less time at the movies or beach during final exam week? Doing these things is more costly, that's why. Using valuable study time to go to the beach would most likely mean foregoing a passing grade in history, although a student's grade in economics might be unaffected if he or she kept up during the semester and developed the economic way of thinking.

By now you should have the idea. Choosing one thing means giving up others that might have been chosen. Opportunity cost is the highest valued option sacrificed as the result of choosing an alternative.

THE PRODUCTION POSSIBILITIES CURVE

The resources of every individual are limited. Purposeful decision-making and economizing behavior imply that individuals seek to get the most out of their limited resources. They do not deliberately waste resources.

The nature of the economizing problem can be brought into clearer focus by the use of a production possibilities diagram. A **production possibilities curve** reveals the maximum amount of any two products that can be produced from a fixed quantity of resources.

Production Possibilities Curve: A curve that outlines all possible combinations of total output that could be produced, assuming (a) the utilization of a fixed amount of productive resources, (b) full and efficient use of those resources, and (c) a specific state of technical knowledge.

Exhibit 1 illustrates the production possibilities curve for Susan, an intelligent economics major. It indicates the combinations of grades possible for two alternative amounts of study time—six and eight hours. If she uses her six hours of study time efficiently, she can choose any grade combination along the six-hour production possibilities curve. However, when her study time is limited to six hours per week, Susan is able to raise her grade in one of the subjects only by accepting a lower grade in the other. If she wants to improve her overall performance (raise at least one grade without lowering the other), she will have to apply more time to academic endeavors. For example, she might increase her weekly study time from six to eight hours. Of course, this would require her to give up something else—leisure.

Can the production possibilities concept be applied to the entire economy? The answer is yes. You cannot have both guns and butter, as the old saying goes. An increase in military expenditures will require the use of resources that otherwise could be applied to the production of nonmilitary goods. If scarce resources are being used efficiently, more of one thing will require the sacrifice of others. Exhibit 2 illustrates the concept of the production possibilities curve for an economy producing only two goods: food and clothing.

What restricts the ability of an economy to produce more of everything?

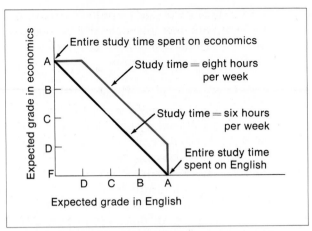

EXHIBIT 1   The production possibilities curve for grades in English and economics

The production possibilities, in terms of grades, for Susan are illustrated for two alternative quantities of total study time. If she studied 6 hours per week, concentrating entirely on economics, she would expect an A, but would flunk English because she spent all of her time studying economics. On the other hand, studying 6 hours per week, she could attain (a) a D in English and a B in economics, (b) a C in both, (c) a B in English and a D in economics, or (d) an F in economics but an A in English. The black line represents her production possibilities curve for 6 hours of studying.

A higher grade in one subject costs a grade reduction in the other. Could she make higher grades in both? Yes, if she were willing to apply more resources, thereby giving up some leisure. The colored line indicates her production possibilities curve if she studied 8 hours per week.

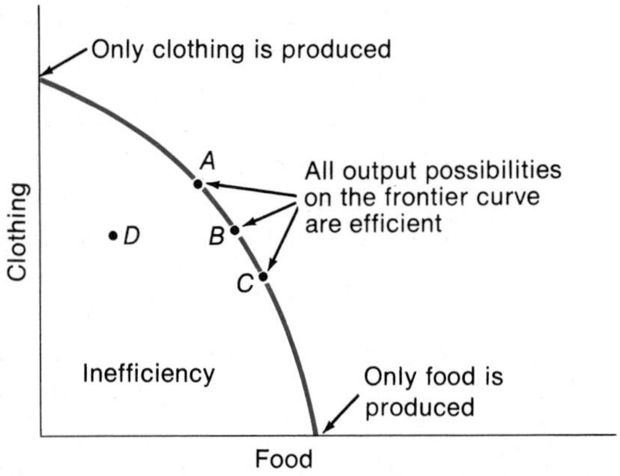

EXHIBIT 2   The concept of the production possibilities curve for an economy

When an economy is using its limited resources efficiently, it is at the edge of its production possibilities frontier (for example, points *A, B,* and *C*). Thus, production of more clothing requires the economy to give up some other goods—food in this simple example. *With time,* a technological discovery or expansion of the economy's resource base could make it possible to produce more of both, shifting the production possibilities curve outward. Or the citizens of the economy might decide to give up some leisure for more of both goods. These factors aside, however, limited resources will constrain the production possibilities of an economy.

The same thing that kept Susan from making a higher grade in *both* English and economics—lack of resources. There will be various maximum combinations of goods that an economy will be able to produce when:

1. it uses some fixed quantity of resources,
2. the resources are not wasted or used inefficiently, and
3. the level of technology is constant.

When these three conditions are met, the economy will be at the perimeter of its production possibilities frontier (points such as *A, B,* and *C,* Exhibit 2). The production of more of one good, clothing, for example, will necessitate less production of other goods (for example, food).

When the resources of an economy are used wastefully and inefficiently, the economy is operating at a point inside the production possibilities curve—point *D,* for example. Why might this happen? It happens because the economy is not properly solving the economizing problem. A major purpose of economics is to ensure that we are getting the most out of the resources available, that we move to the perimeter of the production possibilities curve. We will return to this problem again and again.

Shifting the Production Possibilities Curve Outward

Could an economy ever have more of all goods? Could the production possibilities curve be shifted outward? The answer is yes, under certain circumstances. There are three major methods.

1. An Increase in the Economy's Resource Base Would Expand Our Ability to Produce Goods and Services. If we had more and better resources, we could produce a greater amount of all goods. Many resources are man-made. If we were willing to give up some current consumption, we could invest a greater amount of today's resources into the production of long-lasting physical structures, machines, education, and the development of human skills. This **capital formation** would provide us with better tools and skills in the future and thereby increase our ability to produce goods and services. Exhibit 3 illustrates the link between capital formation and the *future* production possibilities of an economy. Initially, the two economies illustrated confront an identical production possibilities curve (*RS*). However, since Economy A (Exhibit 3a) allocates more of its resources to investment than Economy B, with the passage of time A's production possibilities curve shifts outward by a greater amount. The growth rate of A—the rate of expansion of the economy's ability to produce goods—is enhanced because the economy allocates a larger share of its output to investment. Of course, it is costly to shift the production possibilities curve of an economy outward. As more of today's resources are used to produce "tools" that will make us more productive tomorrow, fewer will be available for producing current consumer goods. More investment in machines and human skills will necessitate less current consumption.

2. Advancements in Technology and Human Knowledge Would Expand the Economy's Production Possibilities. **Technology** defines the relationship between resource inputs and the output of goods and services. Technological improvements make it possible for a given base of resources to generate a greater output.[4]

Capital Formation: The production of buildings, machinery, tools, and other equipment that will enhance the ability of future economic participants to produce. The term can also be applied to efforts to upgrade the knowledge and skill of workers and thereby increase their ability to produce in the future.

Technology: The body of skills and technical knowledge available at any given time. The level of technology establishes the relationship between inputs and the output they can generate.

---

[4]Without modern technical knowledge it would be impossible to produce the vast array of goods and services responsible for our standard of living. Thomas Sowell makes this point clear when he notes:

> The cavemen had the same natural resources at their disposal as we have today, and the difference between their standard of living and ours is a difference between the knowledge they could bring to bear on those resources and the knowledge used today.

See Thomas Sowell, *Knowledge and Decisions* (New York: Basic Books, 1980), p. 47.

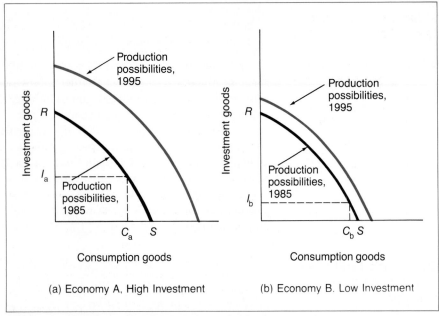

EXHIBIT 3   Investment and production possibilities in the future

Here we illustrate two economies that initially confront identical production possibilities curves (*RS*). The economy illustrated on the left allocates a larger share of its output to investment (*I*$_a$, compared to *I*$_b$ for the economy on the right). As a result, the production possibilities of the high-investment economy will shift outward by a larger amount than will be true for the low-investment economy.

For example, the discovery of drought-resistant hybrid seeds has led to vast expansions in the output of corn per acre (and per worker-hour of labor). Thus, a technological improvement also shifts the production possibilities curve outward. If we were to devote more resources now to research and development, we would speed up the rate of technological change. Of course, this would mean giving up current consumption, capital formation, or leisure.

3. By Working Harder and Giving Up Current Leisure, We Could Increase Our Production of Goods and Services.   Strictly speaking, this is not an expansion in the production frontier because leisure is also a good. We are giving up some of that good to have more of other things.

The work effort of individuals not only reflects their personal preferences but is also a function of public policy. For example, high tax rates may induce individuals to reduce their work time. The basic economic postulate implies that as high tax rates reduce the *personal* payoff from working (and earning taxable income), individuals will shift more of their time to other areas, including the consumption of leisure, and the production possibilities curve for material goods will shift inward.

It is apparent that the production possibilities curve for material goods is not fixed. It is influenced by both individual preferences and public policy. We will discuss this topic more thoroughly as we proceed.

Division of Labor and Production Possibilities

Division of Labor: A method that breaks down the production of a commodity into a series of specific tasks, each performed by a different worker.

In a modern economy, individuals do not produce all, or even most, of the items that we consume. Instead, we sell our labor services (usually agreeing to perform specified productive functions) and utilize the derived income to purchase desired goods. We are induced to follow this course because **division of labor** and exchange allow us to produce far more goods and services through cooperative effort than would be possible if each household sought to produce its own food, clothing, shelter, transportation, and other desired goods.

Observing the operation of a pin manufacturer more than 200 years ago, Adam Smith noted that specialization and division of labor permitted people to attain a far greater output than would have been possible if each worker alone had performed all of the functions necessary to produce a pin. When each worker specialized in a productive function, ten workers were able to produce 48,000 pins per day, or 4800 pins *per worker*. In the absence of specialization and division of labor, Smith doubted an individual worker would have been able to produce as many as 20 pins per day.[5]

The division of labor permits us to break production tasks into a series of related operations. Each worker performs a single task that may be only one of hundreds of tasks necessary for the production of a commodity. There are several reasons why the division of labor often leads to enormous gains in overall output per worker. First, specialization permits individuals to take advantage of their existing abilities and skills. (Put another way, specialization permits an economy to take advantage of the fact that individuals have different skills.) Productive assignments can be undertaken by those individuals who are able to accomplish them most efficiently. Second, when individual workers specialize in just one task (or one narrow area), they become increasingly proficient, acquiring knowledge and experience in the specific task with the passage of time. The most important source of gain from the division of labor, however, is probably the facilitation of alternative production techniques, particularly those that rely upon the intensive use of machinery and high-level technology. The division of labor allows us to adopt complex, large-scale production techniques unthinkable for an individual household. As our knowledge of technology and the potential of machinery expand, capital-intensive production procedures and the division of labor permit us to attain living standards undreamed of just a few decades ago.

TRADE TIPS AND COMPARATIVE ADVANTAGE

Economizing means getting the most out of the resources available. How can this be accomplished? How can we move the perimeter of the economy's production possibilities curve? In answering these questions, we must understand several important principles.

First, let us consider the economizing problem of Woodward and Mason, individuals in the construction business. Exhibit 4 presents certain facts about the abilities of Woodward and Mason. Woodward is highly skilled, fast, and reliable. During a month, Woodward can build either four frame houses or two

---

[5]See Adam Smith, *An Inquiry into the Nature and Causes of the Wealth of Nations* (1776; Cannan's ed., Chicago: University of Chicago Press, 1976), pp. 7–16, for additional detail on the importance of the division of labor.

EXHIBIT 4 Comparative advantage and producing a much-needed vacation

The monthly production possibilities of Woodward and Mason are:

Frame Houses per Month		Brick Houses per Month	
Woodward	Mason	Woodward	Mason
4	1	2	1

Initially, they worked all year, each of them producing both frame and brick houses. Annually, Woodward was able to produce 16 of each, and Mason only 6 of each. Thus, their beginning total output was 22 frame and 22 brick units.

After both specialized in their areas of greatest comparative advantage, Mason produced only brick houses. During the first 11 months, Mason produced 11 brick houses. Woodward worked 5½ months producing 22 frame houses and another 5½ months producing 11 brick houses. As the chart shows, after specialization, Woodward and Mason were able to match last year's joint output in just 11 months. The law of comparative advantage made it possible for them to maintain their previous output level and still take a much-needed vacation.

	Annual Output before Specialization		11-Month Output after Specialization	
	Frame Houses	Brick Houses	Frame Houses	Brick Houses
Woodward	16	16	22	11
Mason	6	6	0	11
Total	22	22	22	22

brick houses. By way of comparison with Woodward, Mason is less skilled. It takes Mason an entire month to build either a frame or a brick house. Thus, Mason is slower than Woodward at building both kinds of houses.

Last year, both builders worked the entire 12 months. Woodward spent 8 months producing 16 brick houses and the other 4 months producing 16 frame houses. Mason was able to produce only 6 frame and 6 brick houses during the year. Their joint output was 22 frame and 22 brick houses.

Since Woodward has an *absolute advantage* (Woodward can build both frame and brick houses more rapidly than Mason) in the production of houses, few observers would believe that Woodward and Mason could gain from specialization and trade of products. However, they would indeed gain. Suppose Mason specialized in the production of brick houses. In 11 months Mason could produce 11 brick houses. Simultaneously, suppose that Woodward spent 5½ months producing each type of house. Woodward could produce 22 frame houses (4 per month) in those 5½ months, and 11 brick houses (2 per month) in another 5½ months. After they specialize, it would be possible for Mason and Woodward to produce 22 frame houses (11 each) and 22 brick houses (all by Woodward) with just 11 months of work. If 5 of Mason's 11 brick houses were traded to Woodward for 6 frame houses, then Mason would be able to attain last year's individual output rate (6 frame and 6 brick). Similarly, upon receipt of the 5 brick houses from Mason in exchange for 6 frame ones, Woodward would also be left with last year's output rate (16 frame and 16 brick). Thus, with specialization and exchange, Woodward and Mason could both attain last year's production rate with just 11 months of work. They could take a vacation the last month of the year.

Despite the fact that Woodward was better than Mason at producing both frame and brick houses, the two were able to gain from the trade and specialization.[6] Was it magic? What is happening here? Our old friend, opportunity cost, will help us unravel this seemingly paradoxical result. In what sense is Woodward better at producing brick houses than Mason? True, in a month, Woodward can produce twice as many brick houses as Mason, but what is Woodward's opportunity cost of producing a brick house? Two frame ones, right? In the same time required to produce a single brick house, Woodward can produce two frame houses.

Consider Mason's opportunity cost of producing a brick house. It is only one frame house. So who is the cheaper producer of brick houses? Mason is, because Mason's opportunity cost of producing a brick house is one frame house, compared to Woodward's opportunity cost of two frame houses.

The reason that Woodward and Mason could both gain is that their exchange allowed each of them to specialize in the production of the product that, *comparatively* speaking, they could produce cheapest. Mason was the cheaper producer of brick houses. Woodward was the cheaper producer of the frame ones. They were able to economize—get more out of their resources—by trading and specializing in the thing that each did comparatively better.

This simple example demonstrates a basic truth known as the law of comparative advantage, which lies at the heart of economizing behavior for any economy. Initially developed in the early 1800s by the great English economist David Ricardo, the **law of comparative advantage** states that the total output of a group, an entire economy, or a group of nations will be greatest when the output of each good is produced by the person (or firm) with the lowest opportunity cost.

If a product, any product, is produced by one producer when it could have been produced by another with a lower opportunity cost, the economy gives up more than is necessary. It is not economizing. Economizing, or maximum economic efficiency, requires that output always be generated by the producer who has the lowest opportunity cost.

Perhaps one additional example will help to drive home the implications of the law of comparative advantage. Consider the situation of an attorney who can type 120 words per minute. The attorney is trying to decide whether or not to hire a secretary, who only types 60 words per minute, to complete some legal documents. If the lawyer does the typing job, it will take four hours; if a secretary is hired, the typing job will take eight hours. Thus, the lawyer has an absolute advantage in typing compared to the prospective employee. However, the attorney's time is worth $50 per hour when working as a lawyer, whereas the typist's time is worth $5 per hour as a typist. Although a fast typist, the attorney is also a high opportunity cost producer of typing service. If the lawyer types the documents, the job will cost $200, which is the opportunity cost of four hours of lost time as a lawyer. Alternatively, if the typist is hired, the cost of having the documents typed is only $40 (eight hours of typing service at $5 per hour). Thus, the lawyer's comparative advantage lies in practicing law. The attorney

Law of Comparative Advantage: A principle which states that individuals, firms, regions, or nations can gain by specializing in the production of goods that they produce cheaply (that is, at a low opportunity cost) and exchanging those goods for other desired goods for which they are high opportunity cost producers.

---

[6]Throughout this section we will assume that individuals are equally content to produce either product. Dropping this assumption would add to the complexity of the analysis, but it would not change the basic principle.

will gain by hiring the typist and spending the additional time specializing in the area of comparative advantage.

DIVISION OF LABOR, SPECIALIZATION, AND EXCHANGE IN ACCORDANCE WITH THE LAW OF COMPARATIVE ADVANTAGE

It is difficult to exaggerate the gains derived from specialization, division of labor, and exchange in accordance with the law of comparative advantage. These factors are the primary source of our modern standard of living. Can you imagine the difficulty involved in producing one's own housing, clothing, and food, to say nothing of radios, television sets, automatic dishwashers, automobiles, and telephone services? Yet most families in the United States, Western Europe, Japan, and Australia enjoy these conveniences. They are able to do so largely because their economies are organized in such a way that individuals can cooperate, specialize, trade, and therefore reap the benefits of the enormous increases in output—both in quantity and diversity—thus produced. An economy that fails to realize potential gains stemming from the division of labor and specialization in accordance with the law of comparative advantage is operating inside of its production possibilities curve, at a point such as *D* of Exhibit 2. This is the case for most so-called less developed economies. For various reasons, production in these economies is primarily centered in the individual household. Therefore, the output level per worker of these economies falls well below the level that could be attained if labor were applied in a more efficient manner.

Comparative Advantage and Regional Specialization

We have emphasized that parties can gain from exchange even if one of them is more skilled in the production of both items traded. This principle holds true for trade between regions and nations as well as between individuals. Parties will find it particularly advantageous to trade those goods that they can produce most efficiently for commodities that would be extremely costly to produce on a personal or local level.

Why are oranges not grown in Kansas? Why don't more southern California orange growers raise wheat? Comparative advantage explains a great deal about the regional specialization that we often take for granted. Relative to California, Kansas is far more efficient in the production of wheat than it is in the growing of oranges. Similarly, the endowments of southern California give it a comparative advantage in the production of oranges rather than wheat. Thus, California oranges tend to be exchanged for Kansas wheat.

Since the endowments of land, labor skills, and capital differ among regions, so, too, does the opportunity cost of producing different products. In the open spaces of the Great Plains, fertile land is cheap. Consequently this region tends to specialize in feed grains, beef, and dairy products. Florida, with its mild winter climate and sunny beaches, specializes in citrus crops and tourism. In the East and upper Midwest, the transportation network is highly developed, and raw materials are readily accessible. Manufacturing and trade dominate these regions. Residents of each region tend to specialize in those things that they do best.

Comparative Advantage and Trade between Nations

The principle of comparative advantage applies to trade between nations as well. Whenever differing natural endowments, labor skills, or other factors result in differences in the opportunity cost of producing goods, a nation can gain by specializing in the production of products for which it is best equipped (that is, the low opportunity cost producer) and exporting these goods in exchange for those products that the country is least able to produce. Countries with an abundance of rich farmland, such as Canada, Australia, Argentina, and even the United States, export feed grains, beef, and other agricultural products. Switzerland, a country with a labor force that has passed precision skills down from generation to generation, exports watches and scientific instruments. When highly skilled diamond cutters immigrated to Israel, this small nation without a single diamond mine utilized this comparative advantage to become the world's largest exporter of cut diamonds.

The list is seemingly endless. Japan, with few material resources but a highly efficient labor force, imports many raw materials and exports radios, small appliances, cameras, and small manufactured goods. India and Korea, countries with an abundance of labor relative to land, export products such as textiles, which require large amounts of labor. All of these countries gain by selling products they can produce at a low opportunity cost and buying products for which their production opportunity cost would be high.

When one begins to think about it, the law of comparative advantage is almost common sense. Stated in layman's terms, it merely means that if we want to accomplish a task with the least effort, each of us should specialize in that component of the task that we do best.

The principle of comparative advantage is universal. It is just as valid in socialist countries as it is for capitalists. If socialist planners are interested in getting the most out of available resources, they, too, should apply the principle of comparative advantage.

Dependence, Specialization, and Exchange

Specialization and mutual interdependence are directly related. If the United States specializes in the production of agricultural products and Middle East countries specialize in the production of oil, the two countries become mutually interdependent. Similarly, if Texas specializes in production of cotton and Michigan in production of wheat, mutual interdependence results. In some cases this dependence can have serious consequences for one or both of the parties. The potential costs of mutual interdependence (for example, vulnerability to economic pressure applied by a trading partner who supplies an important economic good) and its potential benefits (for example, economic interaction that may well increase international understanding and reduce the likelihood of war) should be weighed along with the mutual consumption gains when one is evaluating the merits of specialization.

Specialization and Work Alienation

Specialization clearly makes it possible to produce more goods. But it also may result in many workers performing simple, boring, and monotonous functions. Our friend Woodward may get tired of building just frame houses, and Mason's life may lose a certain zest because he does nothing but produce brick ones. On a more practical level, specialization often results in assembly-line production techniques. Workers may become quite skilled because they perform identical tasks over and over again, but they may also become bored if the work is personally unrewarding. Thus, strictly speaking, some of the gains associated with the expansion of physical output may result in worker dissatisfaction.

You may be thinking that economists consider nothing but material goods and ignore the importance of human beings. It may seem that they do not care if a worker hates a job because it is repetitive, unchallenging, and boring. Our initial approach to the topic of specialization is vulnerable to this charge. We stressed only physical production because it makes the principle simpler to communicate. However, specialization could be considered strictly from the viewpoint of utility, in which both output and job satisfaction are taken into account. After all, job satisfaction is an economic good.

An individual's opportunity cost of producing a good (or performing a service) includes the sacrifice of both physical production of other goods and any reduction (or improvement) in the desirability of working conditions. This approach does consider both material goods for one's satisfaction and the job satisfaction that is important to any human being. It does not, however, alter the basic principle. Individuals could still gain by producing and selling those things for which they have a comparatively low opportunity cost, including the job satisfaction component, while buying other things for which their opportunity cost is high. They would tend to specialize in the provision of those things they *both* do well and enjoy most. Persons with a strong aversion to monotonous work would be less likely to choose such work even though they might be skilled at it. Those with a smaller comparative advantage, measured strictly in terms of physical goods, might have a lower opportunity cost because they find the work more rewarding.

The introduction of working conditions and job preferences does not invalidate the basic concept. It is still true that maximum economic efficiency, in the utility sense, requires that each productive activity be performed by those persons with the lowest opportunity cost, including costs associated with their personal evaluation of other jobs.

Personal Motivation and Gaining from Specialization and Exchange

What motivates people to act? How does the purposeful decision-maker choose? Economic thinking implies that people will choose an option only if they expect the benefits (utility) of the choice to exceed its opportunity cost. Purposeful decision-makers will be motivated by the pursuit of personal gain. They will never knowingly choose an alternative for which they expect the opportunity cost to exceed the expected benefits. To do so would be to make a choice with the full awareness that it meant the sacrifice of another, preferred course of action. That simply would not make sense. To say that people are motivated by personal gain does not, of course, mean that they are inconsiderate of others. Other people's feelings will often affect the personal benefit received by a decision-maker.

When an individual's interests, aptitudes, abilities, and skills make it possible to gain by exchanging low opportunity cost goods for those things that he or she produces at a high opportunity cost, pursuit of the potential gain will motivate the individual to trade precisely in this manner. If free exchange is allowed, it will not be necessary for people to be assigned the "right" job or to be told that, comparatively speaking, they should trade A for B because they are good at producing A but not so good at producing B. In a market setting, individuals will voluntarily specialize because they will gain by doing so. Thus, when people simply follow their own interests, the goods (or resources) they sell will be produced primarily by means of skills with which they are heavily endowed. Similarly, decision-makers seeking personal gain will tend to buy those things that require skills they do not possess and let others do the productive activities they find unrewarding (relative to the payment for those services).

THREE ECONOMIZING DECISIONS FACING ALL NATIONS: WHAT, HOW, AND FOR WHOM?

We have outlined several basic concepts that are important if one is to understand the economizing problem. In this section we outline three general economizing questions that every economy, regardless of its structure, must answer.

1. What Will Be Produced?   All of the goods that we desire cannot be produced. What goods should we produce and in what quantities? Should we produce more food and less clothing, more consumer durables and less clean air, more national defense and less leisure? Or should we use up some of our productive resources, producing more goods today even though it will mean fewer goods in the future? If our economy is operating efficiently (that is, on its production possibilities curve), the choice to produce more of one commodity will reduce our ability to produce others. Sometimes the impact may be more indirect. Production of some goods will not only require productive resources but may, as a by-product, reduce the actual amount of other goods available. For example, production of warmer houses and more automobile travel may, as a by-product, increase air pollution, and thus reduce the availability of clean air (another desired good). Use of natural resources (water, minerals, trees, etc.) to produce some goods may simultaneously reduce the quality of our environment. Every economy must answer these and similar questions about what should be produced.

2. How Will Goods Be Produced?   Usually, different combinations of productive resources can be utilized to produce a good. Education could be produced with less labor by the use of more television lectures, recording devices, and books. Wheat could be raised with less land and more fertilizer. Chairs could be constructed with more labor and fewer machines. What combinations of the alternative productive resources will be used to produce the goods of an economy?

   The decision to produce does not accomplish the task. Resources must be organized and people motivated. How can the resources of an economy be transformed into the final output of goods and services? Economies may differ as to the into the final output of goods and services? Economies may differ as to the combination of economic incentives, threats of force, and types of competitive behavior that are permissible, but all still face the problem of how their limited resources can be utilized to produce goods.

3. For Whom Will Goods Be Produced?   Who will actually consume the products available? This economic question is often referred to as the distribution problem. Property rights for resources, including labor skills, might be established and resource owners permitted to sell their services to the highest bidder. Goods would then be allocated to those who could meet the bids. Prices and private ownership would be the determining factors of distribution. Alternatively, goods might be split on a strict per capita basis, with each person getting an equal share of the pie. Or they might be divided according to the relative political influences of citizens, with larger shares going to persons who are more persuasive and skillful than others at organizing and obtaining political power. They could be distributed according to need, with a dictator or an all-powerful, democratically elected legislature deciding the various "needs" of the citizens.

The Three Decisions Are Interrelated

One thing is obvious. These three questions are highly interrelated. How goods are distributed will exert considerable influence on the "voluntary" availability of productive resources, including human resources. The choice of what to produce will influence how and what resources are used. In reality, these three basic economic questions must be resolved simultaneously, but this does not alter the fact that all economies, whatever their other differences, must somehow answer them.

TWO METHODS OF MAKING DECISIONS—THE MARKET AND GOVERNMENT PLANNING

Market Mechanism: A method of organization that allows unregulated prices and the decentralized decisions of private-property owners to resolve the basic economic problems of consumption, production, and distribution.

Collective Decision-Making: The method of organization that relies on public sector decision-making (that is, voting, political bargaining, lobbying, etc.). It can be used to resolve the basic economic problems of an economy.

In general, there are two methods of organizing economic activity—a **market mechanism** and **collective decision-making.** There is, of course, some overlap between these two classifications and some variation within them. The rules and guidelines for a market economy will be established at the outset by the public decision-making process. The accepted forms of competition may vary among market economies. There may be some differences in how the rights and responsibilities of property owners are defined. Once the rules of the game are established, however, a market economy will rely on the unregulated pricing mechanism to direct the decisions of consumers, producers, and owners of productive resources. The government will not prevent a seller from using price reductions and quality improvements as a method of competing with other sellers. Nor will the government prevent a buyer from using price as a method of bidding a product or productive resource away from another potential buyer. Legal restraints (for example, government licensing) will not be utilized to limit potential buyers or sellers from producing, selling, or buying in the marketplace. The free interplay and bargaining between buyers and sellers will establish the conditions of trade and answer the three basic economic questions. The government's role is secondary—only that of the referee and rule-maker.

As an alternative to market organization, economic decisions can be made by collective decision-making—by elected representatives, direct referendum, or some other governmental mechanism (for example, military force). Central planning and political factors replace market forces. The decision to expand or contract the output of education, medical services, automobiles, electricity, steel, consumer durables, and thousands of other commodities is made by government officials and planning boards. This is not to say that the preferences of individuals are of no importance. If the government officials and central

"In exchange, when someone gains, someone else must lose. Trading is a zero-sum game."

People tend to think of making, building, and creating things as productive activities. Agriculture and manufacturing are like this. They create something genuinely new, something that was not there before. Trade, however, is only the exchange of one thing for another. Nothing is created. Therefore, it must be a zero-sum game in which one person's gain is necesarily a loss to another. So goes a popular myth.

Voluntary exchange is productive for three reasons. First, it channels goods and services to those who value them most. People have fallen into the habit of thinking of material things as wealth, but material things are not wealth until they are in the hands of someone who values them. A highly technical mathematics book is not wealth to a longshoreman with a sixth-grade education. It becomes wealth only after it is in the hands of a mathematician. A master painting may be wealth to the art connoisseur but of little value to a cowboy. Wealth is created by the act of channeling goods to persons who value them highly.

When a good is exchanged for money, it is being channeled toward the person who values it most. When you pay $300 per month for the use of an apartment, rented from the owner for that amount, a good is channeled toward the party who values it most. You value the apartment more than the $300 or you would not have agreed to the transaction. Thus, you gain. No one values it more highly or they would bid more than $300 for it. The apartment owner places greater value on the $300 than on the use of the apartment, otherwise he or she would not rent to you. The owner, too, gains. The trade makes both you and your landlord better off.

Second, exchange can be advantageous to trading partners because it permits each to specialize in areas in which they have a comparative advantage. For example, exchange permits a skilled carpenter to concentrate on building house frames while contracting for electrical and plumbing services from others who have comparative advantages in those areas. Similarly, trade permits a country such as Canada to specialize in the production of wheat, while Brazil specializes in coffee. Such specialization enlarges joint output and permits both countries to gain from the exchange of Canadian wheat for Brazilian coffee.

Third, voluntary exchange makes it possible for individuals to produce more goods through cooperative effort. In the absence of exchange, productive activity would be limited to the individual household. Self-provision and small-scale production would be the rule. Voluntary exchange permits us to realize gains derived from the division of labor and the adoption of large-scale production methods. Production can be broken down into a series of specific operations. This procedure often leads to a more efficient application of both labor and machinery. Without voluntary exchanges, these gains would be lost.

The motivating force behind exchange is the pursuit of personal gain. Unless *both* parties expect to gain from an exchange, it will not take place. Mutual gain forms the foundation for voluntary exchange. Trade is a positive-sum game.

planners are influenced by the democratic process, they have to consider how their actions will influence their election prospects. If they do not, like the firm that produces a product that consumers do not want, their tenure of service is likely to be a short one.

In most economies, including that of the United States, a large number of decisions are made through both the decentralized pricing system and public sector decision-making. Both exert considerable influence on how we solve fundamental economic problems. Although the two arrangements are different, in each case the choices of individuals acting as decision-makers are important. Economics is about how people make decisions; the tools of economics can be applied to both market and public sector action. Constraints on the individual and incentives to pursue various types of activities will differ according to whether decisions are made in the public sector or in the marketplace. But people are people. Changes in personal costs and benefits will still influence their choices. In turn, the acts of political participants—voters, lobbyists, and politicians—will influence public policy and its economic consequences.

David Ricardo (1772–1823) and the Early Followers of Smith

Following the pioneering work of Adam Smith, other economists developed economic principles and applied them to the social problems of their day. The contributions of three Englishmen, David Ricardo, Thomas Malthus, and John Stuart Mill, were particularly important.

By 1800, the Industrial Revolution had begun to transform the Western world. Most economists of that time believed that gains from specialization, expansion in trade among nations, and industrialization would significantly improve people's living standards. Thomas Malthus was an exception.

Malthus did not see how humankind could escape the "population trap." If wages temporarily rose above the subsistence level, fewer people would die of starvation and families would have more children. Thus, economic progress would trigger a population explosion, leading merely to an increase in the number of people seeking to consume the existing supply of food. An expansion in the production of goods would increasingly necessitate the use of land that was less fertile. Thus, Malthus perceived that food production would, at best, increase arithmetically (1,2,3, 4,5, and so on), whereas the population, if unchecked by starvation, would expand geometrically (1,2,4,8, 16, and so on).

Because Malthus used economic analysis to arrive at his gloomy prediction, economics soon earned the title "the dismal science," a label that persists to this day. Although the view of Malthus may have some applicability to less developed countries, the experience of the industrial world during the last 200 years is clearly in conflict with the heart of Malthusian analysis. Malthus failed to perceive the explosion of production that could be generated by technological improvements and capital formation.

David Ricardo is generally recognized as the greatest of the early post-Smith economists. The work of Ricardo lacked the social insight and breadth of knowledge that characterized Smith's writings, but his approach was more systematic. The rigorous logic of his presentation was a major reason for the enormous influence that he had on the direction of economics.

A successful stockbroker prior to his becoming an economist, Ricardo literally invented economic model building. His major work, *The Principles of Political Economy and Taxation* (1817), was published just six years before his untimely death.

Ricardo is best known for his rigorous proof of the law of comparative advantage. Using a simple numerical example, he demonstrated that it would benefit England to specialize in cloth even if Portugal could produce both cloth and wine more cheaply, provided that England was the *relative* low-cost producer of cloth. Ricardo went on to illustrate that if Portugal specialized in wine, for which it possessed an even greater cost advantage than for cloth, it, too, would be better off. Thus, both countries would gain if they specialized in the production of those products for which they were the *relative* low-cost producers. Ricardo's ideas comprised the heart of the nineteenth-century free-trade doctrine.

John Stuart Mill was the leading economist of the post-Ricardo era. Mill's father was James Mill, an economist and intimate friend of Ricardo. At the age of 13, John Stuart was introduced to the writings of Smith, Ricardo, and Malthus. Mill's major contribution as an economist was his ability to organize and synthesize the analyses of earlier writers. His *Principles of Political Economy* (1848) was a masterful summation of economic analysis as it had developed from Smith through Malthus and Ricardo. The two-volume work served as the standard economics text at English universities for several decades.

Much has changed since the days of these early economists. Economics is now more systematic, more mathematical, and, some would say, more rigorous. Nonetheless, it is still based on the postulate that incentives matter (Smith's self-interest). Economic gain stemming from the division of labor and specialization in production is no less important now than it was when Smith articulated the idea 200 years ago. The law of comparative advantage is as significant today as it was when Ricardo developed it in 1817. Modern economics owes an enormous debt to these pioneers in the field.

LOOKING AHEAD   The following chapter presents an overview of the market sector. Chapter 4 focuses on how the public sector, the democratic collective decision-making process, functions. It is not enough merely to study how the pricing system works.

If we are to understand fully the forces that exert a powerful influence on the allocation of economic resources in a country such as the United States, we must apply the tools of economics to both market and public sector choices.

We think that this approach is important, fruitful, and exciting. How does the market sector really work? What does economics say about what activities should be handled by government? What types of economic policies are politically attractive to democratically elected officials? Is sound economic policy sometimes in conflict with good politics? We will tackle all these questions.

1 Because of scarcity, when an individual chooses to do, to make, or to buy something, the individual must simultaneously give up something else that might otherwise have been chosen. The highest valued activity sacrificed is the opportunity cost of the choice.

2 A production possibilities curve reveals the maximum combination of any two products that can be produced with a fixed quantity of resources, assuming that the level of technology is constant. When an individual or an economy is operating at maximum efficiency, the combination of output chosen will be on the production possibilities curve. In such cases, greater production of one good will necessitate a reduction in the output of other goods.

3 The production possibilities curve of an economy can be shifted outward by (a) current investment that expands the future resource base of the economy, (b) technological advancement, and (c) the foregoing of leisure and an increase in work effort. The last factor indicates that the production possibilities constraint is not strictly fixed, even during the current time period. It is partly a matter of preferences.

4 Production can often be expanded through division of labor and cooperative effort among individuals. With division of labor, production of a commodity can be broken down into a series of specific tasks. Specialization and division of labor often lead to an expansion in output per worker because they (a) permit productive tasks to be undertaken by the individuals who can accomplish those tasks most efficiently, (b) lead to improvement in worker efficiency as specific tasks are performed numerous times, and (c) facilitate the efficient application of machinery and advanced technology to the production process.

5 Joint output of individuals, regions, or nations will be maximized when goods are exchanged between parties in accordance with the law of comparative advantage. This law states that parties will specialize in the production of goods for which they are low opportunity cost producers and exchange these for goods for which they are high opportunity cost producers. Pursuit of personal gain will motivate people to specialize in those things that they do best (that is, for which they are low opportunity cost producers) and sell their products or services for goods for which they are high opportunity cost producers.

6 Exchange is productive. Voluntary exchange (a) channels goods into the hands of people who value them most, (b) permits individuals to specialize in the areas of their greatest comparative advantage, and (c) creates the opportunity for greater productive efficiency and increased output through specialization, division of labor, and large-scale production techniques. Trade is a positive-sum game that improves the economic well-being of each voluntary participant.

7 Every economy must answer three basic questions: (a) What will be produced? (b) How will goods be produced? (c) How will the goods be distributed? These three questions are highly interrelated.

8 There are two basic methods of making economic decisions: the market mechanism and public sector decision-making. The decisions of individuals will influence the result in both cases. The tools of economics are general. They are applicable to choices that influence both market and public sector decisions.

1 "The principle of comparative advantage gives individuals an incentive to specialize in those things that they do best." Explain in your own words why this is true.

2 Economists often argue that wage rates reflect productivity. Yet the wages of house-painters have increased nearly as rapidly as the national average, even though these workers use approximately the same methods that were applied 50 years ago. Can you explain why the wages of painters have risen substantially even though their productivity has changed little?

3 It takes one hour to travel from New York City to Washington, D.C., by air but five hours by bus. If the airfare is $55 and the bus fare $35, which would be cheaper for someone whose opportunity cost of travel time is $3 per hour? for someone whose opportunity cost is $5 per hour? $7 per hour?

4 Explain why the percentage of college-educated women employed outside of the home exceeds the percentage of women with eight years of schooling who are engaged in outside employment.

5 Explain why parking lots in downtown areas of large cities often have several decks, whereas many of equal size in suburban areas usually cover only the ground level.

6 Is exchange productive? If so, what does it produce? Who gains when goods are voluntarily exchanged?

7 (a) Do you think that your work effort is influenced by whether or not there is a close link between personal output and personal compensation (reward)? Explain.
(b) Suppose that the grades in your class were going to be determined by a random draw at the end of the course. How would this influence your study habits?
(c) How would your study habits be influenced if everyone in the class were going to be given an A grade? if grades were based entirely on examinations composed of the multiple-choice questions in the *Coursebook?*
(d) Do you think that the total output of goods in the United States is affected by the close link between productive contribution and individual reward? Why or why not?

3

SUPPLY, DEMAND, AND THE MARKET PROCESS

I am convinced that if it [the market system] were the result of deliberate human design, and if the people guided by the price changes understood that their decisions have significance far beyond their immediate aim, this mechanism would have been acclaimed as one of the greatest triumphs of the human mind.[1]
Nobel laureate Friedrich Hayek

Consider the awesome task of coordinating the economic activity of the United States, a nation with 80,000,000 household-consumer units. The labor force is composed of approximately 105,000,000 workers, each possessing various skills and job preferences. There are more than 15,000,000 business firms, which currently produce a vast array of products ranging from hairpins to jumbo jets.

How can the actions of these economic participants be coordinated in a sensible manner? How do producers know how much of each good to produce? What keeps them from producing too many ballpoint pens and too few bicycles with reflector lights? Who directs each labor force participant to the job that best fits his or her skills and preferences? How can we be sure that the business firms will choose the correct production methods? In this chapter we analyze how a market-directed pricing system answers these questions.

In a market economy, no individual or planning board tells the participants what to do. Markets are free, some would say competitive, in the sense that there are no legal restrictions limiting the entry of either buyers or sellers. The economic role of government is limited to defining property rights, enforcing contracts, protecting people from fraud, and similar activities that establish the rules of the game. Although centralized planning is absent, it does not follow that the participants are without direction. As we shall see, the decentralized decision-making of market participants provides direction and leads to economic order.

In the real world, even economies that are strongly market oriented, such as ours in the United States, use a combination of market and public sector answers to the basic economic questions. In all economies, there is a mixture of market sector and government allocation. Nevertheless, it is still quite useful to understand how the free-market pricing system functions, how it motivates people, and how it allocates goods and resources.

---

[1]Friedrich Hayek, "The Use of Knowledge in Society," *American Economic Review* 35, (September, 1945), pp. 519–530.

SCARCITY NECESSITATES RATIONING

Rationing: An allocation of a limited supply of a good or resource to users who would like to have more of it. Various criteria, including charging a price, can be utilized to allocate the limited supply. When price performs the rationing function, the good or resource is allocated to those willing to give up the most "other things" in order to obtain ownership rights.

When a good (or resource) is scarce, some criterion must be set up for deciding who will receive the good (or resource) and who will do without it. Scarcity makes **rationing** a necessity.

There are several possible criteria that could be used for rationing a limited amount of a good among citizens who would like to have more of it. If the criterion were First come, first served, goods would be allocated to those who were fastest at getting in line or to those who were most willing to wait in line. If beauty were used, goods would be allocated to those who were thought to be most beautiful. The political process might be utilized, and goods would be allocated on the basis of ability to manipulate the political process to personal advantage. One thing is certain: Scarcity requires that some method be established to decide who gets the limited amount of available goods and resources.

Competition Is the Result of Rationing

Competition is not unique to a market system. Rather, it is a natural outgrowth of scarcity and the desire of human beings to improve their conditions. Competition exists in both capitalist and socialist societies. It exists both when goods are allocated by price and when they are allocated by other means—collective decision-making, for example.

Certainly the rationing criterion will influence the competitive techniques utilized. When the rationing criterion is price, individuals will engage in income-generating activities that enhance their ability to pay the price. The market system encourages individuals to provide services to others in exchange for income. In turn, the income will permit them to procure more of the scarce goods.

A different rationing criterion will encourage other types of behavior. When the appearance of sincerity, broad knowledge, fairness, good judgment, and a positive TV image are important, as they are in the rationing of political positions, people will dedicate resources to the projection of these qualities. However, competition cannot be eliminated by changing the way in which it manifests itself or the form in which it is displayed. No society has been able to eliminate competition, because no society has been able to eliminate the necessity of rationing. When people who want more scarce goods seek to meet the criteria established to ration those goods, competition occurs.

The market is one method of rationing and allocating scarce goods and resources. Let us investigate how it works.

CONSUMER CHOICE AND THE LAW OF DEMAND

The income of consumers is almost always substantially less than their wants. The authors have desires for backyard tennis courts, European vacations, and summer homes in the mountains, but we have not purchased any of them. Why? Because given the restriction of limited income, our desire for other goods is even more urgent. Our incomes would allow us to purchase backyard tennis courts only if we spent less on food, trips to the beach, housing, books, clothes, and other forms of recreation. We have a choice and have chosen to forego the courts instead of the other goods.

How do consumers decide which things to buy and which things to forego? Sensibly, they want to get the most satisfaction from the spending of their money. Economizing behavior suggests that rational consumers will spend their limited incomes on the things from which they expect the most satisfaction. Given personal tastes, they will choose the best alternatives that their limited incomes will permit. Prices influence consumer decisions. An increase in the price of a good will increase a consumer's opportunity cost of consuming it. More of other things must be given up if the consumer chooses the higher-priced commodity.

According to the basic postulate of economics, an increase in the cost of an alternative will reduce the likelihood that it will be chosen. This basic postulate implies that higher prices will discourage consumption. Lower prices will reduce the cost of choosing a good, stimulating consumption of it. This inverse relationship between the price of a good and the amount of it that consumers choose to buy is called the **law of demand.**

Law of Demand: A principle which states that there is an inverse relationship between the price of a good and the amount of it buyers are willing to purchase.

The availability of substitutes—goods that perform similar functions—helps to explain the logic of the law of demand. No single good is absolutely essential. Margarine can be substituted for butter. Wood, aluminum, bricks, and glass can be substituted for steel. Insulation, car pools, slower driving, bicycling, and small cars are substitute products that allow households to reduce their gasoline consumption. As the price (and therefore the consumers' opportunity cost) of a good increases, people have a greater incentive to turn to substitute products and economize on their use of the more expensive good. Prices really do matter.

Exhibit 1 is a graphic presentation of the law of demand. In constructing a demand curve, economists measure price on the vertical or y axis and amount demanded on the horizontal or x axis. The demand curve will slope

EXHIBIT 1   The law of demand

As the price of beef rose during 1977–1979, consumers substituted chicken, fish, and other food products for beef. The consumption level of beef (and other products) is inversely related to its price.

The numerical data used in this example are from *Statistical Abstract of the United States—1980* (Washington D.C.: U.S. Government Printing Office), pp. 131, 705.

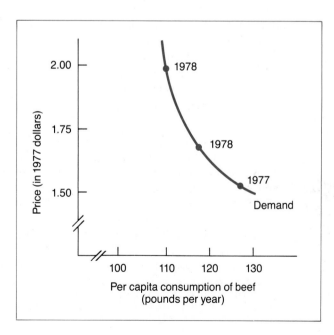

downward to the right, indicating that the amount demanded of a good, beef in this example, will increase as price declines. During 1977–1979, there was a sharp increase in the price of beef. Consumers responded, no doubt unhappily, by using less of it. In 1977, when the average price of beef was $1.48 per pound, the per capita annual beef consumption was 125.9 pounds. As the beef price rose to $1.69 per pound in 1978, annual consumption declined to 120.1 pounds. By 1979, the average price of beef had risen to $1.88 per pound; the annual consumption of beef declined still more, to 107.6 pounds, as consumers substituted chicken, fish, and other products for the more expensive beef.[2]

Some commodities may be much more responsive to a change in price than others. Consider a good for which there are several good substitutes—a Florida vacation, for example. If the price of a Florida vacation increases, perhaps because of higher gasoline prices, consumers will substitute more movies, local camping trips, baseball games, TV programs, and other recreational activities for the vacation. As illustrated by Exhibit 2, since good substitutes are available, an increase in the price of Florida vacations will cause a sharp reduction in quantity demanded. Economists say that demand for Florida vacations is *elastic*,[3] the term used to indicate that quantity demanded is quite responsive to a change in price.

Other goods may be much less responsive to a change in price. Suppose the price of physician services were to rise 15 percent, as indicated by Exhibit 2. What impact would this price increase have on the quantity demanded? The higher prices would cause some people to prescribe their own medications for colds, flu, and minor illnesses. Others might turn to painkillers, magic potions, and faith healers for even major medical problems. Most consumers, however, would consider these to be poor substitutes for the services of a physician. Thus, higher medical prices would cause a relatively small reduction in the quantity

EXHIBIT 2 Responsiveness of demand to a price change

A 15 percent increase in the price of Florida vacations (D_1) caused the quantity demanded to decline from Q_0 to Q_1, a 50 percent reduction. In contrast, a 15 percent increase in the price of physician services (D_2) resulted in only a 5 percent reduction in quantity demanded (from Q_0 to Q_2). Economists would say that the demand for Florida vacations is elastic, but the demand for physician services is inelastic.

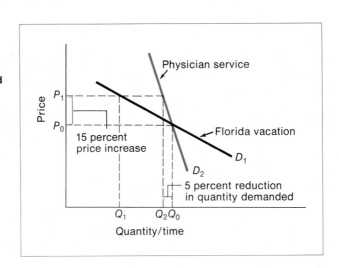

[2]The per capita annual consumption of both poultry and fish products rose during 1977–1979.

[3]The mathematical formula for price elasticity of demand is (a) percent change in quantity demanded divided by (b) percent change in price. If the absolute value of this expression exceeds 1, demand is elastic. If it is less than 1, demand is inelastic. For those in a microeconomics course, this is explained in more detail in the chapter on demand and consumer choice.

demanded. The demand for medical service is thus *inelastic,* the term used to indicate that the amount demanded is *relatively* unresponsive to a change in price.

However, despite differences in the degree of responsiveness, the fundamental law of demand holds for all goods. A price increase will induce consumers to turn to substitutes, leading to a reduction in the amount purchased. A price reduction will make a commodity relatively cheaper, inducing consumers to purchase more of it as they substitute it for other goods.

The demand schedule is not something that can be observed directly by decision-makers of a business firm or planning agency. Nonetheless, when prices are used to ration goods, consumer reactions to each price communicate information about the preferences of consumers—how they value alternative commodities. The height of the unseen demand curve indicates the maximum price that consumers are willing to pay for *an additional unit* of the product. If consumers value *additional units* of a product highly, they will be willing to pay a large amount (a high price) for it. Alternatively, if their valuation of *additional units* of the good is low, they will be willing to pay only a small amount for it.

PRODUCER CHOICE AND THE LAW OF SUPPLY

How does the market process determine the amount of each good that will be produced? We cannot answer this question unless we understand the factors that influence the choices of those who supply goods. Producers of goods and services, often utilizing the business firm,

1. organize productive inputs, such as labor, land, natural resources, and intermediate goods,
2. transform and combine these factors of production into goods desired by households, and
3. sell the final products to consumers for a price.

Profit: An excess of sales revenue relative to the cost of production. The cost component includes the opportunity cost of all resources, *including those owned by the firm.* Therefore, profit accrues only when the value of the good produced is greater than the sum of the values of the individual resources utilized.

Production involves the conversion of resources to commodities and services. Producers will have to pay the owners of scarce resources a price that is at least equal to what the resources could earn elsewhere. Stated another way, each resource employed will have to be bid away from all alternative uses; it (or its owner) will have to be paid its opportunity cost. The sum of the amount paid by the producer to each of the productive resources, including the cost of production coordination and management, will equal the product's opportunity cost.

All economic participants have a strong incentive to undertake activities that generate profit. **Profit** is a residual "income reward" granted to decision-makers who carry out a productive activity that increases the value of the resources. If an activity is to be profitable, the revenue derived from the sale of the product must exceed the cost of employing the resources that have been converted to make the product. Profitability indicates that consumers value the product more than any other which could be produced from the resources. Sometimes decision-makers use resources unwisely. They convert resources to a product that consumers value less than the opportunity cost of the resources utilized. **Losses** result, since the sales revenue derived from the project is insufficient to pay for the employment cost of the resources.

Loss: Deficit of sales revenue relative to the cost of production, once all the resources utilized have received their opportunity cost. Losses are a penalty imposed on those who misuse resources. Losses occur only when the value of the good produced is less than the sum of the values of the individual resources utilized.

Entrepreneur: A profit-seeking decision-maker who decides which projects to undertake and how they should be undertaken. If successful, an entrepreneur's actions will increase the value of resources.

Persons who undertake production organization, those who decide what to produce and how to produce it, are called **entrepreneurs.**[4] The business of the entrepreneur is to figure out which projects will, in fact, be profitable. Since the profitability of a project will be affected by the price consumers are willing to pay for a product, the price of resources required to produce it, and the cost of alternative production processes, successful entrepreneurs must be either knowledgeable in each of these areas or obtain the advice of others who have such knowledge.

Prosperous entrepreneurs must convert and rearrange resources in a manner that will increase their value. An individual who purchases 100 acres of raw land, puts in streets and a sewage disposal system, divides the plot into 1-acre lots, and sells them for 50 percent more than the opportunity cost of all resources used is clearly an entrepreneur. This entrepreneur "profits" because the value of the resources has been increased. Sometimes entrepreneurial activity is less complex. For example, a 15-year-old who purchases a power mower and sells lawn service to the neighbors is also an entrepreneur, seeking to profit by increasing the value of resources. In a market economy, profit is the reward to the entrepreneur who undertakes the project. It is also a signal to other entrepreneurs to enter a highly productive market, competing for the original entrepreneur's profit.

How will producer-entrepreneurs respond to a change in product price? Other things constant, a higher price will increase the producer's incentive to supply the good. New entrepreneurs, seeking personal gain, will enter the market and begin supplying the product. Established producers will expand the scale of their operation, leading to an additional expansion in output. Higher prices will induce producers to supply a greater amount. The direct relationship between the price of a product and the amount of it that will be supplied is termed the **law of supply.**

Law of Supply: A principle which states that there will be a direct relationship between the price of a good and the amount of it offered for sale.

Exhibit 3 presents a graphic picture of this law. The supply curve summarizes information about production conditions. Unless the profit-seeking producer receives a price that is at least equal to the opportunity cost of the resources employed, the producer will not *continue* to supply the good. The height of the supply curve indicates both (a) the minimum price necessary to induce producers to supply a specific quantity and (b) the valuation of the resources utilized in the production of the marginal unit of the good. This minimum supply price will be high (low) if the opportunity cost of supplying the marginal unit is high (low).

MARKETS AND THE COORDINATION OF SUPPLY AND DEMAND

Consumer-buyers and producer-sellers make decisions independent of each other, but markets coordinate their choices and direct their actions. To the

---

[4]This French-origin word literally means "one who undertakes." The entrepreneur is the person who is ultimately responsible. Of course, this responsibility may be shared with others (partners or stockholders, for example) or partially delegated to technical experts. Nonetheless, the success or failure of the entrepreneur is dependent on the outcome of the choices that he or she makes.

Market: An abstract concept which encompasses the trading arrangements of buyers and sellers that underlie the forces of supply and demand.

economist a market is not a physical location. A **market** is an abstract concept that encompasses the forces generated by the buying and selling decisions of economic participants. A market may be quite narrow (for example, the market for razor blades). Alternatively, it is sometimes useful to aggregate diverse goods into a single market, such as the market for "consumer goods." There is also a broad range of sophistication among markets. The New York Stock Exchange is a highly computerized market in which buyers and sellers who never formally meet exchange corporate ownership shares worth millions of dollars each weekday. In contrast, the neighborhood market for lawn-mowing services may be highly informal, since it brings together buyers and sellers primarily by word of mouth.

Equilibrium: A state of balance between conflicting forces, such as supply and demand.

Equilibrium is a state in which conflicting forces are in perfect balance. When there is a balance—an equilibrium—the tendency for change is absent. Before a market equilibrium can be attained, the decisions of consumers and producers must be brought into harmony with one another.

Short-Run Market Equilibrium

Short Run: A time period of insufficient length to permit decision-makers to adjust fully to a change in market conditions. For example, in the short run, producers will have time to increase output by utilizing more labor and raw materials, but they will not have time to expand the size of their plants or install additional heavy equipment.

The great English economist Alfred Marshall pioneered the development of supply and demand analysis. From the beginning, Marshall recognized that time plays a role in the market process. Marshall introduced the concept of the **short-run,** a time period of such short duration that decision-makers do not have time to *adjust fully* to a change in market conditions. During the short run, producers are able to alter the amount of a good supplied only by utilizing more (or less) labor and raw materials with their *existing* plant and heavy equipment. In the short run, there is insufficient time to build a new plant or obtain new "made-to-order" heavy equipment for the producer's current facility.

As Exhibit 1 illustrates, the amount of a good demanded by consumers will be inversely related to its price. On the other hand, a higher price will

EXHIBIT 3   The supply curve

As the price of a product increases, *other things constant,* producers will increase the amount of product supplied.

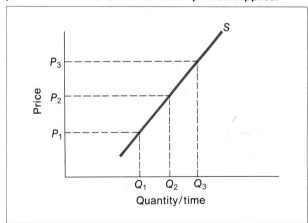

induce producers to utilize their existing facilities more intensively in the short run. As Exhibit 3 depicts, the amount of a good supplied will be directly related to its market price.

The market price of a commodity will tend to bring these two conflicting forces, supply and demand, into balance. This means that unless the quantity supplied by producers is already precisely equal to the quantity demanded by consumers, there will be a tendency for the market price to change until a balance is reached.

Exhibit 4 illustrates both supply and demand curves in the short run for a hypothetical commodity—smoos. At a high price, $12 for example, smoo producers will plan to supply 600 units per month, whereas consumers will choose to purchase only 450. An excess supply of 150 units will result. The inventories of smoo producers will rise. Rather than continue to accumulate undesired inventories, some smoo producers will cut their price. This reduction in price will make smoo production less attractive to producers. Some of the marginal producers will go out of business, and other firms will reduce their current output. Simultaneously, the lower price will induce consumers to purchase more smoos. Eventually, after the smoo price has declined to $10, the quantity supplied by producers and the quantity demanded by consumers will be brought into balance at 550 units per month. At this price ($10), the production plans of producers will be in harmony with the purchasing plans of consumers.

What will happen if the price of smoos is low—$8 for example? The amount demanded by consumers (650 units) will exceed the amount supplied by producers (500 units). An excess demand of 150 units will be present. Some consumers who would like to purchase smoos at $8 per unit will be unable to do so because of the inadequate supply. Rather than do without the good, some will be willing to pay a higher price. Recognizing this fact, producers will raise their price. As the price increases to $10, producers will expand their output and consumers will cut down on their consumption. At the $10 price, short-run equilibrium will be restored.

Long-Run Market Equilibrium

Long Run: A time period of sufficient length to enable decision-makers to adjust fully to a market change. For example, in the long run, producers will have time to alter their utilization of all productive factors, including the heavy equipment and physical structure of their plants.

In the **long run,** decision-makers will have time to adjust fully to a change in market conditions. With the passage of time, producers will be able to alter their output; not only will they use their current plant more intensively, but given sufficient time, they will be able to change the size of their production facility. The long run is a time period of sufficient duration to permit producers to expand the size of their capital stock (the physical structure and heavy equipment of their plant).

A balance between amount supplied and amount demanded is the only prerequisite for market equilibrium in the short run. However, if the current market price is going to persist in the future, an additional condition must be present: The opportunity cost of producing the product must also be equal to the market price.

If the market price of a good is greater than the opportunity cost of producing it, suppliers will gain from an expansion in production. Profit-seeking entrepreneurs will be attracted to the industry, and output (supply) will increase until a lower market price eliminates profits.[5] In contrast, if the market price is

EXHIBIT 4 Supply and demand

The table below indicates the supply and demand conditions for smoos. These conditions are also illustrated by the graph on the right. When the price exceeds $10, an excess supply is present, which places downward pressure on price. In contrast, when the price is less than $10, an excess demand results, an excess demand results, which causes the price to rise. Thus, the market price will tend toward $10, at which point supply and demand will be in balance.

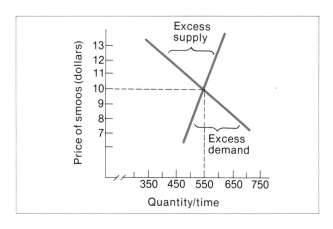

Price of Smoos (Dollars)	Quantity Supplied (Per Month)	Quantity Demanded (Per Month)	Condition in the Market	Direction of Pressure on Price
13	625	400	Excess supply	Downward
12	600	450	Excess supply	Downward
11	575	500	Excess supply	Downward
10	550	550	Balance	Equilibrium
9	525	600	Excess demand	Upward
8	500	650	Excess demand	Upward
7	475	700	Excess demand	Upward

less than the opportunity cost of a good's production, suppliers will lose money if they continue to produce the good. The losses will drive producers from the market. Supply will decline, pushing prices upward until the losses are eliminated.

SHIFTS IN DEMAND AND CHANGES IN QUANTITY DEMANDED

A demand curve isolates the impact that price has on the amount of a product purchased. Of course, factors other than price—for example, consumer income, tastes, prices of related goods, and expectations as to the future price of a product—also influence the decisions of consumers. If any one of these factors change, the entire demand curve shifts. Economists refer to such shifts in the demand curve as a *change in demand*.

---

[5] Bear in mind that economists utilize the opportunity cost concept for *all* factors of production, including those owned by the producers. Therefore, the owners are receiving a return equal to the opportunity cost of their investment capital even when profits are zero. Thus, zero profits mean that the capitalist owners are being paid precisely their opportunity cost, precisely what they could earn if their resources were employed in the highest valued alternative that must be foregone as the result of current use. Far from indicating that a firm is about to go out of business, zero economic profits imply that each factor of production, including the capital owned by the firm and the managerial skills of the owner-entrepreneur, is earning the market rate of return.

Let us take a closer look at some of the factors that would cause the demand for a product to change. Expansion in income makes it possible for consumers to purchase more goods. They usually respond by increasing their spending on a wide cross section of products. Changes in prices of closely related products also influence the choices of consumers. If the price of butter were to fall, many consumers would substitute it for margarine. The demand for margarine would decline (shift to the left) as a result. Our expectations about the future price of a product also influence our current decisions. For example, if you think that the price of automobiles is going to rise by 20 percent next month, this will increase your incentive to buy now, before the price rises. In contrast, if you think that the price of a product is going to decline, you will demand less *now*, as you attempt to extend your purchasing decision into the future, when prices are expected to be lower.

Failure to distinguish between a change in *demand* and a change in *quantity demanded* is one of the most common mistakes of introductory economics students.[6] A change in demand is a shift in the entire demand curve. A change in quantity demanded is a movement along the same demand curve.

Exhibit 5 clearly demonstrates the difference between the two. The demand curve D_1 indicates the initial demand (the entire curve) for doorknobs. At a price of $3, consumers would purchase Q_1. If the price declined to $1, there would be an increase in quantity demanded from Q_1 to Q_3. Arrow A indicates the change in *quantity demanded*—a movement along demand curve D_1. Now suppose that there were a 20 percent increase in income, causing a housing boom. The *demand* for doorknobs would increase from D_1 to D_2. As indicated by the B arrows, the entire demand curve would shift. At the higher income level, consumers would be willing to purchase more doorknobs at $3, at $2, at $1, and at other prices than was previously true. The increase in income leads to an increase in *demand*—a shift in the entire curve.

EXHIBIT 5 The difference be-tween a change in demand and a change in quantity demanded

Arrow *A* indicates a change in *quantity demanded,* a move-ment along the demand curve D_1 in response to a change in the price of doorknobs. The *B* arrows illustrate a change in *demand,* a shift of the entire curve.

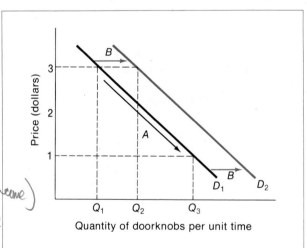

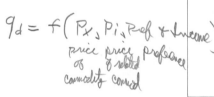
$$q_d = f\left(P_x, P_i, Pref + Income\right)$$
price price preference
of   of related
commodity commodity

---

[6]Questions designed to test the ability of students to make this distinction are favorites of many economics instructors. A word to the wise should be sufficient.

How does the market react to change in demand? What happens to price and the amount supplied of a good if demand increases? Exhibit 6 will help to answer these questions while yielding insight into real-world past events. In the mid-1970s, there was a sharp rise in the price of gasoline. Many car owners attempted to economize on their use of the more expensive fuel by substituting smaller cars for their gas-guzzling, heavier models. There was an increase in *demand* for compact cars. The demand curve for such cars shifted to the right (from D_1 to D_2). At the original equilibrium price, $5000, there was an excess demand for compact cars. The excess demand caused the price of compact cars to rise. Market forces eventually brought about a new balance between supply and demand, establishing a new equilibrium price ($7000, for example) at a higher sales level. The pricing system responded to the increase in demand by granting (a) producers a stronger incentive to supply more compact cars and (b) consumers an incentive to search for other, cheaper substitute methods of conserving gasoline than purchasing compact cars.

SHIFTS IN SUPPLY

The decisions of producers lie behind the supply curve. Other things constant, the supply curve summarizes the willingness of producers to offer a product at alternative prices. However, price is not the only factor that producers consider. Costs are also important. Production requires the use of valuable resources— labor, machines, land, building, and raw materials. Use of these resources is costly to suppliers.

Remember that entrepreneurs will supply only those products for which they expect benefits (primarily sales revenues) to exceed their production cost. Factors that reduce the producer's opportunity cost of production—lower resource prices or a technological improvement, for example—would increase the incentive to supply a larger output. Cost reductions would cause supply to increase (shift to the right). In contrast, higher input prices and changes that

EXHIBIT 6   A shift in demand

As conditions change over time, the entire demand curve for a product may shift. Facing higher gasoline prices, many consumers decided to purchase compact cars in the mid-1970s. The *demand* for compact cars increased, causing both an increase in price and greater sales.

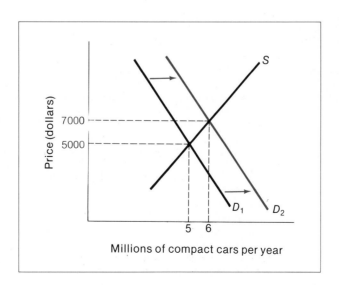

increase the producer's opportunity cost would cause supply to decline (shift to the left).

As with demand, it is important to note the difference between (a) a change in quantity supplied and (b) a change in supply. A change in quantity supplied is a movement along the same supply curve in response to a change in price. A change in supply indicates a shift in the entire supply curve.

How does the market react to a change in supply? Exhibit 7 illustrates the impact of a technological improvement that reduced the cost of producing electronic desk calculators in the 1970s. The reduction in cost made it more

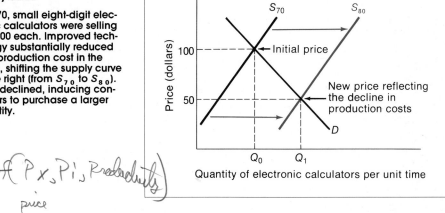

EXHIBIT 7 Improved technology and a shift in the supply curve

In 1970, small eight-digit electronic calculators were selling for $100 each. Improved technology substantially reduced their production cost in the 1970s, shifting the supply curve to the right (from S_{70} to S_{80}). Price declined, inducing consumers to purchase a larger quantity.

$qs = f\left(Px, Pi, Productivity\right)$

price
of
drow

attractive for entrepreneurs to produce these calculators. Several new firms began production. Old firms also expanded their production, contributing to the expansion of supply. At the old $100 price, consumers would not buy the larger supply of electronic calculators. A reduction in price was necessary to bring the wishes of producers and consumers back into balance. By 1980 the price of electronic calculators had fallen to $50.

Sometimes the removal or erection of market restrictions will cause the supply curve to shift. During the 1973 Middle East crisis, Arab oil-producing countries used political action to stop the flow of crude oil to Western nations. Temporarily, the United States was completely cut off from this source of petroleum. The reduction in supply led to a shortage of gasoline *at the original price*.

A market economy eliminates a shortage by allowing the price to rise. The smaller supply is rationed to those willing to pay higher prices (see Exhibit 8). The rise in the price of gasoline induces consumers to use less of it. Sunday leisure trips become more expensive. Unnecessary travel is curtailed. A new, higher equilibrium price, P_2, results, and the quantity demanded (a movement along the demand curve) is reduced at the now higher price. At this new, higher equilibrium price, the consumption decisions of consumers have again been brought into harmony with the quantity supplied by producers.

TIME AND THE ADJUSTMENT PROCESS

The signals that the pricing system sends to consumers and producers will change with market conditions. But the market adjustment process will not be completed instantaneously. Sometimes various signals are sent out only with the passage of time.

The response of consumers to a change in market conditions will generally be more pronounced with the passage of time. Consider the response of consumers to the higher gasoline prices during the 1970s. Initially consumers cut out some unnecessary trips and leisure driving. Some drove more slowly in order

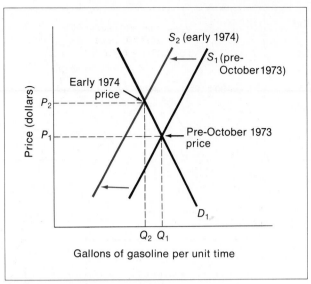

EXHIBIT 8   A decrease in supply

During the October 1973 Middle East conflict the Arab countries reduced the supply of crude oil to the United States and other nations. This action reduced the supply of gasoline. In a market economy such action would cause the price of gasoline to rise, and the smaller supply would be rationed to buyers willing to pay the higher prices.

to get better gasoline mileage. As Exhibit 9 illustrates, these adjustments led to some reduction in gasoline consumption. However, as the high gasoline prices persisted, new car purchases began to shift toward smaller cars that used less gas. Since people usually waited for their current gas-guzzler to wear out before they bought a new, smaller car, it took several years before the full impact of this adjustment was felt. Once people had shifted to higher-mileage automobiles, there was a significantly larger reduction in gasoline consumption than had been initially observed. The adjustment process for gasoline is a typical one. The demand response to a price change will usually be less in the short run than over a longer period of time.

Similarly, the adjustments of producers to changing market conditions will take time. Suppose that there is an increase in demand for radios. How will this change be reflected in the market? Initially, retailers will note that radios move off their shelves more rapidly. Their inventories will decline. During the first few weeks, however, individual radio retailers will be unsure whether the increase in demand is a random, temporary phenomenon or a permanent change. Therefore, they will most likely increase their wholesale orders while leaving the retail price constant. Since all retailers will now be placing larger orders, the sales of manufacturers will increase, and their inventories will decline. A few alert entrepreneurs may anticipate the expansion in demand and develop their production plans accordingly. With the passage of time, other producers, initially oblivious to the increase in demand, will take note of the strong demand for radios. Some will raise their prices. Others will increase their output. Most

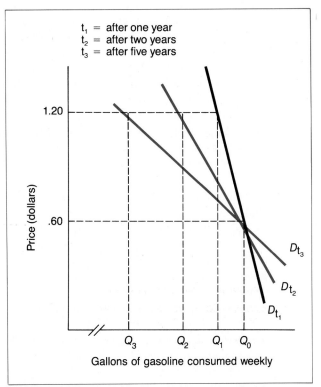

EXHIBIT 9   Time and the buyer's response to a price increase

Usually, the shorter the time period, the less responsive is consumption to a change in price. The gasoline price increases of the 1970s illustrate the point. Initially, gasoline consumption did not decline very much (from Q_0 to Q_1 during the first year) as the price of gasoline rose. However, with the passage of time, consumers adjusted more fully and the consumption of gasoline fell by a larger amount (to Q_3).

manufacturers perceiving the strong demand will do both. Retailers will soon pass the higher prices on to consumers.

Once the increase in demand is widely perceived by suppliers, the price of radios will rise sharply. Profits will exist in the industry. The astute entrepreneurs who anticipated the increase in demand will have expanded their production capacity. They will be rewarded with substantial profits. Other radio suppliers will hastily attempt to expand their production in order to increase their profits. However, instituting a rapid increase in production will be costly for producers who failed to anticipate (and plan for) the higher level of demand. Such firms will have to resort to overtime payments, air shipments of raw materials, and/or the employment of inexperienced workers in order to increase their output rapidly. With the passage of time, output can be expanded in a more orderly fashion and at a lower cost.

Although producers will expand their output at different rates, the profitable opportunities will induce additional supply, which will eventually moderate the price of radios. However, all of these responses will take time, even though economists sometimes talk as if the process were instantaneous.

Price Ceiling: A legally established maximum price that sellers may charge.

Buyers often believe that prices are too high, and sellers generally perceive prices as too low. Unhappy with the prices established by market forces, individuals sometimes attempt to have prices set by legislative action. Fixing prices seems like a simple, straightforward solution. Simple, straightforward solutions, however, often have unanticipated repercussions. Do not forget the secondary effects.

Price ceilings are often popular during a period of inflation, a situation in which prices of most products are continually rising. Many people mistakenly believe that the rising prices are the cause of the inflation rather than just one of its effects. Exhibit 10a illustrates the impact of fixing a price of a product below its equilibrium level. Of course, the price ceiling does result in a lower price than would result from market forces, at least in the short run. However, that is not the end of the story. At the below-equilibrium price, producers will be unwilling to supply as much as consumers would like to purchase. A shortage ($Q_c - Q_p$, Exhibit 10a) of the goods will result. A **shortage** is a situation in which the quantity demanded by consumers exceeds the quantity supplied by producers *at the existing price.* Unfortunately, fixing the price will not eliminate the rationing problem. Nonprice factors will now become more important in the rationing process. Producers will be more discriminating in their sales to eager buyers. Sellers will be partial to friends, buyers who do them favors, even buyers who are willing to make illegal black-market payments.

Shortage: A condition in which the amount of a good offered by sellers is less than the amount demanded by buyers at the existing price. An increase in price would eliminate the shortage.

In addition, the below-equilibrium price reduces the incentive of sellers to expand the future supply of the good. Fewer resources will flow from suppliers into the production of this good. Higher profits will be available elsewhere. With the passage of time, the shortage conditions will worsen as suppliers direct resources away from production of this commodity and into other areas.

What other secondary effects can we expect? In the real world, there are two ways that sellers can raise prices. First, they can raise their money price, holding quality constant. Or, second, they can hold the money price constant while reducing the quality of the good. Confronting a price ceiling, sellers will rely on the latter method of raising prices. Rather than do without the good, some buyers will accept the lower-quality product. It is not easy to repeal the laws of supply and demand (see Myths of Economics, below).

It is important to note that a shortage is not the same as scarcity. Scarcity is inescapable. Scarcity exists whenever people want more of a good than Nature has provided. This means, of course, that almost everything is scarce. Shortages, on the other hand, are avoidable if prices are permitted to rise. A higher, unfixed price (P_0 rather than P_1 in Exhibit 10a) would (a) stimulate additional production, (b) discourage consumption, and (c) ration the available supply to those willing to give up the most in exchange, that is, to pay the highest prices. These forces, an expansion in output and a reduction in consumption, would eliminate the shortage.

Price Floor: A legally established minimum price that buyers must pay for a good or resource.

Surplus: A condition in which the amount of a good that sellers are willing to offer is greater than the amount that buyers will purchase at the existing price. A decline in price would eliminate the surplus.

Exhibit 10b illustrates the case of a **price floor,** which fixes the price of a good or resource above its equilibrium level. At the higher price, sellers will want to bring a larger amount to the market, while buyers will choose to buy less of the good. A **surplus** ($Q_p - Q_c$) will result. Agricultural price supports and minimum wage legislation are examples of price floors. Predictably, nonprice factors will

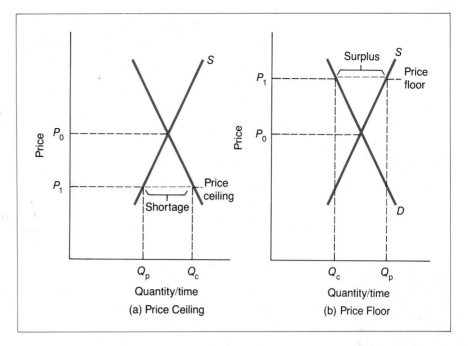

again play a larger role in the rationing process than would be true without a price floor. Buyers can now be more selective, since sellers want to sell more than buyers, in aggregate, desire to purchase. Buyers can be expected to seek out sellers willing to offer them favors (discounts on other products, easier credit, or better service, for example). Some sellers may be unable to market their product or service.[8] Unsold merchandise and underutilized resources will result.

Note that a surplus does not mean the good is no longer scarce. People still want more of the good than is freely available from Nature, even though they desire less, *at the current price,* than sellers desire to bring to the market. A decline in price would eliminate the surplus but not the scarcity of the item.

HOW THE MARKET ANSWERS THE THREE BASIC ECONOMIC QUESTIONS

How does the market's pricing mechanism resolve the three basic economic questions—*what* goods will be produced, *how* will they be produced, and *for whom* will they be produced?

In a market economy, what will be produced is determined by the consumer's evaluation of a good (demand) relative to its opportunity cost (supply). If consumers value a good (in terms of money) more than its opportunity cost, they will choose to purchase it. Simultaneously, profit-seeking producers will

---

[8]Our theory indicates that minimum wage legislation (a price floor for unskilled labor) will generate an excess supply of inexperienced, low-skilled workers. The extremely high unemployment rate of teenagers—a group with little work experience—supports this view.

supply a good as long as consumers are willing to pay a price that is sufficient to cover the opportunity cost of producing the good. The result: There is an incentive to produce those goods, and only those goods, to which consumers attach a value at least as high as the production costs of the goods.

How goods will be produced is determined by the economizing behavior of suppliers. Suppliers have a strong incentive to use production methods that minimize costs, because lower costs will mean larger profits. Thus, producers can be expected to organize production efficiently—to utilize a division of labor, to discover and adapt new technologies, and to choose labor–capital combinations that will result in lower production costs.

What assurances are there that producers will not waste resources or exploit consumers by charging high prices? Competition provides the answer. Inefficient producers will have higher costs. They will find it difficult to meet the price competition of sellers who use resources wisely. Similarly, in a market with many sellers, competition among firms will, on the whole, keep prices from straying much above production costs. When prices are above the opportunity costs of a good, profits for the producers will result. As we have discussed, the profits will attract additional suppliers into the market, driving the price downward.

To whom will the goods be distributed? Goods will be allocated to consumers willing and able to pay the market price. Of course, some consumers will be more able to pay the market price—they have larger incomes (more "dollar votes") than others. The unequal distribution of income among consumers is directly related to what is produced and how. The income of individuals will reflect the extent of their provision of resources to others. Those who supply large amounts of highly valued resources—resources for which market participants are willing to pay a high price—will have high incomes. In contrast, those who supply few resources or resources that are *not* valued highly by others will have low incomes.

As long as the preferences and productive abilities of individuals differ, a market solution will lead to an unequal distribution of income. Many people are critical of the pricing system because of its method of distribution. But unequal income distribution is not unique to a market economy. Other systems also use unequal income shares to provide the incentive for individuals to undertake activities. Since efforts to alter the distribution of income will also affect supply conditions, this issue is highly complex. As we proceed, we will investigate it in more detail.

THE COMMUNICATING, COORDINATING, AND MOTIVATING FUNCTIONS OF THE MARKET

The mechanics of supply and demand are important because they help us to understand forces present in the real world. However, sometimes we economists have a tendency to focus on the mechanics without fully explaining their importance. Economic activity is conducted by human decision-makers. Knowledge, coordination, and motivation are critical to the operation of every economy. If people do not know where their services are valued highly, what

MYTHS OF ECONOMICS

"Rent controls are an effective method of ensuring adequate housing at a price the poor can afford."

When rents (a price for a good) are set below the equilibrium level, the amount of rental housing demanded by consumers will exceed the amount that landlords will make available. *Initially,* if the mandated price is not set too much below equilibrium, the impact of rent controls may be barely noticeable. However, with the passage of time, their effects will grow. Inevitably controls will lead to the following results.

1. The Future Supply of Rental Houses Will Decline. The below-equilibrium price will discourage entrepreneurs from constructing new rental housing units. Private investment will flow elsewhere, since the controls have depressed the rate of return in the rental housing market. The current owners of such housing may be forced to accept the lower price. However, potential future suppliers of rental housing have other alternatives. Many of them will opt to use their knowledge and resources in other areas.

2. Shortages and Black Markets Will Develop. Since the quantity of housing supplied will fail to keep pace with the quantity demanded, some persons who value rental housing highly will be unable to find it. Frustrated by the shortage, they will seek methods by which they may induce landlords to rent to them. Some will agree to prepay their rent, including a substantial damage deposit. Others will resort to tie-in agreements (for example, they might agree also to rent or buy the landlord's furniture at an exorbitant price) in their efforts to evade the controls. Still others will make under-the-table payments in order to secure the cheap housing.

3. The Quality of Rental Housing Will Deteriorate. Economic thinking suggests that there are two ways to raise prices. The nominal price can be increased, quality being held constant. Alternatively, quality can be reduced, the same nominal price being maintained. When landlords are prohibited from adopting the former, they will utilize the latter. They will paint rental units less often. Normal maintenance and repair service will deteriorate. Tenant parking lots will be eliminated (or rented). Cleaning and maintenance of the general surroundings will be neglected. Eventually, the quality of the rental housing will reflect the controlled price. Cheap housing will be of cheap quality.

4. Nonprice Methods of Rationing Will Increase in Importance. Since price no longer plays its normal role, other forms of competition will develop. Prohibited from price rationing, landlords will rely more heavily on nonmonetary discriminating devices. They will favor friends, persons of influence, and those with life-styles similar to their own. In contrast, applicants with many children, unconventional life-styles, or perhaps dark skin will find fewer landlords who cater to their personal requirements. Since the cost to landlords of discriminating against those with characteristics they do not like has been reduced, such discrimination will become more prevalent in the rationing process.

5. Inefficient Use of Housing Space Will Result. The tenant in a rent-controlled apartment will think twice before moving. Why? Even though the tenant might want a larger or smaller space, or even though the tenant might want to move closer to work, he or she will be less likely to move because it is much more difficult to find a vacancy if rent control ordinances are in effect. As a result, turnover will drop somewhat, and people will end up living in apartments not quite suited to their needs.

Are conditions in the real world consistent with economic theory? More than any other major city in the United States, New York City has experimented with rent controls. The result has been an unusually large number of furniture and housing "package rentals" as both landlords and renters seek to avoid the impact of the controls. Complaints about the failure of landlords to undertake repairs, maintain rental units properly, and provide complimentary services such as garbage pickup and rat control efforts are far more common in New York City than in any other place in the United States. Economic theory helps to explain why this is the case.

During the inflation-plagued 1970s, the popularity of rent controls increased. Washington, D.C., San Francisco, Los Angeles, and several other cities experimented with various types of control schemes. Studies indicate that a three-pronged pattern emerged after the imposition of rent controls. First, investment in new construction came to a standstill after the controls were imposed. Even in cases where newly constructed buildings were exempted from the controls, construction was adversely affected; landlords feared the imposition of the controls once a new apartment dwelling was in place. Second, the rent controls induced many landlords to convert their apartment buildings to condominium complexes. For example, in Washington, D.C., a city that effectively instituted rent controls in 1974, the number of condominiums jumped from 1000 in 1976 to approximately 10,000 in 1979. San Francisco, New York, and other large cities with controls experienced a similar "boom" in conversion to the condominium market. Finally, vacancy rates declined as the rent control communities began to feel the effects of the developing housing shortage.

Although rent controls may appear to be a simple solution, the truth of the matter is that a decline

goods are desired by consumers, or which production methods are efficient, they cannot be expected to economize resources. Similarly, unless actions are coordinated, an economy will come to a standstill. In addition, as many leaders of centrally planned economies have discovered, people must be motivated to act before production plans can be realized. An efficiently operating economy must communicate, coordinate, and motivate the actions of decision-makers. In this section, we will take a closer look at how the pricing system performs these functions.

Communicating Information to Decision-Makers

Communication of information is one of the most important functions of a market price. We cannot *directly* observe the preferences of consumers. How highly do consumers value tricycles relative to attic fans, television sets relative to trampolines, or automobiles relative to swimming pools? Product prices communicate up-to-date information about the consumer's valuation of additional units of these and numerous other commodities. Similarly, we cannot turn to an engineering equation in order to calculate the opportunity cost of alternative commodities. But resource prices tell the business decision-maker the relative importance others place on production factors (skill categories of labor, natural resources, and machinery, for example). With this information, in addition to knowledge of the relationship between potential input combinations and the output of a product, producers can make reliable estimates of their opportunity costs.

Without the information provided by market prices, it would be impossible for decision-makers to determine how intensively a good was desired relative to its opportunity costs—that is, relative to other things that might be produced with the resources required to produce the good. Markets collect and register bits and pieces of information reflecting the choices of consumers, producers, and resource suppliers. This vast body of information, which is almost always well beyond the comprehension of any single individual, is tabulated into a summary statistic—*the market price.* This summary statistic provides market participants with information on the relative scarcity of products.

When weather conditions, consumer preferences, technology, political revolution, or natural disaster alter the relative scarcity of a product or resource, market prices communicate this information to decision-makers. Direct knowledge of why conditions were altered is not necessary in order to make the appropriate adjustment. A change in the market price provides sufficient information to determine whether an item has become more or less scarce.[10]

Coordinating the Actions of Market Participants

Market prices coordinate the choices of buyers and sellers, bringing their decisions into line with each other. If suppliers are bringing more of a product to market than is demanded by consumers at the market price, that price will fall. As the price declines, producers will cut back their output (some may even go out of business), and simultaneously the price reduction will induce consumers to utilize more of the good. The excess supply will eventually be eliminated, and balance will be restored in the market.

Alternatively, if producers are currently supplying less than consumers are purchasing, there will be an excess demand in the market. Rather than do without, some consumers will bid up the price. As the price rises, consumers will be encouraged to economize on their use of the good, and suppliers will be encouraged to produce more of it. Again, price will serve to balance the scales of supply and demand.

Prices also direct entrepreneurs to undertake the production projects that are demanded most intensely (relative to their cost) by consumers. Entrepreneurial activity is guided by the signal lights of profits and losses. If consumers really want more of a good—for example, luxury apartments—the intensity of their demand will lead to a market price that exceeds the opportunity cost of constructing the apartments. A profitable opportunity will be created. Entrepreneurs will soon discover this opportunity for gain, undertake construction, and thereby expand the availability of the apartments. In contrast, if consumers want less of a good—for example, books by Watergate criminals—the opportunity cost of supplying such books will exceed the sales revenue from their production. Entrepreneurs who undertake such unprofitable projects will be penalized.

An understanding of the importance of the entrepreneur also sheds light on the market adjustment process. Since entrepreneurs, like the rest of us, have imperfect knowledge, they will not be able instantaneously to identify profitable opportunities and the disequilibrium conditions that accompany them. However, with the passage of time, information about a profitable opportunity will become more widely disseminated. More and more producers will move to

---

[10]The market adjustment to the destruction of the anchovy crop off the coast of Peru in 1972 provides an excellent example of the role of price as a communication signal. The normal anchovy run off the coast of Peru did not materialize in 1972. Anchovies are a major source of protein for animal feed. Soybeans are a good substitute for anchovies. It was not necessary for American farmers to know any of these things in order to make the correct response. As soybeans were used more intensively in feed grains, the price of soybeans increased during 1972–1974. Responding to the summary statistic (higher soybean prices), farmers increased their production of soybeans, which moderated the adverse effects of the anchovy destruction.

supply the good, which is intensely desired by consumers relative to its cost. Of course, as entrepreneurs expand supply, they will eventually eliminate the profit.

The move toward equilibrium will typically be a groping process. With time, successful entrepreneurial activity will be more clearly identified. Successful methods will be copied by other producers. Learning-by-doing and trial-and-error will help producers sort out attractive projects from "losers." The process, however, will never quite be complete. By the time entrepreneurs discover one intensely desired product (or a new, more efficient production technique), change will have occurred elsewhere, creating other unrealized profitable opportunities. The wheels of dynamic change never stop.

Motivating the Economic Players

One of the major advantages of the pricing system is its ability to motivate people. Prices establish a reward–penalty system that induces the participants to work, cooperate with others, invest for the future, supply goods that are intensely desired by others, economize on the use of scarce resources, and utilize efficient production methods. Pursuit of personal gain is a powerful motivator.

This reward–penalty system will direct the actions of entrepreneurs. They will seek to supply goods that are intensely desired relative to their opportunity cost, because such projects are profitable. In contrast, they will try to avoid using resources to produce things that are valued less than their opportunity cost because such projects will result in losses. No government agency needs to tell decision-makers what to produce or what not to produce. No central authority forces the milkman to deliver milk, the construction firm to produce houses, the farmer to produce wheat, or the baker to produce bread. Producers choose to engage in these and millions of other productive activities because they consider them to be in their self-interest.

Similarly, no one has to tell resource suppliers to acquire, develop, and supply productive inputs. Why are many young people willing to undertake the necessary work, stress, late hours of study, and financial cost to acquire a medical or law degree, a doctoral degree in economics or physics, or a master's degree in business administration? Why do others seek to master a skill requiring an apprentice program? Why do individuals save to buy a business, capital equipment, or other assets? Although many factors undoubtedly influence one's decision to acquire skills and capital assets, the expectation of financial reward is an important stimulus. Without this stimulus, the motivation to work, create, develop skills, and supply capital assets to those productive activities most desired by others would be weakened. Market forces supply this essential ingredient so automatically that most people do not even realize it. Responding to the reward–penalty system of the market, the actions of even self-interested people will be channelled into the areas of production that are most highly desired relative to their opportunity cost.

More than 200 years ago, the father of economics, Adam Smith, first articulated the revolutionary idea that competitive markets bring personal self-interest and general welfare into harmony with each other. Smith noted that the butcher, for example, supplies meat to customers, not out of benevolence, but rather out of self-interest. Emphasizing his point, Smith stated:

Every individual is continually exerting himself to find out the most advantageous employment for whatever capital he can command. It is his own advantage, indeed, and not that of the

society which he has in view. But the study of his own advantage naturally, or rather neces-
sarily, leads him to prefer that employment which is most advantageous to society. . . . He
intends only his own gain, and he is in this, as in many other cases, led by an invisible
hand to promote an end which was no part of his intention. By pursuing his own
interest he frequently promotes that of the society more effectually than when he really
intends to promote it.[11]

Market prices coordinate the decentralized individual planning of economic participants and bring their plans (self-interest) into harmony with the general welfare. This was the message of Adam Smith in 1776. It was an idea whose time had come.

Qualifications

In this chapter, we have focused on the operation of a market economy. The efficiency of market organization is dependent on (a) competitive markets and (b) well-defined private-property rights. Competition, the great regulator, is capable of protecting both buyer and seller. The presence of independent alternative suppliers protects the consumer against a seller who seeks to charge prices substantially above the cost of production. The existence of alternative resource suppliers protects the producer against a supplier who might otherwise be tempted to withhold a vital resource unless granted exorbitant compensation. The existence of alternative employment opportunities protects the employee from the power of any single employer. Competition can equalize the bargaining power between buyers and sellers.

Although property rights are often associated with selfishness, they might be viewed more properly as an arrangement that (a) forces resource users to bear fully the cost of their action and (b) prohibits persons from engaging in destructive forms of competition. When property rights are securely defined, suppliers will be required to pay resource owners the opportunity cost of each resource employed. They will not be permitted to seize and utilize scarce resources without compensating the owner, that is, without bidding the resources away from alternative users.

Similarly, securely defined property rights will eliminate the use of violence as a competitive weapon. A producer you do not buy from (or work for) will not be permitted to burn your house down. Nor will a competitive resource supplier whose prices you undercut be permitted to slash your automobile tires or hammer your head against concrete.

Lack of competition and poorly defined property rights will alter the operation of a market economy. As we proceed, we will investigate each of these problems in detail.

CHAPTER LEARNING OBJECTIVES

1 Because people want more of scarce goods than Nature has made freely available, a rationing mechanism is necessary. Competition is the natural outgrowth of the necessity for rationing scarce goods. A change in the rationing mechanism utilized will alter the form of competition, but it will not eliminate competitive tactics.

----

[11]Adam Smith, *An Inquiry into the Nature and Causes of the Wealth of Nations* (New York: Modern Library, 1937), p. 423.

2   The law of demand holds that there is an inverse relationship between price and amount of a good purchased. A rise in price will cause consumers to purchase less because they now have a greater incentive to use substitutes. On the other hand, a reduction in price will induce consumers to buy more, since they will substitute the cheaper good for other commodities.

3   The law of supply states that there is a direct relationship between the price of a product and the amount supplied. Other things constant, an increase in the price of a product will induce the established firms to expand their output and new firms to enter the market. The quantity supplied will expand.

4   Market prices will bring the conflicting forces of supply and demand into balance. If the quantity supplied to the market by producers exceeds the quantity demanded by consumers, price will decline until the excess supply is eliminated. On the other hand, if the quantity demanded by consumers exceeds the quantity supplied by producers, price will rise until the excess demand is eliminated.

5   When a market is in long-run equilibrium, supply and demand will be in balance and the producer's opportunity cost will equal the market price. If the opportunity cost of supplying the good is less than the market price, profits will accrue. The profits will attract additional suppliers, cause lower prices, and push the market toward an equilibrium. On the other hand, if the opportunity cost of producing a good exceeds the market price, suppliers will experience losses. The losses will induce producers to leave the market, causing price to rise until equilibrium is restored.

6   Changes in consumer income, prices of closely related goods, preferences, and expectation as to future prices will cause the entire demand curve to shift. An increase (decrease) in demand will cause prices to rise (fall) and quantity supplied to increase (decline).

7   Changes in input prices, technology, and other factors that influence the producer's cost of production will cause the entire supply curve to shift. An increase (decrease) in supply will cause prices to fall (increase) and quantity demanded to expand (decline).

8   The constraint of time temporarily limits the ability of consumers to adjust to changes in prices. With the passage of time, a price increase will usually elicit a larger reduction in quantity demanded. Similarly, the market supply curve shows more responsiveness to a change in price in the long run than during the short-term time period.

9   When a price is fixed below the market equilibrium, buyers will want to purchase more than sellers are willing to supply. A shortage will result. Nonprice factors such as waiting lines, quality deterioration, and illegal transactions will play a more important role in the rationing process.

10   When a price is fixed above the market equilibrium level, sellers will want to supply a larger amount than buyers are willing to purchase at the current price. A surplus will result.

11   The pricing system answers the three basic allocation questions in the following manner.

(a) *What goods will be produced?* Additional units of goods will be produced only if consumers value them more highly than the opportunity cost of the resources necessary to produce them.

(b) *How will goods be produced?* The methods that result in the lowest opportunity cost will be chosen. Since lower costs mean larger profits, markets reward producers who discover and utilize efficient (low-cost) production methods.

(c) *To whom will the goods be distributed?* Goods will be distributed to individuals according to the quantity and price of the productive resources supplied in the marketplace. A great number of goods will be allocated to persons who are able to sell a large quantity of highly valued productive resources; few goods will be allocated to persons who supply only a small quantity of low-valued resources.

12   Market prices communicate information, coordinate the actions of buyers and sellers, and provide the incentive structure that motivates decision-makers to act. The information provided by prices instructs entrepreneurs as to (a) how to use scarce resources and (b) which products are intensely desired (relative to their opportunity cost) by consumers. Market prices establish a reward–penalty system, which induces individuals to cooperate with each other and motivates them to work efficiently, invest for the future, supply intensely desired goods, economize on the use of scarce resources, and utilize efficient production methods. Even though decentralized individual planning is a characteristic of the market system, there is a harmony between personal self-interest and the general welfare, as Adam Smith noted long ago. The efficiency of the system is dependent on (a) competitive market conditions and (b) securely defined private-property rights.

THE ECONOMIC WAY OF THINKING — DISCUSSION QUESTIONS

1   What is the purpose of prices? Do prices do anything other than ration goods to those with the most dollar votes? Explain. What factors determine the price of a good?

2   How many of the following "goods" do you think conform to the general law of supply: (a) gasoline, (b) cheating on exams, (c) political favors from legislators, (d) the services of heart specialists, (e) children, (f) legal divorces, (g) the services of a minister? Explain your answer in each case.

3   Which of the following do you think would lead to an increase in the current demand for beef: (a) higher pork prices, (b) higher incomes, (c) higher feed grain prices, (d) a banner-year corn crop, (e) an increase in the price of beef?

4   (a) "The motivating force behind a market economy is individual self-interest."
(b) "Cooperation among individuals is the keystone of a market system. Without cooperation there would be no exchange and economic welfare would suffer drastically."
Are these statements true or false? Explain your answer.

5   "We cannot allow the price of gasoline to go any higher because it is as essential to the poor as to the rich. We cannot allow the rich to bid gasoline away from the poor. I would prefer to ration ten gallons of gas to each driver — both rich and poor." (Overheard during the gasoline shortage of the 1970s.)
(a) Do you agree with this opinion? Why?
(b) Do you think gasoline is more essential than food? Should the rich be allowed to bid food away from the poor? Should food be rationed, equal portions being granted to both rich and poor? Why or why not?
(c) Were your answers to both (a) and (b) consistent? Explain.

6   **What's Wrong with This Way of Thinking?**

"Economists argue that lower prices will necessarily result in less supply. However, there are exceptions to this rule. For example, in 1970 ten-digit electronic calculators sold for $100. By 1980 the price of the same type of calculator had declined to less than $30. Yet business firms produced and sold five times as many calculators in 1980 as in 1970. Lower prices did *not* result in less production and a decline in the number of calculators supplied."

7   A severe frost hit Brazil in July 1975, damaging the coffee crop. The 1976 harvest was 9.5 million bags, down from the 1975 harvest of 23 million bags. Since Brazil is the

world's leading coffee producer, there was a substantial reduction in the world supply of coffee in 1976. Use supply and demand analysis to describe:

   (a) what happened to the price of coffee in 1976;
   (b) the U.S. per capita consumption of coffee in 1976 compared to that in 1975;
   (c) the price of tea in 1976;
   (d) the revenues of coffee producers in 1976 (be careful).

Coffee is allocated by the market. Did the sharp reduction in supply create a shortage? Why or why not?

Industrious students should obtain real-world data to back up their analysis. Information on coffee prices and consumption for the United States is available in the *Statistical Abstract of the United States* (annual).

4

SUPPLY AND DEMAND FOR THE PUBLIC SECTOR

The economic role of government is pivotal. The government sets the rules of the game. It establishes and defines property rights, which are necessary for the smooth operation of markets. As we shall soon see, public policy is an important determinant of economic stability. The government sometimes uses subsidies to encourage the production of some goods while applying special taxes to reduce the availability of others. In a few cases—education, the mail service, and local electric power, for example—the government becomes directly involved in the production process.

Because of government's broad economic role, it is vital that we understand how it works and the circumstances under which it contributes to the efficient allocation of resources. What functions does government perform best? Why does it sometimes fail to perform as we would like? What activities might best be left to the market? Recent work in economics, particularly in the area of public choice, is relevant if we are seeking intelligent answers to these age-old questions.

In this chapter, we focus on the shortcomings of the market and the potential of government policy as an alternate means for resolving economic problems. Issues involving market and public sector organization will be discussed repeatedly throughout this book. Political economy—how the public sector works in comparison with the market—is an integral and exciting aspect of economic analysis.

IDEAL ECONOMIC EFFICIENCY

Economic Efficiency: Econo-
mizing behavior. When ap-
plied to a community, it
implies that (a) an activity
should be undertaken if the
sum of the benefits to the
individuals exceeds the sum of
their costs, and (b) no activity
should be undertaken if the
costs borne by the individuals
exceed the benefits.

We need a criterion by which to judge market and public sector action. Economists use the standard of **economic efficiency.** The central idea is straight-forward. It simply means that *for any given level of effort* (cost), we want to obtain the largest possible benefit. A corollary is that we want to obtain any specific level of benefits *with the least possible effort.* Economic efficiency is simply getting the most out of the available resources.

But what does this mean when applied to the entire economy? Individuals are the final decision-makers of an economy. Individuals will bear the costs and reap the benefits of economic activity. When applied to the entire economy, two conditions are necessary for ideal economic efficiency to exist:

Rule 1. *Undertaking an economic action will be efficient if it produces more benefits than costs for the individuals of the economy.* Such actions result in gain—improvement in the well-being of at least some individuals without creating welfare losses to others. Failure to undertake such activities means that potential gain has been foregone.

Rule 2. *Undertaking an economic action will be inefficient if it produces more costs to the individuals than benefits.* When an action results in greater total costs than benefits, somebody must be harmed. The benefits that accrue to those who gain are insufficient to compensate for the losses imposed on others. Therefore, when all persons are considered, the net impact of such an action is counterproductive.

When either rule 1 or rule 2 is violated, economic inefficiency results. The concept of economic efficiency applies to all possible income distributions, although a change in income distribution may alter the precise combination of goods and services that is most efficient. Positive economics does not tell us *how* income should be distributed. Of course, we all have ideas on the subject. Most of us would like to see more income distributed our way. But for each kind of income distribution, there will be an ideal resource allocation that will be most efficient.

A closer look at supply and demand when competitive pressures are present will help you to understand the concept of efficiency. The supply curve reflects the producer's opportunity costs. Each point along the supply curve indicates the *minimum* price for which the units of a good could be produced without a loss to the seller. Each point along the demand curve indicates the consumer's valuation of the good—the *maximum* amount that the consumer of each unit is willing to pay for the unit. Any time the consumer's valuation exceeds the producer's opportunity cost—the producer's minimum supply price—production and sale of the good can generate mutual gain.

When only the buyer and seller are affected by production and exchange, competitive markets directed by the forces of supply and demand are efficient. Exhibit 1 illustrates why this is true. Suppliers of a good, bicycles in this example, will produce additional units as long as the market price exceeds the production cost. Similarly, consumers will gain from the purchase of additional units as long as their benefits, revealed by the height of the demand curve, exceed the market price. Market forces will result in an equilibrium output level of Q: All units for which the benefits to consumers exceed the costs to suppliers will be produced. Rule 1 is met; all potential gains from exchange (the shaded area) between

EXHIBIT 1   What is good about idealized market exchange?

When competitive forces are present, price will tend toward the supply–demand intersection *P*. At that price, the seller's opportunity cost of producing the last unit will just equal the buyer's evaluation of that unit. All potential mutual gains from production and exchange are realized.

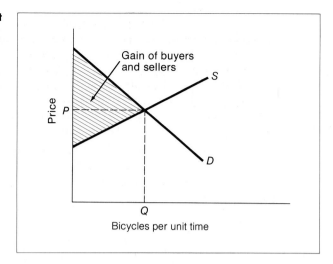

consumers and producers are fully realized. Production beyond *Q*, however, will prove inefficient. If more than *Q* bicycles are produced, rule 2 is violated; consumers value the additional units *less* than their cost. With competitive markets, suppliers will find it unprofitable to produce units beyond *Q* because costs will exceed revenues.

Thus, both consumers and producers will be guided by the pricing system to output level *Q*, just the right amount. The market works beautifully. Individuals, pursuing their own interest, are guided as if by an invisible hand to promote the general welfare. This was the message of Adam Smith, more than 200 years ago.

WHY MIGHT THE INVISIBLE HAND FAIL?

Is the invisible hand still working today? Why might it fail? There are four important factors than can limit the ability of the invisible hand to perform its magic.

Lack of Competition

Competition is vital to the proper operation of the pricing mechanism. It is competition that drives the prices for consumer goods down to the level of their cost. Similarly, competition in factor markets prevents both (a) sellers from charging exorbitant prices to producers and (b) buyers from taking advantage of the owners of productive resources. The existence of competitors reduces the power of both buyers and sellers to rig the market in their own favor.

Modern mass production techniques often make it possible for a large-scale producer to gain a cost advantage over smaller competitors. In several industries—automobiles, steel, aircraft, and aluminum, for example—a few large firms produce the entire output. Because an enormous amount of capital investment is required to enter these industries, existing large-scale producers may be partially insulated from the competitive pressure of new rivals.

Since competition is the enemy of high prices, sellers have a strong incentive to escape from its pressures by colluding rather than competing.

Competition is something that is good for the other guy. Individually, each of us would prefer to be loosened from its grip. Students do not like stiff competitors at exam time, when seeking entry to graduate school, or in their social or romantic lives. Similarly, sellers prefer few real competitors.

Exhibit 2 illustrates how sellers can gain from collusive action. If a group of sellers could eliminate the competition from new entrants to the market, they would be able to raise their prices. The total revenue of sellers is simply the market price multiplied by the quantity sold. The sellers' revenues would be greater if only the restricted output Q_2 were sold rather than the competitive output Q_1. The artificially high price P_2 is in excess of the competitive opportunity cost of supplying the good. The price of the good does not reflect its actual level of scarcity.

It is in the interests of consumers and the community that output be expanded to Q_1, the output consistent with economic efficiency. But it is in the interests of the sellers to make the good artificially scarce and raise its price. If the sellers can use collusion, government action, or other means of restricting supply, they can gain. However, the restricted output level would violate rule 2. Inefficiency would result. There is a conflict between the interests of the sellers and what is best for the entire community.

When there are only a few firms in the industry and competition from new entrants can be restrained, the sellers may be able to rig the market in their favor. Through collusion, either tacit or overt, suppliers may be able to escape competitive pressures. What can the government do to preserve competition? Congress has enacted a series of antitrust laws, most notably the Sherman Antitrust Act and the Clayton Act, making it illegal for firms to collude or attempt to monopolize a product. It established the Federal Trade Commission, which prohibits "certain methods of competition in commerce," such as false advertising, improper grading of materials, and deceptive business practices.

For the most part, economists favor the principle of government action to ensure and promote competitive markets, but there is considerable debate about the effectiveness of past public policy in this area. Few economists are satisfied with the government's role as a promoter of competition.

EXHIBIT 2 Rigging the market

If a group of sellers can restrict the entry of competitors and connive to reduce their own output, they can sometimes obtain more total revenue by selling fewer units. Note that the total sales revenue P_2Q_2 for the restricted supply exceeds the sales revenue P_1Q_1 for the competitive supply.

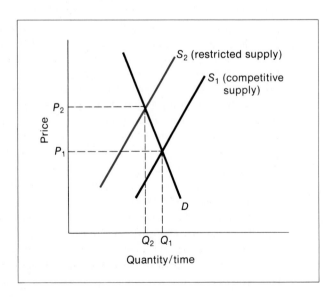

Two general criticisms are voiced. Many suggest that the government should pursue a more vigorous antitrust policy. They believe that antitrust action should be taken to expand the number of rivals in several industries—automobiles and steel, for example—that are currently dominated by a few firms. On the other hand, other critics argue that antitrust policy and business regulation, both past and present, have often, paradoxically, restricted competition. Consumers have been "protected" against *low* prices and producers from new rivals. These critics argue that government regulatory policy has been part of the problem rather than part of the solution. They believe this results from an inherent flaw in the political process—the disproportionate power of special interests.

Externalities—What Have You Been Doing to Your Neighbor?

Externalities: The side effects of an action that influence the well-being of nonconsenting parties. The nonconsenting parties may be either helped (by external benefits) or harmed (by external costs).

Production and consumption of some goods will result in spillover effects that the market will fail to register. These spillover effects, called **externalities,** are present when the actions of one individual or group affect the welfare of others without their consent.

Examples of externalities abound. If you live in an apartment house and the noisy stereo of your next-door neighbors keeps you from studying economics, your neighbors are creating an externality. Their actions are imposing an unwanted cost on you. Driving your car during rush hour increases the level of congestion, thereby imposing a cost on other motorists. If an examination is graded on the curve, cheating creates an externality inasmuch as it raises the class average.

Not all externalities result in the imposition of a cost. Sometimes human actions generate *benefits* for nonparticipating parties. The homeowner who keeps a house in good condition and maintains a neat lawn improves the beauty of the entire community, thereby benefiting community members. A flood-control project that benefits the upstream residents will also generate gain for those who live downstream. Scientific theories benefit their authors, but the knowledge gained also contributes to the welfare of others.

Why do externalities create problems for the market mechanism? Exhibit 3 can help us answer this question. With competitive markets in equilibrium, the cost of a good (including a normal profit for the producer) will be paid by consumers. Unless consumer benefits exceed the opportunity cost of production, the goods will not be produced. But what happens when externalities are present?

Suppose that a firm discharges smoke into the air or sewage into a river. Valuable resources, clean air and pure water, are utilized, but neither the firm nor the consumers of its products will pay for these costs. As Exhibit 3a shows, the supply curve will understate the opportunity cost of production when these external costs are present. Since the producer will consider only the private cost and ignore the cost imposed on secondary parties, supply curve S_1 will result. If all costs were considered, supply would be S_2. The actual supply curve S_1 will not reflect the opportunity cost of producing the good. The producer will be misled into thinking that the opportunity cost is low enough to merit an increase in supply. Output will be expanded beyond Q_2 (to Q_1), even though the community's valuation of the additional units is less than their cost. The second efficiency condition, rule 2, is violated. Inefficiency in the form of excessive air and water pollution results. In the *total* picture, the harm the pollution does outweighs the benefits to some of the people involved.

As Exhibit 3b shows, external benefits can also create problems. When they are present, the market demand curve D_1 will not fully reflect the total

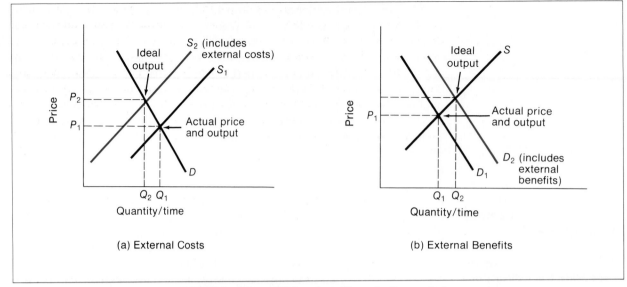

EXHIBIT 3 Externalities and problems for the market

When external costs are present (a), the output level of a product will exceed the desired amount. In contrast, market output of goods that generate external benefits (b) will be less than the ideal level.

benefits, which include those that accrue to secondary parties. Output Q_1 will result. Could the community gain from a greater output of the product? Yes. The demand curve D_2 reflects both the direct benefits of consumers and the secondary benefits bestowed on secondary parties. Expansion of output beyond Q_1 to Q_2 would result in net gain to the community. However, since neither consumers nor producers can capture the secondary benefits, consumption level Q_1 will result. The potential net gain from the greater output level Q_2 will be lost. Rule 1 of our hypothetical efficiency criterion is violated.

Competitive markets will fail to give consumers and producers the right signals when externalities are present. The market will tend to underallocate resources to the production of goods with external benefits and overallocate resources to the production of goods that impose external costs on nonconsenting parties.

Public Goods—More Problems for the Market

Public Goods: Jointly consumed goods. When consumed by one person, they are also made available to others. National defense, poetry, and scientific theories are all public goods.

Some goods cannot be provided though the marketplace because there is no way of excluding nonpaying customers. Goods that must be consumed jointly by all are called **public goods.** National defense, the judicial and legal system, and the monetary system are examples of public goods. The national defense that protects you also protects others. There is no feasible way in which national defense could be provided to some citizens but not to others. Similarly, the actions of a central monetary authority are a public good. The monetary system that influences the prices of things you buy also influences the prices and incomes of others.

Why are public goods troublesome for the market? Typically, in the marketplace, there is a direct link between consumption and payment. If you do not pay, you do not consume. Similarly, the payments of consumers provide the incentive to supply products. Public goods, however, are consumed jointly. If a public good is made available to one person, it is simultaneously made available to others. Since people cannot be excluded, their incentive to reveal their true valuation of the good is destroyed. Why would you voluntarily pay your "fair share" for national defense, the courts, or police protection if these goods were provided in the market? If others contribute a large amount, the public good will be provided pretty much regardless of what you do. If others do not pay, your actions will not make much difference anyway. Thus, each person has an incentive to opt out, to refuse to help pay voluntarily for the public good.

When everybody opts out, what happens? Not very much of the public good is produced. This is precisely why the market cannot handle public goods very well. Resources will be underallocated to the production of public goods because most people, following their self-interest, will refuse to pay for them. Due to the nature of public goods, there is often a conflict between self-interest and the public interest of economic efficiency.

Economic Instability

If markets are to function well, a stable monetary exchange system must be provided. Many market exchanges involve a time dimension. Houses, cars, consumer durables, land, buildings, equipment, and many other items are paid for over a period of months or even years. If the purchasing power of the monetary unit, the dollar in the United States, gyrated wildly, few would want to make long-term transactions, because of the uncertainty. The smooth functioning of the market would be retarded.

The government's spending and monetary policies exert a powerful influence on economic stability. If properly conducted, they can contribute to economic stability, full and efficient utilization of resources, and stable prices. However, improper stabilization policy can cause massive unemployment, rapidly rising prices, or perhaps both.

Economists are not in complete agreement on the extent to which public policy can stabilize the economy and promote full employment. They often debate the impact of various policy tools. All agree, however, that a stable economic environment is vital to a market economy. Those pursuing a course in macroeconomics will find both the potential and the limitations of government action as a stabilizing force in the economy discussed further in Part Two.

THE ECONOMICS OF COLLECTIVE ACTION

The pricing system will fail to meet our ideal efficiency standards if (a) markets are not competitive, (b) externalities are present, (c) public goods necessitate joint consumption, or (d) the aggregate economy is characterized by instability and the resultant uncertainty. If public sector action can correct these deficiencies, net gains for the community are possible. Public policy does not have to be a zero-sum game.

It is important to understand that sometimes public sector action can be expected to improve the efficiency of the market. However, it is also important to recognize that collective action is merely an alternative form of economic organization. Like the market, it is determined by human behavior and the decisions of individuals.

Public Choice Analysis: **The study of decision-making as it affects the formation and operation of collective organizations, such as governments. The discipline bridges the gap between economics and political science. In general, the principles and methodology of economics are applied to political science topics.**

If we are going to make meaningful comparisons between market allocation and collective action, we need to develop a sound theory that will help us understand both forms of economic organization. **Public choice analysis** has significantly advanced our understanding of the collective decision-making process in recent years. Something of a cross between economics and political science, public choice theory applies the principles and methodology of economics to collective choices.

In addition to their market choices, individual voters, politicians, lobbyists, and bureaucrats make "public choices" that affect many others besides themselves. In a democratic setting, individual preferences will influence the outcome of collective decisions, just as they influence outcomes in the market. The government is *not* a supra-individual that will always make decisions in the "public interest," however that nebulous term might be defined. It is merely an institution through which individuals make collective decisions and carry out activities collectively.

Public choice theory postulates that individual behavior in the political arena will be motivated by considerations similar to those that influence market behavior. If self-interest is a powerful motivator in the marketplace, there is every reason to believe it will also be a motivating factor when choices are made collectively. If market choices are influenced by changes in projected *personal* costs relative to benefits, there is every reason to expect that such changes will also influence political choices. Public choice theory, in other words, postulates that the number of saints and sinners in the two sectors will be comparable.

In analyzing the behavior of people in the marketplace, economists develop a logically consistent theory of behavior that can be tested against reality. Through theory and empirical testing we seek to explain various economic actions of decision-makers and, in general, how the market operates.

In the public sphere our purpose should be the same: to explain how the collective decision-making process really operates. This means developing a logically consistent theory linking individual behavior to collective action, analyzing the implications of that theory, and testing these implications against the events of the real world.

Since the theory of collective decision-making is not as well developed as our theory of market behavior, our conclusions will, of course, be less definitive. However, in the last 25 years, social scientists have made great strides in our understanding of resource allocation by the public sector.[1] Currently, this subject is often dealt with at a more advanced academic level. However, even on an introductory level, economic tools can be utilized to shed light on how the public sector handles economic activities.

Differences and Similarities between Market and Collective Action[2]

There are some basic characteristics that influence outcomes in both the market and the public sectors. As we have noted, there is reason to believe that the motivational factors present in both sectors are similar. However, there are basic structural differences. Voluntary exchange coordinated by prices is the

---

[1] The contributions of Kenneth Arrow, James Buchanan, Duncan Black, Anthony Downs, Mancur Olson, and Gordon Tullock have been particularly important.

[2] The "Public Choice" section of this book analyzes the topics of alternative forms of economic organization—market versus collective action—in more detail.

dominant characteristic of a market economy (although, of course, when externalities are present, involuntary exchange may also result). In a democratic setting, the dominant characteristic of collective action is majority rule, effective either directly or through legislative procedures. Let us take a look at both the differences and similarities between the two sectors.

1. Competitive Behavior Is Present in Both the Market and Public Sectors. Although the market sector is sometimes referred to as "the competitive sector," it is clear that competitive behavior is present in both sectors. Politicians compete with each other for elective office. Bureau chiefs and agency heads compete for additional taxpayer dollars. Public sector employees, like their counterparts in the private sector, compete for promotions, higher incomes, and additional power. Lobbyists compete to secure funds, favorable rulings, and legislation for the interest groups they represent. The nature of the competition and the criteria for success do differ between the two sectors. Nonetheless, both sectors must confront the reality of scarcity, and therefore the necessity of a rationing mechanism. Competitive behavior is an outgrowth of the need to ration scarce goods and resources.

2. Public Sector Organization Can Break the Individual Consumption–Payment Link. In the market, a consumer who wants to obtain a commodity must be willing to pay the price. For each person there is a one-to-one correspondence between consuming the commodity and paying the purchase price. In this respect, there is a fundamental difference between market and collective action. The government usually does not establish a one-to-one relationship between the tax bill of an individual consumer and the amount of political goods that that individual consumes.

Your tax bill will be the same whether you like or dislike the national defense, agriculture, or antipoverty policies of the government. You will be taxed for subsidies to higher education, sugarbeet growers, airlines, cultural centers, and many other **political goods**[3] regardless of whether you consume or use them. In some cases you may even be made worse off by a government program, but this fact will not alter the amount of your payment (taxes) for political goods. In other cases, you may receive very large benefits (either monetary or subjective) from a governmental action without any significant impact on your tax bill. The direct link between individual consumption of the good and individual payment for the good is not required in the public sector.

Political Good: Any good (or policy) supplied by the political process.

3. Scarcity Imposes the Aggregate Consumption–Payment Link in Both Sectors. Although the government can break the link between payment for the good and the right to consume the good for an *individual,* the reality of the *aggregate consumption–aggregate payment link* will remain. Provision of scarce goods requires the foregoing of alternatives. Someone must cover the cost of providing scarce goods regardless of the sector utilized to produce (or distribute) them. There are no free lunches in either the private or the public sector. Free goods provided in the public sector are "free" only to individuals. They are most

---

[3]"Political good" is a broad term used to designate any action supplied through the public sector. Note that political goods may be either private goods or public goods.

certainly not free from the viewpoint of society. Taxpayers must pay for goods that the government might choose to distribute free to individual consumers.

An increase in the amount of goods provided by the public sector will mean an increase in the total costs of government. More political goods will mean more taxes. Given scarcity, the link between aggregate consumption and aggregate costs of production cannot be broken by public sector action.

4. The Element of Compulsion Is Present in the Public Sector. As we have already discussed, voluntary exchange is the dominant characteristic of market organization. Except when externalities are present, involuntary exchange is absent. In the marketplace, a minority need not yield to the majority. For example, the views of the majority, even an overwhelming majority, do not prevent minority consumers from purchasing desired goods.

Governments possess an exclusive right to the use of coercion. Large corporations like Exxon and General Motors are economically powerful, but they cannot require you to buy their products. In contrast, if the majority (either directly or through the legislative process) decides on a particular policy, the minority must accept the policy and help pay for its costs, even if that minority strongly disagrees. If representative legislative policy allocates $10 billion for the development of a superweapon system, the dissenting minority is required to pay taxes that will help finance the project. Other dissenting minorities will be compelled to pay taxes for the support of welfare programs, farm subsidies, foreign aid, or hundreds of other projects on which reasonable people will surely differ. When issues are decided in the public sector, dissidents must, at least temporarily, yield to the current dominant view.

The right to compel is sometimes necessary to promote social cooperation. For example, legislation compelling individuals to stop when the traffic light turns red or to drive on the right side of the road clearly enhances the safety of us all. Thus, sometimes it will be possible to increase social cooperativeness and even expand the available options by public sector actions or policies that place some limitation on our choices.

5. When Collective Decisions Are Made Legislatively, Voters Must Choose among Candidates Who Represent a Bundle of Positions on Issues. The legislative voter cannot choose the views of Representative Free Lunch on poverty and business welfare and simultaneously choose the views of challenger Ms. Austerity on national defense and tariffs. Inability to separate a candidate's views on one issue from his or her views on another greatly reduces the voter's power to register preferences on specific issues. Since the average representative is asked to vote on approximately 2000 different issues during a two-year term, the size of the problem is obvious.

To the average individual, choosing a representative is a bit like choosing an agent who will both control a substantial portion of one's income and regulate one's activities. The specific agent preferred by an individual voter may or may not be elected. The voter's agent will be only one voice within the legislative body that will make many decisions that affect the voter's welfare. Simultaneously, the agent has the responsibility to represent hundreds of thousands of other persons on each legislative issue. There is no way that the agent can articulate the positions of both group A and group B on a specific issue. Similarly, it will be impossible for the voter to select one agent to represent views on issue X and another agent to represent views on issue Y. As a result of the "bundle-purchase" nature of the political process, the likelihood that a collective decision will reflect the precise views of an individual voter is low.

6. Income and Power Are Distributed Differently in the Two Sectors. In the marketplace, individuals who supply more highly valued resources have larger incomes. The number of dollar votes available to an individual reflect her or his abilities, ambitions, skills, perceptiveness, inheritance, and good fortune, among other things. An unequal distribution of consumer power results.

In the public sector, ballots call the tune when decisions are made democratically. One citizen, one vote is the rule. However, this does not mean that political goods and services—those resources that make up political power or political income—are allocated equally to all citizens by the collective decision-making process. Some individuals are much more astute than others at using the political process to obtain personal advantage. The political process rewards those who are most capable of delivering votes—not only their own individual votes but those of others as well. Persuasive skills (i.e., lobbying, public speaking, public relations), organizational abilities, finances, and knowledge are vital to success in the political arena. Persons who have more of these resources can expect to benefit more handsomely, in terms of both money and power, from the political process than individuals who lack them.

The Supply of and Demand for Public Sector Action

In the marketplace, consumers demand goods with their dollar votes. Producers supply goods. The actions of both are influenced by personal self-interest. In a democratic political system, voters and legislators are counterparts to consumers and producers. Voters demand political goods with their political resources—votes, lobbying, contributions, and organizational abilities. Vote-conscious legislators are suppliers of political goods.

How does a voter decide which political supplier to support? Many things influence the voter's decision, but personal self-interest surely must be high on the list. Will the policies of Senator Snodgrass or those of the challenger, Ms. Good Deal, help *me* most? Where do they stand on the major issues? What are their views on those issues that may seem unimportant to others but are of vital importance to *me?* Are they likely to raise or lower *my* taxes? All of these factors influence the voter's personal benefits and costs from public sector action. Economic theory suggests that they influence choices among the candidates.

Other things constant, voters will support those candidates whom they expect to provide them with the most benefits, net of costs. The greater the expected gains from a candidate's election, the more voters will do to ensure the candidate's success. A voter, like the consumer in the marketplace, will ask the supplier, "What can you do for me and how much will it cost?"

The goal of the political supplier is to put together a majority coalition—to win the election. Vote-seeking politicians, like profit-conscious business decision-makers, will have a strong incentive to cater to the views of their constituents. The easiest way to win votes, both politically and financially, is to give the constituents, or at least appear to give them, what they want. A politician who pays no heed to the views of his or her constituents is as rare as a business-person selling castor oil at a football game.

There are two major reasons that voters are likely to turn to public sector economic organization: (1) to reduce waste and inefficiency stemming from non-competitive markets, externalities, public goods, and economic instability and (2) to redistribute income. Public sector action that corrects, or appears to correct, the shortcomings of the market will be attractive. If properly conducted, it will generate more benefits to the community than costs. Much real-world public policy is motivated by a desire to correct the shortcomings of the market. Anti-trust action is designed to promote competition. Government provision of national defense, crime prevention, a legal system, and flood-control projects is related to the public-good nature of these activities. Similarly, externalities account for public sector action in such areas as pollution control, education, pure research, and no-fault insurance. Clearly, the tax, spending, and monetary policies of the government are utilized to influence the level of economic activity in most Western nations.

Demand for public sector action may also stem from a desire to change the income distribution. There is no reason to presume that the unhampered market will lead to the most desirable distribution of income. In fact, the ideal distribution of income is largely a matter of personal preference. There is nothing in positive economics that tells us that one distribution of income is better than another. Some persons may desire to see more income allocated to low-income citizens. The most common scientific argument for redistribution to the poor is based on the "public-good" nature of adequate income for all. Alleviation of poverty may help not only the poor but also those who are well-off. Middle- and upper-income recipients, for example, may benefit if the less fortunate members of the community enjoy better food, clothing, housing, and health care. If the rich would gain, why will they not voluntarily give to the poor? For the same reason that individuals will do little to provide national defense volun-tarily. The antipoverty efforts of any single individual will exert little impact on the total amount of poverty in the community. Because individual action is so insignificant, each person has an incentive to opt out. When everybody opts out, the market provides less than the desired amount of antipoverty action.

Others may desire public sector redistribution for less altruistic reasons—they may seek to enhance their own personal incomes. Sometimes redistribution will take the form of direct income transfers. In other cases, the redistribution strategy may be indirect; it may simply increase the demand for one's service. Regardless of the mechanism, higher taxes will generally accompany income redistribution.

Substantial income redistribution may adversely affect the efficiency of resource allocation and the incentive to produce. There are three major reasons why large-scale redistribution is likely to reduce the size of the economic pie. First, such redistribution weakens the link between productive activity and reward. When taxes take a larger share of one's income, the benefits derived from hard work and productive service are reduced. The basic economic postulate suggests that when the benefits allocated to producers are lowered (and benefits of nonproducers are raised), less productive effort will be supplied. Second, as public policy redistributes a larger share of income, individuals will allocate

Rent Seeking: Actions by individuals and interest groups designed to restructure public policy in a manner that will either directly or indirectly redistribute more income to themselves.

more resources to **rent seeking.**[4] Rent seeking is a term used by economists to classify actions designed to change public policy—tax structure, composition of spending, or regulation—in a manner that will redistribute income to oneself. Resources allocated to rent seeking (perhaps "favor seeking" would be more descriptive) will be unavailable to increase the size of the economic pie. Third, higher taxes to finance income redistribution and an expansion in rent-seeking activities will generate a response. Taxpayers will be encouraged to take steps to protect their income. More accountants, lawyers, and tax shelter experts will be retained as people seek to limit the amount of their income that is redistributed to others. Like the resources allocated to rent seeking, resources allocated to protecting one's wealth from public policy will also be wasted. They will not be available for productive activity. Therefore, given the incentive structure generated by large-scale redistributional policies, there is good reason to expect that such policies will reduce the size of the economic pie.

CONFLICTS BETWEEN GOOD ECONOMICS AND GOOD POLITICS

What reason is there for believing that political action will result in economic inefficiency? Current economic and political research is continually yielding knowledge that will help us to answer this question more definitively. We deal with it in more detail in a later chapter, but three important characteristics of the political process are introduced here.

1. The Rationally Ignorant Voter. Less than one-half of the American electorate can correctly identify the names of their congressmen and women, much less state where their representatives stand on various issues. Why are so many people ignorant of the simplest facts regarding the political process? The explanation does not lie with a lack of intelligence of the average American. The phenomenon is explained by the incentives confronting the voter. Most citizens recognize that their vote is unlikely to determine the outcome of an election. Since their vote is highly unlikely to resolve the issue at hand, citizens have little incentive to seek costly information in order to cast an intelligent vote. Economists refer to this lack of incentive as the **rational ignorance effect.**

Rational Ignorance Effect: Voter ignorance that is present because individuals perceive their votes as unlikely to be decisive. Voters rationally have little incentive to inform themselves so as to cast an intelligent vote.

The rationally ignorant voter is merely exercising good judgment as to how her or his time and effort will yield the most benefits. There is a parallel between the voter's failure to acquire political knowledge and the farmer's inattention to the factors that determine the weather. Weather is probably the most important factor determining the income of an individual farmer, yet it makes no sense for the farmer to invest time and resources attempting to understand and alter the weather. An improved knowledge of the weather system will probably not enable the farmer to avoid its adverse effects. So it is with the average voter. The average voter stands to gain little from acquiring more information about a wide range of issues that are decided in the political arena.

[4]See James M. Buchanan, Robert D. Tollison, and Gordon Tullock, *Toward a Theory of the Rent-Seeking Society* (College Station: Texas A & M University Press, 1981), for additional detail on rent seeking.

Since the resolution of these issues, like the weather, is out of their hands, voters have little incentive to become more informed.

Thus, most voters simply rely on information that is supplied to them freely by candidates and the mass media. Conversations with friends and information acquired at work, from newspapers, from TV news, and from political advertising are especially important because the voter has so little incentive to incur any personal information-gathering cost. Few voters are able to describe accurately the consequences of, for example, raising tariffs on automobiles or abolishing the farm price support program. This should not surprise us. In using their time and efforts in ways other than studying these policy issues, they are merely responding to economic incentives.[5]

Special Interest Issue: An issue that generates substantial *individual* benefits to a small minority while imposing a small *individual* cost on other voters. In total, the net cost to the majority might either exceed or fall short of the net benefits to the special interest group.

2. The Problem of Special Interest. A **special interest issue** is one that generates substantial personal benefits for a small number of constituents while imposing a small individual cost on a large number of other voters. A few gain a great deal *individually,* whereas a large number lose a little *as individuals.*

Special interest issues are very attractive to vote-conscious politicians (that is, to those most eager and most likely to win elections). Voters who have a small cost imposed on them by a policy favoring a special interest will not care enough about the issue to examine it, particularly if it is complex enough that the imposition of the cost is difficult to identify. Because of the cost of information, most of those harmed will not even be aware of the legislator's views on such an issue. Most voters will simply ignore special interest issues. The special interests, however, will be vitally concerned. They will let the candidate (or legislator) know how important an issue is to them. They will help politicians, both financially and otherwise, who favor their position, and will oppose those who do not.

What would you do if you wanted to win an election? Support the special interest groups. Milk them for financial resources. Use those resources to "educate" the uninformed majority of voters about how you support policies that are in their interest. You would have an incentive to follow this path even if the total community benefits from the support of the special interest were less than the cost. The policy might cause economic inefficiency, but it could still be a political winner.

Why stand up for a large majority? Even though the total cost may be very large, each person bears only a small cost. Most voters are uninformed on the issue. They do not care much about it. They would do little to help you get elected even if you supported their best interests on this issue. Astute politicians will support the special interest group if they plan to be around for very long.

The political process tends to be biased in favor of special interest groups. There is thus sometimes a conflict between good politics and ideal public policy. Throughout, as we consider public policy alternatives, we will remind you to consider how public policy is likely to operate when special interest influence is strong.

3. Political Gains from Shortsighted Policies. The complexity of many issues makes it difficult for voters to identify the future benefits and costs. Will a tax

---

[5]Anthony Downs, in *An Economic Theory of Democracy* (New York: Harper, 1958), and Gordon Tullock, in *Toward a Mathematics of Politics* (Ann Arbor: University of Michigan Press, 1967), among others, have emphasized this point.

cut reduce the long-run rate of unemployment? Are wage–price controls an efficient means of dealing with inflation? Can pro-union legislation raise the real wages of workers? These questions are complex. Few voters will analyze the short-run and long-run implications of policy in these areas. Thus, voters will have a tendency to rely on current conditions. To the voter, the best indicator of the success of a policy is, How are things now?

OUTSTANDING ECONOMIST
James Buchanan (1919–   )

Twenty-five years ago, most economists were content to concentrate on the workings of the marketplace, its shortcomings, and what government action might do to correct these deficiencies. Both political scientists and economists envisioned the public sector as a type of supra-individual, a creature making decisions in the public interest. James Buchanan set out to change all of this. He, perhaps more than anyone else, is responsible for what some have called the "public choice revolution."

Buchanan perceives government to be an outgrowth of individual behavior. Individual human beings are the ultimate choice-makers, shaping and molding group action as well as private affairs. By means of the tools of economics, theories are developed to explain how the political process works. Real-world data are used to test the theories. Buchanan's approach is that of scientific politics.

Noting that approximately 40 percent of every dollar earned in the United States in channeled through the public sector, Buchanan argues:

It just doesn't make any sense to concentrate, as traditional economic theory does, on the 60 percent of your income and product that's related to the private sector and to provide no explanation of why the remainder is used in the way it is. So the extension of the highly sophisticated tools of analysis that economics has developed over the past 200 years to the realm of political choices was a natural and logical one.[6]

In their widely acclaimed book, *The Calculus of Consent,*[7] Buchanan and Gordon Tullock develop a theory of constitutions and analyze

---

[6]Quoted in Judith Scott-Epley, "From Constitutions to Car Inspections: Looking for a Better Way," *Virginia Tech Magazine* (September/October 1981), p. 230.

[7]J.M. Buchanan and G. Tullock, *The Calculus of Consent* (Ann Arbor: University of Michigan Press, 1962).

political behavior under alternative decision rules (for example, simple majority, legislative procedure, etc.). With the individual always used as the foundation of the analysis, they develop theories concerning special interests, logrolling, and the types of activities that are most likely to be provided through the public sector. Empirical work testing many·of the implications of the book continues today. In a more recent book, *The Limits of Liberty,*[8] which Buchanan considers complementary to the earlier book with Tullock, Buchanan applies his individualistic perspective to explain the emergence of property rights, law, and government itself, with a view toward unraveling some of the problems of the 1970s.

A past president of the Southern Economic Association, Buchanan has also written widely on externalities, public goods, and public finance. His doctoral degree is from the University of Chicago, and he is a member of the Mont Pelerin Society. He taught at Florida State, Virginia, UCLA, and Virginia Polytechnic Institute before accepting his present position as Distinguished Professor of Economics and general director of the Center for the Study of Public Choice at George Mason University.

---

[8]J.M. Buchanan, *The Limits of Liberty* (Chicago: University of Chicago Press, 1975).

Political entrepreneurs seeking to win an election have a strong incentive to support policies that generate current benefits in exchange for future costs, particularly if the future costs will be difficult to identify on election day. Therefore, public sector action will be biased in favor of legislation that offers immediate (and easily identifiable) current benefits in exchange for future costs that are complex and difficult to identify. Simultaneously, there is a bias against legislation that involves immediate and easily identifiable costs (for example, higher taxes) while yielding future benefits that are complex and difficult to identify. Economists refer to this bias inherent in the collective decision-making process as the **shortsightedness effect**.

Shortsightedness Effect: Mis-allocation of resources that results because public sector action is biased (a) in favor of proposals yielding clearly defined current benefits in exchange for difficult-to-identify future costs and (b) against proposals with clearly identifiable current costs yielding less concrete and less obvious future benefits.

The nature of democratic institutions restricts the planning horizon of elected officials. Positive results must be observable by the next election, or the incumbent is likely to be replaced by someone who promises more rapid results. Policies that will *eventually* pay off in the future (after the next election) will have little attractiveness to vote-seeking politicians if those policies do not exert a beneficial impact by election day. As we shall subsequently see, the short-sighted nature of the political process reduces the likelihood that governments will be able to promote economic stability and a noninflationary environment.

What if shortsighted policies lead to serious problems after an election? This can be sticky for politicians; but is it not better to be an *officeholder* explaining why things are in a mess than a *defeated candidate* trying to convince people who will not listen why you were right all the time? The political entrepreneur has a strong incentive to win the next election and worry about what is right later.

LOOKING AHEAD

In the following chapter, we will take a look at the government's actual spending and tax policies. In subsequent chapters, the significance of economic organization and issues of political economy will be highlighted. The tools of economics are used with a dual objective. We will attempt to point out what government *ideally should do,* but we will also focus on what we can *expect government to do.* Not surprisingly, these two are not always identical. Political economy—the use of economic tools to explain how both the market and the public sectors actually work—is a fascinating subject. It helps us to understand the "why" behind many of today's current events. Who said economics is the dismal science?

CHAPTER LEARNING OBJECTIVES

1 Two conditions must be met to achieve economic efficiency: (a) All activities that produce more benefits than costs for the individuals within an economy must be undertaken, and (b) activities that generate more costs to the individuals than benefits must not be undertaken. If only the buyer and seller are affected, production and exchange in competitive markets are consistent with the ideal-efficiency criteria.

2 Lack of competition may make it possible for a group of sellers to gain by restricting output and raising prices. There is a conflict between (a) the self-interest of sellers that leads them to collude, restrict output, and raise product prices above their production costs and (b) economic efficiency. Public sector action—promoting competition or regulating private firms—may be able to improve economic efficiency in industries in which competitive pressures are lacking.

3 The market will tend to underallocate resources to the production of goods with

external benefits and overallocate resources to those products that generate external costs.

4 Public goods are troublesome for the market to handle because nonpaying customers cannot easily be excluded. Since the amount of a public good that each individual receives is largely unaffected by whether he or she helps pay for it, most individuals will contribute little. Thus, the market will tend to undersupply public goods.

5 The public sector can improve the operation of markets by providing a stable economic environment.

6 The public sector is an alternative means of organizing economic activity. Public sector decision-making will reflect the choices of individuals acting as voters, politicians, financial contributors, lobbyists, and bureaucrats. Public choice analysis applies the principles and methodology of economics to group decision-making in an effort to help us understand collective organizations.

7 Successful political candidates will seek to offer programs that voters favor. Voters, in turn, will be attracted to candidates who reflect the voters' own views and interests. In a democratic setting, there are two major reasons why voters will turn to collective organization: (a) to reduce waste and inefficiency stemming from noncompetitive markets, externalities, public goods, and economic instability and (b) to alter the income distribution.

8 Public sector action may sometimes improve the market's efficiency and lead to an increase in the community's welfare, all individuals considered. However, the political process is likely to conflict with ideal economic efficiency criteria when (a) voters have little knowledge of an issue, (b) special interests are strong, and/or (c) political figures can gain from following shortsighted policies.

THE ECONOMIC WAY OF THINKING—DISCUSSION QUESTIONS

1 Explain in your own words what is meant by external costs and external benefits. Why may market allocations be less than ideal when externalities are present?

2 If producers are to be provided with an incentive to produce a good, why is it important for them to be able to prevent nonpaying customers from receiving the good?

3 Do you think that real-world politicians adopt political positions in order to help their election prospects? Can you name a current political figure who consistently puts "principles above politics"? If so, check with three of your classmates and see if they agree.

4 Do you think that special interest groups exert much influence on local government? Why or why not? As a test, check the composition of the local zoning board in your community. How many real estate agents, contractors, developers, and landlords are on the board? Are there any citizens without real estate interests on the board?

5 "Economics is a positive science. Government by its very nature is influenced by philosophical considerations. Therefore, the tools of economics cannot tell us much about how the public sector works." Do you agree or disagree? Why?

6 Which of the following are public goods: (a) an antimissile system surrounding Washington, D.C., (b) a fire department, (c) tennis courts, (d) Yellowstone National Park, (e) elementary schools?

7 "Political organization cannot reform human beings. We should not expect it to. The public sector is an alternative to the market. Political organization will influence the direction of human action primarily by modifying the incentive structure. For some types of activity, public sector organization is likely to improve on the market, and for others, the market is likely to be superior." Do you agree or disagree? Why?

PART TWO

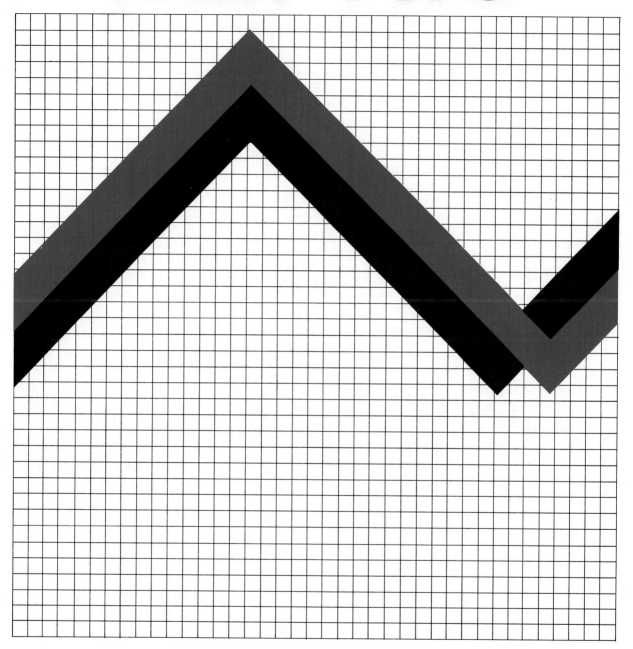

MACROECONOMICS

TAKING THE NATION'S ECONOMIC PULSE

Ours is a society that is infatuated with measurement. We seek to measure everything from the figure of Miss America to the speed of Goose Gossage's fastball. Therefore, the fact that we have devised methods for measuring something as important as the performance of our economy is not surprising. However, it is surprising that we waited so long to do so. In the early 1930s, the Department of Commerce for the first time systematically developed and published data on the performance of the economy. Before that, there were no generally accepted methods or procedures for taking "the pulse of our economy."

MICRO- AND MACROECONOMICS

As we examine the nation's economic pulse, we must keep in mind that the gross national product (GNP) is primarily a macroeconomic concept. That is, it deals with more than one producing or consuming unit.

In Chapter 3, we discussed how the forces of supply and demand interact to influence the output level of a specific commodity. Analysis that focuses on a single commodity, or at most a single industry, is referred to as **microeconomics**. The unit of analysis in microeconomics is one single producing or consuming unit. For example, in microeconomic analysis we examine the price of oil or the demand for wheat instead of focusing on general price levels or total demand for all goods and services in the economy.

Macroeconomics, like microeconomics, is concerned with markets, prices, and the determination of equilibrium; but in macroeconomics, the markets are

Microeconomics: That branch of economics that focuses on the determination of price, output, and equilibrium in narrowly defined markets, such as the market for a specific product or resource.

Macroeconomics: That branch of economics that focuses on the economy as a whole or on highly aggregated markets. Macroeconomics examines such factors as total demand for all goods and services in the economy or total employment in the economy.

[1]Kenneth Boulding, "Fun and Games with the Gross National Product—The Role of Misleading Indicators in Social Policy," in *The Environmental Crisis,* ed. Harold W. Helfrich, Jr. (New Haven, Connecticut: Yale University Press, 1970), p. 157.

considered together as a whole. For example, we might deal with the market for all current goods and services as a single entity, even though this market contains commodities ranging from apples to education. Macroeconomics deals with the overall picture—what determines the level of aggregate income, output, and employment in the economy as a whole.

Although macroeconomics focuses on aggregated markets, changes that affect the decisions of microunits (individual firms, consumers, and workers, for example) are still important. Many contemporary economists believe that in the past some macroeconomic theories failed to recognize the significance of changes in the behavior of microunits. Therefore, even though we will be focusing on highly aggregated markets, we will continue to pay heed to such microeconomic factors as changes in individual prices and the incentives confronting persons who make decisions at the microlevel. In the following pages we will learn to measure the pulse of the entire economy. While this is clearly a macroeconomic view, we must remember that the overall pulse is made up of millions of individual pulses lumped together.

THE CONCEPT OF GNP

Gross National Product: The total market value of all final-product goods and services produced during a specific period, usually a year.

The **gross national product** is a measure of the market value of all final goods and services produced during a specific time period. GNP is a "flow" concept and is typically measured in terms of an annual rate. It is designed to measure the market value of production that flows through the economy's factories and shops each year. Thus, GNP is similar to a water gauge that measures the amount of water that flows through a pipe each hour.

What Counts toward GNP?

The gross national product includes only currently produced final goods measured in dollars. Since measurement is restricted to *current production*, many transactions that take place in the country have to be excluded.

1. Only Final Goods Count. A *final good* is a good in the hands of its ultimate user. Goods go through many stages of production. But GNP counts only the dollar market value of all final goods and services produced during a year.

Exhibit 1 will help to clarify this important point. Before the final good, bread, is in the hands of the consumer, it will go through several stages of production. The farmer produces a pound of wheat and sells it to the miller for 20 cents. The miller grinds the wheat into flour and sells it to the baker for 35 cents. The miller's actions have added 15 cents to the value of the wheat. The baker combines the flour with other ingredients, makes a loaf of bread, and sells it to the grocer for 60 cents. The baker has added 25 cents to the value of the bread. The grocer stocks the bread on the grocery shelf and provides a convenient location for consumers to shop. The grocer sells the loaf of bread for 60 cents, adding 9 cents to the value of the final product. Only the market value of the final product—69 cents for the loaf of bread—is counted by GNP. The market value of the final product is the amount added to the value of the good at each stage of production—the 20 cents added by the farmer, the 15 cents added by the miller, the 25 cents added by the baker, and the 9 cents added by the grocer.

If the market value of the product at each intermediate stage of produc-

EXHIBIT 1   GNP and stages of production

Most goods go through several stages of production. This chart illustrates both the market value of a loaf of bread as it passes through the various stages of production (column 1) and the amount added to the value of the bread by each intermediate producer (column 2). GNP counts only the market value of the final product. Of course, the amount added by each intermediate producer (column 2) sums to the market value of the final product.

Stages of Production	Market Value of the Product (Dollars) (1)	Amount Added to the Value of the Product (Dollars) (2)
Stage 1: farmer's wheat	0.20	0.20
Stage 2: miller's flour	0.35	0.15
Stage 3: baker's bread (wholesale)	0.60	0.25
Stage 4: grocer's bread (retail)	0.69	0.09
Amount added to GNP		0.69

tion (for example, the sum of column 1) were added to GNP, double counting would result. GNP would overstate the value of the final products available to consumers. To avoid this problem, GNP includes only the value of final goods and services.

2. Only Goods Produced during the Period Count.   Keep in mind that GNP is a measure of current production. Therefore, exchanges of goods or assets produced during a preceding period do not contribute to current GNP.

The purchase of a used car produced last year will not enhance current GNP, nor will the sale of a "used" home constructed five years ago. Production of these goods was counted at the time they were produced. Current sales and purchases of such items merely involve the exchange of existing goods. Since they do not involve current production of additional goods, they are not counted in GNP.

Purchases or sales of stocks, bonds, and U.S. securities also do not count in GNP for the same reason. They represent exchange of current assets, not production of additional goods. The same can be said of private gifts and government transfer payments like welfare and social security. They are not counted because they do not enhance current production.

3. Goods and Services Are Measured in Dollars.   Literally millions of different commodities and services are produced each year. How can the production of houses, movies, legal services, education, automobiles, dresses, heart transplants, astrological services, and many other items be added together? These vastly different commodities and services have only one thing in common: someone pays for each of them in terms of dollars. Dollars act as a common denominator; units of each different good are weighted according to their dollar selling price. For example, production of an automobile adds 80 times as much to GNP as production of a briefcase, since the new automobile sells for $8,000 compared to $100 for the new briefcase. The total spending on all final goods produced during the year is summed, in dollar terms, to obtain the annual GNP.

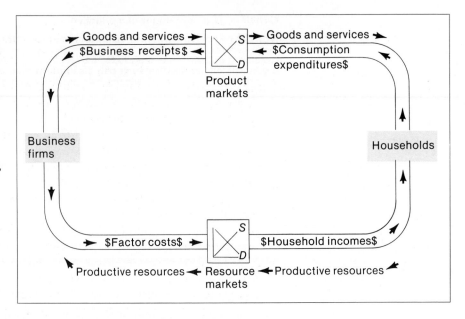

The Circular Flow of Expenditures and Resource Costs

There are two ways of looking at GNP, as shown in Exhibit 2. Only two economic sectors, businesses and households, are included in this simple model. The dollar flow of expenditures and receipts is demonstrated within the circular flow diagram. The flow of real products and resources is indicated by the arrows outside the circular flow loops. Goods and services produced in the business sector are sold to consumers in the household sector. Households supply the factors of production and receive income payments in exchange for their services. In turn, all the income of households is expended on the purchase of goods and services.

The bottom loop of Exhibit 2 illustrates the dollar flow of factor cost payments (wages, rents, interest, and profits) from the business sector to the household sector in exchange for productive resources (labor, land, capital equipment, and entrepreneurship). These factor payments constitute the income of households. The price of the productive resources is determined by the forces of supply and demand operating in resource markets. Businesses utilize the services of the productive resources to produce goods and services.

The top loop of Exhibit 2 illustrates the dollar flow of consumer expenditures from households to businesses in exchange for goods and services. Business firms derive their revenues from the sale of products (food, clothing, medical services, and so forth) that they supply to households. The prices of these goods and services are determined in product markets.

TWO MEASURES OF GNP AND WHY THEY ARE EQUAL

The GNP of the simple two-sector economy depicted in Exhibit 2 can be measured in two ways. First, it can be calculated by adding up the total expenditures on the final goods and services supplied to household–consumer units (the top loop of Exhibit 2). The dollar flow of these consumer expenditures on goods and services is equal to the GNP of this two-sector economy.

Second, GNP can be determined by adding up the total cost of supplying the goods and services, including the residual–income profit of the producer—entrepreneurs (the bottom loop of Exhibit 1). Business revenues derived from the sale of goods and services will be either paid to resource suppliers or held by capitalist—entrepreneurs in the form of profits. Therefore, the two methods of calculating GNP will yield identical outcomes. Note that profits are considered a cost of production. Business decision makers would be unwilling to supply the capital assets utilized in the production process and undertake the risk of loss if they did not anticipate being rewarded with profit. Similarly, wage payments induce workers to supply labor services. Both wages and profits are necessary to induce decision makers to engage in the production process.

Of course, modern economies are much more complicated than our simple two-sector circular flow model. The model does not yet include the actions of government, foreign economies, or investment by businesses. These factors will be examined in later chapters. Nonetheless, the general principle still holds. Gross national product can be determined by either (a) summing the total expenditures on the final-product goods and services produced during a period or (b) summing the total cost incurred as a result of producing the goods and services supplied during the period. GNP obtained by adding up the dollar value of final goods and services purchased will equal GNP obtained by adding up the total of all "cost" items, including the producer's profits, associated with the production of final goods. Exhibit 3 summarizes the components of GNP for both the expenditure approach and the resource cost—income approach.

From an accounting viewpoint, the total payments to the factors of production, including the producer's profit or loss, must be equal to the sale price generated by the good. This is true for each good or service produced, and it is also true for the aggregate economy. It is a fundamental accounting identity.

The Expenditure Approach

As Exhibit 3 indicates, when the expenditure approach is used to calculate GNP, four basic components of final products purchased must be considered. The left side of Exhibit 4 presents the value of these four components of GNP for 1980.

EXHIBIT 3 The two ways of measuring GNP

Even though modern economies are far more complicated than the two-sector circular flow model of Exhibit 1, there are still two methods of calculating GNP. It can be calculated by either summing the expenditures on the final-product goods and services of each sector (left side of chart) or summing the costs associated with the production of these goods and services (right side of chart).

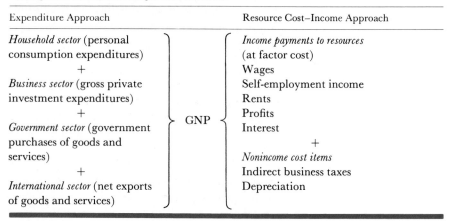

Expenditure Approach		Resource Cost–Income Approach
Household sector (personal consumption expenditures)		*Income payments to resources* (at factor cost)
+		Wages
Business sector (gross private investment expenditures)		Self-employment income
		Rents
+	GNP	Profits
Government sector (government purchases of goods and services)		Interest
		+
+		*Nonincome cost items*
International sector (net exports of goods and services)		Indirect business taxes
		Depreciation

EXHIBIT 4 Two ways of measuring GNP—1981 data (billions of dollars)

The left side shows the flow of expenditures and the right side the flow of resource costs. Both procedures yield GNP.

Expenditure Approach			Resource Cost– Income Approach	
Personal consumption		1858	Employee compensation	1772
Durable goods	232		Proprietors' income	135
Nondurable goods	743			
Services	883		Rents	34
			Corporate profits	192
Gross private investment		450		
Fixed investment	434		Interest income	215
Inventories	16			
			Indirect business taxes	
Government purchases		591	(includes transfers)	255
Federal	230			
State and local	361		Depreciation (capital	
			consumption)	322
Net exports		26		
Gross national product		2925	Gross national product	2925

U.S. Department of Commerce. These data are also available in the *Federal Reserve Bulletin,* which is published monthly.

1. Consumption Purchases. Personal consumption purchases are the largest component of GNP. In 1981 they amounted to $1858 billion. Most consumption expenditures are for nondurable goods or services. Items such as food, clothing, medical services, and education are included in this category. These items are used up or consumed in a relatively short time. Durable goods, such as appliances and automobiles, are also part of consumption and are enjoyed over a longer period, even though they are fully counted at the time they are purchased.

2. Investment Purchases. Investment or capital goods provide a flow of *future* consumption or production services. Unlike food or medical services, they are not immediately used. A house is an investment good because it will provide a stream of services long into the future. Similarly, business plants and equipment are investment goods because they, too, will provide productive services in the future. Changes in business inventories are also classified as an investment good, since they will provide future consumer benefits. It is important to note that this last component of investment purchases fluctuates substantially. When business conditions are improving, inventories often decline. On the other hand, during a recession, inventories sometimes increase rapidly because firms are unable to sell all of their current production. In 1981, for example, total investment expenditures were $450 billion, including a $16 billion expansion in inventory stock.

3. Government Purchases. The government component includes both investment and consumption services. Items such as education, police protection, national defense, and government buildings are included in this category. Since transfer payments are excluded from this account, the amount actually spent by the government on goods and services is smaller than its total expenditures.

4. Net Exports. Exports are domestic goods and services purchased by foreigners. Imports are foreign goods and services purchased domestically. To measure GNP in terms of total purchases, we (a) add the dollar value of domestic goods purchased by foreigners and (b) subtract the dollar value of foreign goods purchased by Americans.

$$\text{Net exports} = \text{total exports} - \text{total imports}$$

The Resource Cost–Income Approach

Exhibit 4 shows how, rather than adding up the flow of expenditures on final goods and services, we could add up the flow of costs incurred in their production. Let's take a closer look at each of these costs.

1. Employee Compensation. Labor services play a very important role in the production process. Thus, it is not surprising that employee compensation, $1772 billion in 1981, is the largest cost incurred in the production of goods and services.

2. Proprietors' Income. Self-employed proprietors undertake the risks of owning their own businesses and simultaneously provide their own labor services to the firm. Their earnings in 1981 contributed $135 billion to GNP, 4.6 percent of the total. Together, employees and self-employed proprietors accounted for two-thirds of GNP.

3. Rents. Machines, buildings, land, and other physical assets also contribute to the production process. Rents, corporate profits, and interest are payments to persons who provide either physical resources or the financial resources with which to purchase physical assets. For example, rents are payments to resource owners who permit others to utilize their assets during a time period.

4. Corporate Profits. Corporate profits are compensation earned by stockholders who both bear the risk of the business undertaking and provide the financial resources with which the firm purchases resources.

5. Interest. Interest is a payment to parties who extend loans to producers. Not all cost components of GNP result in an income payment to a resource supplier. There are two major indirect costs.

6. Indirect Business Taxes. Taxes, such as sales and excise taxes, are imposed on the sale of many goods. These taxes are clearly passed on to the consumer. Indirect business taxes are directly included in the price of goods when GNP is calculated by the expenditure approach. They are a cost of doing business when looked at from the factor cost viewpoint.

7. Depreciation. Utilizing machines to produce goods causes the machines to wear out. Thus, capital is "used up" in the production process. Depreciation of capital is a cost of producing current goods. In 1981, depreciation amounted to $322 billion or approximately 11 percent of GNP.

Gross National Income or Gross National Cost?

As indicated by Exhibit 4, both the cost and the expenditure approaches lead to the same estimate of GNP, $2925 billion in 1981. They are simply two ways of calculating the same thing. Considering the two approaches together helps to keep the GNP in perspective. From the purchaser's viewpoint, it is indeed a gross national product. "Good things," as seen through the eyes of a purchaser, were produced and households, investors, foreigners, or the government paid for them. However, production also involves costs. The owners of labor services, capital goods, and managerial skills made the sacrifices necessary to bring the final products into existence. Viewed from the producer's position, GNP might be better termed a gross national cost, since resource owners had to forego things in order to produce goods and services. Stated another way, the actual total supply of goods and services to the various sectors of the economy must be equal to the actual total income of resource suppliers.

Total output (supply) and total income are merely alternative methods of viewing the same thing. Aggregate output is the value of the final-user goods and services supplied to the household, business, government, and foreign sectors during the period. Aggregate income is the sum of the payments to the resource suppliers who produced those goods. They must equal one another.

The Real Income– Real Output Link

The two methods of measuring GNP also highlight the linkage between real output and real income. National income accounting methods illustrate that the flow of goods and services to the household, business, government, and foreign sectors must equal the flow of income to the resource suppliers. Obviously, since aggregate output and aggregate income must be equal, one cannot change without the other changing. The only way in which a nation can increase its real income is to increase its real output. Unless there is an expansion in the production of goods and services valued by consumers, businesses, governments, and foreigners, there will not be an expansion in the real income of a nation. Growth of real income is entirely dependent on the growth of real output.

When evaluating policy alternatives designed to stimulate the growth of income, one must keep the link between aggregate income and aggregate output clearly in focus. Proponents of such policies as tax reductions, public-sector employment, higher minimum wages, and increased unionization generally argue that their proposals will lead to either a higher level of income or more rapid economic growth. In evaluating these and other policy alternatives, the careful researcher will ask, "How will the proposal affect output?" Unless there is a reason to believe that the policy will stimulate the production of desired goods and services, it will not increase income.

DEPRECIATION AND NET NATIONAL PRODUCT

The inclusion of depreciation in GNP points out that it is indeed a "gross" rather than a "net" measure of economic production. Since GNP fails to make an allowance for capital goods that wear out during the year, it overstates the net output of an economy.

Net National Product: Gross national product minus a depreciation allowance for the wearing out of machines and buildings during the period.

The **net national product** (NNP) is a concept designed to correct this deficiency. NNP is the total market value of consumption and government goods and services produced plus any net additions to the nation's capital stock.

In accounting terms, net national product is simply GNP minus depreciation.

Since NNP counts only the net additions to the nation's capital stock, it is less than GNP. Net investment—the additions to capital stock—is always equal to gross investment minus depreciation. NNP counts only net investment.

OTHER RELATED INCOME MEASURES

Although GNP and NNP are the most frequently quoted indices of economic performance, economists sometimes refer to three other related concepts. Exhibit 5 shows how each of them is determined. Remember that NNP measures the total flow of consumption and government expenditures plus the net additions to the capital stock. It measures the production of goods and services of the economy, *valued at market prices.* However, these prices include indirect business taxes, which boost market prices but do not represent a cost of utilizing a factor of production. When economists subtract these indirect taxes from the NNP, the resulting figure is called **national income.**

National Income: The total income payments to owners of human (labor) and physical capital during a period. It is also equal to NNP minus indirect business taxes.

National income represents net output valued at factor cost. As Exhibit 5 shows, national income can be determined in two ways: as NNP minus indirect business taxes (and business transfers) or as the income payments to all factors of production. Thus, the sum of employee compensation, interest, self-employment income, rents, and corporate profits also yields national income.

Personal Income: The total income received by individuals that is available for consumption, saving, and payment of personal taxes.

Although national income represents the earnings of all resource owners, it is not the same as **personal income.** Personal income is the total of all income received by individuals—income with which they consume, save, and pay taxes. It differs from national income in two respects. First, some income is earned but not *directly* received. Stockholders do not receive all the income generated by corporations. Corporate tax takes a share. Additional profits are channeled back into the business, remaining undistributed to the stockholders. Social

EXHIBIT 5 Five indicators of economic performance: gross national product and four related concepts—1981

Economic Indicator	Billions of Dollars
Gross national product	2925.5
Subtract: Depreciation	321.6
Net national product	2603.9
Subtract: Indirect business taxes	251.1
Business transfers	5.6
National income	2347.2
Subtract: Corporate profits	191.7
Social security contributions	238.9
Add: Government transfer payments	321.6
Net interest paid	93.1
Dividends	61.3
Business transfer payments	11.6
Personal income	2404.2
Subtract: Personal taxes	388.2
Disposable income	2016.0

U.S. Department of Commerce, *Survey of Current Business* (April 1982).

security taxes are deducted from employees' paychecks, forming a component of income earned but not directly received. In order to calculate personal income, these factors must be subtracted.

Second, some income is received even though it was not earned during the current period. Government transfer payments, such as social security, in addition to government interest payments or the national debt are included in this category. By the same token, dividends received add to personal income, regardless of when they are earned. These components must be added to yield personal income.

As anyone who has ever worked on a job knows, the amount of your paycheck is not equal to your salary. Personal taxes must be deducted. **Disposable income** is the income that is yours to do with as you please. It is simply personal income minus personal taxes.

Disposable Income: The income available to individuals after personal taxes. It can be either spent on consumption or saved.

Thus, there are five alternative measures of national product and income:

1. Gross national product
2. Net national product
3. National income
4. Personal income
5. Disposable income

Each of the five measures something different, but they are all closely related. Movement of one of the income measures nearly always parallels the movement of the other indicators. *Since the five measures move together,* economists often use only GNP or the terms "income," "output," or "aggregate production" when referring to the general movement of all five of the indicators of productive activity.

WHAT GNP DOES NOT CONSIDER

As we will emphasize below, GNP is not a measure of how much "better off" we are. There are both positive and negative sides to it. Perhaps it might be best thought of as an index of current productive activity—activity that results in the goods and services that we desire but at the expense of work, waiting, risk, and depreciation, which we do not desire.

GNP is not a perfect device for measuring current production and income. Some items such as household production are excluded, even though they would be properly classed as "current production." Sometimes production results in harmful side effects that are not fully accounted for. In this section, we will focus on some of the limitations and shortcomings of GNP as a measure of economic performance.

Prices Change over Time

We often like to compare GNP during two different years in order to measure increases or decreases in production. Price changes, however, make such comparisons more complex. GNP will increase if either (a) more goods and services are produced or (b) prices rise. Often both (a) and (b) will contribute to an increase in GNP. Since we are usually interested in isolating differences in output or actual production during two different time intervals, GNP must be adjusted for the change in prices.

GNP Deflator: A price index that reveals the cost of purchasing the items included in GNP during the period relative to the cost of purchasing these same items during a base year (currently 1972). Since the base year is assigned a value of 100, when the GNP deflator takes on values greater than 100, it indicates that prices have risen.

Money GNP: GNP valued at the current prices of the period.

Real GNP: GNP in current dollars deflated for changes in the prices of the items included in GNP. Mathematically, real GNP_2 is equal to money GNP_2 multiplied by (GNP Deflator$_1$/GNP Deflator$_2$). Thus, if prices have risen between periods 1 and 2, the ratio of the GNP deflator in period 1 to the deflator in period 2 will be less than 1. Therefore, this ratio will deflate the money GNP for the rising prices.

How can we determine how much the prices of items included in GNP have risen during a specific period? We answer this question by constructing a price index called the **GNP deflator.** The Department of Commerce estimates how much of each item included in GNP has been produced during a year. This bundle of goods will include automobiles, houses, office buildings, medical services, bread, milk, entertainment, and all other goods included in the GNP, *in the quantities that they are actually produced during the current year.* The Department then calculates the ratio of the value of this bundle of goods at current prices divided by the value of the bundle *at the prices that were present during the designated earlier base year.* When prices are rising (or falling), this ratio will be greater (or less) than 1. The chosen base year (currently 1972 for the GNP deflator) is assigned the value of 100. The GNP deflator is equal to the calculated ratio multiplied by 100. When the GNP deflator exceeds 100, this indicates that, on average, prices are higher than they were during the base period.

We can use the GNP deflator to measure GNP in dollars of constant purchasing power. If prices are rising, we simply deflate the **money GNP** during the latter period to account for the effects of inflation. When GNP is stated in terms of constant dollars, economists call it **real GNP.**

Exhibit 6 illustrates how real GNP is measured and why it is important to adjust for price changes. Money GNP increased 146.6 percent between 1972 and 1981. Does this mean that output expanded by 146.6 percent during the period from 1972 to 1981? Indeed not. The GNP deflator in 1981 was 193.7, compared to 100.0 in 1972. Prices rose by 93.7 percent during the period. In determining the real GNP for 1981 in terms of 1972 dollars, we deflate the 1981 money GNP for the rise in prices:

$$\text{Real GNP}_{81} = \text{money GNP}_{81} \times \frac{\text{GNP deflator}_{72}}{\text{GNP deflator}_{81}}$$

Because prices were rising, the latter ratio is less than 1. In terms of 1972 dollars, the real GNP in 1981 was $1510 billion, only 27.3 percent more than in 1972. Thus, although money GNP expanded by 146.4 percent, real GNP increased by only 27.3 percent.

A change in money GNP tells us nothing about what happened to the rate of real production unless we also know what happened to prices. If prices more than doubled during the time period, money income could have doubled while production actually declined. Conversely, if prices fell, money income

EXHIBIT 6   Changes in prices and the real GNP

Between 1972 and 1981, GNP increased by 146.6 percent. But when the 1981 GNP was deflated to account for price increases, real GNP increased by only 27.3 percent.

	GNP (Billions of Dollars)	Price Index (GNP Deflator)	Real GNP (1972 Dollars)
1972	1186	100.0	1186
1981	2925	193.7	1510
Percent increase	146.6	93.7	27.3

U.S. Department of Commerce.

could have remained constant while real GNP increased. Data on both money GNP and price changes are essential for a meaningful comparison of real income between two time periods.

Nonmarket Production

The GNP fails to count household production because such production does not involve a market transaction. Thus, the household services of 100 million people are excluded. If you mow the yard or perform similar household productive activities, your labor services add nothing to GNP, since no market transaction is involved. Such nonmarket productive activities are sizable—10 or 15 percent of total GNP, perhaps more.

The Underground Economy

Many economic transactions go unreported because they involve either illegal activities or tax evasion (which is illegal, although the activities generating the income may not be). Many of these "underground" activities produce goods and services that are valued by purchasers. Nonetheless, since the activities are unreported, they do not contribute to GNP. Estimates of the size of the underground economy in the United States range from 10 to 15 percent of total output. Most observers, as we have noted, believe that these unrecorded transactions have grown much more rapidly than measured output in recent years. If this is true, it implies that the published GNP figures are actually understating the growth rate of output, since an expanding proportion of total output is being excluded.

Production of Economic "Bads" or Disproduct

GNP counts only work that was paid for or goods that were purchased. It does not count goods that were used up, destroyed, or diminished in value *if there was not a market transaction.* Junk piles, garbage, and cancer created by air and water pollution—and all of the other "disproducts" associated with current consumption—are excluded because they do not go through the market. These undesirable items are clear deductions from our total available goods and resources. Their total might be called the gross national disproduct.

When production generates harmful side effects, these side effects reduce either the availability of a current good (for example, clean air, good health, or a noncongested environment) or our ability to produce future goods (as, for example, in the case of the depletion of natural resources). GNP does not account for these negative side effects. Thus, it tends to overstate our "real output" of desired goods.

Leisure

Simon Kuznets, the "inventor" of the GNP, indicated that the failure to include human cost fully was one of the grave omissions of national income accounting. GNP excludes leisure, a good that is valuable to each of us. One country might attain a $6000 per capita GNP with an average work week of 30 hours. Another might attain the same per capita GNP with a 50 hour work week. In terms of total output, the first country has the greater production because it "produces" more leisure, or sacrifices less human cost. Yet GNP does not reflect this fact.

The average number of hours worked per week in the United States has declined steadily. The average nonagricultural production worker spent only 35 hours on the job in 1980, compared to more than 40 hours in 1947; this is a 12 percent reduction in weekly hours worked. Clearly, this reduction in the length of the work week increased the standard of living of Americans, even though it did not enhance GNP.

GNP also fails to take ito account such human costs as the physical or mental strain that is associated with many jobs. While, on average, jobs today are less physically strenuous and less exhausting, they are perhaps more monotonous than they were 30 years ago. These shortcomings—the failure to consider leisure and other human costs of employment—reduce the significance of longitudinal GNP comparisons.

New and Changing Goods

New goods are always being introduced and the quality of existing goods changed. In 1900, there were no jet planes, television sets, or automobiles. On the other hand, there were plenty of open spaces, trees, pure-water rivers, cheap land, and areas with low crime rates. Obviously, things are quite different today.

The introduction of new goods and the changes in the quality of current commodities present a problem even when one is comparing GNP between two time periods separated by only a decade or two. For example, there have been tremendous changes in the convenience, packaging, and preparations of foods since the mid 1960s. Perhaps, more significantly, oral contraceptives have changed the alternatives available to an entire generation of women (and men) since the early 1960s. GNP simply cannot measure such changes, which obviously affect the quality of life, and thus it may sometimes be a highly imperfect indicator of economic output at two widely separated points in time or between two countries.

WHAT GNP MEASURES

GNP does not measure welfare, happiness, or even social progress. These subjective concepts are all influenced by many factors other than economic goods. Until recently, popular opinion often associated a rising GNP with progress and improvement in the quality of life. GNP was never intended to be such an index of social progress.

GNP does not say anything about the usefulness of an activity. If individuals, corporations, or the government purchase an item, it counts as product. A dollar spent for the schooling of an orphan child counts no more or no less than the alcoholic's dollar spent on another bottle of cheap wine. GNP makes no distinction. The only criterion is whether someone wants the good or service enough to pay for it.

What, then, does GNP measure? The greatest contribution of GNP (measured in constant prices) is its precision, despite all of its limitations, as an indicator of short-term changes in productive activity.

GNP Can Measure Swings in the Economic Pendulum

During the last 50 years, real GNP has been increasing at a rate of approximately 3.5 percent annually. However, the rate of growth has not been steady. One of the major objectives of macroeconomics is to determine the cause of extreme fluctuations in GNP growth and thereby suggest policy alternatives that would reduce this economic instability.

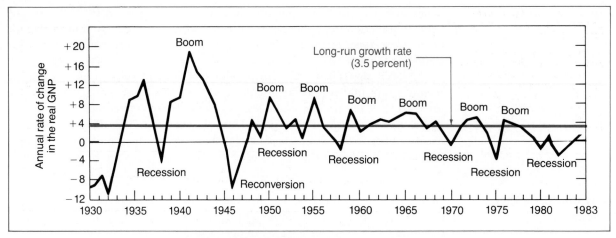

EXHIBIT 7 Instability in the growth of real GNP

Note that, while fluctuations are present, the periods of positive growth outweigh the periods of declining real income. The long-run real GNP in the United States has grown approximately 3.5 percent annually.

Exhibit 7 illustrates the fluctuation in real GNP during the last 50 years. The annual growth of aggregate real output exceeded 8 percent for several short periods. In a number of other years, output as measured by real GNP actually declined. In 1938, it fell by nearly 5 percent. From 1929 to 1939, a period of time referred to as the Great Depression, economic growth came to a complete standstill. In fact, between 1929 and 1933, real GNP actually declined by more than 25 percent! The 1929 level of real GNP was not reached again until 1939. Since the 1930s, growth has been more stable, but economic ups and downs still occur. For example, World War II was characterized by a rapid expansion of GNP, which was followed by a decline after the war. The real GNP did not reach its 1944 level again until 1951, although the output of consumer goods did increase significantly in the years immediately after the war as the conversion was made to a peacetime economy. The years 1954, 1958, 1960, 1970, 1974, and 1979–1980 were characterized by downswings in economic activity. Upswings in real GNP came in 1950, 1955, most of the 1960s, 1972–1973, and 1976–1977.

EMPLOYMENT AND ECONOMIC INSTABILITY

As we noted in the previous section, fluctuations in GNP have, over time, been uneven. This, in turn, has had a great effect on conditions in the aggregate labor market. A key measure of labor market conditions, the rate of unemployment, has fluctuated widely during the last several decades, primarily in relation to changes in GNP. In the midst of the Great Depression, when GNP declined sharply, one out of every four persons in the labor force was looking for a job but was unable to find one. With the expansion of GNP and the wartime economy from 1940 to 1945, unemployment fell sharply. During the years from 1943 to 1945, the rate fell to less than 2 percent (see Exhibit 8). Since World War II, the GNP and the rate of unemployment have been more stable, but

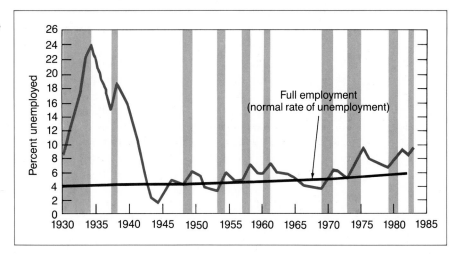

significant fluctuations continue even today. Conditions in the aggregate labor market, like those in the aggregate product market, have been characterized by instability.

THREE TYPES OF UNEMPLOYMENT

Unemployed: The term used to describe a person, not currently employed, who is either (a) actively seeking employment or (b) waiting to begin or return to a job.

Frictional Unemployment: Unemployment due to constant changes in the economy that prevent unemployed workers from being immediately matched up with existing job openings for which they are qualified. It results because of scarce information and efforts by job seekers to acquire employment information.

In a dynamic economy, there is a constant flow of workers in and out of the labor force, from job to job, and from employment to unemployment and back to employment. In 1980 alone, approximately 10 million workers changed jobs. Many moves stem from expansions and contractions in the economy, many others result from the efforts of employees to improve their economic status by better matching their skills with the requirements of the economy. In many instances, these moves actually improve the operational efficiency of the economy and the real income of the participants. Nonetheless, periods of unemployment are often an inevitable result of this mobility.

The Bureau of Labor Statistics, which assembles the official labor force data for the United States, classifies a person who is not working as **unemployed** if he or she is either (a) actively seeking employment or (b) waiting to begin or return to a job.[2] This classification deals with the who but not the why of unemployment. In order to get at the why, economists like to divide unemployment into three categories: frictional, structural, and cyclical. Let us take a closer look at these three classifications.

Frictional Unemployment

Unemployment that is caused by the constant change in the labor market is called **frictional unemployment.** Frictional unemployment occurs because (a) employers are not fully aware of all available workers and their job qualifications and (b) workers are not fully aware of the jobs being offered by

---

[2]More precisely, persons are counted among those actively seeking employment if they have looked for a job at any time during the preceding four weeks. Persons who are available for work but are not working because they are on layoff or are waiting to start a new job within the next 30 days are also counted among the unemployed.

employers. There may be 20 qualified plumbers in a city seeking employment and 20 or more firms trying to hire plumbers. Until the firms and plumbers find each other, frictional unemployment exists. The basic cause of frictional unemployment is imperfect information. It takes time for qualified job seekers to identify firms demanding their services, and vice versa.

Employers looking for a new worker seldom hire the first applicant who walks into their employment office. They want to find the "best available" worker to fill their opening. It is costly to hire workers who perform poorly. Sometimes it is even costly to terminate their employment. So employers search— they expend time and resources trying to screen applicants and choose only those who have the desired qualifications.

Similarly, persons seeking employment usually do not take the first job available. They too, search among potential alternatives, seeking the best job available as they perceive it. They undergo search cost (submit to job interviews, use employment agencies, and so on) in an effort to find out about opportunities. As job seekers find out about more and more potential job alternatives, the benefits of additional job search diminish. Eventually, the unemployed worker decides that the benefit of additional job search is not worth the cost and chooses the "best" of the current alternatives. All of this takes time, and during that time, the job seeker is contributing to the frictional unemployment of the economy.

Structural Unemployment

Structural Unemployment: Unemployment due to structural changes in the economy that eliminate some jobs while generating job openings for which the unemployed workers are *not* well qualified.

Structural unemployment occurs because of changes in the basic characteristics of the economy that prevent the "matching up" of available workers with available jobs. Employment openings continue to exist because the unemployed workers do not possess the necessary qualifications to fill them. There may be 20 plumbers looking for work and firms may have jobs open for 20 nuclear engineers.

There are many causes of structural unemployment. Dynamic changes in demand may change the skill requirements of some jobs. Some skills may become obsolete, whereas others may be in short supply relative to demand. An influx of younger, less experienced workers who fail to meet the requirements of available jobs could cause structural unemployment. Dramatic shifts in defense and other government expenditures often promotes excess demand and job vacancies in one area while generating excess supply and unemployment in another. Institutional factors, such as minimum wage legislation, might reduce the incentive of business firms to offer on-the-job training, which would have improved the matchup between job openings and available employees.

Cyclical Unemployment

Cyclical Unemployment: Unemployment due to recessionary business conditions and inadequate aggregate demand for labor.

Cyclical unemployment results when GNP contracts and there is a decline in demand for labor in the aggregate. As GNP expands, we could expect cyclical unemployment to fall somewhat. Previously, we saw that when there is a decline in demand in some industries and expansion in others, some frictional unemployment arises, since workers and employers have imperfect information about job openings and potential employees. As Exhibit 9 illustrates, imperfect information also helps to explain why a decline in the aggregate demand for labor results in unemployment. When the demand for labor declines, some workers are laid off (or fail to be hired) at the existing wage rate.

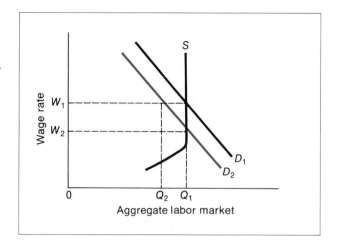

The greater the reduction in aggregate demand, the greater will be the reduction in wages necessary to eliminate the cyclical unemployment. Therefore, substantial reductions in aggregate demand will lead to sharp increases in the rate of unemployment and long periods of unemployment above the "normal rate."

Macroeconomics is concerned primarily with cyclical unemployment. In a later chapter, we will investigate potential sources of cyclical unemployment and consider policy alternatives to reduce it.

WHAT IS FULL EMPLOYMENT?

Full Employment: The level
of employment that results
from the efficient use of the
civilian labor force allowing
for structural and frictional
unemployment. For the United
States, full employment is
thought to exist when between
94 and 95 percent of the labor
force is employed.

Clearly, when most people speak of **full employment,** they do not mean zero unemployment. In a dynamic economy there will always be some structural and frictional unemployment. Currently, most economists believe that full employment exists when between 94 and 95 percent of the labor force is employed.

Even the economist's concept of full employment is not entirely clear cut. It incorporates the idea that at a given time there is some normal rate of unemployment in a dynamic exchange economy. This normal rate of unemployment results from both frictional and structural factors. The normal rate of unemployment is influenced by both the characteristics of the labor force and social institutions.

Two Factors that Affect the Normal Rate of Unemployment

Normal Rate of Unemploy-
ment: The long-run average
rate of unemployment due to
the frictional and structural
conditions of labor markets.

Characteristics of the Labor Force.   Young workers, in their search to find a desirable permanent occupation, change jobs more often and are more likely to shift from the labor force to schooling and back to the labor force than are older workers. Therefore, their rate of unemployment will exceed the average for older, more established workers. Thus, an increase in youthful workers, as a percentage of the total labor force, will cause the normal rate of unemployment to rise.

Public Policy.   Policies that reduce barriers to entry into the labor market and improve the flow of information about jobs (and about the availability of workers) will tend to reduce the normal rate of unemployment. In contrast, public policies that (a) encourage workers to reject job offers and continue to search for employment, (b) prohibit employers from offering wage rates that would induce them to employ (and train) low-skill workers, and (c) reduce the employer's opportunity cost of using layoffs to adjust rates of production will increase the normal rate of unemployment. The actual rate of employment that it will be possible to attain and sustain in the future during normal times is very much a function of public policy. Full employment, however, is an empty concept if it means employment at unproductive jobs. The meaningful goal of full employment is productive employment—employment that will generate goods and services desired by workers at the lowest possible cost.

Actual and Potential GNP

Potential Output: The level of output that can be attained and sustained into the future, given the size of the labor force, the expected productivity of labor, and the normal rate of unemployment consistent with the efficient operation of the labor market. For periods of time, the actual output may differ from the economy's potential.

If an economy is going to realize its potential, full employment is essential. When the actual rate of unemployment exceeds the normal level, the actual output of the economy will fall below its potential. Some resources that could be productively employed will be underutilized.

The Council of Economic Advisors defines the **potential output** as:

the amount of output that could be expected at full employment. . . . It does not represent the absolute maximum level of production that could be generated by wartime or other abnormal levels of aggregate demand, but rather that which could be expected from high utilization rates obtainable under more normal circumstances.

The concept of potential output emcompasses two important ideas: (a) full utilization of resources, including labor, and (b) a **supply-constrained economy.** Potential output might be properly thought of as the maximum sustainable output level consistent with the economy's resource base, given its institutional arrangements.

Supply-Constrained Economy: An economy for which the ability to produce output will be constrained by (a) the scarcity of resources and (b) the economy's institutional arrangements. Given these two factors, there will be a maximum output rate that the economy will be able to sustain into the future.

Estimates of the potential output level involve three major elements—the size of the labor force, the quality (productivity) of labor, and the normal rate of unemployment. Since these factors cannot be estimated with certainty, there is not uniform agreement among economists as to the potential rate of output for the U.S. economy. Relying upon the projections of potential output developed by the Council of Economic Advisors, Exhibit 10 illustrates the record of the U.S. economy since 1954. During the 1950s, the rate of unemployment was above the "normal rate." Excess capacity was present because the level of aggregate demand was insufficient to maintain full employment. The gap between potential and actual GNP was particularly large during the recessions of 1954, 1958, and 1961. During the 1960s, the gap narrowed as the economy approached and temporarily exceeded its capacity. Actual output again failed to approach its potential during the recessions of 1970, 1974–1975, and 1979–1981.

THE ECONOMICS OF INFLATION

Inflation: A rise in the general level of prices of goods and services. The purchasing power of the monetary unit, such as the dollar, declines when inflation is present.

In recent years, much public attention has been focused on both the concepts of employment and **inflation.** While we have discussed changes in GNP and employment, we have not up to now examined the macroeconomic role played by inflation.

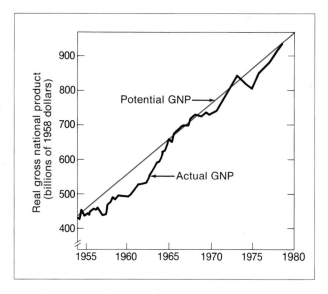

Consumer Price Index: An indicator of the general level of prices. It attempts to compare the cost of purchasing the market basket bought by a typical consumer during a specific period with the cost of purchasing the same market basket during an earlier period.

Inflation is a rise in the general level of prices. When inflation is present the cost of purchasing the bundle of goods and services consumed by the typical American household will rise. We have already explained how the GNP deflator is used to adjust money GNP for rising prices during a period. However, suppose we want to measure the impact of inflation on household income. The **consumer price index** is the most common means of measuring the inflation rate for items purchased by the typical household unit. The CPI, calculated monthly by the Bureau of Labor Statistics, is an estimate of how much it costs to buy the typical market basket purchased by urban middle-income families in comparison to the cost in an earlier year. (Actually, the Bureau of Labor Statistics publishes two indexes of consumer prices. One for "all urban households" and the other for "urban wage earners and clerical workers." The two differ slightly because the typical bundles of goods purchased by the two groups are not identical.) The CPI representative market basket includes eggs, bread, housing, entertainment, medical services, and other goods in the amounts that they are purchased by most middle-income families. As prices rise, the cost of purchasing this representative market basket will go up, reflecting the high prices.

To calculate the current consumer price index, a base year is chosen, and the CPI for that year is arbitrarily assigned a value of 100. For example, the present base year is 1972–1973. Thus, the current cost of purchasing the typical market basket is compared to its cost during the base year. If it now costs $1000 to purchase the same market basket that could have been purchased for $500 in the base year, the price index is 200. A price index of 200 indicates that prices are now 100 percent higher than during the base year.

The annual inflation rate for consumer goods and services is the percentage change in the consumer price index from one year to the next. Mathematically, the inflation rate (i) can be written as

$$i = \frac{\text{This year's CPI} - \text{last year's CPI}}{\text{last year's CPI}} \times 100$$

Thus, if the CPI in year 2 was 220 compared to 200 during year 1, the inflation rate would equal 10 percent, that is [(220 − 200)/200] × 100. Since the CPI is calculated monthly, we often compare its value during a specific month with its value during that same month one year earlier in order to calculate the inflation rate during the most recent 12 months.

During the 1950s and into the mid-1960s, the annual rate of inflation in the United States was usually less than 2 percent. During the period from 1967 to 1978, the annual rate of inflation averaged 6.8 percent, compared to only 1.4 percent during 1952–1965 (see Exhibit 11). Clearly, the rate of inflation in our economy accelerated during the 1970s. While this acceleration in the rate of inflation is alarming, it might also be informative to consider the matter in comparison to other world economies.

The rate of inflation among countries varies widely. As Exhibit 12 shows, inflation has been a way of life for some time in such South American countries as Chile, Argentina, and Brazil. During the period from 1955 to 1968, the rate of inflation in most Western industrial nations was 5 percent or less. Since that time, the rate of inflation has risen sharply in Italy, the United Kingdom, France, and most other industrial nations. Among the European nations, Switzerland and West Germany have done the best job of controlling inflation during recent years.

WHO GAINS AND WHO LOSES FROM INFLATION?

Inflation reduces the purchasing power of money income received in the future (for example, payments from pensions, life insurance policies, and receipts from outstanding loans). If decision makers do not consider inflation when they agree to a contract, debtors will gain at the expense of lenders. Does this mean that inflation helps poor people? Not necessarily. We must remember that people need reasonably good credit before they can borrow money. This limits the ability of persons in the lowest income brackets to acquire debt. Most studies in this area suggest that unanticipated inflation results in a moderate redistribution from recipients of both low (less than $5000) and high (more than $50,000) incomes to those in the middle-income groupings.

A more important redistributional effect of unanticipated inflation is between age groupings. Persons under 35 years of age are more likely to be debtors. Inflation helps them pay back their housing mortgages, car loans, and other outstanding debts if their interest rates are less than the rate of inflation. In contrast, those over 50 years of age are more likely to have savings, paid-up life insurance policies, bonds, and other forms of fixed future income. Inflation eats away at the purchasing power of these savings. Thus, it tends to redistribute income from the old to the young.

However, the biggest gainer from unanticipated inflation is the federal government. Households are net lenders, and the government is the largest debtor. Therefore, unanticipated inflation tends to transfer wealth from households to the government.[3]

---

[3]See G. L. Bach, "Inflation: Who Gains and Who Loses?" *Challenge* (July/August 1974), pp. 48–55, for evidence supporting this view.

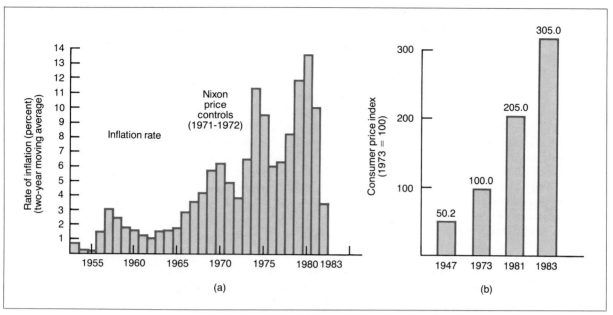

EXHIBIT 11   Inflation in our times

During the period from 1952 to 1965, the annual rate of inflation never exceeded 3 percent. Since 1966, the annual rate of inflation has never fallen below 3 percent, even for
a single year. During 1952-1965, the annual rate of inflation was 1.4 percent; during 1967-
1978, it was 6.8 percent. As graph (b) illustrates, consumer prices doubled in just 12 years
during the latter period.

EXHIBIT 12   Worldwide inflation

Country	Compound Annual Rate of Change in Consumer Prices	
	1970–1975	1975–1980
Chile	266	82
Argentina	72	211
Brazil	21	51
Colombia	18	25
Ecuador	14	12
Peru	13	51
France	9	10
West Germany	6	4
Italy	12	16
Japan	13	7
Switzerland	8	2
United Kingdom	13	14
Australia	10	11
Canada	7	9
United States	7	9

International Monetary Fund, *International Financial Statistics* (monthly).

DOES THE CPI OVERSTATE THE INFLATION RATE?

Many economists believe that the consumer price index (CPI) is seriously flawed. They believe that it has often overstated the rate of inflation. The wages of approximately 25 percent of the labor force and the expenditures of more than half of the federal budget are tied to the CPI. Therefore, this is a serious matter. There are two major reasons why economists believe that the CPI is flawed.

1. Failure to Account for Consumer Substitution Away from Goods That Rise in Price. The CPI assumes that consumers purchase the market basket consumed during an earlier base period, currently 1972–1973. However, as the prices of various products rise at different rates, consumers will shift their purchases away from products that have become more expensive toward goods that have become relatively cheaper. Thus, the more expensive products tend to comprise a smaller proportion of the typical market basket.

However, the CPI makes no allowance for this shift. For example, when the price of gasoline rose sharply during the 1970s, people drove less and shifted to smaller, higher mileage automobiles. The proportion of personal consumption expenditures allocated to gasoline fell from 3.5 percent in 1972 to 2.8 percent in 1980. Despite this decline in gasoline consumption, the CPI continues to weight gasoline as if consumers were still purchasing the base-year amount.

Consumers reduce the burden of inflation by purchasing less of goods that rise in price most rapidly. Failure of the CPI to consider this fact results in an overstatement of the inflation rate.

2. The Overstatement of Housing Costs. The most serious shortcoming of the CPI is probably its treatment of home ownership costs. The home ownership component accounts for nearly 25 percent of the market basket on which the index is based. The CPI treats the price of a house and the mortgage interest payments of the house as separate transactions. The price of housing is counted *once* when it is purchased and *again* as the interest rate component on the mortgage.

Mortgage interest costs are not included for households that did not buy a house during the survey year. However, for those who did buy a house, *all* mortgage interest due for the first half of the term of the mortgage (usually a period of 10 to 15 years) is included. This procedure makes it seem as if all homeowners refinanced their mortgages each month. Thus, when interest rates rise, as they did during the 1970s, the CPI tells us how much home ownership costs rose, assuming that everyone bought a new home during the period. However, this is not the case. Most homeowners have home mortgages of fixed interest rates. Thus, their home ownership costs do not rise, as the CPI implies they do.

With billions of dollars of both wage payments and government expenditures hanging upon the CPI, it is imperative that these flaws be corrected.

Anticipated Inflation: An increase in the general level of prices that is expected by economic decision makers. Past experience and current conditions are the major determinants of an individual's expectations with regard to future price changes.

An analysis of the debtor–creditor impact of inflation is incomplete without the recognition that, after a period of inflation, individuals eventually begin to incorporate the expectation of future inflation into their decision making. **Anticipated inflation** is a change in the level of prices that is expected by decision makers. Once both borrowers and lenders anticipate inflation, they will adjust their behavior to account for it. For example, lenders will demand and borrowers will grant a higher interest rate on loans because both parties expect the value of the dollars paid back to depreciate. A borrower and a lender might agree to a 5 percent interest rate if they anticipate stable prices during the course of the loan. However, if both expect prices to rise 10 percent annually, they might agree instead to a 15 percent interest rate. The higher interest rate would compensate the lender for the expected decline in the purchasing power of the dollar during the course of the loan.

When inflation is fully and accurately anticipated, debtors do not benefit at the expense of lenders. Debtors gain at the expense of creditors only if the actual rate of inflation exceeds the rate expected at the time the terms of the transaction are agreed upon.

When inflation is widely anticipated, the redistribution of wealth is likely to be minor. Wealth will be primarily distributed away from persons who are least able (or lack the knowledge) to make adjustments to protect themselves against price increases toward those who are best able to do so. Persons will adopt a variety of economic arrangements to protect their wealth and income against erosion by inflation. For example, collective bargaining agreements will incorporate **escalator clauses** or contain a premium for the expected rate of inflation. Home mortgage interest rates will rise to incorporate the inflationary factor. Similarly, life insurance premiums will decline, since the money interest rate of the insurance company's current assets will rise as a result of inflation. Once the inflation is fully anticipated, generalizations about wealth transfers among groups will no longer hold true.

Inflation will affect the prices of the things we sell as well as the prices of the goods we buy. Both wages and prices will rise during a period of inflation. Before we become too upset about inflation "robbing us of the purchasing power of our paychecks," we should recognize that inflation influences the size of those paychecks. The weekly earnings of employees would not have doubled during the period from 1969 to 1979 if the rate of inflation had not been in excess of 7 percent. Given the rate of output during the period, it would clearly be wrong to argue that Americans could have doubled their consumption of goods and services between 1969 and 1979 had it not been for inflation.

Escalator Clause: A contractual agreement that periodically and automatically adjusts the wage rates of a collective-bargaining agreement upward by an amount determined by the rate of inflation.

The Dangers of Inflation

Merely because money income initially tends to rise with prices, it does not follow that there is no need to be concerned about inflation, particularly high rates of inflation. Three negative aspects of inflation are particularly important.

1. Price Changes Can Frustrate the Intent of a Long-Term Contract. Most market exchanges, including long-term contracts, are made in money terms. If unanticipated inflation takes place, it can change the result of long-term contracts, such as mortgages, life insurance policies, pensions, bonds, and other arrangements that involve a debtor–lender relationship.

2. Rapid Price Changes Cause Uncertainty. If one is not sure whether prices are going to increase, decrease, or remain the same, any contract that has a time dimension becomes hazardous because of uncertainty. The builder does not know whether to tack on a charge of 2, 5, or 10 percent to a contract, even though inflation is bound to increase building costs by some amount during the time necessary for construction. Union workers do not know whether to accept a contract calling for a 5 percent wage increase for the next two years. Inflation could partially or completely negate the increase. Long-term money exchanges must take into account the uncertainty created by inflation.

3. Real Resources Are Used Up As Decision Makers Seek to Protect Themselves from Inflation. Failure to anticipate accurately the rate of inflation can have a substantial effect on one's wealth. Individuals, therefore, divert scarce resources from the production of desired goods and services to the acquisition of information on the future rate of inflation. Inflation forecasting and financial consulting become booming industries during inflationary times. This process of seeking information and adjusting one's decision making is costly.

For example, firms are unable to establish list prices for any length of time. Catalogues have to be continually updated and reissued. Business planning is unnecessarily frustrated by the need for continuous reassessment of factor and product prices.

The Causes of Inflation and Stagflation

What causes inflation? We must acquire some additional tools before we can analyze this question in detail, but we can outline a couple of theories. First, economists emphasize the link between aggregate demand and supply. If aggregate demand rises more rapidly than supply, prices will rise. Second, nearly all economists believe that a rapid expansion in a nation's stock of money will cause inflation. The old saying is that prices will rise because "there is too much money chasing too few goods." The hyperinflation experienced by South American countries has been mainly the result of monetary expansion.

As recently as a decade ago, most economists thought that inflation was generally associated with prosperity and rapid economic growth. During the 1970s, however, the United States and other industrial nations experienced several inflationary recessions. Economists have coined the term **stagflation** to describe the phenomenon of rapid inflation and sluggish economic growth. One of the challenges of the 1980s will be to develop a solution to the problem of stagflation—to develop economic policies that will reduce the rate of inflation, lead to a more efficient utilization of resources, and increase the future production possibilities available to economic participants. Again and again, we will return to this issue as we probe deeper into macroeconomics.

Stagflation: A period during which an economy is experiencing both substantial inflation and a slow growth in output.

CHAPTER LEARNING OBJECTIVES

1   Gross national product is a measure of the market value of the final goods and services produced during a specific time period.

2   Dollars act as a common denominator for GNP. Production of each final product is weighted according to its selling price. Alternatively, GNP can be calculated by adding up the dollar factor cost of producing the final goods. The two methods sum to an identical result.

3   When the expenditure approach is utilized, there are four major components of GNP: (a) consumption, (b) investment, (c) government, and (d) net exports.

4   The major components of GNP as calculated by the resource cost–income approach are (a) wages and salaries, (b) self-employment income, (c) rents, (d) interest, (e) corporate profits, and (f) nonincome expenses, primarily depreciation and indirect business taxes.

5   GNP may increase because of an increase in either output or prices. Price indexes are used to measure the impact of price changes. Real GNP can be determined by adjusting money GNP to account for price changes between periods.

6   GNP is an imperfect measure of current production. It excludes household production. It fails to account for such negative side effects of current production as air and water pollution, adverse impacts on health, depletion of natural resources, and other factors that do not flow through markets. It imperfectly adjusts for quality changes. GNP comparisons are less meaningful when the typical bundle of available goods and services differs widely between two time periods (or between two nations).

7   Despite all its limitations, GNP is of tremendous importance because it is an accurate tool enabling us to identify short-term economic fluctuations. Without such a

reliable indicator, economic theory would be unable to determine the cause of economic slowdowns and economic policy would be helpless against them. Elimination of this limitation on both theory and policy is the great contribution of GNP.

8   Economists frequently refer to four other income measures that are related to GNP: net national product, national income, personal income, and disposable income. All of these measures of income tend to move together.

9   When GNP increases, the unemployment rate usually declines and output increases rapidly. Declining GNP is characterized by increasing unemployment, declining business conditions, and a low rate of growth.

10   Even an efficient exchange economy will experience some unemployment. Frictional unemployment results because of imperfect information about available job openings and qualified applicants. Structural unemployment results because there are factors that prevent the "matching up" of available applicants with available jobs. Currently, frictional and structural unemployment in the United States are thought to involve between 5 and 6 percent of the labor force.

11   Cyclical unemployment results because aggregate demand for labor is insufficient to maintain full employment. A primary concern of macroeconomics is how cyclical unemployment can be minimized. If unemployment resulting from deficient aggregate demand could be eliminated, the actual output of the economy would be able to reach its full potential.

12   Full employment results when the rate of unemployment is normal, given the dynamic change and structural characteristics of the economy. Both public policy and changes in the composition of the labor force affect the full-employment level. The meaningful goal of full employment is employment that produces desired goods and services. It is not employment just for the sake of keeping people working.

13   Inflation is a general rise in the level of prices as measured by a price index. The rate of inflation in the 1970s for almost all Western nations was substantially higher than the rates during the 1950s and 1960s.

THE ECONOMIC WAY OF THINKING — DISCUSSION QUESTIONS

1   Why does a pound of beef add more to GNP than a pound of wheat? Does it reflect demand or costs? Comment.

2   What is real GNP? How is it determined? Calculate the change in real GNP between 1972 and 1981.

3   Indicate which of the following activities are counted as part of GNP and why:
(a) The services of a housewife
(b) Frank Murry's purchase of a 1979 Chevrolet
(c) The purchase of 100 shares of AT&T stock
(d) Family lawn services purchased from the neighbor's 16 year old who has a lawn mowing business
(e) Deterioration of the water quality of Lake Michigan

4   Why might the GNP be a misleading index of changes in output between 1900 and 1980 in the United States? Why might it be a misleading index of differences in output between the United States and Mexico?

5   Explain why even an efficiently functioning economic system will have some unemployed resources.

6   "My money wage rose by 6 percent last year, but inflation completely erased these gains. How can I get ahead when inflation continues to wipe out my increases in earnings?" Evaluate. Do you agree with the view implicit in this question?

7   Explain why it matters whether inflation is accurately anticipated.

AGGREGATE DEMAND AND EQUILIBRIUM IN A SIMPLE KEYNESIAN MODEL

What people sought to save, in Keynes's view, had still to be brought to equal what they wanted to invest. If efforts to save exceeded the desire to invest, the resulting shortage of purchasing power or demand caused output to fall. And it kept falling until employment and income had been so reduced that savings were brought into line with investment![1]
John Kenneth Galbraith

In Chapter 5, we indicated that the GNP and employment rates of our economy have often fluctuated. Now we want to develop and examine a model of national income determination that helps explain why this happens. To do this, we will examine aggregate demand in a theoretical structure that was first developed by John Maynard Keynes.

The concept of planned aggregate demand is a key element of Keynesian economic theory. Keynes argued that producers would supply only the quantity of goods sufficient to meet the planned demand of consumers, investors, government, and foreigners. Therefore, subject to the constraint imposed by the scarcity of resources, planned aggregate demand (the total expected spending on consumption, investment, government, and net exports) would determine the level of output and employment. If producers expect demand to be strong enough for purchasers to buy their products, they will produce the goods. On the other hand, if they perceive that demand is so weak that there will be no market for their output, business decision makers will not produce the goods, even if this means idle machines and workers. Therefore, in the Keynesian framework, (a) aggregate demand (total spending) and (b) total output and employment will vary directly. Aggregate demand determines the level of output and employment.

In this framework, **aggregate demand** is comprised of the total spending on goods and services. For a purely private domestic economy, the sum of the consumption and investment expenditures constitutes aggregate demand. When government and foreign trade are integrated into the analysis, aggregate demand has four components: (a) consumption, (b) investment, (c) government expenditures, and (d) net exports (exports minus imports). Let us examine the major components of aggregate demand.

Aggregate Demand: Total current spending for goods and services. It has four components: (a) consumption, (b) investment, (c) government, and (d) net exports.

---

[1]John Kenneth Galbraith, "The Coming of J. M. Keynes," *Business and Society Review* (Fall 1975), p. 34.

Consumption: Household spending on consumer goods and services during the current period. Consumption is a "flow" concept.

Saving: Disposable income that is not spent on consumption. Saving is a "flow" concept.

When we receive a paycheck, what do we usually do with it? Literally, there are two possibilities. We can either spend it or save it. You will recall from Chapter 5 that household spending on current goods and services is called **consumption.**

That portion of income that is not used to purchase consumption goods is called **saving.** Saving is the difference between one's current income and the amount spent on current goods and services. This can be expressed in three ways.

$$\text{Disposable Income} = \text{consumption} + \text{saving}$$

or

$$\text{Consumption} = \text{disposable income} - \text{saving}$$

or

$$\text{Saving} = \text{disposable income} - \text{consumption}$$

Dissaving: Consumption expenditures that are in excess of disposable income and that are made possible by either borrowing or drawing on past savings.

Sometimes our current spending on goods exceeds our income. When that is the case, we are **dissaving.** Dissaving is negative saving.

Both consumption and saving are flow concepts. One's consumption might be $500 per month or $6000 per year. Similarly, saving (without an s) is the amount saved during a specific time period.

Income: The Main Determinant of Consumption

Consumption Function: A fundamental relationship between disposable income and consumption. As disposable income increases, current consumption expenditures will rise, but by a smaller amount than the increase in income.

According to Keynes, the primary determinant of consumer spending is disposable income. There is a strong positive relationship between the amount spent on consumption and the disposable income of households. This relationship between consumption spending and disposable income is called the **consumption function.** It occupies a central position in the model of income determination developed by John Maynard Keynes.

Exhibit 1 illustrates the relationship between disposable income and consumption for U.S. families in 1980. The consumption spending of low-income families exceeded their incomes. They were dissaving. As income increased, the consumption spending of households also increased, although not quite as rapidly as saving. High-income families spent a smaller percentage of their disposable income on consumption. A larger share was allocated to saving.

The consumption function suggests that as income rises individuals will increase both their current consumption and saving. Families will use some, but not all, of the additional income for current consumption. By the same token, if income should fall, the consumption function implies that families will not absorb the entire reduction by contracting their current consumption. Saving will also be reduced, cushioning the decline in consumption.

A Closer Look at Income and the Consumption Function

Keynes used the expression "propensity to consume" to describe the relationship between an individual's or family's current consumption and income. The propensity to consume can be either an average or a marginal concept. The **average propensity to consume** (APC) of your household is your current consumption spending divided by your disposable income. Obviously, the APC tells you what portion of your total income is spent on consumption.

EXHIBIT 1 The estimated consumption function in the short run

The percentage of income saved in the short run increases with income level.

U.S. Department of Agriculture. The 1973 data were inflated to account for the change in the value of the dollar during the period.

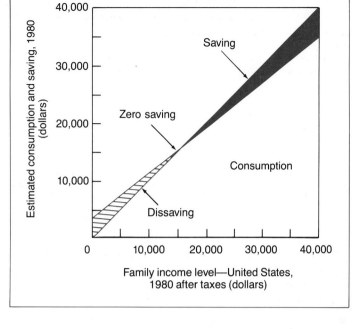

Family income level—United States, 1980 after taxes (dollars)

Average Propensity to Consume: Current consumption spending divided by current disposable income.

$$APC = \frac{\text{current consumption}}{\text{current disposable income}}$$

For example, if you had a disposable income of $20,000 and spent $19,000 on current consumption items, you would have an APC of 0.95.

As income increases, your average propensity to consume usually declines in the short run. This results because, on a short-term basis, you usually spend a smaller than average portion of your additional, or marginal, income on consumption. A greater share of the additional income is allocated to saving. The **marginal propensity to consume** (MPC) of a household is the fraction of *additional* disposable income that is allocated to consumption. The MPC tells you what portion of each *additional* dollar of income is spent on consumption.

Marginal Propensity to Consume: *Additional* current consumption divided by *additional* current disposable income.

$$MPC = \frac{\text{additional consumption}}{\text{additional disposable income}}$$

For example, if your income increases by $100 and you therefore increase your current consumption expenditures by $80, your marginal propensity to consume is 0.80. Eight-tenths of the extra $100 is spent on current consumption. The remainder is allocated to saving.

Exhibit 2 uses the family income-consumption data shown in Exhibit 1 to illustrate both the average and the marginal propensity to consume. American families with $5000 of income in 1980 spent $7000 on current consumption. They were dissaving. Their average propensity to consume—current consumption divided by income—was 1.40. As income rose to $10,000, consumption increased from $7000 to $11,000. Therefore, their average propensity to consume was 1.10. They were still dissaving, but less so than at the $5000 level. As family income expands, a smaller percentage of income is allocated to current consumption. Thus, as Exhibit 2 shows, APC falls as income increases.

EXHIBIT 2 The short-run averge and marginal propensity to consume

This table uses the estimated family income and consumption data for 1980 (see Exhibit 1) to illustrate how the APC, MPC, and MPS are determined.

Family Income (Dollars) (1)	Current Consumption (Dollars) (2)	Additional Consumption, Δ(2) (Dollars) (3)	APC (2) ÷ (1) (4)	APS (1) − (2) ÷ (1) (5)	MPC (3) ÷ Δ(1) (6)	MPS 1 − MPC (7)
5,000	7,000	—	1.40	−0.40	—	—
10,000	11,000	4,000	1.10	−0.10	0.80	0.20
15,000	15,000	4,000	1.00	0	0.80	0.20
20,000	19.000	4,000	0.95	0.05	0.80	0.20
25,000	23,000	4,000	0.92	0.08	0.80	0.20
30,000	27,000	4,000	0.90	0.10	0.80	0.20
35,000	31,000	4,000	0.89	0.11	0.80	0.20
40,000	35,000	4,000	0.88	0.12	0.80	0.20

Marginal Propensity to Save: **The fraction of *additional* disposable income that is saved.**

Remember that saving is merely income that is not spent on current consumption. The **marginal propensity to save** (MPS) is the fraction of additional disposable income that is saved.

$$\text{MPS} = \frac{\text{additional saving}}{\text{additional disposable income}}$$

Exhibit 2 (column 7) also shows MPS for the United States in 1980. As income increased the proportion of additional income allocated to saving also increased. Since disposable income must be either spent on consumption or saved, MPC plus MPS must equal 1.

Exhibit 3 presents a graphic representation of hypothetical *aggregate* consumption and saving functions. Both saving and consumption increase with disposable income. Consumption and disposable income are just equal at $1.7 trillion (Exhibit 3a). Of course, saving would be zero at this income level (Exhibit 3b). As income rises, consumption increases less rapidly. For example, as income increases from $1.7 trillion to $1.9 trillion, consumption expands to $1.8 trillion. A $200 billion increase in disposable income leads to a $100 billion expansion in consumption. Thus, MPC = 0.50. When disposable income is $1.9 trillion, households will save $100 billion. The saving schedule is merely the difference between the 45-degree line and the consumption function C. When disposable income is less than $1.7 trillion, consumption spending will exceed income (Exhibit 3a). Thus, households will be dissaving (Exhibit 3b). Positive saving will take place when disposable income exceeds $1.7 trillion.

Although Keynes considered income to be the primary determinant of consumption, other factors may also exert an influence. As we proceed with our analysis, four additional factors will prove to be of significance.

1. Expectation of Inflation Affects Consumption. When consumers perceive that the prices of goods and services are going to rise in the future, they have an incentive to move their consumption expenditures forward. They want to "buy now before prices go higher." Thus, the expectation of an acceleration in the rate of inflation will stimulate current spending on goods and services.

2. Expectations about Future Business Conditions Affect Consumption. If people expect their income to rise in the future, they will most likely spend a larger portion of their current incomes. In contrast, pessimism about future prospects will probably cause households to reduce their current spending.

3. Taxes Affect Consumption. The disposable income of consumers is directly affected by the level of taxation. An increase in tax rates will reduce the disposable income of consumers, inducing them to cut back on consumption. On the other hand, a reduction in taxes will enlarge the disposable income of consumers, providing an indirect stimulus for current consumption.

4. The Interest Rate Affects Consumption. Although Keynes rejected the view that the interest rate exerted significant impact on consumption, recent work has shown that spending on consumer durables, such as major appliances and automobiles, is quite sensitive to the interest rate. Since these items are often financed by borrowing, higher interest rates increase the monthly payments necessary for their purchase and thereby discourage people from buying them.

EXHIBIT 3 The consumption and saving schedules

Graph (a) pictures the positive relationship between consumption spending and disposable income. The 45-degree line outlines all points for which consumption and disposable income are equal. The vertical distance between the 45-degree line and the consumption function C indicates the level of saving (or dissaving). Graph (b) shows the saving function alone. Note that the amount of saving at an income level (graph b) will always equal the difference between the 45-degree line and the consumption function (graph a) for the corresponding level of income.

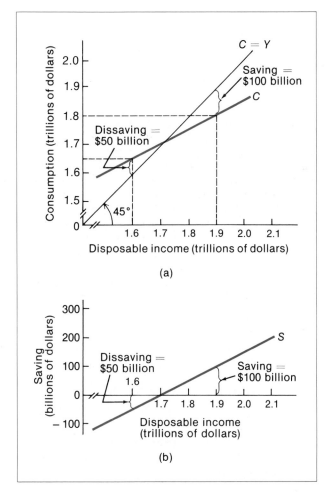

INVESTMENT AS A COMPONENT OF AGGREGATE DEMAND

Investment: The flow of expenditures on durable assets (fixed investment) plus the addition to inventories (inventory investment) during a period. These expenditures enhance our ability to provide consumer benefits in the future.

Fixed Investment: Expenditures on new durable assets, such as buildings and equipment, that increase our ability to produce goods and services in the future.

Inventory Investment: Changes in the stock of unsold goods and raw materials held during a period.

Net Investment: The addition to the nation's capital goods and business inventories during a period.

Investment—like consumption and saving—is also a flow concept. Investment is the flow of expenditures on durable assets that either increase our ability to produce products *in the future* or yield *future* consumer benefits. Current expenditures on assets such as new plant facilities, machines, tools, and additions to inventories are counted as investment since they enhance our ability to supply goods and services in the future. Household expenditures on long-lasting goods such as housing are also included in investment.

Investment is divided into two major subcategories: fixed investment and inventories. **Fixed investment** consists of those durable assets (sometimes called capital goods) that are designed to enhance our productive capacity in the future. **Inventory investment** consists of the *additions* to raw materials and final products not yet sold. At any given time, firms generally hold a stock of raw materials and finished goods. With the passage of time, they often add to or subtract from these inventories. The change in these inventory holdings during a period form the inventory component of investment.

Investment does not include financial transactions, such as the purchase of stocks or bonds. Such transactions involve only the transfer of an asset. They do not create additional productive equipment that will increase our ability to produce goods and services in the future.

Net investment is the addition to the nation's capital goods and business inventories during a period. Additions to capital stock will increase the capacity of the nation to produce goods *in the future.* Capital goods are not an "end" in themselves, but rather a means to produce an end. Machines are produced today so that our output of consumer goods can be increased in the future.

Spending on investment goods will increase aggregate demand during the current period. Production of investment goods, like production of consumption goods, requires labor, natural resources, and other factors of production. Additional investment means more employment of both people and machines.

The Determinants of Investment

What determines the level of investment? Three factors are particularly important.

1. The Relationship between Current Sales and Plant Capacity. When businesses are selling more than their capital stock (plant and equipment) has the ability to produce, business decision makers will want to invest in expanding plant capacity. If, however, sales drop far below capacity, the existing capital stock can produce all that the firms can sell and there will be no incentive to increase investment.

2. Expected Future Sales. Individuals in business invest in buildings and machines because they expect to be able to sell the products produced at a profit. If they expect the future sales for their products to decline, their incentive to invest is sharply reduced. If they expect future sales to increase sharply, they will expand investment. Expectation about future business conditions will exert a powerful influence on investment.

3. The Interest Rate. Interest is nothing more than the price of borrowing money. To invest, a firm must either (a) borrow and pay interest or (b) use its own funds and forego the interest it could have earned by lending to others. The higher the interest rate, the more costly it is to invest and the less incentive businesses have to invest. As interest rates decline, investment becomes cheaper, increasing the incentive to invest. This, however, does not always hold true under all conditions. When an economy is in a recession and future business prospects are bleak, even a sharp decline in the interest rate may not have much impact on investment. Writing against the background of the depression of the 1930s, Keynes emphasized that when economic conditions are depressed, a decline in the interest rate may exert little impact upon the rate of investment undertaken by business decision makers.

GOVERNMENT EXPENDITURES AS A COMPONENT OF AGGREGATE DEMAND

Governments purchase a wide variety of goods and services. Some government purchases (highways, flood-control projects, aircraft, and office buildings, for example) are similar to investment in that they are long lasting and yield a stream of benefits over time. Other government purchases are basically consumption goods and are used up during the current time period. School lunch programs, police and fire protection, and meals for the elderly are examples of government purchases of this variety.

Both investment and consumption types of government expenditures require labor and the use of other scarce resources. They add to aggregate demand—the total spending figure. However, government transfer payments, such as social security, welfare payments, and agriculture subsidy programs, do not directly contribute to demand. They merely "redistribute" demand from taxpayer donors to government beneficiaries.

The level of government spending is a policy variable, subject to alteration by the political process. Of course, economic conditions will exert varying degrees of influence upon both the level and composition of government expenditures chosen. Nonetheless, policy-makers have substantial discretionary power to alter the rate of government spending to suit their political needs, in ways that reflect political, rather than purely economic, priorities. As we proceed, we will investigate in detail the significance of changes in government expenditures—how they affect aggregate demand, output, and employment.

NET EXPORTS AS A COMPONENT OF AGGREGATE DEMAND

Net exports, the purchases of domestic goods by foreigners minus the goods imported from foreigners, usually comprise only 1 or 2 percent of the gross national product in the United States. However, since these are net figures—that is, they are exports minus imports—they substantially understate the importance of the international trade sector and its potential impact on aggregate demand. In 1980, gross exports of goods and services constituted nearly 13 percent of our GNP, and imports summed to 12 percent of GNP. The international sector appears to be growing as a share of total U.S. output.

Equilibrium (Macro):
Condition that exists when planned aggregate demand is equal to total income (aggregate supply). At this level of income, the planned injections into the income stream will just equal the planned leakages from the income stream. Since there is a balance of forces, the equilibrium income level will be sustained, even if it does not coincide with full employment.

Now that we have an understanding of the major components of aggregate demand, we have the necessary tools with which to explain the **equilibrium** levels of output, income, and employment. When an economy is in equilibrium, there is no tendency for output either to expand or to decline.

In order to make our analysis of equilibrium more readily understandable, we will initially employ several simplifying assumptions. First, we will begin by focusing on the operation of a purely private economy. The impact of government expenditures and taxes will be introduced as we proceed. Second, the analysis of monetary factors and their importance will be deferred until a later chapter. Third, we will assume that the price level remains constant until full employment is reached. Therefore, changes in total income will lead to changes in both *real* output and employment as long as the economy has not yet approached its capacity. For the short-run time period, the assumption of stable prices may approximate real-world conditions. Fourth, we will assume an economy with no foreign trade.

The Aggregate Demand–Aggregate Supply Approach— Planned Expenditures Must Equal Total Output

Aggregate Supply: The total value of current output produced. In the Keynesian model, the aggregate supply of goods and services is always equal to income for all possible levels of income.

Planned Aggregate Demand: The total planned consumption and investment expenditures on goods and services during the period.

As we have already stated, economists refer to the total expenditures on goods and services as aggregate demand. For a purely private economy, the sum of the consumption and investment expenditures constitutes aggregate demand.

Aggregate supply is composed of the total output of all goods and services produced during the period. The business sector utilizes the services of labor, land, machines, and other resources to produce output. The payments to the factor suppliers (which constitute income to the resource owners) are equal to the value of the goods and services produced during the period. Aggregate income and aggregate supply (output) are merely opposite sides of the same set of transactions. They are always equal.

When an economy is in equilibrium, **planned aggregate demand** must be just equal to the value of the total output produced (aggregate supply). In equation form, the equilibrium condition for a purely private economy is

$$\underbrace{\text{Total output}\atop\text{(or total income)}}_{\text{aggregate supply}} = \underbrace{\text{planned consumption} + \text{planned investment}}_{\text{planned aggregate demand}}$$

In other words, an economy is in equilibrium when the flow of income generated from the goods and services produced gives rise to a level of spending that is just sufficient to purchase the existing level of output.

Equilibrium and Disequilibrium—The Circular Flow Approach

The circular flow diagram originally presented in Chapter 5 (Exhibit 1) can be modified to help illustrate the concept of Keynesian macroequilibrium. Exhibit 4 modifies the diagram to include saving and investment. (The government and foreign sectors are excluded for now.) In order to simplify the analysis, we will assume that all saving originates from the household sector. In reality, some of the profit of business firms may be retained as business saving. However, the bulk of the nation's saving is derived from the household sector; so our simplifying assumption is largely consistent with the real world.

EXHIBIT 4 The circular flow with saving and investment

When saving and investment are included, there are two pathways by which funds can travel from households to product markets: (a) directly through household consumption expenditures or (b) indirectly through the loanable funds market (saving), the extension of loans to businesses for investment expenditures. In equilibrium, the flow of consumption and investment expenditures (top loop) will equal the flow of income to resource owners (bottom loop).

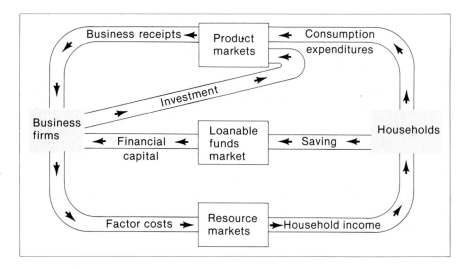

Loanable Funds Market: A general term used to describe the market arrangements that coordinate the borrowing and lending decisions of business firms and households. Commercial banks, savings and loan associations, the stock and bond markets, and life insurance companies are important financial institutions in this market.

While most saving takes place in the household sector, business firms are the major source of investment expenditures. Thus, investors and savers are different people. Their actions are directed through the **loanable funds market,** a market that reflects the borrowing and lending decisions of business firms and individuals. The loanable funds market is composed of a variety of financial institutions, including commercial banks, savings and loan associations, and other financial institutions. As Exhibit 4 illustrates, households supply funds to the loanable funds market, and business firms desiring funds for investment purposes demand funds from it.

With the addition of saving and investment to the circular flow diagram, there are now two ways in which funds can flow from households to product markets. Households will spend some of their income on consumer goods. However, the portion of household income that is saved will flow into the loanable funds market. Firms will utilize these funds to finance new investments. In turn, these investment expenditures will combine with household expenditures to create the total flow of expenditures (demand) into product markets.

If the planned expenditures of consumers and investors (the top loop of Exhibit 4) are just equal to the value of the goods and services produced during the period (the bottom loop), there is no tendency for output to change. The spending plans of consumers and investors mesh precisely with the production plans of business decision makers. The economy is in equilibrium. However, when total spending is unequal to total income, change will ensue. If the planned expenditures of consumers and investors (aggregate demand) are less than the value of the products that the businesses produce during a specific period (aggregate supply), business firms will be unable to sell all of the output produced. Inventories will rise. The abnormally large inventories will induce business decision makers to reduce production during the next period. Thus, when planned aggregate demand is less than planned output, future output will decline.

On the other hand, if the spending of consumers and investors exceeds the value of the output produced during the period, business firms will be selling more goods and services than they are producing. Inventories will decline. This unplanned reduction in inventories will cause firms to expand output during the next period.

EXHIBIT 5   Equilibrium level of income, output, and employment

Possible Levels of Employment (Millions of Persons) (1)	Aggregate Supply (Output and Income) (NNP = DI) (Billions of Dollars) (2)	Planned Consumption (Billions of Dollars) (3)	Planned Saving (Billions of Dollars) (4)	Planned Investment (Billions of Dollars) (5)	Unplanned Inventory Changes (Billions of Dollars) (6)	Planned Aggregate Demand, C + I (Billions of Dollars) (7)	Tendency of Employment, Output, and Income (8)
80	2900	2750	150	200	−50	2950	Increase
90	2950	2775	175	200	−25	2975	Increase
100	3000	2800	200	200	0	3000	Equilibrium
110	3050	2825	225	200	+25	3025	Decrease
120	3100	2850	250	200	+50	3050	Decrease

Equilibrium and Disequilibrium—Tabular Presentation

The equilibrium levels of output, income, and employment are sometimes easier to grasp when the major components are presented in tabular form. Exhibit 5 presents data for hypothetical consumption, saving, and investment schedules. Investment is assumed here to be determined by such factors as business expectations and technological change. Thus, it is not dependent on the level of income. Consumption, as we have already noted, is positively related to income, however. Aggregate equilibrium for the economy is present when output is $3000 billion. At that output level, consumers plan to spend $2800 billion for current goods and services and save $200 billion. Business decision makers also plan to invest $200 billion. The total planned level of spending (C + I), $3000 billion, is just equal to income at that output level. The plans of producers, investors, and consumers are perfectly consistent with one another. The equilibrium rate of output, $3000 billion, can be sustained in the future.

The plans of business and household decision makers will, however, come into conflict at income levels other than equilibrium. What will happen if the output of the economy temporarily expands to $3050 billion? Employment will increase from 100 to 110 million. At this higher income level, households will plan to save $225 billion, spending $2825 billion on consumption. Business decision makers will plan to invest $200 billion. Aggregate demand will be $3025, $25 billion less than aggregate supply. The spending of consumers and investors will be insufficient to purchase the total output produced. Business decision makers will be unable to sell as much as they had planned, and inventories will rise. The actual investment of the business sector will be $225 billion, $200 billion in planned investment and a $25 billion unplanned and unwanted inventory investment.[2] Business decision makers will respond to these now excess inventories by cutting back production and planned investment next year. Output and income will decline toward the equilibrium level. Employment will decline and unemployment will rise.

An economy is able to sustain only the equilibrium level of income. When aggregate income (supply) is greater than aggregate demand, unwanted inven-

---

[2]The reader should note the distinction between planned investment and actual investment. Actual investment must always equal actual saving. Investment necessitates saving—that is, a reduction in consumption. But planned investment will not equal planned saving when business firms find that their inventories are rising or falling in an unplanned manner.

tories will accumulate. Business firms will therefore cut back production and employment and income will fall. When aggregate income (supply) is less than aggregate demand, inventories will decline. Business firms will therefore expand production and employment and income will rise. The economy will always tend to move toward equilibrium where planned aggregate demand is just equal to income (supply).

Equilibrium and Disequilibrium—Graphic Presentation

Equilibrium can also be readily envisioned graphically. Exhibit 6 shows a graph for which planned aggregate demand, consumption plus investment, is measured on the y axis and total income (NNP) on the x axis. The 45-degree line extending from the origin shows all points that are equidistant from the x and y axes. Therefore, all points on the 45-degree line represent output levels for which aggregate demand and total income are equal.

The 45-degree line can also be thought of as an aggregate supply schedule. Remember that aggregate supply (output) and aggregate income must be equal. The market value of all final goods and services must equal the income payments received by those who produced them. The aggregate supply schedule outlines the willingness of producers to offer alternative levels of output.

Business firms will produce (supply) a level of output only if they expect consumers and investors to spend enough to purchase that output level. The 45-degree line indicates all levels of output (income) for which total spending will be sufficient to purchase the output level and thereby sufficient to induce business firms to supply it. Aggregate demand will equal aggregate supply for all points on the 45-degree line. Thus, the 45-degree line maps out all possible equilibrium levels of output. Note that there are many possible equilibrium levels of total income, output, and employment, not just one.

Exhibit 7 graphically depicts the consumption and aggregate demand schedule for the data presented in Exhibit 5. Consumption is positively related to income. As income rises, planned consumption increases, although by a smaller amount than income. Thus, the consumption function will be flatter than the 45-degree line. Since investment is determined independent of income,

EXHIBIT 6 Aggregate equilibrium

Total spending (aggregate demand) will equal aggregate income for *all levels* of spending and income along a 45-degree line from the origin. Thus, all points along the 45-degree line represent equilibrium levels of output (aggregate supply).

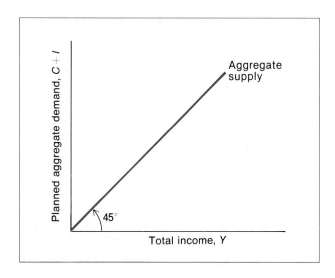

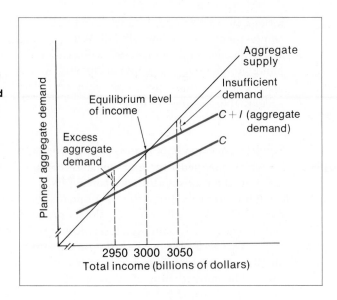

when planned investment ($200 billion) is added (vertically) to the consumption schedule, the result yields aggregate demand.

The equilibrium level of total income (NNP) will be at the point where planned aggregate demand is just equal to aggregate supply (total income). Consequently, the equilibrium level of income will be at $3000 billion, where the aggregate demand function $(C + I)$ crosses the 45-degree line. Under the conditions that we have outlined, no other level of income could be sustained.

Using the graphic analysis, let us consider why total income will move toward the $3000 billion equilibrium level. When total income exceeds $3000 billion—for example, at $3050 billion—the aggregate demand function lies below the 45-degree line. Remember that the $C + I$ line indicates how much people want to spend at each income level. When the $C + I$ line is below the 45-degree line, total spending is less than total income (output). Thus, unwanted inventories will accumulate and businesses will reduce their future production. Employment will decline. Income will fall back from $3050 billion to the equilibrium level of $3000 billion.

In contrast, if total income is temporarily below equilibrium, there is a tendency for income to rise. Suppose that income is temporarily at $2950 billion. At this income level, the $C + I$ function lies above the 45-degree line. Aggregate demand exceeds aggregate supply (income). Businesses are selling more than they are currently producing. Inventories are falling. Businesses will react to this by hiring more workers and expanding production. Income will rise to the $3000 billion equilibrium. Only at the equilibrium level, the point at which the $C + I$ (aggregate demand) function crosses the 45-degree line, will the plans of consumers and investors sustain the existing income level into the future.

Adding Government Demand

Thus far, we have focused on a purely private economy. For a mixed economy, the government, like private consumers and investors, demands resources and contributes to income. Government expenditures contribute to total spending on goods and services, thereby forming the third major component of aggregate

EXHIBIT 8 Equilibrium for a mixed economy

Given the current level of aggregate demand, only the income level Y_e could be maintained over time. What if full employment required an income level greater than Y_e—for example, Y_f? Continual unemployment would result, unless something happened to change the level of aggregate demand.

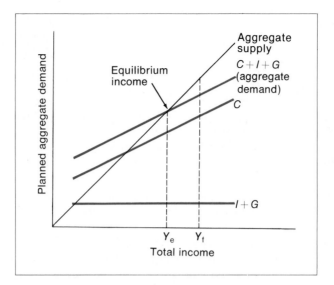

demand. Government taxes *reduce* the amount of income available for consumption spending. Therefore, taxes, like saving, are a withdrawal from the national income scheme.

The total aggregate demand for a mixed economy like that of the United States is the sum of consumption (C), investment (I), and government (G) spending on goods and services.[3] It is often referred to as $C + I + G$. In equilibrium, aggregate income (supply), often referred to as Y, must still equal aggregate demand. Exhibit 8 illustrates the equilibrium level of income for a mixed private–government economy. Planned aggregate demand is equal to aggregate supply at income level Y_e. At this level, the total spending of consumers, business investors, and the government is just equal to the income payments to factor suppliers.

If national income were temporarily greater than Y_e, it would tend to fall because of insufficient demand. On the other hand, if income were temporarily less than Y_e, then aggregate demand would exceed income, causing businesses to expand production during the next period. The plans of business decision makers, consumers, and government could all be realized simultaneously only at income level Y_e, given the current demand. Thus, there would be a tendency for income to converge on Y_e.[4]

---

[3]This is true for a closed economy, one that does not trade with other nations.

[4]There is another method of analyzing equilibrium: In equilibrium, the planned leakages (saving and taxes) must be equal to the planned injections (investment and government spending). Any level of income for which leakages and injections are not equal cannot be maintained. When planned injections are in excess of planned leakages, government spending and private investment are putting more into the income stream than saving and taxes are taking out. Business decision makers will expand future output in order to replenish their inventories. As output expands, employment will increase. When planned leakages are in excess of injections, taxes and saving are taking more out of the income stream than investment and government spending are injecting back into it. Output will exceed current consumption demand and undesired inventories will rise. Firms will respond by reducing production, and employment and income will decline.

What if full employment required a higher income level, such as Y_f? If this were the case, the economy would experience unemployment. Aggregate demand would be insufficient to maintain income level Y_f. Within the Keynesian type of analysis we have developed in this chapter, aggregate equilibrium need not coincide with full employment. In fact, for a purely private economy, Keynesians argue that there is no reason to expect that full employment will be present when the economy is in equilibrium. Therefore, prolonged periods of unemployment are not surprising.

What happens if aggregate demand is so strong that the economy is unable to supply the equilibrium level of income even when all resources are fully employed? Full employment places a ceiling on the production capacity of an economy. Excess aggregate demand at full employment merely results in rising prices—in other words, in inflation.

The introduction of government into the model provides several policy alternatives that might be used to regulate aggregate demand. To a great extent, the level of government spending is a policy variable. The government might spend more (or less) on such things as highways, defense, education, and cleaning up the environment in order to ensure the proper level of aggregate demand. The government's taxing policy can also be utilized to influence demand. In subsequent chapters, we will analyze both the potential for and limitations of public policy as a tool with which to control aggregate demand and promote full employment with price stability.

THE MULTIPLIER PRINCIPLE

We have seen in earlier sections of this chapter that changes in spending in areas such as consumption, investment, or government will change the equilibrium level of income in the economy. We now want to take a closer look at this process. In so doing, we will not only examine how and why such changes take place but also what determines the magnitude of the changes.

Suppose that a business firm decided to undertake a $1 million investment project. Since investment is a component of aggregate demand, the project should directly increase demand by $1 million. The investment project would require plumbers, carpenters, masons, lumber, cement, and many other resources. The incomes of the suppliers of these resources would be increased by $1 million. What would they do with this additional income? We know that there are two possibilities, some of the income would be spent and some of it would be saved. The portion that was spent would increase the incomes of retailers and others who supply these additional consumption products and services. After setting aside a portion of this additional income, these retailers and others would also spend some of their additional income on current consumption. Their consumption spending would result in still more additional income for other product and service suppliers.

An initial investment sets off a chain reaction of additional rounds of spending. Income increases by some multiple of the initial investment. This amplified effect of investment on income is called the multiplier principle.

The **multiplier** is the number by which the initial investment would be multiplied in order to obtain the total amplified increase in income. If the $1 million investment resulted in $4 million of additional income, the multi-

Multiplier: The ratio of the change in the equilibrium level of income to the independent change in investment, consumption, or government spending that brings about that change. Numerically, the multiplier is equal to $1/(1 - MPC)$.

plier would be 4—income increased by four times the amount of the initial increase in spending. Similarly, if total income increased by $3 million, the multiplier would be 3.

MPC Determines the Size of the Multiplier

The size of the expenditure multiplier is dependent on the marginal propensity to consume. This is true because the multiplier process depends on income received being passed on to others in the form of consumption spending. The MPC obviously measures how much income is passed on at each level of spending. Exhibit 9 illustrates this point using the data from our previous example. Suppose that the MPC for the economy were $3/4$, indicating that consumers spend 75 percent of any additional income. We know that a $1 million investment would initially result in $1 million of additional income in round 1. Since the MPC is $3/4$, consumption would increase by $750,000, contributing that amount to income in round 2. The recipients of the round-2 income would spend three-fourths of it on current consumption. Thus, their spending would increase income by $562,500 in round 3. In total, income would eventually increase by $4 million, given an MPC of $3/4$. Therefore, the multiplier would be 4.

If the MPC had been greater, income recipients would have spent a larger share of their additional income on current consumption. Thus, the additional income generated in each round would have been greater, thereby increasing the size of the multiplier. There is a precise relationship between the expenditure multiplier and the MPC. The *expenditure multiplier M* is

$$M = \frac{1}{1 - \text{MPC}}$$

Since income is either consumed or saved, $1 - \text{MPC}$ is also the MPS. Therefore, the expenditure multiplier is also

$$M = \frac{1}{\text{MPS}}$$

Merely inverting the MPS yields the multiplier. If households saved $1/10$ of their additional income, the multiplier would be 10. If MPS were equal to $1/2$, the multiplier would be 2. Exhibit 10 illustrates the relationship between MPS, MPC, and the multiplier for several alternative values.

EXHIBIT 9   The multiplier principle

Expenditure Stage	Additional Income (Dollars)	Additional Consumption (Dollars)	Marginal Propensity to Consume
Round 1	1,000,000	750,000	3/4
Round 2	750,000	562,500	3/4
Round 3	562,500	421,875	3/4
Round 4	421,875	316,406	3/4
Round 5	316,406	237,305	3/4
All others	949,219	711,914	3/4
Total	4,000,000	3,000,000	–

EXHIBIT 10   The relationship between MPS, MPC, and the multiplier

MPS	MPC	Multiplier
1/10	9/10	10
1/5	4/5	5
1/4	3/4	4
1/3	2/3	3
1/2	1/2	2
2/3	1/3	1.5

A higher MPC (lower MPS) means a larger multiplier.

Although we have used an increase in investment spending to demonstrate the multiplier concept, the general principle applies to all categories of spending. Any independent shift in the level of government, consumption, or investment spending will have the *same amplified impact* on income. It is because the multiplier principle has the ability to explain why even relatively small changes in any one of these components of aggregate demand can induce much larger changes in national income that it occupies a central position in the Keynesian model.

A Graphic Illustration of the Multiplier

It is also possible to demonstrate the multiplier graphically within the framework of the Keynesian model. Suppose that the economy is initially in equilibrium at the $2.7 trillion income level. Exhibit 11 illustrates that aggregate demand is just equal to income at $2.7 trillion. Let us assume that business decision makers suddenly become more optimistic and plan to spend an additional $50 billion on investment. This additional investment will cause the aggregate demand function, $C + I_1 + G$, to shift upward $50 billion. At every income level, $50 billion of additional investment is planned, as indicated by the new $C + I_2 + G$ aggregate demand schedule. A new equilibrium will result in which aggregate demand is now equal to income.

How much will equilibrium income increase? This will depend on the MPC. Graphically, MPC, the fraction of additional income that is consumed, is the slope of the consumption function. Exhibit 11 illustrates the multiplier when MPC is $2/3$. The $50 billion of additional investment will directly increase income by that amount (first round). Persons receiving the $50 billion will increase their spending by $33.3 billion (50 billion multiplied by $2/3$ — the MPC) during the second round, causing an additional expansion in income. Of course, this additional consumption spending in round 2 will generate additional income for others. During round 3, the round-2 income recipients will increase their spending, triggering an additional expansion in income. After the process has continued through successive rounds, income will have increased by $150 billion. In this example, the multiplier is 3, since income rose by three times the initial expansion in investment.

If the MPC were greater than $2/3$, the slope of the consumption (and aggregate demand) schedule would be steeper. The $50 billion of new investment would have an even larger multiple impact on total income because more income would have been passed along at each level of spending.

The multiplier can also function in reverse. Exhibit 11 can be used to illustrate this point. Suppose that the economy is initially at the full-employment

EXHIBIT 11 Graphic illustration of the multiplier

This diagram illustrates how an increase in planned investment triggers successive rounds of additional consumption spending, causing income to rise by a multiple of the initial increase in aggregate demand. When the MPC is ⅔, a $50 billion increase in planned investment will cause income to expand from $2.20 trillion to $2.35 trillion, an increase of $150 billion. Hence, the multiplier is 3.

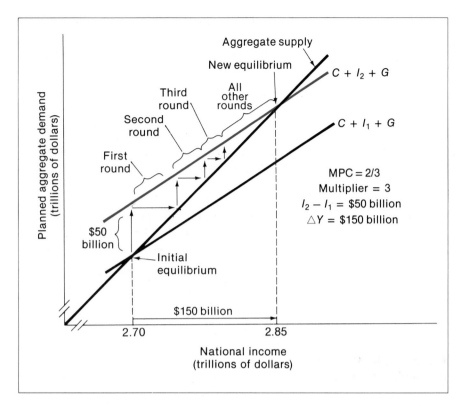

income level of $2.85 trillion. Despite the high level of income, something happens to disturb the expectations of business decision makers. Maybe the stock market takes a turn for the worse or diplomatic relations with a potential enemy are strained. For whatever reason, business decision makers expect that the future market for their product will be weak. Thus, they decide to cut back on their current investment by $50 billion. The investment schedule shifts down by this amount (a shift from I_2 to I_1 in Exhibit 11). Aggregate demand also declines by $50 billion.

How much will the equilibrium level of income fall? The multiplier principle will magnify the impact of the change in business investment plans. Given an MPC of ⅔, the $50 billion decline in investment will result in a $150 billion reduction in the equilibrium level of income. Because of the multiplier principle, the comparatively small reduction in planned investment will be amplified. Income will fall sharply and depressed economic conditions will permeate the economy. As forecasters, the business decision makers were on target. The future is not bright. Their prophecy of a future recession has been fulfilled.

Reality and the Multiplier

Do events in the real world conform to the multiplier principle? We will deal with this question in more detail as we go along, but two points should be made now.

1. It Takes Time for the Multiplier to Work. Within the model, it appears that the multiplier has an instantaneous impact. In the real world, however, this is not the case. The income will be spent over a period of weeks or even months. Thus, there will be some delay before secondary parties receive their additional income. It is usually thought that approximately one-half of the multiplier effect will be felt during the first six months. Thus, if the total multiplier is 4, a multiplier effect of approximately 2 should be felt during the first six-month period.

2. Idle Resources Are Necessary before the Multiplier Can Increase Real Income. It is important to recognize the distinction between an economy with idle resources, unemployed labor and machines, and one without them. When resources are idle, each round of additional spending generated by the multiplier will expand real output and employment. However, when there are no idle resources, the expansion in income will be merely inflationary. The increased spending will result in higher prices, not an expansion in real production.

THE PARADOX OF THRIFT

Paradox of Thrift: An apparent contradiction between the desire of households to increase saving and their ability to realize a higher rate of saving *in aggregate*. In the Keynesian model, when households *in aggregate* plan to save more, consumption will decline, causing income to fall by the amount of the reduction in consumption times the multiplier. At the lower income level, *actual* saving may be no greater (it might even be less) than the level that would have occurred had households not tried to be more thrifty.

Most of us usually think of saving as a good thing. The Keynesian model, however, suggests that what is good for the individual household may not always be good for the entire economy. Although saving is sometimes the route to fortune for an individual, too much aggregate saving can result in unemployed resources and a decline in national income.

Exhibit 12 illustrates what economists call the **paradox of thrift.** Suppose that the economy is initially in equilibrium at $3.0 trillion of income. At this income level, the economy is just able to maintain full employment. Suppose that the planned saving of households increases by $25 billion. Because households now planned to save more, the saving schedule will shift upward to S_2, a $25 billion increase. But saving is merely income not consumed. An increase in planned savings means a reduction in planned consumption. Thus, the aggregate demand schedule will shift downward by the $25 billion as a result of the thriftiness of individuals. This sets off the multiplier chain reaction.

EXHIBIT 12   The paradox of thrift

Suppose that the initial full-employment equilibrium income level is $3.0 trillion and that consumers suddenly decide to increase their saving by $25 billion. What will happen to the equilibrium level of income? It will fall by $75 billion because the multiplier will amplify the impact of the decline in aggregate demand.

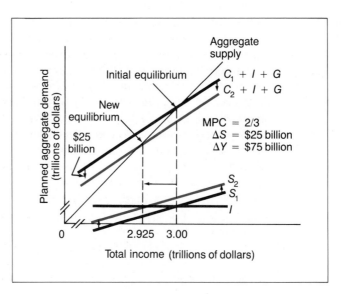

With an MPC of ⅔, the reduced consumption of $25 billion will eventually reduce equilibrium income by $75 billion. When households in the aggregate attempt to save more, their actions cause aggregate demand and the equilibrium level of income to fall!

The *actual* saving at income level $2.925 trillion is the same as for the initial equilibrium level of income. Even though consumers attempt (plan) to save more, the reduction in income caused by their efforts to be more thrifty foil their efforts. From the individual viewpoint, saving adds to wealth. It permits a higher level of future spending. From society's viewpoint, however, a dollar saved is a dollar not spent. The reduction in spending could have disastrous consequences leading to declining income, production, and employment.

In the real world, efforts to be more thrifty are likely to come at times when they will be most damaging. For example, when individuals anticipate the onset of a recession, most will reduce their spending in an effort to prepare for possible layoffs and general hard times. While this makes sense for individuals, increased saving on an aggregate level may actually bring about the recession everyone feared. From society's viewpoint, the remedy of individuals—an increase in thriftiness—becomes part of the problem. When an economy is operating at less than full employment, the paradox of thrift can become a reality.

INVESTMENT INSTABILITY AND THE ACCELERATOR

The multiplier principle emphasizes that changes in investment can generate substantial additional income and consumption. What about a possible link in the other direction? Can additional consumption induce changes in the level of investment?

Accelerator Principle: The proposition that an increase in consumer demand will result in an expansion in investment because a larger capital stock will be necessary to produce the higher level of consumer goods. The principle also implies that when consumption is growing, a mere *slowing down* in the rate of growth in consumer demand will cause gross investment to decline. Thus, the principle suggests that investment will be highly volatile.

According to the **accelerator principle,** rising consumption will result in more investment because a larger capital stock will be necessary to produce the additional consumption. The accelerator principle postulates a constant relationship between the economy's capital stock and the level of consumption output. Thus, more consumption necessitates more investment—that is, additions to the nation's capital stock.

Let us apply this principle to a simple example. Assume, for the moment, that the economy consumes 10,000 loaves of bread per year. (Keep in mind that both investment and consumption are flow concepts.) To produce 10,000 loaves of bread per year takes 10 ovens. Let us assume that one oven wears out each year, so gross investment in the first year is one replacement oven. Now, if the economy in year 2 consumes 11,000 loaves, it will take 11 ovens to produce that much bread. New investment in year 2 will be one replacement oven and one new oven to meet the inrease in consumption demand. Note that a 10 percent increase in consumption (that is, 1000 loaves/10,000 loaves) has brought about a 100 percent increase in investment (two ovens compared to one in the previous period). Obviously, however, the economy in year 2 now has the capital stock necessary to produce 11,000 loaves of bread. Thus, investment will only increase by the one replacement oven during the subsequent year. If consumption does not increase again, investment will actually decline from two ovens to one—a 50 percent decline in investment.

As long as consumption increases, investment will grow, but if consumption just levels off, investment will fall and equilibrium income will also fall. If consumption actually declines, investment and equilibrium income will decline drastically.

Because of the accelerator, rising consumption will induce additional investment, causing income to rise rapidly during an upswing. However, if consumption merely slows down, investment will decline, causing total income to fall. Thus, according to this theory, private investment will be very volatile, shooting up during an expansion and plummeting during a business slowdown.

THE ACCELERATOR–MULTIPLIER INTERACTION AND THE ROLE OF INVENTORIES

It should be noted here that some contemporary economists, as well as Keynesians, believe that the multiplier and accelerator concepts interact strongly to make swings in the business cycle more severe. An expansion in consumption will reduce inventories. Business decision makers will read this signal and step up investment spending, which in turn, through the multiplier, will produce multiplied increases in income and consumption spending. This increased consumption further reduces inventories and the investment accelerator–multiplier process continues until the full employment of resources is reached. When this occurs, it is not possible to increase output, since there are no additional resources available. Therefore, the price of existing and already utilized resources must rise. This triggers price increases, lowering consumers' real income and subsequently reducing consumption. Inventories pile up and producers respond by cutting back investment spending, setting off the multiplier–accelerator process in the negative direction. Remember, in the Keynesian model, inventories are the barometer that businesses use to guide their investment decisions.

The Keynesian theory of the business cycle emphasizes the role of inventories in fluctuations in GNP. This view is not accepted by all economists. The monetarists believe that economic fluctuations originate from a different source. They warn that association is not causation. As we will discuss in a later chapter, the monetarists believe that changes in investment are the result, not the cause, of fluctuations in the supply of money.

THE CENTRAL THEME OF KEYNES

Before closing this chapter, it is important to reiterate the concept of equilibrium introduced by the Keynesian model. Equilibrium within the Keynesian model is not dependent on full employment. There is no reason to expect that full employment will necessarily be associated with the equilibrium income level. The Keynesian model implies that the level of aggregate demand reached by the unhampered market mechanism, which coordinates millions of individual economic decisions, will often be insufficient to ensure full employment.

Aggregate demand is the catalyst of this underemployment Keynesian model. When aggregate demand changes, income and employment levels also change. Until full employment is attained, supply is always accommodative. An increase in aggregate demand will thus lead to an increase in output and real income. The pre-Keynesian view was that "supply creates its own demand." The Keynesian view simply turns this statement around. Until the full-employment capacity of an economy is reached, demand creates its own supply.

Although Keynes emphasized that a market economy, on its own, will often be unable to provide a level of demand consistent with full employment, he did offer us some hope for achieving that level by other means. According to Keynes, government spending can directly contribute to aggregated demand since taxation influences disposable income directly and therefore consumer spending indirectly. Thus, if full employment is desired, governments can take an active role in bringing it about. This was the positive side of Keynes' message.

In subsequent chapters, we will analyze the ability of governments to use their spending and taxation policies to provide a level of demand consistent with full employment and economic stability.

CHAPTER LEARNING OBJECTIVES

1 The primary determinant of consumption is disposable income. As disposable income increases, consumption expenditures will rise, although in the short run they will generally rise less rapidly than income.

2 The major determinants of investment are (a) current sales relative to the productive capacity of the existing productive facilities, (b) expectations about future sales, and (c) the interest rate. Keynes perceived that during a period of depressed economic conditions, investment would be largely unresponsive to changes in the interest rate.

3 In the Keynesian model, which includes government, planned aggregate demand is the sum of the planned consumption, investment, and government expenditures. Aggregate demand is the moving force in the Keynesian model.

4 When an economy is in equilibrium, planned aggregate demand will be just equal to aggregate supply. If planned aggregate demand is temporarily less than output, businesses will be unable to sell as much as they had anticipated (planned). Rather than continue to accumulate undesired inventories, they will reduce future output. Income will decline to the equilibrium level. If planned aggregate demand is temporarily in excess of output, businesses will sell more of their products than they anticipate. Their inventories will be depleted below the desired level. In an effort to restore the depleted inventories, they will expand future output, and income will rise to the equilibrium level.

5 In the Keynesian model, there are many potential equilibrium levels of income, depending on the level of aggregate demand. Equilibrium may exist at an income level less than or greater than full employment.

6 Aggregate demand determines income, output, and employment in the Keynesian model. Until the full-employment capacity is reached, increases in aggregate demand will generate higher levels of real output and employment. Thus, policies that affect aggregate demand can, at least potentially, be utilized to promote full employment with stable prices.

7 According to the multiplier principle, independent changes in planned investment, government expenditures, and consumption have a magnified impact on income. Income will increase by some multiple of the initial change in spending. The multiplier is the number by which the initial investment is multiplied in order to obtain the total amplified increase in income. The size of the multiplier increases with the marginal propensity to consume.

8 It takes time for the secondary effects of the multiplier to be felt. It is usually thought that approximately one half of the multiplier effect will be felt during the first six months after an independent change in spending.

9   When resources are idle, each round of additional spending generated by the multiplier will expand real output and employment. When there are few idle resources, the increased spending will be inflationary.

10   The Keynesian model suggests that an increase in planned aggregate saving could cause problems. Higher planned saving would mean a reduction in planned consumption. Other things constant, aggregate demand would decline, causing the equilibrium level of income to fall. Since households often try to save more at the beginning of a recessionary period, their actions may push the economy further into a recession and complicate the recovery process.

11   Interaction between the multiplier and accelerator enhances the potential for economic instability. During expansion, an increase in investment serves to increase consumption, which in turn increases the demand for additional investment. Consumption and investment feed each other, and the economy booms. However, full employment places a ceiling on growth and eventually the expansion levels off. The accelerator principle explains why, as growth and consumption level off, net investment often declines sharply, plunging the economy toward recession.

THE ECONOMIC WAY OF THINKING — DISCUSSION QUESTIONS

1   Explain why it sometimes may be impossible for the plans of savers and investors to be fulfilled simultaneously.

2   When is an economy in aggregate equilibrium? Explain in your own words why an economy will return to aggregate equilibrium from a position of excess aggregate demand or from a position of insufficient aggregate demand.

3   How will each of the following factors influence the consumption schedule?
(a) The expectation that consumer prices will rise more rapidly in the future
(b) Pessimism about future employment conditions
(c) A reduction in income taxes
(d) An increase in the interest rate
(e) A decline in stock prices
(f) A redistribution of income from older workers (aged 45 and over) to the young (under 35)
(g) A redistribution of income from the wealthy to the poor

4   "The best cure for unemployment and recession is for everybody, including the government, to tighten their belts, cut down on unnecesary spending, and forego luxury items until the recession is over." Do you agree? Why or why not?

5   Explain in your own words how the multiplier and accelerator reinforce each other to generate cyclical business conditions.

6   Explain the paradox of thrift.

7   What is the multiplier principle? What determines the size of the multiplier? Does the multiplier principle make it more or less difficult to stabilize the economy? Explain.

FISCAL POLICY AND DEMAND MANAGEMENT

Government is responsible for too much total spending (which results in demand inflation) as well as too little total spending (which results in depression). Among its other purposes, government spending increases total expenditures while taxing decreases it, so that fiscal policy is an instrument for regulating total spending[1]
Professor Abba Lerner

According to Keynesian theory, economic instability is caused by erratic fluctuations in aggregate demand. When aggregate demand is deficient, unnecessary and abnormally high unemployment results. On the other hand, when an economy is already operating at capacity, excess aggregate demand generates inflation. If aggregate demand could be managed properly, full employment and economic stability could be attained.

Since the government's taxation and expenditure policies can influence aggregate demand, the federal budget is a useful weapon to combat economic instability, unemployment, and inflation. Government spending is a component of aggregate demand. It can directly influence the level of demand. Taxes alter the disposable income of consumers and the profitability of business firms. Thus, taxation policy has an indirect impact on the consumption and investment components of aggregate demand. Taxes and government expenditures are fiscal policy tools. **Fiscal policy** is the use of government spending and taxation policy as a vehicle for managing the determinants of aggregate output.

Fiscal Policy: The use of government taxation and expenditure policies to influence aggregate demand and output.

FISCAL POLICY IN HISTORICAL PERSPECTIVE

Despite the enormous prosperity that has been achieved at various times by market economies, spurts of economic growth seem inevitably to be followed by recession. Having confronted and analyzed the massive unemployment and idle productive capacity of the 1930s, Professor Keynes believed that he had discovered both the cause of and remedy for economic instability and recession. According to the Keynesian view, fluctuations in aggregate demand are the major source of economic disturbance. Therefore, if demand could be stabilized

---

[1]Personal communication to the authors, 1979.

and maintained at a level consistent with the economy's full-employment productive capacity, the most serious shortcoming of a market economy could be eliminated. With a message like this, is it any wonder that Keynes became the most influential economist of the twentieth century?

The Keynesian analysis highlights the potential importance of the government's budget. Whether we like it or not, the sheer size of the budget provides policy-makers with a powerful tool capable of influencing the economy. However, the federal budget is much more than merely a revenue and expenditure statement of a large organization. The determinants of the federal budget differ from the determinants of the revenues and expenditures of a private business organization.

Prior to the 1960s, the desirability of a balanced federal budget was widely accepted among business and political leaders. Keynesian economists were highly critical of this view. They argued that the government's taxation and expenditure policies should be determined by the demand requirements of the economy rather than the desire to equalize revenues with expenditures. Keynesian theory implies that budgetary (fiscal) policy can be a stabilizing device, a regulatory tool, to ensure that the rate of spending is sufficient to provide for full employment, but not so large as to trigger an inflationary price rise. The economy's demand requirements, according to this view, are not necessarily related directly to a balanced budget.

The 1964 tax cut ushered in a new era of fiscal policy management. Even though Keynesian theory had dominated academic circles for some time, the 1964 tax cut provided the first clear application of the theory to public policy in the United States. When the tax cut was initially considered in 1963, the economy was sluggish. The price level was virtually stable, and the unemployment rate hovered around 6 percent. The federal budget was running a deficit. It was against this background that Walter Heller, the chairman of the Council of Economic Advisers, convinced a reluctant President Kennedy to propose lower tax rates in spite of the budget deficit. The major argument of Chairman Heller and other economists was that a tax cut would stimulate consumer and business spending, increasing aggregate demand and employment. In 1964, the tax cut was enacted; economic growth and high employment did indeed follow.

Economists were very optimistic about the potential of "real-world" fiscal policy to assure a high level of employment and economic stability. However, economic events did not continue to unfold as anticipated. The 1970s were a period of inflation and sluggish growth. Fiscal management of the economy was not as easy as many economists had imagined it to be during the euphoria following the 1964 tax cut.

The economic experience of the 1970s made economists increasingly aware of two important points. First, the proper timing of modifications in fiscal policy is both more important and more difficult than was believed during the 1960s. If a change in fiscal policy direction is adopted 12 months too late, the effects may be substantially different than those that would have been derived from an earlier adoption. Second, fiscal policy is more complex than was previously thought. Political as well as economic considerations influence the timing, direction, and structure of fiscal changes. The simultaneous combination of unemployment and inflation makes the proper fiscal strategy far less clear-cut. There are both demand and supply factors to consider. Fiscal policy changes may exert undesired side effects in other markets, particularly the loanable funds and capital goods markets. All of these factors add to the complexity of fiscal policy and, in some cases, limit its effectiveness.

We will begin by focusing on the mechanics of fiscal policy, considering its potential as an economic stabilization tool. Alternative fiscal strategies and the conditions under which they are most likely to be effective will be discussed. Initially, our focus will be on the demand-side impacts of fiscal policy. Later, we will integrate supply-side considerations more fully into our model and analyze the impact of fiscal policy on aggregate supply.

DEMAND STIMULUS TO COMBAT RECESSION

Recessionary Gap: The amount by which aggregate demand falls short of the full-employment level of income, when the nation's resources are not being fully utilized.

Exhibit 1 presents a graphic picture of an economy operating below its full-employment productive potential. The economy is experiencing an abnormally high rate of unemployment because of deficient aggregate demand. When the resources of the economy are fully employed, the equilibrium rate of income is $3.32 trillion. But the initial level of aggregate demand $(C + I + G_1)$ results in an actual equilibrium income level of $3.20 trillion, $120 billion below capacity. There is a **recessionary gap** between actual aggregate demand and the level of aggregate demand necessary to expand real output to the economy's full-employment potential. The amount by which aggregate demand falls short of the full-employment level of income, the recessionary gap, is the *vertical* distance by which the aggregate demand schedule falls short of the aggregate supply schedule at the full-employment level of income. For the economy pictured by Exhibit 1, the recessionary gap would be $30 billion. (Note: The recessionary gap is *not* the difference between full-employment income and actual income).

EXHIBIT 1   Government expenditures as a route to full-employment equilibrium

A $30 billion increase in autonomous government expenditures, *holding taxes constant,* would increase income from $3.20 trillion to the full-employment level of $3.32 trillion, a $120 billion expansion.

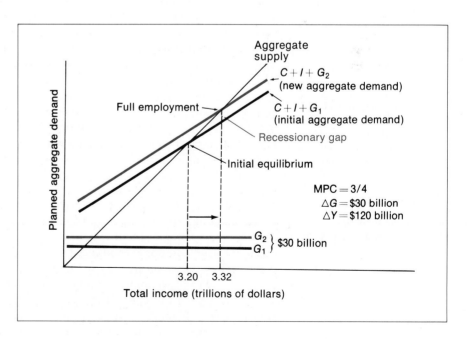

Increased Government Spending

How could public policy combat the recession, stimulate aggregate demand, and push the economy to its full-employment capacity level of output? One way would be to increase government expenditures *while holding taxes constant.* If the government increased its demand for such things as education, national defense, recreation areas, office buildings, training programs, and public housing, the *aggregate* demand for goods and services would rise. Suppose that the government spent an *additional* $30 billion on these goods. Aggregate demand would shift upward by $30 billion to $C + I + G_2$. The additional government spending would increase the income of newly employed workers, setting off a multiplier effect. Since the marginal propensity to consume for the economy is 3/4, the expenditure multiplier would be 4. Thus, the $30 billion of additional government spending would stimulate $120 billion of additional output, pushing the economy to full employment. Since unemployed resources are present, the expansion in demand would not cause rising prices until the economy's full-employment capacity ($3.32 billion) was reached. Given the excess capacity *initially* available, supply constraints would not restrict the effectiveness of the expansionary fiscal policy. Both real and nominal output would expand by $120 billion.

Should the government raise taxes to finance the additional expenditures? From the standpoint of policy effectiveness, it is important that the additional government spending does not merely replace private consumption and investment. If income taxes were raised, this would reduce the disposable income available to households, causing consumption to decline. Higher business taxes would discourage investment. Higher taxes would at least partially offset the expansionary effect of the increased level of government expenditures.

Budget Deficit: The amount by which government expenditures exceed tax revenues.

If the increased spending is to have a maximum expansionary effect, deficit financing should be used. The government should plan a **budget deficit,** recognizing that its tax revenues will be less than expenditures. Like a private business, the government cannot spend money that it does not have. If taxes are not raised, how will the government finance the higher level of current expenditures? Borrowing is the answer. The government can borrow from individuals, firms, and banks in order to cover its planned deficit. The Treasury can issue bonds, U.S. securities, in order to raise the funds necessary to finance the government's deficit.

Expansionary Fiscal Policy: A tax rate structure and level of government expenditures such that a budget deficit would be expected even if the economy were at full employment.

When government uses deficit spending in an attempt to increase aggregate demand and close a recessionary gap, it is using **expansionary fiscal policy.** This is the Keynesian prescription for stimulating an economy operating below full employment. Of course, there are two ways to bring about a deficit. We turn now to the second.

A Tax Cut and the Elimination of Underutilized Capacity

As an alternative to increasing government expenditures, a tax cut can be used to stimulate aggregate demand and combat recessionary conditions. Political decision-makers may feel that consumers, rather than the government, can best determine what additional goods need to be produced when output is expanded. If this is the case, an income tax reduction is the appropriate means of leading an underemployed economy back to its full potential.

An income tax cut will increase the disposable income of households. Lower taxes will mean a larger paycheck for millions of consumers. Since after-tax income is an important determinant of consumption, this increase

EXHIBIT 2   Tax reduction as a route to full employment

When the economy is below full-employment equilibrium, a reduction in taxes can also be utilized as a method of stimulating the economy back to full employment.

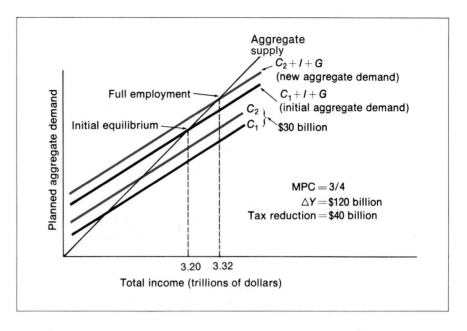

in "take-home pay" will induce households to enlarge their consumption expenditures. Aggregate demand will increase as a result.

As Exhibit 2 illustrates, a reduction in taxes will induce an increase in consumer spending by an amount equal to the change in disposable income times the MPC. A $40 billion tax cut will cause the consumption schedule (and aggregate demand) to shift upward by $30 billion, the amount of the tax cut times MPC (3/4). The increased consumer spending will generate more income for shopkeepers, restaurant owners, travel agencies, gasoline stations, automobile dealers, and many others. Because of the multiplier effect, $30 billion of additional consumer spending (stemming from the $40 billion tax cut) will cause income to expand by $120 billion.[2] Thus, a tax cut, like an expansion in government expenditures, can stimulate aggregate demand and push the economy to the full-employment equilibrium level of income.

Countercyclical Policy: A policy that tends to move the economy in an opposite direction from the forces of the business cycle. Thus, such a policy would stimulate demand during the contraction phase of the business cycle and restrain demand during the expansionary phase.

If taxes are cut, should government expenditures be reduced in order to keep the federal budget in balance? An expenditure reduction would inhibit aggregate demand, preventing it from expanding to the level consistent with the full-employment capacity of the economy. **Countercyclical policy** suggests that the government should couple a budget deficit with the tax cut and thereby stimulate aggregate demand while providing for the attainment of the full-employment equilibrium level of income.

---

[2]The net taxation multiplier (M_t) is the change in income divided by the change in taxes. In the example above, income increases by $120 billion as a result of a $40 billion tax reduction. Therefore, the net tax multiplier is 3. The net tax multiplier can also be calculated by the following formula:

$$M_t = \frac{MPC}{1 - MPC}$$

Thus, when MPC is equal to 3/4,

$$M_t = \frac{3/4}{1 - 3/4} = \frac{3/4}{1/4} = 3$$

As we saw in Chapter 6, private investment often declines sharply during a recession. Policy planners may want to combine an income tax cut with a reduction in business taxes in order to stimulate investment. Policy prescriptions such as more rapid tax write-offs for the depreciation of equipment, reductions in corporate income taxes, and/or larger investment tax credits might be chosen as the means of stimulating private investment. These tax reductions will increase both the after-tax flow of business-firm funds and the after-tax rate of return expected from investment projects. Decision-makers will be induced to undertake additional investment expenditures, shifting the investment schedule upward. The additional investment will have a multiplier effect, causing income to rise by the expansion in investment times the multiplier.

FISCAL POLICY FOR DEALING WITH INFLATION

Full employment places a ceiling on the productive capacity of the economy. What would happen if an economic expansion led to a level of demand that exceeded the economy's potential output? Once the full-employment rate of output has been reached, further increases in demand will cause prices to rise. The excess aggregate demand is inflationary.

Inflationary Gap: The amount by which aggregate demand exceeds the full-employment level of income, when an economy is experiencing rising prices resulting from excess demand.

Exhibit 3 presents a graphic picture of inflationary pressures that stem from excess demand. When aggregate demand is $C_2 + I_2 + G_2$, an inflationary gap AB exists. Specifically, the **inflationary gap** is the amount by which aggregate demand exceeds income at the level of income that is consistent with both full-employment and price stability.

If policy-makers could accurately forecast the coming inflation, **restrictive fiscal policy** could be used to prevent an inflationary gap and combat the rising prices. A reduced level of government expenditures would diminish aggregate demand directly, maintaining total spending at $C_1 + I_1 + G_1$. Alternatively, taxes could be increased. An increase in personal taxation would reduce disposable income, causing consumption to decline. An increase in business taxes would dampen investment.

Restrictive Fiscal Policy: A tax rate structure and level of government expenditures such that a budget surplus would be expected if the economy were at full employment.

Budget Surplus: The amount by which tax revenues are in excess of government expenditures.

Higher taxes and a reduction in government expenditures may result in a **budget surplus.** When a budget surplus is present, taxation is taking more out of the income stream than government expenditures are putting back into it. The Keynesian analysis suggests that this is precisely the proper policy prescription with which to combat inflation generated by excess demand.

However, if anti-inflation policy is going to work in this way, as illustrated by Exhibit 3, it is vital that the policy of restraint be instituted *prior* to the increase in the price level. Remember, following the Keynesian tradition, our model assumes that prices are inflexible downward. Therefore, once the price level has risen (that is, once the inflation rate has accelerated), restrictive fiscal policy and the accompanying lower rate of demand will, at least initially, exert their primary impact upon output rather than upon prices.[3]

---

[3]The recession of 1970 illustrates this point. After the inflation rate accelerated to 6 percent, up from 2 to 3 percent in the mid-1960s, during 1968–1969 the Nixon administration shifted to a policy of fiscal restraint. The more restrictive macroeconomic policy contributed to the recession of 1970.

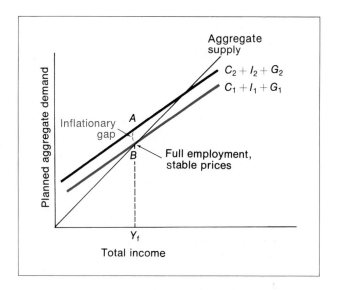

EXHIBIT 3 **Restrictive fiscal policy to offset inflationary pressure**

Excessive aggregate demand, such as that pictured by $C_2 + I_2 + G_2$, would cause rising prices. If policy-makers could anticipate the excessive demand, its inflationary impact could be offset by a restrictive fiscal policy. For example, government expenditures might be cut in order to maintain aggregate demand at $C_1 + I_1 + G_1$.

Our analysis highlights the importance of proper timing. If inflationary forces are anticipated, offsetting restrictive policy is a highly effective weapon against the inflation. However, if the restrictive fiscal policy is not instituted until after the inflationary forces are at work, undesired negative side effects on real output are likely to accompany the anti-inflationary strategy.

FISCAL POLICY AND BUDGET DEFICITS

Most politicians and budget planners in the 1950s thought of taxes as merely a tool with which to raise revenues for the financing of government expenditures. The budgetary problem, as has been noted, was conceived as one of matching revenues with expenditures.

According to the Keynesian view, it is often imprudent to seek a balanced budget. Rather, a planned budget deficit (expansionary fiscal policy) is more appropriate when economic conditions are slack, and a planned budget surplus (restrictive fiscal policy) is called for when policy-makers anticipate an inflationary boom. The general economic conditions replace the concept of the annual balanced budget as the proper criterion for determining budget policy.

Planned and Actual Deficits

Not only does the budget policy of the government exert an influence on economic conditions, but economic conditions also influence the revenue and expenditure level of the government, and not always in accordance with policy. Or, to put it another way, budget policy can have unplanned, counterproductive effects. When an economy is at less than full employment, a tax reduction may result in a deficit that is smaller than anticipated. This happens when the planned government deficit, by stimulating a rise in income, also stimulates an increase in tax revenues. Thus, despite the reduction in tax *rates*, tax *revenues* may decline by only a small amount. There is considerable evidence that this is what happened as a result of the much-heralded 1964 tax cut in the United States. Beginning in March 1964, the tax rates on personal income were slashed across the board by approximately 20 percent. The basic tax rate on corporate earnings was reduced from 52 percent to 48 percent. A planned annual deficit of between $10 billion and $15 billion was initially expected during fiscal years 1965 and 1966. However, GNP grew rapidly during the period immediately following the tax cut. Measured in dollars of constant purchasing power, revenues from the personal and corporate income taxes during fiscal year 1965 (which began four months after the tax cut) actually exceeded those of 1963 and 1964! The total taxes collected at the higher income levels were greater than anticipated. The actual government deficits were $1.6 billion in 1965 and $3.8 billion in 1966, much lower than the planned deficits for the two years.

How Not to Reduce the Deficit

In the reverse situation, when taxes are increased or expenditures reduced in an effort to avoid a budgetary deficit, a deficit may still result. Exhibit 4 illustrates why this is true. Suppose that the government is initially running a deficit because total income is at less than the full-employment level. Balanced-budget-minded politicians increase taxes and reduce government expenditures in order to bring the budget into balance. Such a policy will cause economic conditions to deteriorate even further. The tax increase will reduce disposable income, leading to a decline in consumption and aggregate demand. The reduction in government spending will directly reduce aggregate demand. As demand declines, the $C + I + G$ line will shift down, causing the equilibrium level of income to fall by some multiple of the decline in aggregate demand. At the lower income level, tax revenues will be less than expected, even though tax rates have been increased. An *actual* budget deficit may still result, even though the policy was designed to avoid it.

There is strong evidence that the 1958–1959 budgetary policies of the Eisenhower administration resulted in precisely this type of unplanned deficit. In 1958, the unemployment rate was 6.8 percent, and the economy was performing far below capacity. The Eisenhower administration *planned* a balanced budget despite the state of the economy at that time. The result was a continuation of high unemployment levels through 1961, a slow rate of growth in income, and a $12.9 billion budget deficit. Even though a balanced budget was *planned*, the actual deficit for the 1958–1959 fiscal year was the largest of any single year between World War II and 1968. It was primarily the result of *planning* a balanced budget when lower tax rates and a budget deficit were called for to stimulate income and employment.

The Full-Employment Budget Concept

The budget is complex, and no single indicator can reflect its precise impact on the economy. The actual budget deficit (surplus) does not reveal its source: It may or may not be indicative of the direction of economic policy. If a deficit, for example, does exist, it is important to know whether it is a *planned* deficit—the result of expansionary policy—or an *unplanned* deficit—the result of an inappropriate policy in combination with an economic recession, as was the case with the Eisenhower administration deficit in 1958–1959.

In an attempt to solve this problem, economists have devised a summary statistic designed to isolate (a) the impact of the budget on the economy from (b) the impact of the economy on the budget deficit or surplus. This summary

EXHIBIT 4   Trying to balance the budget can make things worse

If an economy were operating at less than full employment, reduced government expenditures and/or higher tax rates would cause aggregate demand to fall (shift to $C_2 + I_2 + G_2$). Income would decline. At the lower level of income, unemployment would rise, and tax revenues would be less than expected. An actual budget deficit would still be likely to result.

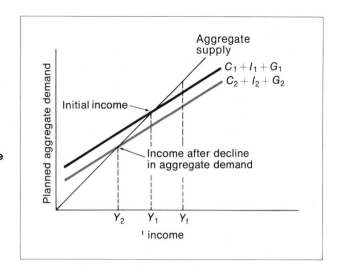

Full-Employment Budget: An estimate of what government revenues and expenditures would be if the economy were at full employment.

statistic, called the **full-employment budget,** is an estimate of what the revenues and expenditures of the government would be if the economy were at full employment, the level of activity associated with 5.0 to 5.5 percent unemployment. The full-employment budget standardizes budget estimates to a long-run, high-employment norm and thereby removes the impact of variations in economic activity that influence the actual budget deficit or surplus.

When the economy is operating at its full-employment norm, the actual budget and the full-employment budget are equal. The full-employment budget concept is most significant when the actual level of economic activity differs substantially from the long-run, full-employment norm. If there is a full-employment budget deficit, this indicates that fiscal policy is expansionary; policy-makers *planned* the budget deficit. Similarly, a surplus in the full-employment budget implies that fiscal policy is restrictive. In contrast, if the estimated full-employment budget is roughly in balance (or running a surplus), this indicates the absence of fiscal stimulus, *even though the actual budget deficit might be substantial.* Under these circumstances, the actual budget deficit is clearly *unplanned* and is not indicative of expansionary fiscal policy.

Economists are not in complete agreement on the precise guidelines to be used for calculating the full-employment budget estimate. Since there is no rigid definition of full employment, calculations based on alternative assumptions are clearly possible. Although the full-employment budget estimate provides us with a somewhat reliable indicator of fiscal policy, it may not be a *perfect* indicator of fiscal stimulus or restraint. Most economists believe that it performs its most useful function when utilized in conjunction with the actual budget deficit or surplus data.

PRACTICAL LIMITATIONS OF DEMAND-MANAGEMENT STRATEGY

Instituting fiscal changes that will promote high employment and at the same time reduce economic instability is far more difficult than most economists envisioned in the mid-1960s. With the benefit of hindsight, it is clear that past fiscal modifications have sometimes been destabilizing. Fiscal restraint, imposed to combat inflation, has sometimes overrestricted the economy and thus has contributed to the onset and the severity of recessions; expansionary macroeconomic policies, on the other hand, have sometimes overstimulated the economy and promoted inflation.

Why have policy-makers failed to create dependable, consistent policies and to achieve economic stability, given what they know about demand management? This question is not easily answered. It is important to recognize that maintaining the proper level of aggregate demand is a highly complex task. Both economic and political factors are involved. Although fiscal policy is an effective tool for combating a serious recession, the likelihood that it will entirely override the business-cycle forces is greatly reduced by the following four factors.

1. Forecasting Errors and Time Lags Make It Difficult to Time Fiscal Policy Properly. Policy-makers, like other decision-makers, must make choices without perfect information. Our ability to forecast a forthcoming recession or inflationary acceleration is very limited. Thus, the economic conditions that call for a change in fiscal policy may already be present and be worsening before they are widely recognized. Even after the need for a policy change is recognized, there is generally an additional time lag before the change can be instituted. Experts must study the problem. Congressional leaders must hold hearings. Legislators may choose to delay action if they can use their positions to obtain special favors for their constituencies. A majority of the lawmakers must be convinced that a proposed action is in the interest of the country and that of their own districts and supporters. All of these things take time.

Even after a change is instituted, its major impact will not be felt immediately. If government expenditures are going to be increased, time will be required for competitive bids to be submitted and new contracts granted. Contractors may be unable to begin work right away. Although a tax reduction will usually stimulate the economy more quickly, the secondary effects of the multiplier process will only be felt with time.

In summary, it is extremely difficult to synchronize demand-management policies with real-world economic conditions because of the unavoidable delays involved in instituting the policies and interpreting their effects.

2. If the Economic Slump Is Localized within a Specific Geographical Area or Labor Force Group, Generalized Economic Stimuli May Be Relatively Ineffective. The stimulation effects of a tax cut or general increase in government expenditures will tend to be felt throughout the economy, causing an increase in demand for virtually every product. If the economic slowdown is widespread, this generalized economic stimulus will be an advantage. On the other hand, if the depressed economic conditions are localized within a specific industry (such as the aerospace or automobile industry), a specific geographical region (for example, the industrial Northeast or Appalachia), or a specific labor force group (such as youthful blacks or unskilled workers), the general stimulus may generate inflationary pressure in other economic sectors while failing to relieve conditions in the specifically depressed areas. For example, if unemployment is high in West Virginia, a generalized increase in demand will probably do little to relieve the situation.

When depressed economic conditions are localized, a microeconomic approach is necessary. Fiscal policy must be carefully targeted if it is to be

effective. Under such circumstances, well-designed government expenditure projects have a clear advantage over a generalized tax cut. In theory, there is no reason why much or most fiscal stimuli cannot be of this variety. However, the economics of this approach are better than the politics. In the real world, representatives from low-unemployment areas are predictably more concerned with steering government projects toward their own constituencies than with voting funds to assist high-unemployment areas that make up other legislators' constituencies. Political factors impose a constraint on what we can realistically expect to attain through targeted fiscal policy.

3. Public Choice Theory Indicates That Discretionary Fiscal Policy Will Have an Inflationary Bias. If fiscal policy is to exert a countercyclical influence, it must be even-handed and attuned to changing economic conditions. As the economy stops contracting and begins expanding, fiscal policy should be responsive: Ideally, it should shift from stimulus to restraint. But economists sometimes forget that real-world fiscal policy is instituted by means of the legislative decision-making process. Political entrepreneurs are generally interested in how fiscal policy will affect their own election prospects. Like other policy choices, fiscal choices provide incumbent legislators with a tool for furthering their political objectives and personal ambitions. Fiscal policy choices will be influenced by political considerations. It is naive to expect otherwise.

Public choice theory indicates that fiscal policy prescriptions are asymmetrical—that political entrepreneurs are more likely to follow an expansionary course than to institute restrictive budget policy. Tax reductions and spending programs (and, thus, budget deficits) permit political entrepreneurs to provide benefits to their constituents. These benefits, of course, will be popular with voters. Given the popularity of spending programs and tax reductions, we should expect politicians to be quick, perhaps too quick, to institute economic stimuli. In contrast, budget cuts and tax increases will require political entrepreneurs to vote for either a reduction in the dollar amount of public sector goods provided to their constituents or the imposition of higher taxes. Politicians will be reluctant to undertake the unpleasant tasks of imposing higher taxes and cutting government expenditures, even when appropriate.

Thus, political considerations—concerns with popularity among constituents—tend to make expansionary policies more attractive than restrictive policies to political decision-makers. This reduces the likelihood that appropriate, balanced fiscal action will be instituted.[4]

4. Secondary Effects of a Fiscal Policy May Undercut the Policy's Desired Effects. Suppose policy-makers desire to expand government expenditures in order to stimulate demand. If the additional government expenditures are financed by borrowing, the demand for loanable funds will rise. Upward pressure will be exerted on interest rates. The higher interest rates may, especially with the passage of time, cause the level of private investment and purchase of durable goods to decline. Any such decline in private spending will at least partially undercut the expansionary effect generated by the additional government expenditures. Alternatively, if taxes are raised in order to finance the additional spending, this, too, will crowd out private spending. The higher tax rates will reduce disposable income, causing the level of consumer spending to fall.

Secondary effects may also dampen the impact of restrictive fiscal policy. Suppose the government reduces its expenditures and/or increases taxes in order to achieve a budget surplus. As the result of the surplus, the government's demand for loanable funds will decline, placing downward pressure on interest rates. In turn, the lower interest rates will stimulate private investment, at least partially undercutting the government's more restrictive policy.

AUTOMATIC STABILIZERS

There are a few fiscal programs that automatically tend to help stabilize the economy. No discretionary legislative action is needed, and the problem of proper timing can be minimized.

Automatic stabilizers, even without legislative action, tend to contribute to a budget deficit during bad times and to a surplus during an economic boom. When unemployment is rising and business conditions are slow. these stabilizers automatically reduce taxes and increase government expenditures, giving the economy a shot in the arm. On the other hand, automatic stabilizers help to apply the brakes to an economic boom, increasing tax revenues and decreasing government spending. Three of these built-in stabilizers deserve specific mention.

1. Unemployment Compensation. When unemployment is high, the receipts from the unemployment compensation tax will decline because of the reduction in employment. Payments will increase because more workers are now eligible to receive benefits. The program will automatically run a deficit during a business slowdown. In contrast, when the unemployment rate is low, tax receipts from the program will increase because more people are now working. The amount paid in benefits will decline because fewer people are unemployed. The program will automatically tend to run a surplus during good times. Thus, without any change in policy, the program has the desired countercyclical effect on aggregate demand.[5]

Automatic Stabilizers: Built-in features that tend automatically to promote a budget deficit during a recession and a budget surplus during an inflationary boom, even without change in policy.

---

[4]See James M. Buchanan and Richard E. Wagner, *Democracy in Deficit—The Political Legacy of Lord Keynes* (New York: Academic Press, 1977), for additional discussion of this topic.

[5]Although unemployment compensation has the desired countercyclical effects on demand, it also reduces the incentive to accept available employment opportunities. As a result, researchers have found that the *existing* unemployment compensation system actually increases the long-run normal unemployment rate. This issue is discussed in detail later.

When James Tobin was appointed to the Council of Economic Advisers by President John F. Kennedy in 1961, he warned the young president, "I'm a sort of ivory tower economist." "That's all right," replied Kennedy, "I'm a sort of ivory tower president."[6]

Tobin helped design President Kennedy's famous tax-cut program of the 1960s and was responsible for the incorporation of the investment tax credit into the legislation. A former president of the American Economic Association, Tobin was an undergraduate at Harvard in the 1930s, when the ideas of Keynes began to sweep across the United States. To this day, Tobin continues to be an unabashed Keynesian.

Not surprisingly, Tobin is a strong critic of the Reagan economic program of tax reductions coupled with a deceleration in the growth rate of the money supply. He argues that the tax cuts will stimulate consumption and the tight money policies will generate high interest rates that will hold back investment. This, according to Tobin, will lead to feeble growth. In contrast, Tobin favors tight fiscal policy coupled with aggressive monetary policy. He believes that this strategy would lower interest rates, stimulate investment, and promote economic growth.

[6]Conversation reported in "Keynesian Yalie," *Time,* October 26, 1981, p. 68.

The Sterling Professor of Economics at Yale University since 1957, Tobin was awarded the Nobel Prize in economics in 1981. His best-known work, and that which caught the attention of the Nobel committee, is his theory of portfolio selection. His work in this area has revolutionized our understanding of how people and institutions choose between various available combinations of risk and yield. By emphasizing the logic of building a diverse "portfolio" of various kinds of financial assets, Tobin forced economists to recognize as simplistic the assumption that investors would always choose the highest rate of return (profit or interest). Characteristically, Tobin refers to his theory as "just the principle of not putting all your eggs in one basket."[7]

The Nobel Prize has not significantly changed Tobin's life. He still enjoys teaching and lunching with Yale undergraduates. Students may not realize that their shy professor is considered by some to be the greatest living Keynesian economist.

[7]Quoted by William D. Marbach, in "Laurels for an Old Roman," *Newsweek,* October 26, 1981, p. 62.

2. Corporate Profit Tax. Tax studies show that the corporate profit tax is the most countercyclical of all the automatic stabilizers. This results because corporate profits are highly sensitive to cyclical conditions. Under recessionary conditions, corporate profits will decline sharply and so will corporate tax payments. This sharp decline in tax revenues will tend to enlarge the size of the government deficit. During economic expansion, corporate profits typically increase much more rapidly than wages, income, or consumption. This increase in corporate profits will result in a rapid increase in the "tax take" from the business sector during expansion. Thus, the corporate tax payments will go up during expansion and fall rapidly during a contraction if there is no change in tax policy.

3. Progressive Income Tax. During economic expansion, the disposable income of consumers increases less rapidly than total income. This results because, with higher incomes, the progressive income tax pushes more people into the higher tax brackets. Thus, tax revenues increase because (a) income is higher and (b) tax rates on marginal income have increased. On the other hand, when income

(Continued on page 147.)

PERSPECTIVES IN ECONOMICS

FACT AND FICTION ABOUT THE NATIONAL DEBT

Keynesian analysis suggests that a budget deficit may often be an appropriate means of stimulating the economy. When the federal budget runs a deficit, the difference between expenditures and revenues is financed by borrowing. The U.S. Treasury issues interest-bearing bonds, which are sold to financial investors. These interest-bearing bonds comprise the national debt. In effect, the national debt is a loan from financial investors to the U.S. Treasury.

For years, laymen, politicians, and economists have debated about the burden of the national debt. One side has argued that we are mortgaging the futures of our children and grandchildren. Future generations will pay the consequences of our fiscal irresponsibility. The other side has retorted, "We owe it to ourselves." Since most of the national debt is held by U.S. citizens in the form of bonds, it represents an asset as well as a future liability. Not only will we pass along a tax burden associated with the interest payments on the debt, but we will also bequeath to our children and grandchildren a valuable asset — interest-bearing U.S. bonds. The asset will offset the liability of the debt. Has time, the ultimate judge, declared a winner of this debate? What is fact and what is fiction about the national debt?

1. FACT: *The national debt is owned by U.S. citizens, foreigners, U.S. government agencies, and the Federal Reserve System.* Exhibit 5 gives the breakdown on who owns the debt. The biggest share of it, some 55.5 percent, is held internally by U.S. citizens and private institutions, such as insurance companies and commercial banks. Thirteen percent of the national debt is held by foreigners. The portion owned by foreigners is sometimes referred to as external debt. Approximately 19 percent of the debt is held by agencies of the federal government. For example, surplus social security trust funds are often used to purchase U.S. bonds. When the debt is owned by a government agency, it is little more than an accounting transaction indicating that one government agency (for example, the Social Security Administration) is making a loan to another (for example, the U.S. Treasury). Even the interest payments, in this case, represent little more than an internal government transfer. Approximately one-eighth of the public debt is held by the Federal Reserve System. As we will see in the next chapter, this portion of the debt is an important determinant of the stock of money in the United States.

2. FICTION: *The national debt must be paid off.* Borrowing is an everyday method of doing business. Many of the nation's largest and most profitable corporations continually have outstanding debts to bondholders. Yet these corporations, particularly the profitable ones, will have no trouble refinancing the outstanding debt if they so wish. What is necessary is that the borrower have sufficient assets or income to pay both the interest and principal as they come due. As long as General Motors has billions of dollars worth of assets and corporate income, it will have no trouble borrowing a few million and refinancing the debt, and refinancing it again and again, because lenders know that GM will be able to pay off the loan. Similarly, as long as the U.S. government can raise huge revenues through taxes, lenders can be very sure that the government will be able to return their money plus interest when due. Therefore, there is no date in the future on which the national debt must be repaid.

3. FICTION: *The national debt has grown so fast that the U.S. government is or the verge of bankruptcy.* As we just indicated, what is important is the government's ability to raise revenues to meet its debt obligation. Actually, by this standard, the debt has declined in recent years. In 1946, the national debt was 120 percent of GNP. By 1955, it was only 70 percent of GNP. By 1974, the national debt was only 35 percent of GNP. In recent years the national debt has risen slightly relative to GNP. As of 1980, it was approximately 37 percent of GNP.

4. FACT: *The interest burden on the debt has risen significantly in recent years.* Exhibit 6 represents the interest payments on the debt as a percentage of GNP for the period from 1954 to 1980. After World War II, interest on the debt declined relative to GNP. During the period from 1954 to 1973, the ratio of interest payments on the national debt divided by GNP was virtually constant at 1.5 percent. The high interest rates and the large deficits during the period from 1974 to 1980 pushed the interest payment/GNP ratio upward. The interest payments

EXHIBIT 5 Ownership of the national debt (February 1982)

Ownership of U.S. Securities	Dollar Value (Billions)	Percentage
U.S. government agencies	201.1	19.2
Federal Reserve Banks	125.4	12.0
Domestic investors	581.7	55.5
Foreign investors	140.0	13.3
Total	1048.2	100.0

Board of Governors of the Federal Reserve System.

on the national debt in 1980 were 2.6 percent of GNP. The federal government must levy taxes in order to meet the interest payments on the debt. If the interest payments should continue to rise relative to total income, additional taxes to meet this obligation could exert a significant negative impact on the incentive to earn taxable income. Clearly, excessive debt can lead to serious economic problems. However, the probability of default by the federal government is vastly different from that for municipal and state governmental units. Unlike the latter, the federal government can create money. Thus, excessive federal debt would be far more likely to lead to inflation than to bankruptcy.

5. FACT: *Since the Korean War, private debt has grown faster than the national debt.* The growth of the national debt should be kept in perspective. During the last 27 years, public debt has increased much more slowly than private debt. Exhibit 7 shows that between 1953 and 1980 the national debt increased 238 percent, compared to a more than 1043 percent increase in private indebtedness. To the extent that excessive debt is a problem, it is clearly a problem for both the public and private sectors.

6. FACT: *For federal debt that is financed internally, future generations of Americans will inherit both a higher tax liability and additional bonds.* The U.S. debt is a liability to future taxpayers, who will pay higher taxes in order to meet the interest payments on the debt. Simultaneously, it is an asset to owners or future owners of U.S. securities, who will receive principal and interest payments. For internal debt, both of these parties are U.S. citizens, either current or future.

7. FACT: *External debt has increased in recent years.* In 1970, only $20 billion of U.S. securities, 5 percent of the total, were held by foreigners. By 1980, the figure had jumped to $138 billion, representing almost 18 percent of the total national debt. Even external debt can potentially improve the economic welfare of future generations. It depends on how the government uses the borrowed funds.

8. FACT: *The true measure of how the debt influences the welfare of future generations requires knowledge of how it influences the future capital stock.* The economic welfare of future generations will be determined by how much capital stock—houses, factories, machines, and other productive assets—is bequeathed to them. When the government borrows, it tends to raise the interest rate and discourage private investment. This reduction in private capital formation can be offset if the government spends the borrowed funds on long-lasting capital assets, such as hospitals, schools, highways, and airplanes, that will yield future income greater than future interest payments. On the other hand, if the borrowed funds are spent primarily on current consumption items (for example, income transfers and administrative expenses), the capital assets available to future generations will be reduced and the burden of the debt increased. This is true for both the internal and the external debt.

9. FACT: *When deficit spending is necessary to push the economy to full employment, it will contribute to the future capital stock and therefore improve the economic welfare of future generations.* If there are unemployed resources that could be used to produce houses, factories, and other assets, as well as current consumer goods, a government deficit may help put these resources to work. When a deficit results in the employment of otherwise idle resources, there can be little doubt that it will help future generations despite the future tax liability. For example, consider the 1930s. Between 1930 and 1934, gross private investment was less than 3 percent of GNP. Once allowance was made for depreciation, the nation's capital stock actually declined. Were future generations helped because the federal government incurred little debt (either with the public or the Federal Reserve) during this period? The answer clearly is no. Future generations would have been better off if the government had incurred a deficit

EXHIBIT 6 Interest payments as a percentage of gross national product

During the period from 1954 to 1973, the interest payments on the portion of the national debt held by the public comprised approximately 1.5 percent of GNP. In recent years, the percentage has risen. The interest on the national debt now totals 2.6 percent of GNP.

Budget of the United States (annual).

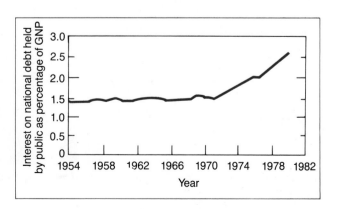

while using monetary and fiscal tools to put idle manpower and resources to work. The future capital stock would have been greater, to say nothing of current output during that period.

10. FACT: *In the 1970s, deficit spending drained a substantial share of the funds from the private loanable funds market.* There is some evidence that most of these funds were allocated to current consumption rather than to capital formation. The consequence seems to have been a slowing in the U.S. growth rate. In many respects, *changes* in the national debt, particularly in that portion held by private investors, are more important than the actual size of the debt. Rapid growth of the privately held portion of the national debt implies that the government is draining a substantial amount of funds from the private capital market. Potential investment funds are being bid away from businesses and state and local governments in the process. During the period from 1946 to 1966,

U.S. Treasury borrowing from private sources expanded from $208 billion to $219 billion, an $11 billion increase in 20 years. Federal borrowing from the private loanable funds market increased from $219 billion in 1966 to $657 billion in 1980, a $438 billion *increase* in just 14 years! Whereas during the period from 1946 to 1966 less than 1 percent of the funds raised in the domestic loanable funds market were used to cover the Treasury's deficit, more than 15 percent of the funds raised during the period from 1967 to 1980 were allocated to the federal deficit.

As we indicated, if the borrowed funds are directed into capital formation, they will have little negative effect on the U.S. economic growth rate and the well-being of future generations. However, this has not been the case in recent years. The share of federal spending allocated to capital formation has been steadily declining, reflecting a vast increase in transfer payments. The proportion of funds channeled into investment in

the private sector is substantially greater than that for the public sector. Therefore, there is good reason to suspect that the vast expansion of federal borrowing from private sources during the period from 1967 to 1980 drained funds away from capital formation. To the extent that this has been true, our current capital stock is lower than it otherwise would have been. Our growth rate has suffered in the process.

Discussion

1. Can the government or a private corporation have continual debt outstanding? Explain.

2. Do we owe the national debt to ourselves? Does this mean that the size of the debt is of little concern? Why or why not?

3. "The national debt is a mortgage against the future of our children and grandchildren. We are forcing them to pay for our irresponsible and unrestrained spending." Evaluate.

EXHIBIT 7   Private and public debt, 1953 and 1980

Private debt has increased much more rapidly than the national debt.

Federal Reserve Board.

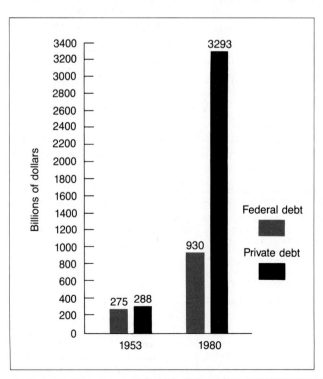

declines, many taxpayers are assigned lower tax rates, reducing the government's tax take. However, when inflation is present during a recession, the normal countercyclical impact on the progressive tax structure is eliminated. The inflation pushes taxpayers into higher tax brackets, even though their *real* incomes are declining. During an inflationary recession, the progressive income tax actually exerts a perverse (negative) effect on aggregate demand.[8]

LOOKING AHEAD

Thus far, we have concentrated on the demand side of the aggregate market for goods and services. We must more fully integrate aggregate supply into our analysis. This will be our goal in Chapter 8.

CHAPTER LEARNING OBJECTIVES

1 Fiscal policy is a tool that can be used to moderate economic disturbances that arise from fluctuations in aggregate demand.

2 When an economy's resources are underutilized, an increase in government expenditures, holding taxes constant, will increase aggregate demand and push the economy to a higher level of real income and employment.

3 A tax reduction can also be used to push an economy toward full employment. When taxes are reduced, the disposable income of consumers will increase, stimulating consumption. At the higher level of consumption, both real income and employment will expand. Tax reductions can usually influence consumption rapidly because the tax-withholding system affects disposable income almost immediately.

4 Restrictive fiscal policy (higher taxes or reduced government expenditures) can be used to combat inflationary pressure. In the face of inflation, a planned government surplus would be in order.

5 The Keynesian view rejects the idea that the government's budget should be balanced annually. Keynesian analysis implies that general economic conditions should be the prime determinant of fiscal policy. When the economy is slack, budget authorities should plan a deficit. In contrast, when the economy is experiencing an inflationary boom, a budget surplus is in order.

6 Proper timing is vital for the success of fiscal policy. If a fiscal action is not properly timed, it may be counterproductive. Restrictive fiscal policy, if applied during a recession, will lengthen the recession's duration and heighten its severity. Similarly, if expansionary fiscal policy is followed despite an ongoing or approaching inflation, the inflationary conditions will worsen.

---

[8]Beginning in 1985, the federal personal income tax is scheduled to be indexed for inflation. Indexing will eliminate the ability of inflation to push individuals into higher tax brackets when their real incomes have not increased. Thus, with indexing, personal income tax revenues, as a share of income, will fall if real personal income declines during an inflationary recession. Similarly, revenues will expand, as a share of income, when *real* incomes increase during an economic boom. Therefore, indexing will make the personal income tax a more consistent automatic stabilizer.

7 The full-employment budget is a measure of what expenditures and revenues would be if the economy were at full employment. It provides a useful summary statistic on the degree to which deficits or surpluses are the result of fiscal policy. The full-employment budget generally reveals the impact of fiscal policies on the economy more clearly than the actual budget.

8 Economic theory indicates that there are limitations on the expected effectiveness of discretionary fiscal policy as a stabilization tool. There is often a lag between the time when a policy change is needed and the time when legislative authority is granted. Even after a fiscal policy change has been instituted, it may take time for the policy to exert its major effects. If an economic slump is localized to a specific geographical area or labor force group, a generalized fiscal stimulus may be relatively ineffective. The effectiveness and timing of fiscal policy may also suffer as a result of political considerations. Political entrepreneurs find spending attractive but dislike imposing taxes. Thus, they will find budget deficits more attractive than surpluses. Therefore, an inflationary bias is likely to characterize the conduct of fiscal policy. The secondary effects of fiscal policy (for example, higher interest rates due to a budget deficit) may, at least partially, undercut the policy's desired effects. Each of these factors complicates the effective use of countercyclical fiscal policy.

9 Unemployment compensation, corporate taxes, and the progressive income tax act as automatic stabilizers because they automatically contribute to a budget deficit during slack times and to a budget surplus when the economy is at full employment.

10 The burden of the national debt has long been a controversial issue. It is not true that the debt will eventually have to be paid off. Nor does the debt indicate that the federal government is about to go bankrupt. Since the Korean War, private debt has grown more rapidly than the federal debt. The debt affects future generations through its impact on capital formation. During the period from 1946 to 1966, federal borrowing had little impact on the private loanable funds market. In contrast, during the period from 1967 to 1980, there was a vast increase in the growth of Treasury borrowing in the private credit market. Given the declining share of government expenditures allocated to capital investment, there is reason to believe that the borrowing during the period from 1967 to 1980 retarded capital formation and economic growth.

THE ECONOMIC WAY OF THINKING — DISCUSSION QUESTIONS

1 Suppose that you are a member of the Council of Economic Advisers. The president has asked you to prepare a statement on "What is the proper fiscal policy for the next 12 months?" Prepare such a statement, indicating (a) the current state of the economy (that is, unemployment rate, growth in real income, and rate of inflation) and (b) your fiscal policy suggestions. Should the budget be in balance? Present the reasoning behind your suggestions.

2 If an economy were experiencing 7 percent unemployment while prices were rising at a 2 percent annual rate, indicate your view on appropriate fiscal policy. Explain your reasons.

3 "In the real world, it is wrong to expect that fiscal policy will be symmetric. Politicians will be glad to run a deficit during bad times to stimulate the economy, but they will surely fail to plan a surplus when it is needed to halt inflationary pressures. Thus, fiscal policy has an inflationary bias." Do you agree with this view? Why or why not?

4 What are automatic stabilizers? Explain the major advantage of automatic stabilizers.

5 What's Wrong with This Way of Thinking?

"Keynesians argue that a budget deficit will stimulate the economy. The historical evidence is highly inconsistent with this view. A $12 billion budget deficit in 1958 was associated with a serious recession, not expansion. We experienced recessions in both 1961 and 1974–1975, despite budget deficits. The federal budget ran a deficit every year from 1931 through 1939. Yet the economy continued to wallow in the Depression. Budget deficits do not stimulate GNP and employment."

AGGREGATE SUPPLY, FISCAL POLICY, AND STABILIZATION

Tax reductions have two principal effects. On the one hand, individuals and firms will buy more goods and services [the demand effect]. . . . But tax cuts also increase the supply of goods and services. Since lower tax rates allow individuals and firms to keep a larger fraction of their income after taxes, the lower rates affect incentive to work, to save, and to invest the savings, increasing potential GNP.[1]
Council of Economic Advisers
(1980–1981)
Charles L. Schultze, Chairman

For years, microeconomists have recognized that both demand and supply are important and that it is a mistake to focus on one to the near-exclusion of the other. Heavily influenced by the Great Depression, macroeconomists, on the other hand, have generally focused on aggregate demand. Balance is rapidly being restored, however. Like demand, supply is an important component of the macro- as well as the microeconomic way of thinking.

Classical economic analysis of price, output, and employment focused primarily on the supply side of the market. The classical economists believed that total output was determined by the conditions affecting supply. Furthermore, they argued that an expansion in aggregate demand would not alter total output but would merely lead to inflation. Similarly, they argued that a reduction in aggregate demand would primarily affect the price level, leaving real output more or less unchanged.

The Great Depression and other economic downturns provide strong evidence that the classical view of aggregate demand was incorrect. Downward price flexibility does not quickly and painlessly restore full employment in the face of declining demand. However, the economic conditions prevalent in the 1970s indicate that the classical view on the importance of aggregate supply was essentially correct. Supply factors *do* limit our ability to expand output. Supply is not the *only* thing that matters, but that it does matter is undeniable.

In this chapter, we will investigate the determinants of aggregate supply and incorporate more fully the concept of a supply constraint into our macro-economic model. We will consider the major factors likely to alter the economy's supply constraint. Finally, we will discuss one of the more controversial current issues, the impact of taxes on output, employment, and prices.

---

[1] *Economic Report of the President, 1981,* p. 79.

THE DETERMINANTS OF AGGREGATE SUPPLY

Goods are not gifts from nature. Human energy and knowledge must be applied to physical resources before goods become available to consumers, investors, and governments. What determines the supply of goods and services? The three major determinants of aggregate supply are (1) the quantity (and quality) of resources used in the production process, (2) the efficiency with which the applied resources are used, and (3) the current state of production technology. Let us take a closer look at each of these three factors.[2]

Resource Utilization

Other things constant, as the quantity (and quality) of resources contributing to the production process expands, aggregate supply will increase. But resources are scarce. At any point in time, the size of the economy's resource base will constrain aggregate supply. With the passage of time, the economy's resource base will change. Capital goods wear out with usage and time. Some investment will be necessary just to replace the machines, structures, and other capital assets worn out during a period. In addition, *net* investment can expand the availability of physical capital, loosening the aggregate supply constraint. The knowledge and skills of the work force—the supply of human labor resources—will also affect the productive capacity of an economy. Investment in education, training, and skill-enhancing experience is an essential ingredient for the maintenance and enlargement of the human resources that play such a vital role in the production process.

Potentially productive resources will not enhance aggregate supply unless they actually become engaged in the productive process. Just as physical-resource scarcity limits the economy's resource base, so, too, do human-imposed restrictions and individual decisions that reduce the *effective* availability of resources. For example, a worker who is unemployed because the combination of unemployment compensation, welfare benefits, and leisure is preferred to any of the available jobs adds no more to current production than a person who is *not* part of the labor force at all. Similarly, a potential youthful worker priced out of employment by minimum wage legislation is *not* part of the *effective* resource base of the economy. Thus, the size of the effective resource base of the economy is influenced by both scarcity and the human-created barriers that discourage the utilization of resources.

Economic Efficiency

The efficiency of resource utilization will also affect aggregate supply. Political and economic institutions that encourage individuals to specialize in those areas where they have the greatest comparative advantage and to engage in mutually advantageous exchange are necessary ingredients for the efficient use of resources. Without the gains from the division of labor and cooperative effort by participants, aggregate supply will fall far short of its potential. Public policy can enhance the efficiency of resource use if it provides (a) a stable environment under which competitive markets can flourish, (b) an effi-

---

[2]The analysis of aggregate supply is closely related to the concept of the production possibilities curve discussed in Chapter 2 (see pp. 21–25). This would be an excellent time to review that material.

cient remedy in instances where externalities (spillover effects) would otherwise be a source of waste, and (c) the desired level of public goods.[3]

However, public policy can also be a source of inefficiency. For example, if the tax structure encourages individuals to purchase goods and services that cost more to produce than their true consumer value, economic waste results. Similarly, regulatory actions that generate greater costs than benefits will reduce the size of the economic pie. As we proceed, we will analyze the impact of public policy on economic efficiency and aggregate supply in greater detail.

Technology

A technological improvement is the discovery of a new and better way of doing something—a new production technique that reduces costs or a new product that is economically superior to those previously available. Scientific breakthroughs play an important role in the advancement of technology. For example, when scientists discovered a new, low-cost method of converting sand into a silicon chip with computing power a thousand times greater than the human brain, our production capacity (aggregate supply) expanded. Sometimes technological advances merely involve the dissemination and adoption of a new idea that enables us to get more out of our existing resources. For example, when Ray Kroc, a West Coast equipment salesman, transformed an idea into a chain of stores to provide fast-service, low-cost hamburgers, his technological advance increased aggregate supply. The consumption opportunities available to millions of persons were improved as Kroc's idea became the fast-food restaurant chain that the world knows today as McDonald's.

An efficient economic system must provide a method of validating and disseminating technological advances. In a market economy, prices and competition serve this function. If consumers are willing to buy a new product at a price that will cover the product's resource cost, the idea behind the product— the technological advance it represents—is validated by the market. In contrast, if resource costs exceed the market price of a product, economic losses provide the decision-maker with swift if painful proof that the idea is unsound or untimely, economically speaking.

THE AGGREGATE SUPPLY CURVE FOR THE CONSTRAINED ECONOMY

Real Aggregate Supply Curve: A curve indicating the relationship between total real output and the price level. The term may also be used to describe the relationship between aggregate expenditures and the real income level of an economy.

Supply-side factors restrain our ability to produce additional output. Exhibit 1 incorporates a **real aggregate supply curve** into the now-familiar Keynesian income–flow model. Until the economy's full-employment supply constraint (income Y_f) is reached, *real* output will be fully responsive to an expansion in aggregate demand. Therefore, in this range, sometimes referred to as the Keynesian range, the real aggregate supply curve is merely the 45-degree line. Since demand stimulus will lead to the employment of additional resources rather than rising prices in the Keynesian range, real aggregate supply and nominal aggregate supply are equal.[4]

---

[3]See Chapter 4 for additional detail on the potential positive role of government in each of these areas.

[4]As we discussed earlier, the constancy of prices in the Keynesian range reflects both the assumption of downward price inflexibility and the absence of rising prices because unemployed resources are available.

EXHIBIT 1   The constrained aggregate supply curve

Here we illustrate the shape of the *real* aggregate supply curve for a supply-constrained economy within the Keynesian framework. The real aggregate supply curve is merely the 45-degree line until the supply-constrained output rate, Y_f, is attained. Since output rates beyond Y_f cannot be sustained, the real aggregate supply curve becomes vertical at Y_f.

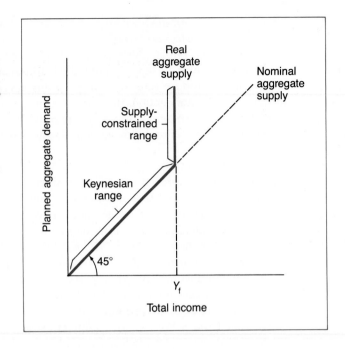

Supply-Constrained Output: The maximum output that can be sustained in the long run, given public policy and the current availability of resources. It is similar to the full-employment constraint, except that it also encompasses the concept of economic efficiency. Public policies that lead to an inefficient use of resources will decrease an economy's supply-constrained output rate.

Microincentive Structure: The incentive factors that influence *if* and *how* resources are used. In addition to market conditions, these factors will be influenced by public policy. For example, the economy's tax and income transfer policies will influence the personal benefits derived from work, saving, and investing and thereby affect the incentive of individuals to undertake these activities.

However, once the **supply-constrained output** (Y_f) is attained, the real aggregate supply curve becomes vertical. It will *not* be possible to sustain real output rates greater than Y_f. As the dotted 45-degree line indicates, nominal supply (income) may expand beyond Y_f as prices rise in response to demand conditions. But the higher levels of nominal income will be unable to push real income beyond the economy's supply capacity.

An economy's supply constraint encompasses the concepts of both full employment and economic efficiency. Given the **microincentive structure** of an economy, the supply constraint indicates the maximum real output that can be sustained by demand-stimulus policies.

It is important to recognize that public policy, as well as resource scarcity, influences an economy's attainable output rate. Idle resources do not always imply deficient aggregate demand.[5] Some resources may remain idle or be used inefficiently because public policy generates an incentive structure that encourages such activity. A supply constraint reflecting the economy's micro-structure will be no more responsive to demand-stimulation policies than con-straints imposed by the actual unavailability of resources.

Exhibit 2 illustrates how changes in aggregate demand affect the level of output and prices in our supply-constrained model. Given the availability of unemployed resources, "demand creates its own supply" in the Keynesian range. As aggregate demand increases from $C_1 + I_1 + G_1$ to $C_2 + I_2 + G_2$, real output expands via the multiplier process to Y_f. Prices remain constant, since both real and nominal income increase by identical amounts.

---

[5]Remember, full employment, the employment rate associated with the "normal rate of unemploy-ment," reflects both frictional unemployment and the structural conditions of the economy. Thus, public policies that contribute to structural unemployment will influence an economy's full-employment rate. See pp. 97–98 for additional detail on this topic.

EXHIBIT 2   Changes in demand and the aggregate supply constraint

If an economy is currently operating at Y_1, an income level well below its full-employment capacity Y_f, an increase in aggregate demand from $C_1 + I_1 + G_1$ to $C_2 + I_2 + G_2$ will cause both real and nominal income to increase to Y_f. In this Keynesian range, additional demand will lead to additional real (and nominal) output. However, once income has been pushed to the full-employment capacity, still more demand (for example, $C_3 + I_3 + G_3$) will merely cause inflation. Nominal income will increase because of the higher prices, but real income will be constrained at Y_f.

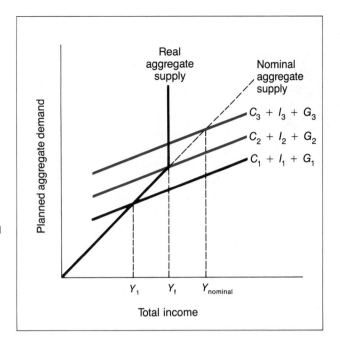

Given the economy's full-employment supply constraint, aggregate demand $C_2 + I_2 + G_2$ elicits the maximum rate of output consistent with stable prices. An increase in aggregate demand beyond this rate (for example, an increase to $C_3 + I_3 + G_3$) leads only to higher prices. Nominal income increases but real income remains unchanged (at Y_f). Employees get more nominal dollars in their paychecks, but these dollars only buy the same amount of goods as before the price increase.

Is it really true that supply constraints will prevent any increase in output beyond Y_f? The 45-degree portion of the aggregate supply curve is a simplification intended to reinforce the idea that changes in demand exert little impact on prices (and a great deal of impact on output) when substantial excess capacity is present. Similarly, the vertical portion of the aggregate supply curve is a simplifying assumption meant to illustrate the concept that there is an attainable output rate beyond which increases in demand will lead almost exclusively to price increases (and only small increases in real output).

The vertical portion of the aggregate supply curve should not be taken to imply that it would be impossible to expand output *temporarily* beyond Y_f. *For a short period of time,* expansionary demand policies may well lead to an output rate greater than Y_f. Unemployment may fall below its long-run normal rate. Employees may work abnormally large amounts of overtime. Employers may operate their plants beyond their normal productive rates. But these abnormally high utilization rates will not continue in the long run. Output rates beyond the supply constraint Y_f will *not* be sustainable. As decision-makers adjust the utilization rates of their resources to their desired long-run level, output will eventually fall back to Y_f.[6]

---

[6]In Chapter 11, we will analyze more fully the implications of utilizing demand-stimulus policies to attain output rates beyond the economy's supply constraint and explain why such a strategy will often be ineffective (and even counterproductive) in the long run. See pp. 224–235.

The 1970s highlighted the importance of aggregate supply. Aggregate demand was strong during the decade, pushing up *nominal* income at a very rapid rate. Nonetheless, *real* income grew slowly. Supply-side factors limited the ability of demand-stimulus policies to promote *real* economic growth.

Shifts in the Aggregate Supply Curve

Changes in (a) the quantity of resources utilized, (b) the efficiency with which they are applied, and/or (c) the level of technology will cause the aggregate supply curve to shift. These determinants of supply will be influenced by individual and collective choices, as well as by the forces of Nature—unfavorable weather conditions, for example.

Let us first consider factors that will increase aggregate supply. With the passage of time, net capital formation may expand the availability of machines and other capital assets. Additional natural resources may be discovered. The size of the labor force may expand. The education and skill level of workers may improve. Technological advancements may make it possible to squeeze a larger output from the available resources. Each of these factors would expand the production possibilities (the supply-constrained output capacity) of the economy.

Exhibit 3 illustrates the impact of an increase in aggregate supply within the framework of our income–flow model. The expansion in aggregate supply (AS) will shift the real AS curve to the right, indicating that a larger real income level (Y_2 rather than Y_1) is now attainable. If aggregate demand increases to $C_2 + I_2 + G_2$, the equilibrium income level Y_2 will be consistent with stable prices. Both real and nominal income of the economy will expand. If aggregate supply did not expand (that is, if it remained at real AS_1), an increase in aggregate demand to $C_2 + I_2 + G_2$ would be inflationary. However, when aggregate supply does increase, the higher level of aggregate demand will be in harmony with both price stability and an expansion in real income (to Y_2).

Sometimes unfavorable natural or economic events or imprudent economic policies cause aggregate supply to decline. A drought reduces the supply of agriculture products. Bad weather slows production on construction projects. Excessive regulatory actions and/or a decline in the competitiveness of markets may reduce the efficiency of an economy and thereby retard aggregate supply.

The sharp increases in crude-oil prices during 1973–1974 and again in 1979–1980 provide a vivid illustration of changing conditions adversely affecting supply. The higher oil prices meant that oil-importing nations like the United States had to give up a larger amount of other goods in exchange for each barrel of imported oil. The result was a transfer of wealth from the oil-importing nations to the oil-exporting countries. The resource base of the oil-importing nations was contracted—cheap oil was no longer available. Thus, aggregate supply fell.

Exhibit 3b illustrates the impact of such a reduction in aggregate supply. The vertical portion of the real aggregate supply curve will shift to the left (to AS_2), reflecting the decline in the attainable output rate. Real income will decline to Y_2. If aggregate demand remains unchanged at $C_1 + I_1 + G_1$, prices will rise.

The implication of our theory is that a reduction in aggregate supply will exert an inflationary impact upon the economy, unless it is offset by a decline in aggregate demand. The experience of the United States during the

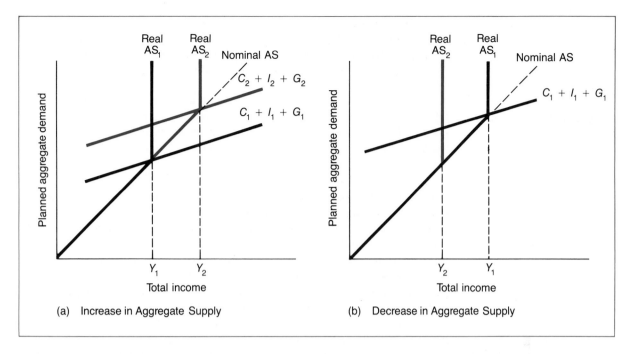

(a) Increase in Aggregate Supply   **(b)** Decrease in Aggregate Supply

EXHIBIT 3 Shifts in aggregate supply

If aggregate supply increases to real AS_2 (frame a), an accompanying increase in aggregate demand (shift to $C_2 + I_2 + G_2$) will permit the economy to attain a higher equilibrium rate of real output (Y_2) while maintaining price stability. Frame (b) illustrates the impact of a decline in aggregate supply (from AS_1 to AS_2). If aggregate demand remains unchanged at $C_1 + I_1 + G_1$, the reduction in supply will cause prices to rise. *Real* income will decline to Y_2. Unless aggregate demand also declines, inflation will accompany the fall in aggregate supply.

periods of rising crude-oil prices is consistent with this view. Following the oil embargo and sharply rising crude-oil prices of 1973–1974, the U.S. economy slipped into a recession in 1974–1975; at the same time the inflation rate was accelerating to 11 percent in 1974, up from 6.2 percent in 1973. The pattern was repeated during 1979–1980. Real GNP was virtually unchanged during 1979–1980, while the inflation rate rose from 7.6 percent in 1978 to more than 12 percent during 1979 and 1980. Of course, other factors may also have contributed to the inflationary pressures during these periods. Nonetheless, our analysis indicates that the sharp oil price increases and the accompanying decline in aggregate supply played important roles in the acceleration of the inflation rate during 1973–1975 and again during 1978–1980.

FISCAL POLICY, AGGREGATE DEMAND, AND AGGREGATE SUPPLY

In the past, macroeconomists have often ignored the supply-side effects of taxes. However, it has become very clear that alteration of tax rates will affect aggregate supply as well as aggregate demand. Tax rates, in addition to affecting disposable income to be spent on consumption, also alter relative prices and thereby affect the incentive of individuals to work, invest, save, and utilize resources efficiently. The *marginal tax rate* is particularly important because it determines the breakdown of one's additional income into tax payments on the one hand and disposable income on the other. Changes in marginal tax rates will influence the incentive of individuals to use the resources at their disposal.

When marginal tax rates are reduced, there is an increased reward derived from added work, investment, saving, and other activities that become less heavily taxed. People shift into these activities away from leisure (and leisure-intensive activities), tax shelters, consumption of tax-deductible goods, and other forms of tax avoidance. These substitutions both enlarge the effective resource base and improve the efficiency with which the resources are applied.

Other things constant, these incentive effects lead to an increase in aggregate supply. In contrast, higher tax rates reduce the reward derived from productive activities while making tax avoidance more attractive. This encourages a shift of resources from productive activities to tax avoidance, which will retard aggregate supply.

Fiscal policy affects aggregate demand and aggregate supply differently. Fiscal policy affects aggregate demand through its impact on disposable income and the flow of expenditures. It affects aggregate supply through changes in marginal tax rates, which influence the relative attractiveness of productive activity in comparison to leisure and tax avoidance.

Of course, tax revenues provide support for public sector expenditures. Public goods such as police and fire protection, the legal system, national defense, provision of roads, and the monetary system provide the infrastructure for the efficient operation of markets. The efficiency gains derived from collective action in these and other areas may outweigh the negative effects of the tax rates necessary to finance these public goods. In such instances, aggregate supply increases despite the negative effects of the taxation on incentive. However, as the size of the public sector expands, funds are likely to be allocated into areas (increased transfer payments, for example) where they exert less and less positive impact on aggregate supply. Simultaneously, the "disincentive effects" and supply-side inefficiencies will become more important as marginal tax rates rise. Eventually, the adverse impact of the higher tax rates will dominate.

The Supply-Side Effects of Changes in Tax Rates

Let us consider in detail the economic distortions and supply-side effects arising from high marginal tax rates. We will then be able to analyze the impact of various fiscal policies on aggregate supply as well as on aggregate demand. There are three major reasons that rising marginal tax rates may retard aggregate supply.

1. High Marginal Tax Rates May Decrease the Supply of Labor and Reduce Its Productive Efficiency. An increase in marginal tax rates encourages individuals to shift their labor resources away from activities that generate taxable income toward activities that are untaxed. In the process, the gains stemming from specialization, exchange, and the law of comparative advantage will be diminished.[7] Aggregate supply will be retarded, unless the benefits from government-provided goods and services outweigh these disincentive effects.

How will rising marginal tax rates influence labor supply? First, they encourage individuals to substitute leisure for work. Economists refer to this as the **leisure–work substitution effect.** The higher marginal tax rates will induce some individuals to opt out of the labor force.[8] Others will simply work less. People will decide that productive effort yielding so little personal return is

---

[7]Students who do not understand this point should review the material on specialization, exchange, and the law of comparative advantage for a detailed explanation of the impact of these factors on the production possibilities of an economy. See Chapter 2, pp. 25–31.

[8]Empirical studies have suggested that higher marginal tax rates may *not* measurably alter the hours worked of prime-age males. However, the labor supply of married women, older workers, and youthful workers is more responsive. A recent study by Michael Evans estimated that a 10 percent reduction in personal income tax rates increases the hours worked of non-prime-age males by 3.7 percent. See Michael Evans, "An Econometric Model Incorporating the Supply-Side Effects of Economic Policy" (Paper presented at a conference on "The Supply-Side Effects of Economic Policy," Washington University and Federal Reserve Bank of St. Louis, October 24–25, 1980).

simply not worthwhile. Many of them will decide to take more lengthy vacations, forego overtime opportunities, retire earlier, be more particular about accepting jobs when unemployed, or forget about pursuing that promising but risky business venture. These substitutions of "leisure" for taxable work effort will reduce the available labor supply, causing aggregate supply to fall.[9] In addition to hours of work, the effectiveness of work time can also be influenced. Since workers are unable to capture as large a proportion of a larger paycheck, they may be *less willing* to work intensively and productively on a job, accept additional responsibility, work under less pleasant conditions, and make similar sacrifices in order to gain a higher pay rate.

High marginal tax rates will also result in inefficient utilization of labor. Some individuals will substitute less productive activities that are not taxed (or that are taxed at a lower rate) for work that is taxed at a higher rate. Here the possibilities abound. Untaxed household production may be substituted for taxed activities. Self-employment generally affords the individual a greater opportunity to legally consume tax-deductible goods (in this context, they are called "expenses"). Therefore, rising marginal tax rates will encourage individuals to allocate more labor to self-employment activities (because of the tax shelter benefits rather than its high productivity) and away from more productive but more highly taxed employee labor services. Similarly, high marginal tax rates will channel labor resources into the underground economy Waste and economic inefficiency result.

2. High Marginal Tax Rates May Decrease the Supply of Capital and Reduce Its Productive Efficiency. An individual can use disposable income for either additional consumption or for increased savings and investments. The expectation of future income derived from savings and investments provides the reward that induces individuals to forego current consumption. However, high marginal tax rates reduce that reward, making it less attractive for individuals to save and invest: The greater their future income, the more it will be taxed. Correspondingly, the high tax rates make current consumption cheap. Individuals will be encouraged to channel funds away from savings and investments toward current consumption.

Perhaps the following example will make this point clear. Suppose one is considering the purchase of a $30,000 Mercedes for business purposes. If the current interest rate is 10 percent, one would have to give up $3000 of additional *before-tax* income per year in order to purchase the Mercedes. However, if one is in the 50 percent marginal tax bracket, since half of one's additional income is taxed, the Mercedes could be enjoyed at a cost of only $1500 of *after-tax* income per year. Still higher increases in marginal tax rates would make

---

[9]Some economists have argued that higher marginal tax rates may induce individuals to work more in order to maintain their usual standard of living. The problem with this view is that it ignores the reason the taxes are levied. Taxes are levied so that public services can be provided. Higher tax rates and an expansion in public sector goods will generate a negative income effect *only* if the public sector projects are inefficient—that is, only if they reduce real income. If public sector projects are efficient, *on average,* the benefits derived from the public sector spending will at least offset the reduction in income caused by the higher taxes. Persons will *experience* a reduction in income (which might induce them to work more) only if their valuation of what the government provides with the tax revenues is less than their valuation of the revenues given up to the tax collector. Levying taxes to finance true income-destroying activities is hardly defensible, even if it does force those hurt by the inefficiency to work more to regain lost income. See James Gwartney and Richard Stroup, "Labor Supply and Tax Rates: A Correction of the Record," *American Economic Review* (forthcoming), for additional detail on this point.

the cost of the Mercedes to the consumer (but not to society) even lower. As marginal tax rates on investment earnings in England rose to 98 percent in the 1970s, the sales of Rolls-Royces and Mercedes soared.[10] Such marginal tax rates made it cheap, in terms of after-tax future income, for wealthy consumers to enjoy expensive automobiles.

Not only do high marginal tax rates retard the growth of saving and investment; they also encourage investors to turn to projects that shelter current income from taxation and to turn away from projects with a higher rate of return but fewer tax-avoidance benefits. Investments in depreciable assets can often provide substantial tax advantages. Projects that supply investors with rapid depreciation write-offs and paper losses can be utilized to (a) put off tax liability until some future date and (b) transform regular income into capital gains income, which is taxed at a lower rate. Resources with valuable alternative uses are channeled into the **tax shelter industry,** an industry that owes its prosperity, if not its existence, to high marginal tax rates. Many of our most intelligent citizens are becoming tax lawyers, accountants, and investment consultants as the tax shelter industry expands and prospers. Other individuals are going into business largely because of the associated tax advantages. Lawyers, physicians, college professors, plumbers, and electricians, among others, are spending less time working professionally and more time trying to figure out how to reduce their tax liability. All of this activity consumes real resources, which would be applied to more valuable, more productive activities were it not for the high marginal tax rates.

3. High Marginal Tax Rates May Encourage Individuals to Substitute Less-Desired, Tax-Deductible Goods for More-Desired, Nondeductible Goods. This is a side effect of high tax rates that often goes unnoticed. High marginal tax rates make **tax-deductible expenditures** cheap for those with large taxable incomes. Of course, people will adjust their expenditure patterns accordingly. By substituting tax-deductible purchases for nondeductible goods, they can reduce their tax burden.

Most corporate earnings in the United States are taxed at a 46 percent marginal rate. In addition, the owners of a corporate business must pay personal income tax on the dividends paid out by the firm. For a corporate owner-manager whose marginal personal income tax rate is 44 percent, the implied tax on corporate earnings paid out to the owner is 70 percent, when both the corporate (46 percent) and personal income tax (44 percent of the 54 percent of the corporate earnings remaining after taxation) are considered. Under these circumstances, the *personal cost* of purchasing tax-deductible goods becomes very low. Luxury automobiles for business use, a company airplane, company membership in a country club, a business-related vacation in Hawaii, a plush business office, and numerous other business-related goods can be enjoyed at a fraction of their production cost since they are business expenses. The cost of a tax-deductible item is reduced by the amount of the marginal tax rate. The higher the consumer's tax bracket, the greater the reduction in the item's cost to that consumer. Thus, for example, if one were in the 50 percent marginal tax bracket, the *personal cost* of a $5000 tax-deductible vacation with all the trimmings (accommodations

Tax Shelter Industry: Business enterprises that specialize in offering investment opportunities designed to create a short-term accounting or "paper" loss, which can then be deducted from one's taxable income; at the same time, future "capital gain" income is generated, which is taxable at a lower rate.

Tax-Deductible Expenditures: Expenditures that the taxing authorities permit taxpayers to subtract from their income, thereby reducing the size of their taxable income. These are usually either (a) costs associated with one's business or profession or (b) expenditures on goods that public policy designates as meritorious (medical services, interest on home mortgages, and charitable contributions, for example).

---

[10]Measured in terms of future after-tax annual income foregone, what is the cost of a $30,000 automobile for a businessperson in the 98 percent marginal tax bracket when the interest rate is 10 percent? How does it compare with the cost of a bicycle that must be purchased with after-tax earnings?

WHAT IS SUPPLY-SIDE ECONOMICS?

As the economic program of the Reagan administration unfolded, we were told that it embodied the principles of supply-side economics. The term was widely used by the mass media. As is often the case with a popularized expression, supply-side economics was used quite loosely. Many people, including policymakers, used the expression without really understanding the idea. The expression began to mean different things to different people.

Supply-side economics stresses the role of relative prices. If a product becomes more expensive relative to an alternative, the supply-side approach emphasizes that people will choose less of the higher-priced product and more of the substitute products that have become relatively cheaper. For example, an increase in the price of beef causes people to choose less beef and more chicken. Similarly, supply-side economists emphasize that fiscal policy, especially the tax and income transfer components, change relative prices and thereby alter aggregate supply. Three relative prices are of particular importance.

First, marginal tax rates affect the allocation of existing income between (a) current consumption and (b) saving and investing for future consumption. Rising marginal tax rates reduce the individual's *after-tax* reward derived from saving and investing. Thus, decision-makers will tend to substitute current consumption for saving and investment

projects that will yield future *taxable* income. The result is a decline in capital formation and future output (aggregate supply).

Second, higher marginal tax rates make it (a) less rewarding for an individual to devote time, effort, and capital more diligently to the production of goods and services most desired by others, and (b) more attractive to employ a more leisurely pace and attitude, centered directly on what the producer personally enjoys. The higher tax rate makes it more difficult for buyers to get what they want, since more of the payment they offer to producers for added value is diverted from producers to the tax collector.

Third, marginal tax rates will influence the relative prices of (a) activities that reduce (shelter) one's current income and (b) projects that yield taxable income. As marginal tax rates rise, the benefit derived from tax shelters increases, while the after-tax rewards to projects yielding taxable income fall. Thus, investment decisions will be distorted. Low productivity projects with tax shelter benefits will be substituted for projects yielding a higher pretax rate of return. Inefficiency results, causing aggregate supply to fall (or grow at a slower rate).

The supply-side view is not monolithic. There are at least two supply-side perspectives. One—we might call it the "quick-fix view"—believes that lower tax rates will stimulate output rapidly and will often lead to an increase in tax revenues. Although this view may

have some validity for exceedingly high marginal tax rates, there is little evidence to support it in the lower range of tax rates, say marginal rates of less than 25 percent. The U.S. experience during 1981–1982 indicates that a tax cut is not a quick fix.

The dominant supply-side view is that the incentive effects emanating from a reduction in marginal rates will work more slowly. In the first place, the decision-makers will have to be convinced that the new incentive structure is permanent rather than temporary before they can be induced to undertake long-term projects. Even after they are convinced, it will take time for them to adjust fully to the new reward structure—to opt out of tax shelters and into more socially productive investments, for example. According to this view, supply-side economics is clearly a long-run strategy.

The supply-side perspective adds another dimension to fiscal policy. The Keynesian view emphasizes that fiscal policy operates on the economy by changing disposable income and thus demand; supply-side economics emphasizes that fiscal policy affects the economy by changing relative prices. While our understanding of the potency of the demand-side income effects and the supply-side relative price effects is incomplete, one thing is certain. The current interest in supply-side economics will trigger additional research designed to help us understand more fully the effects of fiscal policy on both aggregate demand and aggregate supply.

at the finest hotels, dining at the best restaurants, flying first-class, renting a luxury car) would be only $2500. Even if this (business-related) vacation is only worth $3000, it will nevertheless be purchased and supplied at a cost to society of $5000.

Here, the inefficiency stems from the fact that individuals do not bear the full cost of tax-deductible purchases. Since the customers do not bear the full cost of tax-deductible purchases, they are substituted for more highly valued nondeductible goods whose price tags are more directly determined by their production costs. Waste and inefficiency are by-products of this incentive structure.

Fiscal Policy Possibilities Once aggregate supply constrains an economy, it is important to consider both the demand and supply effects of fiscal policy. With regard to the expansionary and restrictive fiscal policies that can be applied to an economy, four general possibilities emerge: (1) a tax reduction coupled with an increase in the planned budget deficit; (2) a tax increase coupled with a planned budget surplus (or decline in the size of the deficit); (3) a tax increase coupled with an increase in the planned deficit; and (4) a tax reduction coupled with a planned budget surplus (or decline in the size of the deficit).

1. Lower Tax Rates and an Expansion in the Budget Deficit. Clearly, this fiscal strategy is expansionary. The budget deficit, as we have seen, stimulates aggregate demand, since government expenditures are injecting more spending into the income stream than tax revenues are draining out. Simultaneously, the lower marginal tax rates enhance aggregate supply, since they increase the incentive to utilize resources productively and efficiently. If the economy is operating below its supply-constrained income level, this fiscal strategy is a sound one. The increase in aggregate demand permits real income and output to expand toward the supply constraint of the economy, and the lower tax rates increase aggregate supply, further enlarging the potential noninflationary output of the economy.

However, once output has increased to the economy's supply constraint, the wisdom of this strategy is questionable. If the expansionary impact of the budget deficit is large, and the positive effects of the lower tax rates on aggregate supply are small, the strategy will be inflationary. Exhibit 4 illustrates this point. Initially, the economy is presumed to be in equilibrium at output level Y_1. The tax reduction coupled with a budget deficit is instituted. The budget deficit stimulates aggregate demand, causing it to expand (to $C_2 + I_2 + G_2$). This increase in aggregate demand triggers the multiplier process and causes nominal income to expand to Y_{2n}. The lower tax rates improve the microstructure of the economy, causing aggregate supply to expand (to AS_2). Real income increases from Y_1 to Y_2. However, the demand effect dominates. Thus, the increase in real income is smaller than the expansion in nominal income, indicating that inflation is a side effect of this fiscal strategy.

It is important to distinguish between changes in tax *rates* and changes in tax *revenues*. Individuals will adjust their work efforts and tax-avoidance activities in response to the lower tax rates. Their response will increase the size of the tax base. Therefore, tax revenues will generally decline by a smaller percentage than that by which the tax rates are reduced. If the supply-side effects are quite strong, the revenue reduction accompanying the lower rates may be small, particularly in the long run.[11] Thus, only a small increase in the size of the deficit may occur. If this is the case, the demand-stimulus effects will be dampened, reducing the inflationary side effects of this policy.

---

[11]When marginal rates are extremely high, a rate reduction *in high tax brackets* might actually lead to an *increase* in tax revenue.

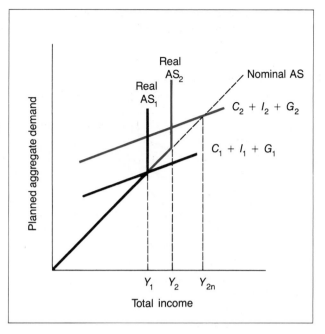

2. Higher Tax Rates and a Planned Budget Surplus (or Smaller Deficit). This strategy will cause both aggregate demand and aggregate supply to decline. It has often been advocated to combat inflation. Suppose an economy is experiencing inflation because aggregate demand is greater than aggregate supply. Policy-makers institute a tax increase and plan a budget surplus. The budget surplus causes aggregate demand to decline, since the budget injects less spending into the income stream than tax revenues drain out. Simultaneously, the higher tax rates induce resource users to move away from activities that generate taxable income and toward tax avoidance. Aggregate supply decreases as a result. If the budget surplus is substantial, the demand effects will dominate, and the strategy will retard the inflation. However, real income will also decline. Essentially, this strategy leads to an economic slowdown—a recession—in an effort to control the inflationary pressures.

3. Higher Tax Rates and a Planned Budget Deficit. In this case, the impact of the budget on aggregate demand is the reverse of the impact of tax rates on aggregate supply. This strategy depends upon the presence of a budget deficit, even when tax rates are increased. For this to be true, (a) government expenditures must increase sharply, and/or (b) tax revenues must decline (or expand by only a small amount) as tax rates are increased.

Exhibit 5 illustrates the impact of fiscal policy characterized by a budget deficit and rising tax rates. Initially, the economy is assumed to be in equilibrium. Aggregate demand ($C_1 + I_1 + G_1$) is equal to aggregate supply (real AS_1) at output Y_1. The budget deficit stimulates the economy, causing the aggregate demand curve to shift upward to $C_2 + I_2 + G_2$. Simultaneously, the rising marginal tax rates cause people to substitute leisure and tax avoidance for productive activities. Real aggregate supply declines (shifts to the left) to AS_2. This combination—an increase in aggregate demand coupled with higher tax rates—will be highly inflationary. While nominal income expands to Y_{2n}, real

EXHIBIT 5 The impact of a budget deficit coupled with rising tax rates

The budget deficit causes aggregate demand to shift upward to $C_2 + I_2 + G_2$. The higher tax rates alter incentives, causing real aggregate supply to decline, shifting to AS_2. The result is inflation—an increase in nominal income to Y_{2n} and a decline in real income to Y_2. Some economists believe that this is what happened during the 1970s.

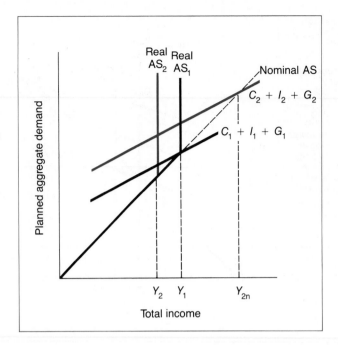

income is slowed (to Y_2) as the result of the negative impact of the high marginal tax rates on aggregate supply. This fiscal policy leads to inflation accompanied by recession and sluggish economic growth.

Some economists believe that this is precisely what happened during the 1970s. Government spending, particularly transfer payments, increased sharply as the Great Society programs of the latter half of the 1960s were put into place and expanded. Budget policy was expansionary. The federal budget was in deficit every year during the 1970s. Simultaneously, the inflation of the decade pushed taxpayers into higher and higher marginal tax brackets. Economists who believe that the adverse incentive effects of high marginal tax rates on aggregate supply are highly significant argue that fiscal policy was a major contributing factor to the economic sluggishness of the 1970s.

Of course, the rising marginal tax rates of the 1970s were not the only factor influencing aggregate supply. As we discussed earlier in this chapter, higher worldwide oil prices reduced the efficiency of much of the capital stock in the United States, further retarding supply. Viewed from this perspective, the 1970s seem much less puzzling. Given (a) the impact of soaring oil-import prices and the rising marginal tax rates on aggregate supply and (b) the impact of the budget deficits on aggregate demand, the inflation and sluggish growth of the 1970s are not particularly surprising.

4. Lower Tax Rates and a Budget Surplus (or Smaller Deficit). A budget surplus tends to retard aggregate demand, while lower tax rates induce an expansion in aggregate supply. In order to institute this strategy, (a) policy-makers must reduce government expenditures (or at least cut expenditure growth significantly), and/or (b) tax *revenues* must remain relatively unresponsive to the reduction in marginal tax rates.

The viability of this strategy is one of today's most divisive issues among

EXHIBIT 6   The Reagan fiscal
policy—proponents and critics

When the Reagan administration assumed office; it confronted an economy characterized by both inflation and a
high rate of unemployment. A
reduction in tax rates coupled
with cuts in government expenditures was proposed and
adopted. As illustrated by
(a) above, the proponents of
the Reagan strategy argued
that the tax rate reduction
would stimulate aggregate
supply (to AS$_2$), while the budget cuts and the planned eventual budget surplus would curtail demand (shift to $C_2 + I_2 +$
G_2). The expected outcome:
substantial real growth and deceleration in the inflation rate.
As illustrated by (b) above,
critics argued that the lower tax
rates would result in a substantial loss of tax revenues, large
budget deficits, and an increase in aggregate demand
relative to supply. The result:
an acceleration in the inflation
rate.

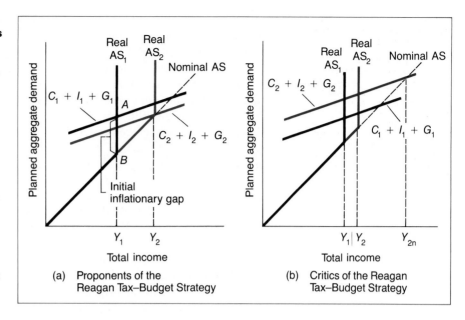

(a)   Proponents of the
      Reagan Tax–Budget Strategy

(b)   Critics of the Reagan
      Tax–Budget Strategy

economists. Economists who believe that the relative price incentive effects are
quite important argue that a reduction in tax *rates* will expand the tax base
and stimulate substantial economic growth. Therefore, the lower tax rates will
not lead to a substantial reduction in tax revenues, at least not in the long run.

Traditional Keynesian economists reject this view. They do not believe
that lower tax rates will exert much impact on aggregate supply. Thus, they
argue that a substantial tax cut will result in a large decline in the Treasury's
tax revenues, a huge budget deficit, and an acceleration in the inflation rate.

The Reagan Tax Cut— The Proponents and the Critics

The responsiveness of aggregate supply to lower tax rates lies at the heart of
the controversy over the Reagan fiscal policy. When President Reagan assumed
office in 1981, he inherited an economy experiencing high rates of both inflation
and unemployment. The inflation rate during 1980 exceeded 12 percent. The
unemployment rate at the beginning of 1981 stood at 7.5 percent. Following
through on a campaign promise, Reagan advocated budget cuts and a 30 percent
across-the-board reduction in tax rates spread over three years. Congress modified the Reagan plan, limiting the tax rate reduction to 23 percent and spreading
it over 39 months. The proponents of the Reagan strategy believed that the lower
tax rates would exert a strong positive impact on aggregate supply, but the
critics rejected this view.

Exhibit 6 presents a graphic illustration of the logic behind the views of
both the proponents and critics of the Reagan plan. Initially, the economy
was assumed to be characterized by excess demand and inflation. An inflationary gap of *AB* was present. As Exhibit 6a indicates, the proponents of the Reagan
policy believed that the reduction in tax rates would lead to a substantial
increase in aggregate supply (shift from real AS$_1$ to AS$_2$). They expected real
income to increase, causing an expansion in the tax base. At the higher rate
of real income, they believed that the loss of tax revenue would be relatively
small. They also believed that if significant budget cuts were made, the size

of the budget deficits could be reduced. The budget cuts would reduce demand-side pressures, causing aggregate demand to decline to $C_2 + I_2 + G_2$, according to this view. The result would be an increase in the real growth rate accompanied by a deceleration in the inflation rate.

Following the traditional demand-side Keynesian view, the critics of the plan argued that the supply-side effects of the tax rate reduction would be small. They believed that the reduction in tax rates would lead to a substantial decline in the tax revenue of the Treasury, causing large budget deficits. As Exhibit 6b illustrates, the critics believed that the budget deficits would overwhelm the supply-side effects; the large deficits would cause aggregate demand to rise (shift upward to $C_2 + I_2 + G_2$), while aggregate supply would expand only to AS_2. As frame (b) illustrates, this increase in aggregate demand relative to aggregate supply would cause the inflationary pressures to worsen. This is why the critics charged that the Reagan strategy would be counterproductive.

The Great Unanswered Question.   Who is right—the traditional demand-side Keynesians or the supply-side Reaganites? The answer to this question is critical, but there is no consensus among economists. Some believe that the supply-side incentive effects are quite important and argue that a strategy like Reagan's is at least a step in the right direction. Others believe, as we have seen, that the impact of aggregate demand will always overwhelm any possible supply-side effects and that the Reagan strategy was destined to failure from the outset.

One point is clear. The Reagan experiment is both interesting and important. It should go a long way toward helping us understand one of today's "great unanswered questions" in macroeconomics.

WHAT DO WE KNOW ABOUT FISCAL POLICY?

In light of the experience of the last decade, what do we know about fiscal policy? Four major points emerge.

1. Fiscal Policy Can Be an Effective Weapon with Which to Confront a Serious Recession Generated by Deficient Demand.   Tax reductions and/or increases in government expenditures are capable of preventing a recurrence of anything like the experience of the 1930s. This is a major accomplishment that those who grew up during the *relatively* stable post-World War II era often fail to appreciate.

2. The Use of Countercyclical Fiscal Policy Is Difficult and Highly Complex.   Both economic and political factors make it difficult. Our limited knowledge of the future and the presence of real-world time lags reduce our ability to time fiscal policy changes properly. The incentive structure under which political decisions are made reduces the likelihood that fiscal policy will be applied evenly. Our knowledge of the relative importance of the demand and supply effects of fiscal policy is inadequate. Thus, our attempts to create and structure fiscal policy that will combat a combination of inflation and unemployment are characterized by uncertainty.

3. Once the Inflation Rate Has Accelerated, It Is Difficult for Fiscal Policy to Return the Economy to a Condition of Stable Prices.   If properly timed, restrictive fiscal policy could prevent a demand-induced acceleration in the inflation. However, *once the inflation rate has begun to accelerate,* the application of an anti-inflationary fiscal policy will be more costly. Its initial impact is likely to be on output; its decelerating influence on the price level will be delayed.

4. It Is Important to Consider the Impact of Fiscal Policy on Aggregate Supply. Supply conditions generally inhibit the growth of real output and income. The impact of fiscal policy upon the supply and efficient use of resources must not be ignored. The tools of microeconomics can help us understand the macroeconomic impact of fiscal policy.

THE DUAL PROBLEMS OF MACROECONOMICS

In Chapters 6 and 7, we noted that instability in aggregate demand can be an important source of unemployment and economic inefficiency. In this chapter, we have indicated that limited supply constrains our ability to expand real income. These chapters highlight the twin policy objectives of macroeconomics:

    1. The provision of a stable economic environment, characterized by steady economic growth, a high level of employment, and a stable price level.

    2. The allocation of resources in an efficient manner that minimizes waste so that the supply of goods and services available can be maximized.

The first could be called the "stability problem" and the second "the efficiency problem." The two are closely intertwined. We will return to these objectives repeatedly. They provide effective criteria for evaluating macroeconomic policy.

LOOKING AHEAD

We are now ready to integrate the monetary system into our analysis. The following chapter will focus on the operation of the banking system and the factors that determine the supply of money. In Chapter 10, we will analyze the ways in which monetary policy affects the interest rate, price level, and output.

CHAPTER LEARNING OBJECTIVES

1 Both aggregate demand and aggregate supply influence the levels of output, employment, and prices.

2 The three major determinants of aggregate supply are (a) the utilization level of resources, (b) the efficiency with which the resources are applied, and (c) the current state of technology. An alteration in any one of these three factors will induce a change in aggregate supply. The constraints on aggregate supply involve both resource scarcity and the incentive structure—the ways in which, and the degree to which, people are motivated to work, save, and invest—resulting from public policy.

3 If an economy is operating at its supply-constrained output level, an increase in aggregate demand will lead to higher prices rather than to a larger sustained rate of real output.

4 It is useful to divide a real aggregate supply curve into two distinct segments: (a) a Keynesian range, within which output can be fully responsive to an increase in aggregate demand, and, beyond this, (b) a supply-constrained range, where an increase in aggregate demand will lead, in the long run, only to an increase in price levels. The Keynesian range is a simplification of the idea that *when excess capacity is present,* an increase in aggregate demand will exert its primary impact on output, and prices will remain relatively stable. Similarly, the supply-constrained portion of the aggregate

supply curve simplifies and reinforces the important concept of an attainable output rate beyond which increases in aggregate demand will lead almost exclusively to price increases and exert little impact on real output.

5   With the passage of time, factors such as net capital formation, discovery of additional natural resources, technological advances, improvements in the skill (and educational) level of the work force, and improvements in the operational efficiency of markets will increase aggregate supply. An increase in aggregate supply will make it possible for real output to expand and price stability to be maintained.

6   Factors such as unfavorable weather conditions, a decline in capital assets, a decline in the average skill (or educational) level of the labor force, higher prices for imported goods, and falling prices for exported goods will cause a decline in aggregate supply. A decrease in aggregate supply will cause real output to fall. It will also lead to inflation, unless it is accompanied by a reduction in aggregate demand.

7   Changes in marginal tax rates alter the incentive of individuals to work, invest, save, and pay taxes. Other things constant, an increase in marginal tax rates will (a) decrease the supply of labor and reduce its productive efficiency, (b) decrease the supply of capital and reduce its productive efficiency, and (c) encourage individuals to substitute less-desired, tax-deductible goods for more-desired, nondeductible goods.

8   When fiscal policy alters marginal tax rates, it will thus exert an impact on aggregate supply as well as on aggregate demand. Other things constant, higher marginal tax rates tend to reduce aggregate supply; lower rates will increase supply.

9   The economic policy of the 1970s was characterized by budget deficits and rising marginal tax rates. The budget deficits added to aggregate demand, while the higher tax rates reduced aggregate supply. This combination of factors contributed to the inflationary pressures of the decade.

10   When the Reagan administration took office in 1981, its fiscal strategy was to reduce government expenditures and tax rates. Since the proponents of the Reagan plan believed that lower tax rates would stimulate income, they expected that the tax cut would lead to only a small reduction in tax revenues. Thus, if government expenditures were reduced, the size of the budget deficit could also be reduced (or at least maintained within manageable proportions). The proponents of this strategy believed it would stimulate aggregate supply while retarding aggregate demand and thereby reduce the inflationary pressures.

11   The critics of the Reagan plan charged that the loss of tax revenues would be substantial, leading to huge budget deficits. They believed that the plan would exert little impact on aggregate supply, while stimulating aggregate demand. Thus, the critics argued that the plan would cause the already high rate of inflation to accelerate.

THE ECONOMIC WAY OF THINKING—DISCUSSION QUESTIONS

1   Indicate the impact of each of the following on aggregate supply in the United States:

(a) An increase in the world price of wheat, a major export product of the United States

(b) The discovery of a major oil field in Utah

(c) A sharp reduction in the import price of Japanese automobiles stemming from the adoption of new, improved production techniques

(d) A drought causing a 40 percent loss of the Midwest corn crop

(e) A 20 percent increase in unemployment compensation benefits to help alleviate hardships of unemployment

(f) A discovery of an additional $20 billion of gold misplaced in the vaults at Fort Knox

2 "An increase in aggregate expenditures will always lead to more income because one person's spending is another person's income. Maintenance of a high level of expenditures is the key to maintenance of a high level of income." Evaluate.

3 If unemployed resources are present, an economy is not operating on the vertical portion of its aggregate supply curve. True, false, or uncertain? Discuss.

4 Empirical studies indicate that males in their prime earning years do not adjust their work time significantly in response to a change in their after-tax wage rates. Do these findings indicate that marginal tax rates exert little influence on aggregate supply? Why or why not? Discuss.

6 When the Reagan administration took office, its fiscal strategy was to cut taxes and government expenditures. The administration believed that this strategy, with time, would effectively combat the high rate of inflation without causing a major recession. Evaluate the Reagan strategy. Has it reduced the inflation rate? The unemployment rate? Has the administration followed its announced strategy or has it changed course? Indicate why you judge the Reagan fiscal policy as either a success or failure. Be specific.

7 Given current economic conditions, how would an increase in aggregate demand influence output, employment, and price? Discuss.

ADDENDUM

MACROEQUILIBRIUM WITHIN THE PRICE–QUANTITY FRAMEWORK

We have utilized the traditional Keynesian income–flow approach to analyze the aggregate market for goods and services. However, the flow of total spending, which comprises aggregate demand in the Keynesian framework, is actually nothing more than the sum of price times quantity for all goods and services produced during a given period. Therefore, the relationship between price (level) and quantity (of output) can also be used to analyze highly aggregated markets. We can view the price and output relationship for the entire economy, if the purchases of consumers, investors, and government are considered as a single market, the market for goods and services. Since the price variable represents the average price of all goods and services, it is really the price level of the economy. An increase in price in the aggregate goods and services market is indicative of inflation. Similarly, the quantity variable in the aggregate goods and services market represents the total real output of the economy. An increase in quantity indicates an expansion in real output.

Using the price–quantity framework, Exhibit A-1 illustrates the general shapes of the aggregate demand and aggregate supply curves for the macro-economic model that we have developed. As Exhibit A-1a reveals, aggregate demand is inversely related to price. As the price level decreases, the value of money and assets representing future income measured in money terms (for example, government bonds and savings deposits) will rise. These monetary assets will buy more goods and services as the price level declines. Thus, other things constant, a lower price level will induce individuals to demand more of everything. For a single good, as we discussed in Chapter 3, there is also an inverse relationship between price and amount demanded; but in that case it is because

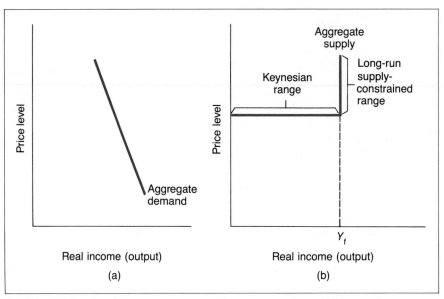

EXHIBIT A-1 Aggregate demand and supply: the price—quantity framework

Here we view the aggregate demand and supply curves within the framework of the price—quantity relationship. The aggregate demand curve (above, left) will slope downward to the right. As prices fall, money (and assets that represent a fixed amount of money) become worth more in purchasing-power terms. Therefore, individuals increase their purchases (amount demanded) as prices decline. The aggregate supply curve (above, right) will (a) have a flat portion reflecting inflexible prices and excess capacity for output rates below the full-employment (Y_f) level and (b) a vertical portion beginning at Y_f, reflecting the supply constraints of the economy.

consumers substitute lower-priced for higher-priced products. When the demand curve is for all goods, this substitution effect is not present. However, though the explanations are somewhat different, both the aggregate demand curve and the demand curve for a single commodity will slope downward to the right, indicating the inverse relationship of amount demanded to price.

Exhibit A-1b illustrates the aggregate supply curve. Remember, our model assumes that the existing level of prices will remain unchanged until the supply-constrained output, Y_f, is reached. Therefore, for output rates less than Y_f, the aggregate supply curve is perfectly horizontal, indicating that an expansion in aggregate demand will induce the flow of available idle resources into the production process at the existing level of prices, P_1. Given the resource base and the economy's incentive structures, it will not be possible to maintain output rates greater than Y_f. Thus, the aggregate supply curve becomes vertical at Y_f.

In Exhibit 2, we illustrated the impact of changing demand conditions within the framework of the Keynesian income–flow diagram. Exhibit A-2 illustrates that same analysis for the price—quantity model. As aggregate demand increases from D_1 to D_2, output is fully responsive to the demand stimulus. Real income expands to Y_f, while prices remain stable at P_1. In this range, the additional output is generated by drawing previously unemployed resources into the production process. However, once the unemployed resources are in use, the supply constraint of the economy is confronted. Although an increase in demand from D_2 to D_3 might expand output temporarily, output levels beyond Y_f cannot be maintained in the long run. An expansion in aggregate demand to

EXHIBIT A-2 Aggregate output: the price–quantity framework

Here we present the changes in aggregate demand from Exhibit 2, as viewed within the price–quantity framework. Initially, the economy is operating at price level P_1 and at output Y_1, well below the full-employment capacity Y_f. Given these Keynesian underemployment conditions, an increase in aggregate demand from D_1 to D_2 will cause real output to expand to Y_f; prices will remain stable. However, once the full-employment output level has been attained, an additional increase in demand to D_3 will merely cause higher prices (price level increases to P_2) rather than additional real output.

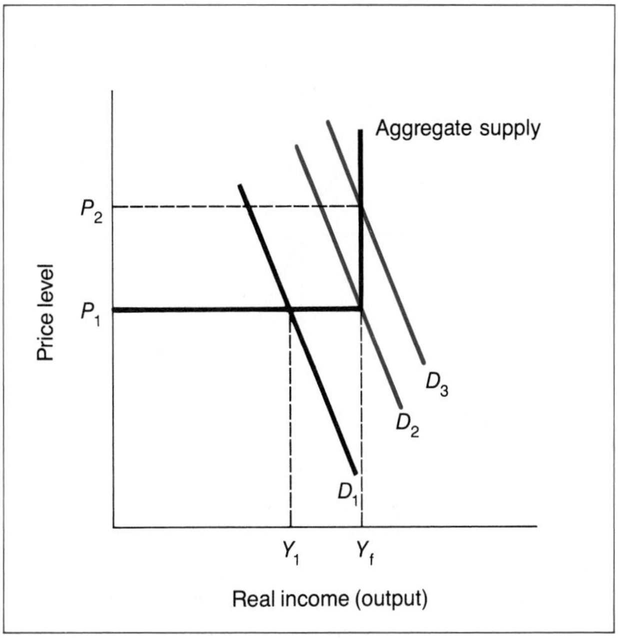

D_3 will be inflationary. When the adjustment process is complete, the new equilibrium will be at a higher level of prices (P_2), and the rate of real output will still be constrained at Y_f.

Suppose that an expansion in demand pushed that price level upward. What would happen if the inflationary rise in prices were followed by a period of declining demand? Our Keynesian assumption of downward price rigidity implies that once a price level is attained, a decline in aggregate demand will induce a fall in real output. Thus, although an increase in demand beyond the supply constraint merely results in inflation—a higher level of prices—a decrease in demand will *not* result in lower prices.

We can also demonstrate the impact of a change in aggregate supply within the price–quantity framework. Exhibit A-3a illustrates the case of an increase in aggregate supply. When accompanied by an increase in aggregate demand (D_2), the increase in aggregate supply (to AS_2) leads to a higher level of real income at Y_2; price stability is maintained.

Exhibit A-3b illustrates the impact of a decline in aggregate supply. If the level of demand remains unchanged (at D), the fall in supply will cause real income to decline (to Y_2). The price level will rise, since the demand (D) has increased *relative* to the new, smaller supply of goods.

The price–quantity framework, like the Keynesian income–flow model, can be utilized to analyze changes in macroeconomic markets. They are simply alternative methods of looking at problems. The price–quantity framework illustrates more clearly what is happening to prices; the income–flow model highlights the importance of equilibrium between total spending and total output. It can often be profitable to employ both approaches when analyzing the impact of macroeconomic changes.

CHAPTER 8 AGGREGATE SUPPLY, FISCAL POLICY, AND STABILIZATION **171**

EXHIBIT A-3   Changes in aggregate supply

As frame (a) illustrates, when aggregate supply increases (to AS₂), an expansion in demand (to D₂) leads to an increase in real income (to Y₂); price stability is maintained. Frame (b) illustrates the case of a decline in aggregate supply. A fall in real income and in higher prices results, unless aggregate demand declines also.

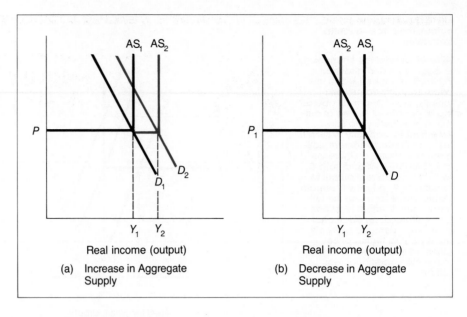

(a)   Increase in Aggregate Supply

(b)   Decrease in Aggregate Supply

There have been three great inventions since the beginning of time: fire, the wheel, and central banking.
Will Rogers

MONEY AND THE BANKING SYSTEM

The purposes of this chapter are to explain the operation of our banking/finance system and to analyze the determinants of the money supply. Later, we will consider the influence of money on prices, employment, output, and other important economic variables.

To many economists, analyzing the determinants of national income without considering money is like playing football without a quarterback. The central moving force has been excluded. Although the majority would assign a somewhat lesser role to money, almost all economists believe that money, and therefore monetary policy, matters a great deal.

WHAT IS MONEY?

Money makes the world go around. Although this is an exaggeration, money is nonetheless an important cog in the wheel that makes trade go around. Without money, everyday exchange would be both tedious and costly. Of course, money today is issued and controlled by governments, but the use of money arose thousands of years ago, not because of government decree, but because money simplified exchange. Money performs three basic functions.

1. Money Serves as a Medium of Exchange. If one desires to exchange labor services for clothing, one first sells one's labor for money and then uses the money to buy clothes. Similarly, if a farmer wants to exchange a cow for electricity and medical services, the cow is sold for money, which is then used to buy the electricity and medical services. In a barter economy, such simple exchange would necessitate finding a buyer for one's goods who was willing to sell precisely those things one wanted to purchase. Exchange would be enormously time-consuming. In an exchange economy with money, money trades in all markets, simplifying exchange and oiling the wheels of trade.

2. Money Serves as an Accounting Unit. Consumers want to compare the prices of widely differing goods and services so that they will be able to make sensible choices. Similarly, cost-conscious businesspeople want to compare the prices of vastly different productive resources. Since money is widely used in exchange, it certainly makes sense that we also use it as the accounting unit, the yardstick by which we compare the value of goods and resources.

3. Money Is Used as a Store of Value. Money is a financial asset, a form of savings. There are some disadvantages of using money as a vehicle for storing value (wealth). Most methods of holding money do not yield an interest return. During a time of inflation, the purchasing power of money will decline, imposing a cost on those who are holding wealth in the form of money. However, money has the advantage of being a perfectly **liquid asset.** It can be easily and quickly transformed into other goods at a low transaction cost and without an appreciable loss in its nominal value. Thus, most people hold some of their wealth in the form of money because it provides readily available purchasing power for dealing with an uncertain future.

Liquid Asset: An asset that can be easily and quickly converted to purchasing power without loss of value.

Why Is Money Valuable?

Neither currency nor checking-account deposits have significant intrinsic value. A dollar bill is just a piece of paper. Checkable deposits are nothing more than accounting numbers. Coins have some intrinsic value as metal, but it is considerably less than their value as money.

From what does money derive its value? The confidence of people is important. People are willing to accept money because they are confident that it can be used to purchase real goods and services. This is partly a matter of law. The government has designated currency as "legal tender"—acceptable for payment of debts.

However, the major source of the value of money is the same as that of other commodities. Economic goods are more or less valuable because of their scarcity relative to the amount that people desire. Money is no exception.

If the purchasing power of money is to remain stable over time, the supply of money must be controlled. The value of a dollar is measured in terms of what it will buy. Therefore, its value is inversely related to the level of prices. An increase in the level of prices and a decline in the purchasing power of money are the same thing. Assuming a constant rate of use, if the supply of money grows more rapidly than the growth in the real output of goods and services, prices will rise. This happens because the quantity of money has risen *relative* to the availability of goods. In layman's terms, there is "too much money chasing too few goods."

The linkage between rising prices and a *rapid* growth of the supply of money was demonstrated dramatically in post-World War I Germany. The supply of German marks increased by 250 percent *per month* for a time. The German government was printing money almost as fast as the printing presses would run. Since money became substantially more plentiful in relation to goods and services, it quickly lost its value. As a result, an egg cost 80 billion marks and a loaf of bread 200 billion. Workers picked up their wages in suitcases. Shops closed at lunch hour to change price tags. The value of money was eroded.

How Is the Supply of Money Defined?

Demand Deposits: Deposits in a bank that can either be withdrawn or payable on demand to a third party via check. In essence, they are "checkbook money" because they permit transactions to be paid for by check rather than currency.

NOW Accounts: Interest-earning savings accounts on which the account holder is permitted to write checks. They may be offered by savings and loan associations, credit unions, and mutual savings banks, as well as by commercial banks.

Money Supply (M-1): The sum of (a) currency in circulation (including coins), (b) demand deposits of commercial banks, (c) other *checkable* deposits of depository institutions, and (d) traveler's checks.

Determining what should be included in the supply of money is not as easy as it might appear to be. At one time, only gold and silver coins were considered money. Eventually, paper currency and **demand deposits** (checking-account balances) replaced metal coins as the major means of exchange. In defining money, it makes sense to rely on its basic functions as a medium of exchange, a unit of account, and a store of value. On the basis of these criteria, it is clear that currency (including both coins and paper bills) and demand deposits should be included in the supply of money. Most of the nation's business—more than 75 percent—is conducted by check. Demand deposits are freely convertible to currency. The amount of currency in circulation at any given time is merely a reflection of the public's preferences for "checking-account money" versus cash. In addition to demand deposits, financial institutions also offer combination savings/checking accounts. NOW (negotiable order of withdrawal) accounts are the most common such deposits. **NOW accounts** earn interest, but the depositor is also permitted to write checks against the account. Thus, deposits in NOW accounts and similar combination savings/checking deposits are also part of the money supply. Like currency and demand deposits, funds in these checkable accounts are immediately available for use as a medium of exchange. Traveler's checks can also be freely converted to cash at parity and may be used as a means of payment.

The **money supply (M-1)** in its narrowest definition is composed of (a) currency in circulation, (b) demand deposits, (c) other checkable deposits, and (d) traveler's checks. Economists use the term M-1 when referring to this narrowly defined money supply. As Exhibit 1 shows, the total money supply (M-1) in the United States was $452.3 billion in April 1982. Demand and other checkable deposits account for approximately 70 percent of the total money supply. Unless otherwise noted, throughout this text, when we speak of the money supply, we will be referring to the M-1 definition.

EXHIBIT 1   Composition of the money supply in the United States

Components of the Money Supply	Amount in Circulation, April 1982	
	Total (Billions of Dollars)	Percentage of Total Money Supply (M-1)
Currency (in circulation)	126.3	27.9
Demand deposits	233.0	51.5
Other checkable deposits[a]	88.6	19.6
Traveler's checks	4.4	1.0
Total money supply, M-1	452.3	100.0
Total money supply, M-2	1879.7	
Total money supply, M-3	2256.6	

[a]Includes NOW accounts and automatic transfer system balances in all institutions, credit union share-draft balances, and demand deposits at mutual savings banks.

The Board of Governors of the Federal Reserve System, June 1982.

Thrift Institutions: Traditional savings institutions, such as savings and loan associations, mutual savings banks, and credit unions.

Money Supply (M-2): Equal to M-1 plus (a) savings and time deposits (accounts of less than $100,000) of all depository institutions, (b) money market mutual fund shares, (c) overnight loans from customers to commercial banks, and (d) overnight Eurodollar deposits held by U.S. residents.

Eurodollar Deposits: Deposits denominated in U.S. dollars at banks and other financial institutions outside of the United States. Although this name originated because of the large amounts of such deposits held at banks in Western Europe, similar deposits in other parts of the world are also called Eurodollars.

Money Supply (M-3): Equal to M-2 plus time deposits (accounts of more than $100,000) at all depository institutions and (b) longer-term (more than overnight) loans of customers to commercial banks and savings and loan associations.

Near Monies and Broader Definitions. Several financial assets resemble money in many ways. Noncheckable time deposits in commercial banks and **thrift institutions** are a highly liquid means of holding purchasing power into the future. Although these deposits are not legally available on demand (without payment of a penalty), they can often be withdrawn on short notice. Some noncheckable savings accounts can even be transferred to one's checking account upon request without penalty. Similarly, money market mutual fund shares can generally be quickly transformed to cash at (or very near) their parity value.

The line between money and "near monies" is a fine one. Some economists prefer to use a broader definition of the money supply than M-1. In various degrees, these broader definitions incorporate savings and other liquid assets into the money supply. The most common broad definition of the money supply is M-2. The **money supply (M-2)** includes M-1 plus (a) savings and small-denomination time deposits at all depository institutions, (b) money market mutual fund shares, (c) overnight loans of customers to commercial banks (they are called *repurchase agreements*) and (d) overnight **Eurodollar deposits** of U.S. residents. In each case, these financial assets can be easily converted to checking-account funds. Their owners may perceive them as funds available for use as payment. In some cases, the assets may even be directly used as a means of exchange. Thus, regardless of whether or not they are counted as part of the money supply, it is clear that the additional assets incorporated into M-2 are close substitutes for money.

There is a third method of measuring the money supply, M-3. Under this definition, the **money supply (M-3)** is composed of M-2 plus (a) large-denomination (more than $100,000) time deposits at all depository institutions and (b) longer-term (more than overnight) loans of customers to commercial banks and savings and loan associations. These additional assets included in M-3 are not quite as liquid as the items that comprise M-2.

As Exhibit 1 notes, M-2 and M-3 are roughly four to five times larger than M-1. Exhibit 2 illustrates the paths of the three measures of the money supply during the period from 1964 to 1982. Although all three have increased substantially in recent years, they have not always moved together. In general, the growth rates of M-2 and M-3 have been more rapid than the rate for M-1. We will take note of these differences, but our attention will be focused primarily on the narrowest definition, M-1.

THE BUSINESS OF BANKING

We must understand a few things about the business of banking before we can explain the factors that influence the supply of money. As we have indicated, the banking industry in the United States operates under the jurisdiction of the Federal Reserve System. Not all banks belong to the Federal Reserve, but recent legislation leaves only a nominal difference between member and nonmember banks.

Since 1933, almost all commercial banks—state and national—have had their deposits insured with the Federal Deposit Insurance Corporation (FDIC). The FDIC fully insures each account up to $100,000 against losses due to bank failure. The Federal Savings and Loan Insurance Corporation and the National Credit Union Administration provide identical coverage for deposits of savings

EXHIBIT 2 Three alternative measures of the money supply

The graph illustrates the growth of the money supply (1964–1982) according to three alternative definitions. The narrowest and most widely used definition, M-1, includes currency, demand deposits, other checkable deposits in all institutions, and traveler's checks. M-2 includes M-1 plus money market mutual fund shares, savings and time deposits of less than $100,000, overnight Eurodollar deposits, and overnight repurchase agreements issued by commercial banks. M-3 includes M-2 plus time deposits of $100,000 or more and longer-term repurchase agreements issued by banks and savings and loan institutions.

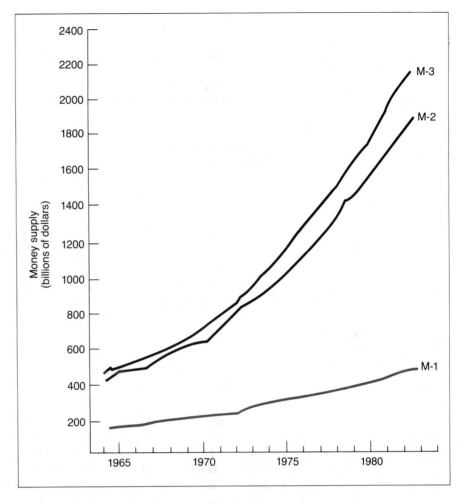

and loan associations and credit unions. Since the establishment of the FDIC, bank failures have become a rare, although not impossible, occurrence.

Banks are in business to make a profit. They provide checking- and savings-account services to their customers. However, interest-earning investments are the major source of income for most banks. Banks use a sizable share of both their demand and time deposits for interest-earning purposes—primarily the extension of loans and the undertaking of financial investments.

The consolidated balance sheet for all commercial banks (Exhibit 3) illustrates the major banking functions. It shows that the major liabilities of banks are demand and time deposits. *From the viewpoint of a bank,* these are liabilities because they represent an obligation of the bank to its depositors. Outstanding interest-earning loans comprise the major class of banking assets. In addition, most banks own sizable amounts of interest-earning securities, both government and private.

Banking differs from most businesses in that a large portion of its liabilities are payable on demand. However, even though it would be possible for all depositors to demand the money in their checking accounts on the same day, the probability of this occurring is quite remote. Typically, while some

EXHIBIT 3   The functions of commercial banks

Banks provide services and pay interest to attract demand and time deposits (liabilities). A portion of their assets is held as *reserves* (either cash or deposits with the Fed) to meet their daily obligations toward their depositors. Most of the rest is invested and loaned out, providing interest income for the bank.

Consolidated Balance Sheet of Commercial Banks—May 1982
(Billions of Dollars)

Assets		Liabilities	
Reserves	43.0	Capital accounts	132.5
Loans outstanding	1007.5	Demand deposits	327.9
U.S. government securities	114.3	Time deposits	958.2
Other securities	236.6	Other liabilities	393.4
Other assets	410.6		
Total	1812.0	Total	1812.0

Federal Reserve Bulletin, June 1982.

individuals are making withdrawals, others are making deposits. These transactions tend to balance out, eliminating sudden changes in demand deposits.

Thus, banks maintain only a fraction of their assets in reserves to meet the requirements of depositors. As Exhibit 3 illustrates, on average, **reserves**—vault cash and deposits with the Federal Reserve—were only 13 percent as large as the demand deposit obligation of member banks in 1982.

Reserves: Vault cash plus deposits of the bank with Federal Reserve Banks.

Recent Changes in Financial Institutions and the Banking System

Commercial Banks: **Financial institutions that offer a wide range of services (for example, checking accounts, savings accounts, and extension of loans) to their customers. Commercial banks are owned by stockholders and seek to operate at a profit.**

Savings and Loan Associations: **Financial institutions that accept deposits in exchange for shares that pay dividends. Historically, these funds have been channeled into residential mortgage loans. Under recent banking legislation, S & L's are now permitted to offer checkable deposits (NOW accounts) and extend a broad range of services similar to those of commercial banks.**

Prior to the 1980s, commercial banks, savings and loan associations, and credit unions performed distinctly different functions. If one wanted a checking account, a personal or business loan, or a credit card, one would go to a **commercial bank.** For maximum interest on a savings account, or to obtain funds to buy a home, one would patronize a **savings and loan association. Credit unions** specialized in small personal loans, frequently offering the advantage of automatic deductions from one's paychecks.

In recent years, changes in the rules issued by the authorities regulating depository institutions have blurred the traditional distinctions among commercial banks, savings and loan associations, credit unions, and **mutual savings banks.** Under the Depository Institutions Deregulation and Monetary Control Act of 1980 (see feature, page 190), all of these depository institutions are permitted to offer NOW checking accounts. Simultaneously, the Depository Act lifted various restrictions on the types of loans and investments that savings and loan associations, mutual savings banks, and credit unions could make and provided for the phasing out of interest-rate ceilings on time and savings deposits by 1986. In addition, *all* depository institutions were placed under the jurisdiction of the Federal Reserve System and eventually will be required to meet similar regulatory requirements. As the result of these changes, the functions performed by commercial banks, savings and loan associations, mutual savings banks, and credit unions are now quite similar. In essence, recent legal and regulatory changes have transformed thrift institutions into banks. All of these depository institutions now offer both checking and savings accounts, and extend a wide variety of loans to their customers. Therefore, when we speak

Credit Unions: Financial cooperative organizations of individuals with a common affiliation (such as an employer or labor union). They accept deposits, including checkable deposits, pay interest (or dividends) on them out of earnings, and channel their funds primarily into loans to members.

Mutual Savings Banks: Financial institutions that accept deposits in exchange for interest payments. Historically, home mortgages have constituted their primary interest-earning assets. Under recent banking legislation, these banks, too, are authorized to offer interest-bearing checkable accounts. They exist in only 18 states and are concentrated in the Northeast.

EXHIBIT 4   A thumbnail sketch of the major depository institutions in the United States

Type of Institution	Number (Approximate)	Assets—March 1982 (Billions of Dollars)
Commercial banks	14,700	1819.9
Savings and loan associations	4,700	678.0
Mutual savings banks	500	174.8
Credit unions	22,300	81.1

Federal Reserve Bulletin, June 1982.

of the banking industry, we are referring not only to commercial banks but to savings and loan associations, credit unions, and mutual savings banks as well.

Exhibit 4 provides a thumbnail sketch of the depository institutions that comprise the banking industry. The assets of commercial banks are nearly twice as large as the combined total of those of the other three banking/depository institutions. In turn, the assets of savings and loan associations are substantially greater than those of either mutual savings banks or credit unions. Credit unions are more numerous (22,300) than any other type of depository institution, but their total assets came to only $81.1 billion in 1982.

Fractional Reserve Goldsmithing

Economists often like to draw an analogy between the goldsmith of the past and our current banking system. In the past, gold was used as the means of making payments. It was money. People would store their money with a goldsmith for safekeeping, just as many of us open a checking account for safety reasons. Gold owners received a certificate granting them the right to withdraw their gold anytime they wished. If they wanted to buy something, they would go to the goldsmith, withdraw gold, and use it as a means of making a payment. Thus, the money supply was equal to the amount of gold in circulation plus the gold deposited with goldsmiths.

The day-to-day deposits of and requests for gold were always only a fraction of the total amount of gold deposited. A major portion of the gold simply lay idle in the goldsmiths' "vaults." Taking notice of this fact, goldsmiths soon began loaning gold to local merchants. After a time, the merchants would pay back the gold plus an interest payment for its use. What happened to the money supply when a goldsmith extended loans to local merchants? The deposits of persons who initially brought their gold to the goldsmith were not reduced. Depositors could still withdraw their gold anytime they wished (as long as they did not all try to do so at once). The merchants were now able to use the gold they borrowed from the goldsmith as a means of payment. As goldsmiths lent gold, they increased the amount of gold in circulation, thereby increasing the money supply.

It was inconvenient to make a trip to the goldsmith every time one wanted to buy something. Since people knew that the certificates were redeemable in gold, certificates began circulating as a means of payment. The depositors were pleased with this arrangement because it eliminated the need for a trip to the goldsmith every time something was exchanged for gold. As long as they had confidence in the goldsmith, sellers were glad to accept the gold certificates as payment.

Since depositors were now able to utilize the gold certificates as money, the daily withdrawals and deposits with goldsmiths declined even more. Local goldsmiths would keep about 20 percent of the total gold deposited with them so they could meet the current requests to redeem gold certificates that were in circulation. The remaining 80 percent of their gold deposits would be loaned out to business merchants, traders, and other citizens. Therefore, 100 percent of the gold certificates was circulating as money; and that portion of gold that had been loaned out, 80 percent of the total deposits, was also circulating as money. The total money supply, gold certificates plus gold, was now 1.8 times the amount of gold that had been originally deposited with the goldsmith. Since the goldsmiths issued loans and kept only a fraction of the total gold deposited with them, they were able to increase the money supply.

As long as the goldsmiths held enough reserves to meet the current requests of their depositors, everything went along smoothly. Most gold depositors probably did not even realize that the goldsmiths did not have *their* actual gold and *that of other depositors,* precisely designated as such, sitting in the "vaults."

Goldsmiths derived income from loaning gold. The more gold they loaned, the greater their total income. Some goldsmiths, trying to increase their income by extending more and more interest-earning loans, depleted the gold in their vaults to imprudently low levels. If an unexpectedly large number of depositors wanted their gold, these greedy goldsmiths would have been unable to meet their requests. They would lose the confidence of their depositors, and the system of fractional reserve goldsmithing would tend to break down.

Fractional Reserve Banking

Fractional Reserve Banking: A system that enables banks to keep *less than* 100 percent reserves against their deposits. Required reserves are a fraction of deposits.

Required Reserves: The minimum amount of reserves that a bank is required by law to keep on hand to back up its deposits. Thus, if reserve requirements were 15 percent, banks would be required to keep $150,000 in reserves against each $1 million of deposits.

In principle, our **fractional reserve banking** system is very similar to goldsmithing. The early goldsmiths did not have enough gold on hand to pay all of their depositors simultaneously. Nor do our banks have enough cash and other reserves to pay all of their depositors simultaneously (see Exhibit 3). The early goldsmiths expanded the money supply by issuing loans. So do present-day bankers. The amount of gold held in reserve to meet the requirements of depositors limited the ability of the goldsmiths to expand the supply of money. The amount of cash and other **required reserves** limit the ability of present-day banks to expand the supply of money.

How Bankers Create Money. How do banks expand the supply of money? In order to answer this question, let us consider a banking system without a central bank and in which only currency acts as reserves against deposits. Initially, we will assume that all banks are required by law to maintain vault currency equal to at least 20 percent of the checking accounts of their depositors.

Suppose that you found $1000, which apparently your long-deceased uncle had hidden in the basement of his house. How much would this newly found $1000 of currency expand the money supply? You take the bills to the First National Bank, open a checking account of $1000, and deposit the cash with the banker. First National is now required to keep an additional $200 in vault cash, 20 percent of your deposit. However, they received $1000 of additional cash, so

Excess Reserves: Actual reserves that exceed the legal requirement.

after placing $200 in the bank vault, First National has $800 of **excess reserves,** reserves over and above the amount they are required by law to maintain. Given their current excess reserves, First National can now extend an $800 loan. Suppose that they loan $800 to a local citizen to buy a car. At the time the loan is extended, the money supply will increase by $800 as the bank adds the funds to the checking account of the borrower. No one else has less money. You still have your $1000 checking account, and the borrower has $800 for a new car.

When the borrower buys a new car, the seller accepts a check and deposits the $800 in a bank, Citizen's State Bank. What happens as the check clears? The temporary excess reserves of the First National Bank will be eliminated when it pays $800 to the Citizen's State Bank. But when Citizen's State Bank receives $800 in currency, it will now have excess reserves. It must keep 20 percent, an additional $160, in the reserve against the $800 checking-account deposit of the automobile seller. The remaining $640 could be loaned out. Since Citizen's State, like other banks, is in business to make money, it will be quite happy to "extend a helping hand" to a borrower. As the second bank loans out its excess reserves, the deposits of the persons borrowing the money will increase by $640. Another $640 has now been added to the money supply. You still have your $1000, the automobile seller has an additional $800, and the new borrower has just received an additional $640. Because you found the $1000 that had been stashed away by your uncle, the money supply has increased by $2440.

Of course, the process can continue. Exhibit 5 follows the *potential* creation of money resulting from the initial $1000 through several additional stages. In total, the money supply can increase by a maximum of $5000, the $1000 initial deposit plus an additional $4000 in demand deposits that can be created by the process of extending new loans.

Deposit Expansion Multiplier: The multiple by which an increase (decrease) in reserves will increase (decrease) the money supply. It is inversely related to the required reserve ratio.

The multiple by which new reserves increase the stock of money is referred to as the **deposit expansion multiplier.** In our example, the potential deposit expansion multiplier is 5. The amount by which additional reserves can increase the supply of money is determined by the ratio of required reserves to demand deposits. In fact, the deposit expansion multiplier is merely the reciprocal of the required reserve ratio. In our example, the required reserves are 20 percent, or

EXHIBIT 5   Creating money from new reserves

When banks are required to maintain 20 percent reserves against demand deposits, the creation of $1000 of new reserves will potentially increase the supply of money by $5000.

Bank	New Cash Deposits (Actual Reserves) (Dollars)	New Required Reserves (Dollars)	Potential Demand Deposits Created by Extending New Loans (Dollars)
Initial deposit	1000.00	200.00	800.00
Second stage	800.00	160.00	640.00
Third stage	640.00	128.00	512.00
Fourth stage	512.00	102.40	409.60
Fifth stage	409.60	81.92	327.68
Sixth stage	327.68	65.54	262.14
Seventh stage	262.14	52.43	209.71
All others	1048.58	209.71	838.87
Total	5000.00	1000.00	4000.00

only 10 percent reserves were required, the deposit expansion multiplier would be 10, the reciprocal of 1/10.

The lower the percentage of the reserve requirement, the greater is the potential expansion in the supply of money resulting from the creation of new reserves. The fractional reserve requirement places a ceiling on potential money creation from new reserves.

The Actual Deposit Expansion Multiplier.   Will the introduction of the new currency reserves necessarily have a full deposit expansion multiplier effect? The answer is no. The actual deposit multiplier may be less than the potential for two reasons.

First, the deposit expansion multiplier will be reduced if some persons decide to hold the currency rather than deposit it in a bank. For example, suppose that the person who borrowed the $800 in the preceding example spends only $700 and stashes the remaining $100 away for a possible emergency. Then only $700 can end up as a deposit in the second stage and contribute to the excess reserves necessary for expansion. The potential of new loans in the second stage and in all subsequent stages will be reduced proportionally. When currency remains in circulation, outside of banks, it will reduce the size of the deposit expansion multiplier.

Second, the deposit multiplier will be less than its maximum when banks fail to utilize all the new excess reserves to extend loans. However, banks have a strong incentive to loan out most of their new excess reserves. Idle excess reserves do not draw interest. Banks want to use most of these excess reserves so they will generate interest income. Exhibit 6 shows that this is indeed the case. In recent years, excess reserves have comprised less than 1 percent of the total reserves of banks.

Currency leakages and idle excess bank reserves will result in a deposit expansion multiplier that is less than its potential maximum. However, since most people maintain most of their money in bank deposits rather than as currency, and since banks typically eliminate most of their excess reserves by extending loans, strong forces are present that will lead to multiple expansion.

THE FEDERAL RESERVE SYSTEM

The Federal Reserve System is the central monetary authority or "central bank" for the United States. Every major country has a central banking authority. The Bank of England and Bank of France, for example, perform central banking functions for their respective countries.

Central banks are charged with the responsibility of carrying out monetary policy. The major purpose of the Federal Reserve System (and other central banks) is to regulate the supply of money and provide a monetary climate that is in the best interest of the entire economy.

The Fed, a term often used to refer to the Federal Reserve System, was created in 1913. As Exhibit 7 illustrates, the policies of the Fed are determined by the Board of Governors. This powerful board consists of seven members, each appointed to a staggered 14-year term by the president with the advice and consent of the Senate. Since a new member of the governing board is appointed only every other year, each president has only limited power over the Fed.

EXHIBIT 6 Banking and excess reserves

Profit-maximizing banks use their excess reserves to extend loans and other forms of credit. Thus, excess reserves are very small, less than 1 percent of the total in recent years.

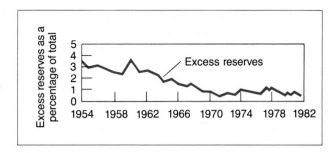

Because the Fed operates with considerable independence of both Congress and the executive branch, it often becomes the "whipping boy" for legislative leaders and presidents during difficult times.

The Board of Governors establishes rules and regulations applicable to all depository institutions. It sets the reserve requirements and regulates the composition of the asset holdings of depository institutions. The board is the rule-maker, and often the umpire, of the banking industry.

Two important committees assist the Board of Governors in carrying out monetary policy. First, the Federal Open Market Committee (FOMC) is a powerful policy-making arm of the system. This committee is made up of (a) the seven members of the Board of Governors, (b) the president of the New York District Bank, and (c) four (of the remaining eleven) additional presidents of the Fed's District Banks, who rotate on the committee. The FOMC determines the Fed's policy with respect to the purchase and sale of government bonds. As we shall soon see, this is the Fed's most frequently used method of controlling the money supply in the United States. Second, the Federal Advisory Council meets periodically with the Board of Governors to express its views on monetary policy. The Federal Advisory Council is composed of 12 commercial bankers, one from each of the 12 Federal Reserve districts. As the name implies, this council is purely advisory.

EXHIBIT 7 The structure of the Federal Reserve System

The Board of Governors of the Federal Reserve System is at the center of the banking system in the United States. The board sets the rules and regulations for the banking system and other depository institutions, thereby controlling the supply of money.

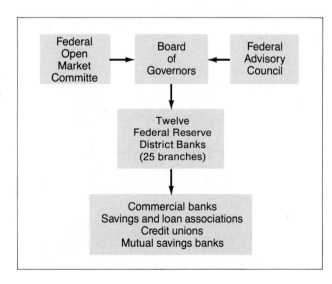

The 12 Federal Reserve District Banks operate under the control of the Board of Governors.[1] These district banks handle approximately 85 percent of all check-clearing services of the banking system. Federal Reserve District Banks differ from commercial banks in several important respects.

1. *Federal Reserve Banks Are Not Profit-Making Institutions.* Instead, they are an arm of the government. All of their earnings, above minimum expenses, belong to the Treasury.

2. *Unlike Other Banks, Federal Reserve Banks Can Actually Issue Money.* Approximately 90 percent of the currency in circulation was issued by the Fed. Look at the dollar bill in your pocket. Chances are that it has "Federal Reserve Note" engraved on it, indicating that it was issued by the Federal Reserve System. The Fed is the only bank that can issue money.

3. *Federal Reserve Banks Act as Bankers' Banks.* Private citizens and corporations do *not* bank with Federal Reserve Banks. Commercial depository institutions and the federal government are the only banking customers of the Fed. Most depository institutions, regardless of their membership status with the Fed, usually maintain some deposits with the Federal Reserve System. Of course, deposits with the Fed count as reserves. The Fed audits the books of depository institutions regularly so as to assure regulatory compliance and the protection of depositors against fraud. The Fed also plays an important role in the clearing of checks through the banking system. Since most banks maintain deposits with the Fed, the clearing of checks becomes merely an accounting transaction.

Initially, the Fed was made independent of the executive branch so that the Treasury would not use it for political purposes. However, the policies of the Treasury and the Fed are usually closely coordinated. For example, the chairman of the Board of Governors of the Federal Reserve, the Secretary of the Treasury, and the chairman of the President's Council of Economic Advisers meet weekly to discuss and plan macroeconomic policy. In reality, it would be more accurate to think of the Fed and the executive branch as equal partners in the determination of policies designed to promote full employment and stable prices.

How the Fed Controls Our Money Supply

The Fed has three major means of controlling the money stock: (a) establishing reserve requirements for depository institutions, (b) buying and selling U.S. government securities in the open market, and (c) setting the interest rate at which it will loan funds to commercial banks and other depository institutions. We will analyze in detail how each of these tools can be used to regulate the amount of money in circulation.

Reserve Requirements. The Federal Reserve System requires banking institutions (including credit unions and savings and loan associations) to maintain reserves against the demand deposits of its customers. The reserves of banking

---

[1]Federal Reserve District Banks are located in Boston, New York, Philadelphia, Cleveland, Richmond, Atlanta, Chicago, St. Louis, Minneapolis, Kansas City, Dallas, and San Francisco. There are also 25 district "branch banks."

institutions are composed of (a) currency held by the bank and (b) deposits of the bank with the Federal Reserve System. A bank can always obtain additional currency by drawing on its deposits with the Federal Reserve. Thus, both cash on hand and the bank's deposits with the Fed can be used to meet the demands of depositors. Therefore, both count as reserves.

Required Reserve Ratio: A percentage of a specified liability category (for example, transaction accounts) that banking institutions are required to hold as reserves against that type of liability.

Transaction Accounts: Accounts including demand deposits, NOW accounts, and other checkable deposits against which the account holder is permitted to transfer funds for the purpose of making payment to a third party.

Nonpersonal Time Deposits: Time deposits owned by businesses or corporations.

Exhibit 8 indicates the **required reserve ratio**—the percentage of each deposit category that banks are required to keep in reserve (that is, their cash plus deposits with the Fed). The reserve requirement for **transaction accounts,** primarily checkable deposits, was set at 3 percent for amounts under $26 million and 12 percent for amounts in excess of $26 million as of June 1982.[2] A reserve ratio of 3 percent is applicable for **nonpersonal time deposits** with a maturity date during the next 3½ years. Currently, no reserves are required against nonpersonal time deposits with a maturity date of more than 3½ years in the future. Banks are also required to maintain 3 percent in reserve against Eurodollar liabilities.

Why are commercial banks required to maintain assets in the form of reserves? One reason is to prevent imprudent bankers from overextending loans and thereby placing themselves in a poor position to deal with any sudden increase in withdrawals by depositors. The quantity of reserves needed to meet such emergencies is not left totally to the judgment of individual bankers. The Fed sets the rules.

However, the Fed's control over reserve requirements is important for another reason. By altering them, the Fed can alter the money supply. The law does not prevent commercial banks from holding reserves over and above those required by the Fed, but, as we have noted, profit-seeking banking institutions prefer to hold interest-bearing assets such as loans rather than large amounts of excess reserves. Since reserves draw no interest, banks seek to minimize their excess reserves.

Exhibit 9 shows the actual reserve position of commercial banks (see also Exhibit 6). Not surprisingly, the actual reserves of these banks are very close to the required level. Since the excess reserves of banks are very small, when the

EXHIBIT 8 The required reserve ratio of banking institutions

Banking institutions are required to maintain 3 percent reserves against transaction-account deposits of less than $26 million and 12 percent reserves for transaction deposits over $26 million (in effect June 1982). Other required reserve ratios are also shown below.

	Transaction Accounts		Nonpersonal Time Deposits		Eurocurrency Liabilities
	$0–26 Million	Over $26 Million	Less Than 3½ Years Maturity	3½ Years or More Maturity	All Types
Required reserves as a percent of deposits	3	12	3	0	3

Federal Reserve Bulletin, June 1982.

[2]The $26 million dividing point is adjusted each year by 80 percent of the change in total transaction account deposits in all banking institutions, beginning in 1982.

EXHIBIT 9 The reserves of banks

In 1982, the actual reserves of banks were only slightly in excess of their required reserves. The required reserves average out at approximately 9 percent against demand deposits plus 1 percent against time deposits.

Total—Commercial Banks
March 1982
(Billions of Dollars)

Total demand deposits	350.8
Total time deposits	944.2
Actual reserves	41.09
Required reserves	40.91
Excess reserves	.18

Federal Reserve Bulletin, June 1982.

Fed changes the required reserve ratio, banks respond in a manner that changes the money supply.

If the Fed reduced the required reserve ratio, it would free additional reserves that banks could loan out. Profit-seeking banks would not allow these excess reserves to lie idle. They would extend additional loans. The extension of the new loans would expand the money supply.

What would happen if the Fed increased the reserve requirements? Since banks typically have very few excess reserves, they would have to extend fewer loans in the future. This reduction in loans outstanding would cause a decline in the money supply.

Reserve requirements are an important determinant of the money supply because they influence both the availability of excess reserves and the size of the deposit expansion multiplier. Higher reserve requirements will reduce the size of the deposit expansion multiplier and force banks to extend fewer loans. Therefore, an increase in the required reserve ratio will reduce the money supply. On the other hand, a decline in the required reserve ratio will increase the potential deposit expansion multiplier and the availability of excess reserves. Banks will tend to extend additional loans, thereby expanding the money supply.

In recent years, the Fed has seldom utilized its regulatory power over reserve requirements to alter the supply of money. Because of the deposit expansion multiplier, small changes in reserve requirements can cause large changes in the money supply. In addition, the precise magnitude and timing of a change in the money stock that will result from a change in reserve requirements are difficult to predict. For these reasons, the Fed has usually preferred to use other monetary tools.

Open Market Operations: The buying and selling of U.S. government securities (national debt) by the Federal Reserve.

Open Market Operations.   **Open market operations,** the buying and selling of U.S. securities in the open market, is by far the most important mechanism that the Fed utilizes to control the stock of money. When the Fed enters the market and buys U.S. government securities, it expands the reserves available to banking institutions. The sellers of the securities receive a check drawn on a Federal Reserve Bank. As the check is deposited in a bank, the bank acquires a deposit or credit with the Federal Reserve. The banking system has increased its reserves, and the Fed has purchased part of the national debt. Since the deposit with the Fed, like currency, counts as reserves, banks can now extend more loans. The money supply will eventually increase by the amount of the securities purchased by the Fed times the actual deposit expansion multiplier.

Let us consider a hypothetical case. Suppose that the Fed purchases $10,000 of U.S. securities from commercial bank A. Bank A has fewer securities, but it now has additional excess reserves of $10,000; put another way, $10,000 has been added to the economy's *potential* reserves. The bank can extend new loans of up to $10,000 while maintaining its initial reserve position. This $10,000 expansion of loans will contribute directly to the money supply. Part of it will eventually be deposited in other banks, and they will also be able to extend additional loans. The creation of the $10,000 of new bank reserves will cause the money supply to increase by some multiple of the amount of U.S. securities purchased by the Fed.

The reserve requirements in effect in the early 1980s suggest that the *potential* deposit multiplier could be 9 or 10. Of course, as new reserves are injected into the banking system, there is some leakage either because of potential currency reserves circulating as cash or because some banks may be accumulating

EXHIBIT 10 How big is the actual money deposit multiplier?

In recent years the actual deposit expansion multiplier has been between 2.5 and 3.0. Of course, if the reserve requirements were lowered (raised), the deposit expansion multiplier would rise (fall).

Year (December)	Money Supply (M-1)[a]	Total Potential Reserves[a,b]	Money Deposit Expansion Multiplier
1970	216.8	73.1	2.97
1972	252.4	85.8	2.94
1974	278.0	100.6	2.76
1976	311.1	114.3	2.72
1978	364.2	134.9	2.70
1979	390.5	145.3	2.69
1980	415.6	158.2	2.63
1981	441.9	166.0	2.66

[a]Billions of dollars.

[b]Economists refer to the total potential reserves as the monetary base.

Board of Governors of the Federal Reserve System and *Economic Report of the President, 1982.*

Potential Reserves: The total Federal Reserve credit outstanding. Most of this credit is in the form of U.S. securities held by the Fed.

excess reserves. Exhibit 10 shows that during the 1970s the money supply was between 2.6 and 3.0 times greater than the **potential reserves**[3], suggesting that the actual deposit expansion multiplier is about 2.75. Therefore, when the Fed purchases U.S. securities, injecting additional reserves into the system, *on average,* the money supply tends to increase by approximately $2.75 for each dollar of securities purchased.

Open market operations can also be used to reduce the money stock, or its rate of increase. If the Fed wants to reduce the money stock, it will sell some of its current holdings of government securities. When the Fed sells securities, the buyer will pay for them with a check drawn on a commercial bank. As the check clears, the reserves of that bank with the Fed will decline. The reserves available to commercial banks are reduced, and the money stock will fall.

Since open market operations have been the Fed's primary tool of monetary control in recent years, the money stock and the Fed's ownership of U.S. securities have followed similar paths. When the Fed increases its purchases of U.S. securities at a rapid rate, the money stock will grow rapidly. A slowdown in the Fed's purchases of government bonds will tend to reduce the rate of monetary expansion.

As we indicated earlier, the Federal Open Market Committee (FOMC), a special committee of the Fed, decides when and how open market operations will be used. The members meet every three or four weeks to map out the Fed's policy concerning the purchase and sale of U.S. securities.

The Discount Rate—The Cost of Borrowing from the Fed. Banking institutions can borrow from the Federal Reserve, but when they do they must pay interest on the loan. The interest rate that banks pay on loans from the Federal Reserve is called the **discount rate.** When the newspapers announce that the discount rate has increased by 0.5 percent, many people think this means their

Discount Rate: The interest rate that the Federal Reserve charges banking institutions that borrow funds from it.

[3]Currency in circulation plus the actual reserves of commercial banks comprise the total potential reserves. Economists often use the term "monetary base" when referring to the total potential reserves.

local banker will (or must) now charge them a higher interest rate for a loan.[4] This is not necessarily so. The major source of loan funds of commercial banks is reserves acquired through demand and time deposits. Borrowing from the Fed contributes less than 0.5 of 1 percent to the available loan funds of commercial banks. Thus, an increase in the discount rate does not necessarily cause your local bank to raise the rate at which it will lend money to you.

The Fed does not have to loan funds to banking institutions. Banks rely on this source of funds primarily to meet a short-run shortage of reserves. They are most likely to turn to the Fed as a temporary method of meeting their reserve requirements while they are making other adjustments in their loan and investment portfolios.

An increase in the discount rate makes it more expensive for banking institutions to borrow from the Fed. Borrowing is discouraged, and banks are more likely to build up their reserves to ensure that they will not have to borrow from the Fed. Thus, an increase in the discount rate is restrictive. It will tend to discourage banks from shaving their excess reserves to a low level.

In contrast, a reduction in the discount rate is expansionary. At the lower interest rate, it costs banks less if they have to turn to the Fed to meet a temporary emergency. Thus, banks are more likely to reduce their excess reserves to a minimum, extending more loans and increasing the money supply, as the cost of borrowing from the Fed declines.

However, the general public has a tendency to overestimate the importance of a change in the discount rate. Since it applies to such a small share of total reserves, a 0.5 percent change in the discount rate has something less than a profound impact on the availability of credit and the supply of money. The influence of a change in the discount rate is not completely negligible, but usually the open market operations of the Fed are a much better index of the direction and magnitude of monetary policy.

Also, if a bank has to borrow in order to meet its reserve requirements, it need not turn to the Fed. Instead, it can go to the **federal funds market.** In this market, banks with excess reserves extend short-term (sometimes for as little as a day) loans to other banks seeking additional reserves. If the federal funds rate (the interest rate in the federal funds market) is less than the discount rate, banks seeking additional reserves will tap this source rather than borrow from the Fed. In recent years the Fed has kept its loans to banking institutions at a low level by altering the discount rate to match the federal funds rate more closely. As a result, the federal funds rate and the discount rate tend to move together. If the federal funds rate is significantly above the discount rate, banks will attempt to borrow heavily from the Fed. Typically, when this happens, the Fed will raise its discount rate, removing the incentive of banks to borrow from the Fed rather than from the federal funds market.

Summarizing the Tools of the Fed. Exhibit 11 summarizes the monetary tools of the Federal Reserve. If the Fed wants to follow an expansionary policy, it can decrease reserve requirements, purchase additional U.S. securities, and/or lower the discount rate. If the Fed wants to reduce the money stock, it can

Federal Funds Market: A loanable funds market in which banks seeking additional reserves borrow short-term (generally for seven days or less) funds from banks with excess reserves. The interest rate in this market is called the federal funds rate.

---

[4]The discount rate is also sometimes confused with the prime interest rate, the rate at which banks will loan money to low-risk customers. The two rates are different. A change in the discount rate will not necessarily affect the prime interest rate.

EXHIBIT 11 Summary of the monetary tools of the Federal Reserve

Federal Reserve Policy	Expansionary Monetary Policy	Restrictive Monetary Policy
1. Reserve requirements	*Reduce reserve requirements,* because this will free additional excess reserves and induce banks to extend additional loans, which will expand the money supply	*Raise reserve requirements,* because this will reduce the excess reserves of banks, causing them to make fewer loans; as the outstanding loans of banks decline, the money stock will be reduced
2. Open market operations	*Purchase additional U.S. securities,* which will expand the money stock directly, and increase the reserves of banks, inducing bankers in turn to extend more loans; this will expand the money stock indirectly	*Sell U.S. securities,* which will reduce both the money stock and excess reserves; the decline in excess reserves will indirectly lead to an additional reduction in the money supply
3. Discount rate	*Lower the discount rate,* which will encourage more borrowing from the Fed; banks will tend to reduce their reserves and extend more loans because of the lower cost of borrowing from the Fed if they temporarily run short on reserves.	*Raise the discount rate,* thereby discouraging borrowing from the Fed; banks will tend to extend fewer loans and build up their reserves so they will not have to borrow from the Fed

increase the reserve requirements, sell U.S. securities, and/or raise the discount rate. Since the Fed typically seeks only small changes in the money supply (or its rate of increase), it usually utilizes only one or two of these tools at a time to accomplish a desired objective.

The Fed's Monetary Growth Targets

Prior to October 1979, the Fed judged the appropriateness of monetary policy primarily by looking at interest rates. In the face of rapid inflation and monetary expansion, the Fed announced that henceforth it would seek to control the monetary aggregates more closely while permitting the interest rates to fluctuate according to market forces.

With the passage of time, the money supply, like the GNP, generally expands. In a dynamic setting, therefore, monetary policy might best be gauged by the rate of change in the money supply. When economists say that monetary policy is expansionary, they mean that the rate of growth of the money stock is rapid. Similarly, restrictive monetary policy implies a slow rate of growth or a decline in the money stock.

At the beginning of each year, the Fed announces its target range for the rate of growth of various measures of the money supply. For 1982, the Fed's target growth range for M-1 was 3.5 to 6 percent. The Fed seeks to utilize its policy tools—particularly open market operations—to maintain the supply of

THE DEREGULATION AND MONETARY CONTROL ACT

"This act is the most significant banking legislation before Congress since the passage of the Federal Reserve Act in 1913."
Senator William Proxmire, Chairman, Senate Committee on Banking, Housing, and Urban Affairs (1980)

As Senator Proxmire indicated, the Depository Institutions Deregulation and Monetary Control Act of 1980 was an extremely important piece of legislation. In effect, it restructured the banking industry, eroding the distinction between banking institutions and thrift institutions, such as savings and loan associations and credit unions. The act marked the culmination of several years of study by members of Congress, regulatory agencies, and financial institutions. As the title implies, the legislation had a twofold purpose: (1) deregulation designed to enhance the competitiveness of the financial industry and (2) imposition of uniform rules, applicable to all depository institutions, that would improve the Fed's ability to control the money supply accurately.

Prior to the passage of the act, different types of financial institutions operated under different sets of regulations, which were designed to segment the financial market. There were specific restrictions on the kinds of deposit accounts each type of institution could offer and the variety of loans and investments each could undertake. As a result, competition between depository institutions was limited.

Let us consider the major elements of the act and analyze their impact upon the financial industry.

1. The Fed Sets the Reserve Requirements for All Depository Institutions. The act granted the Federal Reserve the power to regulate the reserves of savings and loan associations, mutual savings banks, credit unions, and nonmember commercial banks, as well as those of the system's member banks. The Fed was instructed to apply reserve requirements uniformly to all depository institutions. The act provided for the phasing in of these requirements over periods of up to eight years. It was believed that expansion of the Fed's power over the reserve requirements of all depository institutions would permit the agency to control the supply of money with greater precision.

2. The Right to Offer NOW Accounts Was Extended to All Depository Institutions. The Banking Act of 1933 granted commercial banks a virtual monopoly over checking accounts. The 1980 act dismantled the earlier legislation and thereby permitted all thrift institutions to compete for checking-account deposits.

3. Various Restrictions on the Types of Loans and Investments That Nonbanking Thrift Institutions Could Make Were Revoked. Most thrift institutions were authorized to hold a larger share of their assets in the form of consumer loans, corporate securities, commercial paper, and various other types of unsecured loans. This removal of restrictions placed depository institutions on a more equal footing; all can now offer a wide range of loanable fund services.

4. Interest-Rate Ceilings on Time and Savings Deposits at Depository Institutions Will Be Phased Out by 1986. Interest rates rose during the 1970s; regulated interest ceilings imposed on the financial industry discouraged people from saving, impeded the ability of many depositors to compete for funds, and created inequities among institutions. The phaseout of these "interest-rate controls" will permit all depository institutions to compete more effectively for funds. The act also provided for the overriding of state usury laws to varying degrees. Thus, it is a move toward a competitive market in the loanable funds industry.

The act removed a number of artificial distinctions among financial institutions. With time, the competitive process should improve the efficiency of the financial industry. However, the transition period may well be fraught with danger and instability. In the short run, some financial institutions may find it difficult to meet the new competitive pressures. In addition, as funds flow in and move out of institutions and different types of accounts, the Fed may find it more difficult, *during the transition period,* to maintain monetary stability. Even positive, desirable change usually involves growing pains.

money within the target range. Currently, the Fed has announced that it plans gradually to reduce the growth rate of the money supply (M-1) by .5 percent a year for the next four to six years. Presumably, this slower rate of growth will help control inflation.

Although the concept of announced monetary targets is generally applauded among economists, there is one problem with it. Thus far, the Fed has not been very good at hitting its announced targets. For short time periods of six to nine months, the growth rate of the money supply in recent years has often either soared above the announced maximum growth target or fallen well short of even the minimum growth rate target. The Federal Reserve has come under intense criticism for these fluctuations, the implication of which we will investigate as we proceed.

The Fed and the Treasury

Many students have a tendency to confuse the Federal Reserve and the U.S. Treasury, probably because both sound like monetary agencies. The Treasury is a budgetary agency. If there is a budgetary deficit, the Treasury will *issue* U.S. securities as a method of financing the deficit. Newly issued U.S. securities are almost always sold to private investors (or invested in government trust funds). Bonds issued by the Treasury to finance a budget deficit are seldom purchased directly by the Fed. In any case, the Treasury is interested primarily in obtaining funds so it can pay Uncle Sam's bills. Except for nominal amounts, mostly coins, the Treasury does not issue money. Borrowing—the public sale of new U.S. securities—is the primary method used by the Treasury to cover any excess of expenditures in relation to tax revenues.

Whereas the Treasury is concerned with the revenues and expenditures of the government, the Fed is concerned primarily with the availability of money and credit for the entire economy. The Fed does not *issue* U.S. securities. It merely purchases and sells government securities issued by the Treasury as a means of controlling the money supply of the economy. The Fed does not have an obligation to meet the financial responsibilities of the U.S. government. That is the domain of the Treasury. The Fed's responsibility is to provide a stable monetary framework for the entire economy. Thus, although the two agencies cooperate with each other, they are distinctly different institutions established for different purposes.

LOOKING AHEAD

In this chapter we focused on the mechanics of monetary control. In the following chapter we will analyze the impact of monetary policy on output, growth, and prices.

CHAPTER LEARNING OBJECTIVES

1 Money is anything that is widely accepted as a medium of exchange. It also acts as a unit of account and provides a means of storing current purchasing power for the future. Without money, exchange would be both costly and tedious.

2 There is some debate among economists as to precisely how the money supply should be defined. The narrowest and most widely used definition of the money supply (M-1) includes only (a) currency in the hands of the public, (b) demand deposits with commercial banks, (c) other checkable deposits in depository institutions, and (d) traveler's checks. None of these categories of money have significant intrinsic value. Money derives its value from its scarcity relative to its usefulness.

3   Banking is a business. Banks provide their depositors with safekeeping of money, check-clearing services on demand deposits, and interest payments on time deposits. Banks derive most of their income from the extension of loans and investments in interest-earning securities.

4   Recent legislation and regulatory changes have altered the structure of the banking industry. Currently, savings and loan associations, mutual savings banks, and credit unions offer services, including checking accounts, similar to those of commercial banks. The Federal Reserve System now regulates all of these depository institutions and is legally required to apply uniform reserve requirements to each. In essence, these changes have integrated the three classes of thrift institutions into the banking industry.

5   The Federal Reserve System is a central banking authority designed to provide a stable monetary framework for the entire economy. It establishes regulations that determine the supply of money. It issues most of the currency in the United States. It is a banker's bank.

6   The Fed has three major tools with which to control the money supply.
    (a) *Establishment of the Required Reserve Ratio.* Under a fractional reserve banking system, reserve requirements limit the ability of banking institutions to expand the money supply by extending more loans. When the Fed lowers the required reserve ratio, it creates excess reserves and allows banks to extend new loans, expanding the money supply. Raising the reserve requirements has the opposite effect.
    (b) *Open Market Operations.* The open market operations of the Fed can directly influence both the money supply and available reserves. When the Fed buys U.S. securities, the money supply will expand because bond buyers will acquire money and the reserves of banks will increase as checks drawn on Federal Reserve Banks are cleared. When the Fed sells securities, the money supply will contract because bond buyers are giving up money in exchange for securities. The reserves available to banks will decline, causing banks to issue fewer loans and thereby reducing the money supply.
    (c) *The Discount Rate.* An increase in the discount rate is restrictive because it discourages banks from borrowing from the Fed in order to extend new loans. A reduction in the discount rate is expansionary because it makes borrowing from the Fed less costly.

7   At the beginning of each year the Fed announces a target range for the growth of monetary aggregates. In a dynamic setting, monetary policy can best be judged by the rate of change in the money supply. A rapid growth rate in the money supply is indicative of expansionary monetary policy while a slower rate indicates that monetary policy is more restrictive.

8   The Federal Reserve and the U.S. Treasury are two distinct, different agencies. The Fed is concerned primarily with the money supply and the establishment of a stable monetary climate. The Treasury focuses on budgetary matters—tax revenues, government expenditures, and the financing of government debt.

9   The Deregulation and Monetary Control Act of 1980 (a) dismantled many of the regulations that restricted competitiveness among depository institutions and (b) imposed uniform reserve requirements on all depository institutions, placing them under the jurisdiction of the Fed. All depository institutions were granted the right to offer NOW accounts. Various limitations on the types of loans that thrift institutions could extend were relaxed. The act mandated the phasing out of interest-rate ceilings on time and savings deposits. Essentially, it removed many of the artificial distinctions among financial institutions.

1 Why can banks continue to hold reserves that are only a fraction of the demand deposits of their customers? Is your money safe in a bank? Why or why not?

2 What makes money valuable? Does money perform an economic service? Explain. Could money perform its function better if there were twice as much of it? Why or why not?

3 "People are poor because they don't have very much money. Yet central bankers keep money scarce. If poor people had more money, poverty could be eliminated." Explain the confused thinking this statement reveals and why it is misleading.

4 Explain how the creation of new reserves would cause the supply of money to increase by some multiple of the newly created reserves.

5 How will the following actions affect the money supply?
(a) A reduction in the discount rate
(b) An increase in the reserve requirements
(c) Purchase by the Fed of $10 million of U.S. securities from a commercial bank
(d) Sale by the U.S. Treasury of $10 million of newly issued bonds to a commercial bank
(e) An increase in the discount rate
(f) Sale by the Fed of $20 million of U.S. securities to a private investor

6 What's Wrong with This Way of Thinking?

"When the government runs a budget deficit, it simply pays its bills by printing more money. As the newly printed money works its way through the economy, it waters down the value of paper money already in circulation. Thus, it takes more money to buy things. The major source of inflation is newly created paper money resulting from budget deficits."

Money is only a machine, but is an extraordinarily efficient machine. Without it, we could not have begun to attain the astounding growth in output and the level of living we have experienced in the past two centuries. . . . But money has one feature that other machines do not share. Because it is so pervasive, when it gets out of order, it throws a monkey wrench into the operation of all other machines.[1]
Milton Friedman

10

MONEY, KEYNESIANISM, AND MONETARISM

Now that we have an understanding of the banking system and the determinants of the money supply, we can investigate the impact of money on the level of output, prices, and employment.

After reviewing the importance of money from a historical viewpoint, we will present the Keynesian view of how monetary policy works. While there is broad agreement among modern economists that "money matters," the consensus view is an outgrowth of professional debate. Areas of controversy remain with regard to details and points of emphasis. During the 1960s, the monetarists, a group of economists who believe that monetary policy has been an important source of both economic instability and inflation, arose to challenge the dominant Keynesian view. The latter part of this chapter presents the monetarist position, comparing and contrasting it with the Keynesian perspective.

HISTORICAL BACKGROUND ON THE IMPORTANCE OF MONEY

Money is involved in almost every exchange. Usually, the purchaser receives goods, and the seller receives money. If we add together the purchases of all final products and services, they are equal to the GNP. The GNP is merely the sum of the price P times the quantity Q of each final product purchased. When the existing money stock M is multiplied by the number of times V that money is used to buy final products, this too yields the economy's GNP. Therefore,

$$PQ = GNP = MV$$

Velocity of Money: The average number of times a dollar is used to purchase final goods and services during a year. It is equal to GNP divided by the stock of money.

The V represents velocity, or the annual rate at which money changes hands in the purchase of final products. The **velocity of money** is merely GNP divided

---

[1]Milton Friedman, "The Role of Monetary Policy," *American Economic Review* (March 1968): 12

by the size of the money stock. For example, in 1981, GNP was $2.92 trillion, and the average money stock (currency plus demand deposits), was $429 billion. On the average, each dollar was used 6.8 times to purchase a final product or service. Therefore, the velocity of money was 6.8.

The Classical View— Money Does Not Matter

Equation of Exchange: $MV = PQ$, where M is the money supply, V is the velocity of money, P is the price level, and Q is the quantity of goods and services produced.

Quantity Theory of Money: A theory, based on the equation of exhange, that hypothesizes that a change in the money supply will cause a proportional change in the price level beause velocity and real output are unaffected by the quantity of money.

The **equation of exchange,** $MV = PQ$, is simply an identity, or a tautology. The equation is defined in such a way that it must be true. Classical economists, articulating the consensus view prior to the time of Keynes, formulated a theory—the quantity theory of money—using this equation. Put crudely, the **quantity theory of money** hypothesized that V and Q do not change very much. Thus, an increase in M, the money supply, would cause a proportional increase in prices P. For example, according to the classical view, if the money stock were increased by 5 percent, the price level would rise by 5 percent.

On what did the classical economists base these conclusions? They thought that institutional factors, such as the organization of banking and credit, the rapidity of transportation and communication, and the frequency of income payments were the primary determinants of velocity. Since these factors would change very slowly, for all practical purposes the velocity or "turnover" rate of money in the short run was constant. The classicists also thought that flexible wages and prices would ensure full employment. Thus, a change in the money supply could not affect real output.

For classical economists, the link between prices and the money supply was straightforward and quite mechanical. An increase in the money stock meant a proportional increase in prices. The real income of the economy was determined by other factors, such as capital accumulation, technology, and the skill of the labor force. They did not believe that money had any independent effect on real production, income, or employment.

The View of the Early Keynesians—Money Still Does Not Matter Much

The Great Depression undermined the simple classical theory and laid the foundation for the Keynesian revolution. The classical theory could not explain widespread unemployment. Strongly influenced by the massive unemployment that existed during the Great Depression, the early Keynesians emphasized the role of spending (demand) to the exclusion of almost everything else. Noting that the marginal propensity to consume declined (and the marginal propensity to save increased) with income, most early Keynesians believed that saving would rise as income increased over time. They feared that excess saving (and insufficient consumption) would lead to a persistent and chronic deficiency in aggregate demand, unless government stimulated spending.

During the 20 years after the publication of *The General Theory,* Keynesians paid little attention to money as a potential vehicle for stimulating demand. During the 1950s, it was popular to draw an analogy between monetary policy and the workings of a string. Like a string, monetary policy could be used to *pull* (hold back) the economy and thereby control inflation. However, just as one cannot *push* with a string, monetary policy could not be used to push (stimulate) aggregate demand.

In *The General Theory,* Keynes offered a plausible explanation for his belief that monetary policy might be an ineffective method of stimulating demand. What if the direction of changes in velocity were opposite to the direction of changes in the money stock? If a 5 percent increase in money led to a 5 percent reduction in velocity, money would fail to change anything. It would directly influence neither real income nor the price level.

Lord Keynes himself was *not* an advocate of the extreme position that money does not matter.[2] However, he did point out that under unusual conditions, as in the case where the demand schedule of individuals for money balances was perfectly horizontal, the interest rate would be unresponsive to a change in the supply of money. In the shadow of the Great Depression, many of his early followers took the unusual to be the typical.

HOW MONETARY POLICY WORKS—THE MODERN KEYNESIAN VIEW

Demand for Money: At any given interest rate, the amount of wealth that people desire to hold in the form of money balances; that is, cash and checking-account deposits. The quantity demanded is inversely related to the interest rate.

What factors underlie the **demand for money**?[3] That is, why do people want to maintain part of their wealth in the form of cash and checking account money? Keynes stressed three major reasons for this tendency: the transactions motive, the precautionary motive, and the speculative motive.

The reasoning behind the *transactions motive* is that money helps each of us make everyday purchases. However, the time when we receive our income does not match up perfectly with the time when we want to buy things. So, we keep a little cash or money in the bank in order to bridge the gap between everyday expenses and payday. Similarly, the *precautionary motive* is based on the premise that most of us keep a little money in the bank or in our billfold to handle unforeseen contingencies—such as an automobile accident or Junior breaking his arm. Keynes felt that these two motives for holding money balances were determined primarily by the level of income. The third major reason, the *speculative motive,* is based on the reasoning that individuals and businesses may want to maintain part of their wealth in the form of money so that they will be in a position to take ready advantage of changes in prices, particularly prices of bonds, stocks, and other financial assets. Money is the most liquid form in which to hold wealth. Unlike land or houses, it can be quickly traded for other assets. Thus, people may want to hold some money so that they can quickly respond to a profit-making opportunity.

Interest Rate: The price paid for the use of money or loanable funds for a period of time. It is stated as a percentage of the amount borrowed. For example, an interest rate of 10 percent means that the borrower pays 10 cents annually for each dollar borrowed.

The speculative demand for money is strongly affected by the existing and expected level of interest rates. When interest rates are high, the opportunity cost of holding idle money balances is greater. High interest rates induce people to hold less money, whereas low interest rates have the opposite effect.

Exhibit 1a illustrates the negative relationship between the demand for money and the **interest rate.** The Keynesian view emphasizes that during normal times, the curve representing the demand for money is like the demand curve for any other good. When the price (the interest rate) of holding money

---

[2]Keynes thought that money did matter, even during a recession. He stated, "So long as there is unemployment, employment will change in the same proportion as the quantity of money, and when there is full employment, prices will change in the same proportion as the quantity of money."[*The General Theory of Employment, Interest, and Money* (New York: Harcourt, 1936), p. 296.]

[3]Be careful not to confuse (a) the demand for money balances with (b) the desire for more income. Of course, all of us would like to have more income, but we may be perfectly satisfied with our holdings of money in relation to our holdings of other goods, given our current level of wealth. When we say that people want to hold more (or less) money, we mean that they want to *restructure* their wealth toward larger (smaller) money balances.

EXHIBIT 1   The demand and supply of money

The demand for money is inversely related to the interest rate (a). The supply of money is determined by the monetary authorities (the Fed) through their open market operations, discount rate policy, and reserve requirements (b).

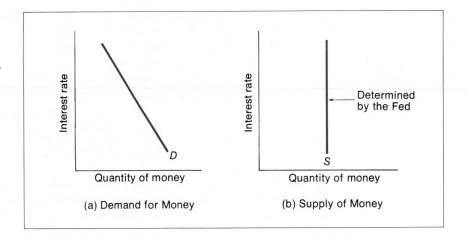

(a) Demand for Money

(b) Supply of Money

rises, the quantity of money demanded will decline. The supply of money is determined by the monetary authorities, the Fed in the United States. The money supply is not affected by interest rates. Hence, as Exhibit 1b shows, it is represented by a vertical line.

When the money market is in equilibrium, the quantity of money demanded at the existing interest rate will just equal the quantity supplied. Monetary policy can influence the rate of interest, *at least in the short run*. Suppose that the money market were initially in equilibrium, since the public was just willing to hold the existing money stock at the market rate of interest. As Exhibit 2 illustrates, an increase in the supply of money will cause the interest rate to fall. The expansionary monetary policy, a shift from M to M', creates an excess supply of money. People have larger money balances than they desire to hold at the 10 percent interest rate. The public will attempt to reduce their money balances by purchasing interest-bearing substitutes, primarily bonds. The demand for bonds will increase, causing bond prices to rise.

There is a negative relationship between bond prices and interest rates. Higher bond prices are the same thing as lower interest rates. Thus, when people reduce their cash balances by purchasing more bonds, the interest rate will fall, reducing the opportunity cost of holding money. Eventually, at the lower rate of interest, 5 percent in the example of Exhibit 2, the public will be content to hold the larger supply of money (M').

When open market operations are used to expand the money supply, the impact on interest rates is even more straightforward. How do the open market purchases by the Fed affect the money supply? The Fed buys interest-bearing bonds from the public, bidding up bond prices and lowering interest rates. The public acquires money balances, funds that can be used to extend credit to private investors. This increase in the supply of funds available to finance private investment will also place downward pressure on interest rates. Of course, lower interest rates will eventually restore equilibrium in the money market.

What happens to interest rates when the Fed sells bonds to the public, thereby reducing the money stock? The Fed's action increases the supply of bonds, causing lower bond prices (higher interest rates). Temporarily, the reduction in the supply of money will create an excess demand for money bal-

EXHIBIT 2   The determination
of interest rates—Keynesian
model

If the demand for money remains fixed, an increase in
supply will cause interest
rates to decline.

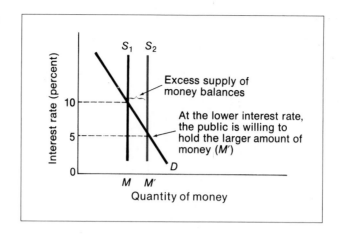

ances. The public will attempt to restore their money balances to the desired level. How can this be done? By selling bonds, extending fewer loans, or borrowing. However, all of these actions will place upward pressure on the interest rate. As interest rates rise, the opportunity cost of holding money will increase. Eventually, equilibrium will be restored in the money market, since the public will be satisfied with their smaller money balances at a new, higher interest rate.

In summary, the modern Keynesian view stresses that monetary policy can influence interest rates. If the demand for money remains constant, expansionary monetary policy will push interest rates downward. In contrast, a restrictive monetary policy will cause interest rates to rise.

Interest Rates and Investment

Interest rates influence the cost of each new investment project. Regardless of whether a business produces doorknobs or razor blades, lamp posts or refrigerators, or some other product, the interest rate will have either a direct or indirect effect on the cost of investment. If one has to borrow, there will be a direct interest cost. Even if borrowing is unnecessary, undertaking an investment project will mean foregoing interest income that could have been earned with the same funds. Since the interest rate contributes to the cost of each new investment, we would expect an inverse relationship between the level of investment and the interest rate.

When an entrepreneur considers an investment, he or she will compare the expected rate of return with the interest rate. If it exceeds the interest rate, the project is profitable—it will be undertaken. In contrast, a profit-seeking entrepreneur will not invest in a project for which the expected rate of return is less than the interest rate.

Exhibit 3 pictures the relationship between investment and the interest rate for both a single firm and the entire economy. As a firm undertakes more investment projects, the expected rate of return from each additional investment opportunity will decline. For the firm depicted in Exhibit 3a, project A is expected to yield more than a 20 percent rate of return, B about 17 percent, C approximately 15 percent, and so on. If the interest rate were 10 percent, projects A, B, C, and D would be undertaken. If the interest rate fell to 5 percent, E (but not F) would also be carried out. However, if the interest rate rose to 16 percent, only projects A and B would be profitable.

EXHIBIT 3 When business
firms invest

If the interest rate were 10 percent, Firm A [graph (a)] would
undertake projects A, B, C, and
D. For the entire economy,
investment would be I. [graph
(b)]. There would be a negative relationship between the
amount of investment and the
interest rate for both individual
firms and the conomy as a
whole (assuming other factors
are held constant).

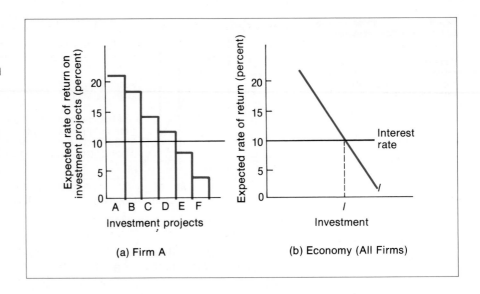

(a) Firm A

(b) Economy (All Firms)

As more capital is invested (that is, more projects are undertaken), it
will be necessary to include some of the less attractive projects. The rate of return on additional investment will decline. This will be true for an individual
firm and, in aggregate, for the entire economy. Thus, as Exhibit 3b shows, for
an economy, there is a negative relationship between total investment and the
interest rate.

Expansionary and Restrictive Monetary Policy

**Expansionary Monetary
Policy: A policy that results in
a rate of change in the supply
of money that exceeds the
long-run average rate.**

**Restrictive Monetary Policy:
A policy that results in a rate
of change in the money supply
that is less than the long-run
average rate.**

The central monetary authorities can influence the supply of money. If the
central monetary planners wanted to follow an **expansionary monetary policy,**
they could do one or more of the following: (a) purchase government bonds,
(b) reduce the reserve requirements of banks, or (c) reduce the discount rate.
All of these changes would tend to increase the supply of money, making credit
more readily available to the economy. In contrast, if the monetary authorities
sold government bonds, increased bank reserve requirements, or raised the discount rate, the supply of money would tend to decline (or increase at a slower
rate). Monetary planners would be following a **restrictive monetary policy,**
causing interest rates to rise in the short run.

Keynesian economists believe that expansionary monetary policy can
be used to reduce interest rates. Because of the lower rate, business entrepreneurs
will undertake a larger number of investment projects. The "easy money"
policy can thereby stimulate private investment.

Exhibit 4 illustrates the Keynesian view of expansionary monetary
policy. The monetary authorities—via open market purchases, for example—
expand the supply of money from M to M' (Exhibit 4a). At the initial interest
rate i_1, the public has more money than it desires to hold. It will attempt to
reduce its money balances by buying bonds and other financial assets. The
interest rate will decline. What effect will this decline have on private investment? Investment will rise, as businessmen and women find that more projects
are profitable at the lower interest rate. Aggregate investment will increase
from I_1 to I_2 (ΔI in Exhibit 4b and c). The additional investment (ΔI) will

cause aggregate demand to expand (Exhibit 4c). By how much will the equilibrium level of income increase? The new investment will have a multiplier effect, causing income to rise by a larger amount than the increase in aggregate demand.

Thus, Keynesian theory suggests that expansionary monetary policy will lower the interest rate and induce additional investment. The expansion in investment will increase aggregate demand and, working via the multiplier, cause aggregate income to rise. Of course, it will take time for the process to work. As we discussed in Chapter 6, the multiplier effect will not take place instantaneously. Several months may pass before the full effects of the expansionary monetary policy are felt. Nonetheless, the directional impact of expansionary monetary policy is straightforward. Expansionary monetary policy provides an additional tool that macroplanners can use to ensure sufficient aggregate demand and full employment.

Monetary policy also presents planners with another tool with which to combat inflation. When aggregate demand exceeds full-employment income, prices tend to rise. The excess demand is inflationary. Monetary policy can be utilized to reduce aggregate demand to a level that is consistent with full employment and stable prices.

Within the Keynesian framework, the effect of restrictive monetary policy is transmitted through its impact on the interest rate. Suppose that the Federal Reserve decides to sell government bonds. The private purchasers of the bonds will pay for them by giving up deposits (money). The supply of money will be reduced. The smaller supply of money (and larger supply of bonds) will cause bond prices to fall and interest rates to rise. As the rate of interest increases, investors will choose to forego some of their less profitable investment projects. The higher interest rates will increase the opportunity cost of investing in physical capital. Private investment will decline as some potential investors choose to purchase bonds instead of capital goods. The decline in private investment will reduce both aggregate demand and the inflationary pressure. Restrictive monetary policy can help to stem the tide of inflation.

Some industries—construction, for example—are much more sensitive to changes in interest rates than others. Higher interest rates increase the monthly payments necessary to finance construction costs. At the higher interest rates

EXHIBIT 4 How monetary poliy can stimulate demand

Within the Keynesian model, an increase in the supply of money (a shift from S_1 to S_2) would cause the interest rate to decline (from i_1 to i_2), stimulating additional investment (ΔI). Because of the multiplier, the equilibrium level of income would increase by a much larger amount [ΔY in graph (c)] than investment. Monetary policy works through the interest rate in the Keynesian model. Of course, it will take time for the full effects of the monetary expansion to be felt.

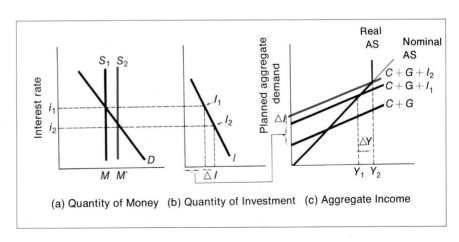

(a) Quantity of Money   (b) Quantity of Investment   (c) Aggregate Income

(and monthly housing payments), many households will decide to put off housing construction into the future. Thus, restrictive monetary policy may have an uneven impact. Widespread unemployment and little new capital investment may dominate some sectors such as construction, while the inflationary pressures continue in other sectors. Some economists have criticized reliance on monetary policy as an anti-inflationary weapon because of this uneven impact.

Combining Monetary and Fiscal Policies

When the government incurs a budget deficit, it must borrow funds to finance the deficit. There are two ways in which the government can finance the deficit. First, the Treasury can sell U.S. securities to the public. When the deficit is financed entirely in this manner, it is a pure fiscal action. The supply of money will be left unchanged.[4] The demand deposits of private parties will decline, but the Treasury's demand deposits will rise by an offsetting amount. With time, the Treasury will use the newly acquired funds to purchase such things as highways, education, bombs, and airplanes. This method of financing the deficit will reduce the supply of loanable funds available for financing private investment. Higher interest rates will result, dampening the expansionary impact of the budget deficit. However, Keynesians believe that, *in the short run,* the negative impact of the interest rate on current investment will be relatively minor. Thus, Keynesians stress that the net effect of a budget deficit will be expansionary, even when it is financed by borrowing from the public.[5]

Second, the budget deficit can be financed by issuing bonds that are purchased, perhaps secondhand, by the Federal Reserve. This method of financing combines fiscal and monetary policies. When the Treasury borrows indirectly from the Fed, the budget deficit is financed by newly created money. This action will leave the funds of potential private bondholders undisturbed and available for financing private investment. The monetary expansion will also exert downward pressure on the short-run interest rate, further stimulating investment and aggregate demand. If stimulus is desired, the combination of expansionary fiscal and monetary policies will clearly exert more intense pressure than a budget deficit financed entirely by borrowing from the public.

THE MODERN MONETARIST VIEW

While the Keynesian view dominated the news media in the 1960s, many professional economists were engaged in research designed to help us better understand the importance of monetary factors. A large part of this research was undertaken by monetarists, economists who believed that the Keynesian analysis failed to grasp the significance of erratic monetary policy as a source of economic instability. Led by Nobel Prize recipient Milton Friedman, the monetarists have substantially influenced the thinking of professional economists.

Like the classicists, the modern monetarists emphasize that money plays a role in each exchange. Unlike the classicists, however, the monetarists treat money not simply as a medium of exchange but as a valuable good that house-

---

[4]Be careful not to confuse (a) bond sales by the Treasury to the public and (b) bond sales by the Federal Reserve to the public. Only the latter will affect the money supply.

[5]As we will soon discuss, many monetarists disagree with this view.

holds demand, just as they demand other goods. Money is valuable because it facilitates exchange and is an alternative method of holding wealth. Households make decisions about how much of their wealth they want to hold (or demand) in the form of houses, cars, clothes, stocks, insurance policies and money. Money, like other goods, is demanded because it yields a stream of services.

The Impact of Money— The Monetarist View

Monetarists believe that the basic aggregate markets—current goods and services, labor resources, loanable funds, and money—are highly interrelated. Supply and demand work together to determine both prices and output levels in these markets. Whereas Keynesians believe that monetary policy reduces the interest rate and thereby stimulates private investment, monetarists argue that there is a much more direct link between output and changes in the supply of money.

Excess Supply of Money: Situation in which the actual money balances of individuals and business firms are in excess of their desired level. Thus, decision-makers will spend money buying other assets and goods as they reduce their actual balances to the desired level.

Monetarists believe that expansionary monetary policy creates an **excess supply of money.** People adjust by increasing their spending on a wide range of goods, causing aggregate demand to expand. Similarly, monetary restriction creates an **excess demand for money,** causing people to reduce their spending. In their view, monetary policy is not dependent on the interest rate for its effectiveness.

Excess Demand for Money: Situation in which the actual balances of individuals and business firms are less than their desired balances. Thus, decision-makers will reduce their spending as they expand their actual balances.

Unlike the classical economists, monetarists do not believe that prices adjust easily and rapidly. They believe that the market process will bring about equilibrium only with the passage of time. The role of time in the adjustment process explains why monetarists believe that the short-run impact of monetary policy differs substantially from its impact in the long run. According to monetarists, short-run fluctuations in the trend rate of growth of the money supply will exert their primary effect on output. Although this "output effect" will be significant, it will be temporary. In the long run, as markets have time to adjust more fully, the impact on monetary factors will be almost exclusively on prices. Output will be largely unaffected, since it will be determined by such factors as changes in the labor force, capital stock, natural resources, and technology.

Expanding the Money Supply and Aggregate Demand

What would happen if the Federal Reserve decided to follow a more expansionary policy? For example, suppose that it bought bonds at a record rate, expanding the money supply at an annual rate of 8 percent, up from 4 percent. As Exhibit 5 shows, these actions would create an excess supply of money balances. People would attempt to adjust by reducing their money holdings. Everybody knows how this could be accomplished—through increased spending! The aggregate demand for current goods would rise as people spent more on consumer goods, capital goods, education, and other items.

If the economy were operating below the constraint imposed by full employment, the expansionary monetary policy would push the economy toward its long-run capacity (Q_1). Real output would expand as previously unemployed manpower and machinery were brought into use. Since the economy would be operating below its long-run capacity, prices would not necessarily rise.

What would happen if the monetary acceleration continued once the long-run, full-employment capacity of the economy had been attained? Stated

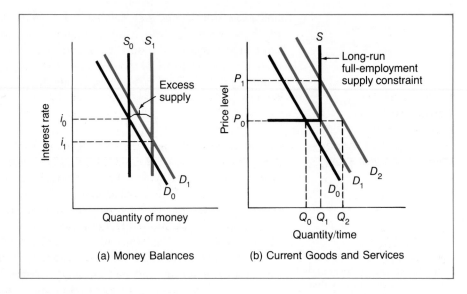

EXHIBIT 5 Money and expanding aggregate demand

An increase in the supply of money [shift from S_0 to S_1 in graph (a)] will generate a temporary excess in holdings of money, which will cause persons to increase their spending on goods and services. Aggregate demand will expand. If the output rate is below the long-run capacity level, for example, Q_0 [graph (b)], full employment with price stability can be attained. However, efforts to push output beyond the long-run supply constraint of the economy (Q_1) will be successful only in the short run. Expansionary monetary policy may *temporarily* push sales to Q_2. Output will expand. But with time, inflation will result (prices will rise to P_1), and output will fall back to the long-run, full-employment output level (Q_1). At this higher level of money income (P_1Q_1), the demand for money will increase (shift from D_0 to D_1), thereby restoring equilibrium in the money market.

(a) Money Balances

(b) Current Goods and Services

another way, what would happen if an expansionary monetary course were followed even though the economy were already at its long-run, full-employment level (Q_1 of Exhibit 5)? According to the monetarist view, in the short run, the long-run, full-employment level of output would be temporarily surpassed. Similarly, the rate of unemployment would temporarily fall below its long-run normal rate.

In order to understand fully the monetarist position, it is necessary to reflect on the market adjustment process. Suppose that you were a radio manufacturer and that there was an increase in demand for your product. How would you know it? You would probably first note that your monthly sales were up. However, sales sometimes rise for several months and then tumble downward for a month or so. Several good months do not necessarily indicate a *permanent* expansion in demand. Therefore, if you were a typical business decision maker, you would initially attempt to expand production in order to accommodate the strong demand and keep your inventories from declining sharply. Several months of the strong demand would be necessary to convince you that market conditions merited a price increase. You would not want to raise prices until you were convinced that the expansion in demand for your product was permanent. An unmerited price rise would drive customers to your competitors. In addition, some of your customers would have contracts specifying price and delivery for as many as 6 to 12 months into the future. Thus, contractually you would be unable to raise these prices, even after you became convinced that the demand for your product had increased.

As a result of these forces, the initial impact of the expansion in demand is primarily on output, even when the economy is at its long-run capacity level. *Initially,* business decision makers will hire more employees, cut down on maintenance time, and assign more overtime. Unemployment will fall below its normal rate. However, this pace cannot be maintained. After 6 to 18 months, the excess demand in markets will cause prices to rise, and output will fall back to a long-run equilibrium level. Thus, the monetarist view stresses that, although expansionary monetary policy can temporarily push unemployment below its normal rate (and capacity beyond its long-run level), in the long run, such a policy will cause inflation without permanently reducing the rate of unemployment.

Disaster and a Reduction in the Money Stock

What would happen if someone, perhaps a mischievous Santa Claus, destroyed half of the U.S. money stock? Suppose that when we get up one morning half of the cash in our billfolds and deposits in our banks are gone! Ignore, for the sake of analysis, the liability of bankers and the fact that the federal government would take corrective action. Just ask yourself, "What has changed because the money supply has been drastically reduced?" The work force is the same. Our buildings, machines, land, and other productive resources are untouched. There are no consumer durables missing. The gold is still in Fort Knox. Only the money, half of it, is gone.

Exhibit 6 sheds some light on the situation. In order to make things simple, let us assume that, before the calamity, individuals were holding their desired level of money balances for current needs. The reduction in the supply of money, the shift from S_0 to S_1, would result in an excess demand for money. Individuals would try to restore at least part of their depleted money holdings.

How do people build up their money balances? All poor, struggling college students should know the answer. They spend less. With almost everybody spending less, the aggregate demand for current goods and services will fall (the shift from D_0 to D_1 in Exhibit 6b).

If prices and wages were perfectly flexible, as the classicists thought, this would not cause any big problem. Both product and resource prices would be cut in half, but real GNP would remain unchanged (that is, would stay at Q_0). In the real world, however, things are not so simple. In the short run, wages and prices tend to be inflexible, particularly downward. As a result of the decline in the aggregate demand, sales would fall to Q_1. An excess supply of many products would exist. Business inventories would rise. Factories would operate at levels far below capacity and unemployment would rise. Our mischievous

EXHIBIT 6 A reduction in the supply of money

When the stock of money declines, an excess demand for money balances results. Individuals seek to restore their money balances by spending less. Aggregate demand declines from D_0 to D_1, and sales fall to Q_1 when prices are inflexible downward. With time, the excess supply in the market for goods and services will cause prices to decline, to P_1, for example. However, this method of restoring equilibrium will be a painful process, beset by economic recession or even a depression.

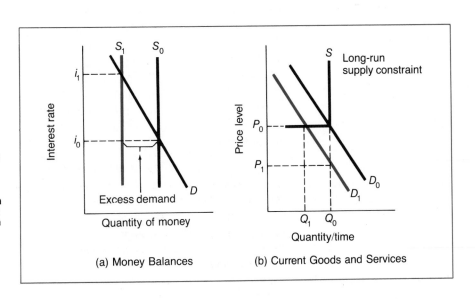

(a) Money Balances

(b) Current Goods and Services

Santa Claus would have brought about disaster without even touching any of our real assets. With time, the excess supply would result in declining prices, but recessionary conditions would permeate the economy long before falling prices would be able to restore equilibrium at price level P_1 and output Q_0.

Why do prices not fall in response to the decline in demand? In the first place, several months may pass before business decision makers recognize that there has been a genuine reduction in demand for their product. Even after they recognize it, additional time will be necessary before contract and catalogue prices can be adjusted to reflect more accurately the new demand conditions.

Similarly, job seekers will not initially recognize that there has been a decline in demand for their services. Thus, they too, will initially be reluctant to accept jobs paying a lower money wage. Anticipating that they will soon find a job at their old money wage, they will extend their employment search time, thereby increasing the duration of their unemployment. Therefore, prices and wage rates will not immediately adjust to the reduction in the money supply and the accompanying decline in demand. Rather, rising unemployment and a business slowdown will result from monetary restriction.

THE BASIC PROPOSITIONS OF MONETARISM

In order to delineate the monetarist position in the clearest way, it is useful to break it down into basic components. Although monetarists believe that money is highly important, it does not follow that they believe monetary policy to be a cure-all for economic ills; in fact, they stress that discretionary monetary policy is more likely than not to be destablizing. Let us consider the basic propositions of the monetarist position in relation to economic stability and discretionary policy.

> **Proposition 1.** Economic instability is almost exclusively the result of fluctuations in the money supply. If erratic monetary policy did not inject demand shocks into the system, the economy would be relatively stable.

Monetarists believe the business cycle is generated largely by inappropriate monetary policy. The problem of economic instability stems from the stop–go nature of our past monetary policy. Rapid monetary expansion generates an economic boom and eventually leads to an increase in the rate of inflation. Typically, the monetary authorities then respond to the inflation by applying the monetary brake. This monetary slowdown thrusts the economy into a recession. Milton Friedman, the leading spokesman for the monetarists, in his presidential address before members of the American Economic Association in 1967, stated:

Every major contraction in this country has been either produced by monetary disorder or greatly exacerbated by monetary disorder. Every major inflation has been produced by monetary expansion.[6]

Monetarists believe that the market economy contains ingredients that minimize economic stability. Consumption spending, in particular, is a stabi-

---

[6]Milton Friedman, "The Role of Monetary Policy," *American Economic Review* (March 1968), p. 12.

lizing element. Since current consumption is largely a function of one's expected future income, consumption spending is relatively stable over the business cycle. According to the monetarist viewpoint, the stability of consumption expenditures will assure that a temporary economic expansion does not spiral into a raging economic boom. Similarly, the strength of consumption expenditures will prevent an uncontrolled economic plunge. If disturbances introduced by monetary fluctuations were eliminated, the monetarists believe that the economy would be relatively stable, at least in comparison with past performance.

> **Proposition 2.** Expansionary monetary policy cannot permanently reduce the unemployment rate and increase the pace of economic growth. In the long run, efforts to use monetary policy to accomplish these goals will not only fail but will be inflationary.

The distinction that monetarists make between the short-run and long-run impact of a change in monetary policy cannot be overemphasized. Although monetarists concede that changes in the supply of money have important short-run effects on output and employment, they do not believe that monetary policy can effectively alter these real variables in the long run.

Even when the economy is operating at its full-employment output rate, monetarists believe that monetary acceleration will *initially* exert its primary impact on output and employment rather than on prices. For a time, decision makers will be fooled by monetary acceleration. *Initially,* as they observe the increase in demand for their product, they will not know whether it reflects a temporary or a permanent change. Similarly, they will be unsure whether there has been (a) an increase in demand for *their product relative to other products* or (b) an increase in demand for all products. The former calls for an expansion in output; the latter does not. Confused by the situation, many producers will choose to expand output and employment. But as producers, in general, attempt to follow this course, they will bid up prices. Eventually, decision makers will discover that there has been a generalized increase in demand, rather than a specific and temporary increase in demand for their product. As they adjust to this situation, incorporating the higher price level (or in the dynamic case, the higher inflation rate) into their market decisions, output and employment will return to their previous rates.

What will happen when the monetary authorities shift gears, deciding to decelerate the growth rate of the money supply in order to fight the inflation? Monetarists stress that, as with monetary acceleration, the initial impact of monetary deceleration will be on output. For a time, many decision makers will believe that the demand for their product has fallen relative to other products. They will cut back output and lay off workers. In the short run, the unemployment rate will rise above its long-run normal level.

1. *Keynesian view*

   Budget deficit or surplus ─────────────────────────────→ aggregate demand

2. *Monetarist view*

   Budget deficit or surplus ──→ interest rate ──→ velocity of money ──→ aggregate demand

Monetarists strongly reject the view that inflation can be traded for a lower rate of unemployment. Although monetary acceleration leads to less unemployment in the short run, it will lead to more unemployment and inflation in the future. According to the monetarists' view, the trade-off is between (a) a lower unemployment rate in the present and the immediate future and (b) an acceleration in the rate of inflation 12 to 24 months in the future and an abnormally high rate of unemployment when inflation subsides.

Proposition 3. The expansionary impact of pure fiscal policy will be largely offset by reductions in private spending caused by rising interest rates, which are an inevitable result of the government borrowing.

Whereas Keynesians stress the effectiveness of fiscal policy, monetarists argue that budget deficits will have only a moderate impact on aggregate demand unless they are accompanied by a change in the money supply.[7] Monetarists stress that expansion by **pure fiscal policy,** a fiscal action that does not alter the money supply, will lead to rising interest rates, which will retard private spending.

Pure Fiscal Policy: A change in taxes or government spending that is not financed by borrowing from the Federal Reserve. Thus, the policy does not change the supply of money.

Suppose that the Treasury is running a $25 billion deficit. If the money supply is to remain unchanged, the deficit will have to be financed by borrowing in the private loanable funds market.[8] What will happen when the Treasury borrows an additional $25 billion in the loanable funds market? According to the monetarist view, the expansion in Treasury borrowing will increase the demand for loanable funds and drive interest rates upward. The rising interest rates will cause private investment and consumption to be partially priced out of the market. Private investors will not undertake some construction and business expansion projects because these are now too expensive. Similarly, higher interest rates (and an increase in taxes necessitated by the interest payments on the enlarged debt) will "squeeze out" private spending on housing, automobiles, and a host of other consumer goods. The anticipated reduction in private spending in response to rising interest rates caused by a budgetary deficit is known as the **crowding-out effect.**

Crowding-Out Effect: A reduction in private spending as a result of high interest rates generated by budget deficits that are financed by borrowing in the private loanable funds market. If this effect is strong, pure fiscal policy loses much of its impact.

---

[7]Milton Friedman, in his *Newsweek* column of August 7, 1967, made this point clear: "Deficits have often been connected with inflation, but they need not be. Whether deficits produce inflation depends on how they are financed. If, as so often happens, they are financed by creating money, they unquestionably do produce inflationary pressure. If they are financed by borrowing from the public, at whatever interest rate is necessary, they may still exert some minor inflationary pressure. However, their major effect will be to make interest rates higher than they otherwise would be."

[8]The only other method of financing the deficit would be an expansion in borrowing from the Federal Reserve. As we noted in Chapter 9, when the Fed buys bonds, whether from the Treasury or from private dealers, the money supply will expand. Thus, a deficit financed by borrowing from the Federal Reserve is not a pure fiscal action.

Monetarists believe that the crowding-out effect will largely offset the impact of an expansionary fiscal action. They argue that deficit spending results mainly in the substitution of public for private sector spending. Of course, if the government could borrow the $25 billion without bidding up the interest rate, private spending would not be crowded out. Monetarists argue that this is unlikely to be the case, however. Few individuals would have excess funds stuffed away in a pillowcase that they would be willing to make available to finance the government deficit.

The monetarists' view of fiscal policy is symmetrical. Just as they question the effectiveness of fiscal expansion, they deny that a budget surplus exerts a significant restraining influence. As a result of the budget surplus, the Treasury's demand for loanable funds will decline, placing downward pressure on the interest rate. The lower interest rate will stimulate additional spending, which will largely offset the restraining influence of the budget surplus.

Although monetarists stress the offsetting effects generated by fiscal action, it is not true that fiscal policy is considered *totally* ineffective within the monetarist framework. Remember that the monetarist view emphasizes that a pure fiscal action will cause the interest rate to rise. At the higher interest rate, businesses and households will find it more costly to hold money balances. Since it will now be more expensive to hold money, decision makers will economize on its use to a greater degree. They will attempt to use their money balances more intensively. The velocity of money will rise. Assuming that the supply of money is constant, an increase in the velocity of money will have an expansionary effect, if only a moderate one, on aggregate demand.

Keynesians and Monetarists—A Summary of Their Views

Keynesians	Monetarists
1. Market economy is inherently unstable; macropolicy can correct this deficiency.	1. Erratic monetary policy is the major source of instability; the market economy has self-correcting, stabilizing features.
2. Policy-makers should plan budget deficits during recessions and budget surpluses during inflationary booms in order to promote full employment and economic stability.	2. Macropolicy cannot *permanently* reduce unemployment and stimulate the pace of economic growth. Efforts to do so with demand-stimulus policies will cause inflation.
3. Fiscal policy is both more potent and more predictable than monetary policy.	3. Fiscal policy is relatively impotent because of the crowding-out effect.
4. Discretionary macroplanning is more likely to lead to stability than are fixed rules.	4. A fixed monetary rule is more likely to lead to stability than is discretionary macropolicy.
5. Monetary policy is transmitted indirectly via the interest rate.	5. Monetary policy exerts a direct impact on the demand for goods and services.
6. Fiscal policy exerts a direct impact via the flow of expenditures.	6. Fiscal policy is transmitted indirectly via the interest rate and the velocity of money.

Just as in the case of monetary policy, the difference between the monetarist and Keynesian views of fiscal policy boils down to the transmission mechanism. Keynesians believe that fiscal policy has a direct effect on aggregate demand, whereas monetarists argue that the impact of a fiscal action is transmitted indirectly to aggregate demand via the interest rate and the velocity of money.

> **Proposition 4.** The difficulties of timing macropolicy properly and the nature of the political process lead one to predict that discretionary macropolicy will be destabilizing.

If macropolicy is going to reduce instability, the effects of expansion or restraint must be felt at the proper time. Given our limited ability to forecast the future accurately, it will be extremely difficult to follow a proper stabilization course. A policy change may be needed before political decision makers recognize the need. The political process will generally lead to additional delays. Even after a policy is instituted, its primary impact may be felt anywhere from 6 to 30 months in the future. By that time, conditions may have changed substantially.

Monetarists believe that since policymakers have limited knowledge about the future and cannot be sure when the major effects of a policy change will be felt, they are highly likely to make errors. For example, acting on the basis of current economic data, policymakers may follow an expansionary course in an attempt to reduce an abnormally high rate of unemployment. However, the major impact of the expansionary monetary policy might not be felt for several months. By the time the policy exerts its primary effect, the economy may have gained strength on its own. Therefore, the primary effect of the expansionary policy may be to cause inflation.

Economic considerations alone are sufficient to make the proper timing of macropolicy extremely difficult, but political pressures make the situation even worse. In a democracy, macropolicy will be designed by elected representatives, an elected president, and officials (such as the Board of Governors of the Federal Reserve) who are appointed by the elected president. The nature of the political process, particularly the shortsightedness effect, makes it extremely likely that an expansionary course will be followed during the period preceding a major election. Economic problems generated by this course will occur later (preferably after the election), and they will be widely diffused among persons who are unlikely to associate the adverse effects with the expansionary policy. If properly timed, expansionary policy can make things look good on election day. Clearly, vote-maximizing political entrepreneurs are under enormous pressure to follow this course.

The summary chart, page 209, gives a thumbnail sketch comparing and contrasting the view of monetarists and Keynesians.

Constant Rate of Monetary Growth — The Monetarist View of Proper Policy

Discretionary policy, in the view of monetarists, is likely to be destabilizing. Our knowledge about the magnitude and timing of macropolicy is inadequate. Our forecasting models often yield incorrect predictions. Political factors are almost sure to influence real-world policy. All of these factors have led monetarists to conclude that discretionary stabilization policy will end up doing more harm than good. According to monetarists, past evidence shows that, in fact, this has been the case.

If discretionary policy is destabilizing because the planners are bound to make mistakes, the solution is straightforward. Eliminate discretionary policy and expand the money supply at a constant, fixed rate. This is precisely what the monetarists advocate. The monetarists favor expanding the money supply at a fixed rate that approximates the long-run rate of growth of the U.S. economy. They believe that this approach would minimize business fluctuations and lead to greater price stability.

Monetarists argue that the fixed growth-rate rule would reduce uncertainty. Long-term contractual agreements could be arrived at with a minimum degree of risk and a maximum degree of confidence. In addition, if the money supply were increased at a steady rate, it would automatically tend to offset short-term economic fluctuations. If there were an economic disturbance (for example, technological change) that resulted in a rapid short-run growth in output, the money would continue expanding only at the designated constant rate. *Relative to output,* this would mean a slower advancement than had previously been the case. Monetary policy would automatically exert a restraining influence on the expansion.

Similarly, during a short-run economic slowdown, the money stock would continue to grow at the constant rate. Because output would be increasing at a slower than normal rate, the money supply would now be increasing more rapidly than usual, *relative to output.* Monetary policy would automatically be expansionary.

Recent changes in the banking industry complicate the institution of a monetary rule. With the availability of checking accounts that earn interest, savings accounts that can be automatically transferred into one's checking account, and financial management accounts that permit one to write checks against stocks, bonds, and money market funds, the precise definition of money has become ambiguous. Critics of the monetary rule argue that these developments illustrate the impracticality of a monetary rule. Monetarists respond that these problems can be worked out. In their view, the important thing is that monetary policy be removed from the hands of discretionary policymakers, who are inevitably prone to error and vulnerable to political pressures.[9]

Money, Output, and Inflation: Explanations of Recent History

The heart of the monetarist position is that monetary acceleration will *initially* stimulate economic growth but will eventually lead to an acceleration in the inflation rate because the economy's supply constraint will be reached. Similarly, a deceleration in monetary growth will *initially* cause an economic slowdown, and the decline in the inflation rate will follow later. If the monetary authorities gyrate from acceleration to deceleration, the result will be economic instability. Does the real world conform to the monetarist theory?

Exhibit 7 presents data on the fluctuations in the supply of money for the 1967–1981 period. During the 1967–1968 period, the money supply grew at an annual rate of 7.4 percent, up from 3.3 percent during 1960–1966. The

[9]Following ideas of the late Henry Simons of the University of Chicago, some monetarists argue that the monetary authorities should be required to target the price level directly. Under this plan, during a period (say three to six months) of rising prices, the monetary authorities would be required to *reduce* the rate of money growth, and during a period of falling prices, *increases* in the rate of monetary growth would be mandated.

EXHIBIT 7   The money supply and economic instability, 1967–1981

Rapid growth in the money supply during 1967-1968 was followed by an acceleration in the rate of inflation in 1969-1970. Similarly, the more rapid monetary growth of 1971-1972 was followed by an inflationary outburst during 1973-1974. How did the monetary growth of 1977-1983 affect the rate of inflation? Just as monetarists predicted, the inflation rate accelerated during 1978-1983. The asterisk (*) signifies a year of double-digit inflation; the shaded areas represent periods of recession.

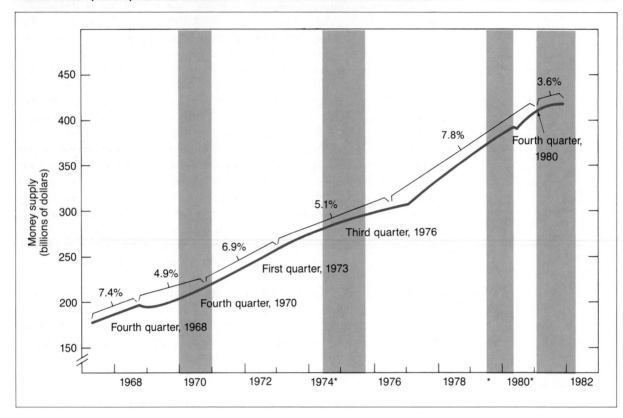

acceleration in the growth rate of the money supply was accompanied by rapid growth and a falling unemployment rate. By 1968 unemployment had declined to 3.6 percent, down from 4.5 percent in 1965. However, just as the monetarist theory predicts, the inflation rate accelerated upward. The inflation rate rose to 4.2 percent in 1968 and to 5.4 percent in 1969, up from only 2.9 percent in 1966 and 1967. By 1969–1970, the monetary authorities had shifted to a restrictive policy in order to combat the inflation. As they decelerated the rate of monetary growth, the result was the inflationary recession of 1970.

Essentially, the pattern was repeated during 1971–1976. The acceleration in the growth rate of the money supply to 6.9 percent during 1971–1972 was followed by deceleration during 1973–1975. The monetary acceleration was accompanied by the economic boom of 1971–1972. Unemployment declined and real output increased sharply. However, by 1973 the inflation rate was again rising, reaching a double-digit rate during 1974. Consistent with the monetarist view, the shift toward deceleration during 1973–1975 was associated with the 1974–1975 recession, the most serious post-war recession that the United States has experienced. Beginning in 1976 (third quarter), monetary policy again shifted toward acceleration. During the 1976–1980 period, the supply of money rose at a 7.8 percent annual rate, the most rapid rate of persistent monetary growth since World War II. Initially, the monetary acceleration exerted a positive impact on the economy. Adjusted for inflation, GNP grew at a 5.6 percent annual rate during 1977–1978. The unemployment rate fell to under 6 percent in 1978, down from 9 percent during the recession of 1975. However, beginning from a base of 6 percent during 1976–1977, the inflation rate jumped sharply to 9 percent in 1978 and 13 percent during 1979–1980. Conforming to the monetarist view, the rapid monetary growth of 1977–1980 was associated with an acceleration in the inflation rate during 1978–1980.

During the six months immediately prior to the 1980 elections, the money supply grew at an annual rate of 14.7 percent, the most rapid growth rate for any period of comparable length since World War II. Beginning in 1981, the Fed abruptly applied the monetary brake. During the 18 months from January 1981 to July 1982, the annual growth rate of the money supply decelerated to only 5.8 percent. Just as the monetarist theory predicts, the monetary deceleration exerted a substantial, immediate impact on output and employment. Real GNP declined by 1.8 percent during 1981–1982, while the unemployment rate soared to more than 10 percent. The rate of inflation also decelerated, falling from 13.5 percent in 1980 to 6.0 percent in 1982. Beginning in July of 1982, the Fed once again reversed its policy. The growth rate of the money supply accelerated during the period of July 1982 through July 1983. Just as the monetarist's theory suggests, economic recovery accompanied this move toward monetary acceleration.

Since the monetarists believe that the initial impact of monetary acceleration will be primarily on output (rather than on prices), they do not expect that the growth rate of the money supply and the inflation rate will always change in the same direction in the short run. However, as Milton Friedman

EXHIBIT 8 Money and inflation in the long run

In the long run, the rate of growth of the money supply and prices are closely linked. Between 1946 and 1966 the money supply grew at an average annual rate of 2.4 percent; price increases averaged 2.5 percent. The acceleration in the rate of growth of the money supply to 6.2 percent during the period from 1967 to 1980 was accompanied by a similar acceleration in the rate of inflation.

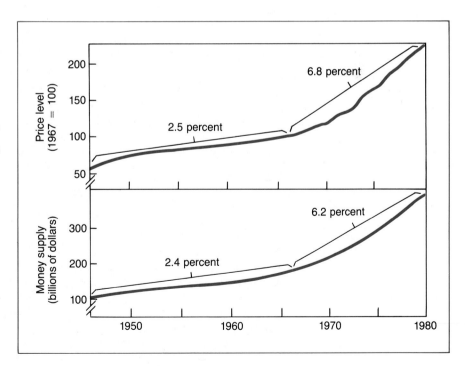

has stated many times, in the long run, monetarists believe that inflation is a monetary phenomenon. They argue that the inflation of the 1970s was the result of the excessive monetary expansion. As Exhibit 8 illustrates, between 1946 and 1966, the monetary authorities expanded the supply of money at an average annual rate 2.4 percent. During that period, prices rose at an annual rate of 2.5 percent. The period since 1966 has been one of monetary acceleration. From 1967 to 1980, the growth of the money supply accelerated to an average rate of 6.2 percent. Consumer prices rose by a similar amount.

Over the long term, the link between monetary acceleration and the rate of inflation is one of the most consistent relationships in all economics. Historically, the relationship has held across time periods and countries. Does this mean Keynesians also accept the monetary explanation of inflation? Keynesians do not find the linkage between monetary expansion and inflation surprising. After all, the Keynesian model also indicates that monetary expansion will be inflationary once an economy has reached its full-employment supply constraint.

However, Keynesians often make two additional points. First, they are less likely to assume that the monetary expansion–inflation linkage denotes cause and effect. Rather than monetary expansion, it may be that strong business conditions cause an economic boom and eventual inflation. For example, as output expands, business demand for loanable funds will increase. Unless offset by action of the Fed, extension of the additional loans will expand the money supply. In contrast, weak demand for loanable funds may cause a monetary deceleration during a recession. Second, Keynesians are more likely to emphasize the importance of supply-side shocks, such as the huge oil-price increases of 1973–1974 (and again during 1979), as sources of inflation. Crop failures, weather conditions, and major strikes may also alter aggregate supply and thereby affect the rate of inflation.

THE MONETARIST–KEYNESIAN CONTROVERSY IN PERSPECTIVE

After nearly two decades of debate, Keynesians and monetarists now differ primarily on questions of emphasis and of how economies function over time rather than on basic tenets of economic faith. The two views have probably influenced each other to some degree. Most economists, monetarists and Keynesians alike, generally believe that both monetary policy and fiscal policy exert an impact on aggregate demand and output. Minor differences about the transmission of macropolicy remain. Keynesians believe that the effect of monetary policy is transmitted through the interest rate, whereas monetarists consider the link to be much more direct. The reverse is true for fiscal policy. The interest rate is the transmitting mechanism for fiscal policy in the monetarists' view; they believe that budget deficits will drive up interest rates, which will cause the velocity of money to increase and thereby generate economic stimulus. In contrast, Keynesians argue that fiscal policy will directly affect aggregate demand. However, these disagreements about the mechanism by which the effects of macropolicy are transmitted do not negate the central point that both monetary policy and fiscal policy work. Both are capable of influencing the direction of the economy.

Similarly, both monetarists and Keynesians recognize that excessive monetary expansion is the primary source of *persistant* inflation. Monetarists might be a bit more inclined to emphasize the consistency of the monetary expansion–inflation link, while Keynesians are more likely to point out that other factors may also contribute to inflation. Nonetheless, general agreement on a linkage has emerged.

Both monetarists and Keynesians have a greater appreciation of the real-world difficulties involved in the steering of a stable macroeconomic course than they did a decade ago. Both recognize that macropolicy errors have been made in the past and are likely to be made in the future. Both recognize that supply-side factors limit the ability of demand-stimulus policies to expand real output. In these areas, differences between monetarists and Keynesians are based on divergent views of—and, of course, differing degrees of faith in—the role of government in formulating economic policy. Monetarists have less faith in the ability of government macroplanners to follow a smooth course. They argue that policymakers, motivated by political considerations and armed only with limited knowledge about the future, will inevitably make mistakes. Thus, unless their hands are tied with a monetary rule, their policies will be a continued source of economic instability.

The monetarists have played a central role in placing monetary policy on an equal footing with fiscal policy. Their skepticism of "fine-tuning" stabilization policies has exerted a moderating influence on professional economists. With these accomplishments to their credit, it now appears that most of the heat has been removed from the monetarist–Keynesian debate.

PERSPECTIVES IN ECONOMICS
BUDGET DEFICITS AND OUR ECONOMY

The thought of budget deficits exceeding $100 billion, not to mention $200 billion, is mind boggling to many Americans. Increasingly, the question is asked, "What impact will these huge deficits have on our economy?" Some people charge that deficits cause inflation. Others believe that they lead to high interest rates. Still others, a distinct minority, argue that there is little reason for alarm, since other countries such as Japan and West Germany have generally experienced only moderate inflation coupled with low interest rates despite larger budget deficits (as a percent of their GNP) than those of the United States.

Rising Budget Deficits

In the midst of the controversy, one thing is clear. Budget deficits have been increasing both in dollar terms

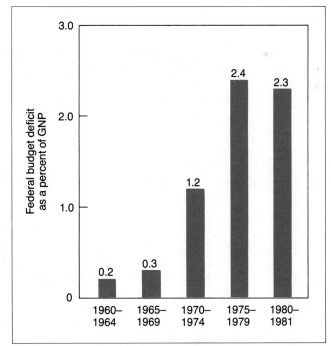

EXHIBIT 9   Increase in budget deficits as a percent of GNP.

Derived from *Economic Report of the President, 1982.*

and, more significantly, *as a percent of GNP* for more than a decade. Exhibit 9 illustrates this point. During the 1960s, federal deficits were only 0.2 or 0.3 percent of GNP. During the first half of the 1970s, they rose to 1.2 percent of GNP, and by the latter half of the decade they had reached 2.4 percent of GNP.

Why has the federal deficit been so large in recent years? The general answer to this question is simple. Federal expenditures have grown more rapidly than the tax base that supports them. During 1969–1980, *measured in real dollars,* federal expenditures expanded at an annual rate of 4.0 percent. Nondefense federal spending grew 6.8 percent annually. In contrast, real national income expanded at only a 2.6 percent annual rate. Since *real* income was growing only about two-thirds as rapidly as *real* federal expenditures, tax revenues lagged behind federal spending, even though tax rates were increased. (This was true primarily because inflation pushed taxpayers into higher tax brackets.) Clearly, during the 1970s, Congress was reluctant to either (a) reduce the growth rate of federal expenditures or (b) levy taxes to finance those expenditures. The result was increasingly large budget deficits.

Not All Deficits Are Alike

It is important to recognize two different types of deficits. First, a deficit may occur because federal spending exceeds tax revenues *during normal business conditions.* Second, a deficit may stem from a decline in tax revenues (and an increase in transfer payments) *during a recession.* The impact of these two types of budget deficits will differ. As we shall see, the first type may indeed place upward pressure on interest rates and even prices. In contrast, deficits during a recession may inject additional demand into the economy, helping to stimulate current consumption, private investments, and total output.

Do Deficits Cause Inflation?

When attempting to answer this question, it is important to isolate the method used to finance the deficit. Deficits may be financed by borrowing from either (a) private investors or (b) the Federal Reserve. If a large deficit is financed primarily by selling bonds to the Federal Reserve, it will accelerate the growth rate of the money supply. Clearly, this method of financing a large deficit will be inflationary.

However, if the deficit is financed by borrowing from the private

sector rather than from the Fed, it will not accelerate the growth rate of the money supply, and it may not generate inflationary pressure. This will be particularly true if the economy is in a recession. This was the case during 1975. The federal deficit jumped to $69.3 billion in 1975, up from $11.5 billion in 1974. The 1975 deficit summed to 4.5 percent of GNP. However, only $7.4 billion (10.7 percent of the deficit) was financed by an expansion in the Fed's holdings of Treasury bonds. The inflation rate actually declined to 7.0 percent during 1975, down from 12.2 percent during 1974.

How has the United States financed its growing deficits? Exhibit 10 provides the answer. During 1970–1974 the Fed financed 21.8 percent of the expansion in the national debt by increasing its holding of U.S. securities. As the deficits ballooned during 1975–1978, the Fed did increase its purchases of bonds, but not nearly as fast as the deficits rose. Therefore, the *proportion* of the deficits financed by the Fed declined (to 11.7 percent). Beginning in 1979, the Fed announced that it was going to focus on the control of the money supply, rather than on other factors such as interest rates. During 1979–1981, the Fed expanded its holdings of U.S. securities very

EXHIBIT 10   The declining proportion of the budget deficits financed by the Federal Reserve

Fiscal Years	Increase in National Debt (Annual Rate in Billions)	Increase in the Fed's Holdings of the National Debt (Annual Rate in Billions)	Expansion in the Fed's Holdings as a Percent of Expansion in the National Debt
1970–1974	24.3	5.3	21.8
1975–1978	74.3	8.7	11.7
1979–1981	69.6	2.7	3.9

Economic Report of the President, 1981, Table B-78, and *Federal Reserve Bulletin* (monthly).

slowly. Thus, most of the deficits during this period were financed by borrowing from private sources.

Deficits and Interest Rates

According to the monetarist view, large budget deficits will lead to rising interest rates that will crowd out private spending. However, when one looks at the historical evidence, the linkage between high interest rates and budget deficits is quite loose. Since World War II, large budget deficits (relative to GNP) were incurred during 1958, 1967–1968, 1971–1972, and 1975–1976. Contrary to the monetarist view, interest rates did not increase sharply during these periods. In fact, interest rates consistently declined during 1971–1972 and 1975–1976, periods characterized by large budget deficits.

When analyzing the crowding-out effect, it is important to (a) consider why the deficits are present and (b) integrate the role of time into the analysis. If a large deficit reflects unfavorable business conditions, then the government may be able to borrow large amounts without pushing interest rates upward, since private demand will generally be weak during an economic downturn. Similarly, if the deficit initially stimulates aggregate demand, business sales will expand more rapidly than expected. Initially, business inventories may fall. This temporary decline in inventories will generate a favorable business cash flow, causing the business demand for loanable funds to fall in the short run. Of course, if the strong demand conditions persist, this situation will reverse itself as business firms seek to borrow to rebuild their abnormally low inventories. During this secondary phase, strong business demand for loanable funds will compete directly with the government's need to finance and refinance its deficit. Rising interest rates are a likely outcome. This appears to be what happened in 1969, 1973, and 1977, when interest rates did eventually rise sharply some 12 to 24 months after large budget deficits were incurred. The linkage between large budget deficits and high interest rates is not as mechanical as the monetarists often imply. Nonetheless, it does seem that large deficits *eventually* place upward pressure on interest rates.

One must also distinguish between *money interest rates* and inflation-adjusted *real interest rates*. High rates of inflation will definitely cause high money interest rates. Therefore, huge deficits financed by borrowing from the Fed (expanding the money supply) will, at least eventually, lead to both inflation and high money interest rates (though not necessarily high real interest rates). In contrast, when the inflation rate is declining, money interest rates will generally fall. Therefore, if the Fed is decelerating the growth rate of the money supply (and thereby slowing the inflation rate), money interest rates may decline even when large deficits are incurred.

Economic analysis does indicate that large budget deficits will increase the demand for loanable funds, causing higher *real* interest rates than would prevail in the absence of the deficits. The big question is how much higher. An increase in the real interest rate will increase the incentive of both domestic savers and foreigners to supply additional funds to U.S. credit markets. Given the mobility of loanable funds across national boundaries, this increase in the quantity of funds supplied could be quite important.

On the other hand, higher interest rates stemming from continuous deficits may also crowd out a sizable amount of capital investment. Herein lies the real problem. Given the sluggish growth rate of the U.S. economy during the 1970s, we can hardly afford the luxury of a lower investment rate, which would reduce our ability to generate future output. Therefore, most economists have been highly concerned about forecasts for *persistently* large deficits.

Are Deficits Inevitable?

Some observers charge that our political system is biased toward both spending and borrowing. Thus, short of major surgery, such as a constitutional amendment limiting spending or mandating a balanced budget, major deficits can be expected in the future. Public-choice analysis indicates that borrowing, as an alternative to taxation, will have considerable popularity with vote-seeking political entrepreneurs. Borrowing eliminates the necessity of voting for higher taxes and postpones payment of the direct cost of government. Interestingly, President Reagan, just like President Carter before him, vigorously criticized budget deficits during the election campaign and promised to balance the budget. Nonetheless, the deficits have continued to mount.

The current deficits are due to a fundamental economic imbalance. It will be difficult to bring the budget into balance in the near future unless the growth rate of government expenditures, particularly of transfer payments (see Chapter 5), is slowed to at least the growth rate of the income base that supports them. Until the White House and Congress face up to this unpleasant reality, the likely outcome is continuing budget deficits, a slow rate of capital formation, and a sluggish economy.

Discussion

1. What are Congress and the President currently doing to reduce the size of budget deficits? What will be the probable effect of their actions?

2. Do you think that elected officials can be counted on to balance the budget, at least during normal economic conditions? Why or why not?

1   The early classical economists thought that the velocity of money was constant and that real output was independent of monetary factors. Therefore, an increase in the stock of money meant proportional increases in prices.

2   Many early Keynesians, influenced by the Great Depression, thought that an increase in the supply of money would be completely offset by a reduction in its velocity. Under these conditions, monetary policy would influence neither aggregate demand nor prices.

3   According to the modern Keynesian view, expansionary monetary policy will reduce the interest rate, thereby stimulating investment and leading to an increase in aggregate demand. A restrictive monetary policy will increase the interest rate, thereby discouraging investment and reducing aggregate demand. The interest rate is the mechanism that transmits monetary policy in the Keynesian model.

4   There are two ways in which the Treasury can finance a deficit: by borrowing from the public and borrowing from the Fed. The former method will increase the supply of bonds (and reduce the availability of loanable funds with which to finance private investment), causing the interest rate to rise. In contrast, borrowing from the Fed will increase the money supply and exert downward pressure on interest rates. It is the more expansionary of the two methods.

5   Monetarists believe that there is a direct link between the money market and other basic aggregated markets. Thus, an increase in the supply of money will create an excess supply of money balances. People will attempt to reduce their money balances by spending the excess supply of money in several markets, including the market for goods and services. The increase in the supply of money will therefore lead directly to an increase in aggregate demand. By parallel reasoning, a reduction in the supply of money will lead to a fall in aggregate demand.

6   Monetarists believe that economic instability is almost exclusively the result of erratic fluctuations in the money supply. Monetary acceleration initially leads to a higher real income, but inflation will eventually result. Responding to the inflation, the monetary authorities will inevitably decelerate monetary growth. This deceleration will lead to an economic slowdown. Monetarists argue that the major economic recessions of the past were the result of monetary contraction and that the major inflationary booms were the result of monetary acceleration. The major cause of the business cycle, in the view of the monetarists, is inept monetary policy.

7   Monetarists do not believe that a pure fiscal policy has much effect on income and employment. Since a pure fiscal action must be financed by borrowing from private investors, monetarists believe that a crowding out of private spending will result.

8   Monetarists believe that, if erratic monetary policy were eliminated, the economy would be relatively stable. They stress that consumption, the major component of national income, is a function primarily of long-run expected income and will tend to moderate temporary fluctuations in income.

9   Given the economic complexities of properly timing macropolicy and the short-sighted bias of the collective decision-making process, monetarists are very pessimistic about the likelihood that macropolicy will be stabilizing. Thus, they favor a monetary rule that would require authorities to expand the money supply at a constant rate. They believe that this policy would reduce the magnitude of business fluctuations since it would eliminate what they perceive to be the major source of instability, namely, the stop–go policies of the monetary authorities.

THE ECONOMIC WAY OF THINKING — DISCUSSION QUESTIONS

1 What impact do Keynesians believe that an increase in the supply of money would have on (a) interest rates, (b) the level of investment, (c) aggregate demand, (d) employment, and (e) prices? Fully explain your answer.

2 Will a budget deficit be more expansionary if it is financed by borrowing from the Federal Reserve or from the general public? Explain.

3 Suppose that you have just been appointed chairman of the Council of Economic Advisers. Prepare a press release outlining your views on unemployment, inflation, and proper macropolicy, both monetary and fiscal, for the next three years.

4 "Inappropriate monetary and fiscal policy was the major cause of economic instability during the 1930s, and it is the major cause of economic instability in the 1970s." Evaluate this view, presenting empirical evidence to defend your position.

5 Indicate how monetarists and Keynesians differ on the following issues:
(a) The impact of monetary policy on the level of output and employment
(b) The impact of fiscal policy on the level of output and employment
(c) The major cause of economic instability
(d) The likelihood that discretionary macropolicy will stabilize the economy

6 Indicate why you either agree or disagree with the position that economic instability would be reduced if a monetary rule requiring the Federal Reserve to increase the money supply at a constant rate (for example, 3 percent annually) were adopted.

Stabilization policy is not a "game" against nature whose reactions do not alter in response to policy stimuli, but a game against intelligent agents whose reactions depend on policy moves.[1]
Neil G. Berkman

11

EXPECTATIONS AND THE LIMITS OF MACROPOLICY

There is one more very important factor that must be incorporated into our "economic way of thinking" about macroeconomics. That factor is expectations—expectations about future prices, future interest rates, and future general economic conditions. What individuals think is going to happen in the future is important because it affects the choices that they make in the present. For example, if individuals expect the price of a product to rise in the future, *current* demand will expand as persons choose to "buy now before the price increases." Our expectations about the future matter today.

In this chapter, we will focus on how expectations affect the operation of our increasingly complex macroeconomic model. We will assume that people adjust their current choices in response to changes in their expectations about the future. The chapter begins with an investigation of why expansionary policies might reduce the unemployment rate, at least temporarily. We then explain why it is unlikely that demand-stimulus policies can permanently reduce unemployment below its long-run, normal rate. The introduction of expectations into our model helps to explain the simultaneous presence of inflation and unemployment, a phenomenon that puzzled many economists during the 1970s. Expectations also help us understand the linkage between interest rates and inflation.

Expectations are important because economics is about people, who think, react, learn from their mistakes, and are capable of altering their behavior as they obtain additional information. Let us investigate the macroeconomic implications of these factors.

---

[1]Neil G. Berkman, "A Rational View of Rational Expectations," *New England Economic Review* (January/February 1980), p. 29.

Economists place strong emphasis on empirical work. In 1958, an English economist, A. W. Phillips, published a very influential paper analyzing the relationship between unemployment and changes in money wages.[2] Using data from the United Kingdom, Phillips found that when the rate of unemployment was low, the rate of change in money wages tended to be large. Theoretically, these findings make sense. A low rate of unemployment implies a tight labor market. Therefore, one would expect that in response to the strong demand, money wages would rise more rapidly than they would if labor markets were "loose" (that is, if the unemployment rate were high).

Building on the work of Phillips, other economists noted that a similar inverse relationship existed between inflation and unemployment. Since wages are the major component of production costs, it is not surprising that a rapid rate of change in the price level, as well as in wages, tends to be associated with a reduction in the rate of unemployment. The curve indicating the relationship between the unemployment rate and the inflation rate (or rate of change in money wages) is termed the **Phillips curve** after its originator.

Phillips Curve: A curve that illustrates the relationship between the rate of change in prices (or money wages) and the rate of unemployment. *In the short run,* the rate of inflation is usually inversely related to the rate of unemployment.

Exhibit 1 illustrates a short-run Phillips curve. When the rate of unemployment is high, the rate of price (and wage) inflation is low. Correspondingly, a reduction in the rate of unemployment is associated with a higher rate of inflation. Thus, the Phillips curve slopes downward and to the right, indicating that *in the short run* an inverse relationship exists between unemployment and inflation.

This helps to explain why during the 1960s economists were highly optimistic that a lower rate of unemployment could be "purchased" at the price of moderate inflation. The late Arthur Okun, chairman of the Council of Economic Advisers during the Johnson years, expressed the dominant view of the era:

On an optimistic-realistic view, the best hope is that a 4 percent rate of unemployment and a 2 percent annual rate of price increase will prove compatible and that such a combination will be regarded as a satisfactory compromise by the American public. This was the hope before the Vietnam spurt in mid-1965, and nothing that has happened since then demonstrates that it is unattainable.[3]

The Short-Run Phillips Curve

Suppose an economy is operating at its supply-constrained rate of output. What will happen if macropolicy makers inject additional demand stimulus into the economy? Most economists believe that the expansionary policy will stimulate both employment and output *for a short period of time.* In addition, the inflation rate is likely to accelerate. The reasoning behind this analysis involves both the role of time in the market adjustment process and the dissemination of information to decision makers. Let us consider this issue in more detail.

It is important to recognize that all prices will not *immediately* reflect the new, stronger demand conditions. The price of many goods will be "temporarily

---

[2]A. W. Phillips, "The Relationship between Unemployment and the Rate of Change of Money Wages in the United Kingdom, 1861–1957," *Economica* 25 (1958), pp. 283–299.

[3]Arthur M. Okun, *The Political Economy of Prosperity* (New York: Norton, 1970), p. 102.

EXHIBIT 1   A hypothetical Phillips curve

According to the Phillips curve, a reduction in the unemployment rate will be associated with an increase in the rate of inflation. The experience of the 1970s indicates that the unemployment–inflation trade-off is a short-run phenomenon.

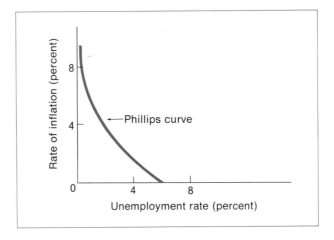

fixed" as a result of business decisions made before the expansion in demand. Catalogue prices, wages determined by earlier collective-bargaining agreements, and other contractually fixed prices will not rise immediately.

In addition, some business decision makers will be reluctant to raise their prices until they are convinced that the strong current sales really represent a permanent change in demand conditions rather than merely a temporary, random occurrence. After all, if the strong short-term sales are only a temporary phenomenon, a price rise may drive potential future customers to competitors. Thus, for a time, the decision makers will hold the line on prices until they have additional information indicating a true increase in demand for their product. *In the short run,* businesses will meet the expansion in demand by using and reducing existing inventories, cutting maintenance time, assigning more overtime, and hiring additional workers.

Of course, if the strong demand persists into the future, the inflation rate will accelerate. However, the rising prices may initially mislead business decision makers. They may mistakenly believe there is an increase in the *relative* price of (and demand for) their product. If this is the case, they will adjust by hiring more workers and expanding output. Their employment and output levels, however, based as they are on inflation, cannot be sustained indefinitely; they are short-run effects.

Similarly, workers may be misled by the wage inflation. Exhibit 2 illustrates what happens to unemployment when inflation pushes money wage rates upward and workers are unaware of it. The number of wage offers that workers *of a specific skill level* might expect to derive from a job search is measured on the y-axis. For the skill category illustrated, most of the job offers fall between $4.50 and $5.50 per hour. When the perceived and actual distributions of wage offers are identical, the job-search time of employees will be normal. Employees will balance the gains associated with additional job search (primarily the expectation of finding a better job) against the cost of the job search. Suppose that when individuals correctly perceive the actual wage-offer distribution, economizing behavior leads them to search until they find a job paying $6 or more per hour. As the normal acceptance range of Exhibit 2 illustrates, there is approximately a 5 percent probability that a wage offer made to employees in this skill category will equal or exceed $6. Thus, the typical job hunter will undertake considerable search time before the $6-per-hour job is found.

EXHIBIT 2   Inflation, mis-information, and the length of job search

If the perceived and actual distributions of wage offers are identical, economizing job search will yield a wage offer of $6 per hour or more *for workers in this skill category.* The normal probability of finding the $6-per-hour job is approximately 5 percent (1 out of 20 job offers). If inflation shifts the actual (but not the perceived) wage-offer distribution to the right, job hunters will quickly find and accept $6-per-hour jobs. Since workers fail to realize that higher-paying jobs are now available, their job-search time will decrease and the unemployment rate will fall.

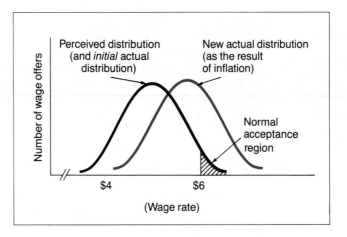

What will happen if inflation shifts the *actual* distribution of wage offers to the right, while job searchers continue to believe that they confront the initial (perceived) wage-offer distribution? Since information is costly and it will take time for the new wage-offer information to be disseminated among job searchers, this is not an unrealistic situation in the short run. Workers will accept or reject job offers still believing they face the initial distribution. Since inflation has shifted the actual distribution to the right, the probability of finding a $6-per-hour job offer has increased substantially. Workers willing to search for the best 5 percent of the available jobs can now get more than $6 per hour. However, *initially* they are unaware that this is the case. Misled by the inflation-induced increase in wage rates, job hunters will quickly find and accept job offers of $6 per hour or more; they will think they are just lucky. The average length of job-search time will decline, causing the actual unemployment rate to fall temporarily below its long-run, normal level.

In the short run, inflationary macrostimulus tends to generate additional output and employment because decision makers are (a) unsure whether the increase in current demand is temporary or permanent, (b) unable to *immediately* adjust previously negotiated long-term contracts, and (c) misled into believing that the inflationary price and wage increases reflect a relative increase in demand for *their* product or service. These factors account for the observed data of Phillips and others who focused on time periods prior to 1970. However, such a situation—rising output and employment due to the failure of decision makers to recognize and adjust to the inflationary *general* increase in demand—will not continue indefinitely into the future. Eventually, decision makers will understand what is happening; they will begin to anticipate the rising prices and wages and to alter their plans and decisions accordingly. Their perception will change to more accurately match reality, causing the perceived and the actual distributions to once again come together.

ADAPTIVE EXPECTATIONS AND THE SHIFTING PHILLIPS CURVE

How are our expectations about the future formed? This is not an easy question to answer. As we proceed, we will consider alternative views.

The simplest theory about the formation of expectations is that people rely upon the past to predict future trends. According to this theory, which

Adaptive Expectations Hypothesis: The hypothesis that economic decision-makers base their future expectations on the actual outcomes observed during recent periods. For example, according to this view, the rate of inflation actually experienced during the last two or three years would be the major determinant of the expected rate of inflation for next year.

economists call the **adaptive expectations hypothesis,** decision makers perceive that the best indicator of the future is what has happened in the recent past.

If prices have been stable for the last four or five years, it is a good bet that they will be fairly stable next year. Similarly, if prices have risen between 4 and 6 percent annually during the last several years, they will probably rise by a similar amount next year. In the face of continuing inflation, the adaptive expectations hypothesis makes it clear why decision makers are unlikely to anticipate stable prices next year.

Exhibit 3 presents a graphic illustration of the adaptive expectations hypothesis. In period 1, prices were actually stable [graph (a)]. Therefore, on the basis of the experience of period 1, decision makers assume that prices will be stable in period 2 [graph (b)]. However, the actual rate of inflation in period 2 jumps to 4 percent. Continuation of the 4 percent rate throughout period 2 (the periods may be several years in length) causes decision makers to change their expectations. Relying on the experience of period 2, decision makers anticipate 4 percent inflation in period 3. When their expectations turn out to be incorrect (the actual rate of inflation during period 3 is 8 percent), they again alter their expectations accordingly. During period 4, the actual rate of inflation declines to 4 percent, less than the expected rate. Again, decision makers adjust their expectations as to the expected rate of inflation in period 5.

Of course, in the real world, one would not expect the precise mechanical link between past occurrences and future expectations that is outlined in Exhibit 3. Nonetheless, the general point is valid. An acceleration or deceleration in the rate of inflation will cause decision makers to change their expectations, but the expectations will lag behind the actual occurrences.

How is the adaptive expectations hypothesis related to the Phillips curve? As we discussed, *in the short run,* macroacceleration will tend to induce an expansion in output and employment. However, with the passage of time, more complete information will be acquired, and individuals will alter their expectations and their actions accordingly. They will not continue to be misled

EXHIBIT 3   The adaptive expectations hypothesis

According to the adaptive expectations hypothesis, the actual occurrence during the last period (or set of periods) will determine people's future expectations. The expected future rate of inflation (b) will lag behind the actual rate of inflation (a) by one period as expectations are altered over time.

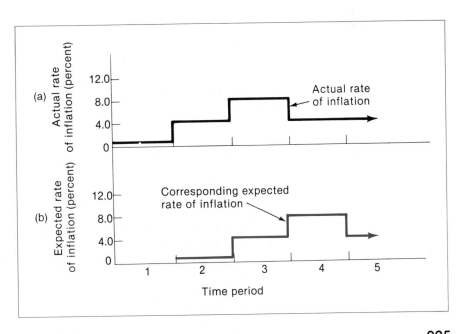

EXHIBIT 4 Adaptive expectations and the shifting Phillips curve

When stable prices are anticipated, expansionary macropolicy will permit macroplanners temporarily to trade off moderate inflation for a lower rate of unemployment (move from A to B). However, with time, decision makers will come to anticipate the inflation, the Phillips curve will shift upward, and the unemployment rate will return to its long-run, normal level (shift from B to C). Once decision makers anticipate a specific rate of inflation, policies that will generate a still higher rate of inflation again will be required to push the unemployment rate below its long-run, normal level. In addition, because of their short-run inverse relationship, any effort to restrain the rate of inflation will temporarily result in an abnormally high rate of unemployment (for example, a move from E to F).

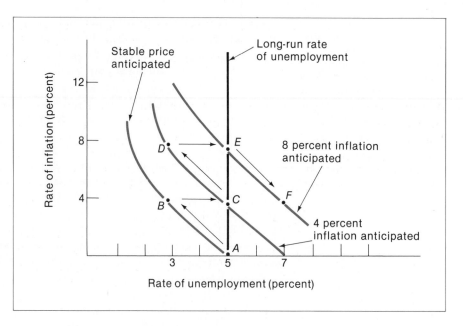

by the expansionary macropolicy. Once it is recognized that the inflation rate has accelerated, workers and their union representatives will incorporate the higher expected rate of inflation into their decision making. They will no longer accept money wage offers that would only be attractive if wages and prices were assumed to be stable (or if the rate of wage and price inflation were lower than the recently experienced rate). Job-search time will increase to its normal average length once workers fully recognize that inflation has shifted the money wage (although not necessarily the real wage) opportunities available to them. Once the inflation is fully anticipated, the rate of unemployment will again rise to its normal, long-run level.

Exhibit 4 illustrates what happens when one incorporates adaptive expectations into the Phillips curve analysis. Beginning from position A, where decision makers anticipate stable prices, expansionary macrostimulus can, in the short run, push the rate of unemployment down while the economy experiences moderate inflation. Suppose that the macroplanners follow a course that leads the economy to point B, 4 percent inflation and only 3 percent unemployment (down from the earlier 5 percent rate). Point B can be temporarily attained, but it is not a sustainable position. After an extended period of 4 percent inflation, decision makers will begin to anticipate the higher rate of inflation. Workers and their union representatives will take the higher expected rate of inflation into account in their job-search and collective-bargaining decision making. Once the rate of inflation is fully anticipated, the economy will confront a new, higher Phillips curve (the one containing points C and D). The rate of unemployment will return to the long-run rate of 5 percent, even though prices will continue to rise at an annual rate of 4 percent (point C). Once the 4 percent rate of inflation is fully anticipated, macroplanners can reduce the rate of unemployment only by accelerating inflation to a still higher level—that is, by inducing another short-run effect. The rate of unemployment can be temporarily reduced to 3 percent only if the macroplanners are willing to tolerate 8 percent inflation (movement from C to D). Of course, once the 8 percent rate has persisted for a while, it, too, will be fully anticipated. The Phillips curve will again shift, unemployment will return to its long-run natural rate, and the inflation will continue at a rate of 8 percent (point E).

Deceleration and the Perverse Short-Run Phillips Curve Trade-Off

Once decision makers fully anticipate the 8 percent rate of inflation, what will happen if macroplanners follow a policy of deceleration in an effort to stabilize prices? As in the case of expansion, the short-term impact of restraint will be primarily on output and employment rather than on prices. Exhibit 5 illustrates the effects of deflation (or a deceleration in the rate of inflation) in the labor market. Initially, workers will fail to recognize that the decline in demand and wage inflation has reduced the attractiveness of the available wage alternatives. For a time, the unexpected deceleration in wage inflation will cause the *actual* wage-offer distribution to lie to the left of the *perceived* distribution. Believing they are unlucky, job hunters will search in vain for job offers in the acceptance region of $6 an hour and above, given the *perceived* wage-offer distribution. As job hunters lengthen their job-search time, the unemployment rate will rise. It will continue above its long-run normal rate until the information about actual wage offers has been fully disseminated among job searchers and has convinced them that the "perceived" more attractive wage offers are no longer available.

Similarly, sales in product markets will slow and inventories will rise until sellers recognize the reduction (relative to their expectations) in product demands. Since long-term contracts for labor and for products were written with higher inflation in mind, existing contracts will imply higher *real* prices than the parties bargained for. This factor will also slow economic activity until the contracts expire or are renegotiated.

It is clear now how macrodeceleration will cause both output and employment to decelerate. As Exhibit 4 shows, once 8 percent inflation is fully anticipated and the rate of unemployment has returned to its normal 5 percent long-run level (point E), an anti-inflationary policy will cause a *temporarily* above-normal rate of unemployment (movement from E to F). The cost of returning to stable prices once the "inflationary psychology" has permeated the economy will be an above-normal rate of unemployment and economic recession.

EXHIBIT 5 Decelerating the inflation rate and prolonging job-search time

Here we present the counterpart of Exhibit 2 for deflation (or a deceleration of the inflation rate). Job-search time will be normal when the actual and perceived wage-offer distributions are identical. An unanticipated deceleration in the inflation rate will shift the actual (but, initially, not the perceived) wage-offer distribution to the left. Given their perceptions of the available wage alternatives, normal job-search time will fail to generate acceptable wage offers for many job hunters. As a result, the average job-search time of workers will lengthen and the unemployment rate will rise.

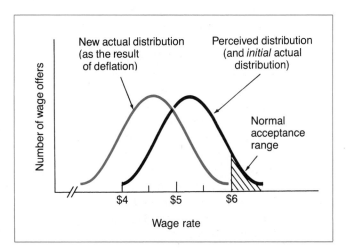

The Phillips Curve: 1959–1981

The adaptive expectations hypothesis implies that the inflation–unemployment trade-off is a short-run phenomenon. When inflationary policies are followed for an extended period of time, the Phillips curve will shift upward to the right. Is the real world consistent with this view? Exhibit 6 presents data on this topic. Inflation and unemployment rates for the 1959–1981 period are mapped. All observed rates from 1959 to 1969 are close to Phillips curve *A*. Each year from 1959 through 1965, prices increased less than 2 percent. Beginning in 1966, prices increased 3 percent or more each year. Despite 3 percent inflation in 1966–1967 and higher rates in 1968–1969, initially the inflation–unemployment trade-off remained consistent with Phillips curve *A*.

However, after the persistent inflation during 1966–1969, the inflation–unemployment picture worsened during 1970–1973. Just as the theory implies, a period of persistent inflation was followed by a shifting of the Phillips curve (to *B*) upward to the right. The measured rates of inflation for 1971 and 1972 are probably biased downward as a result of the Nixon price controls, which were in effect at the time. In January 1973, the controls on most goods were lifted.

EXHIBIT 6   The elusive inflation–unemployment trade-off, 1959–1981

Between 1959 and 1969, the annual rates of inflation and unemployment map out the Phillips curve *A*. The inflation–unemployment trade-off during the period from 1970 to 1973 was consistent with Phillips curve *B*, suggesting that the curve shifted after three or four years of significant inflation during the period from 1966 to 1969. Still higher rates of inflation during the mid-1970s apparently caused the Phillips curve to shift outward again (*C*) during the last half of the decade.

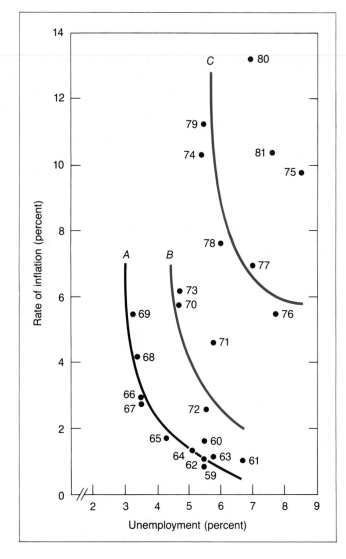

During late 1973 and early 1974, the Organization of Petroleum Exporting Countries (OPEC) decided to quadruple the price of crude oil. These events disrupted the economy and contributed to the high rate of inflation during 1974. As rates of inflation in the 7 to 13 percent range became typical during 1977–1981, the Phillips curve appears to have shifted upward again (to *C*), just as the theory implies that it would. The real-world data are consistent with the view that persistent inflation will cause the Phillips curve to shift upward, generating *high* rates of *both* inflation and unemployment.

The Long-Run Phillips Curve

The shape of the long-run Phillips curve is still the subject of some controversy. However, economists of both Keynesian and monetarist persuasions are increasingly coming to believe that the long-run Phillips curve is perfectly vertical.[4] The experience of the 1970s has shattered the dream that we can *permanently* trade off inflation for a lower rate of unemployment.

There is no evidence that the expansionary policies of the period from 1967 to 1981 generated either a more rapid rate of growth or a lower level of unemployment. The 1950s are often pointed to as a period during which stimulative policies were absent. Except during the Korean War, relative price stability was the norm during the 1950s. Nonetheless, the average annual rate of growth of real GNP during the "stagnating" fifties was 3.9 percent, compared to 2.5 percent during the inflation-plagued period from 1967 to 1981. Similarly, the average rate of unemployment during the 1950s was 4.5 percent, compared to 5.8 percent during 1967 to 1981. Even after we make allowance for the impact of the larger share of youthful and women workers in the 1970s, these data do not suggest that the expansionary policies of the 1970s reduced the long-run rate of unemployment.

To summarize, the adaptive expectations hypothesis points to four basic propositions with regard to the Phillips curve.

1. In the short run, expansionary macropolicies may lead to a *temporary* reduction in the unemployment rate at the expense of an acceleration in the rate of inflation.
2. With time, decision makers adjust to the higher rate of inflation, and the Phillips curve shifts upward until the rate of unemployment returns to its normal, long-run level.
3. Once people anticipate a given rate of inflation, a move to a more restrictive macropolicy will cause the unemployment rate to rise temporarily *above* its long-run, normal rate.
4. In the long run, the Phillips curve is vertical, or nearly vertical. There is no evidence to indicate that expansionary–inflationary policies are able to achieve a reduction in the long-run rate of unemployment—that is, there seems to be no permanent, sustainable trade-off between inflation and unemployment.

---

[4]For example, the two most widely used intermediate macroeconomic texts, one written by two members of the Department of Economics at Massachusetts Institute of Technology (a long-time stronghold of the dominant Keynesian view) and the other by a former student of both Franco Modigliani (a Keynesian) and Milton Friedman (a monetarist), integrate expectations into their analyses and arrive at the conclusion that the long-run Phillips curve is vertical. See Rudiger Dornbusch and Stanley Fischer, *Macroeconomics* (New York: McGraw-Hill, 1978), and Robert J. Gordon, *Macroeconomics* (Boston: Little, Brown, 1978).

POLITICS, EXPECTATIONS, AND THE SPIRALING
UPWARD OF THE INFLATION RATE

In a democratic setting, real-world macropolicy is shaped by political forces, and these forces are highly sensitive to current economic conditions. If unemployment is low (relative to its rate in the recent past) and the rate of inflation is unusually high, political pressure to control inflation will build. On the other hand, if the rate of unemployment is rising, pleas for a more expansionary macropolicy will be widely heard. As we have discussed in earlier chapters, there is a tendency for macropolicy to follow a stop–go pattern, accelerating when unemployment is perceived as the more serious problem and decelerating when political entrepreneurs become increasingly concerned about excessive inflation.

If, as the adaptive expectations hypothesis implies, the initial impact of macropolicy is primarily on output rather than on prices, public choice theory indicates that macropolicy is likely to reflect an inflationary bias. The special interest effect and the shortsightedness effect combine to explain why *real-world* macropolicy makers often choose an inflationary course. The initial effects of such a course will be positive—a decline in unemployment, a more rapid growth rate, and additional tax revenues for spending programs. Although inflationary pressures will build with the passage of time, a shift to an anti-inflationary policy will still be difficult and unlikely. Well-organized interest groups (for example, defense contractors, welfare recipients, the education lobby, public employee unions, and agricultural interests) who would be harmed by a reduction in federal spending (fiscal restraint) will vigorously oppose budget cuts; the beneficiaries of anti-inflationary restraint, on the other hand, are widely dispersed and largely disorganized. Political decision makers will continue to have a strong incentive to respond to the interest groups opposing restraint (or favoring expansion).

In addition, the benefits of anti-inflationary macropolicy measures are difficult to identify and will be realized only in the future. The short-term effects of deceleration—reduction in current demand, rising unemployment, a temporary decline in the growth of output—will be undesirable to most people. The inflation would have to be serious indeed before one would expect a rational political entrepreneur to choose such a painful and politically unrewarding course. It is much easier simply to blame the unions and big corporations that raise their wages and prices (see Chapter 10, pages 270–272). Even when a deceleration policy is chosen, short-term political factors and pressure from interest groups harmed by the restraint are likely to lead to its abandonment as soon as the predictable initial negative effects become visible.[5]

Given adaptive expectations, a stop–go macropolicy with a bias toward inflationary expansion will generate a specific pattern of inflation–unemployment points, resulting in a clockwise upward spiral on the Phillips curve diagram (see Exhibit 7). If an economy is initially positioned at A_1, macroacceleration will reduce the rate of unemployment. Initially, as the economy moves along a short-

---

[5]See James M. Buchanan and Richard Wagner, *Democracy in Deficit: The Political Legacy of Lord Keynes* (New York: Academic Press, 1977), for additional detail on the interaction between public choice theory and discretionary macropolicy.

EXHIBIT 7 Stop–go policy
with an inflationary bias

Macroacceleration temporarily
reduces unemployment while
the inflation rate rises (shifts
from points A to points B). But
with time, the secondary effects
of the expansionary policy will
cause the rates of both unemployment and inflation to rise
(shifts from points B to points
C). If concern about inflation
causes macroplanners to shift
to deceleration, the policy
eventually will retard inflation
while the rate of unemployment
rises (shifts from points C to
points A). If the planners are
concerned more about unemployment than about inflation,
macropolicy will shift to
acceleration well before price
stability is attained. Each new
clockwise pattern will begin at
a successively higher rate of
inflation.

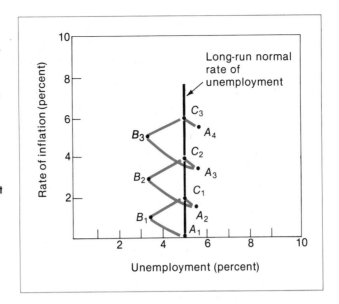

run Phillips curve (to B_1), the rate of inflation will rise by only a moderate amount. As Exhibit 4 illustrated, B_1 is not a stable position. The secondary effects of the macroacceleration, including a rise in the expected future rate of inflation, will cause the rate of unemployment to return to its long-run normal level even while the inflation problem worsens (shift to C_1). As the rate of inflation reaches a high level, pressures for a shift to less macroexpansion will build.

However, the initial effects of a shift to macrodeceleration will also be primarily on output. Economic slowdown and rising unemployment can be expected, even while the inflation rate moderates only slightly (moves to A_2). As political pressures build against the restrictive policy, it will tend to be abandoned long before there is a return to stable prices. As macropolicy shifts back toward acceleration, the cycle will begin again. But this time it will start from a higher base rate of inflation (A_2 rather than A_1). Consecutive cycles will produce a clockwise upward spiral, as shown in Exhibit 7.

Exhibit 8 plots the pattern of the actual inflation–unemployment points for each year from 1959 to 1981. These points are consistent with our theory. With the passage of time, the inflation rate has spiraled upward, just as the model predicts. Higher and higher rates of inflation are experienced, and unemployment continues to fluctuate around its long-run normal rate. Each time, macrodeceleration is abandoned at a higher rate of inflation. Our analysis indicates that a return to price stability by means of macropolicy is likely to be a painful process.

RATIONAL EXPECTATIONS

For some economists, the adaptive expectations hypothesis is too simplistic, assuming as it does that people rely upon a simple rule-of-thumb approach—"the future will tend to be much like the immediate past." These economists argue that expectations are determined rationally; decision makers (a) learn from

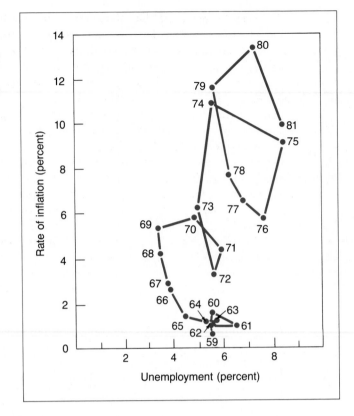

EXHIBIT 8 The ratchet effect and accelerating inflation, 1959–1981

Actual inflation–unemployment has followed the clockwise pattern outlined in Exhibit 7. Macropolicy has switched from restraint to acceleration at successively higher rates of inflation, causing the corresponding rates of inflation in the pattern to spiral upward.

Rational Expectations Hypothesis: This viewpoint expects individuals to weigh all available evidence, including information concerning the probable effects of current and future economic policy, when they formulate their expectations about future economic events, such as the probable future inflation rate.

previous experience and (b) use *all pertinent information* when formulating their views about the future. The **rational expectations hypothesis** assumes that individuals will consider information about the direction of current governmental policy when they formulate their forecasts of inflation and other variables influencing their decisions. The proponents of rational expectations argue that their view is consistent with economizing behavior (see Chapter 1) and that the adaptive expectations hypothesis is not.

Mark Willis, former president of the Federal Reserve Bank of Minneapolis and a proponent of rational expectations, makes this point clear:

With the rational expectations scheme replacing the adaptive expectations scheme, agents in the model take policy changes into account. If a change in policy creates opportunities to make extraordinary profits, they do not ignore them as they do under adaptive expectations. In a rational expectations model of the economy, agents change their decisions to take full advantage of whatever opportunities are produced by a new policy.[6]

Perhaps an example will help clarify the rational expectations hypothesis. Suppose that prices had increased at an annual rate of 6 percent during each

---

[6]Mark H. Willis, "Rational Expectations as a Counterrevolution," *The Public Interest* (special fifteenth anniversary issue on "The Crisis in Economic Theory," 1980.) Also see Thomas J. Sargent, "Rational Expectations and the Reconstruction of Macroeconomics," Federal Reserve Bank of Minneapolis *Quarterly Review* (Summer 1980), and Neil G. Berkman, "A Rational View of Rational Expectations," *New England Economic Review* (January/February 1980), for additional information on this topic.

of the last three years. Decision makers believe that there is a relationship between the growth rate of the money supply and rising prices. Individuals note that the money stock has expanded at a 12 percent annual rate during the last nine months, up from the 7 percent rate of the past several years. According to the rational expectations hypothesis, decision makers will integrate the recent monetary acceleration into their forecast of the future inflation rate. The adaptive expectations hypothesis implies that people will continue to predict that the inflation rate for next period will be like it was for last period (or the last several periods). Rational expectationists argue that decision makers will project an acceleration in the inflation rate, perhaps in the 10 to 12 percent range, since they believe that the inflation rate will eventually respond to the more rapid growth of the money supply.

Contrary to the charges of some critics, the rational expectations hypothesis does *not* assume individuals will never make forecasting errors. However, it does imply that they will *not* continue to make *systematic* errors. For example, sometimes decision makers may overestimate the increase in the inflation rate caused by monetary expansion, and at other times they may underestimate it. However, since people learn from previous experience, they will not continue to make systematic errors.

Macropolicy and Rational Expectations

What are the implications of the rational expectations hypothesis for macroeconomics? There are both positive and negative aspects. The rational expectations hypothesis implies that discretionary macropolicy may be relatively ineffective, *even in the short run*. In the world of rational expectations, individuals can anticipate the impact of policy changes and adjust their actions in a manner that will offset, undercut, or completely paralyze any policy, particularly one that is based on misleading the public about the future. Discretionary macropolicy may, according to this view, be an undependable tool.

Suppose macroplanners decided to accelerate the growth rate of the money supply and enlarge the budget deficit in order to stimulate aggregate demand and promote more rapid short-run growth. The rational expectations hypothesis indicates that people will immediately take steps to adjust to this strategy. The general public may correctly and fully anticipate the effects of this expansionary policy. Expecting a higher rate of inflation in the future, lenders will demand higher interest rates for loanable funds. Union representatives will demand higher wage rates and the inclusion of "cost-of-living adjustments" in order to prevent the erosion of their real wage levels when the inflation rate accelerates in the future.[7] The inflationary premium built into long-term contracts will be enlarged in response to the announcement of the more expansionary macroeconomic course. All of these actions are designed to protect lenders, workers, and business firms from the adverse effects of the expected acceleration in the inflation rate. However, taken collectively, they will quickly generate an increase in wages and prices; the short-run positive effects of the expansionary policy on output and employment will be undercut. The policy

---

[7]The proponents of rational expectations argue that collective-bargaining agreements providing for an automatic upward wage adjustment as the price level rises (so-called "cost-of-living adjustments," which became more and more common in the 1970s) are good examples of rational adjustments to an inflationary environment.

will exert little, or none, of its intended impact. In other words, if people correctly estimate the impact and direction of an expansionary macropolicy on their alternatives and adjust their decision making accordingly, they will render the policy ineffective. Prices will continue to rise—this will be the primary effect; in addition, the unemployment rate will fail to decline, and the short-run Phillips curve will become vertical or almost vertical.

Of course, rational decision makers will not always accurately anticipate the strength of an expansionary policy. If the impact of an expansionary policy is *under*estimated, macrostimulus can exert a positive impact on employment and output in the short run. In contrast, if people *over*estimate the expected inflationary impact of the macrostimulus, their adjustments will not only lead to an acceleration in the inflation rate, but also output and employment will be adversely affected. How can policy makers know whether rational decision makers will over- or underestimate the effects of a policy change? According to the proponents of rational expectations, they cannot. Therefore, policy makers will be unable to accurately anticipate the impact of their actions on real income and employment.

On the positive side, the rational expectations hypothesis indicates that it may be easier to decelerate the inflation rate than the adaptive expectations hypothesis implies. If policy makers can convince the public that they are going to follow a more restrictive course until inflation is brought under control, people will adjust rationally to the expected deceleration in the inflation rate. Interest rates will fall rapidly, reflecting the willingness of lenders to accept lower interest rates because of the anticipated decline in the inflation rate (see the following section, "Interest Rates and the Expected Rate of Inflation"). Money wage demands will be moderated in the anticipation of a lower future inflation rate. As the inflation rate actually decelerates, the cost-of-living adjustments will become smaller and smaller. The "inflationary factor" built into long-term contracts will decline. *If a restrictive policy is really credible,* the rational expectations hypothesis implies that the inflation rate can be decelerated without the economy going through a prolonged period of recession and high unemployment—a situation that is implied by the adaptive expectations hypothesis. However, given their prior record of stop–go policies, it will be difficult for politicians to make a restrictive (anti-inflationary) policy credible. To date, no country has been able to decelerate inflation rapidly without experiencing at least a temporary economic slowdown.

Since the rational expectations hypothesis implies that the effects of discretionary macropolicy are unpredictable, the proponents of this view argue that discretionary macropolicy is destabilizing. The defenders of rational expectations argue that effective policies must be stable, straightforward, and unarbitrary. They must not be continually altered, reversed, or tinkered with. Mark Willis articulates this position:

The government should specify the rules for the economic game—that is, the policies and regulations—so that people know what opportunities are available and understand the probable consequences of their decisions. Tax policies, for example, should be set so that people can know if their relative taxes are going up or down from one year to the next. Spending policies should be announced well in advance and explained so that they don't trick people into making harmful decisions.

An important principle behind this new approach to policy making is that government rules and rule changes should not be based on arbitrary indexes such as the unemployment rate. Rather, they should be based on their ability to improve the general welfare. If a policy can increase efficiency or otherwise make people better off, then use it. But if all it can do is shift some aggregate numbers that may not mean much, why bother?[8]

Certainly, the rational expectations view is not without its critics who contend that the issues are too complex to expect people to make reliable forecasts. They argue that it is unrealistic to assume that most people will (a) develop reliable theories about the operation of a highly complex economy, (b) monitor the necessary policy variables, and (c) consistently make the implied adjustments to changes in macropolicy. Therefore, the critics charge that most people will find a backward-looking rule of thumb, such as that implied by the adaptive expectations hypothesis, to be both sensible and "rational."

The debate about how people develop expectations about the future is likely to continue throughout the 1980s. A synthesis will no doubt emerge with the passage of time, but one point is already clear. It is important to integrate expectations into our thinking about macroeconomic policy. Economic participants are people, not robots that can always be counted on to respond in the same manner. People may be fooled from time to time; but one can be assured they will generally learn from their previous mistakes. Emphasis of this important point, long ago understood by skilled practitioners of economics, may prove to be the major lasting contribution of the rational expectations school.

INTEREST RATES AND THE EXPECTED RATE OF INFLATION

Most people are impatient. We like to have things now, rather than later. The interest rate is the price, the burden if you will, that borrowers must pay in order to acquire, in their "impatience," *current* purchasing power in exchange for *future* purchasing power. It indicates how much a borrower must give up in the future in order to enjoy more goods (or investment funds) in the present. Similarly, from the lender's viewpoint, the interest rate reflects how much future purchasing power can be acquired for each dollar of current purchasing power given up.

It is useful to think of the interest rate in two senses. First, there is the **money rate of interest,** the percentage of the amount borrowed that must be paid to the lender in the future, in addition to the principal amount borrowed. It is usually referred to in terms of an annual rate. Since the purchasing power of the dollar may change between the time the money is borrowed and the time it is paid back with interest, the money rate of interest reveals little about the *real* burden of borrowing or the payoff from lending.

The **real rate of interest** reflects the real burden to borrowers and the payoff to lenders. The real rate of interest is simply the money rate of interest adjusted for inflation. The real rate of interest is the value of interest in terms of its real purchasing power.

The real interest rate may be computed for the past or the future. Looking back, a borrower could figure out that the real interest rate on a loan was only 2 percent if the loan was taken out at 15 percent a year ago and prices have meanwhile risen 13 percent. But choices made today will be based on what

Money Rate of Interest: The interest rate measured in current dollars. It is usually referred to merely as "the interest rate." When future inflation is anticipated, an inflationary premium will be incorporated into the nominal value of this rate.

Real Rate of Interest: The money rate of interest minus the inflationary premium. This rate reflects the real expected burden (or payoff) associated with the borrowing (or lending) of funds.

---

[8]Mark H. Willis, "Rational Expectations as a Counterrevolution," *The Public Interest* (special fifteenth anniversary issue, 1980).

one expects to happen in the future. The expected burden (and payoff) of persons entering into borrowing and lending agreements *today* will be determined by the money rate of interest and the expected rate of inflation. Suppose that an inflation rate of 10 percent is anticipated during the next 12 months. Under these circumstances, a 15 percent money interest rate is expected to impose only a 5 percent real interest burden on the borrower (or yield only a 5 percent real interest payoff to the lender). The difference between the money interest rate and the real interest rate is often referred to as an **inflationary premium.** In equation form, this could be stated as

Real interest rate = money interest rate − inflationary premium

The size of the inflationary premium, of course, varies directly with the expected rate of future inflation.

Since one's expectations about the future rate of inflation exert such an important impact on the attractiveness of money interest rates, we must incorporate this factor into our macroeconomic way of thinking. In Chapter 10 we argued that expansionary monetary policy would cause a reduction of interest rates. Thus far, we have ignored the importance of expectations. We will now amend our analysis, making allowance for changes in the expected rate of inflation.

Typically, expansionary monetary policy will *temporarily* reduce the money rate of interest because it makes potential loanable funds more readily available. Nevertheless, as is often the case in economics, the immediate impact may be a misleading indicator of what will happen in the long run. The monetary expansion will generate forces that may reverse the initial decline in money interest rates. First, the expansionary monetary policy will cause an increase in current spending. Aggregate demand and money income will expand. At higher levels of money income, the demand for loanable funds will rise, placing upward pressure on interest rates. Second, when an economy is operating

Inflationary Premium: A component of the money interest rate that reflects compensation to the lender for the expected decrease due to inflation in the purchasing power of the principal and interest during the course of the loan. It is equal to the expected rate of future inflation.

EXHIBIT 9   The money interest rate and inflation

The expectation of inflation will cause the demand for loanable funds to increase (shift from D_1 to D_2) and the supply of loanable funds to decrease (shift from S_1 to S_2). The result will be higher money interest rates.

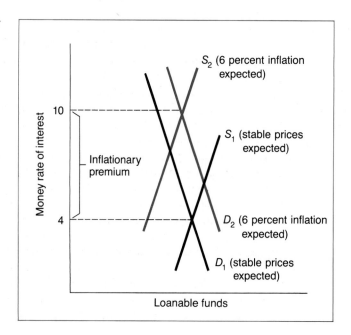

EXHIBIT 10 The money supply, inflation, and interest rates

Time Period	Annual Rate of Change in Money Stock[a]	Annual Rate of Change in Consumer Prices		Interest Rate (AAA Corporate Bond)	
		Initial Year	Terminal Year	Initial Year	Terminal Year
1950–1963	2.2	1.0	1.2	2.6	4.3
1964–1967	4.2	1.3	2.9	4.4	5.5
1968–1973	6.4	4.2	6.2	6.2	7.4
1974–1976	5.0	11.0	5.8	8.6	8.4
1977–1980	7.7	6.5	13.5	8.0	11.9

[a]The money supply data are for M-1.

at its full-employment output rate, monetary acceleration will lead to rising prices. If the expansionary monetary course is continued in order to keep interest rates low, inflation will result. As the inflation persists, both borrowers and lenders come to expect it.

As Exhibit 9 illustrates, the expectation of inflation will lead to higher *money* interest rates. The demand for loanable funds will rise as borrowers anticipate a 6 percent future inflation rate. Business decision makers, willing to pay a 4 percent interest rate when they expect stable prices, will also be willing to pay 10 percent when they expect prices to rise at an annual rate of 6 percent.

Simultaneously, the anticipation of inflation will cause the supply of loanable funds to decline. Lenders will tack a 6 percent inflationary premium onto the real interest rate, in order to compensate themselves for the reduction in the purchasing power of both the principal and the interest earned during the course of the loan. They may also shift their funds to real assets (for example, land or buildings) that are expected to increase in value with inflation.

Thus, when monetary expansion leads to an acceleration in the inflation rate, the added inflation will cause money interest rates to rise, not fall. Exhibit 10 illustrates the impact of monetary policy on the rates of inflation and interest in the United States for the 1950 to 1980 period. During the 1950 to 1963 period, the money supply grew at a moderate rate, 2.2 percent annually. Both the inflation rate and interest rate fluctuated within a very narrow band during this period. The average annual yield on corporate bonds (AAA) never exceeded 4.4 percent during the 14 years. Beginning in the mid-1960s, monetary policy became more expansionary. The annual growth rate of the money supply rose to 4.2 percent during 1964 to 1967. The monetary acceleration was accompanied by increases in the inflation rate, to 2.9 percent annually, and in the interest rate, to 5.5 percent. The trend continued during 1968 to 1973. More rapid monetary growth led to still higher rates of both inflation and interest. The monetary acceleration was reversed during 1974 to 1976. A decline in both the rate of inflation and the rate of interest accompanied the move toward a more restrictive monetary policy. Beginning in 1977, the monetary authorities again reversed their course. The money supply grew at an annual rate of 7.7 percent for 1977 to 1980. A sharply higher inflation rate and rising interest rates accompanied the monetary acceleration during this period. Just as the incorporation of expectations into our analysis indicates, when monetary expansion leads to inflation, it will also result in rising money rates of interest.

The importance of monetary policy to the rates of inflation and interest can be observed worldwide. The highest interest rates in the world are found in countries like Chile, Brazil, and Argentina, where the supply of money has often expanded at annual rates in excess of 30 percent. Low interest rates will be found in countries like Switzerland (or the United States during the 1950s and 1960s), where monetary expansion is moderate, 3 to 4 percent annually.

How quickly will financial markets respond to a change in the direction of monetary policy? The adaptive expectations hypothesis implies that interest rates will lag behind both the monetary acceleration and the inflation rate. In the 1970s, as the inflation rate accelerated, interest rates did appear to lag behind. Thus, looking backward, the real rate of interest was actually negative throughout much of the 1970s.

The rational expectations hypothesis implies that people will adjust rapidly, as soon as they perceive a change in policy direction. There is some recent evidence indicating individuals are beginning to react more promptly to changes in monetary policy. For example, during the six-month period from May to November 1980, there was a rapid acceleration in monetary growth from approximately 6 percent to a 16 percent annual rate. Financial markets, anticipating an acceleration in the inflation rate, responded quickly. The prime interest rate, the rate banks charge their best customers, soared from 11 percent in July 1980 to 21.5 percent in December 1980. In this instance, the temporary period of lower interest rates was quite short. The sharply higher rates lagged behind the monetary acceleration by only a few months, just as would be implied by the rational expectations hypothesis.

PULLING IT ALL TOGETHER

For 30 years following the Keynesian revolution, most economists thought economic conditions would be relatively stable if macropolicy injected demand stimulus into the system during a recession and exercised demand restraint during an inflationary boom. Now expectations theories, public choice analysis, and recent history indicate that stabilization policy is far more complex.

Our knowledge of exactly how expectations are determined and when and why they change is imprecise. Nonetheless, economic theory indicates they are highly important. Incorporation of expectations into our model points to the limitations of macropolicy. To the extent that people eventually adjust to demand-stimulus policies, persistent expansionary macropolicy may generate inflation without *permanently* reducing unemployment below its normal, long-run rate. Similarly, a shift to a more restrictive policy in order to combat inflation is most likely to cause output to slow and unemployment to rise, at least *temporarily,* to abnormally high rates. There are no easy solutions. Finding ways to accelerate the rate of economic growth and promote a high rate of employment is difficult. Once again, economics might be called the dismal science. The debate between the proponents of adaptive and rational expectations does not greatly alter our understanding of macropolicy's limitations, although it does have important implications for the timing and pattern of the adjustment process. And public choice theory has shown that we can expect discretionary macropolicy to have an inflationary bias and to be used as much for political purposes as for economic stabilization.

The bottom line of our analysis is that steering a stable course is substantially more difficult than was envisioned at the beginning of the 1970s. Recognition that there are limits on what can be accomplished with macro-policy does *not* necessarily mean instability and a high rate of unemployment will persist in the future. It does imply, however, that we must change the focus of our search for solutions. We will look at some possibilities for new directions in the final sections of this chapter.

NEW DIRECTIONS IN MACROECONOMIC POLICY

The ideas that will influence economic policy in the 1980s and beyond will be very different from the dominant ideas of the past 35 years.[9]

The approach of economists to macroeconomic problems has changed dramatically during the last decade. The 1970s, like the 1930s, are sure to exert a lasting imprint upon macroeconomics. We have already integrated many of the recent developments into our macroeconomic way of thinking. In the closing sections of this chapter we will summarize the major problems that plague the U.S. economy and consider policy alternatives to deal with these problems. As macroeconomists have become increasingly aware of the limitations of monetary and fiscal policies, their interest in the microstructure of our economy has grown. For the first time since the Keynesian revolution, the development of a microeconomic approach to traditional macroeconomic issues is attracting widespread interest among economists. We will discuss several microeconomic policy suggestions to promote economic growth, high employment, and stable prices.

The Troubled U.S. Economy

As the 1970s began, economists were optimistic about our ability to follow policies that would generate rapid growth, high employment, and economic stability. Clearly, the subsequent economic record fell far short of the optimistic expectations. In 1981, five major problems existed in the U.S. economy.

The Inflation Rate. Exhibit 11 illustrates the inflation rate for the 1960 to 1983 period as measured by the consumer price index. Beginning from an inflation rate of under 2 percent in the early 1960s, the rate rose to 6 percent in 1969. After receding to approximately 3 percent in 1971–1972, the inflation rate jumped all the way to 12.2 percent during the inflationary recession of 1974–1975. By 1976, the rate had again declined to 4.8 percent. However, it began to climb again in 1977, reaching 13.3 percent in 1979 and 12.4 percent in 1980.

Sluggish Economic Growth. In addition to the inflation problem, the decade of the 1970s was marred by sluggish economic growth. Measured by real GNP, the performance of the U.S. economy during the 1970s was the worst of any decade since the 1930s. Exhibit 12 presents a graphic illustration of the growth rate problem. During the 25 years following World War II, real GNP per capita

---

[9]Martin Feldstein, "The Retreat from Keynesian Economics," *The Public Interest* (Summer 1981), p. 93.

EXHIBIT 11   The rising inflation rate, 1960–1983

This graph shows the December-to-December change in the consumer price index for all urban consumers. Shaded areas indicate periods of recession. The inflation rate has been spiraling upward since the mid-1960s.

U.S. Department of Labor.

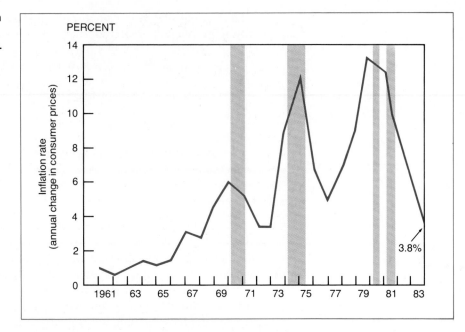

in the United States expanded at an annual rate of 2.3 percent. At a growth rate like this, per capita GNP doubles approximately every generation. Thus, each successive generation is expected to be about twice as wealthy as the preceding generation. During the 1973 to 1980 period, this long-term growth rate fell by approximately a third, to only 1.5 percent. At this slower growth rate, nearly two generations are required for real per capita income to double.

EXHIBIT 12   The declining growth rate of real GNP

During the 1970s the growth rates of real GNP per capita and per employee fell.

U.S. Department of Commerce.

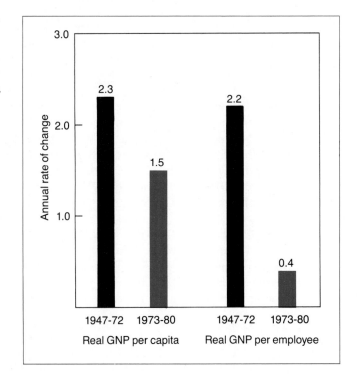

One can build a strong case that even the sluggish growth rate of per capita GNP *understates* the economic decline. As the "baby boom" generation, born following World War II, entered the work force during the 1970s, employment grew rapidly. As a result, the annual growth rate of real GNP *per employee* during 1973 to 1980 fell to only 0.4 percent, down from 2.2 percent during 1947 to 1972.

Not only was the U.S. growth rate poor by historical standards, but it was also poor compared to other major industrial nations. As Exhibit 13 illustrates, the United States and the United Kingdom rank at the bottom among Western economies. The growth rate of real GNP for Japan, France, West Germany, and Canada surpassed that of the United States during the 1970 to 1980 period. Only the United Kingdom ranked below the United States. When one focuses on the growth of output per worker, the picture is even bleaker. Japan, West Germany, and France experienced a growth rate of real GNP per employee of 3 percent or more during 1970 to 1980; the United States lagged far behind, at a rate of only 0.7 percent. Even the growth rate per employed worker of the United Kingdom exceeded that of the United States.

Low Saving and Investment Rates. Saving is important because it provides the funds with which to finance investment. If people do not save, capital investment projects cannot be carried out, and capital formation is an important determinant of economic growth. There are two reasons why a low investment rate will tend to retard economic growth. First, when capital investment expenditures are low, the plant capacity and modern machinery that allow greater output per labor hour will not be available for workers in the future. Without expanding output (supply) per labor hour, real wage rates will come to a standstill. Second, a low rate of investment means that the capital stock of a nation will only be able to incorporate new technological breakthroughs very slowly. Thus, when new, improved methods of producing goods are discovered, it takes a long time for them to be widely adopted by low-investment nations. The result: a slower growth of real output and income for the low-investment nations.

Many economists believe the sluggishness of the U.S. economy during the 1970s was largely the result of our failure to allocate a larger share of our aggregate income to saving, investment, and technological development. As Exhibit 14 illustrates, the saving and investment rates of the United States lag well behind other major industrial nations. During the 1970s, the saving rate

EXHIBIT 13 The growth rates of real GNP and GNP per employee for selected countries, 1970–1980.

Country	Growth Rate of Real GNP, 1970–1980	Growth Rate of Real GNP per Employed Worker, 1970–1980
Japan	5.0	4.2
West Germany	2.8	3.1
France	3.9	3.5
Canada	3.9	1.6
United Kingdom	2.2	2.0
United States	2.5	0.7

Derived from *International Economic Conditions: Annual Data 1961–1980*, Federal Reserve Bank of St. Louis (released June 1981), and *Statistical Abstract of the United States—1980*, Table 1589.

EXHIBIT 14 The lagging saving and investment rates of the United States

United Nations, *Monthly Bulletin of Statistics* (various issues, 1970–1979).

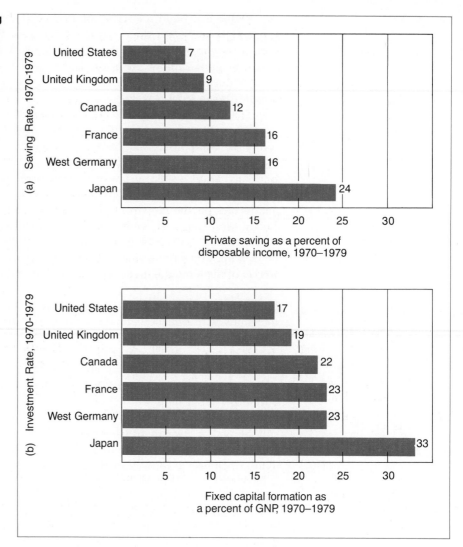

of the United States was less than one-third that of Japan; it was less than one-half the rates of France and West Germany. The low saving rates restricted the availability of funds for capital formation. The capital formation rate of the United States was also well below the rates of Canada, France, West Germany, and Japan (Exhibit 14b). Only the United Kingdom had saving and investment rates roughly similar to those of the United States. Predictably, the growth of GNP in the United Kingdom, like that of the United States, also lagged well behind that of the "high-investment" major Western economies (see Exhibit 13).

High and Unstable Money Interest Rates. From 1950 through 1965, the interest rate on corporate (AAA) bonds fluctuated within a narrow range—between 2.86 percent and 4.49 percent. In sharp contrast, interest rates have been both high and extremely volatile in recent years. In 1974, short-term money interest rates soared to 12 percent, only to fall back to 6 percent less than 12 months later. In 1980, short-term rates rose to the 15 to 17 percent range in February, plummeted to near 8 percent in July, and jumped back to 18 percent at the year's end. Things were not much better in 1981; short-term rates fluctuated between 12 percent and 21.5 percent throughout the year. Such wide interest-rate fluctuations make business investments very risky and long-range financial planning virtually impossible.

Continual Large Deficits. As we previously discussed, budget deficits, *as a percent of GNP,* rose sharply during the 1970s. During the 1975 to 1981 period, the federal deficit averaged 2.4 percent of GNP, up from 0.2 percent of GNP during the 1960s. Prior to the 1970s, large peacetime deficits had been experienced for a year or two during an economic recession. However, the economy was not beset by *continual* large deficits (relative to GNP) until the mid-1970s.

Large deficits pose two major problems. First, they place upward pressure on interest rates because of the strong government demand for loanable funds. Second, as the national debt increases, the interest payments to finance the debt constantly go up.

By 1981, the interest payments on the debt had risen to 2.5 percent of GNP, up from 1.5 percent throughout most of the 1950 to 1975 period. Obviously, the rising interest payments require the government either to (a) raise tax rates or (b) cut expenditures in other areas.

A MICROECONOMIC APPROACH TO MACROECONOMIC PROBLEMS

The 1930s taught us that deficient demand can produce economic recession and high unemployment. The 1970s proved that there can be other causes of sluggish growth and high unemployment. As we search for answers to the economic problems of the 1980s, it is clear that microeconomics will play a far greater role in the shaping of macroeconomic policy than has been true in the past. Economists of all persuasions—Keynesians, monetarists, supply siders, and various hybrids—are developing an increasing appreciation of the importance of the microstructure underlying aggregate markets.

What are the ingredients of this new microapproach to traditional macroeconomic policy matters? First, much closer attention is being paid to incentives and their importance as determinants of unemployment, investment, long-term growth, and inflation. Changes in relative prices do matter. If rapid growth and price stability cannot be attained with macropolicy, perhaps policies that alter the incentive to save, invest, work, and produce can improve the picture.

Second, the new microapproach analyzes changes in the components of the economy more carefully. Changes in the composition of the labor force, the structure of industry, or the functions of government may influence the rates of saving, investment, and economic growth. In the past, the importance of the microcomponents of aggregate markets have often been overlooked.

Third, the new microapproach stresses the importance of the long run. Policy prescriptions that exert positive short-run effects sometimes have harmful side effects in the long run. Since micropolicy prescriptions usually affect the economy by changing relative prices, decision makers must be given time to adjust to the new incentive structure. Clearly, the microapproach is a long-run strategy, not a quick fix.

The microapproach to the macroeconomic problems of the 1980s yields interesting insights and suggests several policy alternatives. We will proceed to take a closer look at some of the implications of this approach.

A Comparison of Unemployment in the 1930s and 1980s

The unemployment problem of the 1980s differs from that of the 1930s. When the unemployment rate soared to nearly 25 percent in 1933, most of those counted among the unemployed were adult men who had lost their jobs. There were few two-earner families. Unemployment compensation and layoff benefits were virtually nonexistent. There were no food stamp or welfare programs to assist unemployed workers.

The unemployment of the post-World War II period, particularly that of the last decade, was markedly different. In the late 1970s nearly half of the unemployed workers were under age 25. Approximately one in four was a teen-ager.[10] Another substantial share of the unemployed were members of families with other employed earners. Unemployment compensation and various assistance programs were in place to cushion the effects of unemployment, particularly for job losers. The sluggish growth and high unemployment rate of the 1980s differ considerably from the conditions in the 1930s. A different type of policy approach is required for the 1980s.

Solving the Investment–Saving Problem

The current U.S. tax structure subsidizes borrowing and penalizes saving. Individuals are permitted to deduct interest costs from their taxable income. Thus borrowing, including borrowing for the purchase of consumer goods, is encouraged. In contrast, income allocated to savings will generally be taxed twice, once as regular income when it is earned, and once again when it earns interest. Even the inflation premium built into the interest rate is taxed as though it represented real income instead of a correction for inflation. This incentive structure—subsidizing borrowing and taxing saving—increases consumer demand for loanable funds while discouraging saving and investment.

This proconsumption and antisaving incentive structure is an outgrowth of the Keynesian view of saving. Influenced by the Great Depression, early Keynesians believed that excessive saving and deficient consumption demand were a constant threat to prosperity. The role of saving as a source of funds for capital formation was generally de-emphasized.

Given the current economic situation, excessive saving is not a problem. If the United States wants to accelerate its sagging growth rate, most economists believe that both saving and investment must be increased. In fact, one could argue that the official statistics actually understate the bleak picture of capital formation. The official statistics make no allowance for the impact of energy price increases on the productivity of the U.S. capital stock. The sharp jump in crude-oil prices during the last decade has rendered much of our capital stock economically obsolete long before it would normally have worn out.

How can economic policy encourage saving and capital formation? The microeconomic answer to this question is: Change relative prices in a manner that will make saving and investment more attractive relative to borrowing and current consumption. There are several policy options. For example, income derived from savings could be made wholly or partially exempt from taxation. Individuals might be permitted to deduct the *net additions* to the personal savings (at least up to some maximum amount) from their taxable income.[11] The

---

[10]In 1979, 48.7 percent of the total persons unemployed were between the ages of 16 and 24; 26 percent of the unemployed workers were teenagers.

[11]The recent tax legislation providing for favorable tax treatment of funds paid into Individual Retirement Accounts is a step in this direction.

deductibility of interest expenses, particularly interest incurred through the use of credit cards and borrowing for consumer purchases, might be eliminated. Such proposals would encourage individuals to supply additional funds to the loanable funds market and discourage them from borrowing to finance consumption expenditures. A lower *real* interest rate would result. This strategy, particularly if accompanied by a reduction in government borrowing, would encourage capital formation. Capital and business income might also be treated more favorably from a tax viewpoint. Corporate tax rates could be reduced. The government might rely more heavily on consumption taxes and reduce taxes on personal and business income. All of these actions would affect relative prices in a manner that would promote more saving, lower real interest rates, and higher rates of capital formation.

A low investment (and saving) rate is inconsistent with a rapid growth rate. If we want to grow faster—to enhance the productivity of our work force more rapidly—a high investment rate is essential. If the U.S. investment rate continues to sag, sluggish growth of productivity and real income will result.

The Macroeconomic Side Effects of Demographic Changes

The microapproach suggests that demographic changes can exert an important influence on saving, unemployment, and growth of real income. There is reason to believe that recent demographic changes exerted an influence on the performance of the U.S. economy during the 1970s. Similarly, analysis of the continuing changes in the age composition during the 1980s will enhance our understanding of what lies ahead.

Exhibit 15 points out the essentials of the demographic changes during the 1970s. There was a tremendous bulge in the 18-to-34 age grouping, in which new job seekers are concentrated and job switching in search of a career path is most common. Undoubtedly, this bulge increased the normal rate of unemployment during the 1970s. Workers in the under-35 age categories are inexperienced and relatively unproductive at this stage of their careers. Growth of real income per capita is retarded when these youthful workers comprise an increasing proportion of the total work force, as was true during the 1970s.

There is also reason to believe that demographic factors during the 1970s adversely affected the saving rate in the United States. In addition to the 18-to-34 age grouping, the number of people aged 65 and over also grew quite rapidly. There is good reason to expect that both of these age groupings have a low saving rate. Youthful individuals often borrow to establish their households, and save only a small percentage of their relatively low incomes. Similarly, the elderly generally dissave in order to meet their current living expenses. In contrast, the 35-to-54 age grouping, which generally saves a high proportion of current income, grew very slowly during the 1970s. These demographic trends contributed to the low saving rate in the United States during the 1970s.

By the end of the 1980s, the situation will differ considerably. As Exhibit 15 shows, there will actually be a decline in the number of people in the 15-to-24 age category and only a moderate expansion in the 25-to-34 age grouping. During the 1980s, the big bulge will be in the 35-to-44 category, where stable employment patterns are far more common. As this latter group acquires a substantial amount of job experience, their incomes will grow rapidly. Economic theory indicates that these demographic trends will both reduce the normal rate of unemployment and contribute to a more rapid growth of real income. In fact, given the sharp decline in the number of workers under age 25, the United

EXHIBIT 15 The changing age composition of the U.S. population, 1970–1980 and 1980–1990

Age	Percent Change in Population Grouping	
	1970–1980	1980–1990
Under 15	−13.8	10.6
15–17	3.4	−20.1
18–24	22.5	−14.6
25–34	45.4	13.5
35–44	11.3	42.4
45–54	−2.2	11.5
55–64	14.0	−1.9
Over 65	25.6	19.6

U.S. Bureau of the Census.

States may well experience a relative shortage of unskilled workers by the end of the 1980s. These changing demographic patterns will lead to an increase in demand for labor-saving capital equipment as producers seek to substitute capital for the increasingly scarce unskilled labor. Clearly, this will be a reversal of the trend present during the 1970s.

The demographic trends will also exert a positive impact on the saving rate during the 1980s. Fewer young people and more individuals in the middle-age categories should push the economy's saving rate upward.

In summary, based on life cycle patterns, there is good reason to expect that the maturing and more gradual growth of the U.S. labor force during the 1980s will reduce the normal rate of unemployment while exerting a positive impact on saving, investment, and the growth of real income.

Employment and Unemployment Compensation

The unemployment compensation system was designed to reduce the hardships of unemployment. As desirable as this program is from a humanitarian standpoint, it diminishes the opportunity cost of job search, leisure, nonproductive activities, and continued unemployment. The conflict between high benefit levels and low rates of unemployment should therefore not be surprising.

The current unemployment compensation system causes the rate of unemployment to rise for two reasons. First, it greatly reduces, and in some cases virtually eliminates, the personal cost of unemployment. The benefits in most states provide covered unemployed workers with *tax-free* payments of 50 to 60 percent of their *previous gross earnings*. Since these benefits are tax free for most workers,[12] they often replace 75 percent or more of the employee's *net* loss of income. Benefit levels in this range greatly reduce the employee's incentive to accept employment at lower wages or in other locations.

Second, unemployment compensation acts as a subsidy to employers who offer unstable or seasonal employment opportunities. Employees would be more reluctant to work for such employers (for example, northern contractors who generally lay off workers in the winter) were it not for the fact that these employees can supplement their earnings with unemployment compensation

---

[12]Persons with incomes in excess of $20,000 (25,000 if they are filing a joint return) must pay tax on 50 percent of their income derived from unemployment compensation. In addition, social security and state income taxes are not collected on this income.

benefits during layoffs. The system makes seasonal, temporary, and casual employment opportunities more attractive than would otherwise be the case. Excessive unemployment results, because employers (and employees) are encouraged to adopt production methods and work rules that rely extensively on temporary employees and supplementary layoff benefits.

There is little doubt that the current unemployment compensation system increases the normal rate of unemployment and thereby retards aggregate supply. Most researchers in the area believe that the long-run rate of unemployment is between 0.5 and 1.0 percent higher than it would be if the negative employment effects of the system could be eliminated. Since more than 80 percent of the work force is now covered by the program, compared to 56 percent in 1960, the impact of the system on the normal rate of unemployment has probably been increasing.

How can the unemployment compensation system be reformed without undercutting the original humanitarian objectives of the program? Several policy alternatives exist. After a specified period of time, three months, for example, unemployment compensation recipients might be required to accept available jobs (including public sector employment) that provide wage rates equal to their unemployment compensation benefits. Under current legislation, persons who refuse to accept suitable work are denied benefits. However, "suitable work" is usually defined as a job similar to the claimant's previous employment, in terms of pay rate, occupation, and work responsibilities. Thus, most claimants can draw benefits for up to 26 weeks (or 39 weeks in some cases) without accepting available jobs that differ from their previous positions.

In addition, the tax structure could be changed in a manner that would reduce the perverse incentive effects. Currently, except for a few high-income workers, unemployment compensation income is not taxed when it is received. If such income were taxed, two things would be accomplished. First, unemployed workers would have a greater incentive to accept available jobs, because income received from *both* earnings and unemployment compensation (not just the former) would now be taxable. Second, people with the same annual income would pay the same tax bill. The current system results in lower taxes as the proportion of income received from unemployment compensation increases. Only a perverse concept of equity could justify taxing an employed person more than an unemployed person with the same income.

Dealing with Youth Unemployment

Nearly one-half of all unemployed workers were under 25 years of age in the early 1980s. The teenage unemployment rate usually runs about 2.5 times the rate for adults. The unemployment problem among black teenagers is particularly acute. The unemployment rate of black teenagers rose to 35.8 percent in 1980, compared to an overall rate of 7.1 percent.

As we discussed previously, since youthful workers are still in the process of deciding what career they want to pursue and how much schooling they need or want, they shift back and forth between jobs and educational opportunities more often than their older counterparts. A higher rate of unemployment for youthful workers results. However, many economists believe that other factors also contribute to the enormous gap between the rates of unemployment for older and younger workers. The experience of other countries, notably West Germany and Britain, indicates that high youth unemployment rates can be avoided. Two specific proposals deserve mention.

1. Exemption from Minimum Wage Legislation. Many younger workers are searching for a path to a good job in the future. This is why so many choose formal education. However, training and skill-building experience can also provide the ticket to future success. Often these attributes are best learned on the job, but they are costly for an employer to provide. The minimum wage law often makes it infeasible for an employer to (a) provide training to inexperienced workers and (b) pay the legal minimum wage at the same time. Thus, there are few (temporarily) low-paying jobs offering a combination of informal (or formal) training and skill-building experience. While we subsidize formal education, this aspect of public policy clearly discriminates against on-the-job training.

2. Youth Work Scholarships. Martin Feldstein has suggested that we provide youthful workers, those under 25 years of age, for example, with a **youth work scholarship.** A wide variety of alternatives are possible. At one extreme, individuals could be provided with monthly subsidies, in addition to wage benefits from their employers as long as they are employed. Under this plan, it would be up to each worker to choose his or her most preferred combination of current wage and on-the-job training. A maximum duration—two years, for example—could be established for each scholarship. An additional reward for continual employment could be provided.

Another possibility would be to provide the scholarship only for jobs that involved approved training. Jobs that resulted in the development of craft, clerical, operative, and perhaps even managerial skill could be high-priority targets. The long-run goal would be to improve the quality of the labor force and the quality and quantity of output, so that real income could be increased without inflation.

Youth Work Scholarship: A proposed scholarship providing subsidies to younger workers who maintain jobs. Some scholarships would limit the subsidies to employment that offered on-the-job training.

PERSPECTIVES IN ECONOMICS
THE REAGAN TAX CUT AND WELFARE FOR THE RICH[13]

The 1981 tax legislation has often been criticized as "welfare for the rich." It is easy to understand why. Not only is the dollar amount of the tax reduction greater for those with higher incomes, but these people will also receive a larger percentage increase in their after-tax marginal earnings. For example, at the top of the income ladder, marginal tax rates are reduced from 70 percent to 50 percent. Thus, after the tax cut, high-income recipients in the top tax bracket are permitted to keep 50 cents of every *additional* dollar earned, compared to only 30 cents under prior legislation. Their after-tax income from an extra dollar of earning will increase by 66.7 percent as the result of the tax cut. Similarly, the marginal tax rate of a married couple with a joint *taxable* income of $60,000 to $85,600 will decline from 54 percent in 1980 to 42 percent in 1984. A couple in this tax bracket will be permitted to keep 58 cents of each *additional* dollar earned in 1984, compared to only 46 percent in 1980—an increase of 26 percent. In contrast, the marginal tax rate in the lowest income category will fall from 14 percent to 11 percent. Thus, the after-tax marginal income in the lowest tax bracket will increase from 86 percent to 89 percent, an increase of only 3 percent.

If *taxable* incomes remain unchanged, tax revenues will decline and high-income taxpayers will reap a disproportionately large "windfall" reduction in the size of their tax bill. Clearly, this is the way that the major news media and most citizens viewed the tax cut. However, the situation is far more complicated. There is good reason to believe that the layperson's view of the distributional aspects of the tax cut is at least misleading, if not incorrect.

The problem arises because of a failure to distinguish between changes in tax *rates* and changes in the *revenues.* Since high-income taxpayers experienced the largest increase in after-tax income *per additional dollar earned,* the incentive effects of the tax cut will be

[13]This piece is based on a larger study done by the authors, which was supported by The Center for Political Economy and Natural Resources at Montana State University. See James Gwartney and Richard Stroup, "Tax Cuts: Who Shoulders the Burden?" Federal Reserve Bank of Atlanta *Economic Review* (March 1982), pp. 19–27, for additional details on this topic.

greatest in this area. The lower rates will also reduce the profitability of tax shelters, inducing high-income taxpayers to allocate less of their income to this area. As a result, more of their income will be taxable. Predictably, *taxable* income in the upper brackets will grow more rapidly than in lower-income brackets. Therefore, lower tax *rates* will not result in a proportional decline in tax *revenues,* at least not in the high marginal tax brackets where the incentive effects of the tax cut will be largest.

The Kennedy–Johnson tax cut provides evidence in support of this view. The 1964 tax cut sliced the top marginal bracket from 91 percent to 70 percent, leading to a 233 percent increase (from 9 cents to 30 cents per additional dollar of earnings) in take-home pay from marginal income in this bracket. The bottom rate was cut from 20 percent to 14 percent. Therefore, after-tax income per dollar of additional earnings in the bottom bracket rose from 80 percent to 86 percent, an increase of only 7.5 percent. Thus, the Kennedy–Johnson tax cut, like the 1981 legislation, resulted in both larger dollar reductions

in tax liability and larger increases in after-tax earnings for high-income taxpayers.[14] However, as Exhibits 16 and 17 illustrate, this does not necessarily mean that the proportion of tax revenue collected from high-income recipients declined. Just as one would expect given the incentive effects, *taxable incomes* grew rapidly in the upper tax brackets after the tax cut. Exhibit 16 presents data on the growth of adjusted gross income (AGI) and tax revenues collected from tax returns with an AGI of $50,000 or more for the 1960 to 1966 period. The adjusted gross income derived from these high-income taxpayers grew at a 7 percent annual rate during the three years immediately prior to the tax cut. The picture was quite different for 1964 to 1966. During the three years following the rate reductions, the AGI (measured in constant 1963 dollars) derived

---

[14]This results because both the 1964 and 1981 tax reductions were approximately "across-the-board" tax cuts. Tax rates were cut by a similar *percentage* for all brackets. However, since the percentage reduction of high-income taxpayers is calculated from their higher marginal tax rate, it will be a larger *nominal* rate reduction.

from returns on incomes of $50,000 or more rose at an annual rate of 17.5 percent.

The growth rate of tax revenues derived from these taxpayers followed, of course, a similar pattern. For the 1961 to 1963 period, the real tax revenue collected from returns with an income of $50,000 or more rose at an annual rate of 6.1 percent. In the three years following the tax cut, tax revenues collected from these taxpayers grew at an annual rate of 14.1 percent. Even though the tax rates of these high-income taxpayers were cut sharply, the constant dollar growth rate of revenues collected in this category rose substantially as the result of the rapid growth of taxable income.

Exhibit 17 presents data on tax revenue before and after the 1964 tax cut according to percentile income groupings. For the bottom 50 percent of income earners, tax revenues (measured in 1963 dollars) declined from $5.01 billion in 1963 to $4.55 billion in 1965, a reduction of 9.2 percent. Clearly, there is no reason to think that this group is on the backward-bending portion of the Laffer

---

EXHIBIT 16   The growth rate of adjusted gross income and tax revenue for high-income returns

These data are for tax returns reporting incomes of $50,000 or more, prior to and subsequent to the 1964 tax cut. Data are measured in constant 1963 dollars. Note the rapid growth in both income and tax revenue collected from these high-income taxpayers following the 1964 tax cut.

Year	Adjusted Gross Income (Billions of Constant 1963 Dollars) Returns with AGI Greater than $50,000	Tax Revenue Collected (Billions of Constant 1963 Dollars) Returns with AGI Greater than $50,000
1960	11.99	4.54
1961	13.75	5.21
1962	13.62	5.04
1963	14.60	5.38
1964	17.67	6.08
1965	21.33	7.20
1966	23.65	7.97
Average Growth Rate (Percent)		
1961–1963 (before tax cut)	7.0	6.1
1964–1966 (after tax cut)	17.5	14.1

Internal Revenue Service, *Statistics of Income: Individual Income Tax Returns* (annual).

EXHIBIT 17 Tax revenue from various income groupings

The tax revenues are ranked according to adjusted gross income prior to and subsequent to the 1964 reduction in tax rates.

Percentile of All Returns (Ranked from Lowest to Highest Income)	Tax Revenues Collected from Group (in Billions of 1963 Dollars)[a]		Percent Change
	1963	1965	
Bottom 50 percent	$ 5.01	$ 4.55	−9.2
50th to 75th percentile	10.02	9.61	−4.1
75th to 95th percentile	16.00	15.41	−3.7
Top 5 percent	17.17	18.49	+7.7
Total	$48.20	$48.06	−0.3

[a]These estimates were derived by interpolation.

Internal Revenue Service, *Statistics of Income: Individual Income Tax Returns* (1963 and 1965).

curve.[15] Revenue collections from returns in the 50th to 75th percentile and in the 75th to 95th percentile also declined, albeit by a smaller percentage than for the lowest income grouping. In all three of these income categories, the negative impact of the rate reductions on tax revenues was dominant over the positive impact of income growth on tax revenues. Therefore, tax revenues collected in these income categories in 1965 were lower than was true for 1963.

The picture for the 5 percent of taxpayers with the highest incomes was quite different. The tax rates of these high-income taxpayers were reduced from the 30 to 91 percent range in 1963 to the 25 to 70 percent range in 1965. In this highest income category, *real* federal tax revenue collections from personal income rose from $17.17 billion in 1963 to $18.49 billion in 1965, a healthy increase of 7.7 percent. Tax revenues collected from these high-income taxpayers grew because the rapid expansion in their taxable income had more impact than the loss of tax revenue associated with the rate reductions. *The 1964 tax cut actually shifted the tax burden to-*

ward the rich, despite the fact that this group received larger *nominal* rate reductions than other groups. The top 5 percent of taxpayers paid 38.5 percent of the federal personal income tax in 1965, up from 35.6 percent in 1963.

Where are we on the Laffer curve? The correct answer will vary for different income brackets. For persons with low marginal tax rates, 10 percent for example, there is little reason to expect that a 20 percent rate reduction (from 10 percent to 8 percent) will have much impact on their incentive to earn and report additional taxable income. After all, at the margin, take-home pay will only increase from 90 percent to 92 percent in this bracket, not a very large increase. Under these conditions, there is every reason to expect that lower tax rates will lead to an approximately proportional reduction in tax revenues.

However, the implications of the same 20 percent reduction in *high* marginal tax rates are dramatically different. A 20 percent cut in a 70 percent marginal rate (to 56 percent), will increase the taxpayer's after-tax income per additional dollar earned from 30 cents to 44 cents, an increase of 47 percent. In this bracket, the incentive effects of the 20 percent reduction will be substantial.

Thus, there is reason to believe that the *taxable* income of individuals

in high marginal tax brackets will be far more sensitive to changes in marginal tax rates than the taxable income of those with lower marginal rates. A reduction in high marginal rates may result in only a small reduction in tax revenues. At very high rates, we may even see an increase in tax revenues, as the backward-bending Laffer curve implies. Therefore, even if the larger *nominal* rate reductions go to high-income (and therefore high-marginal-rate) taxpayers, it does not follow that they will carry a smaller share of the personal income tax burden. In fact, an analysis of the 1964 tax cut indicates that this is unlikely to be the case.

Discussion

1. Do you think the rich should pay a *higher percentage* of their income in taxes than do the poor? Why or why not?

2. Do you think that the marginal earnings of persons with high incomes should be taxed at rates of 50 percent or more? Why or why not?

3. If the highest marginal rates could be reduced 10 percent without any loss of tax revenue to the Treasury, would you favor the reduction? Why or why not?

---

[15]The backward-bending portion of the Laffer curve indicates that for tax rates above a certain level, an increase in tax rates leads to a *reduction* in tax revenues (see Chapter 5, pp. 93–96).

1 Prior to the 1970s, there was evidence to suggest that higher rates of inflation were associated with lower rates of unemployment. This relationship could be mapped out on a curve, known as the Phillips curve.

2 Expansionary macropolicy may be able to reduce *temporarily* the rate of unemployment, because decision makers are (a) unsure whether the increase in current demand is temporary or permanent, (b) unable to adjust previously negotiated long-term contracts *immediately,* and (c) misled into believing that the inflationary price and wage increases reflect a relative increase in demand for *their* product or service.

3 According to the adaptive expectations hypothesis, individuals base their expectations on the immediate past. The expectations in the short run lag behind actual events. In this view, if an inflationary course is pursued, the *short-run* trade-off of lower unemployment for an accelerated inflation rate holds true. However, individuals will *eventually* come to expect the higher inflation rate and alter their decisions accordingly. This will cause the rate of unemployment to return in the long run to its normal level.

4 The initial effects of macrodeceleration, according to the adaptive expectations hypothesis, will also be on output rather than on prices. The macrodeceleration will cause output to slow and the unemployment rate to rise temporarily above its normal, long-run rate. The primary impact of macrorestraint on prices may come later, perhaps several months after the rate of growth of output begins to slow.

5 In the long run, there is no evidence that inflationary policies can reduce the unemployment rate—that inflation can be "traded off" for unemployment. Thus, the long-run Phillips curve is vertical, or nearly vertical.

6 Collective choice theory indicates that strong political pressures exist that are likely to lead to a stop–go macropolicy with an inflationary bias. Such a policy will cause the annual inflation–unemployment points plotted on a Phillips curve diagram to rotate in a clockwise manner and spiral upward. The actual inflation–unemployment data imply that this is what happened during the post-1967 inflation.

7 According to the rational expectations hypothesis, people will (a) comprehend the impact of macropolicy changes on prices and employment and (b) adjust their choices accordingly and rapidly. For example, when confronting an expansionary macropolicy, lenders will demand higher interest rates, union representatives higher money wage rates, and business firms higher prices on long-term contractual sales. According to the rational expectations theory, these actions will cause the inflation rate to rise almost immediately while largely offsetting the employment and output effects of the expansionary policy.

8 Given rational expectations, the anticipated impact of a macropolicy change is unpredictable. Discretionary macropolicy is likely to be a major source of instability. The implication of this theory is that policy makers should seek to follow a consistent, stable course.

9 The critics of the rational expectations view argue that it is unrealistic to assume that people possess the knowledge necessary to respond consistently to changes in macropolicy. Thus, they believe decision making that is based on a simple rule of thumb (in the future, things will be very similar to what they have been in the recent past) is most common and more probable in the real world.

10 Expectations as to the future rate of inflation will influence money interest rates. During a time of inflation, money interest rates will include an inflationary premium. Although expansionary macropolicy may temporarily reduce the money rate of interest, if pursued persistently it will lead to inflation and high interest rates. The high money interest rates in the United States during the 1970s are consistent with this view.

11 Incorporation of expectations into our macroeconomic thinking indicates the limitations of macropolicy. To the extent that decision makers adjust to demand-stimulus policies, persistent expansionary macropolicy may lead to inflation without *permanently*

reducing the unemployment rate below its long-run, normal rate. Recognition of the limitations of macropolicy forces economists to search more diligently for new ways to deal with instability, inflation, and unemployment.

12 During the 1970s, the economy of the United States was plagued by a declining growth rate and an accelerating inflation rate. The growth rate of the U.S. economy was poor not only by historical standards but also in comparison to other industrial nations.

13 In recent years, there has been an upsurge in interest in microeconomic policy designed to deal with problems of sluggish economic growth, high unemployment, and inflation. The microapproach emphasizes (a) relative price effects, (b) the microstructure of the economy, and (c) long-run rather than short-run policy prescriptions.

14 Unemployment in the 1980s differs from that of the 1930s in several respects. In the 1930s, unemployment generally involved the loss of jobs by prime-age workers who were solely responsible for the income of their families. Unemployment compensation, layoff benefits, and welfare programs were generally unavailable to cushion the impact of unemployment. In contrast, in the early 1980s, nearly half of the unemployed workers were under age 25. Multi-earner families were much more common, and various types of income transfer programs were available to assist the unemployed.

15 If the United States wants to accelerate its sagging growth rate, most economists believe that a higher rate of capital formation will be necessary. Currently, the U.S. tax structure tends to subsidize borrowing and penalize saving. A reversal of this incentive structure would encourage saving, reduce current consumption, and help supply the funds necessary for an expansion in capital formation.

16 During the 1970s there was a rapid growth in the number of people under age 35 and over age 65. These demographic changes increased the normal rate of unemployment, retarded the growth of real income, and reduced the rate of saving. In contrast, during the 1980s, there will be a decline in the youthful (under age 25) segment of the population, while the 35-to-54 age group will expand rapidly. Other things constant, this will reduce the normal rate of unemployment, lead to a more rapid growth rate of income, and result in a higher rate of saving.

17 The unemployment compensation program was designed to minimize the hardship of unemployment. Unfortunately, the system also encourages unemployment, since it (a) induces employers to make more extensive use of temporary layoffs and (b) makes longer periods of unemployment (and job search) cheaper to workers relative to the acceptance of available employment opportunities. The system could be reformed so as to retain its original objective but minimize its adverse impact on the normal rate of employment.

18 Exemption of youthful workers from minimum wage legislation and the institution of youth work scholarships are two reforms that many economists believe would effectively combat the high rate of unemployment among youthful workers.

THE ECONOMIC WAY OF THINKING — DISCUSSION QUESTIONS

1 "In order to achieve the nonperfectionist's goal of high enough output to give us no more than 3 percent unemployment, the price index might have to rise by as much as 4 to 5 percent per year." (Paul Samuelson and Robert Solow, American Economic Association meetings, December 1959)

(a) Do you think that a rate of inflation of 4 or 5 percent would enable us to achieve the nonperfectionist's goal of 3 percent unemployment today? Why or why not?

(b) Would a rate of inflation of 15 or 20 percent enable us to achieve the goal? If so, could the 3 percent unemployment level be maintained? Why or why not?

2 State in your own words the adaptive expectations hypothesis. Explain why adaptive expectations imply that macroacceleration will only *temporarily* reduce the rate of unemployment.

3 Compare and contrast the rational expectations hypothesis with the adaptive expectations hypothesis. If expectations are formed "rationally" rather than "adaptively," will it be easier or more difficult to decelerate the inflation rate without causing an economic recession? Explain.

4 "The high rates of interest during the 1970s are reflective of the Fed's tight money policies. If the Fed would loosen monetary growth a little more, lower interest rates and more rapid economic growth would result." Indicate why you either agree or disagree with this view.

5 The analysis summarized by Exhibits 7 and 8 assumes adaptive expectations. How would the outcome differ if people adjusted quickly to changes in macropolicy, as the rational expectations hypothesis implies?

6 Outline the major economic problems that plagued the U.S. economy during the 1970s. How would each of the following explain these problems: (a) Keynesians, (b) monetarists, (c) supply-side economists, and (d) proponents of the rational expectations view? Are there substantial points of agreement among these alternative views? Explain.

7 The chairman of the Council of Economic Advisers has requested that you write a short paper on how we can permanently reduce the rate of unemployment. Be sure to make specific proposals. Indicate why your recommendations will work. Submit the paper to your instructor, and she or he will pass it along to the CEA.

8 The early part of this chapter outlined the economic conditions present when Ronald Reagan became president. How have conditions changed? Has his program effectively combated inflation, unemployment, instability, and high interest rates? What grade would you give the president's economic program?

9 "The economic events of the 1970s illustrate the failure of macroeconomic policy. If economists were as smart as they let on, we would have experienced neither the high rate of unemployment nor the business instability of the decade." Indicate why you either agree or disagree with this view.

10 How does the microeconomic approach to the problems of unemployment and economic growth differ from the traditional emphasis on monetary and fiscal policy? Is the microeconomic approach a substitute for traditional monetary and fiscal policy? Explain.

11 Why do you think that the economic growth rate of the United States has been so slow compared to that of other industrial nations? Should we be concerned about our sagging growth rate? Why or why not?

12 Why was the unemployment rate so high during the 1970s? Was the high unemployment rate indicative of a sluggish demand for labor? What do you think will happen to the unemployment rate in the late 1980s?

PART THREE

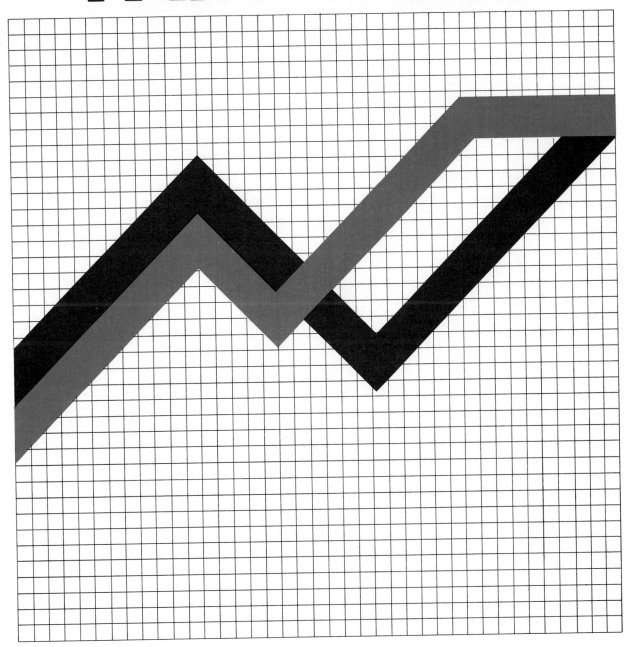

MICROECONOMICS

12

DEMAND AND CONSUMER CHOICE

Macroeconomics focuses on aggregate markets—the big picture. Aggregate outcomes are, of course, the result of many individual decisions. We cannot understand, or successfully influence, the big picture without a solid knowledge of how microeconomic decisions are made. In this section, we will break down the aggregate product market into microeconomic markets for specific products.

Microeconomics focuses on how changes in *relative* prices influence consumer decisions. As we stressed in Chapter 3, the price system guides individuals in their production and consumption decisions.[2] Prices coordinate the vast array of individual economic activities by signaling relative wants and needs and by motivating market participants to bring their own activities into harmony with those of others. Changes in one market affect conditions in others. In this chapter we take a closer look at (a) the interrelationships among markets and (b) the factors underlying the demand for specific products.

CHOICE AND INDIVIDUAL DEMAND

Exhibit 1 shows how consumers allocated their spending among alternative goods in 1950 and 1981. Why did consumers spend more on transportation than medical care, or more on alcoholic beverages than religious and welfare activities? Why have consumer expenditures on food declined (as a percentage of the total) while spending on housing has expanded? If we are to answer these questions, we will need to know something about the factors that influence the behavior of consumers.

---

[1] Henry Fielding, *Tom Jones,* Book VI, Chapter III.

[2] You may want to review Chapter 3 before beginning the study of microeconomics.

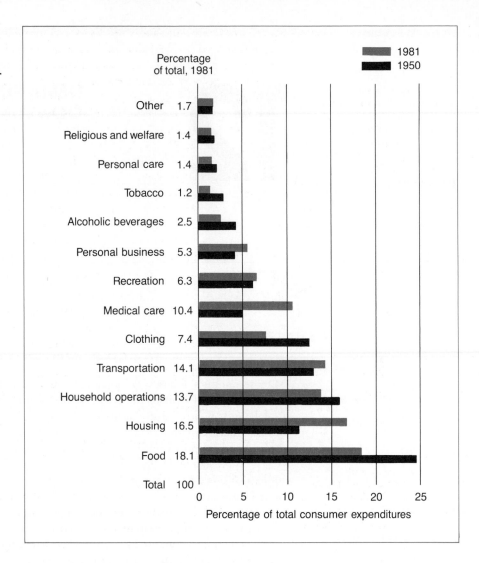

When analyzing the choices of consumers, economists usually make the following assumptions.

1. Limited Income Necessitates Choice.   Most of us are all too aware that our desire for goods far exceeds our limited income. People do not have enough resources to produce everything they would like. A limited income forces each of us to make choices. When one good or service is purchased, many others must be foregone.

2. Consumers Make Decisions Purposefully.   Consumption decisions are made in order to increase personal welfare. A foolish purchase means giving up something more worthwhile. The purpose or goal behind a consumer decision can usually be met in many different ways, so that careful consideration of alternatives is useful. Consumers generally choose the alternative that is expected to increase their personal welfare the most, relative to cost. They do not *consciously* choose a lesser-valued alternative when another of equal cost but projected greater benefit is available.

3. One Good Can Be Substituted for Another. Consumers have many goals, each with alternative means of satisfaction. No single good is so precious that some of it will not be given up in exchange for more of other goods. For example, consumers will give up some fried chicken in order to have more pizza, hamburgers, fish, ham sandwiches, or apple pie. Similarly, reading, watching movies and television, or playing cards can be substituted for playing football. How about our "need" for basic commodities such as water or energy? The "need" of a person for an item is closely related to its cost—what must be given up in order to obtain the item. Southern California residents "need" water from the north, but the individual resident, when faced with a high water cost, finds that cactus gardens can be substituted for lawn, a plumber's bill for a faucet drip, and flow constrictors for full-force showers. The need for water depends on its cost. People living in Montana, where household electricity costs about twice as much as in nearby Washington, use half as much electricity per household. Montanans reduce their "need" for electricity by substituting gas, fuel oil, insulation, and wool sweaters for it.

4. Consumers Must Make Decisions without Perfect Information, but Knowledge and Past Experience Will Help. No human being has perfect foresight. Napoleon did not anticipate Waterloo; Julius Caesar did not anticipate the actions of Brutus. Consumers will not always correctly anticipate the consequences of their choices.

However, consumer choices are not made in a vacuum. You have a pretty good idea of what to expect when you buy a cup of coffee, five gallons of gasoline, or lunch at your favorite diner. Why? Because you have learned from experience—your own and that of others. When you buy a product, your expectations may not be fulfilled precisely (for example, the coffee may be stronger than expected or the gasoline may make your car knock), but even these experiences will give you valuable information that can be used in making future decisions.

Law of Diminishing Marginal Utility: **A basic economic principle which states that as the consumption of a commodity increases, eventually the marginal utility derived from consuming more of the commodity (per unit of time) will decline. Marginal utility may decline even though total utility continues to increase, albeit at a reduced rate.**

5. The Law of Diminishing Marginal Utility Applies: As the Rate of Consumption Increases, the Utility Derived from Consuming Additional Units of a Good Will Decline. Utility is a term that economists use to describe the subjective personal benefits that result from an action. The **law of diminishing marginal utility** states that the **marginal** (or additional) **utility** derived from consuming successive units of a product will *eventually* decline as the rate of utilization increases. For example, the law implies that even though you might like ice cream, your marginal satisfaction from *additional* ice cream will eventually decline. Ice cream at lunchtime might be great. An additional helping for dinner might be even better. However, after you have had it for evening dessert and a midnight snack, ice cream for breakfast will begin to lose some of its attraction. The law of diminishing marginal utility will have set in, and thus the marginal utility derived from the consumption of additional units of ice cream will decline.

Marginal Utility: **The additional utility received by a person from the consumption of an additional unit of a good within a given time period.**

Marginal Utility and Consumer Choice

Consumer choices, like other decisions, are influenced by changes in benefits and costs. If a consumer wants to get the most out of her or his expenditures, how much of each good should be purchased? As more of a good is consumed per unit of time, the law of diminishing marginal utility states that the consumer's marginal benefit per unit of time will decline. A consumer will gain by purchasing more of a product as long as the benefit, or marginal utility (MU), derived from the consumption of an additional unit exceeds the costs of the unit (the expected marginal utility from other consumption alternatives that must now be given up).

Given a fixed income and specified prices for the commodities to be purchased, consumers will maximize their satisfaction (or total utility) by ensuring that the last dollar spent on each commodity purchased yields an equal degree of marginal utility. If consumers are to get the most for their money, the last dollar spent on product A must yield the same utility as the last dollar spent on product B (or any other product).[3] After all, if tickets for football games, for example, yielded less marginal utility *per dollar* than opera tickets did, the obvious thing for a consumer to do would to be cut back spending on football games and allocate more funds for opera tickets. If we assume that people really attempt to spend their money in a way that yields the greatest amount of satisfaction, the applicability of the consumer decision-making theory outlined above is difficult to question.

Price Changes and Consumption Decisions

Demand is the schedule of the amount of a product that consumers would be willing to purchase at alternative prices during a specific time period. The first law of demand states that the amount of a product purchased is inversely related to its price. Why? First, as the price of a product declines, the opportunity cost of consuming it will fall. The lower opportunity cost will induce consumers to buy more of it. However, as they increase their rate of consumption, what will happen to the marginal utility derived from the product? It will fall. Thus, as more of the product is consumed, eventually the benefits (marginal utility) derived from the consumption of still more units will again be less than the cost. Purposeful decision-makers will not choose such units. Thus, a price reduction will induce consumers to purchase more of a product, but the response will be limited because of the law of diminishing marginal utility. Economists refer to this tendency to substitute a *relatively* cheaper product for goods that are now more expensive as the **substitution effect.**

Substitution Effect: That part of an increase in amount consumed that is the result of a good being cheaper in relation to other goods because of a reduction in price.

Second, since the money income of consumers is constant, a reduction in the price of a product will increase their real income—the amount of goods and services that they are able to purchase. Typically, consumers will respond by purchasing more of the cheaper product (as well as other products) because they can now better afford to do so. This factor is referred to as the **income effect.**

Income Effect: That part of an increase in amount consumed that is the result of the consumer's real income (the consumption possibilities available to the consumer) being expanded by a reduction in the price of a good.

Of course, the substitution and income effects will generally cause

---

[3]Mathematically, this implies that the consumer's total utility is at a maximum when his limited income is spent on products such that

$$\frac{MU_a}{P_a} = \frac{MU_b}{P_b} = \cdots = \frac{MU_n}{P_n}$$

where MU represents the marginal utility derived from the last unit of a product, and P represents the price of the good. The subscripts a, b, . . . , n indicate the different products available to the consumer. In the continuous case, the above expression implies that the consumer will get the most for his or her money when the consumption of each product is increased only to the point where the marginal utility from one more unit of the good is equal to the marginal utility obtainable from the best alternative purchase that must now be foregone. For more advanced students, this proposition is developed in an alternative, more formal manner in the Addendum on indifference curves.

consumers to purchase less of a good if its price rises. Why will consumers curtail their consumption of a product that has risen in price? The opportunity cost of consuming the product has risen, making it a less attractive buy. As consumption is reduced, however, the consumer's marginal utility derived from the product will rise. If the price rise is not so great as to price the consumer out of the market completely, a sufficient fall in the rate of consumption will cause enough rise in the product's marginal utility that it will again equal its opportunity cost. With moderate increases in price, the consumer's reduction in consumption will be limited. We must also bear in mind that if we assume that the consumer's money income is constant, the price increase will reduce the individual's real income. A reduction in real income will tend to result in a reduction in the consumption of many goods, including the good that has increased in price.

Exhibit 2 illustrates the adjustment of consumers to a change in a price. In 1978–1979, gasoline prices rose rapidly in the United States. As demand theory would predict, consumers reduced their rate of consumption. As gasoline prices rose from 80 cents to $1.20, Joneses weekly consumption fell from 20 gallons to 18 gallons. Initially, consumers eliminated the least valued uses of gasoline. Less valuable trips were discontinued, shopping trips were combined with other business near shopping centers, and television watching was substituted for leisure driving. At the lower consumption level, the marginal utility of gasoline rose, bringing it into line with the higher price.

Still higher gasoline prices would have elicited an even greater reduction in consumption. The additional decline in consumption would have required consumers to forego still higher valued uses of gasoline. However, if the price had risen to $1.60, for example, the response would have again been limited, because the marginal utility of gasoline would have risen as consumption was reduced.

Time Cost and Consumer Choice

The monetary price of a good is not always a complete measure of its cost to the consumer. Consumption of most goods requires time as well as money. Time,

EXHIBIT 2 Gas prices, consumption, and marginal utility

Individuals will increase their rate of consumption of a product as long as MU exceeds its opportunity cost (principally the price of the good). Higher prices will cause individuals to consume less, but the reduction in consumption will be limited because the MU of the product will rise as consumption falls.

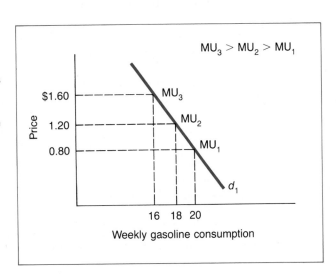

like money, is scarce to the consumer. A lower time cost, like a lower money price, will make a product more attractive to consumers.[4]

Some commodities are demanded primarily because of their ability to reduce the consumer's time cost. Consumers are often willing to pay higher money prices for such goods. The popularity of automatic dishwashers, electric razors, prepared foods, air travel, and taxi service is based on their low time cost in comparison with substitutes.

What is the cost of a college education? Tuition payments and the price of books comprise only a small component. The major cost of a college education is the time cost—approximately 4000 hours. If a student's time is valued at only $3 per hour, the time cost of a college education is $12,000!

Time costs, unlike money prices, differ among individuals. They are higher for persons with greater earning power. Other things being equal, high-wage consumers choose fewer time-intensive (and more time-saving) commodities than persons with a lower time cost. High-wage consumers are overrepresented among air and taxicab passengers but underrepresented among television watchers, chess players, and long-distance automobile travelers. Can you explain why? You should be able to if you understand that both money and time cost influence the choices of consumers.

Consumer Choice and Market Demand

The market demand schedule is the amount demanded by all the individuals in the market area at various prices. Since individual consumers purchase less at higher prices, the amount demanded in a market area is also inversely related to price.

Exhibit 3 illustrates the relationship between individual demand and market demand for a hypothetical two-person market. The individual demand curves for both Jones and Smith are shown. At 50 cents per gallon, both Jones and Smith consume 20 gallons of gasoline weekly. The amount demanded in the two-person market is 40 gallons. If the price rises to $1 per gallon, the amount demanded in the market will fall to 28 gallons, 16 demanded by Jones and 12 by Smith. The market demand is simply the horizontal sum of the individual demand curves.

Market demand reflects individual demand. Individuals buy less as price increases. Therefore, the total amount demanded in the market declines as price increases.

Consumer Surplus

Consumer Surplus: The difference between the maximum amount a consumer would be willing to pay for a unit of a good and the payment that is actually made.

The demand curve reveals how many units consumers will purchase at various prices. However, it also reveals consumers' evaluation of units of a good. The height of the demand curve indicates how much consumers value a particular unit. The difference between the amount that consumers would be willing to pay and the amount they actually pay for a good is called **consumer surplus.** As Exhibit 4 illustrates, it is measured by the area under the demand curve but above the market price level.

Previously, we indicated that voluntary exchange is advantageous to both

---

[4]For a technical treatment of the importance of time as a component of cost from the vantage point of the consumer, see Gary Becker, "A Theory of the Allocation of Time," *Economic Journal* (September 1965), pp. 493–517.

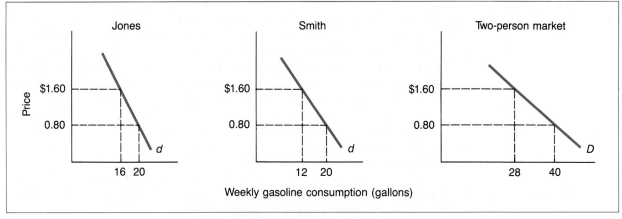

EXHIBIT 3 Individual and market demand curves

The market demand curve is merely the horizontal sum of the individual demand curves. The market demand curve will slope downward to the right just as the individual demand curves do.

buyer and seller. Consumer surplus is a measure of the gain that accrues to the buyer/consumer. Consumer surplus also reflects the law of diminishing marginal utility. Consumers will continue purchasing additional units of a good until the marginal utility is just equal to the market price. Up to that point, however, consumption of each unit will generate a surplus for the consumer, since the valuation of the unit generally exceeds the market price. In aggregate, the total value (utility) consumers place on the units purchased may be far greater than the consumers' total cost.

The size of the consumer surplus is determined by the market price. A reduction in the market price will increase the amount of consumer surplus; an increase in the market price will cause the surplus to decline.

EXHIBIT 4 Consumer surplus

As the shaded area indicates, the difference between the amount consumers would be willing to pay and the price they actually pay is called consumer surplus.

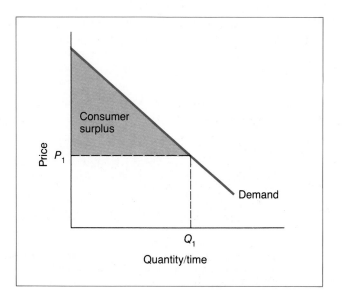

What Causes the Demand Curve to Shift?

The demand schedule isolates the impact of price on amount purchased, assuming other factors are held constant. What are these "other factors"? How do they influence demand?

Changes in the Income of Consumers Influence the Demand for a Product.[5] The demand for most products is positively related to income. As their income expands, consumers typically spend more on consumption. The demand for most products increases. Conversely, a reduction in consumer income usually causes the demand for a product to fall.

Changes in the Distribution of Income Influence the Demand for Specific Products. If more income were allocated to alcoholics and less to vegetarians, the demand for liquor would increase, whereas the demand for vegetables would fall. Consider another example. Suppose that a law were passed that taxed all inheritances over $50,000 at a 90 percent rate. If the law effectively reduced the income of sons and daughters of the wealthy, it would also reduce their demand for yachts, around-the-world cruises, diamonds, and perhaps even Harvard educations. If the revenues from the tax were redistributed to persons with incomes below $5000, the demand for hamburgers, used cars, moderately priced housing, and other commodities that low-income families purchase would increase relative to yachts, cruises, and diamonds.

The Prices of Closely Related Goods Influence the Demand for a Product. Related goods may be either substitutes or complements. When two products perform similar functions or fulfill similar needs, they are **substitutes**. There is a direct relationship between the price of a product and the demand for substitutes. For example, butter and margarine are substitutes. Higher butter prices will increase the demand for margarine as consumers substitute it for the more expensive butter. Similarly, higher coffee prices will increase the demand for such substitutes as cocoa and tea. A substitute relationship exists between beef and pork, pencils and pens, apples and oranges, and so forth.

Other closely related products are consumed jointly. Goods that "go together," so to speak, are called **complements.** For complements, there is an inverse relationship between the price of one and the demand for the other. For example, as the experiences of the 1970s illustrate quite well, higher gasoline prices cause the demand for large automobiles to decline. Gasoline and large automobiles are complementary. Similarly, lower prices for portable radios increase the demand for complementary batteries. Ham and eggs are complementary to each other; so are tents and camping equipment, and automatic dishwashers and electricity.

Changes in Consumer Preferences Influence Demand. Why do preferences change? People are always changing. New information might change their valuation of a good. How did consumers respond to new information linking cigarette smoking to cancer in the mid-1960s? They smoked fewer cigarettes. Annual per capita consumption, which had been increasing, fell more than 6

Substitutes: Products that are related such that an increase in the price of one will cause an increase in demand for the other (for example, butter and margarine, Chevrolets and Fords).

Complements: Products that are usually consumed jointly (for example, lamps and light bulbs). An increase in the price of one will cause the demand for the other to fall.

---

[5]Do not forget that a change in *quantity demanded* is a movement along a demand curve in response to a change in price, but a change in *demand* is a shift in the entire demand curve. Review Chapter 3 if you find this point confusing.

percent between 1965 and 1970. When consumers acquired information that cigarettes were also cancer sticks, many of them changed their preferences.

Changes in Population and Its Composition Influence the Demand for Products. The demand for products in a market area is directly related to the number of consumers. Changes in the composition of the population may also have an impact on demand. If a higher percentage of the population is between 16 and 21 years of age, the demand for movies, stereo equipment and records, sports cars, and college educations will be positively affected. An increase in the number of elderly people will positively affect the demand for medical care, retirement housing, and vacation travel.

Expectations Influence Demand. When consumers expect the future price of a product to rise (fall), their current demand for it will expand (decline). Buy now, before the price goes even higher! When the price of beef rose sharply in 1977–1978, how did shoppers respond? Initially, current sales increased; consumers hoarded the product because they expected its price to continue rising. Conversely, if consumers thought that the price of a product, automobiles, for example, would be 10 percent lower next year, would this influence current actions? Of course; many consumers would defer their purchase of an automobile until next year, so they would be able to buy at bargain prices.

When an economist constructs a demand schedule for a product, it is assumed that factors other than the price of the product are held constant. As Exhibit 5 shows, changes in any of these factors that influence consumer decisions will cause the entire demand curve to shift. The accompanying Thumbnail Sketch (a) points out that *quantity demanded* (but not demand) will change in response to a change in the price of a product and (b) summarizes the major factors that cause a change in *demand* (a shift of the entire curve).

THE ELASTICITY OF DEMAND

If the tuition charges at your school go up 50 percent next year, how many of your classmates will be back? If the price of salt doubles, how much less will you purchase? These are questions about price elasticity of demand.

EXHIBIT 5   Price is not all that matters

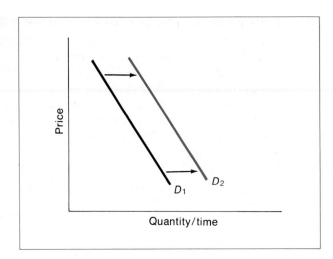

Price Elasticity of Demand: The percent change in the quantity of a product demanded divided by the percent change in its price. Price elasticity of demand indicates the degree of consumer response to variation in price.

Price elasticity of demand[6] is defined as:

$$\frac{\text{Percent change in quantity demanded}}{\text{percent change in price}}$$

This ratio is called the elasticity coefficient. Elasticity of demand refers to the flexibility of consumers' desire for a product—the degree of their responsiveness to a change in a product's price. If the amount of a good that consumers choose falls substantially in response to a small rise in price, the demand for the product is elastic. In contrast, if a substantial increase in price results in only a small reduction in quantity demanded, demand is said to be inelastic. The quantity demanded along an elastic demand curve is highly sensitive to a change in price. In contrast, an inelastic demand curve indicates inflexibility or little consumer response to variation in price.

The precise distinction between elastic and inelastic can be determined by the elasticity coefficient. When the elasticity coefficient is greater than 1 (ignoring the sign), demand is elastic. An elasticity coefficient of less than 1 means that demand is inelastic. "Unitary elasticity" is the term used to denote a price elasticity of 1. The sign of the elasticity coefficient will always be negative, since a change in price will cause the quantity demanded to change in the opposite direction.

---

[6]You might want to distinguish between (a) the elasticity at a point on the demand curve and (b) the *arc* elasticity *between* two points on the demand curve. The formula for point elasticity is:

$$\frac{\text{Change in quantity demanded}}{\text{Initial quantity demanded}} \div \frac{\text{change in price}}{\text{initial price}}$$

The formula for arc elasticity is:

$$[(q_0 - q_1)/\tfrac{1}{2}(q_0 + q_1)] \div [(P_0 - P_1)/\tfrac{1}{2}(P_0 + P_1)]$$

where the subscripts 0 and 1 refer to the respective prices and amounts demanded at two alternative points on a specific demand curve. The arc elasticity is really an average elasticity between the two points on the curve.

Graphic Representation of Demand Elasticity

Exhibit 6 presents demand curves of varying elasticity. A demand curve that is completely vertical is termed "perfectly inelastic." The addict's demand for heroin or the diabetic's demand for insulin might *approximate* perfect inelasticity over a wide range of prices, although no demand curve will be perfectly inelastic at all prices (Exhibit 6a).

The more inelastic the demand, the steeper the demand curve *over any specific price range*. Inspection of the demand for cigarettes (Exhibit 6b), which is highly inelastic, and the demand for portable television sets (Exhibit 6d), which is relatively elastic, indicates that the inelastic curve tends to be steeper. When demand elasticity is unitary, as Exhibit 6c illustrates, a demand curve that is convex to the origin will result. When a demand curve is completely horizontal, an economist would say that it is perfectly elastic. The demand for the wheat of a single wheat farmer, for example, would approximate perfect elasticity (Exhibit 6e).

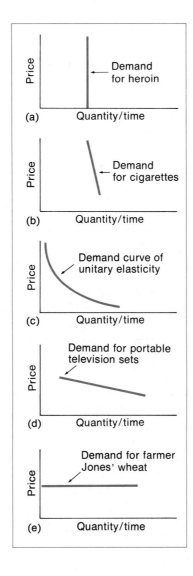

EXHIBIT 6 Demand elasticity

(a) *Perfectly inelastic*—Despite an increase in price, consumers still purchase the same amount. The price elasticity of an addict's demand for heroin or a diabetic's demand for insulin might be approximated by this curve.

(b) *Relatively inelastic*—A percent increase in price results in a smaller percent reduction in sales. The demand for cigarettes has been estimated to be highly inelastic.

(c) *Unitary elasticity*—The percent change in quantity demanded is equal to the percent change in price. A *curve* of decreasing slope results. Sales revenue (price times quantity sold) is constant.

(d) *Relatively elastic*—A percent increase in price leads to a larger percent reduction in purchases. Consumers substitute other products for the more expensive good.

(e) *Perfectly elastic*—Consumers will buy all of farmer Jones's wheat at the market price, but none will be sold above the market price.

Since elasticity is a relative concept, the elasticity of a straight-line demand curve will differ at each point along the line. Thus, as Exhibit 7 illustrates, the elasticity of a straight-line demand curve (one with a constant slope) will range from highly elastic to highly inelastic. For the example of Exhibit 7, when the price rises from $10 to $11, sales decline from 20 to 10. According to the arc elasticity formula, the price elasticity of demand is -7.0. Demand is very elastic in this region. In contrast, demand is quite inelastic in the $1 to $2 price range. As the price increases from $1 to $2, the amount demanded declines from 110 to 100. The arc elasticity of demand in this range is only -0.14; demand is highly inelastic.

Why do we bother with elasticity? Why not talk only about the slope of a demand curve? We use elasticities because they are independent of the units of measure. Whether we talk about dollars per gallon or cents per quart, the elasticities, given in percentages, remain the same. This is appropriate because people do not care what units of measurement are used; they care about what they receive for their money.

Determinants of Elasticity of Demand

Economists have estimated the price elasticity of demand for many products. Exhibit 8 presents some of these estimates. They vary a great deal. The demand for several products—salt, toothpicks, matches, light bulbs, and newspapers, for example—is highly inelastic. On the other hand, the demand for fresh tomatoes, Chevrolet automobiles, and fresh green peas is highly elastic. What factors explain this variation? Why is demand highly responsive to changes in price for some products but not for others?

EXHIBIT 7   The slope of a demand curve is not the same as the price elasticity

With this straight-line (constant-slope) demand curve, demand is more elastic in the high-price range. The formula for arc elasticity (see footnote 6) shows that when price rises from $1 to $2 and quantity falls from 110 to 100, demand is inelastic. A price rise of the same magnitude (but of a smaller percentage), from $10 to $11, leads to a decline in quantity of the same size (but of a larger percentage), so that elasticity is much greater. (Price elasticities are negative, but we typically ignore the sign and look only at the absolute value.)

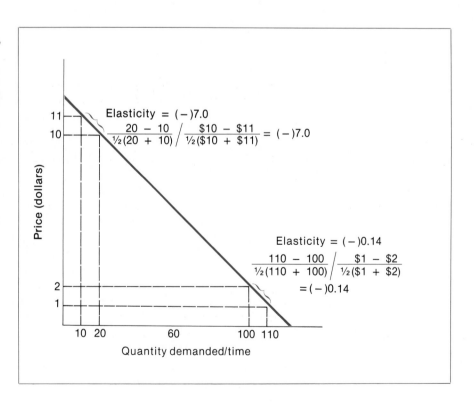

EXHIBIT 8 The estimated price elasticity of demand for selected products

Inelastic	
Salt	0.1
Matches	0.1
Toothpicks	0.1
Airline travel, short run	0.1
Gasoline, short run	0.2
Gasoline, long run	0.7
Residential natural gas, short run	0.1
Residential natural gas, long run	0.5
Coffee	0.25
Cigarettes	0.35
Legal services	0.5
Physician services	0.6
Taxi	0.4
Tires, short run	0.6
Tires, long run	0.4
Automobiles, long run	0.2
Approximate unitary elasticity	
Housing	0.9
Private education	1.1
China and tableware	1.1
Radio and television receivers	1.2
Elastic	
Fresh tomatoes	4.6
Foreign travel, long run	4.0
Airline travel, long run	2.4
Fresh green peas	2.8
Automobiles, short run	1.2–1.5
Chevrolet automobiles	4.0

Hendrik S. Houthakker and Lester D. Taylor, *Consumer Demand in the United States, 1929–1970* (Cambridge, Massachusetts: Harvard University Press, 1966); Douglas R. Bohi, *Analyzing Demand Behavior* (Baltimore: Johns Hopkins University Press, 1981); and U.S. Department of Agriculture.

The Availability of Substitutes.   This factor is the most important determinant of demand elasticity. When good substitutes for a product are available, a price rise simply induces consumers to switch to other products. Demand is elastic. For example, if the price of fountain pens rose, many consumers would switch to pencils, ballpoint pens, and felt-tip pens. If the price of Chevrolets increased, consumers would substitute Fords, Dodges, and Volkswagens.

When good substitutes are unavailable, the demand for a product tends to be inelastic. Medical services are an example. When we are sick, most of us find witch doctors, faith healers, palm readers, and cod-liver oil to be highly imperfect substitutes for a physician. Not surprisingly, the demand for physician services is inelastic.

The availability of substitutes increases as the product class becomes more specific, thus enhancing price elasticity. For example, as Exhibit 8 shows, the price elasticity of Chevrolets, a narrow product class, exceeds that of the broad class of automobiles in general.

The Share of Total Budget Expended on the Product. If the expenditures on a product are quite small relative to the consumer's budget, demand tends to be more inelastic. Compared to one's total budget, expenditures on some commodities are almost inconsequential. Matches, toothpicks, and salt are good examples. Most consumers spend only $1 or $2 per year on each of these items. A doubling of their price would exert little influence on the family budget. Therefore, even if the price of such a product were to rise sharply, consumers would still not find it in their interest to spend much time and effort looking for substitutes.

Time and Adjustment to a Price Change. It takes time for consumers to recognize and to respond fully to a change in the price of a product. Initially, all consumers may not be aware of the price change; more will become aware of it as the price change persists into the future. Consumer response to a price change can also be slow because rapid adjustment of individual consumption patterns is often costly.

Generally, the longer a price change persists, the greater the price elasticity of demand will be. The direct relationship between the elasticity coefficient of demand and the length of the time period allowed for consumer adjustment is often referred to as the second law of demand. According to this law, the elasticity of demand for a product is generally greater in the long run than in the short run.

The case of gasoline provides a vivid illustration of the second law of demand. When gasoline prices rose from 35 cents to 60 cents during 1973–1975, did consumers *immediately* stop driving their 350-horsepower, gas-guzzling automobiles? No. But when their full-sized cars wore out, did many consumers switch to compact cars giving higher gas mileage? Yes. In the short run, consumers responded to higher gas prices by reducing speeds, forming car pools, and driving less. Given more time, however, they substituted compact cars for full-sized models, reducing gasoline consumption even more. Thus, as Exhibit 8 shows, the long-run demand for gasoline (0.7) proved more elastic than the short-run demand (0.2).

Although the demand for most products will be more elastic in the long run than in the short run, there are a few exceptions, primarily durable consumer goods. Often such purchases can initially be "lengthened into the future" as prices rise. The old tires can be driven a few more miles or the old washing machine repaired one more time. Thus, higher prices result in a greater reduction in quantity demanded in the short run than is possible over an extended time period.

Elasticity and Total Expenditures

Price elasticity establishes the relationship between a change in price and the corresponding change in the total expenditures on the product. Let us examine how this relationship works. When demand is inelastic, the percent change in price exceeds the percent reduction in sales. The price effect dominates. Suppose that when the price of beef rises from $2 to $2.40 (a 20 percent increase), the quantity demanded, on average, by consumers falls from 100 pounds to 90 pounds (a 10 percent reduction) per year. Since the percent increase in price exceeds the percent reduction in quantity demanded, we know that demand is inelastic.[7] At the $2 price, the average person spends $200 annually on beef. When the price rises to $2.40, the average annual expenditures rise to $216. The higher beef prices cause total expenditures to increase because demand is inelastic.

When demand is elastic, on the other hand, the percent decline in quantity demanded will exceed the percent increase in price. The loss of sales will exert a greater influence on total expenditures than the rise in price. Therefore, total revenues will fall.

Exhibit 9 summarizes the relationship between changes in price and total expenditures for demand curves of varying elasticity. When demand is inelastic, a change in price will cause total expenditures to change in the same direction. If demand is elastic, price and total expenditures will change in opposite directions. For unitary elasticity, total expenditures will remain constant as price changes.

How Does Income Influence Demand?

Income Elasticity: The percent change in the quantity of a product demanded divided by the percent change in consumer income. It measures the responsiveness of the demand for a good to a change in income.

As income expands, the demand for most goods will increase. **Income elasticity** indicates the responsiveness of the demand for a product to a change in income. It is defined as:

$$\frac{\text{Percent change in quantity demanded}}{\text{percent change in income}}$$

As Exhibit 10 shows, the income elasticity coefficients for products vary, although they are normally positive. In general, goods that people regard as "necessities" will have a low income elasticity of demand. Therefore, it is understandable that items such as fuel, electricity, bread, tobacco, economy clothing, and potatoes have a low income elasticity. A few commodities, such as navy beans, low-quality meat cuts, and bus travel, have a negative income elasticity. Economists refer to goods with a negative income elasticity as **inferior goods.** As income expands, the demand for inferior goods will decline.

Inferior Goods: Goods for which the income elasticity is negative. Thus, an increase in consumer income causes the demand for such a good to decline.

Goods that consumers regard as "luxuries" generally have a high (greater than 1) income elasticity. For example, private education, new automobiles, recreational activities, expensive foods, swimming pools, and air travel are all income-elastic. Thus, as income increases, the demand for these products expands rapidly.

EXHIBIT 9   Demand elasticity, change in price, and change in total expenditures

Price Elasticity of Demand	Numerical Elasticity Coefficient[a]	The Impact of a Change in Price on Total Expenditures (and Sales Revenues)
Elastic	1 to ∞	Price and total expenditures change in opposite directions
Unitary	1	Total expenditures remain constant as price changes
Inelastic	0 to 1	Price and total expenditures change in the same direction

[a]The sign of the elasticity coefficient is negative.

[7]Calculate the elasticity coefficient as an exercise. Is it less than 1?

EXHIBIT 10   The estimated income elasticity of demand for selected products

Low income elasticity	
Fuel	0.38
Electricity	0.50
Food	0.51
Tobacco	0.64
Hospital care	0.69
High income elasticity	
Private education	2.46
New cars	2.45
Recreation and	
amusements	1.57
Alcohol	1.54

Hendrik S. Houthakker and Lester D. Taylor, *Consumer Demand in the United States, 1929–1970* (Cambridge, Massachusetts: Harvard University Press, 1966).

DETERMINANTS OF SPECIFIC PREFERENCES— WHY DO CONSUMERS BUY *THAT*?

Did you ever wonder why a friend spent hard-earned money on something that you would not have even if it were free? Tastes differ, and as we have already shown, they influence demand. What determines preferences? Why do people like one thing but not another? Economists have not been able to explain very much about how preferences are determined. The best strategy has generally been to take preferences as given, using price and other demand-related factors to explain and predict human behavior. Still, there are some observations about consumer preferences worth noting.

First, the preferences behind any one choice are frequently complex. The person looking for a house wants far more than just a shelter. An attractive setting, a convenient location, quality of public services, and a great many other factors will enter the housing decision. Each person may evaluate the same attribute differently. Living near a school may be a high priority for a family with children but a nuisance to a retired couple.

Second, the individual consumer's choice is not always independent of other consumers. Not wanting to be left out, a person might buy an item to "get on the bandwagon"—just because others are buying the same item. Or a good may have "snob appeal," setting owners apart from the crowd or elevating them into an exclusive group. Even relatively inexpensive items may have this appeal.[8]

A third factor influencing consumer choice is advertising. Advertisers would not spend tens of billions of dollars each year if they did not get results. But how does advertising affect consumers? Does it simply provide valuable information about product quality, price, and availability? Or does it use repetition and misleading information to manipulate consumers? Economists are not of one opinion. Let us take a closer look at this important issue.

---

[8]See Harvey Leibenstein, "Bandwagon, Snob, and Veblen Effects in the Theory of Consumer Demand," *Quarterly Journal of Economics* (May 1950), pp. 183–207, and R. Joseph Monsen and Anthony Downs, "Public Goods and Private Status," *Public Interest* (Spring 1971), pp. 64–76, for a more complete discussion of bandwagon and snob effects.

Prolific, innovative, controversial, arrogant, and unconventional are all words that have been used to describe Harvard's John Kenneth Galbraith. Professor Galbraith is a philosopher, poet, social critic, political activist, and economic adviser—all at the same time. He was ambassador to India during the Kennedy administration. He helped Lyndon Johnson plan the war on poverty before splitting with him over the Vietnam issue. Galbraith was one of George McGovern's earliest supporters and served as a McGovern delegate to the Democratic National Convention in 1972.

Galbraith has been a long-time critic of consumer theory in general and advertising in particular. In his best-seller, *The Affluent Society,* Galbraith charged, "The fact that wants can be synthesized by advertising, catalyzed by salesmanship, and shaped by discreet manipulations of the persuaders shows that they are not very urgent."[9]

In Galbraith's view, consumers in affluent Western societies are trapped on a merry-go-round. Artificial wants are created so business firms can sell more goods for profit. Whereas economists typically view production as the means of satisfying wants, Galbraith argues that production necessitates the creation of wants. Advertising and the creation of wants are simply the tools of producers in a modern economy.

The solution to the problem in Galbraith's view is a vast expansion in the role of government.[10] Galbraith favors permanent price controls for sectors of the economy dominated by large corporations, redistribution of income toward greater equality, and socialization of several major industries, such as steel, petroleum, and automobiles. Needless to say, he is not exactly the businessperson's friend. Reflecting on his experience as a price fixer with the Office of Price Administration during World War II, he once remarked, "I always thought that any businessman who left my office smiling indicated that I made some kind of mistake."[11]

For many years, Galbraith was either ignored or treated with scorn by most of his fellow economists. In the late 1960s, however, his undisputed popularity among the general populace began to rub off on his professional peers. In 1971, he served as president of the American Economic Association, an honor that many felt was long overdue.

Galbraith's critics charge that he pays no heed to scientific methods. Most economists make ample use of theory, testing, computers, and statistics. Galbraith will have none of it. He expects his listeners and readers to either have faith or do their own "number grubbing." Although his approach is unlikely to transform the methodology of the profession, he has already caused it to reconsider the foundations of economic analysis.

[9]John Kenneth Galbraith, *The Affluent Society* (Boston: Houghton Mifflin, 1958), p. 123.

[10]See J. K. Galbraith, "Conversations with an Inconvenient Economist," *Challenge* (September/October 1973), pp. 28–37, for a short statement of Galbraith's views on a broad range of issues.

[11]*San Francisco Examiner,* December 29, 1974.

Advertising—How Useful Is It?

What does advertising do for Americans? What were the results of the $54 billion spent on advertising in 1980? Advertising is often used as a sponsoring medium; it reduces the purchase price of newspapers, magazines, and, most obviously, television viewing. However, the consumer of the advertised products pays indirectly for these benefits. Thus, advertising cannot be defended solely on the basis of its sponsorship role.

Advertising does convey information about product price, quality, and availability. New firms or those with new products, new hours, new locations, or new services use advertising to keep consumers informed. Such advertising facilitates trade and increases efficiency. But what about those repetitious television commercials that offer little or no information? The critics charge that such advertising is wasteful, misleading, and manipulative. Let us look at each of these charges.

Is Advertising Wasteful? A great deal of media advertising seems simply to say "We are better" without providing supportive evidence. An advertiser may wish to take customers from a competitor or establish a brand name for a product. A multimillion-dollar media campaign by a soap, cigarette, or automobile manufacturer may be largely offset by a similar campaign waged by a competitor. The consumers of these products end up paying the costs of these battles for their attention and their dollars. However, we must remember that consumers are under no obligation to purchase advertised products. If advertising results in higher prices without providing compensating benefits, consumers can turn to cheaper, nonadvertised products.

A good brand name, even if it has been established by advertising, places additional responsibility on the seller. People value buying from sellers in whom they have confidence. Those who bought from anonymous moonshiners during Prohibition trusted mainly in the skill and integrity of the moonshiner to ensure that the beverages did not contain dangerous impurities. Those who buy Jack Daniels or Jim Beam whiskey today know that besides skill and integrity, distillers have an enormous sum of money tied up in their brands. A distiller would spend a large amount of money, if necessary, to avoid even one death from an impure batch of a brand-name product. Is a brand name, promoted by costly advertising, worth it to the customer? The customer must decide.

Is Advertising Misleading? Unfair and deceptive advertising—including false promises, whether spoken by a seller or packaged by an advertising agency—is illegal under the Federal Trade Commission Act. The fact that a publicly advertised false claim is easier to establish and prosecute than the same words spoken in private is an argument for freedom in advertising. But what about general, unsupported claims that a product is superior to the alternatives or that it will help one enjoy life more? Some believe that such noninformational advertising should be prohibited. They would establish a government agency to evaluate the "informativeness" of advertising. There are dangers in this approach. Someone would have to decide what was informative and what was not, or what was acceptable and what was not. If we could be assured that the special agency would be staffed by "regulatory saints" (borrowing a phrase from George Stigler), it would make sense to follow this course. Past experience, however, indicates that this would not be the case. Eventually, the regulatory agency would most likely be controlled by established business firms and advertising interests. Firms that played ball with the political bloc controlling the agency would be allowed to promote their products. Less powerful and less political rivals would be hassled. Costs would rise as a result of the paperwork created by compliance procedures. If consumers are misled by slick advertisers to part with their money without good reason, might they not also be misled by a slick media campaign to support politicians and regulatory policies that are not in their interest? Why should we expect consumers to make poor decisions when they make market choices but wise decisions when they act in the political (and regulatory) arena? Clearly, additional regulation is not a cure-all. Like freedom in advertising, it has some defects.

Does Advertising Manipulate the Preferences of Consumers? The demand for some products would surely be much smaller without advertising. Some people's preferences may, in fact, be shaped by advertising. However, in evaluating the manipulative effect of advertising, we must keep two things in mind. First, business decision-makers are likely to choose the simplest route to economic gain. Generally, it is easier for business firms to cater to the actual desires of consumers than attempt to reshape their preferences or persuade them to purchase an undesired product. Second, even if advertising does influence preferences, does it follow that this is bad? Economic theory cannot provide an answer. Economic theory does not rank people's desires; it does not assign different values to a person's desires before and after a change in preferences. Suppose that several students of classical music spend an evening at a disco and suddenly find that they like disco music more than Brahms. Were the students' tastes "more natural" or better before being shaped by the disco? Economists may have an opinion, but they have no analytical answer to that question.

LOOKING AHEAD

In this chapter we outlined the mechanism by which consumers' wants and tastes are communicated to producers. Consumer choices underlie the market demand curve. It is the market demand for a product that tells producers how strongly consumers desire each commodity relative to others. In the following chapter, we turn to costs of production, which arise because resources have alternative uses. In fact, the cost of producing a good tells the producer how badly the resources are desired in *other* areas. An understanding of these two topics—consumer demand and cost of production—is essential if we are to understand how markets allocate goods and resources.

CHAPTER LEARNING OBJECTIVES

1 The demand schedule indicates the amount of a good that consumers would be willing to buy at each potential price. The first law of demand states that the quantity of a product demanded is inversely related to its price. A reduction in the price of a product reduces the opportunity cost of consuming it. At the lower price, many consumers will substitute the now cheaper good for other products. In contrast, higher prices will induce consumers to buy less as they turn to substitutes that are now *relatively* cheaper.

2 The market demand curve reflects the demand of individuals. It is simply the horizontal sum of the demand curves of individuals in the market area.

3 In addition to price, the demand for a product is influenced by the (a) level of consumer income, (b) distribution of income among consumers, (c) price of related products (substitutes and complements), (d) preferences of consumers, (e) population in the market area, and (f) consumer expectations about the future price of the product. Changes in any of these six factors will cause the *demand* for the product to change (the entire curve to shift).

4 Consumers usually gain from the purchase of a good. The difference between the amount that consumers would be willing to pay for a good and the amount they actually pay is called consumer surplus. It is measured by the area under the demand curve but above the market price.

5 Time, like money, is scarce for consumers. Consumers consider both time and money costs when they make decisions. Other things constant, a reduction in the time cost of consuming a good will induce consumers to purchase more of the good.

6 Price elasticity reveals the responsiveness of the amount purchased to a change in price. When there are good substitutes available and the item forms a sizable component of the consumer's budget, its demand will tend to be more elastic. Typically, the price

elasticity of a product will increase as more time is allowed for consumers to adjust to the price change. This direct relationship between the size of the elasticity coefficient and the length of the adjustment time period is often referred to as the second law of demand.

7   Both functional and subjective factors influence the demand for a product. Some goods are chosen because they have "snob appeal." Goods may also have a "bandwagon appeal," fulfilling a consumer's desire to be fashionable. Observation suggests that goods are demanded for a variety of reasons.

8   The precise effect of advertising on consumer decisions is difficult to evaluate. The magnitude of advertising by profit-seeking business firms is strong evidence that it influences consumer decisions. Advertising often reduces the amount of time consumers must spend looking for a product and helps them make more informed choices. However, a sizable share of all advertising expenditures is for largely noninformational messages. Although this is a controversial area, it is clearly much easier to point out the shortcomings of advertising than to devise an alternative that would not have similar imperfections.

THE ECONOMIC WAY OF THINKING—DISCUSSION QUESTIONS

1   What impact did the substantially higher gasoline prices of the 1970s have on (a) the demand for big cars, (b) the demand for small cars, (c) the incentive to experiment and develop electric and other non-gas-powered cars, (d) the demand for gasoline (*Be careful*), and (e) the demand for Florida vacations?

2   "As the price of beef rises, the demand of consumers will begin to decline. Economists estimate that a 5 percent rise in beef prices will cause demand to decline by 1 percent." Indicate the two errors in this statement.

3   The following chart presents data on the price of fuel oil, the amount of it demanded, and the demand for insulation. (a) Calculate the price elasticity of demand for fuel oil as its price rises from 30 cents to 50 cents; from 50 cents to 70 cents. (b) Are fuel oil and insulation substitutes or complements? How can you tell from the figures alone?

	Fuel Oil	Insulation
Price per Gallon (Cents)	Quantity Demanded (Millions of Gallons)	Quantity Demanded (Millions of Tons)
30	100	30
50	90	35
70	60	40

4   What are the major factors that influence a product's price elasticity of demand? Explain why these factors are important.

5   Do you think that television advertising—as it is conducted by the automobile industry, for example—is wasteful? If so, what would you propose to do about it? Indicate why your proposal would be an improvement over the current situation.

6   In 1971, residential electricity in the state of Washington cost about 1 cent per kilowatt-hour. In nearby Montana, it cost about 2 cents. In Washington, the average household used about 1200 kilowatt-hours per month, whereas Montanans used about half that much per household. Do these data provide us with two points on the average household's demand curve for residential electricity in this region? Why or why not?

7   **What's Wrong with This Way of Thinking?**

"Economics is unable to explain the value of goods in a sensible manner. A quart of water is much cheaper than a quart of oil. Yet water is essential to both animal and plant life. Without it, we could not survive. How can oil be more valuable than water? Yet economics says that it is."

ADDENDUM

CONSUMER CHOICE AND INDIFFERENCE CURVES

In the text of this chapter, we used marginal utility analysis to develop the demand curve of an individual. In developing the theory of consumer choice, economists usually rely on a more formal technique, indifference curve analysis. Since this technique is widely used at a more advanced level, many instructors like to include it in their introductory course. In this addendum, we use indifference curve analysis to develop the theory of demand in a more formal—some would say more elegant—manner.

WHAT ARE INDIFFERENCE CURVES?

Indifference Curve: A curve, convex from the origin (representing the individual's current consumption), that separates the consumption bundles that are more preferred by an individual from those that are less preferred. The points *on* the curve represent combinations of goods that are equally preferred by the individual.

There are two elements in every choice: (a) preferences (the desirability of various goods) and (b) opportunities (the attainability of various goods). The **indifference curve** concept is useful for portraying a person's preferences. An indifference curve simply separates better (more preferred) bundles of goods from inferior (less preferred) bundles. It provides a diagrammatic picture of how an individual ranks alternative consumption bundles.

In Exhibit A-1, we assume that Robinson Crusoe is initially consuming 8 fish and 8 breadfruit per week (point *A*). This initial bundle provides him with a certain level of satisfaction (utility). However, he would be willing to trade this initial bundle for certain other consumption alternatives if the opportunity presented itself. Since he likes both fish and breadfruit, he would especially like to obtain bundles to the northeast of *A*, since they represent more of both goods. However, he would also be willing to give up some breadfruit if in return he received a compensatory amount of fish. Similarly, if the terms of trade were

EXHIBIT A-1 The indifference curve of Robinson Crusoe

The curve generated by connecting Crusoe's "I do not care" answers separates the combinations of fish and breadfruit that he prefers to the bundle *A* from those that he judges to be inferior to *A*. The *I* points map out an indifference curve.

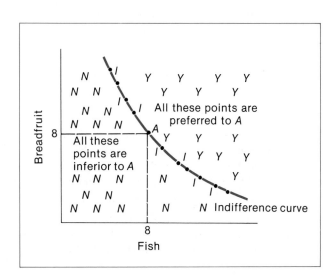

right, he would be willing to exchange fish for breadfruit. These trade-offs would occur *along* the indifference curve.

Starting from point A (8 fish and 8 breadfruit), we ask Crusoe if he is willing to trade that bundle for various other bundles. He answers "Yes" (Y), "No" (N), or "I do not care" (I). Exhibit A-1 illustrates the pattern of his response. Crusoe's "I do not care" answers indicate that the original bundle (point A) and each alternative indicated by an I are valued equally by Crusoe. These I points, when connected, form the indifference curve. This line separates the preferred bundles of fish and breadfruit from the less valued combinations. Note that such a curve may be entirely different for any two people. The preferences of different individuals vary widely.

We can establish a new indifference curve by starting from any point not on the original curve and following the same procedure. If we start with a point (a consumption bundle) to the northeast of the original indifference curve, all points on the new curve will have a higher level of satisfaction for Crusoe than any on the old curve. The new curve will probably have about the same shape as the original.

Characteristics of Indifference Curves

In developing consumer theory, economists assume that the preferences of consumers exhibit certain properties. These properties enable us to make statements about the general pattern of indifference curves. What are these properties, and what do they imply about the characteristics of indifference curves?

1. More Goods Are Preferable to Fewer Goods—Thus, Bundles on Indifference Curves Lying Farthest to the Northeast Are Always Preferred. Assuming the consumption of only two commodities, since *both* commodities are desired, the individual will always prefer to have more of at least one of the goods without loss of any of the other. This means that combinations in the northeast region of an indifference curve diagram will always be preferred to points in the southwest region.

2. Goods Are Substitutable—Therefore, Indifference Curves Slope Downward to the Right. As we indicated in the text of this chapter, individuals are willing to substitute one good for another. Crusoe will be willing to give up some breadfruit if he is compensated with enough fish. Stated another way, there will be some amount of additional fish such that Crusoe will stay on the same indifference curve, even though his consumption of breadfruit has declined. However, in order to remain on the same indifference curve, Crusoe must always acquire more of one good in order to compensate for the loss of the other. Thus, the indifference curve for goods will always slope downward to the right (run northwest to southeast).

3. The Valuation of a Good Declines As It Is Consumed More Intensively—Therefore, Indifference Curves Are Always Convex When Viewed from Below. The slope of the indifference curve represents the willingness of the individual to substitute one good for the other. Economists refer to the amount of one good that is just sufficient to compensate the consumer for the loss of a unit of the other good as the **marginal rate of substitution.** The marginal rate of substitution is equal to the slope of the indifference curve. Reflecting the principle of diminishing marginal utility, the marginal rate of substitution of a good will decline as the

Marginal Rate of Substitution: The change in the consumption level of one good that is just sufficient to offset a unit change in the consumption of another good without causing a shift to another indifference curve. At any point on an indifference curve, it will be equal to the slope of the curve at that point.

good is consumed more intensively relative to other goods. Suppose that Crusoe remains on the same indifference curve while continuing to expand his consumption of fish relative to breadfruit. As his consumption of fish increases (and his consumption of breadfruit declines), his valuation of fish relative to breadfruit will decline. It will take more and more units of fish to compensate for the loss of still another unit of breadfruit. The indifference curve will become flatter and flatter, reflecting the decline in the marginal rate of substitution of fish for breadfruit as Crusoe consumes more fish relative to breadfruit.

Of course, just the opposite will happen if Crusoe's consumption of breadfruit increases relative to that of fish—if he moves northwest along the same indifference curve. In this case, as breadfruit is consumed more intensively, Crusoe's valuation of breadfruit will decline relative to that of fish, and the marginal rate of substitution of fish for breadfruit will rise (the indifference curve will become steeper and steeper). Therefore, since the valuation of each good declines as it is consumed more intensively, indifference curves must be convex when viewed from the origin.

4. Indifference Curves Are Everywhere Dense. We can draw an indifference curve through any point on the diagram. This means simply that any two bundles of goods can be compared by the individual.

5. Indifference Curves Cannot Cross—If They Did, Rational Ordering Would Be Violated. If indifference curves crossed, our postulate that more goods are better than fewer goods would be violated. Exhibit A-2 illustrates this point. The crossing of the indifference curves implies that points Y and Z are equally preferred, since they are both on the same indifference curve as X. However, consumption bundle Y represents more of both fish and breadfruit than bundle Z, so Y must be preferred to Z. Whenever indifference curves cross, this type of internal inconsistency (irrational ranking) will arise. Thus, the indifference curves of an individual must not cross.

EXHIBIT A-2   Indifference curves cannot cross

If the indifference curves of an individual crossed, it would lead to the inconsistency pictured here. Points X and Y must be equally valued, since they are both on the same indifference curve (i_1). Similarly, points X and Z must be equally valued, since they are both on indifference curve i_2. If this is true, Y and Z must also be equally preferred, since they are both equally preferred to X. However, point Y represents more of both goods than Z, so Y has to be preferred to Z. When indifference curves cross, this type of internal inconsistency always arises.

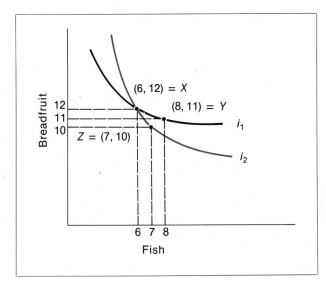

The Usefulness of Indifference Curves

Consumption Opportunity Constraint: **The constraint which separates the consumption bundles that are attainable from those that are unattainable. In a money income economy, it is usually called a budget constraint.**

Together with the opportunity constraint of the individual, indifference curves can be used to indicate the most preferred consumption alternatives available to an individual. The **consumption opportunity constraint** separates consumption bundles that are, in fact, attainable from those that are unattainable.

Assuming that Crusoe could produce only for himself, his consumption opportunity constraint would look like the production possibilities curves that we discussed in Chapter 2. What would happen if natives from another island visited Crusoe and offered to make exchanges with him? If a barter market existed that permitted Crusoe to exchange fish for breadfruit at a specified exchange rate, his options would resemble those of the market constraint illustrated by Exhibit A-3. First, let us consider the case in which Crusoe inhabits a barter economy where the current market exchange rate is 2 fish equal 1 breadfruit. Suppose that as a result of his expertise as a fisherman, Crusoe specializes in this activity and is able to bring 16 fish to the market per week. What consumption alternatives will be open to him? Since 2 fish can be bartered in the market for 1 breadfruit, Crusoe will be able to consume 16 fish, or 8 breadfruit, or any combination on the market constraint indicated by the line between these two points. For example, if he trades 2 of his 16 fish for 1 breadfruit, he will be able to consume a bundle consisting of 14 fish and 1 breadfruit. Assuming that the set of indifference curves of Exhibit A-3 outline Crusoe's preferences, he will choose to consume 8 fish and 4 breadfruit. Of course, it would be possible for Crusoe to choose many other combinations of breadfruit and fish, but none of the other attainable combinations would enable him to reach as high a level of satisfaction. Since he is able to bring only 16 fish to the market, it would be impossible for him to attain an indifference curve higher than i_2.

Crusoe's indifference curve and the market constraint curve will cross at the point at which his attainable level of satisfaction is maximized. At that point (8 fish and 4 breadfruit), the rate at which Crusoe is *willing* to exchange fish for breadfruit (as indicated by the slope of the indifference curve) will be just equal to the rate at which the market will *permit* him to exchange the two (the slope of the market constraint).[12] If the two slopes differ at a point, Crusoe will always be able to find an attainable combination that will permit him to reach a *higher* indifference curve. He will always move down the market constraint when it is flatter than his indifference curve, and up if the market constraint is steeper.[13]

---

[12]This actually is required only if the two goods are available in completely divisible amounts, not just as whole fish or whole breadfruit. For simplicity, we assume here that fractional availability is not a problem.

[13]Mathematically, the satisfaction of the consumer is maximized when the marginal rate of substitution of fish for breadfruit is equal to the price ratio. In utility terms, the marginal rate of substitution of fish for breadfruit is equal to the MU of fish divided by the MU of breadfruit. Therefore, the following expression is a condition for maximum consumer satisfaction:

$$\frac{MU_f}{MU_b} = \frac{P_f}{P_b}$$

This can be rewritten as follows:

$$\frac{MU_f}{P_f} = \frac{MU_b}{P_b}$$

Note that this is precisely the condition of consumer maximization that we indicated earlier in this chapter (see footnote 3).

Suppose that the set of indifference curves shown here
outline Crusoe's preferences.
The slope of the market (or
budget) constraint indicates
that 2 fish trade for 1 breadfruit
in this barter economy. If
Crusoe produces 16 fish per
week, he will trade 8 fish for 4
breadfruit in order to move to
the consumption bundle (8 fish
and 4 breadfruit) that maximizes his level of satisfaction.

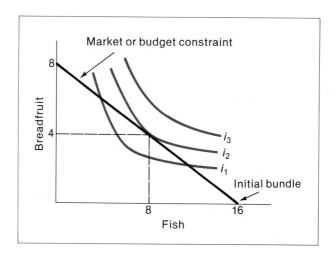

Budget Constraint: The constraint which separates the
bundles of goods that the
consumer can purchase from
those that cannot be pur-
chased, given a limited income
and the prices of products.

Suppose that Crusoe's income
is $16 per day, the price of fish
(P_f) is $1, and the price of
breadfruit (P_b) is $2. Thus,
Crusoe confronts exactly the
same price ratio and budget
constraint as in Exhibit A-3.
Assuming that his preferences
are unchanged, he will again
maximize his satisfaction by
choosing to consume 8 fish
and 4 breadfruit. What will
happen if the price of fish rises
to $2? Crusoe's consumption
opportunities will be reduced.
His budget constraint will turn
clockwise around point A,
reflecting the higher price of
fish. Crusoe's fish consumption
will decline to 5 units. (Note:
Since Crusoe's real income has
been reduced, his consumption
of breadfruit will also decline.)

CRUSOE IN A MONEY ECONOMY

As far as the condition for maximization of consumer satisfaction is concerned,
the movement from a barter economy to a money income economy changes
little. Exhibit A-4 illustrates this point. Initially, the price of fish is $1, and the
price of breadfruit $2. Therefore, the market permits one to exchange 2 fish for
1 breadfruit, just as was the case in Exhibit A-3. In Exhibit A-4, we assume that
Crusoe's money income is $16. At this level of income, he confronts the same
market constraint (we usually call it a **budget constraint** when we are dealing
with a money income economy) as for Exhibit A-3. Given the product prices and
his income, Crusoe can choose to consume 16 fish, or 8 breadfruit, or any
combination indicated by a line (the budget constraint) connecting these two
points. Given his preferences, Crusoe will again choose the combination 8 fish
and 4 breadfruit if he wishes to maximize his level of satisfaction. As was true

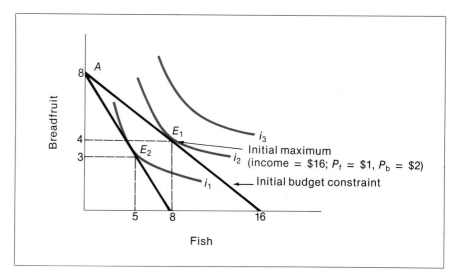

for the barter economy, when Crusoe maximizes his satisfaction (moves to the highest attainable indifference curve), the rate at which he is willing to exchange fish for breadfruit will just equal the rate at which the market will permit him to exchange the two goods. Stated in more technical terms, when his level of satisfaction is at a maximum, Crusoe's marginal rate of substitution of fish for breadfruit, as indicated by the slope of the indifference curve at E_1, will just equal the price ratio (P_f/P_b, which is also the slope of the budget constraint).

What will happen if the price of fish increases? Exhibit A-4 also answers this question. Since the price of breadfruit and Crusoe's money income are constant, a higher fish price will have two effects. First, it will make Crusoe poorer, even though his *money* income will be unchanged. His budget constraint will turn clockwise around point A, illustrating that his consumption options are now more limited—that is, his real income has declined. Second, the budget line will be steeper, indicating that a larger number of breadfruit must now be sacrificed in order to attain an additional unit of fish. It will no longer be possible for Crusoe to attain indifference curve i_2. The best he can do is indifference curve i_1, which he can attain by choosing the bundle 5 fish and 3 breadfruit.

Using the information supplied by Exhibit A-4, we can now locate two points on Crusoe's demand curve for fish. When the price of fish was $1, Crusoe chose 8 fish; when the price rose to $2, Crusoe reduced his consumption to 5 (see Exhibit A-5). Of course, other points on Crusoe's demand curve could also be located if we considered other prices for fish.

The demand curve of Exhibit A-5 is constructed on the assumption that the price of breadfruit remains $2 and that Crusoe's money income remains constant at $16. If either of these factors were to change, the entire demand curve of Exhibit A-5 would shift.

The indifference curve approach is a useful way to illustrate how a person with a fixed budget chooses between two goods. In the real world, of course, people have hundreds, or even thousands, of goods to choose from, and the doubling of only one price usually has only a small impact on a person's consumption and satisfaction possibilities. In our simplified example, the twofold increase in the price of fish makes Crusoe decidedly worse off, since he spends a large portion of his budget on the item.

EXHIBIT A-5 Crusoe's demand for fish

As Exhibit A-4 illustrates, when the price of fish is $1, Crusoe chooses 8 units. When the price of fish increases to $2, he reduces his consumption to 5 units. This gives us two points on Crusoe's demand curve for fish. Other points on the demand curve could be derived by confronting Crusoe with still other prices of fish. [Note: Crusoe's money income ($16) and the price of breadfruit ($2) are unchanged in this analysis.]

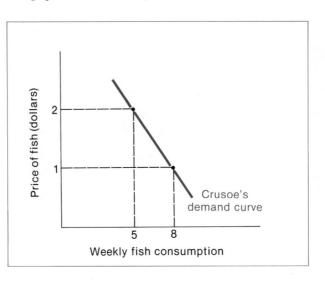

The Income and Substitution Effects

In the text, we indicated that when the price of a product rises, the amount consumed will be altered as a result of both an "income effect" and a "substitution effect." Indifference curve analysis can be used to separate these two effects. Exhibit A-6 is similar to Exhibit A-4. Both exhibits illustrate Crusoe's response to an increase in the price of fish from $1 to $2 when money income ($16) and the price of breadfruit ($2) are held constant. However, Exhibit A-6 breaks down his total response into the substitution effect and the income effect. The reduction in the consumption of fish solely because of the substitution (price) effect can be found by constructing a line tangent to Crusoe's original indifference curve (i_2), the slope of which is indicative of the higher price of fish. This line (the broken line of Exhibit A-6), which is parallel to Crusoe's actual budget constraint (the line containing point E_2), reflects the rise in the price of fish. Since the line is tangent to the original indifference curve i_2, Crusoe's real income is held constant. As this line indicates, Crusoe will reduce his consumption of fish from 8 to 7 strictly because fish are now relatively more expensive. This move from E_1 to F is a pure substitution effect.

However, real income has been reduced. As a result, Crusoe will be unable to attain point F on indifference curve i_2. The best he can attain is point E_2, where his consumption of fish declines by another 2 units to 5. Since the broken line containing F and the budget constraint containing E_2 are parallel, the relative prices of fish and breadfruit are held constant as Crusoe moves from F to E_2. Thus, the move from F to E_2 is a pure income effect. The reduction in the consumption of fish (and breadfruit) is due entirely to the decline in Crusoe's real income.

Indifference curve analysis highlights the assumptions and considerations that enter into consumer decisions. The logic of the proof that there is an inverse relationship between the price and the amount demanded is both elegant and reassuring. It is elegant because of the internal consistency of the logic and the precision of the analysis. It is reassuring because it conforms with our expectations, which are based on the central postulate of economics—that incentives matter in a predictable way.

EXHIBIT A-6 The income and substitution effects

Here we break down Crusoe's response to the rise in the price of fish from $1 to $2 (see Exhibit A-4) into the substitution and income effects. The move from E_1 to F illustrates the substitution effect, whereas the move from F to E_2 reflects the income effect.

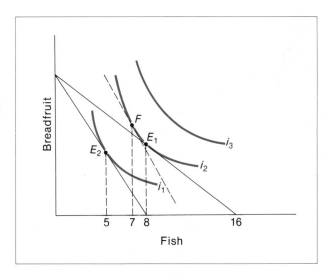

Opportunity cost is the value of the best alternative that must be sacrificed in order to engage in an activity. This is the only relevant cost in economic analysis because it is based on the very nature of the science—the formulation of principles for maximum satisfaction of human wants and scarce resources. The supply curve of any commodity or service consequently reflects opportunity costs which are determined indirectly by consumers clamoring for a myriad of goods.[1]
Marshall Colberg

13

COSTS AND THE SUPPLY OF GOODS

Demand and supply interact to determine the market price of a product. In the last chapter, we illustrated that the demand for a product reflects the preferences of consumers. In this chapter, we focus on costs of production, which are the major determinants of both the nature and the position of the supply curve for a good. If the cost of producing a good exceeds its price, producers will not continue to supply it. Most persons recognize that supply and cost of production are closely linked. For example, if it costs $400 to produce a stereo set, manufacturers will not supply the sets, at least not for very long, at a price of $200. In the long run, the sets will be supplied only if they can command a price of at least $400.

In this chapter, we lay the foundation for a detailed investigation of the link between costs and market supply. The nature and function of costs are central to economic analysis. The economist's measurement of costs sometimes differs from that of business decision-makers and accountants. What do economists mean by costs? Why are costs so important? What is the function of costs in a market economy? We discuss these and related questions in this chapter.

ORGANIZATION OF THE BUSINESS FIRM

The business firm is an entity designed to organize raw materials, labor, and machines with the goal of producing goods and/or services. Firms (a) purchase productive resources from households and other firms, (b) transform them into a different commodity, and (c) sell the transformed product or service to consumers.

---

[1]Marshall R. Colberg, Dascomb R. Forbush, and Gilbert R. Whitaker, *Business Economics* (Homewood, Illinois: Irwin, 1980), p. 12.

Economies may differ in the amount of freedom they allow business decision-makers. They may also differ in the incentive structure that is used to stimulate productive business activity. Nonetheless, every society relies on business firms to organize resources and transform them into products. In Western economies, most business firms choose their own price, output level, and productive techniques. In socialist countries, government policy often establishes the selling price and constrains the actions of business firms in various other ways. However, the central position of the business firm as the organized productive unit is universal to both capitalist and socialist economies.

In capitalist countries, most firms are privately owned. The owners, or entrepreneurs, are the individuals who risk their wealth on the success of the business. If the firm is successful and makes profits, these financial gains go to the owners. Conversely, if things go badly and the firm suffers losses, the owners must bear the consequences. Thus, the wealth of the entrepreneurial owners is directly influenced by the success or failure of the firm.

There are three major legal structures under which business firms may be organized—proprietorships, partnerships, and corporations.

Proprietorships

A proprietorship is a business firm that is owned by a single individual who is fully liable for the debts of the firm. In addition to assuming the responsibilities of ownership, the proprietor often works directly for the firm, providing managerial and other labor services. Many small businesses, including neighborhood grocery stores, barbershops, and farms, are business proprietorships. As Exhibit 1 shows, proprietorships comprised 77 percent of all business firms in 1977. Because most proprietorships are small, however, they generated only 9 percent of all business receipts.

Partnerships

A partnership consists of two or more persons acting as co-owners of a business firm. The partners share both risks and responsibilities in some prearranged manner. There is no difference between a proprietorship and a partnership in terms of owner liability. In both cases, the owners are fully liable for all business debts incurred by the firm. Many law, medical, and accounting firms are organized along partnership lines. This form of business structure accounts for only 8 percent of the total number of firms and 4 percent of all business receipts.

Corporations

Measured in terms of business receipts, the corporate business structure is by far the most important. In 1977, although corporations comprised only 15 percent of all business firms, they accounted for 87 percent of all business receipts. What are the distinctive characteristics of the corporation? What accounts for its attractiveness?

First, the stockholders of the corporation are the legal owners of the firm. Any profits of the firm belong to them. Their liability, however, is strictly limited. They are liable for corporate debts only to the extent of their explicit investment. If a corporation owes you money, you cannot sue the stockholders directly. You can, of course, sue the corporation. But what if it goes bankrupt? Then you and others to whom the firm owes money will simply be out of luck.

EXHIBIT 1   How business firms are organized

	Number (Thousands)	Percentage of All Firms	Percentage of All Business Receipts
Proprietorship	11,346	77	9
Partnership	1,153	8	4
Corporation	2,242	15	87

Statistical Abstract of the United States—1981, Table 896 (the data are for 1977).

Second, the limited liability makes it possible for corporations to attract investment funds from a large number of "owners" who do not participate in the day-to-day management of the firm. The stockholders of many large corporations simply hire managers to operate the firm. Thus, corporations are often characterized by a separation of ownership and operational management.

Third, ownership can easily be transferred. If an owner dies, his or her ownership rights can be sold by the heirs to another owner without disrupting the business firm. Thus, the corporation becomes an ongoing concern. Similarly, if any stockholders become unhappy with the way in which a corporation is run, they can bail out merely by selling their stock.

The managers of a large corporation might be thought of as trained experts hired by the stockholders to run the firm. The decisions of stockholders to buy and sell stock (ownership rights) mirror the confidence of investors in the management of a firm. If both current and prospective stockholders believe that the managers will do a better job, the demand for the firm's stock will increase. Rising stock prices will reflect this increase in demand. Conversely, when a large number of the current stockholders want to sell their shares because they are dissatisfied with the current management, the supply of the firm's stock put up for sale increases, causing its price to tumble. Falling stock prices will often lead to a shake-up in the management of the firm.

THE ROLE OF COSTS

Consumers would like to have more economic goods, but resources are scarce. We cannot produce as much of all goods as we would like. The use of resources to produce one commodity leaves fewer resources with which to produce other desired goods. Thus, the desire for product A must be balanced against the desire for other items, which must now be foregone as a result of the fact that resources have been consumed by the production of A. Every economic system must balance the desire for each good against the scarcity of resources required to produce the good. When decisions are made in the political arena, the budget process performs this balancing function. Congress (or the central committee, or the king) decides how much each good is valued relative to every other good. Taxes and budgets are set accordingly.

In a market economy, consumer demand and cost of production are central to the performance of this balancing function. The desire of consumers for a specific good must be balanced against the *desire for other goods* that could be produced with the resources. Since resources have alternative uses, certain goods that could be produced with these resources must be foregone. It is these foregone opportunities that give rise to costs of production. Resources employed in the production of a good must be paid an amount that will draw them away from their alternative employment opportunities. As resources are bid away from their alternative employment opportunities, costs of production are incurred. Costs of production reveal the value of the resources in their alternative uses.

The demand for a product can be thought of as the voice of consumers instructing firms to produce a good. On the other hand, costs of production represent the voice of consumers saying that other items that could be produced with the resources are also desired. The demand for a product indicates the intensity of consumers' desire for the item. The cost of producing a product indicates the desire of consumers for other goods that must now be foregone because the necessary resources have been employed in the production of the first item.

Calculating Economic Costs and Profits

Explicit Costs: Money paid by a firm to purchase the services of productive resources.

Implicit Costs: The opportunity costs associated with a firm's use of resources that it owns. These costs do *not* involve a direct money payment. Examples include wage income and interest foregone by the owner of a firm who also provides labor services and equity capital to the firm.

Total Cost: The cost, both explicit and implicit, of the resources utilized by the firm. Total cost includes an imputed normal rate of return for the firm's equity capital.

Regardless of their size, business firms give primary attention to profits. But what is profit? Most persons, including many businesspeople, think of profit as that portion of their sales revenues that remains after they have paid for raw materials, labor, machines, and similar inputs. Unfortunately, this concept of profit, which stems from accounting procedures, generally excludes some of the firm's costs.

The key to understanding the economist's concept of profit is our old friend—opportunity cost. The firm incurs a cost whenever it utilizes a resource, thereby requiring the resource owner to forego the highest valued alternative. These costs may be either explicit or implicit. **Explicit costs** result when the firm makes a monetary payment to resource owners. Money wages, interest, and rental payments are a measure of what the firm gives up in order to employ the services of labor and capital resources. Firms usually also incur **implicit costs**—costs associated with the use of resources owned by the firm. Since implicit costs do not involve a direct money or a contractual payment, they are often excluded from accounting statements. For example, the owners of small proprietorships often supply labor services to their businesses. There is an opportunity cost associated with the use of this resource; other opportunities have to be foregone because of the time spent by the owner in the operation of the business. The highest valued alternative foregone is the opportunity cost of the labor service provided by the owner. The **total cost** of production is the sum of the explicit and implicit costs incurred by the employment of all resources involved in the production process.

Profit and the Opportunity Cost of Capital

The most important implicit cost that is generally omitted from accounting statements is the cost of capital. Persons supplying equity capital to a firm expect their financial investment to yield a normal rate of return. By this we mean that they expect to earn at least the rate of return that could be derived from other investment opportunities. If investors do not earn this normal rate of return on their investment, they will not continue to supply financial capital to the business.

Opportunity Cost of Capital:
The implicit rate of return that must be paid to investors to induce them to supply continuously funds necessary to maintain a firm's capital assets.

This normal rate of return is sometimes referred to as the **opportunity cost of capital.** If the normal rate of return on equity capital is 10 percent, investors will not continue to supply funds to firms that are unable to earn a 10 percent rate of return on capital assets. As a result, earning the normal rate of return—that is, covering the opportunity cost of capital—is vital to the survival of a business firm.

Accounting Profit and Economic Profit

Economic Profit: The difference between the firm's total revenues and total costs.

Since economists seek to measure the opportunities foregone as a result of the production of a good or service, they include both explicit and implicit costs in total cost. **Economic profit** is equal to total revenue minus total cost, including both the explicit and implicit cost components. Economic profits will be present only if the earnings of a business are in excess of the opportunity cost of utilizing the assets owned by the firm. Economic losses result when the earnings of the firm are insufficient to cover both explicit and implicit costs. When the firm's revenues are just equal to its costs, both explicit and implicit, economic profits will be zero.

Remember that zero economic profits do not imply that the firm is about to go out of business. On the contrary, they indicate that the owners are receiving exactly the market rate of return on their investment (assets owned by the firm).

Accounting Profits: The sales revenues minus the expenses of a firm over a designated time period, usually one year. Accounting profits typically make allowances for changes in the firm's inventories and depreciation of its assets. However, no allowance is made for the opportunity cost of the equity capital of the firm's owners.

Since accounting procedures often omit implicit costs, such as those associated with owner-provided labor services or capital assets, the accounting costs of the firm generally understate the opportunity costs of production. This understatement of cost leads to an overstatement of profits. Therefore, the **accounting profits** of a firm are generally greater than the firm's economic profits (see feature, following page). When the omission of the costs of owner-provided services is unimportant, as is the case for most large corporations, accounting profits approximate what we refer to as the normal rate of return. High accounting profits (measured as a rate of return on a firm's assets) relative to the average for other firms suggest that a firm is earning an economic profit. Correspondingly, a low accounting rate of profit implies economic losses.

SHORT RUN AND LONG RUN

Short Run (in Production): A time period so short that a firm is unable to vary some of its factors of production. Since substantial time is required to change a firm's plant size, the plant is often considered a "fixed" factor.

A firm cannot adjust its output instantaneously. Time plays an important role in the production process. Economists often speak of the **short run** as a time period so short that the firm is unable to alter its present plant size. In the short run, the firm is "stuck" with its existing plant and heavy equipment. They are "fixed" for a given time period. However, the firm can alter output by applying larger or smaller amounts of variable resources, such as labor and raw materials. Thus, the firm's existing plant capacity can be used more or less intensively in the short run.

In sum, we can say that the short run is that period of time during which at least one factor of production, usually the size of the firm's plant, cannot be varied.

How long is the short run? The length varies from industry to industry. In some industries, substantial changes in plant size can be accomplished in a

ECONOMIC AND ACCOUNTING COST—A HYPOTHETICAL EXAMPLE

The revenue–cost statement for a corner grocery store owned and operated by Terry Smith is presented below.

Terry works full-time as the manager, chief cashier, and janitor. Terry has $30,000 worth of refrigeration and other equipment invested in the store. Last year, Terry's total sales were $75,000; suppliers and employees were paid $50,000. Terry's revenues exceeded explicit costs by $25,000. Did Terry make a profit last year? The accounting statement for the store will probably show a net profit of $25,000. However, if Terry did not have a $30,000 personal investment in equipment, these funds could be collecting 10 percent interest. Thus, Terry is foregoing $3000 of interest each year. Similarly, if the building that Terry owns was not being used as a grocery store, it could be rented for $500 per month. Rental income thus foregone is $6000 per year. In addition, since Terry is tied up working in the grocery store, an $18,000 managerial position with the local A&P is foregone. Thus, when one considers the interest, rental, and salary income that Terry had to forego in order to operate the grocery store last year, Terry's implicit costs were $27,000. The total costs were $77,000. The total revenue of Terry's grocery store was less than the opportunity cost of the resources utilized. Terry incurred a loss of $2000.

Total revenue		
Sales (groceries)		$75,000
Total (explicit) costs		
Groceries, wholesale	$38,000	
Utilities	2,000	
Taxes	3,000	
Advertising	1,000	
Labor services (employees)	6,000	
Total (explicit) costs	50,000	
Net (accounting) profit	25,000	
Additional (implicit) costs		
Interest (personal investment)	$ 3,000	
Rent (Terry's building)	6,000	
Salary (Terry's labor)	18,000	
Total implicit costs	27,000	
Total explicit and implicit costs		77,000
Economic profit (total revenue minus explicit and implicit costs)		− 2,000

Long Run (in Production): A time period of sufficient length to enable the firm the opportunity to vary all factors of production.

few months. In other industries, particularly those that utilize assembly lines and mass production techniques (for example, aircraft and automobiles), the short run might be a year or even several years.

The **long run** is a time period of sufficient length to allow a firm the opportunity to alter its plant size and capacity and all other factors of production. All of the resources of the firm are variable in the long run. In the long run, from the viewpoint of an entire industry, new firms may be established and enter the industry; other firms may dissolve and leave the industry.

Perhaps an example will help to clarify the distinction between the short- and long-run time periods. If a battery manufacturer hired 200 additional workers and ordered more raw materials in order to squeeze a larger output from the existing plant, this would be a short-run adjustment. In contrast, if the manufacturer built an additional plant (or expanded the size of its current facility) and installed additional heavy equipment, this would be a long-run adjustment.

COSTS IN THE SHORT RUN

We have emphasized that in the short run some of a firm's factors of production, such as the size of the plant, will be fixed. Other productive resources will be variable. Thus, in the short run we can break the firm's costs into these two categories—fixed and variable.

Fixed Cost: Cost that does not vary with output. However, fixed cost will be incurred as long as a firm continues in business and the assets have alternative uses.

Fixed cost will remain unchanged even though output is altered. A firm's insurance premiums, its property taxes, and, most significantly, the opportunity cost of utilizing its fixed assets will be present whether the firm produces a large or a small rate of output. Nor will they vary with output. These costs are "fixed" as long as the firm remains in business. Fixed costs will be present at all levels of output, including zero. They can be avoided only if the firm goes out of business.

Average Fixed Cost: Fixed cost divided by the number of units produced. It always declines as output increases.

What will happen to **average fixed cost** (AFC) as output expands? Remember that the firm's fixed cost will be the same whether output is 1, 100, or 1000. The average fixed cost is simply fixed cost divided by output. AFC will decline as output is increased (see Exhibit 2a).

Variable Costs: Costs that vary with the rate of output. Examples include wages paid to workers and payments for raw materials.

Variable costs are those costs that vary with output. For example, additional output can usually be produced by hiring more workers and expending additional funds on raw materials. Variable costs involve expenditures on these and other variable inputs. At any given level of output, the firm's **average variable cost** is the total variable cost divided by output.

Average Variable Cost: The total variable cost divided by the number of units produced.

We have noted that total cost includes both explicit and implicit costs. The total cost of producing a good is also the sum of the fixed and variable costs at each output level. At zero output, total cost will equal fixed cost. As output expands from zero, variable cost must be added to the fixed cost in order to obtain the total cost. **Average total cost** (ATC), sometimes referred to as "unit cost," can be found by dividing the total cost by the total number of units produced. Average total cost is also equal to the sum of the average fixed and average variable costs.

Average Total Cost: Total cost divided by the number of units produced. It is sometimes called per unit cost.

Marginal Cost: The change in total cost associated with a unit change in output.

The economic way of thinking emphasizes the importance of what happens "at the margin." How much does it cost to produce an additional unit? **Marginal cost** is the change in total cost that results from the production of one additional unit. As Exhibit 2 illustrates, in the short run marginal costs will generally decline, eventually reach a minimum, and then increase as output expands. The rising marginal costs simply reflect the fact that it becomes increasingly difficult to squeeze additional output from a plant as the facility's maximum capacity (the dotted line of Exhibit 2b) is approached. The Thumbnail Sketch summarizes the interrelationships among a firm's various costs.

As a firm alters its rate of output in the short run, how will unit cost be affected? Initially, let us look at this question intuitively. In the short run, the firm can vary output by utilizing its fixed plant size more (or less) intensively. As Exhibit 2 illustrates, there are two extreme situations that will result in a high unit cost of output. First, when the output rate of a plant is small relative to its capacity, it is obviously being underutilized. Under these circumstances, average fixed cost will be high, and therefore, average total cost will also be high. It will be costly and inefficient to operate a large plant substantially below its production capacity. At the other extreme, overutilization can also result in high unit cost. An overutilized plant will mean congestion, waiting time for machines, and similar costly delays. As output approaches the maximum

EXHIBIT 2   General character-istics of the short-run cost curves

Average fixed costs (a) will be high for small rates of output, but they will always decline as output expands. Marginal cost (b) will rise sharply as the plant's production capacity *q* is approached. As graph (c) illustrates, ATC will be a U-shaped curve, since AFC will be high for small rates of output and MC will be high as the plant's production capacity is approached.

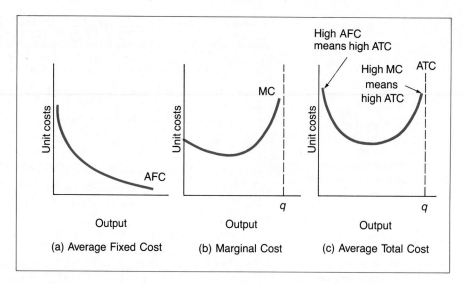

(a) Average Fixed Cost   (b) Marginal Cost   (c) Average Total Cost

capacity of a plant, overutilization will lead to high marginal costs and therefore high average total costs.

Thus, the average total cost curve will be U-shaped, as pictured in Exhibit 2c. Average total cost will be high for both an underutilized plant (because AFC is high) and an overutilized plant (with a high MC).

Diminishing Returns and Production in the Short Run

Law of Diminishing Returns: The postulate that as more and more units of a variable resource are combined with a fixed amount of other resources, employment of *additional* units of the variable resource will eventually increase output only at a decreasing rate. Once diminishing returns are reached, it will take successively larger amounts of the variable factor to expand output by one unit.

Our analysis of the link between unit cost and output rate is corroborated by a long-established economic law, the law of diminishing returns. The **law of diminishing returns** states that as more and more units of a variable factor are applied to a fixed amount of other resources, output will eventually increase by correspondingly smaller amounts. Therefore, measured in terms of their impact on output, the returns to the variable factor will diminish.

The law of diminishing returns was first discovered by the English economist David Ricardo in 1817 (see Outstanding Economist, page 34). It is as famous in economics as the law of gravity is in physics. The law is based on common sense. Have you ever noticed that as you apply a single resource more intensively, the resource eventually tends to accomplish less and less? For example, the gain to a student from the tenth hour of cramming for

---

Thumbnail Sketch—Relationships among a Firm's Costs

1. Total cost includes both explicit and implicit costs.
2. Total cost = fixed cost + variable cost.
3. Marginal cost = change in total cost per unit of output.
4. Average total cost = total cost ÷ output.
5. Average fixed cost = fixed cost ÷ output.
6. Average variable cost = variable cost ÷ output.
7. Average total cost = average fixed cost + average variable cost.

an exam is typically less than the gain from the first or second hour of studying.[2] Similarly, if a farmer applies fertilizer more and more intensively to an acre of land (a fixed factor), the application of additional 100-pound units of fertilizer will expand the wheat yield by successively smaller amounts.

Essentially, the law of diminishing returns is a constraint imposed by nature. If it were not valid, it would be possible to raise all of the world's foodstuffs on an acre of land, or even in a flowerpot. Suppose that we did *not* experience diminishing returns when we applied more labor and fertilizer to land. Would it ever make sense to cultivate any of the less fertile land? Of course not. We would be able to increase output more rapidly by simply applying another unit of labor and fertilizer to the world's most fertile flowerpot! But, of course, that would be a fairy tale; the law of diminishing returns applies in the real world.

Exhibit 3 illustrates the law of diminishing returns numerically. Column 1 indicates the quantity of the variable resource, labor in this example, that is combined with a specified amount of the fixed resource. Column 2 shows the **total product** that will result as the utilization rate of labor increases. Column 3 provides data on the **marginal product,** the change in total output associated with each additional unit of labor. Without the application of labor, output would be zero. As additional units of labor are applied, total product (output) expands. As the first three units of labor are applied, total product increases by successively larger amounts (8, then 12, then 14). However, beginning with the fourth unit, diminishing returns are confronted. When the fourth unit is added, marginal product—the change in the total product—declines to 12 (down from 14, when the third unit was applied). As additional units of labor are applied, marginal product continues to decline. It is increasingly difficult to

Total Product: The total output of a good that is associated with alternative utilization rates of a variable input.

Marginal Product: The change in the total product resulting from a unit change in the employment of a variable input. Mathematically, it is the ratio of (a) change in total product divided by (b) change in the quantity of the variable input.

EXHIBIT 3   The law of diminishing returns (hypothetical data)

(1) Units of the Variable Resource, Labor (per Day)	(2) Total Product (Output)	(3) Marginal Product	(4) Average Product
0	0		—
1	8	8	8.0
2	20	12	10.0
3	34	14	11.3
4	46	12	11.5
5	56	10	11.2
6	64	8	10.7
7	70	6	10.0
8	74	4	9.3
9	75	1	8.3
10	74	1	7.4

---

[2]Why does each additional hour of study time improve your grade less than previous ones? What do you study first? The most important material. As you continue studying, you allocate more and more time to less important tasks, the study of less relevant material. Thus, your return from *additional* hours of study will diminish.

squeeze a larger total product from the fixed resources (for example, plant size and equipment). Eventually, marginal product becomes negative (beginning with the tenth unit).

Column 4 of Exhibit 3 provides data for the **average product** of labor. The averge product is simply the total product divided by the units of labor applied. Note the average product increases as long as the marginal product is greater than the average product. This is true through the first four units. However, the marginal product of the fifth unit of labor is 10, less than the average product for the first four units of labor (11.5). Therefore, beginning with the fifth unit, average product declines as additional labor is applied.

Utilizing the data from Exhibit 3, Exhibit 4 illustrates the law of diminishing returns graphically. Initially, the total product curve (Exhibit 4a) increases quite rapidly. As diminishing marginal returns are confronted (beginning with the fourth unit of labor), total product increases more slowly. Eventually a

Average Product: The total product (output) divided by the number of units of the variable input required to produce that output level.

EXHIBIT 4 The law of diminishing returns

As units of variable input (labor) are added to a fixed input, total product will increase, first at an increasing rate and then at a declining rate (graph a). This will cause both the marginal and average product curves (graph b) to rise at first and then decline. Note that the marginal product curve intersects the average product curve at its maximum.

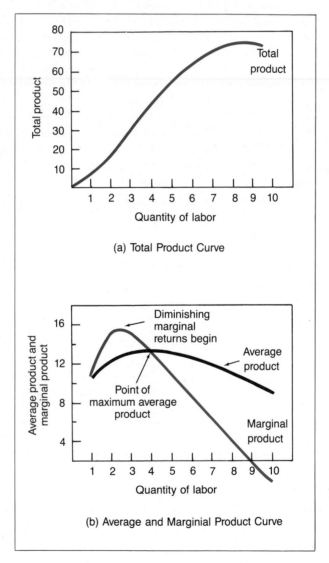

(a) Total Product Curve

(b) Average and Marginial Product Curve

maximum output (75) is reached with the application of the ninth unit of labor. The marginal product curve (Exhibit 4b) reflects the total product curve. Geometrically, marginal product is the slope of the total product curve. Marginal product reaches its maximum with the application of three units of labor. Beyond three units, diminishing returns are present. Eventually, marginal product becomes negative at ten units of labor. When marginal product becomes negative, total product is necessarily declining. The average product curve will rise as long as the marginal product curve is above it. Average product will reach its maximum at four units of labor. Beyond that, average product will decline as the utilization of labor increases.

Diminishing Returns and Cost Curves

What impact will diminishing returns have on a firm's costs? Once a firm confronts diminishing returns, successively larger amounts of variable factors will be required to expand output by an additional unit. Marginal costs will rise until, eventually, they exceed average total cost. When marginal costs are greater than ATC, ATC will increase. It is easy to see why. What happens when an above-average student is added to a class? The class average goes up. What, then, would happen if a unit of above-average cost were added to output? Average total cost would rise. Therefore, the firm's marginal cost curve crosses the ATC curve at the ATC's lowest point. For output rates beyond the minimum ATC, the rising marginal cost will cause average total cost to increase. Again, we will find the average total cost curve to be U-shaped.

Exhibit 5 illustrates numerically the implications of the law of diminishing returns for a firm's short-run cost curves. Here, we assume that Royal Roller Skates, Inc., combines units of a variable input with a fixed factor to produce units of output (skates). Columns 2, 3, and 4 indicate how total cost schedules are altered as output is expanded. Total fixed costs, representing the opportunity cost of the fixed factors of production, are $50 per day. For the first four units of output, total variable costs increase at a *decreasing rate*. This

EXHIBIT 5   Numerical short-run cost schedules of Royal Roller Skates, Inc.

| (1) | Total Cost Data (per Day) | | | Average/Marginal Cost Data (per Day) | | | |
| | (2) | (3) | (4) | (5) | (6) | (7) | (8) |
Output per Day	Total Fixed Cost	Total Variable Cost	Total Cost, (2)+(3)	Average Fixed Cost, (2)÷(1)	Average Variable Cost, (3)÷(1)	Average Total Cost, (4)÷(1)	Marginal Cost, Δ(4)÷Δ(1)
0	$50	$ 0	$ 50	—	—	—	
1	50	15	65	$50.00	$15.00	$65.00	$15
2	50	25	75	25.00	12.50	37.50	10
3	50	34	84	16.67	11.33	28.00	9
4	50	42	92	12.50	10.50	23.00	8
5	50	52	102	10.00	10.40	20.40	10
6	50	64	114	8.33	10.67	19.00	12
7	50	79	129	7.14	11.29	18.43	15
8	50	98	148	6.25	12.25	18.50	19
9	50	122	172	5.56	13.56	19.11	24
10	50	152	202	5.00	15.20	20.20	30
11	50	202	252	4.55	18.36	22.91	50

occurs because, in this range, increasing returns to the variable input are present. However, beginning with the fifth unit of output, diminishing marginal returns are present. From this point on, total variable costs and total costs increase by successively larger amounts as output is expanded.

Columns 5 through 8 of Exhibit 5 reveal the general pattern of the average and marginal cost schedules. For small output rates the average total cost of producing skates is high, primarily because of the high AFC. Initially, marginal costs are less than ATC. However, when diminishing returns set in for output rates beginning with five units, marginal cost will rise. Eventually marginal cost will exceed average variable cost (beginning with the sixth unit of output), causing AVC to rise. Beginning with the eighth unit of output, MC will exceed ATC, causing it to rise also. Thus, ATC will be a minimum at seven units of output. Observe the data of Exhibit 5 carefully to make sure that you fully understand the relationships among the various cost curves.

Utilizing the numeric data of Exhibit 5, Exhibit 6 illustrates graphically both the total and the average/marginal cost curves. Note that the marginal cost curve intersects both the average variable cost and average total cost curves at the minimum points (Exhibit 6b). As marginal costs continue to rise above average total cost, unit costs rise higher and higher as output is expanded (beyond seven units).

In sum, the firm's short-run cost curves are merely a reflection of the law of diminishing marginal returns. Assuming that the price of the variable resource is constant, marginal costs will decline as long as the marginal product of the variable input is rising. This results because, in this range, less and less of the variable input is required to produce each additional unit of output. However, this situation is eventually reversed when diminishing returns are confronted. Once diminishing returns set in, more and more units of the variable factor are required to generate each additional unit of output. Marginal cost will rise, because the marginal product of the variable resources is declining.

EXHIBIT 6   Costs in the short-run

Using data of Exhibit 5, graph (a) illustrates the general shape of the firm's short-run total cost curves; graph (b) illustrates the general shape of the firm's average and marginal cost curves. Note that when output is small (for example, 2 units), average total cost will be high because the average fixed costs are so high. Similarly, when output is large (for example, 11 units) per unit cost (ATC) will be high because it is extremely costly to produce the marginal units. Thus, the short-run ATC curve will be U-shaped.

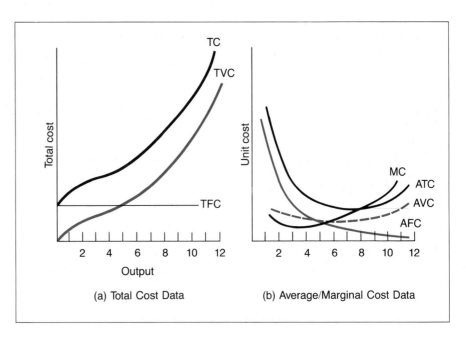

(a) Total Cost Data

(b) Average/Marginal Cost Data

Eventually, marginal cost will exceed average variable and average total costs, causing these costs to rise also. A U-shaped short-run average total cost curve results.

COSTS IN THE LONG RUN

The short-run analysis relates costs to output *for a specific size of plant*. However, firms are not committed forever to their existing plant. In the long run a firm is able to alter its plant size and all other factors of production. All of the resources of the firm are variable in the long run.

How will the firm's choice of plant size affect production costs? Exhibit 7 illustrates the short-run average total cost curves for three plant sizes, ranging from small to large. If these three plant sizes were the only possible choices, which one would be best? The answer would depend on the rate of output that the firm expected to produce. The smallest plant would have the lowest cost if an output rate of less than q_1 were produced. The medium-sized plant would provide the least-cost method of producing output rates between q_1 and q_2. For any output level above q_2, the largest plant would be cost-efficient.

The long-run average total cost curve shows the minimum average cost of producing each output level when the firm is free to choose among all possible plant sizes. It can best be thought of as a "planning curve," because it reflects the expected per unit cost of producing alternative rates of output while plants are still in the blueprint stage.

Exhibit 7 illustrates the long-run average total cost curve when only three plant sizes are possible. The planning curve *ABCD* is mapped out. However, given sufficient time, firms can usually choose among many plants of various sizes. Exhibit 8 presents the long-run planning curve under these circumstances. A smooth planning curve results. Each short-run average total cost curve will be tangent to the long-run planning curve. However, the tangency will occur at the least-cost output level for the short-run curve only when the long-run curve is parallel to the *x* axis (for example, q_n, Exhibit 8).

No single plant size could produce the alternative output rates at the costs indicated by the planning curve. The long-run average total cost curve merely outlines the expected average costs of production for each of a large number of plants that differ in size.

EXHIBIT 7   The long-run average cost

The short-run average cost curves are shown for three alternative plant sizes. If these three were the only possible plant sizes, the long-run average curve would be *ABCD*.

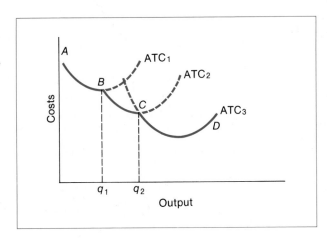

EXHIBIT 8 The planning curve

When many alternative plant sizes are possible, the long-run average total cost curve LRATC is mapped out.

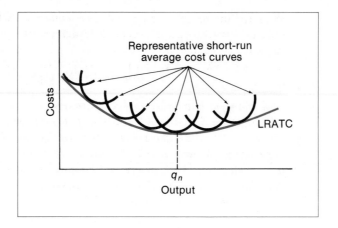

Size of Firm and Unit Cost in the Long Run

Do larger firms have lower minimum unit costs than smaller ones? The answer to this question depends on which industries are being considered. However, there is a sound basis for *initially* expecting some cost reductions from large-scale production methods. Why? Large firms typically produce a large total volume of output.[3] Volume of output denotes the total number of units of a product that the firm expects to produce.[4] There are three major reasons why unit costs initially decline as firms plan a larger total volume of output (and a larger size of plant).

1. Adoption of Mass Production Techniques. Large firms are often able to utilize mass production techniques that are economical *only* when large volumes of output are planned. Mass production usually involves large development and setup costs. However, once the production methods are established, marginal costs are low. Because of the large setup costs, mass production techniques are uneconomical for small volumes of output. For example, the use of molds, dies, and assembly line production methods reduces the per unit cost of automobiles only when the planned volume is in the millions. In contrast, these methods would result in high per unit costs if they were utilized to produce only a few thousand automobiles.

2. Specialization. Large-scale operation results in a greater opportunity for specialized use of both labor and machines. Adam Smith noted 200 years ago that the output of a pin factory is much greater when one worker draws the wire, another straightens it, a third cuts it, a fourth grinds the point, a fifth makes

---

[3]Throughout this section, we assume that larger plants necessarily plan a larger volume of output than their smaller counterparts. Reality approximates these conditions. Firms choose large plants because they are planning to produce a large volume.

[4]Note the distinction between rate and volume of output. *Rate* of output is the number of units produced during a specific period (for example, the next six months). *Volume* is the total number of units produced during all time periods. For example, Boeing might produce two 747 airplanes per month (rate of output) while planning to produce a volume of one hundred 747s during the expected life of the model. Increasing the rate (reducing the time period during which a given output is produced) tends to raise costs, whereas increasing the volume (total amount produced) tends to lower costs. For additional information on production and costs, see Armen Alchian, "Costs," in *International Encyclopedia of the Social Sciences* (New York: Macmillan, 1968), pp. 404–415, and Jack Hirshleifer, "The Firm's Cost Function: A Successful Reconstruction," *Journal of Business* (July 1962), pp. 235–255.

the head of the pin, and so on.[5] In economics, the whole can sometimes be greater than the sum of the parts. Specialization provides the opportunity for persons to become exceptionally proficient at performing small but essential functions. When each of them acts as a specialist, more is produced than if each made the final product from start to finish.

3. Learning by Doing. As a firm increases the number of units manufactured, both labor and management learn from their past mistakes. Improvements in the production process result. Performance improves one's skills. Baseball players improve by playing, and musicians improve by performing. Similarly, workers and management improve their skills as they "practice" productive techniques. This factor has been found to be tremendously important in several areas, including the aircraft and automobile industries.

Economies and Diseconomies of Scale

Economies of Scale: Reductions in the firm's per unit costs that are associated with the use of large plants to produce a large volume of output.

Economic theory suggests that, at least initially, larger firms have lower unit costs. When unit cost declines as output expands, **economies of scale** are present. The long-run average total cost curve is falling.

Are diseconomies of scale possible—that is, are the long-run averge costs ever greater for large firms than for small ones? The economic justification for diseconomies of scale is less obvious (and less tenable) than that for economies of scale. However, as a firm gets bigger and bigger, bureaucratic inefficiencies *may* result. Code book procedures will tend to replace managerial genius. Problems associated with coordinating activities, conveying information, and carrying out managerial directives may multiply. These factors will combine to cause rising long-term average total cost in some, although certainly not all, industries.

Economies and diseconomies of scale stem from different sources than do increasing and diminishing returns. Economies and diseconomies of scale are long-run concepts. They relate to conditions of production when all factors are variable. In contrast, increasing and diminishing returns are short-run concepts. They are applicable only when the firm has a fixed factor of production.

Exhibit 9 outlines three different long-run average total cost (LRATC) curves that describe real-world conditions. For Exhibit 9a, both economies and diseconomies of scale are present. Higher per unit costs will result when firms choose a plant size other than the one that minimizes the cost of producing output q, the ideal size of plant for this industry. Both plants that are larger and those that are smaller than the ideal size will experience higher unit costs. A very narrow range of plant sizes would be possible in industries with the LRATC depicted by Exhibit 9a. Some lines of retail sales and agriculture might approximate these conditions.

Exhibit 9b demonstrates the general shape of the LRATC that economists believe to exist in most industries. Initially, economies of scale exist, but once a minimum efficient scale is reached, wide variation in firm size is possible. Firms smaller than the minimum efficient size would have higher per unit costs, but

---

[5]Smith went on to state: "I have seen a small manufactory of this kind where ten men only were employed, and where some of them consequently performed two or three distinct operations. Those ten persons, therefore, could make among them upwards of forty-eight thousand pins in a day. But if they had all wrought separately and independently, and without any of them having been educated to this peculiar business, they certainly could not each of them have made twenty, perhaps not one pin in a day." (Adam Smith, *An Inquiry into the Nature and Causes of the Wealth of Nations,* 1776 [Cannan's edition, Chicago: University of Chicago Press, 1976], pp. 8–9).

EXHIBIT 9 Three different types of long-run average cost curves

Graph (a) indicates that for output levels less than q, economies of scale are present. Immediately beyond q, diseconomies of scale dominate. Graph (b) indicates that economies of scale are important until some minimum output level q_1 is attained. Once the minimum has been attained, there is a wide range of output levels (q_1 to q_2) that are consistent with the minimum ATC for the industry. Graph (c) indicates that economies of scale exist for all relevant output levels. As we will see later, this type of long-run ATC curve has important implications for the structure of the industry.

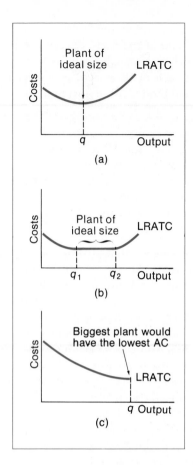

Constant Returns to Scale: Unit costs are constant as the scale of the firm is altered. Neither economies nor diseconomies of scale are present.

firms many times larger than those of the minimum efficient scale would not gain a cost advantage. **Constant returns to scale** are present for a broad range of output rates (between q_1 and q_2). This situation is consistent with real-world conditions in many industries. For example, small firms can be as efficient as larger ones in such industries as apparel, lumber, shoes, and publishing and in many lines of retailing.

Exhibit 9c indicates that economies of scale exist for all relevant output levels. The larger the firm size, the lower the per unit cost. The LRATC in the telephone service industry approximates the curve of Exhibit 9c.

WHAT FACTORS CAUSE THE FIRM'S COST CURVES TO SHIFT?

In outlining the general shapes of a firm's cost curves in both the long and the short runs, we assumed that certain other factors remained constant. What are those other factors, and how will they affect production costs?

1. Prices of Resources. If the price of resources utilized should rise, the firm's cost curves will shift upward. Higher resource prices will increase the cost of producing each alternative output level. As Exhibit 10 illustrates, the firm's cost curves will shift upward. For example, what happens to the cost of producing automobiles when the price of steel rises? The cost of producing automobiles

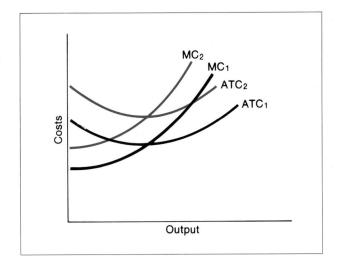

EXHIBIT 10 Higher resource prices and cost

An increase in resource prices will cause the firm's cost curves to shift upward.

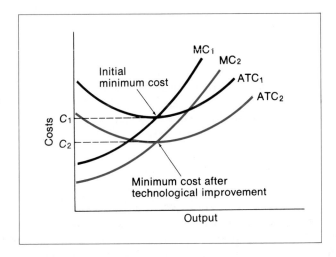

EXHIBIT 11 Egg production, costs, and technological change

Suppose that an egg producer discovers (or develops) a "super" mineral water that makes it possible to get more eggs from the same number of chickens. Because of this technological improvement, various output levels of eggs can now be produced with less feed, space, water, and labor. Costs will be reduced. The egg producer's ATC and MC curves will shift downward.

also rises. Conversely, lower resource prices will result in cost reductions. Thus, the cost curves for any specific plant size will shift downward.

2. Taxes. Taxes are a component of the firm's cost. Suppose that an excise tax of 20 cents were levied on each gallon of gasoline sold by a service station. What would happen to the seller's costs? They would increase. The firm's average total and marginal cost curves would shift upward by the amount of the tax.

3. Technology. Technological improvements often make it possible to produce a specific output with fewer resources. For example, the printing press drastically reduced the number of labor-hours required to print newspapers and books. The spinning wheel reduced the labor-hours necessary to weave cotton into cloth. More recently, electronic calculators, computers, and automated machines have reduced costs in many industries. As Exhibit 11 shows, a technological improvement will shift the firm's cost curves downward, reflecting the reduction in the amount of resources used to produce alternative levels of output.

COSTS AND THE ECONOMIC WAY OF THINKING

When analyzing the firm's costs, economists often present a highly mechanical—some would say unrealistic—view. The role of personal choice tends to be glossed over.

It is important to keep in mind that costs are incurred when choices are made. When business decision-makers choose to purchase raw materials, hire new employees, or renew the lease on a plant, they incur costs. All of these decisions, like other choices, must be made under conditions of uncertainty. Of course, past experience acts as a useful guide, yielding valuable information. Thus, business decision-makers will have a good idea of the costs that will be associated with alternative decisions.

Opportunity costs are actually "expected costs"—they represent that which the decision-maker expects to forego as the result of a choice. Think for a moment of what the cost curves that we developed in this chapter really mean. The firm's short-run marginal cost curve represents the opportunity cost of expanding output, *given the firm's current plant size*. The firm's long-run average total cost curve represents the opportunity cost per unit of output associated with varying plant sizes and rates of output, *given that the alternative plants are still on the drawing boards*. Opportunity costs look forward, reflecting expectations—often based on the past record—as to what will be foregone as a result of current decisions. Strictly speaking, neither the short-run marginal cost nor the long-run average total cost can be determined from accounting records. Accounting costs look backward. They yield valuable information about historical costs.

Sunk Costs

Sunk Costs: **Costs that have already been incurred as a result of past decisions. They are sometimes referred to as historical costs.**

Historical costs associated with past decisions—economists call them **sunk costs**—should exert no direct influence on current choices. The outcome of past choices will provide knowledge that will be relevant to current decisions, but the specific costs themselves are no longer relevant. Past choices cannot be reversed; money that has been spent is gone for good. Current choices should be based on the costs and benefits that are expected in relation to *current* market conditions.

If they are to minimize costs, business decision-makers must recognize the irrelevance of sunk costs. Let us consider a simple example that emphasizes this point. Suppose that the firm of Exhibit 5 pays $100,000 to purchase and install a skate-producing machine. The machine is expected to last ten years. The company's books record the cost of the machine as $10,000 each year under the heading of depreciation. The machine can be utilized to make only roller skates. Since dismantling and reinstallation costs are high, the machine cannot be leased or sold to another firm. It has no scrap value. In other words, there are no alternative uses for the machine. The machine's annual production of roller skates will generate $50,000 of revenues for the firm when it is employed with raw materials and other factors of production that cost $45,000.

Should the firm continue to use the machine? If the annual depreciation cost of the machine is considered, the firm loses $5000 annually on the output of the machine. However, the depreciation cost is a sunk cost. It was incurred when the machine was installed. The current opportunity cost of the machine is precisely zero. The firm is not giving up anything by continuing to operate it. Since the machine generates $5000 of additional net revenue, the firm should

This statement contains a grain of truth. A profit-seeking entrepreneur would not *undertake* a project knowing that the costs could not be covered. However, the view fails to emphasize (a) the time dimension of the production process and (b) the uncertainty associated with business decisions. The production process takes time. Raw materials must be purchased, employees hired, and plants equipped. Retailers must contract with suppliers. As these decisions are made, costs result. Many of the firm's costs of production are incurred long before the product is ready for marketing.

Even a good business decision-maker is not always able to predict the future correctly. Market conditions may change in an unexpected manner. At the time the product is ready for sale, buyers may be unwilling to pay a price that will cover the seller's past costs of production. These past costs, however, are now sunk costs and no longer relevant. Current decisions must be made on the basis of current cost and revenue considerations.

Should a grocer refuse to sell oranges that are about to spoil because their wholesale cost cannot be covered? The grocer's current opportunity cost of selling the oranges may be nearly zero. The alternative may be to throw them in the garbage next week. Almost any price, even one far below past costs, would be better than letting the oranges spoil.

Consider another example. Suppose a couple who own a house plan to relocate temporarily. Should they refuse to rent their house for $200 (if this is the best offer available) because their monthly house payment is $240? Of course not. The house payment will go on, regardless of whether they rent the house. If the homeowners can cover their opportunity costs, perhaps a $60 monthly fee for a property management service, they will gain by renting rather than leaving the house vacant.

Past mistakes provide useful lessons for the future, but they cannot be reversed. Bygones are bygones, even if they resulted in business loss. Only current revenue and cost considerations are relevant to current decisions about price levels and profitability. There is no need to fret over spilt milk, burnt toast, or yesterday's business losses.

continue using it. Of course, given current market conditions, the firm will not purchase a similar machine or replace the machine when it wears out, but this should not influence the decision of whether to continue operating the current machine. The irrelevance of sunk costs helps to explain why it often makes sense to continue operating older equipment (it has a low opportunity cost), even though it might not be wise to purchase similar equipment again.

Costs and Supply

Economists are interested in cost because they seek to explain the supply decisions of firms. A strictly profit-maximizing firm will compare the expected revenues derived from a decision or a course of action with the expected costs. If the expected revenues exceed costs, the course of action will be chosen because it will expand profits (or reduce losses).

In the short run, the marginal cost of producing additional units is the relevant cost consideration. A profit-maximizing decision-maker will compare the expected marginal costs with the expected additional revenues from larger sales. If the latter exceeds the former, output (the quantity supplied) will be expanded.

Whereas marginal costs are central to the choice of short-run output, the expected average total cost is vital to a firm's long-run supply decision. *Before entry into an industry,* a profit-maximizing decision-maker will compare the expected market price with the expected long-run average total cost. Profit-seeking potential entrants will supply the product if, and only if, they expect the market price to exceed their long-run average total cost. Similarly, existing firms will continue to supply a product only if they expect the market price to enable them at least to cover their long-run average total cost.

LOOKING AHEAD

In this chapter, we outlined several basic principles that affect costs for business firms. We will use these basic principles when we analyze the price and output decisions of firms under alternative market structures in the chapters that follow.

CHAPTER LEARNING OBJECTIVES

1 The business firm is used to organize productive resources and transform them into goods and services. There are three major business structures—proprietorships, partnerships, and corporations. Proprietorships are the most numerous, but most of the nation's business activity is conducted through corporations.

2 The demand for a product indicates the intensity of consumers' desire for the item. The (opportunity) cost of producing the item indicates the desire of consumers for other goods that must now be foregone because the necessary resources have been used in the production of the item. In a market economy, these two forces—demand and costs of production—balance the desire of consumers for more of a good against the reality of scarce resources, which requires that other goods be foregone as more of any one specific item is supplied.

3 Economists employ the opportunity cost concept when figuring a firm's costs. Therefore, total cost includes not only explicit (money) costs but also implicit costs associated with the use of productive resources owned by the firm.

4 Since accounting procedures often omit costs, such as the opportunity cost of capital and owner-provided services, accounting costs generally understate the opportunity cost of producing a good. As a result of these omissions, the accounting profits of a firm are generally larger than the firm's economic profits.

5 Economic profit (loss) results when a firm's sales revenues exceed (are less than) its total costs, both explicit and implicit. Firms that are making the market rate of return on their assets will therefore make zero economic profit. Firms that transform resources into products of greater value than the opportunity cost of the resources used will make an economic profit. On the other hand, if the opportunity cost of the resources used exceeds the value of the product, losses will result.

6 The firm's short-run average total cost curve will tend to be U-shaped. When output is small (relative to plant size), average fixed cost (and therefore ATC) will be high. However, as output expands, AFC (and ATC) will fall. As the firm attempts to produce a larger and larger rate of output using its fixed plant size, diminishing returns will eventually set in, and marginal cost will rise quite rapidly as plant capacity is approached. Thus, the short-run ATC will also be high for large output levels because marginal costs are high.

7 The law of diminishing returns explains why a firm's short-run marginal and average costs will eventually rise as the rate of output expands. When diminishing marginal returns are present, successively larger amounts of the variable input will be required to increase output by one more unit. Thus, marginal costs will eventually rise as output expands. Eventually, marginal costs will exceed average total costs, causing the latter to rise also.

8 The ability to plan a larger volume of output often leads to cost reductions. These cost reductions associated with the scale of one's operation result from (a) a greater opportunity to employ mass production methods, (b) specialized use of resources, and (c) learning by doing.

9 The LRATC reflects the costs of production for plants of various sizes. When economies of scale are present (that is, when larger plants have lower per unit costs of production), LRATC will decline. When constant returns to scale are experienced, LRATC will be constant. A rising LRATC is also possible. Bureaucratic decision-making

and other diseconomies of scale may (although not necessarily) cause LRATC to rise.

10 In analyzing the general shapes of a firm's cost curves, we assumed that the following factors remained constant: (a) resource prices, (b) technology, and (c) taxes. Changes in any of these factors would cause the cost curves of a firm to shift.

11 In any analysis of business decision-making, it is important to keep the opportunity cost principle in mind. Economists are interested in costs primarily because costs affect the decisions of suppliers. Short-run marginal costs represent the supplier's opportunity cost of producing additional units with the existing plant facilities of the firm. The long-run average total cost represents the opportunity cost of supplying alternative rates of output, given sufficient time to vary plant size.

12 Sunk costs are costs that have already been incurred. They should not exert a *direct* influence on current business choices. However, they may provide a source of information that will be useful in making current decisions.

THE ECONOMIC WAY OF THINKING — DISCUSSION QUESTIONS

1 What is economic profit? How might it differ from accounting profit? Explain why firms that are making zero economic profit are likely to continue in business.

2 Which of the following do you think reflect sound economic thinking? Explain your answer.
   (a) "I paid $200 for this economics course. Therefore, I'm going to attend the lectures even if they are useless and boring."
   (b) "Since we own rather than rent, housing doesn't cost us anything."
   (c) "I own 100 shares of stock that I can't afford to sell until the price goes up enough for me to get back at least my original investment."
   (d) "It costs to produce private education, whereas public schooling is free."

3 Suppose that a firm produces bicycles. Will the firm's accounting statement reflect the opportunity cost of producing bicycles? Why or why not? What costs would an accounting statement reveal? Should current decisions be based on accounting costs? Explain.

4 Explain in your own words why a firm's short-run average total cost will decline initially but eventually increase as the rate of output is expanded.

5 Which of the following are relevant to a firm's decision to increase output: (a) short-run average total cost; (b) short-run marginal cost; (c) long-run average total cost? Justify your answer.

6 Economics students often confuse (a) diminishing returns to the variable factor and (b) diseconomies of scale. Explain the difference between the two and give one example of each.

7 What's Wrong with This Way of Thinking?

"The American steel industry cannot compete with German and Japanese steel producers. After World War II, these countries rebuilt modern, efficient mills that made use of the latest technology. In contrast, American mills are older and less efficient. Our costs are higher because we are stuck with old facilities."

14

PURE COMPETITION AND MONOPOLY

In Chapter 13 we looked closely at the relationship between the various costs faced by a firm and its rational decisions regarding how much to produce. In this chapter and Chapter 15 we will compare four different industry structures. We will also see how these different structures affect the revenues and output decisions of the firms operating within them. The market structures of pure competition and monopoly will be discussed first in this chapter as a means of comparing the two ends of the market spectrum. Having examined these two types of markets, we will then compare and contrast monopolistic competition and oligopoly in Chapter 15, viewing them as hybrid combinations of competition and monopoly.

COMPETITION, ITS MEANING AND SIGNIFICANCE

Competition as a Dynamic Process: A term that denotes rivalry or competitiveness between or among parties (for example, producers or input suppliers), each of which seeks to deliver a better deal to buyers when quality, price, and product information are all considered. Competing implies a lack of collusion among sellers.

Before we introduce the model of pure competition, a few comments about the usage of the term "competition" are in order. It is important that the function of **competition as a dynamic process** not be overlooked amidst our efforts to explain the mechanics of alternative forms of industrial structure. The competitive process emphasizes the rivalry between firms—the effort on the part of a seller to outperform the competition. Competing firms may use a variety of things—quality of product, style, convenience of location, advertising, and price—to convince consumers that they are offering a better deal. Independent action and rivalry are the essential ingredients of the competitive process.

Competition means that one is not "the only kid on the block." Rivalry among sellers clearly serves the consumer well. Competitive sellers are under

---

[1]Clair Wilcox, *Competition and Monopoly in American Industry,* Monograph no. 21, Temporary National Economic Committee, Investigation of Concentration of Economic Power, 76th Cong., 3rd sess. (Washington, D.C.: U.S. Government Printing Office, 1940), p. 8.

intense pressure to cater to the preferences of consumers. Competition also places pressure on producers to operate efficiently and to avoid waste. Competition weeds out the inefficient—those who are incapable of providing the consumer with quality goods at a low price. Producers who survive in a competitive environment cannot be complacent. They must be forward-looking and innovative. They must be willing to experiment and be quick to adopt improved methods.

Of course, each competitor is in business to make a profit. Rival firms struggle for the dollar votes of consumers. But competition is the taskmaster that forces producers to serve the interests of consumers and to do so at the lowest possible level of profit. As Adam Smith noted more than 200 years ago, competition harnesses the profit motive and puts it to work, elevating our standard of living and directing our resources toward the production of those goods that we desire most intensely relative to their cost. Smith pointed out that aggregate output would be vastly expanded if individuals specialized in those things that they did best and cooperated with others desirous of their services. He believed that self-interest directed by competitive markets would generate precisely these two ingredients—specialization and cooperation. Smith emphasized this theme in Book 1 of *The Wealth of Nations:*

It is not from the benevolence of the butcher, the brewer, or the baker, that we expect our dinner, but from their regard to their own self-interest. We address ourselves, not to their humanity but to their self-love, and never talk to them of our own necessities, but of their advantages.[2]

In Smith's time, as today, many thinkers erred because they did not understand that productive action and voluntary exchange offer potential for mutual gain. Both parties to an economic exchange generally gain (see Myths of Economics, page 33). Bridled by competition, self-interest leads to economic cooperation and provides a powerful fuel for the benefit of humankind. Paradoxical as it seems, although benevolence may be the more admirable attitude, it cannot generate the cooperative effort that is a natural outgrowth of self-interest directed by competition. Thus, the competitive process occupies center stage in economic analysis, which seeks to explain the forces that direct the economic behavior of human beings.

Before we move on to more technical material, two additional points should be made. First, economists also use the term "competition," or more precisely "pure competition," to describe a model of industrial structure. As we shall soon see, this model helps us to understand many aspects of competitive behavior. Nonetheless, the dual usage of the term "competition" to refer to both rivalry among sellers and a model of industrial structure can be confusing. It is important to recognize that firms can be competitive in the industrial-structure sense. In order to avoid confusion, we will use the complete expression "pure competition" when we discuss the competitive model of industrial structure.

Second, we have emphasized the role of competition as the taskmaster forcing sellers to obey the desires of consumers. As is generally the case with those under the thumb of a tough taskmaster, sellers have a strong incentive to

---

[2]Adam Smith, *An Inquiry into the Nature and Causes of the Wealth of Nations* (1776; Cannan's ed., Chicago: University of Chicago Press, 1976), p. 18.

escape the discipline imposed by competitive forces. Business participants can be expected to attempt to avert the discipline of competition. Much of the material on industrial structure will provide a framework within which to analyze both the likelihood of a business firm escaping the directives of competition and the economic implications of its doing so.

THE MODEL OF PURE COMPETITION

Models help us to better organize our thoughts. The polar assumptions of the purely competitive model, which we are about to discuss, are seldom realized in the real world. Nonetheless, mastery of this model can help us better understand the relationship between the decision making of individual firms and market supply. If we understand how competitive economic incentives influence the supply decisions of firms, we will be better able to understand the behavior of firms in less than purely competitive markets.

Pure competition presupposes that the following conditions exist in a market:

1. *All Firms in the Market Are Producing a* **Homogeneous Product.** The product of firm A is identical to the product offered by firm B and all other firms.
2. *A Large Number of Independent Firms Produce the Product.* The independence of the firms rules out joint actions designed to restrict output and raise prices.
3. *Each Buyer and Seller Is Small Relative to the Total Market.* No single buyer or seller is able to exert any noticeable influence on the market supply and demand conditions. For example, a wheat farmer selling 5000 bushels annually would not have a noticeable impact on the U.S. wheat market, where 1,800,000,000 bushels are traded annually. The farmer's sales would be too small to exert a noticeable independent effect.
4. *There Are No Artificial* **Barriers to Entry** *into or Exit from the Market.* Under pure competition, any entrepreneur is free either to produce or to fail to produce in the industry. New entrants need not obtain permission from the government or the existing firms before they are free to compete. Nor does control of an essential resource limit market entry.

THE WORKINGS OF THE COMPETITIVE MODEL

Since a competitive firm by itself produces an output that is small relative to the total market, it is unable to influence the market price. A purely competitive firm must accept the market price if it is to sell any of its product. Thus, competitive firms are sometimes called **price takers,** because they must take the market price in order to sell.

Exhibit 1 illustrates the relationship between market forces [graph (b)] and the demand curve facing the pure competitor [graph (a)].

If a pure competitor sets his or her price above the market level, consumers will simply buy from other sellers. A firm could lower its price, but, since it is small relative to the total market, it can already sell as much as it wants at the market price. A price reduction would merely reduce revenues. Thus, a purely competitive *firm* confronts a perfectly elastic demand for *its* product.

Pure Competition: A model of industrial structure characterized by a large number of small firms producing a homogeneous product in an industry (market area) that permits complete freedom of entry and exit.

Homogeneous Product: A product of one firm that is identical to the product of every other firm in the industry. Consumers see no differences in units of the product offered by alternative sellers.

Barriers to Entry: Obstacles that limit the freedom of potential rivals to enter an industry.

Price Takers: Sellers who must take the market price in order to sell their product. Because each price taker's output is small relative to the total market, price takers can sell all of their output at the market price but are unable to sell any of their output at a price higher than the market price. Thus, they face a horizontal demand curve.

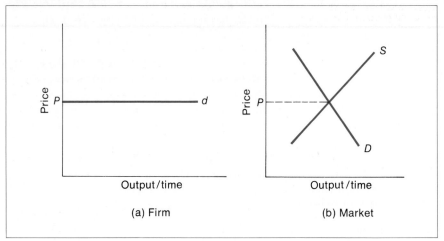

EXHIBIT 1   The firm's demand curve under pure competition

The market forces of supply and demand determine price (b). Under pure competition, individual firms have no control over price. Thus, the demand for the product of the firm is perfectly elastic (a).

(a) Firm

(b) Market

Deciding How Much to Produce— The Short Run

If a firm produces at all, it will continue expanding output as long as the benefits (additional revenues) from the production of the additional units exceed their marginal costs. This decision-making rule will maximize the firm's profits (or minimize its losses).

How will changes in output influence the firm's costs? In Chapter 13 we discovered that the firm's short-run marginal costs will *eventually* increase as output is expanded by working the firm's fixed plant facilities more intensively. The law of diminishing marginal returns assures us that this will be the case. Eventually, both the firm's short-run marginal and average total costs will rise.

What about the benefits or additional revenues from output expansion? **Marginal revenue** (MR) is the change in the firm's total revenue per unit of output. Since the purely competitive firm sells all units at the same price, its marginal revenue will be equal to the market price.

Marginal Revenue: The incremental change in total revenue derived from the sale of one additional unit of a product.

In the short run, the profit-maximizing purely competitive firm will expand output until price (which equals marginal revenue) is just equal to marginal cost. Exhibit 2 helps to explain why. Since the firm can sell as many units as it would like at the market price, the sale of one additional unit will increase revenue by the price of the product. As long as price exceeds marginal cost, revenue will increase more than cost as output is expanded. Since profit is merely the difference between total revenue and total cost, profit will increase as output is expanded as long as price exceeds MC. For the pure competitor, profit will be at a maximum when $P = \text{MR} = \text{MC}$. This would be output level q for the firm depicted in Exhibit 2.

Why would the firm not expand output beyond q? The cost of producing such units is given by the height of the MC curve. The sale of these units would increase revenues by only P, the price of the product. Production of units beyond q would add more to the cost than to revenue. Therefore, production beyond q, the $P = \text{MC}$ output level, would reduce the firm's profits.

A profit-maximizing firm with the cost curves indicated in Exhibit 2 would produce exactly q. The total revenue of the firm would be the sales price

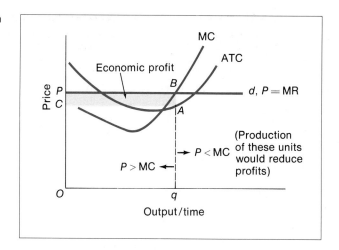

P multiplied by output sold q. Geometrically, the firm's total revenues would be $POqB$. The firm's total cost would be found by multiplying the average total cost by the output level. Geometrically, total costs are represented by $COqA$. The firm's total revenues exceed total costs, and the firm is making short-run economic profit (the shaded area).

A business decision maker who has never heard of the $P = $ MC rule for profit maximizing probably has another rule that yields approximately the same outcome. For example, the rule might be: *produce those units, and only those units, that add more to revenue than to cost.* This ensures maximum profit (or minimum loss). It also takes the firm to the point at which $P = $ MC. Why? To stop short of that point is to fail to produce units that add more (the sales price) to revenue than they do to cost. Similarly, refusal to produce units that cost more than they add to revenue ensures that production will not exceed the $P = $ MC output level. Thus, this commonsense rule leads to the same outcome as the competitive model, even when the decision maker knows nothing of the technical jargon of economics.

Exhibit 3 uses numeric data to illustrate the profit-maximizing decision making for a competitive firm. The firm's short-run total and marginal cost schedules have the general characteristics that we discussed in the previous chapter. Since the firm confronts a market price of $5 per unit, its marginal revenue is $5. Thus, total revenue *increases* by $5 per additional unit of output. The firm maximizes its profit when it supplies an output of 15 units.

There are two ways of viewing this profit-maximizing output rate. First, we could look at the difference between total revenue and total cost, identifying the output rate at which this difference is greatest. Column 6, the profit data, provides this information. For small output rates (less than 11), the firm would actually experience losses. But at 15 units of output, an $11 profit is earned ($75 total revenue minus $64 total cost). Inspection of the profit column indicates that it is impossible to earn a larger profit than $11 at any other rate of output.

Exhibit 4a presents the total-revenue and total-cost approach in graph form. Profits will be maximized when the total-revenue line exceeds the total-cost curve by the largest vertical amount. Of course, that takes place at 15 units of output.

EXHIBIT 3 **Profit maximization of a competitive firm—a numeric illustration**

(1) Output (per Day)	(2) Total Revenue	(3) Total Cost	(4) Marginal Revenue	(5) Marginal Cost	(6) Profit (TR–TC)
0	$ 0.00	$ 25.00	$0.00	$ 0.00	− 20.00
1	5.00	29.80	5.00	4.80	− 24.80
2	10.00	33.75	5.00	3.95	− 23.75
3	15.00	37.25	5.00	3.50	− 22.25
4	20.00	40.25	5.00	3.00	− 20.25
5	25.00	42.75	5.00	2.50	− 17.75
6	30.00	44.75	5.00	2.00	− 14.75
7	35.00	46.50	5.00	1.75	− 11.50
8	40.00	48.00	5.00	1.50	− 8.00
9	45.00	49.25	5.00	1.25	− 4.25
10	50.00	50.25	5.00	1.00	− 0.25
11	55.00	51.50	5.00	1.25	3.50
12	60.00	53.25	5.00	1.75	6.75
13	65.00	55.75	5.00	2.50	9.25
14	70.00	59.25	5.00	3.50	10.75
15	75.00	64.00	5.00	4.75	11.00
16	80.00	70.00	5.00	6.00	10.00
17	85.00	77.25	5.00	7.25	7.75
18	90.00	85.50	5.00	8.25	4.50
19	95.00	95.00	5.00	9.50	0.00
20	100.00	108.00	5.00	13.00	− 8.00
21	105.00	125.00	5.00	17.00	− 20.00

EXHIBIT 4 **Profit maximization—the total and marginal approaches**

Utilizing the data of Exhibit 3, here we provide two alternative ways of viewing profit
maximization. As graph (a) illustrates, the profits of the competitive firm are maximized
at the output level at which total revenue exceeds total cost by the maximum amount.
Graph (b) demonstrates that the maximum-profit output can also be identified by
comparing marginal revenue and marginal cost.

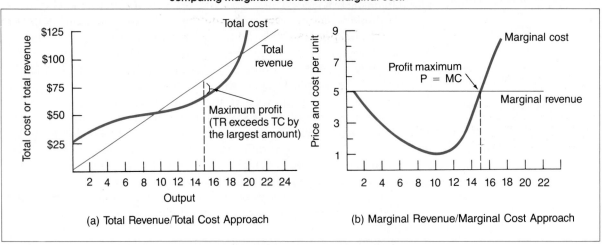

(a) Total Revenue/Total Cost Approach

(b) Marginal Revenue/Marginal Cost Approach

The marginal approach can also be used to determine the profit-
maximizing rate of output for the competitive firm. Remember, as long as
price (marginal revenue) exceeds marginal cost, production and sale of addi-

tional units will add to the firm's profit (or reduce its losses). Inspection of columns 4 and 5 of Exhibit 3 indicates that MR is greater than MC for the first 15 units of output. Production of these units will expand the firm's profit. In contrast, the production of each unit beyond 15 adds more to cost than to revenue. Therefore, profit will decline if output is expanded past 15. Given the cost and revenue schedules of Exhibit 3, the profit-maximizing manager would choose to produce 15 and only 15 units.

Losses and When to Go Out of Business

Suppose that changes take place in the market that depress the price below a firm's average total cost. How will a profit-maximizing (or loss-minimizing) firm respond to this situation? The answer depends on both the firm's current sales revenues relative to its *variable cost* and its expectations about the future. The firm has three options—it can continue to operate in the short run, shut down temporarily, or go out of business.

If the firm anticipates that the lower market price is temporary, it may want to continue operating in the short run, as long as it is able to cover its variable cost. Exhibit 5 illustrates why. The firm shown in this exhibit would minimize its loss at output level q, where $P = $ MC. However, at q, total revenues ($OqBP_1$) are less than total costs ($OqAC$). The firm confronts short-run economic losses. If it shuts down completely, however, it will still incur fixed costs, unless it goes out of business. If the firm anticipates that the market price will increase so that it will be able to cover its average total costs in the future, it may not want to sell out. Therefore, it may choose to produce q units in the short run, even though losses are incurred. At price P_1, production of output q is clearly better than shutting down because the firm is able to cover its variable costs and pay some of its fixed costs. If it were to shut down, but not sell out, the firm would lose the entire amount of its fixed cost.

What if the market price declines below the firm's average variable cost (for example, P_2)? Under these circumstances, a temporary **shutdown** is preferable to short-run operation. If the firm continues to operate in the short run, operating losses merely add to losses resulting from the firm's fixed costs. Therefore, even if the firm expects the market price to increase so that it will be able to survive and prosper in the future, it will shut down in the short run when the market price falls below its average variable cost.

Shutdown: A temporary halt in the operation of a business. The firm does *not* sell its assets. Its variable cost will be eliminated, but the firm's fixed costs will continue. The shutdown firm anticipates a return to operation in the future.

EXHIBIT 5 Operating with short-run losses

A firm will operate in the short run if it (a) can cover its variable costs now and (b) expects price to be high enough in the future to cover all its costs.

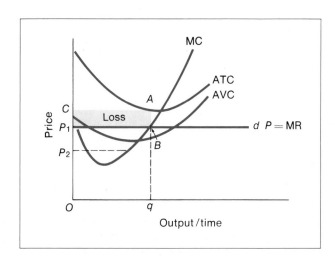

Going Out of Business: The sale of a firm's assets, and its permanent exit from the market. By going out of business, a firm is able to avoid fixed cost, which would continue during a shutdown.

The firm's third option is **going out of business** immediately. After all, even the losses resulting from the firm's fixed costs (remember that if they are costs at all, they must be avoidable) can be avoided if the firm sells out. If it does not expect market conditions to change for the better, this is the preferred option.

Supply and the Competitive Firm

The competitive firm that intends to stay in business will maximize profits (or minimize losses) when it produces the output level at which $P = MC$, as long as it is able to cover its variable costs. Therefore, the portion of the firm's short-run marginal cost curve that lies above its average variable cost is the short-run supply curve of the firm.

Exhibit 6 illustrates that, as the market price increases, the competitive firm will expand output along its MC curve. If the market price were less than P_1, the firm would shut down immediately because it would be unable to cover even its variable cost. However, if the market price is P_1, a price equal to the firm's average variable cost, the firm may supply output q_1 in the short run Economic losses will result, but the firm would incur similar losses if it shut down completely. As the market price increases to P_2, the firm will happily expand output along its MC curve to q_2. At P_2, price is also equal to average costs. The firm is making a "normal rate of return" or zero economic profits. Higher prices will result in a still larger short-run output. The firm will supply q_3 units at market price P_3. At this price, economic profits will result. At still higher prices, output will be expanded even more. As long as price exceeds average variable cost, the firm will expand supply along its MC curve, which therefore becomes the firm's short-run supply curve.

OUTPUT ADJUSTMENTS AND LONG-RUN EQUILIBRIUM

In the long run, firms have the opportunity to alter their plant size and enter or exit from an industry. As long-run adjustments are made, output in the whole industry may either expand or contract.

EXHIBIT 6   The supply curve for the firm and the market

The short-run market supply is merely the sum of the supply produced by all the firms in the market area (b).

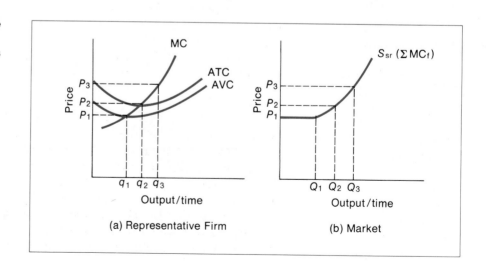

(a) Representative Firm

(b) Market

EXHIBIT 7   Long-run equilibrium in a competitive market

The two conditions necessary for equilibrium in a competitive market are depicted here. First, quantity supplied and quantity demanded must be equal in the market (b). Second, the firm must earn zero economic profit, that is, the "normal rate of return," at the established market price (a).

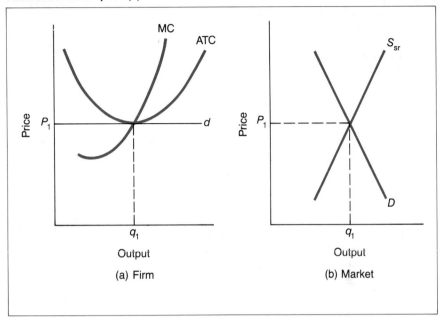

(a) Firm

(b) Market

In addition to the balance between quantity supplied and quantity demanded necessary for short-run equilibrium, the firms in a competitive industry must earn the normal rate of return, and only the normal rate, before long-run equilibrium can be attained. If economic profit is present, new firms will enter the industry, and the current producers will have an incentive to expand the scale of their operation. This will lead to an increase in supply, placing downward pressure on prices. In contrast, if firms in the industry are suffering economic losses, they will leave the market. Supply will decline, placing upward pressure on prices.

Therefore, as Exhibit 7 illustrates, when a competitive industry is in long-run equilibrium, (a) the quantity supplied and the quantity demanded will be equal at the market price and (b) the firms in the industry will be earning normal (zero) economic profit (that is, their minimum ATC will just equal the market price).

How Competitive Firms Respond to Changes in Demand

Suppose that a purely competitive market were in equilibrium. What would happen if there were an increase in demand? Exhibit 8 presents an example. The market demand for a product increases from D_1 to D_2. The price of the product rises from P_1 to P_2. What impact will the higher market price have on the output level of the producing firms? It will increase (from q_1 to q_2, in Exhibit 8) as the firms expand output along their marginal cost curves. In the short run, the producers will make economic profits. The profits will attract new producers to the industry and cause the existing firms to expand the scale of their plants. Hence, the market supply will increase (shift from S_1 to S_2) and

EXHIBIT 8   How the market
responds to an Increase
in demand

The demand for a product
increases to D_2[graph (b)].
Price rises to P_2, inducing firms
to expand output. Firms make
short-run profits [graph (a)],
which draw new competitors
into the industry. Thus, supply
expands (shifts from S_1 to S_2).
If cost conditions are unchanged, the expansion in
supply will continue until the
market price of the product has
declined to its initial level P_1.

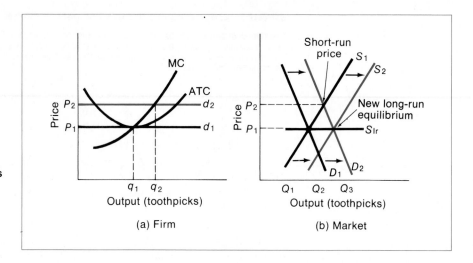

(a) Firm

(b) Market

eventually eliminate the short-run profits. If cost conditions are unchanged in
the industry, the market price for the product will return to its initial level, even
though output has expanded to Q_3.

Whereas economic profits attract new firms to an industry, economic
losses (that are expected to continue) encourage capital and entrepreneurship
to move out of the industry and into other areas where the profitability potential is more favorable. Economic losses mean that the owners of capital in the
industry are earning less than the market rate of return. The opportunity cost
of continuing in the industry exceeds the gain.

Suppose an equilibrium price exists in the industry. The firms are just
able to cover their average costs of production. Now suppose that there is a
reduction in consumer income, causing the market demand for the product to
decrease and the market price to decline. At the new, lower price, firms in the
industry will be unable to cover their costs of production. In the short run, they
will reduce output. This reduction in output by the individual firms will coincide with a reduction in the quantity supplied in the market.

In the face of short-run losses, some firms will leave the industry. Others
will reduce the scale of their operation. These factors will cause the industry
supply to decline. What impact will this have on price? It will raise prices back
up to P_2. In the long run, the market supply will decline until the price rises
sufficiently to permit "normal profits" in the industry.

The Role of Profits in the Competitive Model

In the competitive model, profits and losses are merely signals sent out by consumers to producers. Economic profits will be largest in those areas where consumer wants are greatest relative to costs of production. Profit-seeking entrepreneurs will guide additional resources into these areas. Supply will increase,
driving prices down and eliminating the profits. Free entry and the competitive
process will protect the consumer from arbitrarily high prices. In the long run,
competitive prices will reflect costs of production.

Economic profits result because a firm or entrepreneur increases the
value of resources. The successful business decision maker combines resources
into a product that consumers value more than the sum of the resources used

to produce it. That is why consumers are willing to pay a price in excess of the cost of producing the good.

In contrast, losses result when the actions of a producer reduce the value of resources. The value of the resources used up by such unsuccessful firms exceeds the price consumers are willing to pay for their product. Losses and bankruptcy are the market's way of bringing such wasteful activities to a halt.

Of course, producers, like other decision makers, confront uncertainty and dynamic change. Entrepreneurs, at the time they must make investment decisions, cannot be sure of either future market prices or costs of production. They must base their decisions on expectations. Within the framework of the competitive model, however, the reward–penalty system is clear. Firms that produce efficiently and correctly anticipate products and services for which future demand will be most urgent (relative to production cost) will make economic profit. Those that are inefficient and incorrectly allocate resources into areas of weak future demand will be penalized with losses.

EFFICIENCY AND THE COMPETITIVE MODEL

Economists often seem to be enchanted by the purely competitive model. Sometimes they hold it up as the standard by which to judge other models. What accounts for the special significance of pure competition? Most economists agree that under rather restrictive assumptions the resource allocation within the purely competitive model is ideal from society's viewpoint. In what sense can we say that it is "ideal"?

Production Efficiency (P = ATC)

In the long run, competition forces firms to minimize their average total cost of production and charge a price that is just sufficient to cover production costs. Competitive firms must use production methods that minimize costs if they are going to survive. In addition, they must choose a scale of operation that minimizes their long-run average total cost of production. Consumers of competitively produced goods will benefit, since they will receive the largest quantity at the lowest possible price, given the prevailing cost conditions. Competitive markets will eliminate waste and production inefficiency. Inefficient, high-cost producers will confront economic losses and be driven from a competitive industry.

Allocative Efficiency (P = MC)

Allocative Efficiency: The allocation of resources to the production of the goods and services most desired by consumers. The allocation is "balanced" in such a way that reallocation of resources cannot benefit anyone without hurting someone else.

Allocative efficiency refers to the balance achieved by the allocation of available resources to the production of the goods and services most desired by consumers, given their income. Allocative efficiency is present when all markets are in long-run competitive equilibrium. Each good is produced as long as consumers value it more than the alternative goods that might be produced with the same resources. No unit of the good is produced if a more valuable alternative must be foregone; and any reallocation of resources toward different goods or different combinations of goods—any disturbance of the allocative balance—cannot benefit any one person without hurting someone else.

The profit-maximization rule ($P = MC$) assures allocative efficiency within the competitive model. The market demand (price) reflects consumers' valuation of an additional unit of a good. The seller's marginal cost indicates the value of the resources (in their alternative uses) necessary to produce an additional unit of the good. When the production of each good is expanded, as long as price exceeds marginal cost, each good will be produced if, and only if, consumers value it more than the alternatives that might have been produced. Thus, in purely competitive markets, profit-maximizing producers will be led to produce the combination of goods most desired by consumers.

MONOPOLY—THE OTHER MARKET EXTREME

While pure competition is a market structure with many sellers and competitive forces, monopoly is just the opposite. The word "monopoly," derived from two Greek words, means "single seller."

We will define **monopoly** as a market structure characterized by (a) high barriers to entry and (b) a single seller of a well-defined product for which there are no good substitutes. Even this definition is ambiguous because "high barriers" and "good substitutes" are both relative terms. Are the barriers to entry into the automobile or steel industries high? Many observers would argue that they are. After all, it would take a great deal of financial capital to compete successfully in these industries. However, there are no *legal* restraints that prevent you or anyone else from producing automobiles or steel. The concept of barriers to entry is, in part, subjective.

Similarly, there is always some substitutability among products, even those produced by a monopolist. Is a letter a good substitute for telephone communication? For some purposes—legal correspondence, for example—it is a very good substitute. In other cases, when the speed of communication and immediacy of response are important, telephone communication has a tremendous advantage over letter writing.

Monopoly, then, is always a matter of degree. Pure monopoly, like pure competition, is a rare phenomenon. Nonetheless, there are two reasons why it is important to understand how markets work under pure monopoly. First, the monopoly model will help us understand markets dominated by only a few sellers. A dominant firm in an industry often has a tendency to behave like a monopolist. When there are only two or three producers in a market, they may seek to collude rather than compete with each other and thus together behave like a monopoly. Second, there is only a single producer in a few important industries. Local telephone and electricity services provide examples. The monopoly model will illuminate the operation of such markets.

How Monopoly Comes about—What Creates Barriers to Entry?

What makes it difficult for potential competitors to enter a market? Three factors are of particular importance.

1. Legal Barriers. Legal barriers are the oldest and most effective method of protecting a business firm from potential competitors. Kings once granted exclusive rights to favored citizens or groups. Today, governments continue to establish barriers, restricting the right to buy and sell goods. In the United States, in order to compete in the communications industry (for example, in

Monopoly: A market structure characterized by a single seller of a well-defined product for which there are no good substitutes and by high barriers to the entry of any other firms into the market for that product.

order to operate a radio or television station), one must obtain a government franchise. The Post Office, a government corporation, is granted the exclusive right to deliver first-class mail. Although this is currently being challenged, potential private competitors are eliminated by law.

Licensing, a process by which one obtains permission from the government to enter a specific occupation or business, often limits entry. In many states, a person must obtain a license before operating a liquor store, barbershop, taxicab, funeral home, or drugstore. Sometimes, these licenses cost little and are designed to ensure certain minimum standards. In other cases, they are expensive and designed primarily to limit competition.

Patent: The grant of an exclusive right to use a specific process or produce a specific product for a period of time (17 years in the United States).

Another legal barrier to entry is a **patent,** which grants the owner a legal monopoly on the commercial use of a newly invented product or process for a limited period of time, 17 years in the United States. Once a patent has been granted, other persons are prevented from using the procedures or producing the product unless they obtain permission from the patent holder. Essentially, the patent system is designed to permit inventors to reap the benefits of their inventions. Nonetheless, patents are often used to restrict the entry of rivals into a broad market area. For example, Polaroid's control over patent rights enabled it to exclude all rivals from the instant picture market for years, until Eastman Kodak developed a new process.

2. Economies of Scale. In some industries, a firm is unable to produce at a low cost unless it is quite large, both in absolute terms and relative to the market. Under these circumstances, economies of scale prevent small firms from entering the market, building a reputation, and competing effectively with large firms. The existing firms are thus protected from potential competitors.

3. Control over an Essential Resource. If a single firm has sole control over a resource that is essential for entry into an industry, it can eliminate potential competitors. The famous DeBeers Company of South Africa is a classic case. Since this company has almost exclusive control over all of the world's diamond mines, it can effectively prevent other firms from entering the diamond-producing industry. Its ability to raise the price of new diamonds is limited only by the availability of substitute gems and by the potential sales by current owners of previously produced diamonds.

How Do Monopolists Behave?

Monopolists, like producers in any market, must make rational decisions regarding how much to produce and what price to charge to maximize profits. How they make these decisions has a lot to do with the fact that they are the only producer in their respective market and there are no good substitutes for their products. Since each monopolist is the only firm in the industry, the industry demand curve will coincide with the firm's demand curve. The demand curve will slope downward, indicating that consumers will buy more of the product at a lower price. At high prices, even monopolists will have few customers. Often a price reduction will expand revenues more than costs. If they want to make maximum profits, they should reduce their prices and expand output, as long as the increased sales contribute more to additional revenues than their production adds to cost.

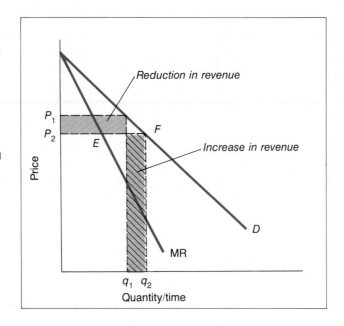

Total Revenue, Marginal Revenue, and Elasticity of Demand

Since the demand curve of a monopolist slopes downward, there will be two conflicting influences on total revenue when the seller reduces price in order to expand output and sales. As Exhibit 9 illustrates, the resultant increase in sales (from q_1 to q_2) will positively influence the total revenue of the monopolist; additional units can now be sold at the lower price that could not have been sold at the higher price. The sale of these units will increase total revenue. However, a price reduction will also tend to *lower* the monopolist's total revenue, simply because the units of the product that *could* have been sold at the higher price are now sold at a lower price (P_1 rather than P_2, as illustrated). The marginal revenue derived from the additional sales will be less than the sales price. Thus, as shown in Exhibit 9, the marginal revenue curve of the monopolist will lie inside (below) the demand curve of the firm.[3]

While the demand curve shows the number of units that can be sold at different prices, it also reveals how revenues vary as price and output are altered. Using a straight-line demand curve, Exhibit 10 illustrates how total and marginal revenue are related to elasticity of demand. At very high prices, the sales of the monopolist will be small. As price is reduced and output is expanded on the elastic portion of the monopolist's demand curve, total revenue will rise. Marginal revenue will be positive. Suppose the monopolist charged $15 for a product and sold 25 units, yielding a total revenue of $375. If the monopolist reduced price to $10, sales would expand to 50 units. Total revenue would rise to $500. Thus, a price reduction from $15 to $10 would increase the total revenue of the monopolist.

Consider the output rate at which elasticity of demand is equal to unity. At that point, total revenue reaches its maximum. Marginal revenue is equal to zero. As price falls below $10 into the inelastic portion of the monopolist's

---

[3]For a straight-line demand curve, the marginal revenue curve will bisect any line parallel to the x-axis. For example, the MR curve will divide the line P_2F into two equal parts, P_2E and EF.

EXHIBIT 10   Price, total revenue, and marginal revenue of a monopolist

In the elastic portion of the monopolist's demand curve (prices greater than $10), a price reduction will be associated with rising total revenue (frame b) and positive marginal revenue. At unitary elasticity (output of 50 units), total revenue will reach a maximum. When the monopolist's demand curve is inelastic (output beyond 50 units), lower prices will lead to declining total revenue and negative marginal revenue.

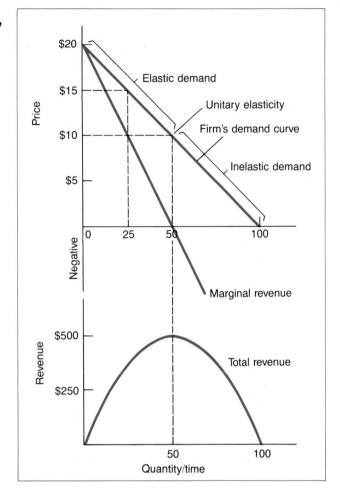

demand curve, total revenue declines as output is expanded. For this range of price and output, marginal revenue will be negative. Thus, marginal revenue goes from positive to negative as the elasticity of demand changes from elastic to inelastic (at output 50 in Exhibit 10).

This analysis has obvious implications. For a monopolist operating on the inelastic portion of its demand curve, a price increase would lead to more total revenue and less total cost (since fewer units would be produced and sold). Thus, we would never expect a profit-maximizing monopolist to push the sales of a product into the range where the product's demand curve becomes inelastic.

The Profit-Maximizing Output

Both cost and revenues must be considered when we analyze the profit-maximization decision rule for the monopolist. The profit-maximizing monopolist will continue expanding output until marginal revenue equals marginal cost. The price corresponding to that output level is given by the demand curve of the monopolist (as in Exhibit 11). The monopolist will be able to sell the profit-maximizing output Q for a price indicated by the height of the demand curve. At any output less than Q, the benefit (marginal revenue) of producing the *additional* units will exceed their cost. The monopolist will gain by expanding output. For any output greater than Q, the monopolist's cost of producing *additional* units will be greater than the benefit (marginal revenue). Production of such units will reduce profits.

Exhibit 11 also depicts the profits of a monopolist. At output Q, the monopolist would charge price P. Price times the number of units sold yields the firm's total revenue ($PAQO$). The firm's total cost would be $CBQO$, the average per unit cost multiplied by the number of units sold. The firm's profits are merely total revenue less total cost (the shaded area of Exhibit 11).

Although both competitive and monopolistic firms expand output until $MR = MC$, there is one important difference. For the competitive firm, price will also equal marginal cost at the maximum-profit output. This will not be true for the monopolist. A profit-maximizing monopolist will choose an output rate at which price is greater than marginal cost. Later we will consider the implications of this difference.

Exhibit 12 provides a numeric illustration of profit-maximizing decision making. At low output rates, marginal revenue exceeds marginal cost. The monopolist will continue expanding output as long as MR is greater than MC. Thus, an output rate of eight units per day will be chosen. Given the demand for the product, the monopolist can sell eight units at a price of $17.25 each. Total revenue will be $138, compared to a total cost of $108.50. Thus, the monopolist will make a profit of $29.50. The profit rate will be smaller at all other output rates. For example, if the monopolist reduces the price to $16 in order to sell nine units per day, marginal revenue will increase by $6. However, the marginal cost of producing the ninth unit is $6.25. Since the cost of producing the ninth unit is greater than the revenue it brings in, profits will decline.

Can the monopolist gain by raising the price above $17.25—to $18.50, for example? Perhaps it may surprise some that the answer is no. Only seven units will be sold at $18.50, for a total revenue of $129.50. The cost of producing seven units will be $102.75. Thus, an output of seven units will generate a profit of $26.75, less than could be attained at the lower price ($17.25) and larger output (eight). The highest price is not always the best price for the monopolist. Sometimes a price reduction will increase the firm's total revenue more than its total cost.

EXHIBIT 11   The short-run price and output of a monopolist

The monopolist will reduce price and expand output as long as MR exceeds MC. Output Q will result. When price exceeds average cost at the output level, profit will accrue.

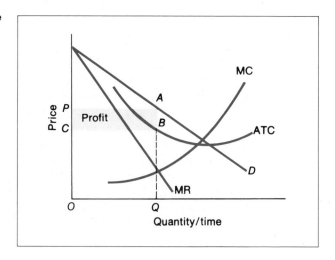

EXHIBIT 12   Profit maximization for a monopolist

Rate of Output (per Day) (1)	Price (per Unit) (2)	Total Revenue (1) × (2) (3)	Total Cost (per Day) (4)	Profit (3) − (4) (5)	Marginal Cost (6)	Marginal Revenue (7)
0	—	—	$ 50.00	$−50.00	—	—
1	$25.00	$ 25.00	60.00	−35.00	$10.00	$ 25.00
2	24.00	48.00	69.00	−21.00	9.00	23.00
3	23.00	69.00	77.00	− 8.00	8.00	21.00
4	22.00	88.00	84.00	4.00	7.00	19.00
5	21.00	105.00	90.50	14.50	6.50	17.00
6	19.75	118.50	96.75	21.75	6.25	13.50
7	18.50	129.50	102.75	26.75	6.00	11.00
8	17.25	138.00	108.50	29.50	5.75	8.50
9	16.00	144.00	114.75	29.25	6.25	6.00
10	14.75	147.50	121.25	26.25	6.50	3.50
11	13.50	148.50	128.00	20.50	6.75	1.00
12	12.25	147.00	135.00	12.00	7.00	− 1.50
13	11.00	143.00	142.25	.75	7.25	− 4.00

Market Forces and the Monopolist

Can market forces eliminate the profits of a monopolist? It is possible—but only over a considerable period of time. The high barriers to market entry insulate a monopolist from competitive pressures, which would otherwise lead to expanded output and reduced prices.

Does this mean that a monopolist can be assured of economic profit? Not necessarily. A monopolist's ability to make profits is limited by the demand for whatever product is produced. In some cases, even a monopolist may be unable to sell for a profit. For example, there are thousands of clever, patented items that are never produced because demand–cost conditions are not favorable enough. Exhibit 13 illustrates this possibility. When the average cost curve of a monopolist is always above its demand curve, economic losses will result.

EXHIBIT 13   When a monopolist incurs losses

Even a monopolist will incur short-run losses if the average cost curve lies above the demand curve.

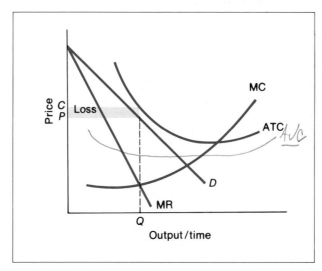

Even a monopolist will not want to operate under these conditions. If market conditions are expected to improve, the monopolist will produce output Q (where MR = MC) and charge price P, *operating in the short run* as long as variable cost can be covered. However, if the loss-producing conditions persist, the monopolist will discontinue production.

Thus far, we have proceeded as if monopolists always know exactly what their revenue and cost curves look like. Of course, this is not true in the real world. A monopolist cannot be sure of the demand conditions for a product. Choices must be made without the benefit of perfect knowledge. Decisions are made on the basis of what is *expected* to happen if prices are increased. The revenue and cost curves illustrated in Exhibits 12 and 13 might be thought of as representing *expected* revenues and costs associated with various output levels. A monopolist usually does not calculate, or is not even aware of, what we have called demand, marginal revenue, and cost curves. Profit-maximizing price and output are usually found by trial and error. However, if profits *are* maximized, the end result will be the same as if MR and MC had been calculated.

PRICE DISCRIMINATION

Price Discrimination: **A practice whereby a seller charges different consumers different prices for the same product or service.**

Until now, we have assumed that the sellers will charge each customer the same price. Sometimes sellers can increase their revenues (and profits) by charging different prices to different groups of consumers. This practice is called **price discrimination.**

If price discrimination is going to be beneficial to a seller, three conditions must be met. First, the firm must confront a downard-sloping demand curve for its product. A monopolist will meet this criterion, a pure competitor will not. Second, there must be at least two identifiable groups of consumers whose price elasticities of demand for the firm's product differ. The seller must be able to identify and separate these consumers at a low cost. Third, the sellers must be able to prevent the customers who are charged a low price from reselling the product to customers who are charged higher prices.

Exhibit 14 illustrates why sellers can sometimes gain from price discrimination. Here, there are two groups of customers for the firm's product. The demand of the first group is less elastic [graph (a)] than the demand of the second group. In each market the seller will maximize profit by equating marginal cost and marginal revenue. The best price for the group with the less elastic demand [graph (a)] is P_a, the output rate at which MR_a = MC. Since the amount purchased by this group is not very sensitive to an increase in price, the higher price (P_a) will generate more revenues (and profit) from this group. In contrast, the demand of the second group [graph (b)] is more sensitive to price. When the price charged the second group decreases, the group purchases substantially more units. Thus, the lower price P_b maximizes the profit from this group.

What easily identifiable characteristics might be linked to the customer's elasticity of demand? Sometimes factors such as age, income, and sex will influence elasticity of demand. For example, the demand of children for movies, airline tickets, and football games is often believed to be more elastic than the demand of adults.

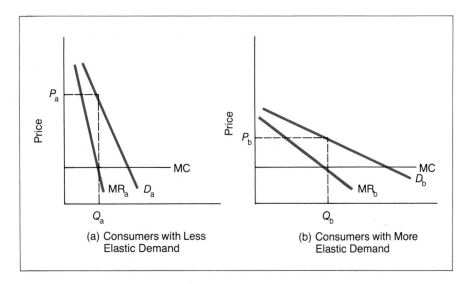

(a) Consumers with Less Elastic Demand

(b) Consumers with More Elastic Demand

Can you think of any examples of price discrimination? Airlines often offer discount fares to individuals willing to travel during off-peak hours, make reservations well in advance, or travel with another person paying full fare. The demand of these consumers is thought to be more elastic than that of other customers, such as business travelers. Thus, the group with the more elastic demand is given the discount, while other customers are required to pay the full fare. Why do professional journals usually charge individual subscribers lower rates than libraries? They generate more revenue by charging higher prices to subscribers with an inelastic demand (libraries). Why are women often charged lower prices for attending nightclubs and baseball games? Again, price discrimination apparently leads to greater increases in revenues than in costs.

A seller need not be a pure monopolist in order to gain from price discrimination. Any firm that faces a downward-sloping demand curve for its product may employ the technique. In fact, competitive weapons such as discounts and economy fares are often indicative of price discrimination. We introduce the concept while discussing monopoly merely to illustrate the general point.

WHY IS MONOPOLY "BAD"?

Through the ages, economists have had few complimentary things to say about monopoly. Most have considered it, at best, a necessary evil. Economists have taken such a dim view of monopoly for three major reasons.

First, monopoly severely limits the options available to consumers. The competition of rivals in a competitive market protects the consumer from the arbitrary behavior of a single seller. But what are your alternatives if you do not like the local telephone service? You can send a letter, deliver your message in person, or write to your elected representatives and complain. However, these are not very satisfactory alternatives to the service of a monopolist. If the monopolist "pushes you around," often you have no feasible alternative but to accept poor service, rude treatment, or high prices.

In the absence of monopoly, the consumer can buy a product either from Firm A or from another firm. In the presence of monopoly, his or her option is to buy from the monopolist or do without. This reduction in the options available to the consumer greatly reduces the consumer's ability to discipline monopolists.

Second, economists have a negative view of monopoly because it results in allocative inefficiency. Efficiency requires a community to undertake an activity when it generates additional benefits that are in excess of the cost. As applied to monopoly, this would require that a firm expand output as long as price exceeds marginal cost. A profit-maximizing monopolist, however, would restrict output below this level.

The demand curve is a measure of how much consumers value additional units of a product. The marginal cost curve represents the opportunity cost of the resources utilized to produce the additional units. Ideally, economic efficiency would require output to be expanded as long as the height of the demand curve exceeded the marginal cost. However, the monopolist will expand output only so long as marginal revenue exceeds marginal cost. At this output, as Exhibit 11 illustrates, price will exceed the marginal cost of producing the additional units. Nonetheless, a profit-maximizing firm will not produce these units (beyond Q in Exhibit 11). Therefore, from this static viewpoint, inefficiency arises because the monopolist produces too few units.

A third shortcoming of monopoly is that profits and losses do not properly induce firms to enter and to exit from industries. When barriers to entry are low, profits induce firms to produce goods for which consumers are willing (because of the expected benefits) to pay prices sufficient to cover costs of production. Losses constrain firms from the production of goods for which consumers are unwilling to cover costs of production. Profits and losses are able to direct factors of production into those activities for which consumer valuation is highest.

For the monopolist, profits play a smaller role because entry barriers are high. Although losses will induce exit from the market, a monopolist's profits are a premium enjoyed at the expense of the consumer.

MONOPOLY AND COMPETITION

The most serious problems raised by a monopoly would be avoided if the monopolist faced the threat of rivals producing the same product or even close substitutes. The presence of competitors would prevent independent firms from restricting output and raising prices.

Why not break up the monopolist into several rival units, substituting competition for monopoly? If it were not for economies of scale, this would be a very good strategy. Many leading economists believe that several industries currently dominated by a few firms (or monopolists) could be made considerably more competitive without sacrificing the potential economies associated with large-scale production.

Exhibit 15 compares competition and monopoly, assuming that economies of scale are unimportant in the industry. Given this assumption, the

Here we assume that a product can be produced by either numerous small firms or a monopolist at the same average total and marginal costs. When there are no cost disadvantages for small-scale production, competition serves to reduce price. For a purely competitive industry (a), supply and demand would dictate price P_c. The firms would just be able to cover their cost. if all the firms merged into a monopoly and *cost conditions remained the same,* the monopolist would restrict output to Q_m (where MC would equal MR). Price would rise to P_m.

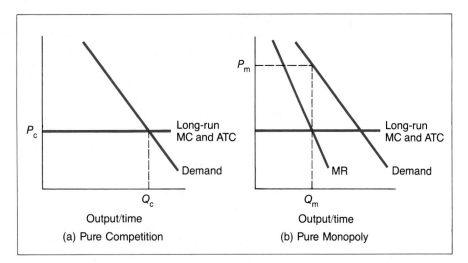

(a) Pure Competition

(b) Pure Monopoly

minimum-cost production conditions for purely competitive firms would not differ from those of a monopolist. If the industry were purely competitive, price would be determined by supply and demand. As Exhibit 15a illustrates, under these conditions competition would drive price down to P_c in the long run. An industry output of Q_c would result. The market price would just equal the marginal opportunity costs of production.

In contrast, if the industry were monopolized, the profit-maximizing monopolist would equate marginal revenue with marginal cost (Exhibit 15b). This would lead to an output level of Q_m. The monopolist would charge P_m, a higher price than would exist in a competitive industry. When economies of scale are unimportant, imposition of competitive conditions on a monopolized industry would result in lower prices, a larger output, and improved economic efficiency.

One Advantage of Monopoly

Unfortunately, it is often unrealistic to expect similar cost conditions for pure competition and monopoly. Economies of scale are often the reason that certain industries tend to be monopolized. If economies of scale are important, larger firms will have lower per unit cost than smaller rivals. Sometimes, economies of scale may be so important that per unit cost of production will be lowest when the entire output of the industry is produced by a single firm. In the absence of government intervention, the "natural" tendency will then be toward monopoly, because increases in firm size through merger or "survival of the fittest" will lead to lower per unit cost. The largest firm will always tend to eliminate smaller rivals because of the economies of scale. Such a firm is referred to as a **natural monopoly**.

Natural Monopoly: **A market situation in which the average costs of production continually decline with increased output. Thus, a single firm would be the lowest-cost producer of the output demanded.**

Note that when a "natural" monopoly exists, a "competitive" market structure will be both costly and difficult to maintain. The telephone industry and local public utilities (water, electricity, etc.) approximate natural monopoly conditions. If there were several telephone companies operating in the same area, each with its own lines, transmission equipment, and home phones, costly duplication would result. In such industries, a large number of firms would not be feasible.

Can the Monopolist Be Controlled?

When monopoly or near monopoly results because of economies of scale, we often turn to government regulation seeking a solution to the problem. Can government regulation improve the allocative efficiency of unregulated monopoly? In theory, the answer to this question is clearly yes. Government regulation can force the monopolist to reduce his or her price, and, at the lower government-imposed price ceiling, the monopolist will voluntarily produce a larger output. Exhibit 16 illustrates why ideal government price regulation would improve resource allocation. The profit-maximizing monopolist sets price at P_o and produces output Q_o, where $MR = MC$. At this output level, however, consumer valuation of additional units clearly exceeds their opportunity cost. How can the regulatory agency improve on the situation that would result from unregulated monopoly?

1. Average Cost Pricing. If a regulatory agency forces the monopolist to reduce price to P_1—the intersection of the firm's ATC curve and the market (and firm) demand curve—the monopolist will expand output to Q_1. Since the firm cannot charge a price above P_1, it cannot increase revenues by selling a smaller output at a higher price. Once the price ceiling is instituted, the firm can increase revenues by P_1, but only P_1, for each unit that it sells. The regulated firm's MR is constant at P_1 for all units sold until output is increased to Q_1. Since the firm's MC is less than P_1 (and therefore less than MR), the profit-maximizing, regulated monopolist will expand output from Q_o to Q_1. The benefits from the consumption of these units (ABQ_1Q_o) clearly exceed their costs (CEQ_1Q_o). Social welfare has improved as a result of the regulative action (we will ignore the impact on the distribution of income). At that output level, revenues are sufficient to cover costs. The firm is making zero economic profit (that is, "normal" profit).

2. Marginal Cost Pricing. Ideally, since marginal cost is still less than price even at the Q_1 output level, additional welfare gains are possible if output is

EXHIBIT 16   Regulation of a monopolist

If unregulated, a profit-maximizing monopolist with the costs indicated here would produce Q_0 units and charge P_0. If a regulatory agency forced the monopolist to reduce price to P_1, the monopolist would expand output to Q_1. Ideally, we would like output to be expanded to Q_2, where $P = MC$, but regulatory agencies usually do not attempt to keep prices as low as P_2. Can you explain why?

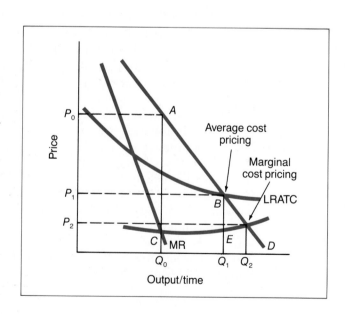

increased to Q_2. However, if a regulatory agency forced the monopolist to reduce his or her price to P_2 (so that price would equal marginal cost at the output level Q_2), economic losses would result. Even a monopolist, unless he or she were subsidized, would not undertake production if the regulatory agency set the price at P_2 or any price below P_1. Usually, problems associated with determining and allocating the necessary subsidy would make this option infeasible.

Why Regulation May Go Astray

The solution of government regulation looks simple on paper. The real world, however, is more complex. Analysis of economic incentives suggests that this solution would usually be less than ideal. Why?

1. Lack of Information.   In discussing ideal regulation, we assume that we know what the firm's cost and demand curve looks like. In reality, of course, this would not be the case.

Because estimates of demand and marginal costs are difficult to obtain, regulatory agencies usually use profits (or rates of return) as a gauge to determine whether the regulated price is too high or too low. The regulatory agency, guarding the public interest, seeks to impose a "fair" or "normal" rate of return on the firm. However, the actual existence of profits is not easily identified. Accounting profit, even allowing for a normal rate of profit, is not the same as economic profit. Regulated firms have a definite incentive to adopt reporting techniques and accounting methods that conceal profits.

2. Cost Shifting.   Not only do monopolists have an incentive to conceal profits, but the *owners* of the regulated firm have less incentive to be concerned about costs than the owners of unregulated firms. If costs decrease, the regulatory agency will force a price reduction. If costs increase, the regulatory agency will allow a price increase. The owners of the regulated firm can expect their long-run rate of profit to be essentially fixed regardless of whether efficient management reduces costs or inefficient management allows costs to increase.

Managers will have a freer hand to pursue personal objectives. They will be more likely to fly first class, entertain lavishly on an expense account, give their relatives and friends good jobs, grant larger wage increases, and perform many other such actions that increase the firm's costs but yield personal benefits to the managers.

3. The Impact of Inflation.   Regulation based on normal rate of return will encounter serious difficulties during inflationary times. If the costs of labor, energy resources, and other factors of production rise along with other prices, the cost of producing the product or service of the regulated firm will increase during the period of inflation. A rate structure based on *last year's cost figures* will not permit the firm to earn a normal rate of return. Of course, as its rate of return drops below normal, the firm's case for a rate increase next year will be strengthened. However, if the inflation continues, the regulated firm's rate of return will continue to be below normal. The firm will be unable to earn the normal rate of return during inflationary times as long as its rate structure is based on historical costs. As a result of its low earnings, the regulated firm will have difficulty raising funds in the capital market. If the normal rate of return on capital is 12 percent, who will want to invest with a firm that is able to earn only 9 percent? Many regulated utilities were caught in precisely this cost-regulated price squeeze as the price of energy and other resources soared during the inflation of the 1970s.

4. Quality Regulation. It is much easier to regulate product price than to regulate quality. Regulated firms desiring to raise the price of their product can often do so by taking cost-reducing steps that result in quality deterioration. Consider the quality dimension of a seemingly uniform good such as telephone service. The speed at which your call goes through, the likelihood that you will have to dial the desired number more than once, the length of time during which your phone is out of order, and the rapidity with which you are able to get it repaired are determinants of the quality of telephone service. Since these factors are hard to control, it is extremely difficult for a regulatory agency to impose a price *per constant quality unit.* During inflationary times, regulated firms caught in a cost-regulated price squeeze may be particularly tempted to lower the quality of their product.

5. Special Interest Effect. The difficulties of government regulation discussed thus far are practical limitations that a regulatory agency, seeking to perform its duties efficiently, would confront. The special interest effect suggests that it is naive to expect regulatory authorities to be guided consistently by the efficiency criterion. Regulatory agencies have a life or death grip on the firms they regulate. These firms will have a strong incentive to ensure that "friendly people" serve as regulators. They will invest political and economic resources to this end.

Consumers, on the other hand, cannot be expected to invest time, resources, votes, and political contributions to ensure that regulatory commissions represent their views. The firms that are regulated will make such investments. Even though the initial stimulus for a regulating agency might come from consumer interests, economic theory suggests that such agencies will eventually reflect the views of the business and labor interests they are supposed to regulate.

Putting the Monopoly Problem into Perspective

Because of its emphasis on competition within an industry, traditional economic theory highlights the market power of monopolists. However, no firm is an island unto itself. Each firm competes with every other firm for the dollar votes of consumers. Vastly different products offer alternative sources of consumer satisfaction. With time, competitors in other markets may limit the power of a monopolist. High prices encourage rivals to develop substitutes. For example, the high price of natural rubber spurred the development of synthetic rubber. High rail shipping rates accelerated the development of long-distance trucking. The exercise of monopoly power by the Organization of Petroleum Exporting Countries (OPEC) has subjected oil to vastly intensified competition from coal, solar, and other energy sources. The search for alternative sources of energy, and the encouragement of petroleum conservation, have led to innovation in areas ranging from home construction to automobile design.

Actually, competition from substitute products—both current and potential—is important for two reasons. First, a monopolist will sometimes choose to produce a larger output and charge a lower price in order to discourage potential rivals from developing substitute products. Second, although the development of substitute products often seems slow and sometimes insignificant, these products reduce the market power of monopolists. With time, broad competition from substitute products will often bring about the destruction of monopoly power.

<table>
<tr><td>

CHAPTER LEARNING OBJECTIVES

</td><td>

1 Pure competition is a model of industrial structure that assumes the presence of a large number of small (relative to the total market) firms, each producing a homogeneous product in a market for which there is complete freedom of entry and exit. Market prices will be determined by supply and demand. In the short-run, firms might make either profits or losses, but, in the long run, competitive pressures will eliminate economic profits (and losses).

2 Under pure competition, firms are price takers—they face a perfectly elastic demand curve. Profit-maximizing (or loss minimizing) firms will expand output as long as the additional output adds more to revenues than to costs. Therefore, the competitive firm will produce at the output level where marginal revenue (and price) equals marginal cost.

3 The firm's short-run marginal cost (above its average variable cost) is its supply curve.

4 If a firm is (a) covering its average variable cost and (b) anticipates that the "below average total cost" price will be temporary, it may operate in the short run even though it is experiencing a loss. However, even if it anticipates more favorable market conditions in the future, loss minimization will require the firm to shut down (temporarily cease operation) if it is unable to cover its average variable cost. If the firm does not anticipate that it will be able to cover its average total cost even in the long run, loss minimization will require that it immediately go out of business.

5 When price exceeds average total costs, a firm will make economic profits. Under pure competition, profits will attract new firms into the industry and stimulate the existing firms to expand. The market supply will increase, pushing price down to the level of average total cost. Competitive firms will be unable to make the long-run economic profits. Losses exist when the market price is less than the firm's average total cost. Losses will cause firms to exit from the industry or reduce their scale of the operation.

6 Economists often argue that pure competition leads to ideal economic efficiency because (a) costs of production are minimized and (b) profit-maximizing producers produce the goods consumers desire most.

7 Monopoly exists when there are high barriers to entry and a single producer of a product for which there are no satisfactory substitutes. A monopolist maximizes profits by expanding output as long as marginal revenue exceeds marginal cost. At this output level, product price exceeds marginal cost.

8 Legal restrictions, economies of scale, and control of an essential resource are the most common sources of barriers to entry.

9 A monopolist might make either profits or losses. If profit results, high barriers to entry will shield the monopolist from competitive pressures. Therefore, long-run economic profits are sometimes possible.

10 Economists are critical of a monopoly because (a) it limits the ability of consumers to "control" the behavior of the producer, (b) the unregulated monopolist produces too little output and charges a price in excess of his or her marginal cost, and (c) profits are less able to induce new entry that will expand the supply of the product until the price declines to the level of production costs.

</td></tr>
</table>

11 Natural monopoly exists when long-run average total costs continue to decline as firm size increases. Thus, a larger firm always has lower costs. Cost of production is lowest in cases in which a single firm generates the entire output of an industry.

12 Monopoly will result in higher prices and less output than would be ideal. Regulation will often fail to meet our ideal efficiency criteria because (a) the regulators will not have knowledge of the firm's cost curves and market demand conditions, (b) firms have an incentive to conceal their actual cost condition and take profits in disguised forms, and (c) the regulators often end up being influenced by the firms they are supposed to regulate.

13 Even a monopolist is not completely free of competitive pressures. All products have some type of substitute. Some monopolists may charge less than the short-run, profit-maximizing price in order to discourage potential competitors from developing substitute products.

THE ECONOMIC WAY OF THINKING — DISCUSSION QUESTIONS

1 If the firms in a competitive industry are making short-run profits, what will happen to the market price in the long run? Explain.

2 What do economists mean when they say that resource allocation is ideal or efficient? Why is it sometimes argued that a purely competitive economy will allocate goods ideally? Explain.

3 "It's wrong to profit from someone else's needs?" Do you agree? (a) Should physicians profit from the illness of their patients? Teachers from the ignorance of their students? Newscasters from their listeners' lack of information about current affairs? Legislators from the needs of their constituents? (b) When is it all right to earn a profit? (c) What role do profits play in a market economy? (d) Do profits and losses actually influence human behavior? (Ignore the issue of whether they should.) Cite evidence with which you are familiar and discuss.

4 Is a monopolist subject to any competitive pressure? Explain. Would an unregulated monopolist have an incentive to operate and produce efficiently? If so, why?

5 Do monopolists charge the highest prices for which they can sell their products? Do they maximize their average profit per sale? Is a monopolistic firm always profitable? Why or why not?

6 Does economic theory indicate that a monopoly forced by an ideal regulatory agency to set prices according to either marginal or average cost would be more efficient than an unregulated monopoly? Explain. Does economic theory suggest that a regulatory agency will follow a proper regulation policy? What are some of the factors that complicate the regulatory function?

*Differences in tastes, desires, in-
comes and locations of buyers,
and differences in the uses which
they wish to make of commodities
all indicate the need for variety
and the necessity of substituting
for the concept of a "competitive
ideal" an ideal involving both
monopoly and competition.[1]
Edward H. Chamberlin*

15

THE INTERMEDIATE CASES: MONOPOLISTIC COMPETITION AND OLIGOPOLY

Most real-world firms operate in markets that fall between the extremes of pure competition and pure monopoly. These firms do not confront numerous competitors all producing a homogeneous product sold at a single price; neither do most firms produce a good or service that is unavailable from other sellers. Instead, most firms face varying degrees of competition. In some cases, there are competitors offering roughly the same product; in other instances, the competitor's product is merely an attractive substitute. There may be numerous competitors; or there may be only a few other sellers in a given market. The models of monopolistic competition and oligopoly have been developed by economists to describe markets that are neither purely competitive nor purely monopolistic.

Monopolistically competitive and oligopolistic firms have different degrees of freedom in setting prices, altering quality, and choosing a marketing strategy than firms in purely competitive or purely monopolistic markets. Most firms, unlike those under purely competitive conditions, will lose some *but not all* of their customers when they increase the price of their product. These firms face a downward-sloping demand curve. They are sometimes called **price searchers** because they must search for the price that is most consistent with their overall goal—maximum profit, for example. But as we have indicated, just as they are not pure competitors, most price searchers are not monopolists, either. Thus, their freedom to raise price is limited by the existence of both actual and potential competitors offering similar products. The difference between monopolistic competition and oligopoly is in one sense a difference in the degree to which a price searcher is limited by competition.

Price Searchers: Firms that face a downward-sloping demand curve for their product.

---

[1]Edward H. Chamberlin, *The Theory of Monopolistic Competition* (Cambridge, Massachusetts: Harvard University Press, 1948), p. 214.

CHARACTERISTICS OF MONOPOLISTIC COMPETITION

Monopolistic Competition: A situation in which there are a large number of independent sellers, each producing a differentiated product in a market with low barriers to entry. Construction, retail sales, and service stations are good examples of monopolistically competitive industries.

During the 1920s, many economists felt that neither pure competition nor pure monopoly was descriptive of markets such as retail sales, construction, service businesses, and small manufacturing, which were generally characterized by numerous firms offering different but closely related products or services. The need for a more accurate model for markets of this type led to the theory of **monopolistic competition.** The theory was developed independently by Joan Robinson, a British economist, and Edward Chamberlin, an American economist. The major work of both Robinson and Chamberlin was published in 1933.[2] Both economists outlined three distinguishing characteristics of monopolistic competition.

Product Differentiation

Differentiated Products: Products that are distinguished from similar products by such characteristics as quality, design, location, and method of promotion.

Monopolistic competitors offer **differentiated products** to consumers. Goods and services of one seller are differentiated from those of another by convenience of location, product quality, reputation of the seller, advertising, and various other product characteristics.

Since the product of each monopolistic competitor is slightly different from that of its rivals, the individual firm faces a downward-sloping demand curve. A price reduction will enable the firm to attract new customers. Alternatively, the firm will be able to increase its price by a small amount and still retain many of its customers, who prefer the location, style, dependability, or other product characteristics offered by the firm. However, the demand curve confronted by the monopolistic competitor is highly elastic. Although each firm has some control over price, that control is extremely limited, since the firm faces competition from rivals offering very similar products. The availability of close substitutes and the ease with which consumers can turn to rival firms (including new firms that are free to enter the market) force a monopolistically competitive firm to think twice before raising its price.

Low Barriers to Entry

Under monopolistic competition, firms are free to enter into or exit from the market. There are neither legal barriers nor market obstacles hindering the movement of competitors into and out of a monopolistically competitive market. Monopolistic competition resembles pure competition in this respect; firms in both these types of markets confront the constant threat of competition from new, innovative rivals.

Many Independent Firms

A monopolistic competitor faces not only the potential threat posed by new rivals but competition from many current sellers as well. Each firm is small relative to the total market. No single firm or small group of firms is able to dominate the market.

Retailing is perhaps the sector of our economy that best typifies monopolistic competition. In most market areas, there are a large number of retail

---

[2]See Joan Robinson, *The Economics of Imperfect Competition* (1933; reprint ed., New York: St. Martin's, 1969), and Edward H. Chamberlin, *The Theory of Monopolistic Competition* (Cambridge, Massachusetts: Harvard University Press, 1933).

stores offering similar products and services. Rivalry is intense, and stores are constantly trying new combinations of price and quality of service (or merchandise) in their effort to win customers. The *free entry* that typifies most retailing makes for rapid change. Yesterday's novelty can quickly become obsolete as new rivals develop still better (or more attractive) products and marketing methods.

PRICE AND OUTPUT UNDER MONOPOLISTIC COMPETITION

How does a monopolistic competitor decide what price to charge and what level of output to produce? Like a pure monopolist, a monopolistic competitor will face a downward-sloping demand curve for its product. Additional units can be sold only at a lower price. Therefore, the marginal revenue curve of the monopolistic competitor will always lie below the firm's demand curve.

Any firm can increase profits by expanding output as long as marginal revenue exceeds marginal cost. Therefore, a monopolistic competitor will lower its prices and expand its output until marginal revenue is equal to marginal cost.

Exhibit 1 illustrates the profit-maximizing price and output under monopolistic competition. A profit-maximizing monopolistic competitor will expand output to q, where marginal revenue is equal to marginal cost. It will charge price P, the highest price at which output q can be sold. For any output level less than q (for example, R), a price reduction and sales expansion will add more to total revenues than to total costs. At output R, marginal revenue exceeds marginal costs. Thus, profits will be greater if price is reduced so output can be expanded. On the other hand, if output exceeds q (for example, S), sale of additional units beyond q will *add* more to costs (MC) than to revenues (MR). The firm will therefore gain by raising the price to P, even though the price rise will result in the loss of customers. Profits will be maximized by charging price P and producing the output level q, where MC = MR.

The firm pictured by Exhibit 1 is making economic profit. Total revenues $PAqO$ exceed the firm's total cost $CBqO$ at the profit-maximizing output level. Since barriers to entry in monopolistically competitive markets are low, profits will attract rival competitors. Other firms will attempt to duplicate the product (or service) offered by the profit-making firms.

EXHIBIT 1 The monopolistic competitor's price and output

A monopolistic competitor maximizes profits by producing output q, for which MR = MC, and charging price P. The firm is making economic profits. What impact will they have?

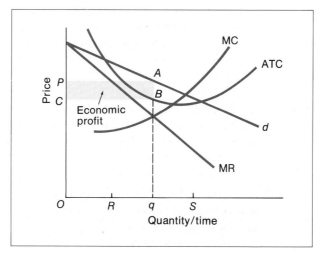

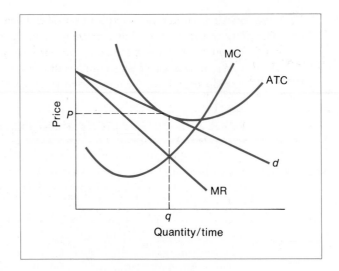

EXHIBIT 2 Monopolistic competition and long-run normal profit

Since entry and exit are free, competition will eventually drive prices down to the level of average total cost.

What impact will the entry of new rivals have on the demand for the products of profit-making firms already in the market? These new rivals will draw customers away from existing firms. As long as monopolistically competitive firms can make economic profits, new competitors will be attracted to the market. Eventually, the competition among rivals will shift the demand curve for monopolistic competitors inward and eliminate the economic profits. In the long run, as illustrated by Exhibit 2, a monopolistically competitive firm will just be able to cover its production costs. It will produce to the MR = MC output level, but the entry of new competition will force the price down to the average per unit cost.

If losses exist in a monopolistically competitive industry, some of the existing firms in the industry will go out of business over a period of time. As such firms leave the industry, some of their previous customers will buy from other firms. The demand curve facing the remaining firms in the industry will shift out until the economic losses are eliminated and the long-run, zero-profit equilibrium illustrated by Exhibit 2 is again restored.

Under monopolistic competition, profits and losses play precisely the same role as they do under pure competition. Economic profits will attract new competitors to the market. The increased availability of the product (and similar products) will drive the price down until the profits are eliminated. Conversely, economic losses will cause competitors to exit from the market. The decline in the availability of the product (supply) will allow the price to rise until firms are once again able to cover their average cost.

In the short run, a monopolistic competitor may make either economic profits or losses, depending on market conditions. In the long run, however, only a normal profit rate (that is, zero economic profits) will be possible because of competitive conditions and freedom of entry.

COMPARING PURE AND MONOPOLISTIC COMPETITION

As you can see, determination of price and output under monopolistic competition is in some ways very similar to that under pure competition. Also, since the long-run equilibrium conditions under pure competition are consistent with ideal economic efficiency, it is useful to compare and contrast other market structures with pure competition. There are both similarities and differences between pure and monopolistic competition.

Similarities between Pure and Monopolistic Competition

Since barriers to entry are low, neither pure nor monopolistic competitors will be able to earn long-run economic profit. In the long run, competition will drive the price of both pure and monopolistic competitors down to the level of average total cost.

In each case, entrepreneurs have a strong incentive to manage and operate their businesses efficiently. Inefficient operation will lead to losses and forced exit from the market. Both pure and monopolistic competitors will be motivated to develop and adopt new cost-reducing procedures and techniques because lower costs will mean higher profits (or at least smaller losses).

The response of pure and monopolistic competitors to changing demand conditions is very similar. In both cases, an increase in market demand leads to higher prices, short-run profits, and the entry of additional firms. With the entry of the new producers, and the concurrent expansion of existing firms, the market supply will increase until the market price falls to the level of average total cost. Similarly, a reduction in demand will lead to lower prices and short-run losses that will force firms from the market. As firms leave the market, supply will decline, permitting the remaining firms to raise prices. Eventually, the short-run losses will be eliminated. Profits and losses will direct the activities of firms under both pure and monopolistic competition.

Differences between Pure and Monopolistic Competition

As Exhibit 3 illustrates, the pure competitor confronts a horizontal demand curve; the demand curve faced by a monopolistic competitor is downward-sloping. This is important because it means that the marginal revenue of the monopolistic competitor will be less than, rather than equal to, price. Thus, when the profit-maximizing monopolistic competitor expands output until

EXHIBIT 3 Comparing pure and monopolistic competition

The long-run equilibrium conditions of firms under pure and monopolistic competition are illustrated here. In both cases, price is equal to average total cost, and economic profit is absent. However, since the monopolistically competitive firm confronts a downward-sloping demand curve for its product, its equilibrium price exceeds marginal cost, and equilibrium output is not large enough to minimize average total cost. *For identical cost conditions,* the price of the monopolistic competitor will be slightly higher than that of the pure competitor. Chamberlin referred to this slightly higher price as the premium a society pays for variety and convenience (product differentiation).

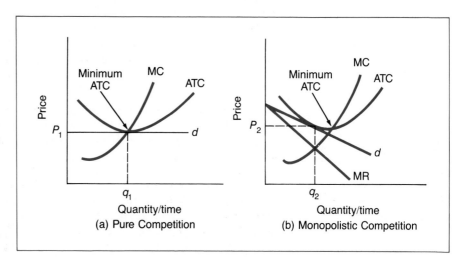

MR $=$ MC, price will still exceed marginal cost (Exhibit 3b). In contrast, in the long-run equilibrium, the price charged by the pure competitor will *equal* marginal cost (Exhibit 3a). Thus, the zero economic profit equilibrium for a monopolistically competitive firm, unlike that for a pure competitor, occurs at an output rate that fails to minimize the firm's long-run average total cost, as Exhibit 3 illustrates. The monopolistic competitor would have a lower per unit cost if a larger output were produced.

Under monopolistic competition, firms produce differentiated products; pure competitors produce homogeneous products. A monopolistically competitive firm will seek to increase the demand for a product by taking steps to convince consumers that the product is both different from and superior to products offered by rivals. Monopolistic competitors often engage in competitive advertising as a means of attracting additional customers. Purely competitive firms do not need to use advertising, since they can already sell all they can produce at the market price.

Allocative Efficiency under Monopolistic Competition

The efficiency of monopolistic competition has been the subject of debate among economists for years. At one time, the dominant view seemed to be that allocative inefficiency results because monopolistic competitors fail to operate at an output level that minimizes their long-run average total cost. Due to the proliferation in the number of monopolistic competitors, the sales of each competitor fall short of their optimal (lowest per unit cost) capacity level. The potential social gain associated with the expansion of production to the P $=$ MC output rate is lost, according to this view, whose advocates point out that if there were fewer producers, they would each be able to operate at a minimum-cost output rate. Instead, there is wasteful duplication—too many producers each operating below their minimum-cost output capacity. According to this traditional view, the location of two or more filling stations, restaurants, grocery stores, or similar establishments side by side is indicative of the economic waste generated by monopolistic competition.

In addition, the critics of monopolistic competition argue that it often leads to self-defeating, wasteful advertising. Firms have an incentive to use advertising to promote artificial distinctions between similar products. Each firm bombards consumers with advertisements proclaiming (or implying) that its own product is fancier, has greater sex appeal, and/or brings quicker relief than any product of rival firms. Firms that do not engage in such advertising can expect their sales to decline. However, advertising results in higher prices for consumers and thus from society's point of view can be argued to be too costly.

In recent years, this traditional view has been seriously challenged. Many economists now believe that such a view is mechanistic and fails to take into account the significance of dynamic competition. Most important, the traditional view assumes that consumers place no value on the wider variety of qualities and styles that results from monopolistic competition. Prices might very well be slightly lower if there were fewer gasoline stations, located farther apart, and offering a more limited variety of service and credit plan options. Similarly, the prices of groceries might very well be slightly lower if there were fewer supermarkets, each a bit more congested and located somewhat less conveniently

Along with Edward Chamberlin, Joan Robinson is given credit for developing the theory of monopolistic competition. In her book *The Economics of Imperfect Competition* (1933), she redefined the market demand curve to account for interdependence among firms.[3] Following Alfred Marshall, she used differences among products to define an industry. Essentially, she viewed each firm as a monopolist facing a downward-sloping demand curve that is affected by the behavior of other "monopolists" in the industry. Unlike Chamberlin, she did not introduce product differentiation and quality competition *within an industry* into her analysis.

Professor Robinson's contribution to economics goes far beyond her role in developing the theory of monopolistic competition. Now professor emerita of economics at Cambridge University, she was one of a select group of economists who worked with Keynes during the developmental stage of his *General Theory*. She fully accepts the Keynesian view that the market economy is inherently unstable. Furthermore, she argues that market economies suffer from other serious defects—income inequality, pollution, business concentration, and manipulation of demand.

Professor Robinson has played a prominent role in continuing the Cambridge tradition of dissent from the traditional orthodoxy. Delivering the Richard T. Ely Lecture to the American Economic Association in 1971, she argued that the economics profession faces a second major crisis. Just as pre-Keynesian economists failed to develop a theory of aggregate employment, Professor Robinson charges that current economists have failed to develop a meaningful theory of "what employment should be for." In her view, "this primarily concerns the allocation of resources between products, but it is also bound up with the distribution of products between people." She feels that the relative earnings of individuals depend on bargaining power and union influence, not primarily on market conditions.

In recent years, she has become a vocal critic of the capitalist system. In many ways, she is something of an English Galbraith. The *Collected Economic Papers* of Professor Robinson now fill four volumes.[4] Her work in economics runs the gamut. Capital theory, international trade, Marxian economics, growth theory, and comparative systems are among the many areas that have felt the touch of her pen.

[3] Joan Robinson, *The Economics of Imperfect Competition* (1933; reprint ed., New York: St. Martin's, 1969).

[4] Joan Robinson, *Collected Papers,* 4 vols. (New York: Humanities Press, 1960–1972).

---

for many customers. However, since customers value diversity in product selection as well as lower prices, it does not follow that consumers are worse off under the conditions created by monopolistic competition. Edward Chamberlin, one of the developers of the theory, argues that the higher prices (and costs) are simply the premium consumers pay for variety and convenience. When consumers receive utility from product diversity, one cannot conclude that pure competition (and the reduction in diversity that would accompany it) would be preferable to monopolistic competition.

The defenders of monopolistic competition also deny that it leads to excessive, wasteful advertising. They point out that advertising often reduces the consumer's search time and provides valuable information on prices. If advertising really raises prices, it must provide the consumer with something that is valuable. Otherwise, the consumer will purchase lower-priced, nonadvertised goods. When consumers really prefer lower prices and less advertising, firms offering that combination do quite well. In fact, the proponents argue, monopolistic competitors actually do often use higher-quality service and lower prices to compete with rivals that may advertise more heavily.

The debate among economists has helped to clarify the issues on this topic. Nonetheless, the efficiency of monopolistic competition continues to be one of the unresolved issues of economics.

REAL-WORLD MONOPOLISTIC COMPETITORS

In our model, we assume that firms have perfect knowledge of both their costs and demand conditions. Real-world firms do not have such information. They must rely on past experience, market surveys, experimenting, and other business skills when they make price, output, and production decisions.

Could profits be increased if prices were raised, or would lower prices lead to larger profits? Real-world business decision-makers cannot go into the back room and look at their demand—cost diagram in order to answer these questions. They must search. They might raise prices for a time and see what would happen to their sales. Or they might lower prices and see if additional sales would expand revenues more than costs. Note that if maximum profit is the goal of the firm, charging prices that are too high can be just as costly as charging prices that are too low. The successful, astute business decision-maker will search and find the profit-maximizing price—the MR = MC output level—that our model assumes is common knowledge.

For real-world entrepreneurs, the problem of uncertainty goes well beyond setting the profit-maximizing price. When considering entry into a monopolistically competitive field, how can entrepreneurs decide whether demand and cost conditions will permit them to make a profit? Just what combination of qualities should be built into the firm's product or service? What location will be best? What forms of advertising will be most effective? Again, past experience, trial and error, and business skill will guide profit-seeking entrepreneurs. Those who have exhibited skill on the basis of past successful experiences will be encouraged to stay and expand. Newcomers can learn by working with others, hiring expert help, or contracting with existing firms, perhaps on a franchise basis.

Despite their high hopes, many firms go out of business every year. In recent years, among corporate establishments alone, the number of firms going out of business has generally exceeded 200,000 annually. A great many of these unsuccessful businesses are small, monopolistically competitive firms that are forced out of business by losses stemming from market competition.

Why do losses result in the real world? Since business decisions must be made without perfect information, mistakes sometimes result. A firm may mistakenly produce a good for which consumers are unwilling to pay a price that will enable the producer to cover the costs of production. Losses are the market's method of bringing such activities to a halt. Economic losses signal that the resources would be valued more highly if they were put to other uses. Losses also provide the incentive to correct this allocative inefficiency.

CHARACTERISTICS OF OLIGOPOLY

Oligopoly: **A market situation in which a small number of sellers comprise the entire industry. It is competition among the few.**

"Oligopoly" means "few sellers." Thus, when there are only a few firms in an industry, the industrial structure is called an **oligopoly.** In the United States, the vast majority of output in such industries as automobiles, steel, cigarettes, and aircraft is produced by only four or five dominant firms. In addition to a small number of producers, there are several other characteristics that oligopolistic industries have in common.

Interdependence among Firms

Since the number of sellers in an oligopolistic industry is small, each firm must take the potential reactions of rivals into account when it makes business decisions. The business decisions of one seller often have a substantial impact on the price of products and the profits of rival firms. The welfare of each oligopolistic seller is dependent on the policies followed by its major rivals.

Substantial Economies of Scale

In an oligopolistic industry, large-scale production (relative to the total market) is necessary to attain a low per unit cost. Economies of scale are significant. A small number of the large-scale, cost-efficient firms will meet the demand for the industry's product.

Using the automobile industry as an example, Exhibit 4 illustrates the importance of economies of scale as a source of oligopoly. It has been estimated that each firm must produce approximately 1 million automobiles annually before its per unit cost of production is minimized. However, when the selling price of automobiles is barely sufficient for firms to cover their costs, the total quantity demanded from the industry as a whole is only 6 million. Thus, in order to minimize costs, each firm must produce approximately one-sixth (1 million of the 6 million) of the output demanded. In other words, the industry can support no more than five or six firms of cost-efficient size.

EXHIBIT 4   Economies of scale and oligopoly

Oligopoly exists in the automobile industry because firms do not fully realize the cost reductions from large-scale output until they produce approximately one-sixth of the total market.

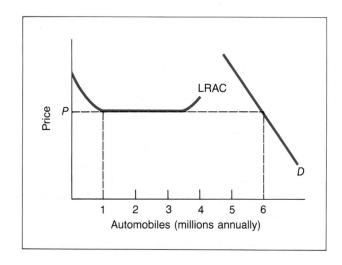

Significant Barriers to Entry

As with monopoly, barriers to entry limit the ability of new firms to compete effectively in oligopolistic industries. Economies of scale are probably the most significant entry barrier. A potential competitor will be unable to start out small and gradually grow to the optimal size, since, as we just explained, a firm in an oligopolistic industry must gain a large share of the market before it is able to minimize per unit cost. Patent rights, control over an essential resource, and government-imposed restraints may also prevent additional competitors from entering oligopolistic industries. Without substantial barriers to entry, oligopolistic competition would be similar to monopolistic competition.

Products May Be Either Homogeneous or Differentiated

The products of sellers in an oligopolistic industry may be either homogeneous or differentiated. However, although the nature of the product does not help us to identify an oligopoly, it influences the competitive strategies of rival firms. When firms produce identical products, there is less opportunity for nonprice competition. On the other hand, rival firms producing differentiated products are more likely to use style, quality, and advertising as competitive weapons.

PRICE AND OUTPUT UNDER OLIGOPOLY

Unlike a monopolist or a pure competitor, an oligopolist cannot determine the product price that will deliver maximum profit simply by estimating demand and cost conditions. An oligopolist must also predict how rival firms (that is, the rest of the industry) will react to price (and quality) adjustments. Since each oligopolist confronts such a complex problem, it is impossible to determine the precise price and output policy that will emerge in oligopolistic industries. However, economics does give signposts that suggest certain behavioral patterns. We can outline the potential range within which prices will lie. We can discuss the factors that will determine whether prices in the industry will be high or low relative to costs of production.

Consider an oligopolistic industry in which seven or eight rival firms produce the entire market output. Substantial economies of scale are present. The firms produce identical products and have similar costs of production. Exhibit 5 depicts the market demand conditions and long-run costs of production of the individual firms for such an industry.

What price will prevail? We can answer this question by making two extreme assumptions. First, suppose that each firm sets its price independently of the other firms. There is no collusion, and each competitive firm acts independently, seeking to maximize profits by offering consumers a better deal than its rivals. Under these conditions, the market price would be driven down to P_c. Firms would just be able to cover their per unit costs of production. What would happen if a *single firm* raised its price? Its customers would switch to rival firms, which would now expand to accommodate the new customers. The firm that raised its price would lose out. It would be self-defeating for any one firm to raise its price if the other firms did not raise theirs.

What would happen if supply conditions were such that the market price was above P_c? Since the demand curve faced by each *individual firm* is highly elastic, rival sellers would have a strong incentive to reduce their price. Any firm that reduced its price slightly, by 1 percent, for example, would gain numerous

EXHIBIT 5 The range of price and output under oligopoly

If oligopolists competed with one another, price-cutting would drive price down to P_c. In contrast, perfect cooperation among firms would lead to a higher price P_m and a smaller output (Q_m rather than Q_c).

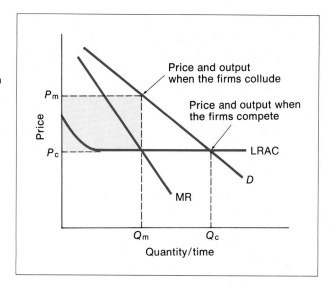

customers. The price-cutting firm would attract some new buyers to the market, but, more important, that firm would also lure many buyers away from rival firms charging higher prices. Total profit would expand as the price-cutter gained a larger share of the total market. But what would happen if all firms attempted to undercut their rivals? Price would be driven down to P_c, and the economic profit of the firms would be eliminated.

When rival oligopolists compete (pricewise) with one another, they drive the market price down to the level of costs of production. However, this is not always the case. There is a strong incentive for oligopolists to collude, raise price, and restrict output.

Cartel: An organization of sellers designed to coordinate supply decisions so that the joint profits of the members will be maximized. A cartel will seek to create a monopoly in the market.

Suppose that the oligopolists, recognizing their interdependence, acted cooperatively in order to maximize their joint profit. They might form a **cartel,** such as OPEC, in order to accomplish this objective. Alternatively, they might collude without the aid of a formal organization. Under federal antitrust laws, collusive action to raise price and maximize the joint profit of the firms would, of course, be illegal. Nonetheless, let us see what would happen if oligopolists followed this course. Exhibit 5 shows the marginal revenue curve that would accompany the market demand D for the product. Under perfect cooperation, the oligopolists would refuse to produce units for which marginal revenue was less than marginal cost. Thus, they would restrict joint output to Q_m, where MR = MC. Market price would rise to P_m. Thus, with collusion, substantial joint profits (the shaded area of Exhibit 5) could be attained. The case of perfect cooperation would be identical with the outcome under monopoly.

In the real world, however, the outcome is likely to fall between the extremes of price competition and perfect cooperation. Oligopolists generally recognize their interdependence and refuse to engage in vigorous price competition, which would drive price down to the level of per unit costs. But there are also obstacles to collusion. Thus, prices in oligopolistic industries do not rise to the monopolistic level. Oligopolistic prices are typically above the purely competitive level but below that for pure monopoly.

EXHIBIT 6   Gaining from cheating

The industry demand (D_i) and marginal revenue curves are shown in graph (b). The joint profits of oligopolists would be maximized at Q_i, where $MR_i = MC$. Price P_i would be best for the industry as a whole. However, the demand curve (d_f) facing each firm (graph a) would be much more elastic than D_i. Given the greater elasticity of its demand curve, an individual firm would maximize its profit by cutting its price to P_f and expanding output to q_f, where $MR_f = MC$. Thus, individual oligopolists could gain by secretly shaving price and cheating on the collusive agreement.

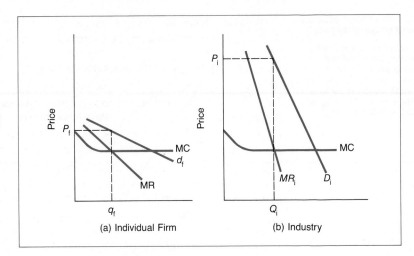

(a) Individual Firm

(b) Industry

Obstacles to Collusion

Collusion: Agreement among firms to avoid various competitive practices, particularly price reductions. It may involve either formal agreements or merely tacit recognition that competitive practices will be self-defeating in the long run. Tacit collusion is difficult to detect. The Sherman Act prohibits collusion and conspiracies to restrain interstate trade.

Collusion is the opposite of competition. It involves cooperative actions by sellers to turn the terms of trade in their own favor against that of buyers. Since oligopolists can profit by colluding to restrict output and raise price, economic theory suggests that they will have a strong incentive to do so.

However, each *individual* oligopolist also has an incentive to cheat on collusive agreements. Exhibit 6 will help us to understand why. An undetected price cut will enable a firm to attract both (a) customers who would not buy from any firm at the higher price *and* (b) those who would normally buy from other firms. Thus, the demand facing the oligopolistic *firm* will be considerably more elastic than the industry demand curve. As Exhibit 6 shows, the price P_i that maximizes the industry's profits will be higher than the price P_f that is best for each individual oligopolist. If a firm can find a way to reduce its price below the collusive agreement prices, expanded sales will more than make up for the reduction in per unit profit margin.

In oligopolistic industries, there are two conflicting tendencies. An oligopolistic firm has a strong incentive to cooperate with its rivals so that joint profit can be maximized. However, it also has a strong incentive to cheat secretly on any collusive agreement in order to increase its share of the joint profit. Oligopolistic agreements therefore tend to be unstable. This instability exists whether the cooperative behavior is informal or formal, as in the case of a cartel.

There are certain situations that work against the tendency of oligopolists to collude. Five major obstacles can limit collusive behavior.

When the Number of Oligopolists Is Fairly Large, Effective Collusion Is Less Likely.   Other things constant, as the number of major firms in an industry increases, it becomes more costly for the oligopolists to communicate, negotiate, and enforce agreements among themselves. Developing and maintaining collusive agreements become more difficult. In addition, the greater the number of firms, the more likely it is that the objectives of individual firms will conflict with those of the industry. Each firm will want a bigger slice of the pie. Costs and the extent of unused plant capacity may differ among firms. Aggressive, less mature firms may want to expand their share of total output. These conflicting interests contribute to the breakdown of collusive agreements.

When It Is Difficult to Eliminate Secret Price Cuts, Collusion Is Less Attractive. Unless a firm has a way of policing the pricing policy of its rivals, it may be the "sucker" in a collusive agreement. Firms that secretly cut prices may gain a larger share of the market, while others maintain their higher prices and lose customers as well as profits. Sometimes price-cutting can be accomplished in ways that are difficult for the other firms to identify. For example, a firm might provide better credit terms, faster delivery, and other related services "free" in order to improve slightly the package offered to the consumer.[5]

When firms sell a differentiated product, improvements in quality and style can be used as competitive weapons. "Price cuts" of this variety are particularly attractive to an oligopolist because they cannot be easily and quickly duplicated by rivals. Competitors can quickly match a reduction in money price, but it will take time for them to match an improvement in quality. When firms can freely use improvements in quality to gain a larger share of the market, collusive agreements on price are of limited value. When cheating (price-cutting) is both profitable and difficult for rivals to police, it is a good bet that oligopolistic rivals will be induced to cheat.

Low Entry Barriers Are an Obstacle to Collusion. Unless potential rivals can be excluded, oligopolists will be unable to make unusually large profits. Temporarily successful collusion will merely attract competitors into the industry, which will eliminate the profits. Even with collusion, long-run profits will not be possible unless entry into the industry can be blocked.

Local markets are sometimes dominated by a few firms. For example, many communities have only a small number of ready-mix concrete producers, bowling alleys, accounting firms, and furniture stores. However, in the absence of government restrictions, entry barriers into these markets are usually low. The threat of potential rivals reduces the gains from collusive behavior under these conditions.

Unstable Demand Conditions Are an Obstacle to Collusion. Demand instability may lead to honest differences among oligopolists about what is best for the industry. One firm may want to expand because it anticipates a sharp increase in future demand. A more pessimistic rival may want to hold the line on existing industrial capacity. Differences in expectations about future demand create still another area of potential conflict among oligopolistic firms. Successful collusion is more likely when demand is relatively stable.

Vigorous Antitrust Action Increases the Cost of Collusion. Under existing antitrust laws, collusive behavior is prohibited. Of course, secret agreements are possible. Simple informal cooperation might be conducted without discussions or collusive agreements. However, like other illegal behavior, all such agreements would be unenforceable by any firm. Vigorous antitrust action can discourage

---

[5]See Marshall R. Colberg, Dascomb Forbush, and Gilbert R. Whitaker, *Business Economics,* 5th ed. (Homewood, Illinois: Irwin, 1975), for an extensive discussion of the alternative methods by which business firms are able to alter price.

firms from undertaking such illegal agreements. As the threat of getting caught increases, participants will be less likely to attempt collusive behavior.

The Kinked Demand Curve

As we noted earlier, since the demand for an oligopolistic firm's product is dependent not only upon market conditions but also upon the reaction of rival firms, the oligopolist must include the possible and probable reactions of rivals in its decisions. How will rivals react to a price change? When there is a dominant firm in an industry, rivals may be willing to follow the leadership of the larger firm. For example, if General Motors raises its prices by 5 percent, the other major automobile manufacturers may cooperate by raising their prices by a similar amount. However, oligopolists can never be sure what rivals will do. Sometimes prospective price increases are announced simply in order to observe the reactions of competitors.

The probable response of rivals is more difficult to determine when there is no single dominant firm in an industry. However, it does appear that rivals will be more likely to match a price reduction than a price increase. If a nondominant firm increases its price, other firms will be able to expand their market share if they maintain their current price. The sales of the firm that increases its price may fall substantially. On the other hand, when a single oligopolist lowers its price, it can be almost certain that rivals will respond. If they do not, their sales will fall sharply. But since the price reduction will be matched by the other firms of the industry, it is not likely to increase sales substantially for any single firm.

Kinked Demand Curve: A demand curve that is highly elastic for a price *increase* but inelastic for a price *reduction*. These differing elasticities are based on the assumption that rival firms will match a price reduction but not a price increase. This demand curve is thought to be descriptive of the situation faced by many oligopolistic firms.

The hypothesis of the **kinked demand curve** is based on these projected reactions. The essential idea of the kinked demand curve is that the oligopolist's demand curve will be (a) very *elastic* for a price increase because other firms will maintain their prices but (b) very inelastic for a price reduction because the other firms will respond by reducing their prices also. The kinked demand curve hypothesis thus implies that prices in oligopolistic industries are likely to be quite stable.

Exhibit 7 illustrates the kinked demand curve. Since the demand curve is kinked at output Q, the marginal revenue curve will be discontinuous. This means that marginal costs could vary substantially at output Q while continuing

EXHIBIT 7   The kinked demand curve

If an oligopolistic firm increases its price, it will lose many customers to rival firms. In contrast, a price reduction, since it will be matched by competitors, will lead to few additional customers. Thus, the oligopolist's demand curve is kinked, and the corresponding MR curve is discontinuous, as shown. The oligopolist will not change price even if MC fluctuates between E and F.

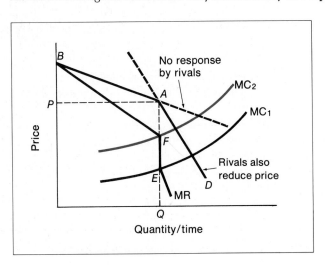

to equal marginal revenue. For example, both MC_1 and MC_2 intersect the MR curve at output Q. Therefore, despite these changes in cost, the profit-maximizing price of the oligopolist will remain at P. When the demand curve of a firm is kinked, the firm's profit-maximizing price may remain unchanged even though there are substantial changes in cost conditions.

Economists continue to debate the importance of the kinked demand curve hypothesis. Initially, the widespread use of price lists and categories that established prices in oligopolistic industries for a significant time period was thought to be consistent with the concept of a kinked demand and stable prices. However, recent studies suggest that price stability in oligopolistic industries may be more apparent than real. These studies have found that even when the *list* price of a product is stable, firms use such factors as discounts, credit terms, and delivery conditions to alter "price" in response to changing market conditions. In any event, it is clear that the kinked demand theory does not offer a complete explanation of price determination. Although the theory predicts tendencies *once a price is established*, it does not explain how the initial price is set.

Limits of the Oligopoly Model

Market Power: The ability of a firm that is not a pure monopolist to earn unusually large profits, indicating that it has some monopoly power. Because the firm has few (or weak) competitors, it has a degree of freedom from the discipline of vigorous competition.

Uncertainty and imprecision characterize the theory of oligopoly. We know that firms will gain if they can successfully agree to restrict output and raise price. However, collusion also has its costs. We have outlined some of the conflicts and difficulties (costs) associated with the establishment of perfect cooperation among oligopolistic firms. In some industries, these difficulties are considerable, and the **market power** of the oligopolists is therefore relatively small. In other industries, oligopolistic cooperation, although probably less than perfect, may permit the firms to turn the terms of trade in their favor. Economists would say that such firms have market power, indicating that even though these firms are not pure monopolists, they do have some monopoly power. Analysis of the costs and benefits of collusive behavior at least allows us to determine when discipline by competitive pressures is more likely for an oligopolist.

CONCENTRATION AND REAL-WORLD OLIGOPOLISTIC POWER

Which industries are dominated by a small number of firms? How important is oligopoly? Economists have developed a tool, the concentration ratio, that will help us to answer these questions.

Concentration Ratio: The total sales of the four (or sometimes eight) largest firms in an industry as a percentage of the total sales of the industry. The higher the ratio, the greater is the market dominance of a small number of firms. The ratio can be seen as a measure of oligopolistic power.

The **concentration ratio** is the percentage of total industry sales that are accounted for by the four (or sometimes eight) largest firms of an industry. This ratio can vary from nearly zero to 100, with 100 indicating that the sales of the four largest firms comprise those of the entire industry.

The concentration ratio can be thought of as a broad indicator of competitiveness. In general, the higher (lower) the concentration ratio, the more (less) likely that the firms of the industry will be able to collude successfully against the interests of consumers. However, this ratio is by no means a perfect measure of competitiveness. Since the sales of foreign producers are excluded, it overstates the degree of concentration in industries for which foreign competition is important. It does not reveal the elasticity of demand for products, although concentration is not as great a problem if good substitutes for a product are available. For example, the market power of aluminum producers is partially limited by competition from steel, plastics, copper, and similar products. Similarly, the monopoly power of commercial airlines is substantially reduced by the availability of automobiles, buses, chartered private flights, and even conference telephone calls. Concentration ratios tend to conceal such competitiveness among products.

The concentration ratio can also overstate the competitiveness in instances in which the relevant market area is a city or region. For example, consider the case of newspaper publishing companies. In 1977, there were more than 7800 such companies in the United States. The sales of the four largest amounted to only 17 percent of the national market. However, most cities were served by only one or two newspapers. In most market areas, newspaper publishing is a highly concentrated industry, even though this is not true nationally. In this instance, the concentration ratio for the nation in the newspaper publishing industry probably overstates the actual competitiveness of the industry.

What do concentration ratios reveal about the U.S. economy? Exhibit 8 presents concentration data for several manufacturing industries in 1947 and 1977. Several industries, including the automobile, steel, aircraft, telephone and telegraph, computer equipment, and soap industries, are dominated by a few

EXHIBIT 8   Concentration ratios for selected manufacturing industries in 1947 and 1977

Industry	1947	1977	Change
High concentration (40 or more)			
Motor vehicles and car bodies	71	93	+22
Blast furnaces and steel mills	50	45	−5
Tires and inner tubes	70[a]	70	—
Aircraft and parts	72	59	−13
Telephone and telegraph	92	99	+7
Farm machinery	36	46	+10
Soap and other detergents	72[a]	59	−13
Photographic equipment and supplies	61	72	+11
Electronic computing equipment	66[a]	44	−22
Medium concentration (20−39)			
Petroleum	37	30	−7
Bread, cake, and related products	16	33	+17
Periodicals	34	22	−12
Gray iron foundries	16	34	+18
Toilet preparations	24	40	+16
Pharmaceuticals	28	24	−4
Low concentration (less than 20)			
Newspapers	21	19	−2
Meat packing	41	19	−22
Bottled and canned soft drinks	12[a]	15	+3
Commercial printing	13[a]	14	+1

[a]Data are for 1963.

U.S. Bureau of the Census, *Census of Manufacturing, 1947* and *1977.*

firms. They are oligopolistic. At the other end of the spectrum, the "big four" accounted for less than 20 percent of the sales of newspapers, meat packing, bottled and canned soft drinks, and commercial printing.

Most research suggests that, on balance, there has been little change in the patterns of business competitiveness over the last several decades. Of course, there have been some changes *within specific industries.* For example, concentration increased in the motor vehicle and photographic equipment industries between 1947 and 1977. The degree of concentration in aircraft, computer equipment, and meat packing has declined significantly in recent years.

Concentration and Mergers

Horizontal Merger: The combining under one ownership of the assets of two or more firms engaged in the production of *similar products.*

During the early stages of the development of American manufacturing, mergers had an important influence on the structure of our economy. The desire of oligopolistic firms to merge is not surprising. A **horizontal merger,** the combining of the assets of two or more firms under the same ownership, provides the firms with an alternative to both the rigors of competition and the insecurity of collusion.

There have been two great waves of horizontal mergers. The first occurred between 1887 and 1904, the second between 1916 and 1929. Many corporations whose names are now household words—U.S. Steel, General Electric, Standard Oil, General Foods, General Mills, and American Can, for example—are the products of mergers formed during these periods. Mergers led to a dominant firm in manufacturing industries such as steel, sugar refining, agricultural implements, leather, rubber, distilleries, and tin cans.

Analysis of these horizontal mergers leads to two interesting observations. First, horizontal mergers can create a highly profitable dominant firm, even if there is freedom of entry into an industry. The entry of new competitors takes time. A firm formed by merger that controls a substantial share of the market for a product can often realize oligopolistic profits for a period of time before the entry of new firms drives prices back down to the level of average cost. Of course, if entry barriers can be established to limit or retard the entry of new rivals, the incentive to merge is further strengthened.[6] Second, with the passage of time, competitive forces have generally eroded the position of the dominant firms created by horizontal mergers. Almost without exception, the market share of the dominant firms created by horizontal mergers began to decline soon after the mergers were consummated. Smaller firms gained ground relative to the dominant firm. This suggests that temporary profits stemming from market power, rather than economies of scale, were the primary motivation for the horizontal mergers. In 1950, the Celler–Kefauver Act made it substantially more difficult to use horizontal mergers as a means of developing oligopolistic power. Today, mergers involving large firms seldom involve former competitors.

Vertical Merger: The creation of a single firm from two firms, one of which was a supplier or customer of the other—for example, a merger of a lumber company with a furniture manufacturer.

Another type of merger, the **vertical merger,** joins a supplier and a buyer—for example, an automobile maker and a steel producer. A vertical merger might simplify the long-range planning process for both firms and reduce the need for costly legal contracting between the two. Even though vertical mergers generally do not increase concentration within industries, some econo-

---

[6]See George Stigler, "Monopoly and Oligopoly by Merger," *American Economic Review* (May 1950), pp. 23–34, for a detailed analysis of this issue.

mists are concerned that such mergers may reduce competition if either the buyer or the supplier grants a market advantage to the other.

Conglomerate Merger: The combining under one ownership of two or more firms that produce *unrelated products*.

A **conglomerate merger** combines two firms in unrelated industries. The stated intent is usually to introduce new and superior management into the firm being absorbed. This type of merger results in increased size but not necessarily in reduced competition. Since the 1960s, when some very large corporations were formed by conglomerate merger, some observers have expressed concern that the concentration of political power created by such mergers and the enormous financial assets available to the operating units may be potentially dangerous. Others have argued that the conglomerate mergers often lead to more efficient management and increased competitiveness within specific industries. The impact of conglomerate mergers on our economy is a topic of current research among economists.

Concentration and Profits

The model of oligopoly implies that if the firms in concentrated industries cooperate with one another, *jointly* they can exercise monopoly power. Is there a relationship between industrial concentration and profitability in the real world? Researchers in this area have not been able to arrive at a definite conclusion. An early study by Joe Bain showed a distinctly positive relationship between concentration and profitability. George Stigler, in a detailed study of manufacturing industries, found that from 1947 to 1954 "the average [profit] rate in the concentrated industries was 8.00 percent, while that in the unconcentrated industries was 7.16 percent." Later, both a study by William Shepherd covering the period from 1960 to 1969 and the White House Task Force on Antitrust Policy presented evidence that the rate of profitability is higher in concentrated industries.

Nonetheless, other researchers remain unconvinced. Sam Peltzman argues that the alleged link "between profitability and concentration is, in fact, attributable to other factors which happen to be correlated with concentration." Yale Brozen argues that the proper test is between concentration and future (not past) profitability. His work indicates that "rates of returns in concentrated industries at a later time . . . turn out to be insignificantly different from those in less concentrated industries."[7]

The weight of the evidence on this topic suggests that the profit rate of firms in concentrated industries is just slightly higher than the profit rate of other firms. The link between industrial concentration and profitability is a weak one. Other factors, such as demand conditions, management efficiency, and entrepreneurship, are the major determinants of business profitability. Thus, the odds are only a little better than 50–50 that a more concentrated industry will be more profitable than a less concentrated one.

[7]For a detailed analysis of this issue, see Joe S. Bain, "Relation of Profit Rate to Industry Concentration: American Manufacturing 1936–40," *Quarterly Journal of Economics* (August 1951); Yale Brozen, "Concentration and Profits: Does Concentration Matter?" in *The Impact of Large Firms on the U.S. Economy,* ed. J. Fred Weston and Stanley I. Ornstein (Lexington, Massachusetts: Heath, 1973); George Stigler, *Capital and Rates of Return in Manufacturing Industries* (Princeton, New Jersey: Princeton University Press, 1963); H. M. Mann, "Seller Concentration, Barriers to Entry, and Rates of Return in Thirty Industries, 1950–1960," *Review of Economics and Statistics* (August 1966); Sam Peltzman, "Profits, Data, and Public Policy," in *Public Policies toward Mergers,* ed. J. Fred Weston and Sam Peltzman (Pacific Palisades, California: Goodyear, 1967); W. G. Shepherd, "Elements of Market Structure," *Review of Economics and Statistics* (February 1972); and "White House Task Force on Antitrust Policy," Report 1, in *Trade Regulation Reports,* Suppl. 415 (May 26, 1969).

Market Power and Profit — The Early Bird Catches the Worm

In the last chapter, we saw that under certain conditions an unregulated monopolist can earn economic profit, even in the long run. Similarly, our analysis of oligopoly suggests that if barriers to entry are high, firms may sometimes be consistently able to earn above-average profits, even in the long run. Suppose that a well-established firm, such as Exxon or General Motors, is able to use its market power to earn consistent economic profits. Do its current stockholders gain because of its monopoly power? Surprisingly, the answer is no. The ownership value of a share of corporate stock for such a corporation long ago began to reflect its market power and profitability. Many of the *present* stockholders paid high prices for their stock because they expected the firm to be highly profitable. In other words, they paid for any above-normal economic profits that the firm might be expected to earn because of its monopoly power.

Do not expect to get rich buying the stock of highly profitable monopolistic or oligopolistic firms. You are already too late. The early bird catches the worm. Those who owned the stock when these firms initially developed their market position have already captured the gain. The value of their stock increased at that time. After a firm's future prospects are widely recognized, subsequent stockholders fail to gain a high rate of return on their financial investment.

MYTHS OF ECONOMICS

"The prices of most goods are unnecessarily inflated by at least 25 percent as a result of the high rate of profit of producers."

During the recent period of inflation, profits have been about as popular with consumers as failing grades are with students at the end of a semester. When food prices rise, the profits of farmers, meat processors, and food store chains are heavily publicized by the news media. When gasoline prices jump, many people believe that they are being pushed up by greedy profiteering on the part of the major oil companies. The casual observer might easily be left with the impression that large profits were the major source of the high rate of inflation of the 1970s.

This issue is clouded by the fact that both the size of profits and their function are largely misunderstood by most people. Surveys show that young people believe that the after-tax profits of corporations comprise between 25 and 30 percent of sales. A recent national sample poll of adults conducted by Opinion Research of Princeton found that the average person thought that profits comprised 29 cents of every dollar of sales in manufacturing. In reality, as Exhibit 9b shows, the after-tax accounting profits of manufacturing corporations are approximately 5 percent of sales. Thus, the public believes that the rate of profit as a percentage of sales is nearly six times greater than the actual figure!

Why are people so misinformed on this issue? The popular media are one source of confusion. The media nearly always report the accounting profits of firms in dollar terms, instead of comparing them to sales, stockholder equity, or the value of the firms' assets. A favorite device is to report that profits, either annually or quarterly, were up by some astonishing percentage.[8] Unless we know

---

[8]This is equally true for large wage increases. Apparently, the extreme example rather than the norm helps to sell newspapers. We should note that such reports do not imply an antibusiness bias. The *Wall Street Journal,* not noted for such bias, regularly headlines its stories in the same manner.

---

whether profits were high, normal, or low during the previous period, this type of statement tells little or nothing about the firm's earnings rate on its capital assets. For example, suppose that a corporation with $100 million of assets earned a profit of $2 million last year, a 2 percent rate of return on its capital assets. Now suppose that the firm's earnings this year are $4 million, generating only a 4 percent rate of return. It would not be unusual for the popular media to report, "The profits of corporation X soared to $4 million, a 100 percent increase over last year." What this statement conceals is that the profits of the firm as as a percentage of its capital assets were less than what you or I could earn on a savings account.

Not only is the average person misinformed about the size of profits, but most individuals do not understand their function. Many believe that if profits were eliminated, our economy would continue to operate as if nothing had happened. This erroneous view indicates a misunderstanding of what accounting profits are. Accounting profits are primarily a monetary return to persons who have

EXHIBIT 9   How great are profits?

After-tax corporate profits average about 12 percent of stockholder equity and 5 percent of sales in the United States.

Economic Report of the President, 1982. As the result of changes in definitions, the data for 1975–1980 are not, strictly speaking, comparable to the figures for the earlier periods.

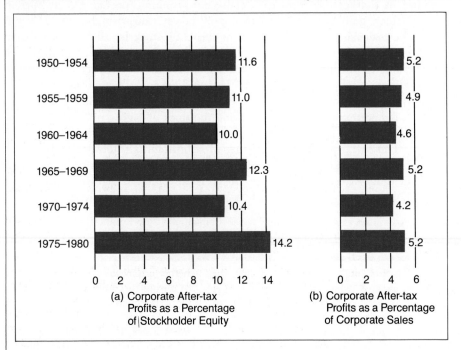

1950–1954   11.6   5.2
1955–1959   11.0   4.9
1960–1964   10.0   4.6
1965–1969   12.3   5.2
1970–1974   10.4   4.2
1975–1980   14.2   5.2

(a) Corporate After-tax
Profits as a Percentage
of Stockholder Equity

(b) Corporate After-tax
Profits as a Percentage
of Corporate Sales

invested in machines, buildings, and nonhuman productive resources. Investment in physical capital involves both risk and the foregoing of current consumption. If profits were eliminated, the incentive of persons to invest and provide the tools that make the American worker the most productive in the world would be destroyed. Who would invest in either physical or human capital (for example, education) if such investments did not lead

to an increase in future income—that is, if investment did not lead to accounting profit?

Profits play an important role in our economy. Persons who increase the value of resources—who produce something that is worth more than the resources that went into it—will be rewarded with economic profit (and generally an above-average accounting profit). Those who allocate resources to a venture that consumers

value less than the opportunity cost of the project will experience economic losses (below-average accounting profits). Without this reward–penalty system, individuals (and firms) would not have the incentive to use resources wisely in the development and production of goods that are most desired by consumers relative to the goods' opportunity cost.

LOOKING AHEAD

The competitiveness of a market economy is influenced not only by the various market structures operating within it but also by public policy. Business activity is often directly regulated by the government. In the following chapter, we will investigate the business structure of the U.S. economy and consider the impact of regulatory activities.

CHAPTER LEARNING OBJECTIVES

1 The distinguishing characteristics of monopolistic competition are (a) firms that produce differentiated products, (b) low barriers to entry into and exit from the market, and (c) a substantial number of independent, rival firms.

2 Monopolistically competitive firms face a gently downward-sloping demand curve. They often use product quality, style, convenience of location, advertising, and price as competitive weapons. Since all rivals within a monopolistically competitive industry are free to duplicate one another's products (or services), the demand for the product of any one firm is highly elastic.

3 A profit-maximizing firm will expand output as long as marginal revenue exceeds marginal cost. Thus, a firm under monopolistic competition will lower its price so that output can be expanded until MR = MC. The price charged by the profit-maximizing monopolistic competitor will be greater than its marginal cost.

4 If monopolistic competitors are making economic profits, rival firms will be induced to enter the market. They will expand the supply of the product (and similar products), enticing some of the customers away from established firms. The demand curve faced by an individual firm will fall (shift inward) until the profits have been eliminated.

5 Economic losses will cause monopolistic competitors to exit from the market. The demand for the products of each remaining firm will rise (shift outward) until the losses have been eliminated.

6 Since barriers to entry are low, firms in a monopolistically competitive industry will make only normal profits in the long run. In the short run, they may make either economic profits or losses, depending on market conditions.

7 Traditional economic theory has emphasized that monopolistic competition is inefficient because (a) price exceeds marginal cost at the long-run equilibrium output level; (b) long-run average cost is not minimized; and (c) excessive advertising is sometimes encouraged. However, other economists have argued more recently that this criticism is misdirected. According to the newer view, firms under monopolistic competition have an incentive to (a) produce efficiently; (b) undertake production if and only if their actions will increase the value of resources used; and (c) offer a variety of products.

8 Oligopolistic market structure is characterized by (a) an interdependence among firms, (b) substantial economies of scale that result in only a small number of firms in the industry, and (c) significant barriers to entry. Oligopolists may produce either homogeneous or differentiated products.

9 There is no general theory of price, output, and equilibrium for oligopolistic markets. If rival oligopolists acted totally independently of their competitors, they would drive price down to the level of cost of production. Alternatively, if they used collusion to obtain perfect cooperation, price would rise to the level that a monopolist would charge. The actual outcome lies between these two extremes.

10 Collusion is the opposite of competition. Oligopolists have a strong incentive to collude and raise their prices. However, the interests of individual firms will conflict with those of the industry as a whole. Since the demand curve faced by individual firms is far more elastic than the industry demand curve, each firm could gain by cutting its price (or raising product quality) by a small amount so that it could attract customers from rivals. If several firms tried to do this, however, the collusive agreement would break down.

11 Oligopolistic firms are less likely to collude successfully against the interests of consumers if (a) the number of rival firms is large; (b) it is costly to prohibit competitors from offering secret price cuts (or quality improvements) to customers; (c) entry barriers are low; (d) market demand conditions tend to be unstable; and/or (e) the threat of antitrust action is present.

12   The kinked demand curve helps to explain why oligopolistic prices may tend to be inflexible. Under the basic assumption of the kinked demand curve—rivals will match price reductions but not increases—a firm's price rise leads to a sharp reduction in its sales, but a price reduction attracts few new customers. Thus, once a price is established, it remains inflexible for extended periods of time.

13   Analysis of concentration ratios suggests that, on balance, there has been little change in the competitiveness of the U.S. economy in several decades.

14   Accounting profits as a share of stockholder equity are probably slightly greater in highly concentrated industries than in those that are less concentrated. The relationship between profits and concentration, however, is not a close one. This suggests that several other factors, such as changing market conditions, quality competition, risk, and ability to exclude rivals, are the major determinants of profitability.

15   The after-tax accounting profits of business firms average about 5 cents of each dollar of sales, substantially less than most Americans believe to be the case. Accounting profits average approximately 12 percent of stockholder equity. This rate of return (accounting profit) provides investors with the incentive to sacrifice current consumption, assume the risk of undertaking a business venture, and supply the funds to purchase buildings, machines, and other assets.

THE ECONOMIC WAY OF THINKING—DISCUSSION QUESTIONS

1   Explain in your own words the meaning of product differentiation. What tactics might be used to differentiate one's product?

2   Why do many economists argue that monopolistic competition is inefficient? If there were fewer small firms in a monopolistically competitive industry (for example, retail groceries), would the *average* selling prices in the industry decline? Why or why not? Would convenience, location, and other quality factors change? Why or why not? Do you think monopolistic competition is inefficient? Explain.

3   It is often charged that competitive advertising among monopolistically competitive firms is wasteful. (a) Do you think that advertising in the following industries is wasteful: retail grocery sales, retail furniture sales, cigarettes, local restaurants, cosmetics, movie theaters, retail department stores? Explain. (b) Does this advertising result in higher prices? (c) Is the advertising valuable to consumers? Explain. (d) Why is it that more firms do not compete by eliminating their advertising and charging lower prices?

4   Explain why decision-makers for firms in an oligopolistic industry have an incentive to collude. What are the factors that influence the success or failure of their collusive efforts?

5   "Effective collusion requires firms to agree on both price and quality. A firm can lower price by raising quality, or it can raise price by lowering quality, even without changing the actual monetary sale price. Unless a firm can keep its competitors from adjusting quality, the gains from price collusion will be short-lived." Do you agree? Why or why not?

6   "High concentration leads to either overt or tacit collusion. Thus, prices in oligopolistic industries will almost surely be rigged against the consumer and to the benefit of the producer." Do you agree? Why or why not?

7   Are profits important in a market economy? Why or why not? Can you think of policies designed to reduce profitability that are consistent with economic efficiency? Explain. Do not forget to consider any secondary effects.

8   **What's Wrong with This Way of Thinking?**

"Firms such as General Motors, AT&T, and General Electric have been using their monopoly power to realize economic profit for years. These high profit rates benefit the current stockholders of these corporations at the expense of the consumers."

If we can avoid the creation of
undue market power, by and large
we expect to achieve better market
performance—better in terms of
lower prices, higher quality products and innovations both in
product and in technology.[1]
Donald F. Turner, former chief
of the Antitrust Division

16

BUSINESS STRUCTURE, REGULATION, AND DEREGULATION

Most contemporary economists believe, just as Adam Smith did, that competition and rivalry among business firms provide benefits to both consumers
and workers. Competition forces producers to operate efficiently and supply
consumers with the goods that they desire most intensely (relative to costs).
Similarly, competition for resources forces each producer to treat workers and
other resource suppliers fairly, offering them pay rates and work environments
that are attractive relative to those available elsewhere.

But in spite of widespread agreement on the desirability of competition,
there are two major aspects of competition about which there is a great deal of
disagreement: the strength and extent of real-world competitive pressures and
the actual effectiveness of governmental regulatory policy. As we have discussed,
both the nature of competition and its intensity vary according to the structure
of the industry under consideration. For example, as we have seen, competitive
elements will eventually be introduced into even highly concentrated oligopolistic industries; at the same time, tendencies toward collusion must also be
considered. Economists often disagree on the ability of unregulated markets to
provide for a strong competitive environment.

As for the argument over the effects of regulation on competition, some
economists point out that regulatory policy, by limiting various types of noncompetitive behavior, effectively increases the discipline of the market. Others
charge that past regulatory policies have often reduced market competitiveness,
contributed to economic inefficiency, and, in general, ignored major concerns of
consumers and workers.

In this chapter we will analyze the structure of the U.S. economy and
consider the effects of regulatory policy on economic behavior in the light of

---

[1]Donald F. Turner, "The Antitrust Chief Dissents," *Fortune* (April 1966), p. 113.

these controversies. How competitive is our economy? Has regulatory policy added to or detracted from its competitiveness? Why have some industries been deregulated? What are the effects of the new "social regulation" designed to provide us with a cleaner, safer, and healthier environment?

THE STRUCTURE OF THE U.S. ECONOMY

The structure of the U.S. economy is extremely diverse. There are approximately 15 million business firms in the United States. Owner-operated farming and service businesses account for more than 6 million of the firms. These businesses are, of course, quite small. In contrast, there are roughly 300,000 corporations with annual business receipts in excess of $1 million. Some of these are giants with thousands of employees and annual sales running into the billions.

The structure of our economy is also continually changing. A century ago, over half of all workers were employed in agriculture, and less than 20 percent worked in manufacturing. Throughout the first half of this century, the relative size of the agricultural sector steadily declined and manufacturing output grew, as a share of total output. By 1950, the manufacturing sector accounted for 30 percent of the total U.S. output; agriculture had declined to less than 10 percent.

Since 1950, a new trend in industrial structure has evolved. The relative sizes of *both* the agricultural and manufacturing sectors have declined, and the government and service sectors (for example, health care, education, professional and repair workers) have expanded. As a share of the total, employment in the government and service sectors rose from 23 percent to more than 34 percent between 1950 and 1980. In contrast, manufacturing employment fell from 30 percent in 1950 to 22 percent in 1980.

During the last two decades, there has also been a movement of industry from the northeast urban centers to the Sunbelt. The composition of the labor force has also changed. Less than a third of all workers were female in 1960; by 1981 more than 43 percent of those at work were women.

How Much of Our Economy Is Competitive?

This is a difficult question to answer. As we have discussed, competition is multidimensional. Dynamic innovation, entrepreneurship, and product-quality competition may be important even in highly concentrated industries. Although the concentration ratio of an industry provides an indication of competitiveness, it is an imperfect measure. The availability of substitutes may substantially limit the monopoly power of firms in some concentrated industries. Other firms may be restrained by the threat of entry from potential rivals. Still other firms in concentrated industries face stiff competition from foreign producers. The relative importance of competitive and noncompetitive sectors within the economy may change with time. Moreover—and perhaps most important—it is not clear where the line should be drawn between competitive and noncompetitive. Most economists would probably classify unregulated industries in which the four largest firms produce less than 20 or 25 percent of the market as competitive. On the other hand, industries in which the largest firms produce more than half of the output would generally be classified as oligopolistic, suggesting the presence of noncompetitive elements. These categories, however, are arbitrary. Exhibit 1 sheds some light on the competitiveness of the U.S. economy.

EXHIBIT 1 The competitiveness of the U.S. economy, 1980

Gross National Product Originating from:	Billions of Dollars	Percentage of Total
Low barriers to entry	1116	42
Agricultural, forestry, and fisheries	77	
Construction	120	
Wholesale and retail trade	422	
Service	344	
Manufacturing (industries with concentration ratios of less than 20 percent)[a]	153	
Medium barriers to entry	95	4
Manufacturing (industries with concentration ratios between 20 and 40 percent)[a]	95	
High barriers to entry (unregulated)	437	17
Manufacturing (industries with concentration ratios greater than 40 percent)[a]	343	
Mining	94	
Primarily regulated industries	626	24
Transportation, communications, and utility	234	
Finance, insurance, and real estate	392	
Government	303	12
All other	49	2
Total	2626	100

[a]The concentration ratios were for the U.S. Bureau of the Census's two-digit industrial classification. The following industries had four-firm concentration ratios of greater than 40 percent: tobacco, chemicals, rubber products, stone, clay, and glass products, primary metals, electrical equipment, transportation equipment (aircraft and automobiles), machinery (except electrical), and instruments and related products.

Derived from the *Statistical Abstract of the United States—1981,* Tables 703, 1423, and 1427.

The table breaks our gross national product down by sector and industrial concentration. Agriculture, construction, wholesale and retail trade, and service industries have traditionally been characterized by small firms and low barriers to entry.[2] These sectors plus manufacturing industries with four-firm concentration ratios of less than 20 percent accounted for more than two-fifths of the total national output in 1980. They now comprise roughly one-half of the private sector. This suggests that competitive forces still play a highly important role in our economy.

On the other hand, business concentration and regulated sectors are also important. Regulated industries and government generate more than one-third of our total output. Highly concentrated manufacturing industries such as tobacco, chemicals, automobiles, aircraft, primary metals, and electrical equipment accounted for 17 percent of our national income in 1980. Most economists believe that firms in these industries are the most capable of escaping the disciplines of competition. Of course, many of these concentrated industries confront stiff foreign competition. For example, although General Motors, Ford,

---

[2]In 1971, proprietorships, partnerships, and corporations with sales of less than $1 million accounted for 81 percent of the income generated by agriculture, 64 percent of income from service, 44 percent of construction income, and 25 percent of wholesale and retail trade income.

Chrysler, and American Motors share a monopoly on *domestic production,* more than one out of every four automobiles sold in the United States is bought from a foreign producer. Foreign competition is also important in other industries, such as steel and petroleum. Product-quality competition may also account for strong rivalry even among a limited number of competitors. Moreover, in a firm as big as General Motors, even the rivalry among the divisions (Buick versus Oldsmobile, for example) may be intense. Direct price competition within the firm is presumably controlled, but competition involving quality remains. Leaders in each division compete for recognition and advancement, and each is judged by monthly sales and profit figures. Thus, competitive forces are not entirely absent even in a concentrated industry.

These data on the U.S. industrial structure indicate that competitive, concentrated, and highly regulated sectors are all sizable. Approximately two-fifths of our national output is generated by roughly competitive industries—that is, industries in which rivalry exists among a substantial number of firms. Another one-fifth of our output originates from industries characterized by a significant degree of industrial concentration. Highly regulated industries account for nearly a quarter of the total output. The government sector generates the remainder of the total output.[3]

Does Big Business Dominate the U.S. Economy?

Bigness and absence of competition are not necessarily the same thing. A firm can be big and yet function in a highly competitive industry. For example, Sears and Montgomery Ward are both large, but they are also part of a highly competitive industry—retail sales.

Exhibit 2 shows the percentage of the U.S. labor force that is employed by the largest corporations. In 1980, the 100 largest corporate giants employed 10 percent of the labor force. More than one in six labor force participants was employed by a corporation that ranked in the top 1000. Other measures of corporate power, such as share of total assets or value added, paint a similar picture.

Has the relative size of the largest corporations grown? As Exhibit 3 shows, the value added[4] of the 200 largest industrial firms grew relative to both manufacturing and total output (GNP) during the 1947–1967 period. Since 1967, the value added of the 200 largest corporations has expanded slightly as a proportion of manufacturing output. However, the relative size of the manufacturing sector has been shrinking in relation to the economy as a whole. As a share of total output, the value added of the 200 largest industrial corporations declined from 11.8 percent in 1967 to 10.6 percent in 1977 (the most recent data available).

What caused the rapid growth of the largest firms during the 1947–1967 period? A study by the Federal Trade Commission found that mergers accounted

---

[3]These data reflect the research on this topic. See George Stigler, *Five Lectures on Economic Problems* (New York: Longman, 1949); G. Warren Nutter and Henry A. Einhorn, *Enterprise Monopoly in the United States: 1899–1958* (New York: Columbia University Press, 1969); and Solomon Fabricant, "Is Monopoly Increasing?" *Journal of Economic History* (Winter 1953), for additional detail on this topic.

[4]Value added is the total value of the firm's sales less the cost of materials and services purchased from resource suppliers and subcontractors. It is a measure of how much the firm's productive efforts have added to the value of its product.

EXHIBIT 2   How many of us work for the giants?

The 1000 largest industrial corporations employ approximately 18 percent of the U.S. work force. The top 100 firms employ one out of every 10 American workers.

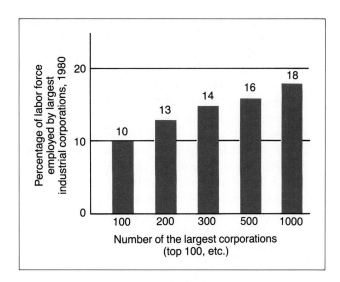

for three-fourths of the relative growth of the 200 largest industrial firms during this period. Most of the mergers were of the conglomerate variety—a collection of diverse enterprises were combined under a single management. Were it not for these mergers, the size of the largest corporations relative to the total economy would have been virtually unchanged during the entire post-World War II period.

The stated objective of public policy has been to restrain various aspects of big business activity, especially when competition seems threatened. Many believe that antitrust action can help to promote efficiency and to keep political power and income more equally distributed. To what extent does the economic and political power of large corporations threaten competitiveness? To what extent does this power need to be restrained? Some observers argue that large firms threaten our decentralized economic institutions and our democratic political structure. Certainly, public choice theory indicates that concentrated business interests, like other special interest organizations, often exert a disproportional influence on the political process. However, we should keep three points in mind as we evaluate this issue and the effectiveness of the government's antitrust policies.

EXHIBIT 3   How big are the giants?

| | The Value Added of the 200 Largest Industrial Corporations | |
Year	Percentage of Manufacturing	Percentage of GNP
1947	30	8.6
1958	38	10.5
1962	40	11.3
1967	42	11.8
1972	43	10.8
1977	44	10.6

Statistical Abstract of the United States—1981, Tables 703 and 918.

First, since the growth of large corporations has resulted mainly from conglomerate mergers, it does not follow that competitiveness within industries has been reduced. In fact, the evidence indicates that there has not been a similar increase in concentration *within* industries (see Exhibit 8 of the previous chapter).

Second, bigness does not ensure greater profitability. The real-world data do not indicate that profits as a percentage of stockholder equity are linked to corporate size.[5] Many of the conglomerates discovered this when their earnings took a nose dive during the 1970s.

Third, the firms that comprise the largest 100 corporations are heterogeneous and constantly changing. As successful management and the vagaries of business fortune exert their influence, some firms are pushed out of the top group and others enter. Of the 100 largest manufacturing corporations in 1909, only 36 remained on the list in 1948. Of the 50 largest manufacturing firms in 1947, only 25 remained in that category in 1972. Of those that dropped out during the period from 1947 to 1972, 5 failed to make even the top 200. With time, even giants stumble and fall, and new competitors arise to take their place. In a world of changing technology and consumer preferences, bigness does not guarantee success or sticking power.

ANTITRUST LEGISLATION—THE POLICY OBJECTIVES

Predatory Pricing: The practice by which a dominant firm in an industry temporarily reduces price in order to damage or eliminate weaker rivals, so that prices can be raised above the level of costs in a later period.

Exclusive Contract: An agreement between manufacturer and retailer that prohibits the retailer from carrying the product lines of firms that are rivals of the manufacturer. Such contracts are illegal under the Clayton Act when they "lessen competition."

Reciprocal Agreement: An agreement between firms whereby the buyer of a product requires the seller to purchase another product as a condition of sale. The practice is illegal under the Clayton Act when it substantially reduces competiton.

Antitrust legislation seeks to (a) ensure that the economy is structured such that competition exists among firms in the same industry (or market area) and (b) prohibit business practices that tend to stifle competition. Once these objectives are accomplished, it is assumed that market forces can be relied on to allocate goods and services.

There are numerous tactics that business entrepreneurs might use in an effort to avoid the rigors of competition. We have already stressed that collusion and price agreements are potential weapons with which to turn the terms of trade in favor of the seller. Potential competitors might also decide to divide a market geographically, agreeing not to compete in certain market areas. Large, diversified firms might use **predatory pricing,** a practice by which a firm *temporarily* reduces its price below cost in certain market areas in order to damage or eliminate the competition of weaker rivals. Once the rivals have been eliminated, the firm uses its monopoly power to raise prices above costs. A competitor might also use exclusive contracts and reciprocal agreements in an effort to maintain an advantage over rivals. An **exclusive contract** (or dealership) is an arrangement whereby the manufacturer of a line of products prohibits retailers from selling any of the products of rival producers. Thus, an established firm, offering many product lines, might use this tactic in order to limit the entry into retail markets of rivals offering only narrow product lines. A **reciprocal agreement** is a situation in which the buyer of a product requires the seller to purchase another product as a condition of sale. For example, General Motors was charged in 1963 with telling railroads that if they did not buy GM locomotives, GM would ship its automobiles by other means. All of these business practices involve the use of market power rather than superior performance to gain at

[5]See William G. Shepherd, *The Economics of Industrial Organization* (Englewood Cliffs, New Jersey: Prentice-Hall, 1979), pp. 270–272, for evidence on this issue. Shepherd found that large corporate size had a mild *negative* impact on the rate of profit of firms during the period from 1960 to 1969.

the expense of rivals. In one form or another, they are all illegal under current antitrust legislation.

Major Antitrust Legislation

A society that wishes to organize economic activity on the basis of competitive markets rather than detailed regulation or socialized planning may need to pursue an antitrust policy. The United States, to a greater extent than most Western countries, has adopted antitrust legislation designed to promote competitive markets. Three major legislative acts—the Sherman Act, the Clayton Act, and the Federal Trade Commission Act—form the foundation of antitrust in the United States.

The Sherman Act. This act was passed in 1890, largely in response to a great wave of mergers. The infamous tobacco, sugar, and Standard Oil trusts enraged Congress and the American people. Action was taken against business concentration. The most important provisions of the act are the following:

Section 1: Every contract, combination in the form of trust or otherwise, or conspiracy, in restraint of trade or commerce among the several states or with foreign nations, is hereby declared illegal.

Section 2: Every person who shall monopolize, or conspire with any other person or persons to monopolize any part of the trade or commerce among the several states, or with foreign nations, shall be guilty of a misdemeanor.

The language of the Sherman Act is vague and subject to interpretation. What does it mean to "attempt to monopolize" or "combine or conspire with another person"? Initially, the courts were hesitant to apply the act to manufacturing corporations. In 1911, however, the Supreme Court ruled that Standard Oil and American Tobacco had used "unreasonable" tactics to restrain trade. At the time, the Standard Oil trust controlled 90 percent of the country's refinery capacity. American Tobacco controlled three-fourths of the tobacco manufacturing market. Both of these firms were broken up into several smaller rival firms.

The Supreme Court, however, did not prohibit monopoly per se. It was the tactics used by Standard Oil and American Tobacco that caused the Court to rule against them. In later cases, the Supreme Court refused to break up other trusts (U.S. Steel and American Can, for example) because it could not be proved that they had followed "unfair or unethical" business practices. But the Sherman Act does not clearly define unfair or unethical business practices, and the courts have been reluctant to enforce it. The ineffectiveness of the act led to the passage of two other antitrust laws in 1914.

The Clayton Act. This act was passed in an effort to spell out and prohibit specific business practices. The following are prohibited by the Clayton Act when they "substantially lessen competition or tend to create a monopoly": (a) *price discrimination*—charging purchasers in different markets different prices that are unrelated to transportation costs; (b) *tying contracts*—a practice whereby the seller requires that the buyer purchase another item; (c) *exclusive dealings*—agreements whereby the seller of a good is forbidden to sell to a competitor of the purchaser; (d) *interlocking stockholding*—one firm purchasing the stock of a competing firm; (e) *interlocking directorates*—the same individual(s) serving on the board of directors of competing firms.

Although somewhat more specific than the Sherman Act, the Clayton Act is still vague. At what point do the prohibited actions actually become illegal? Under what circumstances do these actions "substantially lessen competition"? The task of interpreting this ambiguous phrase still remains with the courts.

The Federal Trade Commission Act. This act declared unlawful all "unfair methods of competition in commerce." The Federal Trade Commission (FTC), composed of five members appointed by the president to seven-year terms, was established to determine the exact meaning of "unfair methods." However, a 1919 Supreme Court decision held that the courts, and not the FTC, had the ultimate responsibility for interpreting the law. Today, the FTC is concerned primarily with (a) enforcing consumer protection legislation, (b) prohibiting deceptive advertising, a power it acquired in 1938, and (c) preventing overt collusion.

When a complaint is filed with the FTC, usually by a third party, the commission investigates. If there is a violation, the FTC initially attempts to settle the dispute by negotiation between the parties. If the attempts to negotiate a settlement fail, a hearing is conducted before one of the commission's examiners. The decision of the hearing examiner may be appealed to the full commission, and the FTC's decision may later be appealed to the U.S. Court of Appeals. The great majority of cases brought before the FTC are now settled by mutual consent of the parties involved.

More Recent Antitrust Legislation

Additional antitrust legislation was passed in the 1930s. The Robinson–Patman Act of 1936 prohibits selling "at unreasonably low prices" when such practices reduce competition. The section of the Clayton Act dealing with price discrimination was aimed at eliminating predatory prices. The Robinson–Patman Act went beyond this. It was intended to protect competitors not just from stronger rivals who might temporarily sell below cost but from more efficient rivals who are actually producing at a lower cost. Chain stores and mass distributors were the initial targets of the legislation. Economists have often been critical of the Robinson–Patman Act, since it has tended to eliminate price competition and protect inefficient producers.

In 1938, Congress passed the Wheeler–Lea Act, which was designed to strengthen sections of the Federal Trade Commission Act that had been weakened by restrictive court decisions. Before the passage of the act, the courts were reluctant to prohibit unfair business practices, such as false and deceptive advertising, unless there was proof of damages to either consumers or rival firms. The Wheeler–Lea Act removed this limitation and gave the FTC extended powers to prosecute and ban false or deceptive advertising.

In 1950, Congress passed the Celler–Kefauver Act (sometimes referred to as the antimerger act), which prohibits a firm from acquiring the assets of a competitor if the transaction substantially lessens competition. The Clayton Act, though it prohibits mergers through stock acquisition, proved unable to prevent business combinations from being formed by sale of assets. The Celler–Kefauver Act has closed this loophole, further limiting the ability of firms to combine in an effort to escape competitive pressures.

Since the intent of the Celler–Kefauver Act is to maintain industrial competition, its applicability to mergers between large firms in the same industry is obvious. The act also prohibits vertical mergers between large firms if competition is reduced by such mergers. For example, the merger of a publishing company with a paper producer is now illegal if the courts find that it lessens competition. However, the applicability of the Celler–Kefauver Act to conglomerate mergers remains ambiguous, primarily because there has not been a clear-cut court decision in this area.

Thumbnail Sketch—Antitrust Legislation

Antitrust laws prohibit the following:
1. Collusion—contracts and conspiracies to restrain trade (Sherman Act, Sec. 1)
2. Monopoly and attempts to monopolize any part of trade or commerce among the several states (Sherman Act, Sec. 2)
3. Persons serving on the board of directors of competing firms with more than $1 million of assets (Clayton Act, Sec. 8)
4. Unfair and deceptive advertising (Federal Trade Commission Act as amended by Wheeler–Lea Act)
5. Price discrimination if the intent is to injure a competitor (Robinson–Patman Act)

The following practices are also illegal when they substantially lessen competition or tend to create a monopoly:
1. Tying contracts (Clayton Act, Sec. 3)
2. Exclusive dealings (Clayton Act, Sec. 3)
3. Interlocking stockholdings and horizontal mergers (Clayton Act, Sec. 7, as amended by Celler–Kefauver Act)
4. Interlocking directorates (Clayton Act, Sec. 8)

The Effectiveness of Antitrust Policy— The Dominant View

Few economists are completely satisfied with all aspects of antitrust policy, but most observers believe that it has exerted a positive, although probably not dramatic, influence on competitive markets. The Sherman and Clayton Acts prohibit the most efficient methods of collusion (for example, mergers, interlocking boards of directors, and interlocking stockholdings) and thereby raise the costs of colluding. Also, since current collusive agreements must thus be tacit and unenforceable, rivals are more likely to cheat. The expected benefits of collusion have been effectively reduced, and economic theory suggests that the magnitude of anticompetitive collusive business practices should therefore be reduced. In addition, counterproductive (from the viewpoint of society) competitive tactics—exclusive contracts, price discrimination, and tying contracts, for example—have been made more costly. Prohibiting such practices has probably served to reduce entry barriers into markets. Since the passage of the Celler–Kefauver Act, most observers believe that antitrust legislation has effectively limited the power of firms to reduce competition *within an industry* through merger. Today, in contrast with earlier periods in American history, the probability of mergers contributing to industrial concentration—and hindering the competition that tends to erode it—is substantially lower.

**Antitrust Policy—
The Dissenting Views**

Like most other areas of policy, antitrust has its critics. Some of the dissenting views are only partially critical. Many economists, though in agreement with overall objectives, disagree with specific aspects of antitrust policy. Many people in business argue that current legislation is vague and that therefore it is difficult to determine whether a firm is in compliance.

There are three major schools of dissent on antitrust policy, which include (a) those individuals who would like deconcentration policies to be pursued more vigorously, (b) those who believe that the strength of competitiveness renders antitrust policy unnecessary, and (c) those who believe that antitrust policy is simply incapable of attacking industrial concentration. We will look briefly at each of these views.

Antitrust Policies Should Be More Vigorously Enforced. The proponents of this position argue that greater effort is required to ensure the existence of competitive markets. They often point out that antitrust policy has functioned primarily as a holding action. That is, it prevents large firms from *increasing* their market share, but it is ineffective as a means for *reducing* industrial concentration. Policy can end up working against its own objectives. For example, established firms controlling 50 or 60 percent of a market are generally left untouched, whereas two smaller firms with a combined market share of as little as 10 percent may be prohibited from merging. Therefore, current policy often protects strong, established firms while weakening their smaller rivals. Those who see current policy as self-defeating typically favor an antitrust policy that would more thoroughly restructure concentrated industries, dividing large firms in such industries into smaller, independent units.

Antitrust Policy Is Unnecessary. The advocates of this position argue that antitrust legislation places too much emphasis on the number of competitors without recognizing the positive role of dynamic competition. They believe that an antitrust policy that limits business concentration will often promote inefficient business organization and therefore higher prices. They reject the notion that pure competition is a proper standard of economic efficiency.[6] As Joseph Schumpeter, an early proponent of this view of competition and regulation, emphasized two decades ago:

It . . . is a mistake to base the theory of government regulation of industry on the principle that big business should be made to work as the respective industry would work in perfect competition.[7]

Like Schumpeter, the current advocates of this position believe that innovative activity is at the heart of competition. An ingenious innovator may forge ahead of competitors, but competition from other innovators will always be present. Competition is a perpetual game of leapfrog, not a process that is dependent on the number of firms in an industry. Bigness is a natural outgrowth of efficiency and successful innovation. One of the leading proponents for this

---

[6]See Dominick T. Armentano, *Antitrust and Monopoly: Anatomy of a Policy Failure* (New York: John Wiley, 1982), for an excellent presentation of this viewpoint.

[7]Joseph Schumpeter, *Capitalism, Socialism and Democracy* (New York: Harper Torchbooks, 1950), p. 106.

position, John McGee, of the University of Washington, argues that concentration is neither inefficient nor indicative of a lack of competition:

Take an industry of many independent producers, each of which is efficiently using small scale and simple methods to make the same product. . . . Suppose that a revolution in technology or management techniques now occurs, so that there is room in the market for only one firm using the new and most efficient methods. Whether it occurs quickly through merger or gradually through bankruptcy, an atomistic industry is transformed into a "monopoly," albeit one selling the same product at a lower price than before. If expected long-run price should rise, resort can still be had to the old and less efficient ways, which were compatible with . . . small firms. It would be incomplete and misleading to describe that process as a "decline of competition." [8]

Antitrust Policy Is Incapable of Dealing with Big Business. The third group of critics argues that antitrust policy is simply incapable of dealing with a modern economy already dominated by a few hundred industrial giants. The leading proponent of this position, John Kenneth Galbraith, charges that monopoly power is far too prevalent for one to expect that market forces could be imposed on large corporations. Galbraith argues that even if this were possible, competition would hinder, not help, economic development. Galbraith states his case against antitrust and competition as follows:

But it will also be evident that the antitrust laws, if they worked as their proponents hoped, would only make problems worse. Their purpose is to stimulate competition, lower prices, otherwise unshackle resource use and promote a more vigorous expansion of the particular industry. But the problem of the modern economy is not inferior performance of the planning system—of the monopolistic or oligopolistic sector, to revive the traditional terminology. The problem is the greater development here as compared with the market system. And the greater the power, the greater the development. Where the power is least—where economic organization conforms most closely to the goals envisaged by the antitrust laws—the development is least. If they fulfilled the hopes of their supporters and those they support, the antitrust laws would make development more unequal by stimulating development further in precisely those parts of the economy where it is now greatest. [9]

New Directions in Antitrust Policy—The AT&T and IBM Cases

Since the days of the Standard Oil trust nearly a century ago, antitrust policy has been strongly influenced by the notion that ideal competitive conditions are characterized by a large number of small firms. This emphasis on the number and size of rival firms has sometimes been pursued with little regard as to how well the interests of consumers are served by a given industry or firm. The Reagan administration seems to be trying to alter the course of antitrust policy. The administration holds the position that bigness does not necessarily mean badness. Under the Reagan antitrust policy, the sheer size of a firm will be less important than has been true in the past. In the enforcement of antitrust legislation, business efficiency and consumer welfare are presumably to be given greater, and industrial concentration less, consideration.

---

[8] John S. McGee, *In Defense of Industrial Concentration* (New York: Praeger, 1971), pp. 21–22.

[9] John Kenneth Galbraith, *Economics and the Public Purpose* (Boston: Houghton Mifflin, 1973), pp. 216–217.

The thrust of the Reagan policy became clear with the settlements in the IBM and AT&T cases on the same day, January 8, 1982. In both of these cases, the government sought to disaggregate the firms into a larger number of smaller firms. Both of the cases had dragged on for years. The filing of the case against IBM in 1969 was one of the last significant acts of the Johnson administration. The AT&T case was filed in 1975 by the Ford administration. The estimated combined costs of these suits to the government and the companies ran in excess of $500 million.

As part of its settlement, AT&T agreed to divest itself of its 22 local telephone companies with assets of $80 billion. These companies are to continue to operate as regulated public utilities. In return, AT&T is to be permitted to enter the fast-growing electronic data and computer fields, from which it had been barred since 1956. After the final divestiture plan is drafted and approved, AT&T is to have 18 months to separate itself from its local operating telephone companies.

In the early 1980s, foreign competitors were severely testing the dominance of AT&T in the telecommunications industry. Although AT&T had maintained substantial market power in the telephone communication industry, technological developments were eroding its position in the broader electronic communications area. Thus, under the terms of the settlement, the research and development arm of AT&T will operate within the forces of market pressure, while the telephone communication arm will be separated and continue to operate in the regulated sector.

Although AT&T operated as a regulated utility, IBM did not. By the late 1960s, IBM was far and away the dominant firm in the computer-manufacturing industry. Like AT&T, IBM had established an image as an aggressive, innovative company. According to the government's position, IBM was hindering competition by charging prices that were too low for the corporation's smaller rivals to meet. However, the government failed to prove adequately that consumers had been harmed by IBM's dominant share of the market.

The passage of time and the competitive process played important roles in the resolution of both of these cases. In the late 1960s, it was quite possible that the competitiveness of the computer-manufacturing industry was being endangered by the near-monopoly position of IBM, but by the latter half of the 1970s this was no longer true. Technological innovations, foreign competition, and the presence of strong rivals (Prime Computer, Wang, Digital, Control Data, Fujitsu, Hitachi, Burroughs, Cray Research, Olivetti, Siemens, and Philips, for example) were eroding IBM's market position. It was not even clear that any American firm would be the leader in the future computer-manufacturing market. It was against this background that the Reagan administration laid the IBM case to rest.

THEORIES OF REGULATION AND REGULATORY POLICY

Antitrust policy seeks to assure that the structure of an industry is competitive. Regulatory policies tend to be somewhat more direct and specific, often dictating pricing or operational policies for business firms. How does regulation work? To date, economists have been unable to develop a complete theory of regulation. Given the complex array of political and economic factors that are involved, this should not be surprising. In regulated markets, predicting what sellers will offer and how much consumers will be willing to buy at various prices is not enough. The regulatory process also represents (a) buyers who are unwilling to pay the full cost, (b) sellers who are inefficient producers, (c) politicians who are simultaneously considering thousands of pieces of legislation, and (d) voters, many of whom are "rationally uninformed" on regulatory issues. It is not easy to predict how such a complex system will deal with economic problems.

We can, however, facilitate our discussion of regulation by breaking it down into two major types: traditional economic regulation and the newer social regulation. We can also draw some conclusions about the decision-making of both economic and political participants in the regulatory process. Economic analysis indicates that decision-makers in the regulatory process, like those in other areas, respond to incentives. There are three incentive-related characteristics of the regulatory process that are important to keep in mind.

1. The Demand for Regulation Often Stems from the Special Interest Effect and Redistribution Considerations Rather Than from the Pursuit of Economic Efficiency. The wealth of an individual (or business firm) can be increased by an improvement in efficiency and an expansion in production. Regulation introduces another possibility. Sellers can gain if competition in their market is restricted. Buyers can gain, at least in the short run, if a legal requirement forcing producers to supply goods below cost is passed. Regulation opens up an additional avenue whereby those most capable of bending the political process to their advantage can increase their wealth.

Our earlier analysis suggested that special interest groups, such as well-organized, concentrated groups of buyers or sellers, exert a disproportionate influence on the political process. In addition, the regulators themselves often comprise a politically powerful interest group. Bureaucratic entrepreneurs are key figures in the regulatory process. Their cooperation is important to those who are regulated. In exchange for cooperation, politicians and bureaucrats are offered all manner of political support.

These factors suggest that there will be demand for economic regulation even if it contributes to economic inefficiency. The wealth of specific groups of buyers, sellers, and political participants may be enhanced, even though the total size of the economic pie is reduced. This is particularly true if the burden of economic inefficiency is widely dispersed among rationally uninformed taxpayers and groups of consumers.

2. Regulation Is Inflexible—It Often Fails to Adjust to Changing Market Conditions. Dynamic change often makes regulatory procedures obsolete. The introduction of the truck vastly changed the competitiveness of the ground transportation industry (previously dominated by railroad interests). Nonetheless, the regulation of price, entry, and route continued for years, even though competitive forces had long since eliminated the monopoly power of firms in this industry. Similarly, city building codes that may have been appropriate when adopted have become obsolete and now retard the introduction of new, more efficient materials and procedures. For example, in many cities, regulatory procedures have prevented builders from introducing such cost-saving materials as plastic pipes, preconstructed septic tanks, and prefabricated housing units. Why does the process work this way? In contrast with the market process, regulatory procedures generally grant a controlling voice to established producers. The introduction of new, more efficient products would reduce the wealth of the existing

"OF COURSE YOU MAY REGISTER A COMPLAINT ABOUT ALL THE GOVERNMENT PAPERWORK, SIR... BUT IT HAS TO BE IN WRITING."

producers of protected products. The political (regulatory) process is often responsive to these producers' charges that substitute materials (or new producers) would create unfair competition, violate safety codes, or be generally unreliable. Hearings are held. Lawsuits are often filed. Regulatory commissions meet and investigate—again and again. All of these procedures result in cost, delay, and inflexibility.

3. With the Passage of Time, Regulatory Agencies Often Adopt the Views of the Business Interests They Are Supposed to Regulate. Although the initial demand for regulatory action sometimes originates with disorganized groups seeking protection from practices that they consider unfair or indicative of monopolistic power, forces are present that will generally dilute or negate the impact of such groups in the long run. Individual consumers (and taxpayers) have little incentive to be greatly concerned with regulatory actions. Often they are lulled into thinking that since there is a regulatory agency, the "public interest" is served. In contrast, firms (and employees) in regulated industries are vitally interested in the structure and composition of regulatory commissions. Favorable actions by the commission could lead to larger profits, higher-paying jobs, and insulation from the uncertainties of competition. Thus, firms and employee groups, recognizing their potential gain, invest both economic and political resources in an effort to influence the actions of regulatory agencies.

How do vote-maximizing political entrepreneurs behave under these conditions? The payoffs from supporting the views of an apathetic public are small. Clearly, the special interest effect is present. When setting policy and making appointments to regulatory agencies, political entrepreneurs have a strong incentive to support the position of well-organized business and labor interests—often the very groups that the regulatory practices were originally designed to police.

There is evidence that regulatory activity in the United States has grown in importance in recent years. The number and the size of regulatory agencies have expanded substantially since the mid-1960s. Murray Weidenbaum, a former chairman of the Council of Economic Advisers, estimated that the various forms of regulation imposed a cost of approximately $500 per person on the U.S. economy during 1979. As Exhibit 4 illustrates, the number of employees involved in the regulatory process has been increasing rapidly.

Traditional Economic Regulation

Regulation of business activity is not a new development. In 1887, Congress established the Interstate Commerce Commission (ICC), providing it with the authority to regulate the railroad industry and, later, the trucking industry. Commissions were established to regulate the commercial airline and the broadcasting industries (the Civil Aeronautics Board and the Federal Communications Commission, respectively). State commissions have regulated the generation of electrical power for many years. All these activities focus on what has been called **economic regulation.**

There are several important elements of traditional economic regulation. First, it is generally industry-specific. For whatever reason, it is deemed that unregulated market forces create various problems in an industry. Sometimes the problem is monopoly. In other cases, excess supply stemming from "cut-throat" competition is alleged to be a problem. In general, it is believed that

Economic Regulation: Regu-lation of product price or industrial structure, usually imposed on a specific industry. By and large, the production processes utilized by the regu-lated firms are unaffected by this type of regulation.

EXHIBIT 4   The growth of the regulatory work force

The rate at which regulation is growing can be seen by the rapidly growing size of the regulatory work force.

Center for the Study of American Business, in *Nation's Business* (February 1981), p. 27.

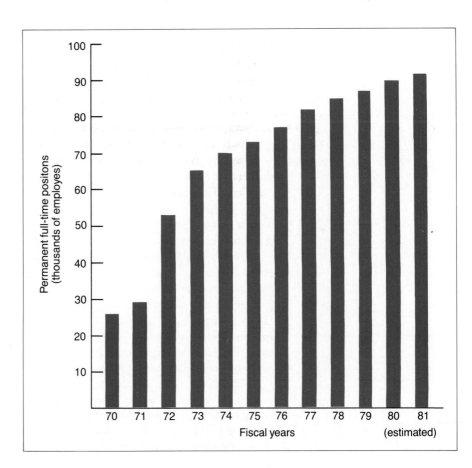

regulation of the industry is necessary to protect the interests of the public and provide for orderly competition. Second, traditional regulation often involves *both* the fixing of price (rates) and the protection of existing firms from potential rivals. Third, as the regulation evolves, it often takes on a cartel-like structure. This is not surprising. As we have discussed, two factors limit the effectiveness of collusive agreements among cartel members. Means must be found to (a) block the entry of potential new competitors and (b) prevent cartel members from cheating on agreements to fix prices. Regulatory agencies are sometimes used to help business firms in a specific industry accomplish both of these objectives.

During the 1970s, widespread dissatisfaction with the traditional regulatory approach developed in several industries. Major steps toward deregulation were taken in the ground and air transportation industries.

Deregulation in the Trucking Industry. The ICC was initially established to regulate rates in the railroad industry. Actually, much of the railroad industry supported the ICC's establishment. For many years, the commission regulated rates and allocated hauls to various rail shippers. However, beginning in the 1930s, the railroads began to confront stiff competition from the developing trucking industry. Since the trucking industry could be entered with relative ease, competitive forces were pushing rates downward. In response to the demands of railroad and large trucking interests, the regulatory control of the ICC was extended to include the trucking industry in 1935.

The ICC influenced the structure of the ground transportation industry in several ways. First, it limited the number of shippers in interstate commerce. Both rail and truck shippers were required to obtain a license from the ICC before they were permitted to compete in the interstate transportation industry. The ICC issued such licenses only when the proposed new service was deemed "necessary for the public convenience." Established shippers were granted the opportunity to present the ICC with counterevidence attesting that the entry of a new shipper was unnecessary or even harmful. The ICC's policies severely limited entry into the trucking industry.

Second, the ICC regulated shipping rates and permitted the rail and truck industries to establish price-fixing rate bureaus. Competitors who wanted to *reduce* their prices below the schedule established by the rate bureau had to ask the ICC to hear their cases. Typically, it would take six to eight months to obtain a ruling from the ICC. These arrangements strongly discouraged price competition in interstate shipping.

Third, the ICC limited the products that carriers could haul, the routes they could travel, and the number of cities along the route that they could serve. Carriers were prohibited from using price reductions as a means to arrange a "return haul." A carrier that was granted a license to haul from St. Louis to Denver might simultaneously have been prohibited from hauling a return shipment from Kansas City. A carrier's assigned route from New Orleans to Chicago might have required an intermediate stop in Atlanta. The result: miles of wasteful travel and trucks that were empty nearly 40 percent of the time.

The ICC's strict regulation of the trucking industry has been relaxed considerably in recent years. The Motor Carrier Act of 1980 now requires established firms opposing the entry of new rivals to show proof that the rivals would fail to serve the public interest. Generally, the act permits competitors to reduce rates as much as 10 percent without obtaining the ICC's approval.

The ICC was instructed to eliminate its prohibition of carriers from serving intermediate points along a route and its restrictions that limited the ability of carriers to arrange return-trip haulage. The antitrust immunity of the rate-setting bureaus was removed.

A recent study by the Federal Trade Commission indicates that the relaxation of entry barriers and rate-fixing policies has exerted a significant impact on the trucking industry.[10] During the first year after passage of the trucking deregulation legislation, the ICC granted 27,960 additional routes to new and existing carriers, compared to only 2710 during fiscal year 1976. Some 2452 new firms entered the trucking industry. Discount rates were widespread, and in general, freight rates fell between 5 and 20 percent during 1980–1981. There was an influx of small, primarily nonunion carriers into the industry. Price competition led to the acceptance of a temporary wage freeze by the Teamsters union. The influx of competition may well eventually lead to a shakedown in the trucking industry. As the profitability rates of trucking firms fall sharply, renewed pressure for stricter regulatory control will be felt. However, as James Miller, chairman of the FTC, has stated, the likelihood of effective noncompetitive practices being reimposed is low because "the deregulation genie is out of the bottle."[11]

Deregulation in the Airline Industry.   The history of the airline industry has followed a similar pattern. For decades, the airline business was operated under the close supervision of the Civil Aeronautics Board (CAB).[12] In effect, the regulatory powers of the CAB imposed a monopolistic structure on the industry. The CAB blocked competitive entry and outlawed competitive pricing. Any carrier that wanted to compete in an interstate route had to convince the CAB that its services were needed. To say that the CAB limited entry on major routes would be an understatement. Despite more than 150 requests, the CAB did not grant a single trunk (long-distance) route to a new carrier between 1938 and 1978. CAB policy also stifled price competition. Carriers that wanted to lower prices were required to present an application to the CAB. A hearing would be held, at which time the firm's competitors would have ample opportunity to indicate why the impending rate reduction was unfair or potentially harmful to their operation.

At least partially in response to evidence that regulatory policies were leading to excessive fares, half-empty planes, and a uniform product offering, airline regulatory policies in the United States were substantially relaxed in the late 1970s. Under the direction of economist Alfred Kahn, the CAB moved toward deregulation. Carriers were permitted to raise prices by as much as 10 percent and lower them by as much as 70 percent merely by giving the CAB notice 45 days in advance. In 1978, Congress passed the Airline Deregulation Act, which reduced the restrictions on price competition and entry into the industry.

---

[10]See James C. Miller III, "First Report Card on Trucking Deregulation," *Wall Street Journal,* March 8, 1982.

[11]James C. Miller III, "First Report Card on Trucking Deregulation," *Wall Street Journal,* March 8, 1982.

[12]Many people incorrectly associate the CAB with regulation of air safety, a function that it did perform in the past. However, since 1958, the Federal Aviation Agency has been responsible for air safety rules.

What has been the result of the move toward deregulation? The number of special plans (night-coach discount fares, preplanned charters, seasonal discounts, and so on) has vastly increased. During 1978, on average, air fares dropped an estimated 20 percent, and the number of passenger-miles traveled shot up by nearly 40 percent. Even corporate airline profits rose initially.[13]

Deregulation also led to an increase in the number of firms. In 1982, there were roughly 70 commercial airlines in the United States, up from 33 prior to deregulation. The major established airlines' share of domestic traffic fell from 92 percent in 1979 to 86 percent in 1981. Air traffic is quite cyclical. The recessions of 1979 and 1981, along with the increased competitiveness of the industry, have hit several airline firms quite hard. Braniff, for example, was forced into bankruptcy; other carriers may well follow. However, as some firms go out of business, the remaining firms in the industry are strengthened. When the economy recovers, there is no reason to believe that a competitive airline industry will not recover as well.

The New Social Regulation

Social Regulation: Legislation designed to improve the health, safety, and environmental conditions available to workers and/or consumers. The legislation usually mandates production procedures, minimum standards, and/or product characteristics to be met by producers and employers.

Along with movement toward deregulation of industrial structure and prices, there has been a sharp increase in what economists call **social regulation.** The new social regulation is comprised of a series of laws in the areas of health, safety, and the environment. Agencies such as the Occupational Safety and Health Administration (OSHA), Consumer Product Safety Commission (CPSC), Food and Drug Administration (FDA), and Environmental Protection Agency (EPA) have grown rapidly. These new agencies as a group are now larger, in terms of both number of employees and size of budgets, than the older regulatory agencies.

There are several significant differences between the two types of regulation. The older economic regulation focuses on a specific industry, whereas the new social regulation applies to the entire economy. Also, though more broadly based, social regulation is much more involved than economic regulation in the actual details of an individual firm's production. Economic regulation confines its attention to price and product quality—the final outcomes of production. The social regulatory agencies, on the other hand, frequently specify in detail the engineering processes to be followed by regulated firms and industries.

The major cost of social regulation is generally felt in the form of both higher production costs and higher prices. Social regulation requires producers to alter production techniques and facilities in accordance with dictated standards—to install more restrooms, to emit less pollution, or to reduce noise levels, for example—and most of the mandated changes increase costs. Of course, there are costs associated with the process of the regulation itself; employment and operating costs of regulatory agencies must be met, which means higher taxes. The higher cost stemming from mandated regulations

---

[13]Even though the regulatory policies stifled both entry and price competition, they did not eliminate other forms of competitive activity. Since firms were generally free to offer additional flights on *existing* routes, the availability of numerous daily flights on a route was often used as a competitive weapon. Given price regulation, this was wasteful, resulting in excessive flights and half-empty planes. This factor, along with the compliance cost of regulatory procedures, drained off much of the potential monopoly profits of the airline companies. Thus, it is not especially surprising that initially the firms' profits increased with deregulation, even though competitive pressures increased and air fares declined.

can also be seen as a tax. As Exhibit 5 illustrates, the higher cost shifts the supply curve for a good affected by the regulation to the left. Higher prices and a decline in the output of the good result.

The primary goal of social regulation is the attainment of a cleaner, safer, healthier environment. Nearly everyone agrees that this is a worthy objective. However, there is considerable disagreement about the procedures that are most likely to accomplish this objective and the price that should be paid to make even marginal improvements. Resources are scarce. More social regulation will mean less of other things. It should not be any more surprising that people differ with regard to the proper consumption level of environmental amenities than it is that they differ with regard to the proper consumption level of ice cream, for example. If one asked 100 people the best rate of consumption for strawberry ice cream, one would expect a wide variety of answers. Similarly, the extent to which we should give up other things to make automobile travel safer, for example, is a question that each person may answer quite differently. One's preferred consumption rate for auto safety, like the preferred rate for strawberry ice cream, will depend in part on expected cost and who pays that cost. Those who expect others to foot the bill will naturally prefer more of any good or amenity, whether it is ice cream or safe highways.

Differing preferences as to how many other goods should be given up in order to attain a safer, cleaner, healthier environment, comprise only part of the problem faced by regulators. An important characteristic of most socially regulated activities is a lack of information about their effects. This is no accident. In most cases, the lack of information contributes directly to the demand for the regulation. For example, if consumers knew exactly what the effect of a particular drug would be, there would be little need for the Food and Drug Administration to keep that drug unavailable. But many people are unaware of the precise effects of drugs, air pollution, or work-place hazards, even when the information is available to experts. It is costly to communicate information, particularly highly technical information. Thus, sometimes there is a potential payoff from letting the experts decide which drugs, how much air pollution, and what forms of work-place safety should be sought. A lack of solid informa-

EXHIBIT 5   The regulation "tax"

Regulation that requires businesses to adopt more costly production techniques is similar to a tax. If the regulation increases per unit costs by t, the supply curve shifts upward by that amount. Higher prices and a smaller output result.

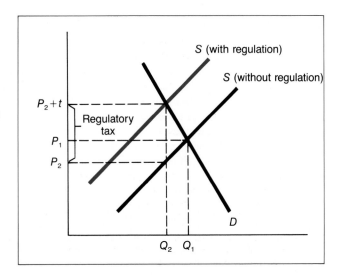

tion generates much of the demand for social regulation. Of course, the lack of information also makes it difficult to evaluate the effectiveness of the regulatory activity.

Future Directions. Nearly everyone concedes that regulation, both economic and social, is an imperfect solution. However, it is often difficult to separate beneficial regulations from those that are counterproductive. Although there is strong support for the continuation and expansion of social regulatory activities, recent experience indicates forces favoring deregulation are also present. Improved empirical evidence on the effectiveness of specific social regulation programs may very well emerge during the next decade.

THE REGULATORY EFFECTS OF MOTOR VEHICLE INSPECTION

As of 1980, 27 states and the District of Columbia imposed some form of mandatory vehicle inspection. The rationale for the required inspections is that improved operational effectiveness of motor vehicles is expected to reduce the incidence of traffic accidents and fatalities. Given that there are approximately 18 million motor vehicle accidents and 50,000 traffic fatalities each year, certainly the objectives of this program are laudable.

However, a recent detailed empirical study by Mark Crain of the Center for Public Choice at George Mason University suggests that the vehicle-inspection programs are failing to exert any detectable impact on the safety of motor vehicle travel. According to Crain, there is no statistical relationship between the number of travel-related accidents, injuries, and deaths in states *with* inspection programs and the number in states *without* such programs. Whether the inspections are required once or twice yearly and whether they are performed by publicly or privately operated inspection stations seem to have no perceptible influence on this finding.

Crain believes there are several reasons why the programs are

ineffective. First, it is not obvious that vehicle inspection is a feasible method of detecting the important potential sources of mechanical failure. Although bad tires and faulty headlights can be observed, drivers are usually well aware of these problems and adjust their driving accordingly. The really important sources of mechanical failure, such as a brake line that will leak or a steering mechanism that will fail *sometime in the near future,* are much more difficult to detect. Given the inspectors' lack of incentive—and the absence of a specific mandate for identifying such potential problems—the inspection system can probably do little to improve the actual operational safety of motor vehicles. Second, Crain points out that even if vehicle inspection *does* initially improve vehicle safety, the potential effect on traffic and travel safety may be offset by drivers who take more risks than they would otherwise because they assume the vehicle to be mechanically sound by virtue of having been inspected. Therefore, they may drive faster and place more confidence in the mechanical ability of the vehicle. These factors may offset the positive effects of the inspections.

Crain places the annual costs of safety-inspection programs at $200 million in fees, $2 to $7 billion in unneeded repairs, $30 million in lost

time for vehicle owners, and $200 million in resources necessary to carry out the inspection program. Given these costs, if the programs are ineffective, why have they not been repealed? Lack of information is, of course, one explanation. Crain's study has had some impact. Thus far, five states have abolished their inspection programs, at least partially in response to Crain's findings. However, it should be noted that the inspection programs do generate beneficiaries. At least some of the expenditures on the program represent gains to various groups and industries involved in providing the inspections, supplying replacement parts, and performing maintenance services. As might be expected, interest groups and trade associations, representing those businesses that perform inspection-related services, have been the most vocal in opposing repeal of the programs and advocating instead a nationally standardized inspection program. Crain's analysis of the inspection program emphasizes the importance of differentiating between stated goals and actual results when evaluating regulatory policy.[14]

---

[14] See W. Mark Crain, *Vehicle Safety Inspection Systems—How Effective?* (Washington, D.C.: American Enterprise Institute, 1980).

1   During the first 50 years of this century, the relative size of the manufacturing sector consistently increased, whereas that of the agricultural sector declined. Since 1950, a new trend has developed. The relative sizes of both the service and government sectors have increased, whereas both agriculture and manufacturing have generated a shrinking share of our national income.

2   It is not easy to categorize each industry as competitive or noncompetitive. Nonetheless, empirical research on industrial structure suggests that roughly 40 percent of our economy is highly competitive, in the sense of rivalry. Another 20 percent of our output is generated by unregulated firms in industries of medium or high concentration. Highly regulated industries account for nearly one-quarter of our total output; public sector firms generate the remainder.

3   The 1000 largest corporations employ approximately 18 percent of the U.S. work force. The size of the largest firms, as measured by value added, has grown relative to total manufacturing since 1947. However, since the size of the entire manufacturing sector relative to the whole economy has simultaneously declined, there has been little actual change in the share of *total output* generated by the 200 largest firms since the 1950s.

4   Antitrust legislation seeks to (a) maintain a competitive structure in the unregulated private sector and (b) prohibit business practices that are thought to stifle competition.

5   The Sherman, Clayton, and Federal Trade Commission Acts form the foundation of antitrust policy in the United States. The Sherman Act prohibits conspiracies to restrain trade and/or monopolize an industry. The Clayton Act prohibits specific business practices, such as price discrimination, tying contracts, exclusive dealings, and mergers and acquisitions (as amended), when they "substantially lessen competition or tend to create a monopoly." As it has evolved through the years, the Federal Trade Commission is concerned primarily with enforcing consumer protection legislation, prohibiting deceptive advertising, and investigating industrial structure.

6   Most economists believe that antitrust policy in the United States has promoted competition and reduced industrial concentration, but not to any dramatic extent.

7   To date, economists have been unable to develop a complete theory of regulation. However, economic analysis does suggest that: (a) the demand for regulation often stems from special interest and redistribution considerations rather than from the pursuit of economic efficiency; (b) regulation often fails to adjust to changing market conditions; and (c) with the passage of time, regulatory agencies are likely to adopt the views of the interest groups they are supposed to regulate.

8   Traditional economic regulation has generally sought to fix prices and/or influence industrial structure. During the 1970s, changing market conditions and recent empirical studies generated widespread dissatisfaction with economic regulation. Significant moves toward deregulation were made in the late 1970s, particularly in the trucking and airline industries. New entrants, intense competition, and discount prices have accompanied the deregulation of these industries.

9   In recent years, economic regulation has been relaxed, and social regulatory activities have expanded rapidly. Social regulation seeks to provide a cleaner, safer, healthier environment for workers and consumers. Pursuit of this objective is costly. Both higher product prices and higher taxes accompany such regulation. Since the costs and particularly the benefits are often difficult to measure and evaluate, the efficiency of social regulatory programs is a controversial topic under current research.

1   "Big business dominates the U.S. economy. Big business uses its power to decide what products we purchase, what jobs we hold, what kind of homes we live in, and even what political candidates we vote for." Evaluate.

2   Do you think that competition can be counted on to discipline the industrial business firms of a modern economy? Explain.

3 Currently, antimerger policy does not restrict conglomerate mergers between large firms if such mergers do not reduce competition in a specific market. Do you think such mergers should be prohibited? Why or why not?

4 "Efficiency requires large-scale production. Yet big businesses mean monopoly power, high prices, and market inefficiency. We must choose between production efficiency and monopoly." Evaluate.

5 Legislation mandating automobiles to be installed with stronger bumpers has presumably made cars both safer and more expensive. Do you think this social regulation has been beneficial? Why or why not? Similar legislation requiring that new automobiles be fully equipped with air bags that would automatically open on impact would have the same effects on safety and price. Do you think this regulation should be imposed? Why or why not?

6 Is there any reason to believe that consumer choice and free markets would provide less than the amount of safety desired by purchasers of a product—lawn mowers, for example? Why or why not?

7 Will social legislation mandating work places and products to be safer reduce the profitability of the regulated firms? Who bears the cost of such legislation? Who receives the primary benefits of the legislation?

8 Some economists argue that if the government lowered the trade barriers that limit the sale of foreign-produced goods in our domestic market, the need for antitrust action would be reduced. Do you agree or disagree? Explain your answer.

17

THE SUPPLY OF AND DEMAND FOR PRODUCTIVE RESOURCES

Thus far we have focused on markets for consumer goods and services. These markets (a) allocate goods and services among competing consumers and (b) determine which consumer goods will be produced. We now turn to an analysis of resource markets, or, as they are sometimes called, factor markets. In a market economy, both the income of resource owners and the value of resources are determined in factor markets. The income available to household units is dependent on the prices of resources and the quantity (and quality) of resources supplied to factor markets. Since the availability of resources can, and does, change with time, our discussion will also consider investment behavior. As is true for consumer-good markets, the tools of supply and demand can be profitably applied to resource markets.

Resources are demanded because they contribute to the production of goods and services. Since resources must be bid away from competitive firms seeking to put them to alternative uses, costs are incurred whenever resources are employed. Profit-seeking firms attempt to utilize resources to make products that can be sold for revenues in excess of the firm's resource costs. Conversely, resource owners are willing to supply their services because they obtain income for them. When choosing among alternative employment opportunities, utility-maximizing resource suppliers seek out those options they believe to be most advantageous.

HUMAN AND NONHUMAN RESOURCES

Broadly speaking, there are two different types of productive inputs—nonhuman and human resources. **Nonhuman resources** are further broken down into the categories of physical capital, land, and natural resources. Capital consists of man-made goods that are used to produce other goods. Tools, machines, and buildings are part of the capital stock.

Increasing the available stock of nonhuman resources involves the sacrifice of current consumption goods. Resources that are used to produce machines, upgrade the quality of land, or discover natural resources could be used to produce current goods and services directly. Why take the roundabout path? The answer is that sometimes indirect methods of producing goods are less costly in the long run. Robinson Crusoe found that he could catch more fish by

Nonhuman Resources: The durable, nonhuman inputs that can be used to produce both current and future output. Machines, buildings, land, and raw materials are examples. Investment can increase the supply of nonhuman resources. Economists often use the term "physical capital" when referring to nonhuman resources.

[1] James E. Meade, "Economic Efficiency and Distributional Justice," in *Contemporary Issues in Economics,* ed. Robert W. Crandell and Richard S. Eckaus (Boston: Little, Brown, 1972), p. 319.

taking some time off from hand fishing to build a net. Although his initial investment in the net reduced his current catch, once the net was completed he was able to more than make up for his earlier loss of output.

Additions to capital stock, whether they are fishing nets or complex machines, involve current sacrifices. Capital-intensive methods of production are adopted only when decision-makers expect the benefits of a larger future output to more than offset the current reduction in the production of consumption goods.

Just as the supply of machines can be increased, so too can wise land-clearing and soil conservation practices be used to upgrade both the quantity and quality of land. Similarly, the supply of natural resources can be increased (within limits) by the application of more resources to discovery and development.

The future productivity of **human resources** can also be increased. Investment in such things as education, training, health, skill-building experience, and migration to areas where jobs are more readily available involves current sacrifice in order to increase future productivity (and income). Economists refer to such activities as **investment in human capital.**[2]

Decisions to invest in human capital involve all the basic ingredients of other investment decisions. Consider the decision of whether to go to college. For most people, it is partly an investment decision. As many students will testify, an investment in a college education requires the sacrifice of current earnings as well as direct expenses for such things as tuition and books. The investment is expected to lead to a better job, *considering both monetary and nonmonetary factors,* and other benefits associated with a college education. The rational investor will weigh the current cost against the expected future benefits. College will be chosen only if the latter are greater than the former.

Some may find it offensive to refer to human beings as though they were machines. Nothing unethical is implied in the term "human capital." Men and women are, of course, not factors of production. They are human beings. However, the effort, skill, ability, and ingenuity of individuals can be applied productively. They can be used to improve human welfare. It is these productive resources that we refer to as human resources, or human capital.

Human resources differ from nonhuman resources in two important respects. First, human capital is embodied in the individual. Choices concerning the use of human resources are vitally affected by working conditions, location, job prestige, and similar nonpecuniary factors. Although monetary factors influence human capital decisions, individuals have some leeway for trading off money income for better working conditions. Second, human resources cannot be bought and sold in nonslave societies. Although the *services* of human resources are bought and sold daily, the right to quit, to sell one's services to another employer or use them in an alternative manner, always exists.

In competitive markets, the price of resources, like the price of products, is determined by supply and demand. In order to develop the theory of price for resource markets, we must first develop a theory for each of these determining factors. Let us begin by focusing on the demand for resources, both human and nonhuman.

Human Resources: The abilities, skills, and health of human beings that can contribute to the production of both current and future output. Investment in training and education can increase the supply of human resources.

Investment in Human Capital: Expenditures on training, education, and skill development designed to increase the productivity of an individual.

---

[2]The contributions of T. W. Schultz and Gary Becker to the literature on human capital have been particularly significant. See B. F. Kiker, ed., *Investment in Human Capital* (Columbia: University of South Carolina Press, 1971), for an excellent collection of readings in this area.

THE DEMAND FOR RESOURCES

Derived Demand: Demand for an item that is based on the demand for products the item helps to produce. The demand for resources is a derived demand.

Producers employ laborers, machines, raw materials, and the other resources required to produce the goods and services that firms hope to sell for a profit. The demand for a resource exists because there is a demand for goods that the resource helps to produce. Thus, the demand for each resource is a **derived demand**; it is derived from the consumer's demand for products.

For example, a service station hires mechanics because customers demand repair service, not because the service station owner receives benefits simply from having mechanics around. If customers did not demand repair service, mechanics would not be employed for long. Similarly, the demand for such inputs as carpenters, plumbers, lumber, and glass windows is derived from the demand of consumers for houses and other consumer products that these resources help to make.

Most resources contribute to the production of numerous goods. For example, glass is used to produce windows, automobiles, dishes, light bulbs, and mirrors, among other things. The total demand for a resource is the sum of the derived demand for it in each of its uses. Consequently, when economists study the demand for factors of production, they must trace changes in resource price to their impacts in the product market.

How will firms respond to an increase in the price of a resource? In the long run, the higher price of a resource will lead to two distinct adjustments, which will ensure an inverse relationship between price and the amount of the resource demanded. First, firms will seek to reduce their utilization of the now more expensive input by substituting other resources for it. Second, the increase in the price of the resource will lead to both higher costs and product prices. Consumers will buy less of the higher-priced product and substitute other goods for it, leading to a decline in the demand for resources used to make it. Therefore, the amount demanded of a factor of production will decline as its price increases. The demand curve for a resource will slope downward.

Let us look a little more closely at both of these adjustments.

1. Substitution in Production. Firms will attempt to use the input combination that minimizes their costs. When the price of a resource goes up, cost-conscious firms will seek to use lower-cost substitutes. The degree to which such substitution can take place will vary. Resources that are good substitutes may exist even though they are not currently being used. Sometimes the style and dimensions of a product can be altered in a manner that will conserve on the use of a more expensive import. The presence of good substitutes in production ensures not only that quantity demanded will be inversely related to price but also that the demand for the resource will be highly elastic.

2. Substitution in Consumption. An increase in the price of a resource will lead to higher prices for products that the input helps to produce. The higher product prices will encourage consumers to purchase substitute goods, reducing the consumption of the more expensive product. When less of that product is produced, however, producer demand for resources (including the one that has risen in price) will decline. The recent experience of the American automobile industry illustrates the point. Throughout much of the 1970s, wages in the U.S. automobile industry increased quite rapidly. The higher wages placed upward pressure on the prices of American-made automobiles. However, as auto prices rose, many consumers switched to substitute products. American auto sales declined, causing a reduction in quantity of labor demanded in the automobile industry and therefore widespread layoffs.

Other things constant, the more elastic the demand for the product, the more elastic the demand for the resource. This relationship stems from the derived nature of resource demand. An increase in the price of a product for which the demand is highly elastic will cause a sharp reduction in the sales of the good. Thus, there will also be a relatively sharp decline in the demand for the resources used to produce the good.

Time and the Demand for Resources

It will take time for producers to adjust fully to a change in the price of a resource. Typically, a producer will be unable to alter a production process or the design of a product *immediately* in order to conserve on the use of a more expensive input or to utilize more efficiently an input whose price has declined. Similarly, consumers may be unable to alter their consumption patterns *immediately* in response to price changes. Thus, the short-run demand for resources is typically less elastic than the demand in the long run.

Using steel as an example, Exhibit 1 illustrates the relationship between time and the demand for resources. Initially, higher steel prices may lead to only a small reduction in usage. If the high price of steel persists, however, automobile manufacturers will alter their designs, moving toward lighter-weight cars that require less steel. Architectural firms will design buildings that permit more substitution of plastics, wood, aluminum, glass, and other resources for steel. Eventually, products made with steel will increase in price, which will encourage consumers to cut back on their use. However, these adjustments will not take place instantaneously. Therefore, the demand (D_{sr}) for steel, like that for most other products, will be more inelastic in the short run than in the long run.

EXHIBIT 1   Time and the demand elasticity of resources

An increase in the price of steel will lead to a much larger reduction in consumption in the long run than in the short run. Typically, the demand for resources will be more inelastic in the short run.

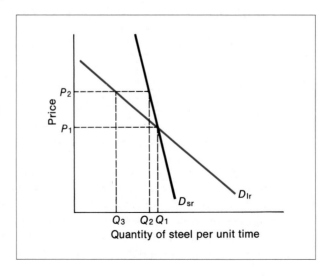

Shifts in the Demand for Resources

The entire demand curve for a resource, like that for a product, may shift, for one of three reasons.

A Change in the Demand for a Product Will Cause a Similar Change in the Demand for the Resources Used to Make the Product. Anything that increases the demand for a consumer good simultaneously increases the demand for resources required to make it; a decline in product demand and price will reduce the demand for the resources embodied in the product. In recent years, the demand for small automobiles has increased, primarily because of higher gasoline prices. The increase in demand for small cars led to an increase in demand for workers to produce them. Even while many auto workers were being laid off at plants producing large cars during the 1970s, employment expanded at plants producing small cars.

Changes in the Productivity of a Resource Will Alter the Demand for the Resource. The higher the productivity of a resource, the greater the demand for it. Several factors combine to determine the productivity of a resource. First, the **marginal product** of any resource will depend upon the amount of other resources with which it is working. In general, additional capital will tend to increase the productivity of labor. For example, someone with a lawn mower can mow more grass than the same person with a pair of shears. A student working with a textbook, class notes, and tutor can learn more economics than the same student without these tools. The quantity and quality of the tools with which we work affect our productivity significantly.

Second, technological advances can improve the productivity of resources, including labor. Advances in the computer industry illustrate this point. Working with computer technology, an accountant and data-entry person can maintain business records and create bookkeeping reports that would have previously required 10 to 15 workers. Similarly, computers have vastly increased the productivity of typesetters, telephone operators, quality-control technicians, and workers in many other occupations.

Third, improvements in the quality (skill level) of a resource will increase productivity and therefore the demand for the resource. As workers obtain valuable new knowledge and/or upgrade their skills, they enhance their productivity. In essence, such workers move into a different skill category, where demand is greater.

All of these factors help explain why wage rates in the United States, Canada, Western Europe, and Japan are higher than in most other areas of the world. Given the skill level of workers, the technology, and the capital equipment with which they work, individuals in these countries produce more goods and services per hour of labor. The demand for labor (relative to supply) is greater because of labor's increased productivity. Essentially, the workers' greater productivity leads to higher wage rates.

A Change in the Price of a Substitute Resource Will Affect the Demand for the Original Resource. An increase in the price of a substitute resource will lead to an increase in demand for the given resource. For example, when the wage rates of unionized workers in a given field or industry increase, the demand for nonunion workers will expand. Conversely, an increase in the price of a resource that is a complement to a given resource will decrease the demand for

> **Marginal Product:** The change in total output that results from the employment of one *additional* unit of a factor of production—one workday of skilled labor, for example.

the given resource. For example, higher prices for computers would most likely cause the demand for computer programmers to fall.

MARGINAL PRODUCTIVITY AND THE FIRM'S HIRING DECISION

Marginal Revenue Product: The change in the total revenue of a firm that results from the employment of one additional unit of a factor of production. The marginal revenue product of an input is equal to its marginal product multiplied by the marginal revenue (price) of the good or service produced.

How does a producer decide whether to employ additional units of a resource? We noted previously that the marginal product of a resource is the increase in output that results when the employment of a resource is expanded by one unit. The resource's marginal product multiplied by the marginal revenue of the product being produced yields what is known as the **marginal revenue product,** or MRP. The MRP is simply the change in the firm's total revenue brought about by the employment of one extra unit of a resource. It reveals how much the employment of the resource adds to revenues.

A profit-maximizing firm, of course, will continue to expand output as long as marginal cost is less than marginal revenue. This rule can be generalized to include the firm's employment of resources. Since firms are usually price takers when they buy resources, the price of a resource is its marginal cost. When a firm has a fixed factor of production—its plant size, for example—the marginal product of a resource will decline as its employment increases, according to the law of diminishing returns. In order to maximize profit, employment of a resource should be expanded as long as MRP exceeds the price of the resource.

Thus, a profit-maximizing firm will hire units of a variable resource up to the employment level at which the price of the resource (its marginal cost) is just equal to the marginal revenue product of the resource. This decision rule applies to all firms, both pure competitors and price searchers.

Value Marginal Product: The marginal product of a resource multiplied by the selling price of the product it helps to produce. Under perfect competition, a firm's marginal revenue product will be equal to the value marginal product.

The marginal product of a resource multiplied by the selling price of the product yields the resource's **value marginal product** (VMP). When a firm sells its product in a competitive market, the selling price and marginal revenue of the product are equal. Thus, under pure competition, the marginal revenue product of a resource is equal to its value marginal product.

Exhibit 2 illustrates the major factors that will influence a firm's hiring decision. SunKissed, Inc., sells prefabricated swimming pools. It also sells installation services, at $1000 per pool. Given the fixed quantity of heavy equipment owned by the firm, column 2 relates the number of expected monthly installations to the level of employment. One laborer could install four pools per month, two laborers eight pools, and so on. Column 3 presents the marginal product schedule for labor. Column 6, the marginal revenue product schedule, shows how the employment of each *additional* unit of labor affects total revenues.

Since SunKissed sells its service competitively, both the marginal revenue product and the value marginal product of labor equal MP (column 3) times the installation price (column 4). What if the firm is not a perfect competitor? The marginal revenue product must always equal MR multiplied by MP. When the firm confronts a downward-sloping demand curve for its product, the marginal revenue of the product will be less than its price. When this is the case, the marginal revenue product of a resource will be less than the value marginal product.

How much labor should SunKissed employ? A profit-maximizing firm compares the cost of a resource with its MRP when making hiring decisions.

EXHIBIT 2   The short-run demand schedule of a firm

SunKissed, Inc., sells and installs swimming pools in a competitive industry. The pools are sold separately. When a pool is sold, the firm receives a $1000 installation fee. Given the firm's current fixed capital, column 2 shows how total output changes as additional units of labor are hired. The marginal revenue product schedule of labor (column 6) is the firm's short-run demand curve for that input.

(1) Units of the Variable Factor (Skilled Labor)	(2) Total Output (Pools Installed per Month)	(3) Marginal Product, Change in (2) Change in (1)	(4) Product Installation Price	(5) Total Revenue, (2) × (4)	(6) Marginal Revenue Product, (3) × (4)
0	0	—	$1000	$ 0	—
1	5.0	5.0	1000	5,000	$5000
2	9.0	4.0	1000	9,000	4000
3	12.0	3.0	1000	12,000	3000
4	14.0	2.0	1000	14,000	2000
5	15.5	1.5	1000	15,500	1500
6	16.5	1.0	1000	16,500	1000
7	17.0	0.5	1000	17,000	500

Employment of labor, as well as other resources, will be expanded as long as MRP exceeds resource costs. Thus, as Exhibit 3 illustrates, the marginal revenue product curve is also the firm's demand curve for the resource.[3] At a monthly wage of $5000, SunKissed would hire only one worker. If the monthly wage dropped to $4000, two workers would be hired. At still lower wage rates, additional workers would be hired.

The location of the firm's MRP curve depends upon (a) the price of the product, (b) the productivity of the resource, and (c) the amount of other resources with which the resource is working. Changes in any other of these three factors will cause the MRP curve to shift. For example, if SunKissed obtained a new machine that made it possible for the workers to install more pools each month, the MRP curve for labor would increase. This increase in the quantity of the other resources working with labor would increase labor's productivity.

Adding Other Factors of Production

Thus far, we have analyzed the firm's hiring decision assuming that it employed one variable resource (labor) and one fixed resource. Of course, production usually involves the use of many resources. When a firm employs multiple resources, how should the resources be combined to produce the product? We can answer this question by considering either the conditions for profit maximization or the conditions for cost minimization.

Profit Maximization When Multiple Resources Are Employed.   The same decision-making considerations apply when the firm employs several factors of production. The profit-maximizing firm will expand its *employment of a resource* as long as the marginal revenue product of the resource exceeds its employment

---

[3]Strictly speaking, this is true only for a variable resource that is employed with a fixed amount of another factor.

EXHIBIT 3   The firm's demand curve for a resource

The firm's demand curve for a resource will reflect the marginal revenue product of the resource. In the short run, it will slope downward because the marginal product of the resource will fall as more of it is used with a fixed amount of other resources. The location of the MRP curve will depend on (a) the price of the product, (b) the productivity of the resource, and (c) the quantity of other factors working with the resource.

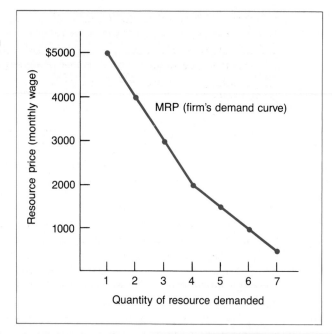

cost. If we assume that resources are perfectly divisible, the profit-maximizing decision rule implies that, in equilibrium, the marginal revenue product of each resource will be equal to the price of the resource. Therefore, the following conditions will exist for the profit-maximizing firm:

$$\text{MRP of skilled labor} = P_{SL} \text{ (wage rate of skilled labor)}$$
$$\text{MRP of unskilled labor} = P_{UL} \text{ (wage rate of unskilled labor)}$$
$$\text{MRP of machine} = P_{M} \text{ (explicit or implicit rental price}$$
$$\text{of machine A)}$$

and so on, for all other factors.

Cost Minimization When Multiple Resources Are Employed.   If the firm is maximizing profits, clearly it must produce the profit-maximizing output at the least possible cost. If the firm is minimizing costs, the marginal dollar expenditure for each resource will have the same impact on output as every other marginal resource expenditure. Factors of production will be employed such that the marginal product per last dollar spent on each factor is the same for all factors.

Suppose that a dollar expenditure on labor caused output to rise by ten units, whereas an additional dollar expenditure on machines generated only a five-unit expansion in output. Under these circumstances, five more units of output would result if the firm spent $1 less on machines and $1 more on labor. The firm's total (and per unit) cost would be reduced if it substituted labor for machines. If the marginal dollar spent on one resource increases output by a larger amount than a dollar expenditure on other resources, costs can always be reduced by substituting resources with a high marginal product *per dollar* for those with a low marginal product *per dollar expenditure.* This substitution should continue until the marginal product per dollar expenditure is equalized—that is, until the resource combination that minimizes cost is attained. When this is true, the proportional relationship between the price of each resource and its marginal product will be equal for all resources. Therefore, the following condition exists when per unit costs are minimized:

$$\frac{\text{MP of skilled labor}}{\text{price of skilled labor}} = \frac{\text{MP of unskilled labor}}{\text{price of unskilled labor}}$$

$$= \frac{\text{MP of machine A}}{\text{price (rental value) of machine A}}$$

and so on, for the other factors.

In the real world, it is sometimes difficult to measure the marginal product of a factor. Businesspeople may not necessarily think in terms of equating the marginal product/price ratio for each factor of production. Nonetheless, if they are minimizing cost, this condition will be present. Real-world decision-makers may use experience, trial and error, and intuitive rules that are nevertheless consistent with cost-minimization and profit-maximizing criteria. However, when profits are maximized and the cost-minimization method of production is attained, regardless of the procedures used, the outcome will be *as if* the employer had followed the profit-maximization and cost-minimization decision-making rules that we have just discussed.

MARGINAL PRODUCTIVITY, DEMAND, AND ECONOMIC JUSTICE

According to the law of diminishing marginal returns, as the employment level of a resource increases, other things constant, the marginal product (and marginal revenue product) of the resource will decline. As we have just seen, a profit-maximizing employer will expand the use of a resource until its marginal revenue product is equal to the price of the resource. If the price of the resource declines, employers will increase their utilization level of that resource. Therefore, as Exhibit 4 shows, the marginal productivity approach can be used to illustrate the inverse relationship between quantity demanded and resource price.

Some observers, noting that under pure competition the price of each resource is just equal to the value of what it produces (that is, input price equals marginal product of the input multiplied by the price of the product), have argued that competitive markets are "just" or "equitable" because each resource gets paid exactly what it is worth. However, there is a major defect in this line of reasoning. The "marginal productivity" of labor (or any other factor) cannot be determined independently of the contribution of other factors. When a product is produced by a combination of factors, as is almost invariably the case, it is impossible to assign a *specific proportion of the total output* to each resource. For example, if one uses a tractor, an acre of land, and seed to produce wheat, one cannot accurately state that labor (or the seed or the land) produced one-half or any other proportion of the output. Hence, those who argue that the factor payments generated by competitive markets are just, because each resource gets paid according to its productive contribution, are assuming one can assign a *specific* proportion of the total output to each resource, which is

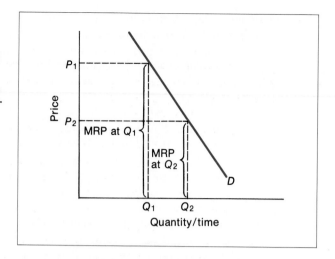

not possible. The marginal product can be used as a measure of the change in total output *associated* with the use of an additional unit of a resource; but this measurement does not *directly* link one resource with one segment of output.

The marginal productivity theory is really a theory about the demand for resources. The central proposition of the theory is that profit-maximizing employers will never pay more for a unit of input, whether it is skilled labor, a machine, or an acre of land, than the input is worth to them. The worth of a unit of input to the firm is determined by how much additional revenue (marginal revenue product) is generated (or seems to be generated) when the unit is used. That is, pursuit of profit will induce employers to hire additional units of each resource as long as the units' marginal productivity generates revenues in excess of costs. Resource prices will tend to reflect—though somewhat roughly in the real world—the marginal productivity of the resource.

However, the price of each resource is determined by conditions of supply as well as demand. Although marginal productivity theory helps us to understand the demand side of the market, it reveals nothing about the *share of the total product* produced by a resource or the justice of a resource price. We must analyze the supply of resources to factor markets in order to complete the picture.

THE SUPPLY OF RESOURCES

In the immediate short-run period, the *total supply* of specific resources, both human and nonhuman, will be virtually fixed. However, resources usually have alternative uses; they can typically be used to help produce a variety of products. Within the fixed total supply there will be some flexibility. The principle of utility maximization implies that resource owners will use their factors of production in a manner that leads to the greatest net advantage to themselves. Of course, both monetary and nonpecuniary considerations will influence their decisions.

In the short run, the quantity of a resource supplied *to a specific use* is directly related to price. Resource owners will shift factors of production toward uses for which compensation has risen and away from areas where resource prices have fallen. Thus, the supply curve for a specific resource (skilled labor, engineering service, or farm land, for example) will slope upward to the right.

The elasticity of supply to a particular use will be dependent on **resource mobility.** Resources that can be easily transferred from one use to another in response to changing price incentives—in other words, those resources with a great many alternative uses or locations—are said to be highly mobile. The supply of such factors to any specific use will be elastic. Factors that have few alternative uses are said to be immobile and will have an inelastic short-run supply.

What can we say about resource mobility in the real world? First, let us consider the mobility of labor. When labor skills can be transferred easily and quickly, human capital is highly mobile. Within skill categories (for example, plumber, store manager, accountant, and secretary), labor will be highly mobile *within the same geographical area*. Movements between geographical areas and from one skill category to another are more costly to accomplish. Thus, labor will be less mobile for movements of this variety.

What about the mobility of land? Land is highly mobile among uses *when location does not matter*. For example, the same land can often be used to raise either corn, wheat, soybeans, or oats. Thus, the supply of land allocated to the production of each of these commodities will be highly responsive to changes in their relative prices. Undeveloped land on the outskirts of cities is particularly mobile among uses. In addition to its value in agriculture, such land might be quickly subdivided and used for a housing development or shopping center. However, since land is totally immobile physically, supply is unresponsive to *changes in price that reflect the desirability of a location*.

Typically, machines are not very mobile among uses. A machine developed to produce airplane wings is seldom of much use in the production of automobiles, appliances, and other products. Steel mills cannot easily be converted to produce aluminum. Of course, there are some exceptions. Trucks can typically be used to haul a variety of products. Building space can often be converted from one use to another. In the short run, however, immobility and inelasticity of supply are characteristic of much of our physical capital.

Resource Mobility: A term that refers to the ease with which factors of production are able to move among alternative uses. Resources that can easily be transferred to a different use or location are said to be highly mobile. In contrast, when a resource has few alternative uses, it is immobile. For example, the skills of a trained rodeo rider would be highly immobile, since they cannot easily be transferred to other lines of work.

Long-Run Supply

In the long run, the supply of resources is not fixed. Machines wear out, human skills depreciate, and even the fertility of land declines with use and erosion. These factors reduce the supply of resources. However, through investment, the supply of productive resources can be expanded. Current resources can be invested to expand the stock of machines, buildings, and durable assets. Alternatively, current resources can be used to train, educate, and develop the skills of future labor force participants. The supply of both physical and human resources in the long run is determined primarily by investment and depreciation.

Price incentives will, of course, influence the investment decisions of both firms and individuals. Considering both monetary and nonmonetary factors, investors will choose those alternatives they believe to be most advantageous. Higher resource prices will induce utility-maximizing investors to supply a larger amount of the resource. In contrast, other things constant, lower resource prices will reduce the incentive to expand the future supply by investing. Therefore, the long-run supply curve for a resource, like the short-run curve, will slope upward to the right.

The theory of long-run resource supply is general. The expected payoff from an investment alternative will influence the decisions of investors in human, as well as physical, capital. For example, the higher salaries of physical and space scientists employed in the expanding space program during the early 1960s induced an expanding number of college students to enter these fields. Similarly, attractive earning opportunities in accounting and law led to an increase in investment and quantity supplied in these areas during the period from 1965 to 1975. When government space efforts tapered off in the late 1960s, the salaries and employment opportunities in physics, aerospace engineering, and astronomy declined. As college enrollments in these areas in the early 1970s attest, human capital investment declined accordingly. In the late 1970s, the demand for petroleum engineers increased. Predictably, salaries rose sharply, as did the number of students graduating in the field of petroleum engineering. As in other markets, people were responding to changes in relative prices.

Considering both monetary and nonmonetary factors, investors will not knowingly invest in areas of low return when higher returns are available elsewhere. Of course, since human capital is embodied in the individual, non-pecuniary considerations will typically be more important for human than for physical capital. Nonetheless, expected monetary payoffs will influence investment decisions in both areas.

The long run, of course, is not a specified length of time. Investment can increase the availability of some resources fairly quickly. For example, it does not take very long to train additional bus drivers. Thus, in the absence of barriers to entry, the quantity of bus drivers supplied will expand rapidly in response to higher wages. However, the gestation period between expansion in investment and an increase in quantity supplied is substantially longer for some resources. It takes a long time to train physicians, dentists, lawyers, and pharmacists. Higher earnings in these occupations may have only a small impact on their *current* availability. Additional investment will go into these areas, but it will typically be several years before there is any substantial increase in the quantity supplied in response to higher earnings for these resources.

Because supply can be substantially expanded over time by investment, the supply of a resource will be much more elastic in the long run than in the short run. This is particularly true when there is a lengthy gestation period between an increase in investment and an actual increase in the availability of a resource. Using nursing services as an example, Exhibit 5 illustrates the relationship between the short- and long-run supply of resources. An increase in the price (wage rate) of nursing services will result in some immediate increase in quantity supplied. Trained nurses may choose to work more hours. Nurses not in the labor force may be drawn back into nursing. With time, the more attractive employment opportunities in nursing will cause the level of investment in human capital in this area to expand (for example, more student nurses). However, since most nursing programs take two to four years, it will be several years before the additional investment will begin to have an impact on supply. In the long run, the quantity of nurses supplied may be quite elastic, but in the short run it is likely to be highly inelastic.

EXHIBIT 5 Time and the elasticity of supply for resources

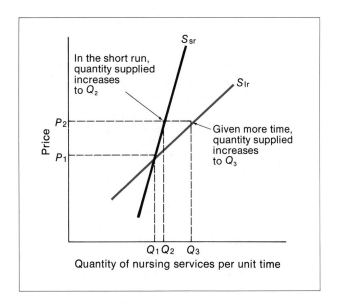

In the short run, quantity supplied increases to Q_2

S_{sr}

S_{lr}

P_2

P_1

Price

Given more time, quantity supplied increases to Q_3

Q_1 Q_2 Q_3

Quantity of nursing services per unit time

SUPPLY, DEMAND, AND RESOURCE PRICES

The theories of both supply and demand for resources have been analyzed. This is all we need to develop the theory of resource pricing in competitive markets. When factor prices are free to vary, resource prices will bring the choices of buyers and sellers into line with each other. The forces of supply and demand operate in precisely the same manner for both resource and product markets. Pressures are present that will push resource prices toward equilibrium, where quantity supplied and quantity demanded are equal. An above-equilibrium price will generate an excess supply, that is, unsold resource services. Since they are unable to sell their services at the above-equilibrium price, some resource owners will reduce their price, pushing the market price toward equilibrium. When a resource price is below equilibrium, excess demand will be present. Rather than do without the resource, employers will bid up the price, eliminating the excess supply.

Resource markets, like product markets, generally go through a series of operations in response to changes. Complete adjustment does not take place instantaneously. Depending on the nature of the resource, a substantial period of time may be necessary before the availability of the resource can be greatly increased. However, the nature of the process is straightforward. For example, at a higher level of demand the price of a resource initially would rise sharply, particularly if the short-run supply was quite inelastic. However, at the higher price, *with time*, the quantity of the resource supplied would expand. If it was a natural resource, individuals and firms would put forth a greater effort to discover and develop the now more valuable productive factor. If it was physical capital, a building or machine, current suppliers would have greater incentive to work intensively to expand production. New suppliers would be drawn into the market. Higher prices for human capital resources would also lead to an expansion in the quantity supplied. With time, more people would acquire the

EXHIBIT 6   Adjusting to dynamic change

An increase in demand for a resource will typically cause price to rise more in the short run than in the long run. Can you explain why?

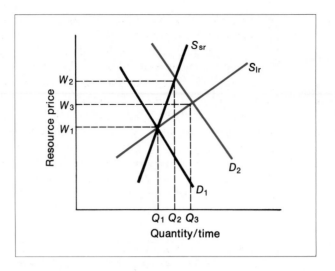

OUTSTANDING ECONOMIST

Gary Becker (1930–   )

This innovative economist is perhaps best known for his ingenious application of economics to several areas that many had previously considered to be noneconomic by nature. Before his pioneering book, *The Economics of Discrimination,*[4] the research of economists

in this area was scanty. Apparently, many felt that something as irrational as prejudice was beyond the realm of a rational science like economics. Becker's book proved otherwise. He developed a general theory that could be used to analyze (and measure) the impact of discrimination in several areas on the status of minorities and women. His work laid the foundation for the burgeoning of research interest in the economics of discrimination that took place during the 1960s and 1970s.

Later, Becker applied economic analysis to such seemingly noneconomic subjects as crime prevention, family development, an individual's allocation of time, and even the selection of a marriage partner.[5] His imaginative work earned him the J. B. Clark Award (1967), granted by the American Economic Association to the "outstanding economist under 40."

The human capital approach

underlies much of Becker's research. His widely acclaimed book, *Human Capital,*[6] is already a classic. This work developed a theoretical foundation for human investment decisions in education, on-the-job training, migration, and health. Becker looks at the individual as a "firm" that will invest in human resources if it is "profitable" to do so. Considering both monetary and nonmonetary factors, the human capital decisions of these profit-maximizing (or utility-maximizing) individuals will be based on the attractiveness (rate of return) of alternative investment opportunities. High rates of return will attract human capital investment to an area, whereas low rates of return will repel it.

Becker has estimated the rate of return for both a high school and college education. His work, along with that of others, suggests that, *on average,* human capital investments in education are highly profitable. A professor at the University of Chicago, Becker also taught at Columbia University for several years.

[4]Gary Becker, *The Economics of Discrimination* (Chicago: University of Chicago Press, 1957).

[5]Gary Becker, *The Economic Approach to Human Behavior* (Chicago: University of Chicago Press, 1976), and Gary Becker and W. M. Landes, *Essays in the Economics of Crime and Punishment* (New York: Columbia University Press, 1974).

[6]Gary Becker, *Human Capital* (New York: Columbia University Press, 1964).

necessary training, education, and experience to develop the skills that would now command a higher price. The expansion of the supply would eventually moderate the price rise. Because of these forces, as Exhibit 6 illustrates, the long-run price increase would be less than the short-run increase.

Similarly, a reduction in demand would cause the price of the resource to fall further in the short run than over a longer period of time. At the lower price, some resource suppliers would use their talents in other areas. The incentive for potential new suppliers to offer the resource would be reduced by the fall in price. With time, the quantity of the resource supplied would become more elastic, moderating the long-run decline in price. Those with the poorest alternatives (that is, lowest opportunity cost) would continue to provide the resource at the lower prices. Those with better alternatives would move to other areas.

LOOKING AHEAD

Now that we have outlined the theoretical underpinnings of factor markets, we can apply the analysis to a broad range of economic issues. The next chapter will focus on the labor market and the determination of wage rates. Later we will focus on the capital market and the allocation of resources over time. The operation of these two markets plays an important role in determining the distribution of income, a topic that will also be analyzed in detail in a subsequent chapter.

CHAPTER LEARNING OBJECTIVES

1 Factor markets, where productive goods and services are bought and sold, help to determine what is produced, how it is produced, and the distribution of income (output). There are two broad classes of productive resources—nonhuman capital and human capital. Both are durable in the sense that they will last into the future, thereby enhancing future productive capabilities. Both yield income to their owners. Investment can expand the future supply of both.

2 The demand for resources is derived from the demand for the products that the resources help to produce. The quantity of a resource demanded is inversely related to its price. If the price of a resource increases, less of it will be used for two reasons. First, producers will substitute other resources for the now more expensive input (substitution in production). Second, the higher resource price will lead to higher prices for products that the resource helps to make, causing consumers to reduce their purchases of those goods (substitution in consumption).

3 The short-run market demand curve will be more inelastic than the long-run curve. It will take time for producers to adjust their production process in order to use more of the less expensive resources and less of the more expensive resources.

4 The demand curve for a resource, like the demand for a product, may shift. The major factors that can increase the demand for a resource are (a) an increase in demand for products that use the resource, (b) an increase in the productivity of the resource, and (c) an increase in the price of substitute resources.

5 Profit-maximizing firms will hire additional units of a resource as long as the marginal revenue product of the resource exceeds its hiring cost, usually the price of the resource. If resources are perfectly divisible, firms will expand their utilization of each resource until the marginal revenue product of each resource is just equal to its price.

6 When a firm is minimizing its costs, it will employ each factor of production up to the point at which the marginal product per last dollar spent on the factor is equal for all factors. This condition implies that the marginal product of labor divided by the

price of labor must equal the marginal product of capital (machines) divided by the price of capital and that this ratio (MP_i/P_i) must be the same for all other inputs used by the firm. When real-world decision-makers minimize per unit costs, the outcome will be *as if* they had followed these mathematical procedures, even though they may not consciously do so.

7 Resource owners will use their factors of production in the manner that they consider most advantageous to themselves. Many resources will be relatively immobile in the short run. The less mobile a resource, the more inelastic its short-run supply. There will be a positive relationship between amount supplied and resource price even in the short run.

8 In the long run, investment and depreciation will alter resource supply. Resource owners will shift factors of production toward areas in which resource prices have risen and away from areas where resource prices have fallen. Thus, the long-run supply will be more elastic than the short-run supply.

9 The prices of resources will be determined by both supply and demand. The demand for a resource will reflect the demand for products that it helps to make. The supply of resources will reflect the human and physical capital investment decisions of individuals and firms.

10 Changing resource prices will influence the decisions of both users and suppliers. Higher resource prices give users a greater incentive to turn to substitutes and stimulate suppliers to provide more of the resource. Since these adjustments take time, when the demand for a resource expands, the price will usually rise more in the short run than in the long run. Similarly, when there is a fall in resource demand, price will decline more in the short run than in the long run.

THE ECONOMIC WAY OF THINKING—DISCUSSION QUESTIONS

1 What is the meaning of the expression "invest in human capital"? In what sense is the decision to invest in human capital like the decision to invest in physical capital? Is human capital investment risky? Explain.

2 (a) "Firms will hire a resource only if they can make money by doing so." (b) "In a market economy, each resource will tend to be paid according to its marginal product. Highly productive resources will command high prices, whereas less productive resources will command lower prices."
Are (a) and (b) both correct? Are they inconsistent with each other? Explain.

3 Use the information of Exhibit 2 to answer the following:
(a) How many skilled laborers would SunKissed hire at a monthly wage of $1200 if it were attempting to maximize profits in its pool installation business?
(b) What would the firm's maximum profit be if its fixed costs were $7000?
(c) Suppose that there was a decline in demand for pools, reducing the market price for installation service to $750. At this demand level, how many employees would SunKissed hire at $1200 per month in the short run? Would SunKissed stay in business at the lower market price? Explain.

4 Are productivity gains the major source of higher wages? If so, how does one account for the rising real wages of barbers, who by and large have used the same technique for half a century? (*Hint:* Do not forget opportunity cost and supply.)

5 "However desirable they might be from an equity viewpoint, programs designed to reduce wage differentials will necessarily reduce the incentive of people to act efficiently and use their productive abilities in those areas where demand is greatest relative to supply." Do you agree or disagree? Why?

6 **What's Wrong with This Way of Thinking?**

"The downward-sloping marginal revenue product curve of labor shows that better workers are hired first. The workers hired later are less productive."

Properly conceived, education produces a labor force that is more skilled, more adaptable to the needs of a changing economy, and more likely to develop the imaginative ideas, techniques, and products which are critical to the processes of economic expansion and social adaptation to change. By doing so—by contributing to worker productivity—the education process qualifies handsomely as a process of investment in human capital.[1]
Burton Weisbrod

18

EARNINGS, SKILL ACQUISITION, AND THE JOB MARKET

The wages of U.S. workers are the highest in the world—and they have been increasing. The compensation for a day of work by the average labor force participant buys far more today than it did 30 years ago. Individual wages, however, vary widely. An unskilled laborer may earn the $3.35 minimum wage, or something close to it. Lawyers and physicians often earn $60 per hour. Dentists and even economists might receive $40 per hour.

Why do some earn more than others? Why are earnings, measured in terms of their purchasing power, so high for Americans? Can high wages be legislated? In this chapter, we analyze these questions.

WHY DO EARNINGS DIFFER?

The earnings of paired individuals in the same occupation or with the same amount of education very often differ substantially. The earnings of persons with the same family background also vary widely. For example, one researcher found that the average earnings differential between brothers was $5600, compared to $6200 for men paired randomly.[2] In addition, the earnings of persons with the same IQ, level of training, or amount of experience typically differ. How do economists explain these variations? Several factors combine to determine the earning power of an individual. Some seem to be the result of good or bad fortune. Others are clearly the result of conscious decisions made by individuals. In the previous chapter, we analyzed how the market forces of supply and demand operate to determine resource prices. The subject of earnings differentials can be usefully approached within the framework of this model.

If (a) all individuals were homogeneous, (b) all jobs were equally attractive, and (c) workers were perfectly mobile among jobs, the earnings of all employees in a competitive economy would be equal. If, given these conditions,

---

[1]Burton A. Weisbrod, "Investing in Human Capital," *Journal of Human Resources* (Summer 1966), pp. 5–21.

[2]Christopher Jencks, *Inequality* (New York: Basic Books, 1972), p. 220.

higher wages existed in any area of the economy, the supply of workers to that area would expand until the wage differential was eliminated. Similarly, low wages in any area would cause workers to exit until wages in that area returned to parity. However, earnings differentials cannot be avoided in the real world, because the conditions necessary for earnings equality do not exist.

Earnings Differentials Due to Nonhomogeneous Labor

Clearly, all workers are not the same. They differ in several important respects, which influence both the supply of and demand for their services.

Worker Productivity. The demand for employees who are highly productive will be greater than the demand for those who are less productive. Persons who can operate a machine more skillfully, hit a baseball more consistently, or sell life insurance policies with greater regularity will have a higher marginal revenue product than their less skillful counterparts. Because they are more productive, their services will command a higher wage from employers.

Workers can increase their productivity by investment in human capital. Formal education, vocational training, skill-building experience, and proper health care to maintain physical fitness can enhance worker productivity. Of course, native ability and motivation will influence the rate at which an individual can transform educational and training experience into greater productivity. Most of us would not be able to hit a baseball with the skill of Steve Garvey even if we practiced every day from the time we were old enough to walk. Individuals differ in the amount of valuable skills they develop from a year of education, vocational school, or on-the-job training. We should not expect a rigid relationship to exist between years of training (or education) and skill level.

In general, more able persons appear to receive more education and training. Not surprisingly, greater investment in human capital leads to higher average annual earnings *once the person enters the labor force full-time*. As Exhibit 1 shows, persons with more education have higher earnings. Similarly, economic research has shown that a positive relationship exists between training and earnings.

Specialized Skills. Investment in human capital and development of specialized skills can protect high-wage workers from the competition of others willing to offer their services at a lower price. Few persons could develop the specialized skills of a Johnny Carson or Tracy Austin. Similarly, skill (and human capital) factors also limit the supply of heart surgeons, trial lawyers, engineers, and business entrepreneurs. As Exhibit 2 illustrates, when the demand for a specialized resource is great relative to its supply, the resource will be able to command a high wage. In 1979, the earnings of engineers were $31,300, almost three times the figure for laborers. Since engineers possess specialized skills that have been developed by both formal education (usually between 16 and 18 years) and experience, laborers are unable to compete directly in the engineering market. In contrast, the training and skill requirements for laborers are possessed by many. Since the supply of laborers is large relative to the demand, their earnings are substantially less.

It is important to keep in mind that wages are determined by demand *relative to supply*. Other things constant, a skilled specialist will command a higher wage than one with less skill, but high skill will not *guarantee* high wages

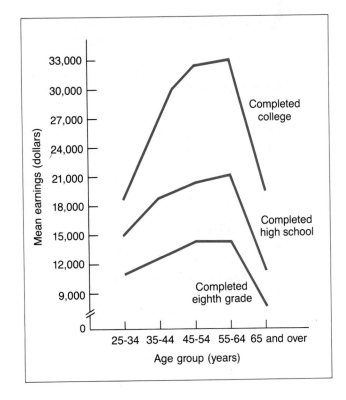

EXHIBIT 2   Supply, demand, and wage differentials

The mean number of years of education for engineers is 16.6 compared to 10.6 for laborers. Because of their specialized skills, high-wage engineers are protected from direct competition with laborers and other persons who do not possess such skills.

Earnings data are from the U.S. Department of Commerce.

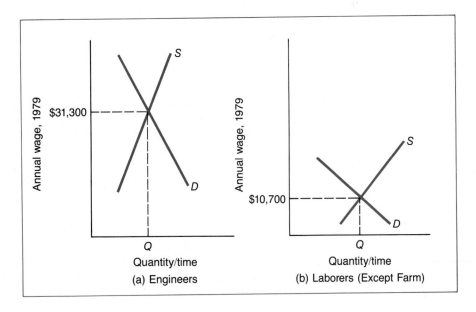

in the absence of demand. For example, expert harness makers and blacksmiths typically command low wages today, even though the supply of these workers is small—because demand even for the services of experts in these areas is low.

Worker Preferences. This very important source of earnings differentials is sometimes overlooked. People have different objectives in life. Some want to make a great deal of money. Many are willing to work long hours, undergo agonizing training and many years of education, and sacrifice social and family life in order to make money. Others may be "workaholics" because they enjoy their jobs. Still others may be satisfied with enough money to get by, preferring to spend more time with their family, the Boy Scouts, the television, or the local tavern keeper.

Economics does not indicate that one set of worker preferences is more desirable than another, any more than it suggests that people should eat more vegetables and less meat. However, economics does indicate that these factors contribute to differences in wages and earnings. Other things constant, persons who are more highly motivated by monetary objectives will be more likely to do the things necessary to command higher wage rates.

Race and Sex. Discrimination on the basis of race or sex contributes to earnings differences among individuals. Employment discrimination may directly limit the earnings opportunities of minorities and women. **Employment discrimination** exists when minority or women employees are treated in a different manner than are similarly productive whites or men. Of course, the earnings of minority employees, for example, may differ from whites for reasons other than employment discrimination. Nonemployment discrimination may limit the opportunity of minority groups and women to acquire human capital (for example, quality education or specialized training) that would enhance both their productivity and earnings. If we want to isolate the impact of current employment discrimination, we must (a) adjust for the impact of education, experience, and skill factors and (b) then make comparisons between *similarly qualified* groups of employees who differ with regard to race (or sex) only.

There are two major forms of employment discrimination—wage rates and employment restrictions. Exhibit 3 illustrates the impact of wage discrimination. When majority employees are preferred to minority and female workers, the demand for the latter two groups is reduced. The wages of blacks and women decline relative to those of white men.

Essentially, there is a dual labor market—one market for the favored group and another for the group against which the discrimination is directed. The favored group, whites for example, are preferred, but the less expensive minority employees are a substitute productive resource. Both white and minority employees are employed, but the whites are paid a higher wage rate.

Exclusionary practices may also be an outlet for employment discrimination. Either in response to outside pressure or because of their own views, employers may hire primarily whites and males for certain types of jobs. When minority and female workers are excluded from a large number of occupations, they are *crowded* into a smaller number of remaining jobs and occupations. If entry restraints prevent people from becoming supervisors, bank officers, plumbers, electricians, and truck drivers, they will be forced to accept other

Employment Discrimination: Unequal treatment of persons on the basis of their race, sex, or religion, restricting their employment and earnings opportunities compared to others of similar productivity. Employment discrimination may stem from the prejudices of employers, consumers, and/or fellow employees.

EXHIBIT 3   The impact of direct wage discrimination

If there is employment discrimination against blacks or women, the demand for their services will decline, and their wage rate will fall from W_w to W_b.

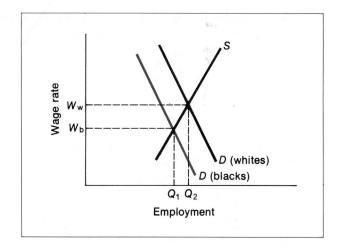

alternatives. The supply of labor in the restricted occupations will increase, causing wage rates to fall. The exclusionary practices will result in higher wages for white males holding jobs from which blacks and females are excluded. The outcome will be an overrepresentation of white males in the higher paying occupations, while a disproportionate number of blacks and women will occupy the low-paying, nonrestricted positions. The impact will be a reduction in the earnings of minorities and women relative to white males.

Earnings Differentials Due to Nonhomogeneous Jobs

Nonpecuniary Job Characteristics: **Working conditions, prestige, variety, location, employee freedom and responsibilities, and other nonwage characteristics of a job that influence how employees evaluate the job.**

When individuals evaluate employment alternatives, they consider working conditions as well as wage rates. Is a job dangerous? Does it offer the opportunity to acquire the experience and training that will enhance future earnings? Is the work strenuous and nerve-racking? Are the working hours, job location, and means of transportation convenient? All of these factors are what economists call **nonpecuniary job characteristics.** Workers are willing to trade off higher wage rates for more favorable nonpecuniary job characteristics. There are numerous examples of this. Because of the dangers involved, aerial window washers (those who hang from windows 20 stories up) earn higher wages than other window washers. Sales jobs involving a great deal of out-of-town travel typically pay more than similar jobs without such inconvenience. Electricians in contract construction are paid more than equally skilled electricians with jobs in which the work and pay are more steady. Because the majority of economists prefer the more independent work environment and intellectual stimulation offered by colleges and universities, the earnings of economists in academia are typically lower than those of economists in business.

Substantial wage differentials exist between similar jobs in (a) large and small firms and (b) urban and rural areas. Nonpecuniary factors, such as transportation costs and locational preferences help to explain these differentials. Large firms must typically draw their labor force from a wider geographical area, resulting in longer average travel time to and from work. Congestion problems are more severe. These factors make employment with large firms less desirable. Thus, they must pay higher wage rates in order to attract the desired size of labor force. Similarly, the lower wages in rural areas probably reflect, at least partially,

IS DISCRIMINATION PROFITABLE TO THE EMPLOYER?

Most people assign the title of "chief discriminator" to the employer. This is because it is the employer who pays lower wages or hires very few minority or female employees even if only in response to consumers, majority employees, union practices, or community pressures. Undoubtedly, however, many employers have followed discriminatory practices of their own volition. Economic theory suggests that it is costly for employers to discriminate when they are merely reflecting their own prejudices. If employers can hire equally productive blacks (or women) at lower wages than for whites (or men), the profit motive gives them a strong incentive to do so. The costs of a discriminator who continues to hire high-wage whites, when similar minority employees are available at a lower wage, will increase. The higher cost will reduce profits.

Major league baseball provides an interesting and easily documented case of an employer paying the cost of discrimination. In the mid-1940s, there were no black players in the "big leagues." Simultaneously, a pool of readily available, proven baseball talent existed in the Negro leagues. The services of most of these players could be purchased at a fraction of the cost of obtaining comparable white players.

Two inputs, white and/or black players, could be used in an effort to win games (an output variable), but the price of an equally productive black player was much lower. Other things constant, firms had an incentive to substitute the less expensive blacks for the higher-priced white players.

After major league baseball had become integrated, the less discriminating employers moved rapidly to employ black players, whereas the highly discriminating teams continued to employ exclusively (or almost exclusively) whites. By the mid-1950s, five teams—the Brooklyn Dodgers, New York Giants, Cleveland Indians, Boston (Milwaukee) Braves, and Chicago White Sox—employed substantially more blacks than the other eleven major league teams.[3] During the period from 1952 to 1956, these five teams were among the top six teams according to won–lost percentage. They won 58 percent of their games, compared to only 46 percent for the highly discriminating teams. Among the teams with few black players, only the New York Yankees were able to compete effectively with the less discriminating teams.

Baseball fans like to watch a winner play. Not only did the less discriminating teams win more games, but their games were also more highly attended. Hiring blacks, largely because of their impact on team performance, paid off nicely at the box office. The less discriminating teams gained, whereas the highly discriminating teams paid a price for their prejudice.

---

[3]See James Gwartney and Charles Haworth, "Employer Cost and Discrimination: The Case of Baseball," *Journal of Political Economy* (June 1974), for a detailed analysis of this topic.

---

employees' willingness to trade off higher wages for jobs in preferred living areas. All of these differences in the nonpecuniary characteristics of jobs contribute to earnings differences among individuals.

Earnings Differentials Due to Immobility of Labor

It is costly to move to a new location or train for a new occupation in order to obtain a job. Such movements do not take place instantaneously. In the real world, labor, like other resources, does not possess perfect mobility. Thus, some wage differentials result from an incomplete adjustment to change.

Since the demand for labor resources is a derived demand, it is affected by changes in product markets. An expansion in the demand for a product causes a rise in the demand for specialized labor to produce the product. Since resources are often highly immobile (that is, the supply is inelastic) in the short run, the expansion in demand may cause the wages of the specialized laborers to rise sharply. This is what happened in the oil-drilling industry in the late 1970s. An expansion in demand triggered a rapid increase in the earnings of petroleum engineers and other specialized personnel. A decline in product demand has the opposite effect. The tapering off of the space program in the late 1960s depressed the wages of engineers, physicists, and space scientists. Demand shifts in the product market favor those in expanding industries but work against those in contracting industries.

Institutional barriers may also limit the mobility of labor. Licensing requirements limit the mobility of labor into many occupations—medicine, taxicab driving, architecture, and undertaking among them. Unions may also follow policies that limit labor mobility and alter the free-market forces of supply and demand. Minimum wage rates may retard the ability of low-skill workers to obtain employment in certain sectors of the economy. All of these restrictions on labor mobility will influence the size of wage differentials among workers.

Thumbnail Sketch—Sources of Earnings Differentials

Differences in workers:
1. Productivity (for example, skills, human capital, native ability, motivation)
2. Specialized skills (primarily human capital plus native ability)
3. Worker preferences (trade-off between money earnings and other things)
4. Race and sex discrimination

Differences in jobs:
1. Location of jobs
2. Nonpecuniary job characteristics (for example, convenience of working hours, job safety, likelihood of temporary layoffs, and working conditions)

Immobility of resources:
1. Temporary disequilibrium resulting from dynamic change
2. Institutional restrictions (for example, occupational licensing and union-imposed restraints)

Summary of Wage Differentials

As the Thumbnail Sketch shows, wage differentials stem from many sources. Many of them play an important allocative role, compensating people for (a) human capital investments that increase their productivity or (b) unfavorable working conditions. Other wage differentials reflect, at least partially, locational preferences or the desire of individuals for higher money income rather than nonmonetary benefits. Still other differentials, such as those related to discrimination and occupational restrictions, are unrelated to worker preferences and are not required to promote efficient production.

PRODUCTIVITY AND THE GENERAL LEVEL OF WAGES

It is also important to understand why the general level of wages varies from one country to another and from one period to another within the same country. Real earnings are vastly greater in the United States than in India or China. In addition, the average real earnings per hour in the United States have approximately doubled during the past 25 years. What factors account for these variations in the general level of wages?

Differences in labor productivity—output produced per worker-hour—are the major source of variation in real wages between nations and between time periods. When the amount produced per worker-hour is high, real wages will be high.

Exhibit 4 illustrates the relationship between real wages and output per

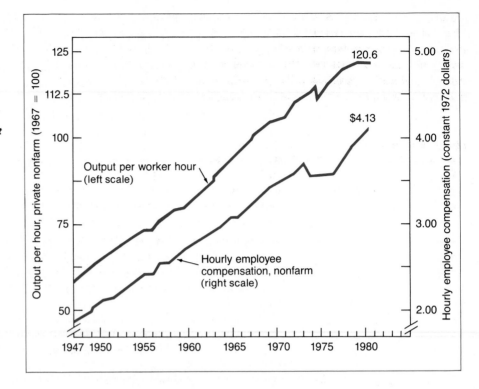

EXHIBIT 4   Productivity and employee compensation, 1947–1980

As the diagram illustrates, productivity of employees per worker-hour is closely related to earnings.

Manpower Report of the President, 1974, Tables C-3, G-1, G-2, and *Economic Report of the President, 1981.*

worker-hour since World War II. Between 1947 and 1980 output per worker-hour rose 111 percent in the nonfarm private sector. What happened to employee compensation? During the same time period, the hourly compensation of employees, measured in constant 1972 dollars, increased from $1.94 to $4.13, an increase of 113 percent.

The close relationship between amount produced and real wages should not be surprising. Do not forget that real income and real output are simply two ways of viewing the same thing. Expansion in real income is totally dependent on expansion of output. Without expansion of output, our money incomes, whatever they may be, will not enable us to purchase more goods and services in aggregate.

In the last chapter, we showed that the productivity of a resource, including labor, is dependent on the amount of the other resources with which it works. Contrary to what many believe, physical capital (for example, modern labor-saving machines) is not the enemy of high real wages (see Myths of Economics, "Automation is the major cause of unemployment"). In fact, just the opposite is true.

Machines make it possible for labor to produce more per worker-hour. Are jobs destroyed in the process? Sometimes *specific* jobs are eliminated, but this merely releases human resources so they can be used to expand output in other areas. Output and productivity, not jobs, are the source of high real wages.

Increasing productivity is brought about by a cooperative process. Investment, both in human and nonhuman capital, is vital to the growth of productivity. For several decades, the educational level of members of the work force in the United States has steadily increased. The median number of years of schooling of persons in the labor force in 1980 was 12.8 compared to 10.6 years in 1949. Simultaneously, the nonhuman capital per worker has expanded (although the *growth rate* of capital investment per worker has slowed considerably in recent years). Both the development and innovative application of improved technological methods are also important determinants of the growth of productivity. Technological improvements make it possible to obtain a larger output from the same resource base. Of course, modern technological advancements are often linked to investments in both physical and human capital.

Investment and the Sagging Rate of Growth of Productivity in the United States

Since investment is so important for the growth of future output (and real income), it is useful to compare investment and growth rates in various countries. Ideally, we should analyze investment in both human and physical capital, including resources utilized to improve the available technology. Investment requires that current consumption be sacrificed in order for more resources to be allocated to the production of nonhuman capital, human capital, and technical knowledge with which to expand future production. Other things constant, countries that allocate more to current *investment* will expand their stock of valuable productive assets more rapidly and experience a more rapid growth in income.

Unfortunately, comparable international investment data for human capital have not been developed. However, Exhibit 5 presents International Monetary Fund data for gross fixed capital formation (physical capital) as a percentage of domestic production for several nations. During the period from 1960 to 1980, the share of GNP allocated to investment was considerably lower for the United States than for other major Western nations. Growth in worker compensation in the United States lagged accordingly. On the other hand, countries such as Japan, West Germany, and France, which allocate a much larger share of their domestic product to capital formation, experienced more rapid wage increases during the period.

Even the data of Exhibit 5 probably understate the lag in capital investment *per worker* in the United States. During the period from 1965 to 1980, there was a vast influx of workers into the labor force as the rate of labor force participation among women increased and the children of the post-World

EXHIBIT 5 Investment and the rate of growth in employee compensation, 1960–1979

Country	Gross Fixed Capital Formation as a Percentage of Gross National Product	Growth Rate of Hourly Employee Compensation Deflated by Consumer Price Index (Percent)
United States	17.8	1.3
United Kingdom	18.5	2.7
Italy	20.5	5.0
Canada	22.7	1.7
France	23.3	5.4
West Germany	24.2	10.5
Japan	32.9	8.6

Capital formation data are from *International Financial Statistics,* 1981 supplement (Washington, D. C.: International Monetary Fund, 1978); the compensation data are from *Economic Report of the President, 1982,* Table B–111.

Automation: A production technique that reduces the amount of labor required to produce a good or service. It is beneficial to adopt the new labor-saving technology only if it reduces the cost of production.

"Automation is the major cause of unemployment. If we keep allowing machines to replace people, we are going to run out of jobs."

Machines are substituted for people if, and only if, the machines reduce costs of production. Why has the automatic elevator replaced the operator, the tractor replaced the horse, and the power shovel replaced the ditch digger? Because each is a cheaper method of accomplishing a task.

The fallacy that **automation** causes unemployment stems from a failure to recognize the secondary effects. Employment may decline in a specific industry as the result of automation. However, lower per unit costs in that industry will lead to either (a) additional spending and jobs in other industries or (b) additional output and employment in the specific industry as consumers buy more of the now cheaper good.

Perhaps an example will help to illustrate the secondary effects of automation. Suppose that someone develops a new toothpaste that actually prevents cavities and sells for half the current price of Colgate. At last, we have a toothpaste that really works. Think of the impact the invention will have on dentists, toothpaste producers and their employees, and even the advertising agencies that give us those marvelous toothpaste commercials. What are these people to do? Haven't their jobs been destroyed?

These are the obvious effects; they are seen to be the direct result of the toothpaste invention. What most people do not see are the additional jobs that will indirectly be created by the invention. Consumers will now spend less on toothpaste, dental bills, and pain relievers. Their real income will be higher. They will now be able to spend *more* on other products they would have foregone had it not been for the new invention. They will in-crease their spending on clothes, recreation, vacations, swimming pools, education, and many other items. This additional spending, which would not have taken place if dental costs had not been reduced by the technological advancement, will generate additional demand and employment in other sectors.

It is undeniable that jobs have been eliminated in the toothpaste and dental industries because of a reduction in consumer spending in these areas. However, *new* jobs have been created in other industries in which consumers have increased their spending as a result of the savings attributable to the new invention.

When the demand for a product is elastic, a cost-saving invention can even generate an increase in employment in the industry affected by the invention. This was essentially what happened in the automobile industry when Henry Ford's mass production techniques reduced the cost (and price) of cars. When the price of automobiles fell 50 percent, consumers bought three times as many cars. Even though the worker-hours *per car* decreased by 25 percent between 1920 and 1930, employment in the industry increased from 250,000 to 380,000 during the period, an increase of approximately 50 percent.

Even if the demand for automobiles had been inelastic, automation would not have caused long-run unemployment. When demand is inelastic, less will be spent on the lower-cost, lower-priced commodity, leaving more to be spent on other goods and services. This spending on other products, which would not have resulted without the new invention, will ensure that there is not a net reduction in employment.

Of course, technological advances that release labor resources may well harm specific individuals or groups. The automatic elevators reduced the job opportunities of elevator operators. Computer technology has reduced the demand for telephone operators. In the future, videotaped lectures may even reduce the job opportunities available to college professors. Thus, the earnings opportunities of specific persons may, at least temporarily, be adversely affected by cost-reducing automated methods. It is understandable why groups directly affected fear and oppose automation.

But focusing on jobs alone can lead to a fundamental misunderstanding about the importance of machines, automation, and technological improvements. Automation neither creates nor destroys jobs. The real impact of cost-reducing machines and technological improvements is an increase in production. Technological advances make it possible for us to produce as much with fewer resources, thereby releasing valuable resources so that production (and consumption) can be expanded in other areas. Other tasks can be accomplished with the newly available resources. Since there is a direct link between improved technology and rising output, automation exerts a positive influence on economic welfare from the viewpoint of society as a whole. In aggregate, running out of jobs is unlikely to be a problem. Jobs represent obstacles, tasks that must be accomplished if we desire to loosen the bonds of scarcity. As long as our ability to produce goods and services falls short of our consumption desires, there will be jobs. A society running out of jobs would be in an enviable position: It would be nearing the impossible goal—victory over scarcity.

War II "baby boom" came of working age. Simultaneously, inflation and the tax treatment of returns to physical capital discouraged private investment.

Economics suggests that a rapid growth in the labor force, accompanied by a sagging rate of capital formation, will adversely affect worker productivity and compensation per worker-hour. As Exhibit 6 shows, this has been precisely the case. During the period from 1948 to 1965, both output per hour and hourly compensation grew annually at a rate slightly in excess of 3.0 percent. Since 1974, there has been a sharp decline in productivity per hour. As the growth rate of output per hour declines, worker compensation per hour must also decline. Real incomes cannot continually increase unless there is an expansion in the production of goods and services. As the growth of productivity sagged during the 1970s, worker compensation per hour, adjusted for inflation, also sagged (Exhibit 6). This lag in the growth rate of productivity is a serious matter. Several leading economists believe that unless the United States begins to allocate a somewhat larger share of its national output to investment, worker productivity and the growth of real income will continue to stagnate.

HOW IS THE ECONOMIC PIE DIVIDED?

We have emphasized that wage rates generally reflect the availability of tools (physical capital) and the skills and abilities of individual workers (human capital). Wages tend to be high when physical capital is plentiful, technology

EXHIBIT 6   The sagging growth of productivity in the United States

Period	Increase in Output per Hour, Private Business Sector (Average Annual Rate)	Increase in Real per Hour Compensation, Private Business Sector (Average Annual Rate)
1948–1955	3.5	3.1
1956–1965	3.1	3.0
1966–1973	2.4	2.8
1974–1981	0.7	1.1

Derived from *Economic Report of the President, 1982,* Table B-41.

is advanced, and the work force is highly skilled. When the equipment available to the typical worker is primitive and most workers lack education and skills, wages are low. Both human capital and physical capital contribute to the productive process.

How is the pie divided between these two broad factors of production in the United States? Exhibit 7 provides an answer. In 1950, approximately 81 percent of the national income was earned by employees and self-employed proprietors, the major categories that reflect the earnings of human capital. In 1980, the share of national income allocated to human capital was also 81 percent. Income earned by nonhuman capital—rents, interest, and corporate profits—currently comprises 18 to 20 percent of the national income.

EXHIBIT 7   The shares of income going to physical and human capital

Including self-employment income, approximately four-fifths of the national income is earned by owners of human capital.

Economic Report of the President, 1981, **Table B-19.**

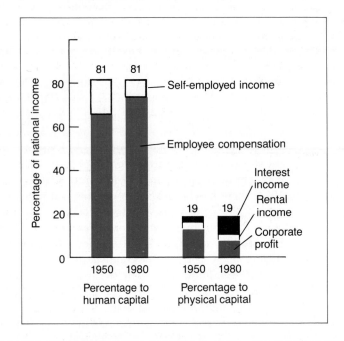

PERSPECTIVES IN ECONOMICS
THE MINIMUM WAGE— AN ECONOMIC APPRAISAL

The legislated minimum wage rates have destroyed beginning jobs for teenagers. These are the jobs in which they normally acquire the skills which make them more productive and enable them to earn far more than the minimum. These [minimum wage] increases have destroyed the stepping-stones to higher wage jobs. [4]

Minimum Wage Legislation: Legislation requiring that all workers in specified industries be paid at least the stated minimum hourly rate of pay.

[4]Yale Brozen, statement before the Illinois Legislature's House Committee on Industrial and Labor Relations, Springfield, Illinois, March 10, 1971.

In 1938, Congress passed the Fair Labor Standards Act, which provided for a national minimum wage of 25 cents per hour. Approximately 43 percent of the private, nonagricultural work force was covered by this legislation. During the last 40 years, the minimum wage has been increased several times, and coverage now extends to 84 percent of the nonagricultural labor force. Currently, federal legislation requires most employers to pay wage rates of at least $3.35 per hour.

Labor Markets and the Minimum Wage

Minimum wage legislation is intended to help the working poor. However, there is good reason to believe that such legislation has the opposite effect. Economic theory indicates that the quantity demanded of labor, particularly a specific skill category of labor, will be inversely related to its wage rate. If a higher minimum wage increases the wage rates of unskilled workers above the level that would be established by market forces, the quantity of unskilled workers employed will fall. The minimum wage will price the services of the least productive (and therefore lowest-wage) workers out of the market.

Exhibit 8 provides a graphic illustration of the direct effect of a $3.35 minimum wage on the employment opportunities of low-skill workers. Without a minimum wage, the supply of and demand for these low-skill workers would be in balance at a wage rate of $2.50. The $3.35 minimum wage makes the low-skill labor service more expensive. Employers will substitute machines and highly skilled workers (whose wages have not been raised by the minimum) for the now more expensive low-productivity employees. Jobs in which low-skill employees are unable to produce a marginal revenue product that is equal to or greater than the minimum will be eliminated. As the cost (and price) of goods and services produced by low-skill employees rises, consumers will rely more heavily on substitute goods produced by highly skilled labor and foreign markets. The net effect of this substitution process will be a reduction in the quantity demanded of low-skill labor.

Of course, some low-skill workers will be able to maintain their jobs, but others will be driven into sectors not covered by the legislation or onto the unemployment and welfare rolls. Workers who retain their jobs will gain. The most adverse effects will fall on those workers who are already most disadvantaged—those whose market earnings are lowest relative to the minimum wage—because it will be so costly to bring their wages up to the minimum.

In summary, the direct results of minimum wage legislation are clearly mixed. Some workers, most likely those whose previous wages were closest to the minimum, will enjoy higher wages. Others, particularly those with the lowest prelegislation wage rates, will be unable to find work.[5] They will often be pushed into the ranks of the unemployed. Many persons in the latter group will eventually give up and drop out of the labor force.

The Minimum Wage, Experience, and Job Training

Minimum wage rates also affect the ability of low-skill workers to acquire experience and training. Many inexperienced workers face a dilemma. They cannot find a job without experience (or skills), but they cannot obtain experience without a job. This is particularly true for youthful workers. Employment experience obtained at an early age, even on seemingly menial tasks, can help one acquire work habits (for example, promptness and self-confidence), skills, and attitudes that will enhance one's value to employers in the future. Since minimum wage legislation prohibits the payment of even a temporarily low wage, it substantially limits the employer's ability to offer employment to inexperienced workers.

---

[5]The impact of minimum wage legislation could differ from the theoretical results that we have outlined if labor markets were dominated by a single buyer. Economists refer to this situation as "monopsony." We choose not to present the monopsony model here because (a) in a modern society, where labor is highly mobile, the major assumptions of the model are seldom met; and (b) the bulk of the empirical evidence in this area is consistent with the competitive model.

EXHIBIT 8 Employment and the minimum wage

If the market wage of a group of employees were $2.50 per hour, a $3.35-per-hour minimum wage would (a) increase the earnings of persons who were able to maintain employment and (b) reduce the employment of others (E_0 to E_1), pushing them onto the unemployment rolls or into less-preferred jobs.

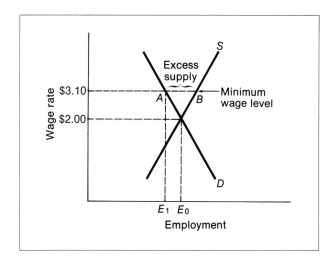

Minimum wage legislation also limits the range of jobs available to low-skill workers. Consider a construction firm that hires "helpers" at $2.50 per hour to work with carpenters and electricians. Since the helpers require close supervision, often make mistakes, and are used on odd jobs during slack periods, initially they are able to command only a low wage. After the minimum wage is introduced, the contractor will receive more applications—including those of workers with experience and past training—but will hire fewer workers at the higher wage. The contractor, now able to be more selective, will hire and train fewer inexperienced helpers. Some **entry-level jobs** will be eliminated.

As entry-level jobs that offer training opportunities to low-productivity workers are eliminated in many sectors of the economy, the positions available to inexperienced workers will be primarily **dead-end jobs.** As Martin Feldstein has pointed out, the minimum wage acts as an institutional barrier limiting the opportunity to acquire on-the-job training.[6] Many leading economists believe that minimum wage legislation is the major reason for the almost complete lack of skill-building jobs at the lower end of the wage spectrum.

Qualifications and Employability

Some people incorrectly argue that inexperienced, low-skill workers have few employment opportunities because they have so few qualifications. Low productivity (skill level) results in low wages, but, in the absence of legal barriers, it need not result in high levels of unemployment. No worker is either qualified or unqualified in an absolute sense. One's qualifications must be considered in relation to one's

wage rate. For example, a carpenter may be "qualified" and in great demand at an hourly wage rate of $5. However, the same carpenter may be "unemployable" at $10 per hour. A $10 minimum wage rate would obviously make many workers unemployable, since many would lack the qualifications (skills) necessary to command such high wages. Although the effects are less widespread, a $3.35 minimum wage does precisely the same thing to low-skill workers; it makes them unqualified, that is, unemployable, at such a high wage rate.

The Impact of the Minimum Wage

Most empirical studies of the minimum wage in the United States have focused on teenagers, since there is a higher proportion of low-wage workers (reflecting their lack of skill-building experience) in this age group. This does not mean that most low-skill workers are teenagers—they are not. However, since the skill level of a *higher proportion* of teenagers is low, researchers are better able to isolate the impact of the minimum wage if they focus on this group.

Not all sectors of the economy are covered by minimum wage legislation. But one of the major effects of the legislation has been to reduce the job opportunities available to teenagers (and presumably other low-skill workers) in industries to which the minimum is applied. In a recently published study, Finis Welch found that after the passage of the 1938 minimum wage, there was a distinct shift in the industrial pattern of teenage employment. Employment among teenagers dropped more than the national average in every industry with above-average coverage by minimum wage legislation. In contrast, every industry with below-average coverage experienced a decline in teenage employment that was less than the national average.[7]

There have been several stud-

Entry-Level Jobs: Jobs that require little training or experience and therefore allow untrained or inexperienced job seekers to enter the work force. These jobs frequently are stepping-stones to better jobs.

Dead-End Jobs: Jobs that offer the employee little opportunity for advancement or on-the-job training.

[6]It is ironic that although we subsidize formal education, we establish barriers that restrict a worker's ability to acquire training. See Martin Feldstein, "The Economics of the New Unemployment," *Public Interest* (Fall 1973), pp. 3–42.

ies on the impact of the minimum wage on the employment opportunities of youth. Most studies indicate that a 10 percent increase in the minimum wage reduces teenage employment by 1 to 3 percent. Of course, the teenage unemployment rate is well above the average for adult workers. Since one would expect youthful workers searching for a career to change jobs more frequently, the teenage–adult unemployment differential is not surprising. However, it is interesting that as the minimum wage has risen and, more importantly, as more fields of employment are covered by the minimum wage, the teenage–adult unemployment differential has widened. For example, the teenage unemployment rate averaged 11.8 percent in 1954–1955, compared to an overall rate of 5 percent—a differential of 6.8 percent. In contrast, throughout most of the 1970s, the teenage minus adult differential exceeded 10 percent.

Is Minimum Wage Legislation Racist?

On the surface, this question may appear to be absurd. However, a closer look at the data reveals that the minimum wage severely restricts the abil-

ity of minorities to acquire experience and skill-building employment opportunities. At the legislated higher minimum, there is an excess supply of low-skill, inexperienced workers. Employers have the opportunity to choose among a surplus of applicants for each opening. They generally choose those workers, *within the low-productivity group,* who have the most skill, experience, and education. If they want to discriminate against minorities, they can do so with impunity. Many low-skill white applicants are available at the artificially high minimum wage. Since all workers must be paid the minimum, the employer's incentive to hire less skilled and less favored groups is destroyed.

Much of the research documenting the adverse impact of the minimum wage on the employment opportunities of blacks has been done by black economists. Walter Williams, economics professor at Temple University, has been at the forefront of those condemning the minimum wage.[8] Andrew Brimmer, a former member of the Federal Reserve Board, has also been among the leading critics of the minimum wage. Brimmer argues:

A growing body of statistical and other evidence accumulated by economists shows that increases in the statutory minimum wage dampen the expansion of employment and lengthen the lineup of those seeking jobs. Advances in the minimum wage have a noticeably adverse impact on young people—with the effects on black teenagers being considerably more severe.[9]

There is strong empirical evidence that the higher rates and expanded coverage of minimum wage legislation have imposed an additional burden on the youthful members of minorities. As Exhibit 9 illustrates, between 1974 and 1981, the average annual rate of unemployment for black teenagers was 35.1 percent, compared to 15.5 percent for white teenagers. This enormous differential has not always existed. Before the minimum wage was raised from 75 cents to $1 in 1956—a 33 percent increase—the rates of unemployment for black and white teenagers were similar (see Exhibit 9, data for 1948–1955). During the period from 1956 to 1981, the black–white unemployment gap steadily widened as the minimum wage rose and as coverage was extended to more and more sectors of our economy.

---

[7]Finis Welch, "The Rising Impact of the Minimum Wage," *Regulation* (November/December 1978), pp. 28–37. See particularly Table 2.

[8]See Walter E. Williams, "Government Sanctioned Restraints That Reduce Economic Opportunities for Minorities," *Policy Review* (Fall 1977), pp. 7–30.

[9]Andrew Brimmer, quoted in Louis Rukeyser, "Jobs Are Eliminated," Naught News Service (August 1978).

EXHIBIT 9 The black–white teenage unemployment differential

Period	Minimum Wage (Dollars)	Percentage of Private Nonagricultural Work Force Covered[a]	Rate of Unemployment for Men, Ages 16–19 (Annual Average Percentage during Period)		
			White	Black	Black Minus White
1948–1949	0.40	53	12.0	13.3	1.3
1950–1955	0.75	53	11.0	11.7	0.7
1956–1960	1.00	58	13.1	21.9	8.8
1961–1962	1.15	62	14.7	24.4	9.7
1963–1966	1.25	69	13.5	24.1	10.6
1967–1973	1.40–1.60	79	12.3	25.4	13.1
1974–1981	2.00–3.35	84	15.5	35.1	19.6

[a]Estimated from data of Employment Standards Administration, U.S. Department of Labor.
Economic Report of the President, 1982, Table B–33.

Not only has the rate of unemployment for black teenagers soared, but the rate of labor force participation for youthful blacks has also been adversely affected. As Exhibit 10 shows, before the large increase in the minimum wage (and expansion in coverage) in 1956, the labor force participation rate for blacks, ages 16 to 24, actually exceeded the rate for whites. During the last two decades, that situation has changed dramatically. By January 1982, the labor force participation rate for blacks, ages 16 and 17, was only 49 percent of the rate for whites of the same age group. Similarly, the participation rates for blacks ages 18 to 19 and 20 to 24 fell substantially below the rates for whites in these age groupings. This suggests that many youthful workers, particularly minority workers, have given up their search for employment at the minimum wage. Since they are no longer searching for employment, they are not counted among the unemployed.

Exhibits 9 and 10 illustrate the tragic facts. Approximately 35 percent of all black teenagers in the labor force are unemployed. Even that figure understates the bleakness of the employment picture for inexperienced black workers, since it does not include those who dropped out of the labor force because they were unable to find a job at the minimum wage. Most labor economists believe that if these discouraged workers were counted, the rate of unemployment for black teenagers would approach 50 percent, twice the rate for the total labor force in the midst of the Great Depression.

Persons from disadvantaged backgrounds are precisely those who are most in need of the employment experience and entry-level, skill-enhancing jobs that are unavailable to them as a result of the minimum wage. Members of disadvantaged minority groups are generally least able to afford formal training beyond high school. What are the long-run implications of a policy that prices low-skill workers out of the job market and thereby prevents them from acquiring the experience and skills necessary for economic success in our modern world? Among other things, future poverty statistics and crime rates will certainly be affected.

The Subminimum Wage for Teenagers

Several bills currently before Congress would provide for a lower minimum wage for teenagers. These proposals would permit employers to pay teenagers wage rates of between 60 percent and 75 percent of the adult minimum wage. Advocates believe this type of legislation will help to alleviate an important side effect of the minimum wage—the low availability of both training and employment opportunities for youthful, inexperienced workers. The major opposition to this legislation comes from labor organizations. This should not be surprising. Low-skill—often nonunion—labor is a substitute for high-skill, (union) labor; a lower minimum wage would enhance the attractiveness of substitute, nonunion labor. Stated another way, the demand for union workers might not be as strong if low-skilled labor were not priced out of the market by the minimum wage.

Discussion

1. How will an increase in the minimum wage affect the welfare of each of the following groups: (a) high-income recipients, (b) food service operators and customers, (c) black teenagers, (d) white teenagers, and (e) college students?

2. Do you think the subminimum wage for teenagers is a good idea? Why or why not?

EXHIBIT 10 The black/white rate of labor force participation for persons 16 to 24 years old

Period	Black/White Labor Force Participation Rate for Youthful Men		
	Ages 16–17	Ages 18–19	Ages 20–24
1954–1955	1.00	1.06	1.05
1956–1960	0.96	1.03	1.03
1961–1962	0.94	1.05	1.02
1963–1966	0.87	1.00	1.04
1967–1973	0.73	0.91	1.00
1974–1976	0.60	0.80	0.93
1977–1980	0.58	0.77	0.90
1982 (January)	0.49	0.72	0.88

Derived from Walter Williams, *Youth and Minority Employment,* a study prepared for the Joint Economic Committee, Congress of the United States (Washington, D.C.: U.S. Government Printing Office, 1977), Table 5, and U.S. Department of Labor, *Employment and Earnings* (February 1982), Table A-3.

Payments to resources are of vital importance because individual incomes are determined by (a) resource prices and (b) the amount of resources that one owns. However, the purchasing power of the income received by resource owners is dependent on productivity. There is nothing magical about the growth of real income; it is dependent on the growth of real output. The real output of a nation is strongly influenced by the capital equipment with which people work.

CHAPTER LEARNING OBJECTIVES

1 There are three major sources of wage differentials among individuals: differences in workers, differences in jobs, and degree of labor mobility. Individual workers differ with respect to productivity (skills, human capital, motivation, native ability, and so on), specialized skills, employment preferences, race, and sex. All these factors influence either the demand for or the supply of labor. In addition, differences in nonpecuniary job characteristics, changes in product markets, and institutional restrictions that limit labor mobility contribute to variations in wages among workers.

2 Productivity is the ultimate source of high wages. High wages in the United States are the result of large amounts of both human and physical capital.

3 The share of GNP allocated to the formation of physical capital is less for the United States than for most other countries. Many economists believe that this low rate of investment is largely responsible for the sluggish growth of income in the United States. Growth in employee compensation is slower in the United States than in other Western nations where the rate of capital formation is higher.

4 Approximately 80 percent of national income in the United States is allocated to human capital (labor) and 20 percent to owners of physical (nonhuman) capital.

5 Automated methods of production will be adopted only if they reduce cost. Although automation *might* reduce revenues and employment *in a specific industry,* the lower cost of production will increase real income, causing demand in other industries to expand. These secondary effects will cause employment to rise in other industries. Improved technology expands our ability to produce. It is expanded production, not the number of jobs, that contributes to our economic well-being.

6 Minimum wage legislation increases the earnings of some low-skill workers, but others are forced to accept inferior employment opportunities, join the ranks of the unemployed, or drop out of the labor force completely. Minimum wage legislation reduces the ability of employers to offer (and low-skill employees to find) work with on-the-job training and skill-building experience. Thus, the jobs available to low-skill workers tend to be primarily dead-end jobs. The most disadvantaged workers, particularly members of minority groups and teenagers, are the hardest hit. Tragically, many youthful workers, particularly blacks, have been priced out of the job market by the minimum wage. Denied the opportunity to obtain entry-level jobs at an early age, many are unable to acquire the job experience and on-the-job training that would provide for more favorable future employment opportunities.

THE ECONOMIC WAY OF THINKING—DISCUSSION QUESTIONS

1 What are the major reasons for the differences in earnings among individuals? Why are wages in some occupations higher than in others? How do wage differentials influence the allocation of resources? How important is this function? Explain.

2 Why are real wages in the United States higher than in other countries? Is the labor force itself responsible for the higher wages of American workers? Explain.

3 What are the major factors that would normally explain earnings differences between (a) a lawyer and a minister, (b) an accountant and an elementary-school teacher, (c) a business executive and a social worker, (d) a country lawyer and a Wall Street lawyer,

(e) an experienced, skilled craftsperson and a 20-year-old high school dropout, (f) a fire fighter and a night security guard, and (g) an upper-story and a ground-floor window washer?

4 What's Wrong with This Way of Thinking?

"Higher wages help everybody. Workers are helped because they can now purchase more of the things they need. Business is helped because the increase in the workers' purchasing power will increase the demand for products. Taxpayers are helped because workers will now pay more taxes. Union activities and legislation increasing the wages of workers will promote economic progress."

5 What's Wrong with This Way of Thinking?

"Jobs are the key to economic progress. Unless we can figure out how to produce more jobs, economic progress will be stifled."

PART FOUR

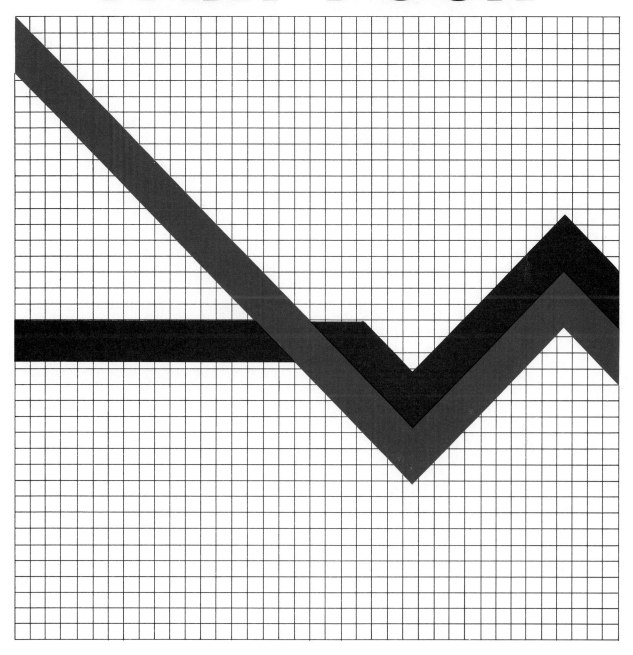

PUBLIC CHOICE

View A: The market coordinates the self-interest of individuals, inducing them to produce a diverse menu of housing structures and food products, convenient shopping centers, completely planned communities with their own police and fire protection, beautiful golf courses, and even the fairyland entertainment center that we call Disney World. The market is a kind of computer that must surely be called one of the wonders of the world.

View B: Personal self-interest working within the framework of a market economy has led to stripped mountainsides, destruction of scenic beauty, pollution of lakes and rivers, air that is a menace to our health, and junkyards that blot our landscape. Unless the market behavior of firms and individuals is altered, environmental disaster cannot be avoided.

Is it possible for the same person to adhere to both of these views? This chapter will help to explain why they need not be inconsistent.

Market Failure: The failure of the market system to attain hypothetically *ideal* allocative efficiency. This means that potential gain exists that has not been captured. However, the cost of establishing a mechanism that could *potentially* capture the gain may exceed the benefits. Therefore, it is not always possible to improve the situation.

We have emphasized that the pricing system coordinates the decisions of buyers and sellers. However, if a market economy is to allocate goods and resources efficiently, certain conditions must be met. First, property rights must be defined so that economic participants will be prohibited from imposing costs on nonconsenting parties. Second, voluntary market behavior requires that productive activity and personal reward be closely linked. Third, both buyers and sellers must be reasonably well informed. Otherwise, one of the parties to an exchange who is misinformed, may unwittingly consent to arrangements that will later be regretted. Fourth, as we emphasized earlier, competition among buyers and sellers must exist.

In this chapter, we focus on **market failure,** economic activity that results in allocative inefficiency relative to the hypothetical ideal of economists. The sources of market failure can be grouped into four general classes: (a) externalities, (b) public goods, (c) conflicts between buyers and sellers *after an exchange,* stemming from poor information and misrepresentation, and (d) monopoly. Since we have already investigated the impact of monopoly on both product and factor markets, we will focus in this chapter on the three other categories of market failure.

Keep in mind that market failure is merely a failure to attain conditions of *ideal* efficiency. Alternative forms of economic organization will also have defects. Market failure creates an opportunity for government to improve the situation. However, in some circumstances, public sector action will not be corrective. Sometimes there may even be good reason to expect that it will be counterproductive. We will analyze market failure in this chapter and focus on the operation of the public sector in the following chapter.

EXTERNAL EFFECTS AND THE MARKET

The genius of a market exchange system lies in its ability to bring personal and social welfare into harmony. Individuals produce and exchange goods because they derive mutual gain from doing so. When only the trading parties are affected, production and voluntary exchange also promote the *social* welfare. Smoothly operating competitive markets lead to economic efficiency as long as all resources and products can be used only with the consent of their owners. Every decision-maker must bear the opportunity cost of any use (or misuse) of scarce resources. Under these conditions, Adam Smith's invisible hand performs its magic.

External Costs: Harmful effects of an individual's or a group's action on the welfare of nonconsenting secondary parties. Litterbugs, drunk drivers, and polluters, for example, create exernal costs.

External Benefits: Beneficial effects of group or individual action on the welfare of non-paying secondary parties.

When production and exchange affect the welfare of nonconsenting secondary parties, externalities are present. The external effects may be either positive or negative. If the welfare of nonconsenting secondary parties is adversely affected, the spillover effects are called **external costs.** A steel mill that belches smoke into the air imposes an external cost on surrounding residents who prefer clear air. A junkyard creates an eyesore, making an area less pleasant for passersby. Similarly, litterbugs, drunk drivers, speeders, muggers, and robbers impose unwanted costs on others. If the spillover effects enhance the welfare of secondary parties, they are called **external benefits.** A beautiful rose garden provides external benefits for the neighbors of the gardener. A golf course generally provides spillover benefits to surrounding property owners.

When external costs and external benefits are present, market prices will not send the proper signals to producers and consumers. This situation results in market failure.

Market Failure: External Costs

Social Costs: The sum of (a) the private costs that are incurred by a decision-maker and (b) any external costs of the action that are imposed on nonconsenting secondary parties. If there are no external costs, private and social costs will be equal.

From the viewpoint of economic efficiency, an action should be undertaken only if it generates benefits in excess of its social costs. **Social costs** include both (a) the private cost borne by the consenting parties and (b) any external cost imposed on nonconsenting secondary parties.

When external costs are present, market prices may fail to register correctly the social cost generated by the use of resources or consumption of products. Decision-makers may not be forced to bear fully the cost associated with their actions. Motivated by self-interest, they may undertake actions that generate a net loss to the community. The harm done to the secondary parties may exceed the net private gain. In such circumstances, private interest and economic efficiency are in conflict.

The hypothetical situation represented in Exhibit 1, which concerns the establishment of a mobile home park in a residential area, highlights the potential conflict. The trading partners—the park owner and those who rent park

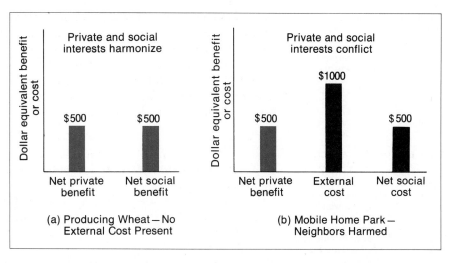

space—gain. Their actions, however, generate congestion and noise (external costs). The harm to the neighboring residents exceeds the private benefits of the park owner and the renters. Social costs exceed social benefits. However, since the residents do not have noise or noncongestion rights, the market fails to register their views. The park owner and renters have an incentive to undertake the project even though it will reduce the community's social welfare.

Why not simply prohibit activities that result in external cost? After all, why should we allow nonconsenting parties to be harmed? This approach has a certain appeal, but closer inspection indicates that it is often an unsatisfactory solution. Automobile exhaust imposes an external cost on bicyclists—and, for that matter, on everyone who breathes. Dogs are notorious for using the neighbor's lawn for bone burying and relief purposes. Motorboats are noisy and frighten fish, much to the disgust of fishermen. Yet few would argue that we do away with cars, dogs, and motorboats. From a social viewpoint, prohibition is often a less desirable alternative than tolerating the inconvenience of the external costs. The gains from the activity must be weighed against the costs imposed on those who are harmed, as well as against practical problems associated with controlling the activity.

External Costs and Ideal Output. Externalities may result from the actions of either consumers or producers. When the actions of a producer impose external costs on others, the costs of the firm, reflecting only private costs, are not an accurate indicator of the total social costs of production.

Exhibit 2 illustrates the impact of external costs on the socially desirable price and output. Suppose that there are a large number of copper-producing firms. They are able to discharge their waste products (mainly sulfur dioxide) into the air without charge, even though the pollution damages people, property, and plants downwind from the discharge. These air pollution costs are external to the copper producers. If allowed to operate freely, the producers have little incentive to adopt either production techniques or control devices that would limit the costs inflicted on other parties. These alternatives would only increase their private production cost.

Since pollutants can be freely discharged into the atmosphere, each copper producer expands output as long as marginal private costs (MC_p) are less than price. This leads to market supply curve S_1, the horizontal summation

EXHIBIT 2 Supply, externality, and minimum-cost production

The supply curve S_1 is the summation of *private* marginal costs when polluting is not costly *to the copper producer*. Since pollution imposes external costs, the social marginal cost is at the level of S_3. Actual output is Q_1 and price is P_1, even though the marginal social cost MC_s is much higher. Curve S_2 shows where social costs could be if producers recognized all social costs and chose production and pollution control methods to minimize private *plus* external costs. *Ideal* output Q^* and price P^* would result if the producers were forced to bear the full cost of resources used, including air pollution damages.

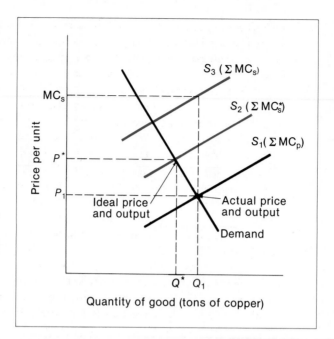

Quantity of good (tons of copper)

of the *private* marginal cost curves of the copper producers. Given the demand, the equilibrium market price for copper is P_1. Producers supply Q_1 units of copper. However, at output level Q_1, the *social* marginal cost of copper is MC_s, an amount substantially in excess of both the private cost and the consumer's valuation (as indicated by the height of the demand curve at Q_1) of copper. As a result of the external costs, output is expanded beyond the ideal efficiency level. From the standpoint of efficiency, the market price, which fails to reflect the external cost, is too low. Additional units of copper are produced even though the value of the resources, as measured by the social marginal costs (and supply curve S_3) required to produce the units, exceeds the consumer's valuation of the units. A deterioration in air quality is a by-product.

If, on the other hand, copper producers used different production techniques and/or efficient pollution control methods, supply curve S_2 (Exhibit 2) would result. Ideal output would be Q^* at price P^*. Customers would buy only the copper for which they were willing to pay all the costs, including the costs imposed on third parties. Since the consumer's benefit derived from the marginal units of copper would be equal to the marginal cost to society of producing copper ($P^* = MC_s^*$), production would be socially efficient.

When a producer's action imposes external costs on secondary parties, the producer's marginal costs will be understated. Therefore, the producer will choose to produce more of a good and charge less for it than the amounts consistent with ideal economic efficiency.

External Costs and Property Rights. Clearly defined and enforced property rights are essential for the efficient operation of a market economy. The problems caused by externalities stem from a failure (or an inability) to define clearly and enforce property rights. Property rights help to determine how resources will be used and who will be allowed to use them. **Private property rights** give owners the exclusive right to control and benefit from their resources as long as their

Private Property Rights: A set of usage and exchange rights held *exclusively* by the owner(s).

actions do not harm others. It is important to recognize that private property rights do not include the right to use one's property in a manner in which injury is inflicted on others. For example, property rights do not grant the owners of rocks the right to throw them at automobiles.

Property rights also provide individuals with legal protection against the actions of parties who might damage, abuse, or steal their property. Although often associated with selfishness on the part of owners, property rights could thus more properly be viewed as a means by which owners (including corporate owners) are protected against the selfishness of others. However, if adequately compensated, property owners often allow others to use their assets, even though the value of the assets will subsequently be lower. Rental car firms sell individuals the right to use their automobiles despite the reduction in the resale value of the car. Housing is often rented, even though normal use by the renter imposes a maintenance and upkeep cost on the homeowner. However, since property rights are clearly defined in these cases, the market exchange system forces persons who use the property to consider fully the costs of their actions.

Some people argue that property should be owned communally. **Communal property rights** (sometimes called common property rights) grant anyone the right to use a resource that is not currently being used by someone else. The rights to use highways, city parks, rivers, and the atmosphere are effectively held communally. If there is more of a resource than persons wish to use, communal property rights work well enough. However, problems arise when scarce resources are owned jointly by all. Since no one has exclusive ownership rights, all individuals (and firms) are free to use communal property as intensively as they wish. Invariably, communal property rights lead to the overutilization of scarce resources (see "The Importance of Communal and Private Property Rights," on the following page).

The problems of air and water pollution stem from the nature of the ownership rights to these resources. Since the atmosphere, rivers, streams, and many lakes are, in effect, owned communally, the users of these resources have little incentive to practice conservation or to use less pollution-intensive methods of production. Any *single user* of our commonly owned air and water resources would be foolish to incur control costs voluntarily in order to reduce the pollutants that that particular user puts into the air (or water). The general level of pollution would be virtually unaffected by one user's actions. However, when *all* users fail to consider how their actions affect air and water quality, the result is overutilization, excessive pollution, and economic inefficiency.

The characteristics of some commodities make it costly or nearly impossible for the government to establish property rights in a manner that will ensure that private parties bear the entire cost or reap all of the benefits of an activity. Exclusive ownership can easily be granted for such commodities as apples, cabbages, waterbeds, cars, and airline tickets, but how would one assign property rights to salmon or whales, which travel thousands of miles each year? Similarly, who owns an oil pool that is located under the property of hundreds of different landowners? In the absence of clearly assigned property rights, spillover costs and overutilization are inevitable. Certain whales are on the verge of extinction because no single individual (or small group) has an incentive to reduce the current catch so that the future catch will be larger. Each tries to catch as many whales as possible now; someone else will catch those whales, the argument goes, if the first person (or group) does not. The same principle applies to oil-pool rights. In the absence of regulation, each oil-well operator

Communal Property Rights:
Rights to property that can be used by all citizens as intensively as they desire. No one has the right to exclude another from the use of such property. These rights are sometimes referred to as common property rights.

has an incentive to draw the oil *from a common pool* as rapidly as possible, but when all operators do so, the commonly owned oil is drawn out too rapidly.

External Benefits and Missed Opportunities

Spillover effects are not always harmful. Sometimes the actions of an individual (or firm) generate external benefits, gains that accrue to nonparticipating (and nonpaying) secondary parties. When external benefits are present, the personal gains of the consenting parties understate the total social gain, including that of secondary parties. Activities with greater social benefits than costs may not be undertaken because no single decision-maker will be able to capture all the gains fully. Considering only personal net gains, decision-makers will allow potential social gains to go unrealized.

THE IMPORTANCE OF COMMUNAL AND PRIVATE PROPERTY RIGHTS

What is common to many is taken least care of, for all men have greater regard for what is their own than for what they possess in common with others.[1]

The point made by Aristotle more than 2000 years ago is as true now as it was then. It is as important in primitive cultures as it is in developed ones. When the property rights to a resource are communally held, the resource invariably is abused. In contrast, when the rights to a resource are held by an individual (or family), conservation and wise utilization generally result. The following examples from sixteenth century England, nineteenth century American Indian cultures, and modern Russia illustrate the point.

Cattle Grazing on the English Commons

Many English villages in the sixteenth century had commons, or commonly held pastures, which were available to any villagers who wanted to graze their animals. Since the benefits of grazing an additional animal accrued fully to the individual, whereas the cost of overgrazing was an external one, the pastures were grazed extensively. Since the pastures were communal property, there was little incentive for an *individual* to conserve grass in the present so that it would be more abundant in the future. When everyone used the pasture extensively, there was not enough grass at the end of the grazing season to provide a good base for next year's growth. What was good for the individual was bad for the village as a whole. In order to preserve the grass, some people organized enclosure movements. After these movements established private property rights, overgrazing no longer occurred.

The Property Rights of American Indians

Among American Indian tribes, common ownership of the hunting grounds was the general rule. Because the number of native Americans was small and their hunting technology was not highly developed, the hunted animals seldom faced extinction. However, there were at least two exceptions.

One was the beaver hunted by the Montagnais Indians of the Labrador Peninsula. When the French fur traders came to the area in the early 1600s, the beaver increased in value and therefore became increasingly scarce. Recognizing the depletion of the beaver population and the animal's possible extinction, the Montagnais began to institute private property rights. Each beaver-trapping area on a stream was assigned to a family, and conservation practices were adopted. The last remaining pair of beavers was never trapped, since the taker would only be hurting his own family the following year. For a time at least, the supply of beavers was no longer in jeopardy. However, when a new wave of European trappers invaded the area, the native Americans, because they were unable to enforce their property rights, abandoned conservation to take the pelts while they could.[2] Individual ownership was destroyed, and conservation disappeared with it.

The second animal that faced extinction was the communally owned buffalo. Once native Americans gained access to both the gun and the white man's market for hides, their incentive and ability to kill the buffalo increased. By 1840, Indians had emptied portions of the

[1]Aristotle, as quoted by Will Durant in *The Life of Greece* (New York: Simon and Schuster, 1939), p. 536.

[2]For an economic analysis of the Montagnais management of the beaver, together with historical references, see Harold Demsetz, "Toward a Theory of Property Rights," *American Economic Review* (May 1967), pp. 347–359.

Great Plains of the area's large buffalo population.[3] In this case, the communal property problem could not be solved by the Indians. Unlike the beaver, the buffalo ranged widely over the Great Plains. Individual, family, and even tribal rights were impossible to establish and enforce. Like oil in a common pool or the sperm whale on the high seas, buffalo were a "fugitive resource," the mobility of which made property rights (and therefore sound management) unattainable. Only the later fencing of the range solved the problem, after most buffalo herds had already been destroyed by both Indians and whites.

Property Rights in the Soviet Union

In the Soviet Union, 97 percent of the farmland is cultivated collectively. The output of the collective farms goes to the state. As a result, most of the benefits derived from wise conservation practices and efficient production techniques accrue to secondary parties (the state) rather than to the individual workers. Families living on collective farms are permitted to cultivate a private plot, the area of which is not to exceed one acre. The "owners" of these private plots are allowed to sell their produce in a relatively free market. Although the private plots constitute approximately 1 percent of the land under cultivation in the Soviet Union, the Communist press reported that about one-quarter of the total value of agricultural output was generated by these plots in 1980. The productivity per acre on the private plots was approximately 40 times higher than that on the collectively farmed land![4] Property rights make a difference even in the Soviet Union. Clearly, the farm workers take better care of the plots they own privately than the land they own communally. Aristotle would surely be satisfied with the long-range accuracy of his observation.

[3]This fascinating part of native American history has been recorded in Francis Haines, *The Buffalo* (New York: Crowell, 1970).

[4]See Hedrick Smith, *The Russians* (New York: New York Times Book Co., Quadrangle, 1976), pp. 199–214, for an informative account of the life on collective farms in the Soviet Union.

As in the case of external costs, external benefits occur when property rights are undefined or unenforceable. Because of this, it is costly—or impossible—to withhold these benefits from secondary parties and retain them for oneself at the same time. The producer of a motion picture has rights to the film and can collect a fee from anyone who sees or rents it. In contrast, a person who produces a beautifully landscaped lot that is visible from the street cannot collect a fee for the enjoyment that others derive from it. Some of the benefits of the landscaper's efforts accrue to secondary parties who will probably not help to cover the cost.

Why should we be bothered if others benefit from our actions? Most of us are not—although it is quite possible, for example, that more people would improve the maintenance of their property if those who derived benefits from it helped pay for it. Generally, external benefits become important only when our inability to capture these potential gains forces us to *forego* a socially beneficial activity. Exhibit 3 illustrates this point. Education adds to students' productivity, preparing them to enjoy higher future earnings. In addition, at least certain types of education reduce the future cost of welfare, generate a more intelligent populace, and perhaps even lower the crime rate. Thus, some of the benefits of education, particularly elementary and secondary education, accrue to the citizenry as a whole. The private market demand curve understates the total social benefits of education. In the absence of government intervention, as shown in Exhibit 3, Q_1 units of education result from the market forces. However, when the external benefits MB are added to the private benefits, the social gain from additional units of education exceeds the cost until output level Q_S is produced. Social welfare could thus be improved if output were expanded beyond Q_1 to

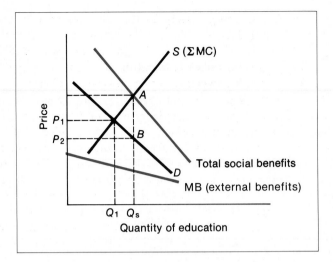

EXHIBIT 3 Adding external benefits

The demand curve D, indicating only private benefits, understates the social benefits of education. At output Q_1, the social benefit of an additional unit of education exceeds the cost. Ideally, output should be expanded to Q_s, where the social benefit of the marginal unit of education would be just equal to its cost. A public subsidy of AB, per unit of education, would lead to this output level.

Q_s, but since educational consumers cannot capture these external gains, they fail to purchase units beyond Q_1. The free market output is too small. A subsidy is required if the ideal output level Q_s is to be achieved.

When external benefits are present, the market demand curve understates the social gains of conducting the beneficial activity. Potential social gains go unrealized because no single decision-maker can appropriate or capture the gains fully; they are seen as "lost" when bestowed on nonpaying secondary parties. Thus, decision-makers lack the incentive to carry an activity far enough to capture the potential social gains.

PUBLIC SECTOR RESPONSES TO EXTERNALITIES

What can the government do to improve the efficiency of resource allocation when externalities are present? Sometimes private property rights can be more clearly defined and more strictly enforced. The granting of property rights to ranchers and homesteaders greatly improved the efficiency of land utilization in the Old West during the 1800s. More recently, the establishment of enforceable property rights to the oyster beds of the Chesapeake Bay improved the efficiency of oyster farming in the area. However, in many instances, it is difficult to delineate boundaries for a resource and determine who owns what portion. This is clearly the case with air and water rights. The air rights of property owners often overlap. Property owners cannot go to court and enforce their property rights to clean air or gain compensation for abuse of clean air unless they can demonstrate three things in court: (a) the extent of the damage inflicted by the pollution, (b) the fact that the pollutant in question actually caused the damage, and (ç) the identity of the party whose emissions caused the damage. It is difficult and costly for property owners to prove these things.

When it is impractical (or impossible) to establish and enforce property rights, as in the case of our air resources, an alternative strategy is necessary. There are two general approaches that government might take. First, a government agency might act as a resource manager, charging the users of the resource a fee. Second, a regulatory agency might establish a maximum pollution emission standard and require all firms to attain at least that standard. We will consider each of these alternatives.

The Pollution Tax Approach

Economists generally favor a user's charge, which we will refer to as a pollution tax. Exhibit 4 utilizes the actual data of a copper smelter to illustrate the economics of this approach. The copper-producing firm has minimum costs of production when it spends nothing on pollution control. The marginal control cost curve reveals the cost savings (control costs avoided) that accrue to the firm when it pollutes. The marginal damage cost curve shows the cost ($32.50 per ton) imposed on parties downwind from the smelter. Without any tax or legal restraints, the smelter would emit 190,000 tons of sulfur dioxide into the air per year, causing $6.2 million in damage. A tax equal to the marginal damage cost of $32.50 per ton emitted would cause the firm to reduce its emissions to 17,100 tons per year and reduce pollution damage from $6.2 million to about $0.6 million per year. The control cost of reducing emissions to this level would be about $2.9 million per year. Total social costs each year would fall from $6.2 million (all borne by those suffering pollution damage) to $3.5 million (combined costs of pollution damage and control, paid entirely by the firm and its customers).

How are the costs of pollution—the damage it causes—and the benefits of controlling pollution to be measured? Any pollution control strategy requires that the control agency make estimates of pollution damage caused by various levels of emission. The agency must be able to compare the benefits gained by controlling emissions at different levels. Unfortunately, the damage inflicted on secondary parties is not easy to measure. It varies among areas. The emission of additional units of sulfur oxides into the environment in Four Corners, Wyoming, is far less damaging than similar emissions in New York City or St. Louis. Economic efficiency requires that a pollution tax rate based on pollution damages be directly related to the population of the area. Thus, densely populated areas would have higher pollution taxes, encouraging high-pollution firms to locate in areas where fewer people would be harmed.

At least in theory, the tax approach would promote efficient resource allocation. Several economic incentives would be altered in a highly desirable way. First, the pollution tax would increase the cost of producing pollution-

EXHIBIT 4   Taxing a smelter's emissions

The marginal control cost curve shows that the firm, if it pays no damage costs itself, will emit 190,000 tons per year while spending nothing on control costs. However, if taxed according to the marginal damages it imposes ($32.50 per ton), it will voluntarily cut back its emissions to 17,100 tons per year, which is the socially efficient level. Further control would cost more than its social benefit.

Richard L. Stroup, "The Economics of Air Pollution Control" (Ph.D. diss., University of Washington, 1970).

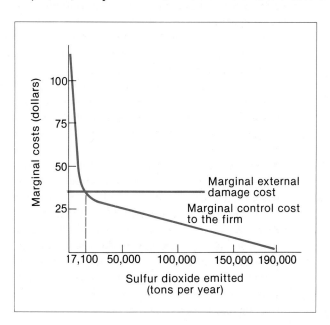

*"In other words, what you'll have us believe,
sir, is that all the fish in the river next to your
plant suddenly died of old age."*

intensive goods, causing the supply in these industries to decline. If the tax was properly set, the ideal price and output conditions illustrated by Exhibit 2 would be approximated. The revenues generated by the tax could be used to compensate the secondary parties harmed by the pollutants or to finance a wide range of projects, including applied research on alternative methods of improving air quality. Second, the pollution tax would give firms an economic incentive to use methods of production (and technology) that would create less pollution. As long as it was cheaper for the firm to control harmful emissions than to pay the emission fee (tax), the firm would opt for control. Third, since firms would be able to lower their tax bills by controlling pollution, a market for new emission-control devices would exist. Entrepreneurs would be induced to develop low-cost control devices and market them to firms that would now have a strong incentive to reduce their level of emissions. Note that measuring levels of emissions is an easier task than measuring the damage done by the emissions.

Given the damage and control cost estimates of Exhibit 4, would it make sense for regulatory authorities to follow a policy that fully eliminated pollution emissions? Clearly, the answer is no. At pollution emission levels of less than 17,100 tons per year, the marginal costs of pollution control would exceed the marginal benefits of the control. In cases such as that illustrated by Exhibit 4, substantial improvement can be made at a modest cost. At some point, however, it will become extremely costly to make additional improvements.

Cleaning up the environment is like squeezing water from a wet towel. Initially, a great deal of water can be squeezed from the towel with very little effort, but it becomes increasingly difficult to squeeze out still more. So it is with the environment. At some point, the benefit of a cleaner environment will simply be less than its cost.

People want clean air and water. Since they want other things as well, those entrusted with the authority to control pollution would have to ask themselves two crucial questions: How many other goods and services are we willing to give up in order to fight the battle against pollution? How much would the public like us to spend, from its pockets, to achieve additional freedom from pollution? Since we all want to obtain the maximum benefit from expenditures on pollution control, it is important that these questions be answered carefully, no matter which control strategy we adopt.

The Maximum Emission Standard Approach

Maximum Emission Standard: The maximum amount of pollution that a polluter is permitted to emit, established by the government or a regulatory authority. Fines are generally imposed on those who are unwilling or unable to comply.

Although economics suggests that the pollution tax approach is highly efficient, in the real world a **maximum emission standard** is generally imposed. In this case, the regulatory agency forces all producers to reduce their emissions to a designated level. Producers who are unable to meet the standard are required to terminate production.

The problem with this approach is that the costs of eliminating pollution emissions generally vary widely among firms. Since the maximum emissions standard approach fails to take account of differences in control costs among polluters, it is generally inefficient in that it results in less pollution control per dollar than, for example, the pollution tax strategy. Many economists consider the maximum emission standard too broad and unspecific for use in attaining minimum-cost pollution control or reduction.

Exhibit 5 illustrates why the standard emissions approach is an inefficient method of reducing the level of pollution. A hypothetical emission control cost schedule is presented for three different producers. In the absence of regulation, each producer will emit 6 units of emissions into the air, for a total of 18 units. Suppose that the regulatory agency wants to reduce the total pollution emissions to six units, one-third of the current level. This can be accomplished by requiring each firm to meet a maximum emission standard of two units. Each producer will have to reduce emissions by four units. However, the cost of meeting this standard will differ substantially among the firms; it will cost producer A $500, producer B $700, and producer C $10,000. If this method is adopted, it will cost society $11,200 in control cost to meet the two-unit maximum pollution standard.

Alternatively, the regulatory agency can levy a pollution tax of $350 per unit and eliminate the same amount of pollution. Confronting the tax, producer A will reduce pollution emissions by six units at a control cost of $1050. Producer B will also cut back emissions by six units, at a cost of $1350. Since it is so costly for producer C to reduce emissions, producer C will choose to pay the tax of $350 per unit and emit six units of pollution into the air. Under the tax strategy, the social cost of eliminating the 12 units of pollution will be only $2400, approximately one-fifth of the cost incurred in the elimination of the same amount of pollution under the maximum control strategy.

Since each polluter would have a different control cost schedule, the pol-

EXHIBIT 5 Controlling pollution—the pollution tax versus the maximum emission standard approach

Consider three firms, each of which currently emits 6 units of pollution. If a maximum standard of 2 units of emissions per producer were imposed, it would cost producer A $500, producer B $700, and producer C $10,000 to meet the standard. The cost of eliminating 12 units of pollution by this method would be $11,200. Alternatively, a pollution tax of $350 would induce the producers to eliminate the same amount of pollution (12 units) at a cost to society of only $2400.

	Units Emitted without Regulation		
	Producer A = 6	Producer B = 6	Producer C = 6
Cost of eliminating first unit	$ 50	$100	$1000
Cost of eliminating second unit	100	150	2000
Cost of eliminating third unit	150	200	3000
Cost of eliminating fourth unit	200	250	4000
Cost of eliminating fifth unit	250	300	5000
Cost of eliminating sixth unit	300	350	6000

Total cost of eliminating 12 units of pollution emissions when:
(a) Maximum emission standard of 2 units is
imposed $500 + $700 + $10,000 = $11,200
(b) Emission tax of $350 is imposed $1050 + $1350 + 0 = $2400

lution tax strategy would result in the most pollution control per dollar. This outcome could be attained because the tax would induce firms that could cut their emissions at the least cost to do so and avoid the tax, but the tax would also permit firms with high control cost to compensate society (pay the tax) and pollute. Some people object to the pollution tax strategy because they believe that it would grant producers a license to pollute. In a sense this is true. Some firms would find it cheaper to pay the tax than to control their emissions. However, the firms with a lower pollution control cost would adopt control techniques. If the tax reflected damage cost at the margin, the remaining damages would impose a lower cost on society than would the cost of control.

In its 1976 report, the President's Council on Environmental Quality estimated that firms (and indirectly the consumers of their products) would spend $250 billion between 1975 and 1984 meeting the requirements of the major federal environmental laws. These laws currently reflect the maximum emission standard approach. They make no use of the pollution tax strategy. How much difference would it make if the tax strategy were substituted for the maximum standard approach? Allen Kneese and Charles Schultze have estimated that pollution taxes could save society between 40 and 90 percent of the costs of pollution control.[5] A savings, over ten years, of from $100 billion to $225 billion seems worthy of serious consideration.

---

[5]Allen V. Kneese and Charles Schultze, *Pollution, Prices, and Public Policy* (Washington, D.C.: Brookings Institution, 1975).

Should the Government Always Try to Control Externalities?

Whenever an externality is present, ideal efficiency of resource allocation cannot be attained. However, it does not follow that the government can always improve the situation and bring the economy closer to its ideal allocation level. In evaluating the case for a public sector response to externalities, one should keep in mind the following three points.

1. Sometimes the Economic Inefficiency Resulting from Externalities Is Small. Therefore, Given the Cost of Public Sector Action, Net Gain from Intervention Is Unlikely. The behavior of individuals often influences the welfare of others. The length of hair, choice of clothing, and personal hygiene care of some individuals may affect the welfare of secondary parties. Should an agency in charge of personal appearance and hygiene be established to deal with externalities in these areas? Persons who value personal freedom would answer with a resounding no. From the standpoint of economic efficiency, their view is correct. The effects of externalities in these and similar areas are small. Thus, the misallocation that results is usually inconsequential. Exhibit 6 provides a graphic illustration. In this instance, if the cost imposed on the secondary parties were fully registered, supply curve S_2 would result. Conditions of ideal efficiency require that output Q_2 be produced and sold at price P_2. Since private decision-makers do not fully consider the economic cost their actions impose on others, a larger output Q_1 and lower price P_1 result from market allocation. However, the difference is small. In fact, the small triangle *ABC* represents the loss that results from the inefficiency created by external cost.

Government intervention would require the use of scarce resources. A regulatory agency would have to be established. No doubt, suits and counter-suits would be filed. These actions would require the use of scarce legal resources. Most public sector decision-makers would lack the information necessary to determine which activities should be taxed and which should be subsidized. Administrative problems such as these greatly reduce the attractiveness of public sector action. When the external effects are small, the cost of government intervention is likely to exceed the loss due to market inefficiency, *relative to the*

EXHIBIT 6   Trivial externalities

Sometimes externalities have only a small impact on the price and output of a good. This graph illustrates the presence of an external cost. Output is slightly larger and price slightly lower than would be ideal, but the loss that results from the inefficiency generated by the externality is only the small triangle *ABC*. Given the costs of the public decision-making process, government intervention would probably not result in a net gain in instances such as this.

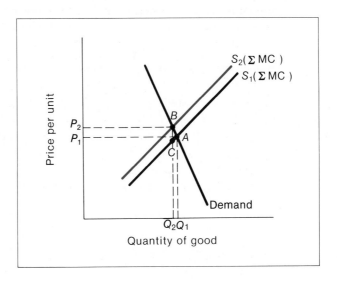

hypothetical ideal. From the standpoint of overall efficiency, under these circumstances, the best approach is to do nothing.

2. The Market Often Finds a Reasonably Efficient Means of Dealing with Externalities. The existence of externalities implies the presence of *potential* gain. If the external effects are significant, market participants have an incentive to organize economic activity in a manner that will enable them to capture the potential gain. If the number of parties affected by the externality is small, they may be able to arrive at a multiparty bargain that will at least partially negate the inefficiency and loss resulting from the externality. Some entrepreneurs have devised ingenious schemes to capture benefits that were previously external to private parties. Community housing developments make it possible to capture benefits that arise when houses are located near a country club, golf course, and/or public park. In these cases, otherwise nonpaying secondary parties can be made to pay for the benefits of trees, gardens, manicured lawns, and so on. If consumers are willing to pay for these amenities, as they often are, developers who provide such services will be able to capture benefits in the form of higher prices on the sale of surrounding lots.[6] Thus, market forces sometimes devise efficient arrangements for dealing with external effects.

3. Government Action May Also Impose an External Cost on Secondary Parties. We have already mentioned that government intervention designed to correct the inefficiencies created by externalities is costly. Often, the costs of public sector intervention exceed the benefits. Therefore, on efficiency grounds, intervention should be rejected. In addition, we should recognize that even democratic public sector action results in the imposition of an externality—the majority imposes an external cost on the minority, which is opposed to the action. Just as an individual may carry an activity too far when some of the costs are borne by others, a majority may also carry an action beyond the point of ideal efficiency. The gains that accrue to the majority may be less than the costs imposed on the minority. Thus, although the government can potentially take corrective measures, counterproductive economic action by the democratic majority may result if the external costs imposed on the minority are not fully considered.

MARKET FAILURE: PUBLIC GOODS

Public goods comprise the extreme case of commodities, the consumption of which results in spillover benefits to secondary parties. In the original formulation by Paul Samuelson, there are two distinctive characteristics of public goods. First, the availability of a public good to one person makes it equally available to all others. Public goods must therefore be consumed jointly by

---

[6]The development of Disney World in Florida is an interesting case in which entrepreneurial ingenuity made it possible to capture external benefits more fully. When Walt Disney developed Disneyland in California, the market value of land in the immediate area soared as a result of the increase in demand for services (food, lodging, gasoline, etc.). Since the land in the area was owned by others, the developers of Disneyland were unable to capture these external benefits. However, when Disney World was developed near Orlando, Florida, the owners purchased an enormous plot of land, far more than was needed for the amusement park. As was the case with Disneyland in California, the operation of Disney World caused land values in the immediate area to rise sharply. However, since the developers of Disney World initially purchased a large amount of land near the attraction, they were able to capture the external benefits by selling prime property to hotels, restaurants, and other businesses desiring a nearby location.

OUTSTANDING ECONOMIST

Allen Kneese (1930–   )

Currently a senior fellow at Resources for the Future (RFF) and adjunct professor of economics at the University of New Mexico, Kneese is a leading authority on environmental economics. He is the author or coauthor of many articles and nearly a dozen books on environmental policy. His recent work in this area has focused on alternative pollution control strategies and quantitative models of environmental economics.[7]

---

[7]See Kneese and Schultze, *Pollution, Prices, and Public Policy,* and Allen V. Kneese, *Economics and the Environment* (London: Penguin, 1977).

Kneese received his doctorate from Indiana University in 1956. He has spent much of his career at RFF, a nonprofit research organization based in Washington, D.C. Currently, he is chairman of the board for the minerals and energy resources program of the prestigious National Academy of Sciences.

Kneese has applied the theory of external cost and public goods to a wide range of environmental problems. In the policy area, in general, he tends to favor an emission charge (pollution tax) control strategy over more direct regulation, such as uniform emission standards.

Kneese recognizes that formulating an efficient control strategy is not an easy task. Control of automobile exhaust, a major source of pollution in many urban areas, presents several special problems. The current approach forces automobile manufacturers to meet certain uniform emission standards on all *new cars* produced. This strategy is highly inefficient for two reasons. First, it forces automobile consumers in sparsely populated areas to pay for the emission control systems on new cars, even though pollution is often not a problem in these areas. Second, the uniform standards approach fails to provide individuals with a personal incentive to keep the control devices operational and their automobiles well tuned in order to reduce exhaust emissions.

In his widely used introductory-

level textbook, *The Economics of Environmental Policy* (coauthored with Myrick Freeman and Robert Haveman),[8] Kneese suggests that we control automobile emissions by means of a "smog tax" rather than national uniform standards. Under the smog tax plan, automobiles would be checked periodically and rated according to their emission levels. The smog tax would then be levied *according to the emissions rating of the vehicle* when gasoline was purchased. The owners of cars with high emission levels would pay higher taxes than the owners of automobiles with lower emission levels.

The smog tax approach would permit regional variation, so that drivers in areas in which pollution was not a problem would not be forced to pay for something that yielded little benefit. Unlike the current system, the tax approach would give individuals a personal incentive to adopt effective pollution control devices (on both new and used cars), keep them in good working order, and keep the motor in tune. If policy planners are interested in adopting effective, efficient control strategies, they would do well to listen to the ingenious ideas of Professor Kneese and other economists who understand the necessity of bringing private and social interests into harmony.

---

[8]A. Myrick Freeman III, Robert Haveman, and Allen V. Kneese, *The Economics of Environmental Policy* (New York: Wiley, 1973).

---

all. Second, because of this joint consumption, it is impossible to exclude nonpayers from the receipt of public goods.[7]

Examples of *pure* public goods are not numerous. National defense is one. The defense system that protects you provides similar protection to all other citizens. Our legal and monetary systems are also public goods. The laws and

---

[9]Note that public and private goods are determined by the characteristics of the good. The consumption benefits of a private good are derived entirely by the individual consumer. The benefits are private. In contrast, the consumption of a public good by a single party makes the benefits of the good equally available to others. Whether the good is produced in the public or private sector of the economy is *not* the factor that determines how the good is classified.

individual rights that are available to one citizen are also provided to others. The policies of the Federal Reserve are provided equally to all citizens. The quality of the atmosphere, and, to a lesser extent, that of rivers and waterways can also be classified as public goods.

The Free Rider Problem

Free Rider: One who receives the benefit of a good without contributing to its costs. Public goods and commodities that generate external benefits offer people the opportunity to become free riders.

Since nonpaying consumers cannot be excluded (at least not at a reasonable cost), a sufficient amount of public goods cannot be provided by the market mechanism. If public goods were provided through the market, each of us would have an incentive to become a **free rider,** one who receives the benefits of a good without contributing to its cost. Why contribute to the cost of supplying a public good? Your actions will have a negligible impact on the supply of clean air, pure water, national defense, and legal justice. The sensible path will lead you to do nothing. As long as you travel that path alone, you will ride along, free and easy. If everyone else joins you, however, the aggregate lack of action will lead to an insufficient quantity of public goods.

Suppose that national defense were provided entirely through the market. Would you voluntarily help to pay for it? Your contribution would have a negligible impact on the total supply of defense available to each of us, even if you made a *large personal* contribution. Many citizens, even though they might value defense highly, would become free riders, and few funds would be available to finance the necessary supply. If the military–industrial complex were dependent on market forces, it would be small indeed!

The harmony between private and social interests tends to break down for public goods. The amount of a public good available to an individual (and others) will be virtually unaltered by whether or not the individual pays for it. Thus, each individual has an incentive to become a free rider. But when numerous individuals become free riders, less than the ideal amount of the public good is produced.

Perhaps another hypothetical example will clarify this important point. Suppose that plans are developed for a flood-control dam. Estimates indicate that the costs of the project will be only one-fifth as great as the benefits to be derived from a reduction in the expected future damage from floods. How will the dam be marketed? Without government action, it will be difficult, because each individual will prefer to be a free rider.

Suppose the flood-control project were proposed for your community. Exhibit 7 shows the options available to you in responding to this public-good project, and the outcomes of each option. The best outcome for you would be the result of option 1. Others would pay the price of the flood-control project, and you would contribute nothing. You would obtain the benefits but would not pay for them. Since others could not provide flood protection for themselves without providing it equally to you, they would have no way of ensuring that you would help pay for the project voluntarily, even though you would derive substantial benefits from it. You would have a strong incentive to become a free rider. However, if everyone, or almost everyone, tried to ride free, the community would fail to purchase the dam because of insufficient funds. This would be the result of option 3.

Unlike option 1, option 2 would be available to all people of the community. If others had preferences like yours, they would prefer option 2 to option 3.

EXHIBIT 7 **Everybody rides free—and loses**

Personal Ranking of Alternative Plans for the Purchase of the Flood-Control Dam (A Public Good)	Personal Alternatives
Option 1	Others pay the purchase price of the flood-control project. You contribute nothing and receive the benefits of flood control. You are a free rider.
Option 2	Jointly, the downstream community residents undertake the flood-control project. You pay your fair share.
Option 3	You fail to contribute. Because others also fail to pay their share, the community does not undertake the project.
Option 4	Because others fail to contribute, the community has insufficient funds to undertake the project. You pay your share but do not receive any protection against future flood damages.

Government action to finance the project through taxation would be preferable to no action at all. However, if the government did not intervene and each person followed personal interests, the community would be left with option 3.

Near Public Goods

Few commodities are pure public goods, but a much larger set of goods are jointly consumed even though nonpaying customers can be excluded. For example, such goods as radio and television broadcasts, national parks, interstate highways, movies, and football games are jointly consumed. Assuming that there is not a congestion problem, additional consumption of these "near public goods," *once they are produced,* is costless to society.

Should nonpaying customers be excluded when the marginal cost of providing the good to them is zero? Many economists argue that such near public goods as highways, national parks, and television programming should be provided free to consumers, at the expense of the taxpayer. Why exclude people from the consumption of these near public goods when their use of the goods does not add to the cost? The argument has a certain appeal.

However, we must be careful. Television programs, highways, parks, and other public goods are scarce. The consumption of other products must be foregone in order to produce such goods. If a zero price is charged, how does one determine whether consumers value additional units enough to cover their opportunity cost? How can an intensely concerned minority communicate its views as to the types of near public goods that should be produced? Taxes will be necessary to cover the costs of making near public goods freely available. Will such taxes lead to inefficiency? All of these factors reduce the attractiveness of public sector provision of jointly consumed commodities when exclusion of nonpaying consumers is possible.

In the real world, market choices, like other decisions, are made with incomplete information. Consumers do not have perfect knowledge about the quality of a product, the price of alternative products, or side effects that may result. They may make incorrect decisions, decisions that they will later regret, because they do not possess good information.

The reality of imperfect knowledge is, of course, not the fault of the market. In fact, the market provides consumers with a strong incentive to acquire information that will help produce satisfying long-run decisions. Because consumers must bear the consequences of their mistakes, they certainly will seek to avoid the deliberate purchase of "lemon" products.

Getting Your Money's Worth

Repeat-Purchase Item: An item purchased often by the same buyer.

The consumer's information problem is minimal if the item is purchased regularly. Consider the problem of purchasing a brand of soap. There is little cost associated with trying out brands. Since soap is a product that is regularly purchased, trial and error is an economical means of determining which brand is most suitable to the consumer's personal needs. It is a **repeat-purchase item.** The consumer can use past experience to good advantage when buying repeat-purchase items, such as soap, toothpaste, most food products, lawn service, and gasoline.

What incentive does the producer have to supply accurate information that will help the customer make a satisfying long-run choice? Is there a conflict between consumer and producer interests? The answers to these questions are critically affected by the seller's dependence on return customers.

If dissatisfaction of *current* customers is expected to have a strong adverse effect on *future* sales, a business entrepreneur will attempt to provide accurate information to help customers make wise choices. The future success of business entrepreneurs who sell repeat-purchase products is highly dependent on the future purchases of currently satisfied customers. There is a harmony of interest because both the buyer and seller will be better off if the customer is satisfied with the product purchased.

Let the Buyer Beware

Major problems of conflicting interests, inadequate information, and unhappy customers arise when goods either (a) are difficult to evaluate on inspection and are seldom repeatedly purchased from the same producer or (b) are potentially capable of serious and lasting harmful side effects that cannot be detected by a layperson. Human nature being what it is, under these conditions, we would expect some unscrupulous producers to sell low-quality, defective, and even harmful goods.

Since customers typically are unable to tell the difference between high-quality and low-quality goods under these conditions, their ability to police quality and price is weakened. Business entrepreneurs have a strong incentive to cut costs by reducing quality. Consumers get less for their dollars; since sellers are not dependent on repeat customers, they may survive and even prosper in the marketplace. The probability of customer dissatisfaction is thus increased because of inadequate information and unexpected poor quality, and the case for an unhampered market mechanism is weakened.[10]

Consider the consumer's information problem when an automobile is purchased. Are most consumers capable of properly evaluating the safety equipment? Except for a handful of experts, most people are not very well equipped to make such decisions. Some consumers might individually seek expert advice. However, it may be more efficient to prevent market failure by having the government regulate automobile safety and require certain safety equipment.

As another example of the problem of inadequate consumer information, consider the case of a drug manufacturer's exaggerated claims for a new product. Until consumers have had experience with the drug or have listened to others' experiences, they might make wasteful purchases. Government regulation might benefit consumers by forcing the manufacturer to modify its claims. Of course, there is no guarantee that the benefits of government action will outweigh the costs. Indeed, as we previously discussed, government regulation itself may be harmful to consumers. Nonetheless, when consumers find it prohibitively expensive to acquire crucial information, the results of government action may be superior to the results of the market.

LOOKING AHEAD

In this chapter, we focused on the failures of the market. In the next chapter, we will use economic analysis to come to a better understanding of the workings of the public sector. We will also discuss some of the expected shortcomings of public sector action. Awareness of both the strengths and weaknesses of alternative forms of economic organization will help us to make more intelligent choices in this important area.

CHAPTER LEARNING OBJECTIVES

1 The sources of market failure can be grouped into four major categories: (a) externalities, (b) public goods, (c) poor information, and (d) monopoly.

2 When externalities are present, the market may fail to confront decision-makers with the proper incentives. Since decision-makers are not forced to consider external cost, they may find it personally advantageous to undertake an economic activity even though it generates a net loss to the community. In contrast, when external benefits are present, decision-makers may fail to undertake economic action that would generate a net social gain.

3 When external costs originate from the activities of a business firm, the firm's cost curve will understate the social cost of producing the good. If production of the good generates external costs, the price of the product under competitive conditions, will be too low and the output too large to meet the *ideal requirements* of economic efficiency.

---

[10]Brand names provide a market solution to information problems that arise from a lack of repeat business. How much would the Coca Cola Company pay to avoid a dangerous bottle of Coke being sold? Surely the answer is, a very large sum. Their reputation is at stake. It is a hostage to quality control. Similarly, franchised food chains make repeat customers of buyers who may never see specific stores twice. The franchise owner polices the control of quality in order to preserve the franchise reputation. That reputation draws customers who are just passing by but know, from reputation, what is being sold. Reputation stimulates repeat business even when a customer only buys once from a *specific* establishment.

4 External costs result from the failure or inability of a society to establish private property rights. Clearly established private property rights enable owners to prohibit others from using or abusing their property. In contrast, communal property rights normally result in overutilization, since most of the cost of overutilization (and misuse) is imposed on others.

5 When external benefits are present, the market demand curve will understate the social gains of conducting the activity. The consumption and production of goods that generate external benefits will tend to be lower than the socially ideal levels.

6 The efficient use of air and water resources is particularly troublesome for the market because it is often impossible to apportion these resources and determine ownership rights. A system of emission charges (a pollution tax) is capable of inducing individuals to make wiser use of these resources. Emission charges (a) increase the cost of producing pollution-intensive goods, (b) grant firms an incentive to use methods of production that create less pollution, and (c) provide producers with an incentive to adopt control devices when it is economical to do so.

7 When the marginal benefits (for example, cleaner air) derived from pollution control are less than the social gains associated with a pollution-generating activity, prohibition of the activity that results in pollution (or other external cost) is not an ideal solution.

8 When the control costs of firms vary, the emission charge (pollution tax) approach will permit society to reduce pollution by a given amount at a lower cost than will the maximum emission standard method, which is currently widely used. The marginal cost of attaining a cleaner environment will rise as the pollution level is reduced. At some point, the economic benefits of a still cleaner environment will be less than the costs.

9 In evaluating the case for government intervention in situations involving externalities, one must consider the following factors: (a) the magnitude of the external effects relative to the cost of government action; (b) the ability of the market to devise means of dealing with the problem without intervention; and (c) the possibility that the political majority may carry the government intervention too far if the external costs imposed on the minority are not fully considered.

10 When it is costly or impossible to withhold a public good from persons who do not or will not help pay for it, the market system breaks down because everyone has an incentive to become a free rider. When everyone attempts to ride free, production of the public good will be lower than the socially ideal level.

11 The market provides an incentive for consumers to acquire information. When a business is dependent on repeat customers, it has a strong incentive to promote customer satisfaction. However, when goods are either (a) difficult to evaluate on inspection and seldom purchased repeatedly from the same producer or (b) have potentially serious and lasting harmful effects, consumer trial and error may be an unsatisfactory means of determining quality. The interests of the consumer and producer are in conflict.

THE ECONOMIC WAY OF THINKING—DISCUSSION QUESTIONS

1 Why may external cost be a cause of economic inefficiency? Why is it important to define property rights clearly? Explain.

2 Devise a tax plan that would (a) reduce the extent of automobile pollution, (b) provide an incentive for entrepreneurs to develop new products that would limit pollution, and (c) permit continued automobile travel for those willing to bear the total social costs. Explain how your plan would influence incentives and why it would work.

3 "When goods generate external benefits, the market is unable to produce an adequate supply. This is why the government must provide such goods as police and fire protection, education, parks, and vaccination against communicable diseases."

   (a) Do you agree? Explain.

(b) Does governmental provision necessarily ensure "an adequate supply"? How would you define "adequate supply"?

(c) Such goods as golf courses, shopping centers, country clubs, neckties, and charity also generate some spillover external benefits. Do you think the government should provide these goods in order to ensure an adequate supply?

4 Which of the following goods are most likely to result in a large number of dissatisfied customers: (a) light bulbs, (b) food at a local restaurant, (c) food at a restaurant along an interstate highway, (d) automobile repair service, (e) used cars, (f) plumbing services, (g) used automatic dishwashers, (h) used sofas, (i) television repair service? Explain your answer.

5 What are public goods? Why does a decentralized pricing system have trouble producing an adequate amount of public goods?

6 Are people more likely to take better care of an item they own jointly (communally) or one they own privately? Why? Does the presence of private property rights affect the behavior of persons in noncapitalist nations? Why or why not?

7 What's Wrong with This Way of Thinking?

"Corporations are the major beneficiaries of our lax pollution control policy. Their costs are reduced because we permit them free use of valuable resources—clean water and air—in order to produce goods. These lower costs are simply added to the profits of the polluting firms."

Nothing is more certain than the indispensable necessity of government; and it is equally undeniable that wherever and however it is instituted, the people must cede to it some of their natural rights, in order to vest it with requisite power [to conduct its assigned responsibilities].[2]
John Jay (1787)

20 PUBLIC CHOICE: GAINING FROM GOVERNMENT AND GOVERNMENT FAILURE[1]

Traditionally, economists have focused on how the market works and what ideal public policy can do to improve economic efficiency. The actual operation of the public sector has been virtually ignored. However, this traditional neglect has become less and less satisfactory in dealing with economics today. Each day, millions of economic decisions are made in the public sector. Approximately two-fifths of our national income is channeled through the various governmental departments and agencies. In addition, the legal framework establishes the "rules of the game" for the market sector. The government's role in defining property rights, enforcing contracts, fixing prices, and regulating business and labor practices has a tremendous impact on the operation of an economy.

This chapter analyzes how various types of economic issues are dealt with through the political process. In studying collective decision-making, we seek to understand the link between individual preferences and political outcomes. The political process is simply an alternative method of making economic decisions. Like the market, it is likely to have defects. When we evaluate the costs and benefits of public sector action, we must also compare the likelihood of achieving our goals through that collective action with the expected outcome of market allocation. In other words, for any economic activity, we must ask ourselves: In which sector will the defects stand least in the way of our goals?

Most political decisions in Western countries are made legislatively. We will focus on a system in which voters choose legislators, who in turn institute public policy. Let us see what the tools of economics reveal about the political process.

VOTERS' DEMAND FOR POLITICAL REPRESENTATION

Individuals express their preferences for types of governmental action through the voting process. Under a legislative system, citizens must express their views through a representative. The impact of voters on the quantity and price of political goods is indirectly felt through their impact on the composition of the body of elected representatives.

How do voters decide whom to support? Many factors undoubtedly

---

[1]Before proceeding with this chapter, you may want to review Chapter 4, which provides an overview of public sector decision-making and introduces the central concepts developed here.

[2]John Jay, "The Dangers of Foreign Force and Influence Threatening the United States," *The Federalist Papers,* no. 2 (New York: Washington Square Press, 1964), pp. 5–6.

influence their decision. The personal characteristics of the candidates are important influences. Criteria such as which candidate is the most persuasive, which presents the best television image, and which appears to be the most honest may determine a voter's choice of whom to support in an election.

The perceived views of candidates on issues, particularly on issues of importance to the individual voter, will also influence the voter's decision. According to economic theory, other things constant, each voter will support the candidate who offers the voter the greatest expected net subjective benefits. Factors other than expected direct economic gain will influence the voter's expected benefits, but personal gain will certainly be an important component.

The greater the perceived net personal economic gain from a particular candidate's platform, the more likely it is that the individual voter will favor that candidate. The greater the perceived net economic cost imposed on a voter by a candidate's positions, the less inclined the voter will be to favor the candidate.

Thus, economics implies that dairy farmers are more likely to prefer candidates who support high prices for dairy products. Support of tax breaks for the oil industry makes a candidate more attractive to oil producers. Welfare recipients typically prefer a candidate who supports increased welfare benefits. And, of course, support of higher teachers' salaries and expanded research funds adds to a politician's rating among college professors and other educators.

Although each of us may have a streak of altruism and concern for the public interest, the opportunity for personal gain influences our evaluation of both political and market alternatives. The greater the expected personal gain, the more likely it is that personal interests will dominate. Moreover, each of us sees the public interest from a different perspective. Since many of us consider our own activities to be important and to contribute to the public interest, we have little trouble equating the benefits to be granted in the name of the public interest with the benefits that would aid us in our individual activities. "rational ignorance effect." (See Chapter 4, pages 75–76.)

The Rational Ignorance Effect

When decisions are made collectively, the direct link between the choice of an individual and the outcome of the issue is broken. The choice of a single voter is seldom decisive when the size of the decision-making group is large. Recognizing that the outcome will not depend on one vote, the individual voter has little incentive to seek information in order to vote more intelligently. Typically, the voter relies on information that is freely supplied by others (candidates, political parties, news media, friends, and interest groups). As we pointed out earlier, economists refer to voters' lack of incentive to acquire information as the "rational ignorance effect." (See Chapter 4, pages 75–76.)

The low probability that one's vote will make any difference also explains why many citizens fail to vote. In the 1980 presidential election, approximately one-half of the eligible population took the time to register and vote. When there is not a presidential election, only about one-third of the eligible voters participate in congressional elections.[3] Voter turnouts for city and county elections are often even lower. These findings should not surprise us; they are precisely what we would expect because the *personal* payoffs from voting are low.

---

[3]Since the probability that a single vote will be decisive is almost zero, one may wonder why even one-third to one-half of U.S. citizens vote. The puzzle is probably explained by the fact that many citizens, maybe even most, receive personal utility from the act of voting.

How does the rational ignorance effect influence the decision-making of voters? Lacking the incentive to acquire information, voters typically consider only a subset of issues about which they feel most strongly. The views of the candidates on these issues of "vital personal importance" influence voting decisions. However, most of the several hundred issues confronting Congress each year are virtually ignored by the typical voter. For example, despite their importance to the nation as a whole, the views of political decision-makers on such things as Japanese fishing rights, appointments to the Interstate Commerce Commission, and allocation of licenses for the operation of television stations are not important enough to command the scrutiny of most citizens. Generally, these issues fail to influence their choices.

Even a voter who manages to follow a politician's previous stands on the hundreds of issues arising each year cannot anticipate all the issues to be faced by elected candidates during their terms of office. In this complex situation, labels such as conservative, liberal, Democrat, and Republican become attractive to the voter. Though oversimplified, such categories allow the rationally ignorant voter to hazard a guess as to a candidate's future stands on future issues. In the world of politics, a candidate's "image," however vague or incorrect, is very important to political success. The details of his or her stand on particular issues simply are not known to most voters. That fact strongly influences the actions of suppliers in the political marketplace.

SUPPLY, PROFITS, AND THE POLITICAL ENTREPRENEUR

The market entrepreneur is a dynamic force in the private sector. The entrepreneur seeks to gain by undertaking potentially profitable projects. In the competitive market process, business entrepreneurs produce commodities that are intensely desired relative to their supply. Similarly, the *political entrepreneur* (or politician) is a dynamic force in the collective decision-making process. The political entrepreneur seeks to offer voters an image and a bundle of political goods that will increase the chances of winning elections. Those who are successful survive and may achieve private power, fame, and even fortune. These goals are as important in the political arena as in the private sector. To increase the chance of being elected, the political entrepreneur must be alert to which political goods and services can attract the most voters. Put another way, in order for the politician to choose and to supply any given political good, the cost, measured in votes lost, must be smaller than the benefits—the votes gained.

This does not mean that politicians always favor the viewpoint of the majority of their constituents on a *specific* issue. In some cases, a candidate may gain more votes among an intensely active minority of people who favor the candidate's position than from a dispassionate and rationally uninformed majority opposed to that position.

Money, Political Advertising, and the Successful Politician

Votes win elections, but the rationally uninformed voters must be convinced to "want" a candidate. What is required to win the support of voters? Both one's positive attributes (for example, honesty, compassion, and effectiveness) and one's position on issues, as we have stressed, are important. However, candidates must bring their strengths to the attention of the voters. Money, manpower, and expertise are required to promote a candidate among the voting population.

"I want NEW promises, Fenwick! When you keep making the same ones over and over, people wise up that you're not keeping them!"

Professor Galbraith and others have stressed the role of product advertising and the mass media in affecting consumer preferences. Since voters have little incentive to acquire information, the impact of the media on the political consumer is even greater than it is on market decisions. The image of a political entrepreneur is determined primarily by an ability to acquire mass media resources and to use these resources to promote his or her positive attributes. Candidates without the financial resources to provide television and other media advertising to rationally ignorant voters are seriously handicapped.[4] Similarly, candidates who are unacceptable to the major communications media face a severe disadvantage.

Being Successful Means Being Political

What does our analysis suggest about the motivation of political decision-makers? Are we implying that they are highly selfish, that they consider only their own pocketbooks and ignore the public interest? The answer is no. When people act in the political sphere, they may genuinely want to help their fellow citizens. Factors other than personal political gain, narrowly defined, influence the actions of many political suppliers. On certain issues, one may feel strongly that one's position is best for the country, even though it may not currently be popular. The national interest as perceived by the political supplier may conflict

---

[4]Political expenditures on advertising and other persuasion techniques indicate that candidates are fully aware of the importance of media exposure. On average, contested candidates for the U.S. Senate or House of Representatives spend between 70 and 80 percent of their campaign resources in this area.

with the position that would be most favorable to reelection prospects. Some politicians may opt for the national interest even when it means political defeat. None of this is inconsistent with an economic view of political choice.

However, the existence of political suicide does not change the fact that *most* political entrepreneurs prefer political life. There is a strong incentive for political suppliers to stake out positions that will increase their vote total in the next election. A politician who refuses to give major consideration to electoral gain increases the risk of replacement by a more astute (and less public-minded) political entrepreneur. Competition—the competition of vote-maximizing political candidates—presents even the most public-spirited politician with a strong incentive to base his decisions primarily on political considerations. Just as neglect of economic profit is the route to market oblivion, neglect of potential votes is the route to political oblivion.

THE DEMAND FOR PUBLIC SECTOR ACTION

People participate in market activity in an effort to obtain more goods and services. People turn to the government for much the same reason.

Voters demand public sector action for two major reasons: (a) to improve economic efficiency and thus capture potential gains lost to market failure, and (b) to redistribute income.

As we discussed in the previous chapter, government can attempt to correct market failure with action that results in more total benefits than costs. Corrective action can increase the size of the economic pie, generating personal benefits for individual voters. Pursuit of this potential gain motivates individuals to turn to government when the market fails. Other things constant, the greater the potential gain accruing to voters from corrective government action, the stronger is the demand for collective action.

Voters may also seek to use the government's taxing, spending, and rule-making powers in order to redistribute income. Government can break the link between what an individual earns and what that individual may consume. Therefore, individual voters may be able to use government action to obtain goods for themselves or favored groups while imposing the cost of the goods on taxpayers in general.

Market Failure and Gaining from Government

Much government action that we take for granted stems from market failure. Government crime-prevention activities provide an example. Of course, there are moral reasons for a society's desire to prohibit crimes such as robbery, arson, and murder. However, these activities can also be viewed from a strictly economic perspective. Clearly, such activities involve external costs. Robbers do not consider the welfare of nonconsenting secondary parties when they seek to transfer wealth from others to themselves. Nonetheless, their actions often impose enormous costs on victims and potential victims. Those who do not have to bear fully the costs that their actions impose on secondary parties will tend to engage in an excessive amount of the activity. There would be more robbers robbing if there were no costs for the criminal. Public policy that imposes costs on criminals—that apprehends and prosecutes robbers and other criminals, reducing the incidence of crime—is socially beneficial.

Almost all individuals, even many of those who occasionally commit crimes, gain from this government action that makes it much more costly for a person to commit such crimes as murder, robbery, kidnapping, rape, arson, and assault. The external costs that these crimes impose on victims are so high that most citizens of the community are quite willing to incur substantial cost in order to obtain the benefits of police protection. Groups could organize in order to pay a private police force cooperatively, but there would be a free-rider problem. Each person would want the others to provide the protection. Anyone whose neighbors were protected would automatically gain without having to pay. Thus, market organization would result in less than the desired amount of police protection. Governmentally provided police protection, paid for by taxes levied on everyone, leads to large personal gains for nearly everyone.

From time to time, politicians debate the merits of terminating government farm price supports, various antipoverty programs, or the minimum wage, but when did you last hear a politician advocate leaving crime prevention to the market? The benefit/cost ratio of government action in this area is very large. Political suppliers have responded to the voters' views.

Government Provision of Public Goods

As we discussed previously, the market fails to allocate public goods efficiently, simply because it is impossible to exclude nonpaying consumers. National defense is probably the most important public good that approximates these conditions. Most people favor some national defense. Because it is a public good, however, it will be produced in less than the desired amount if production is left to the market. There is no feasible way in which nonpaying citizens could be restricted from the consumption of their neighbors' (in this case all of us are neighbors) national defense. There would be few paying customers because personal consumption of national defense would not depend on personal payment. Everyone would have an incentive to become a free rider, but if everybody tried to ride free, little national defense would be produced. As a result, an overwhelming majority of the nation's citizens favor government provision of *some* national defense. Political entrepreneurs who support government action to correct the failure of the market in this area reap more political gain than those who favor leaving defense to the market.

Government Action on Air Pollution. Air quality is also a public good. There is no way in which clean air can be provided to some persons in a neighborhood but not to others. As we explained earlier, the problem of air pollution results from the nature of property rights in this area. Because the atmosphere is, in effect, owned communally, an excessive amount of waste is emitted into it, causing a reduction in air quality. Market signals force users to respond properly to the scarcity of most resources, but this is not the case with communally owned air. For example, an electric utility company will use society's scarce coal resources wisely, since the private owners of coal must be compensated for each ton of the resource consumed. However, without regulation, the same utility will probably fail to conserve air resources, since these are "free" to the firm (but not to the community at large).

If public sector action can bring the private and social costs of using air resources more closely into line, social gain will result. During the last two decades, government intervention in the environmental area has increased.

As industrial output and urbanization have expanded, the problem of pollution has become more severe. At the same time, rising real incomes have encouraged consumers to demand cleaner air. This set of forces has led to a strong environmental movement.

Prompted by the public demand for environmental improvement, Congress passed the Clean Air Act in 1963. The act was reinforced several times, most notably by the Clean Air Amendments of 1970. This comprehensive piece of legislation, sometimes referred to as the Muskie Clean Air Bill, after Senator Edmund Muskie of Maine, contains provisions for maximum emission standards for both automobiles and industrial firms. Since some of the standards are still being set, it has not been possible to assess all the costs and benefits.

How will this public sector pollution control policy affect individual voter-citizens? This is a difficult question to answer. Since air quality is not bought and sold in the market, we cannot be sure of its exact value to individuals. Nonetheless, some researchers have approached the problem. The major beneficiaries of pollution control legislation are the residents of densely populated urban areas, particularly those who are not employed by firms cutting back on employment in order to counterbalance the costs imposed by pollution control standards. The major costs of the Clean Air Amendments are widely dispersed among consumers who must pay higher prices for products that are now more costly to produce.[5]

Summarizing the findings of a detailed study by Henry Peskin of Resources for the Future (Washington, D.C.), Exhibit 1 indicates that the results of the Clean Air program are mixed. People living in densely populated areas such as Jersey City receive the largest gains. In areas that are sparsely populated and where pollution is a smaller problem, Peskin indicates that the costs of higher product prices outweigh the benefits. In fact, he estimates that only 29 percent of the population will experience a gain, while 71 percent will be net losers. For the nation as a whole, the Peskin study estimates that total costs exceed total benefits. Pollution control policy is still evolving, however, and a number of developments could change that outcome. For example, most economists believe that a more flexible, incentive-oriented policy could produce the same benefits at a far lower cost. One such policy might use pollution taxes in such a way that polluters who can control pollution cheaply would reduce emissions more and those for whom control is expensive would pay higher taxes while achieving less pollution control.

Income Redistribution and the Demand for Government Action

Whereas public policy sometimes inadvertently results in income transfers, in other cases public sector programs are specifically designed to redistribute income, either because of a demand for a more equalized distribution of income among *all* citizens or because of a demand for more income by and/or for a

---

[5]Some people believe that the costs of pollution control will be borne by "the big corporations." This view is largely unfounded. There is no more reason to believe that firms will bear the higher cost of pollution control than to believe that they will bear the higher cost of energy, for example. An increase in pollution control costs will reduce the amount of a good supplied at a specific price. This reduction in supply will cause the market price of the product to rise. Higher costs, regardless of their source, will lead to higher prices. There are no free lunches. The consumers of products that are more expensive to produce as a result of pollution regulation control will bear the major burden of the control costs.

EXHIBIT 1 The 1970 clean air amendments—people in some areas gain and others lose

These benefit–cost estimates suggest that some areas, primarily densely populated industrial cities, will have large net benefits, whereas others will pay more than the value they receive in the form of cleaner air.

Rank of Net Gain (or Loss)	County Group or SMSA[a]	Net Benefit (or Cost), Dollars per Family
1	Jersey City SMSA	2284
2	New York SMSA	886
3	Erie SMSA	701
4	Newark SMSA	510
5	Detroit SMSA	385
. . .	. . .	. . .
270	Wyoming, W. Nebraska	−350
271	Santa Barbara SMSA	−362
272	Nevada, S.W. Utah	−379
273	Alaska	−396
274	S.W. Texas	−396

[a]SMSA stands for standard metropolitan statistical area.

Henry M. Peskin, "Environmental Policy and the Distribution of Benefits and Costs," in *U.S. Environmental Policy*, ed. Paul R. Portney (Baltimore: Resources for the Future, Johns Hopkins University Press, 1978), p. 155.

specific group of citizens. As Exhibit 2 illustrates, direct income transfers through the public sector have increased substantially during recent decades. Income transfer payments constituted only 6.3 percent of national income in 1959; they had risen to 12.2 percent by 1979.

Some redistribution of income stems from the inability of the market to reflect fully the preferences of the community for antipoverty efforts. The welfare of many citizens may be adversely affected by the hardship and poverty of others. For example, the economic conditions of ill-clothed children, street beggars, and the elderly poor may impose a cost on many of their fellow citizens. However, private antipoverty efforts, like private-sector national defense, have public-good characteristics. Even though the welfare of a person may be improved if there are fewer poor people, the amount that any one individual contributes to the antipoverty effort exerts little impact on the overall status of the poor. Since the number of poor people, like the strength of our national defense, is largely independent of one's *personal* contribution, individuals have an incentive to become free riders. But when a large number of people become free riders, less than the desired amount of antipoverty effort will be supplied voluntarily.

Under these circumstances, collective action against poverty may improve the general welfare of the community. If everyone is required to contribute through the tax system, the free-rider problem can be overcome. Effective antipoverty efforts may not only help the poor but also encourage donors who are willing to give their fair share if assured that others will do likewise, so that the general level of poverty can actually be reduced.

Self-Interest Redistribution.   Collective action to redistribute income does not always stem from the public-good nature of antipoverty efforts. Rather than seek

EXHIBIT 2 The growth of government transfer payments

Tax Foundation, *Facts and Figures on Government Finance, 1981,* Table 20.

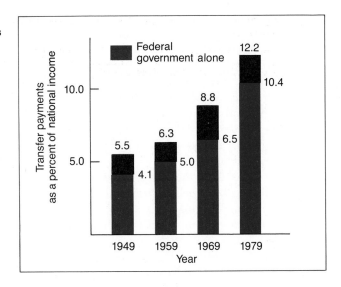

Self-Interest Redistribution: **Redistribution motivated solely by the desire of the members of a group to help themselves. Nonrecipients do not gain from an improvement in the welfare of the recipients.**

to correct what economists call market failure, sometimes people would much rather correct what they see as the market's failure to make them as wealthy as they would like to be. Redistribution motivated solely by the desire of its supporters to help themselves is called **self-interest redistribution** by economists. It is quite common, but it is almost never called redistribution by those who seek it. When farmers lobby for farm subsidies, they may argue that the supports are in our national interest; the supports are also needed to preserve the family farm. When college administrators (and professors) ask for government funds, they typically make their requests on the behalf of students or in the name of scientific advances. Yet, in each case, it is more than a happy coincidence that the desired program also redistributes income to those making the requests. Clearly, a strong element of self-interest is involved.

When are political entrepreneurs most likely to favor self-interest redistribution? We have seen that transfers to the poor, as a public good, might produce benefits greater than their costs. At best, self-interest redistribution results in equally balanced benefits and costs. Political entrepreneurs, however, may be able to gain from such transfers. If transfers are made to well-organized and clearly defined groups, such as the elderly, union members, or shoe producers, strong political support can be obtained from these groups. If those who pay make up a large, unorganized group (for example, taxpayers in general, or all who buy shoes) and the costs are diffused, few votes are lost. This is especially true if the costs can be hidden. Complex programs, debt financing, and money creation are all ways of hiding the cost of providing the redistribution of benefits.

Many who gain the most from self-interest redistribution never receive a check from the government. Dairy producers have successfully invested large sums in order to obtain and maintain federal and state regulation of fresh-milk markets. The gains made by regulated milk producers in the United States are estimated to be over $210 million per year.[6] These gains result from dairy

---

[6]See Richard A. Ippolito and Robert T. Masson, "The Social Cost of Government Regulation of Milk," *Journal of Law and Economics* 21, no. 1 (1978), p. 54.

prices set far above competitive levels. Consumers bear the burden of the producers' benefits—and even pay amounts over and above the gains, since the artificial prices and regulations are inefficient. Of course, the gains made by investors and workers in industries such as this have not been explicitly requested from the government. Rather, requests for various regulations and price controls are made "in the public interest," to avoid "chaos in the market," or "to ensure stable and adequate supplies." The income transfer aspects of each program are at least partially hidden. But, again, the fact that the incomes of those requesting the government intervention happen to increase is surely more than coincidental.

As both the budget and the regulatory powers of government grow, individuals (as well as firms and unions) will find it in their interest to spend more time looking for ways to capture gains bestowed by the government. By the same token, less effort will be devoted to production activities.

Gaining from Government: A Summary

Our analysis is highly simplified. Nonetheless, several important points are clear:

1. Voters seek government action for two major reasons: to capture gains created by market failure and to alter the distribution of income.
2. When market failure is present, government action need not be a zero-sum game in which one person's gain is another's loss. When a majority of voters favor a political action and the benefits are large relative to cost, vote-seeking political entrepreneurs have a strong incentive to back the proposal. The support of such proposals enhances a candidate's election prospects. In these instances, there is harmony between the self-interest of political entrepreneurs and economic efficiency.
3. Point 2 has a corollary: If market failure is not present, the net gains that will accrue to citizens from government intervention will be reduced. There is little reason to believe that the public sector could provide wheat, oranges, shoes, or beef more efficiently than the market sector. Most voters prefer to have such activities conducted in the private sector because it is more efficient and more responsive to their desires.
4. Both government transfer payments and regulation can be used to redistribute income. The demand for public sector redistribution of income may originate from either the public-good nature of antipoverty efforts or from self-interest. In the case of self-interest redistribution, the advocates of government action have a strong incentive to conceal their true motives.

THE ECONOMICS OF GOVERNMENT FAILURE

We no longer expect results from government. What was a torrid romance between the people and government for so long has now become a tired middle-aged liaison which we do not quite know how to break off.[7]

The collective decision-making process is not an ideal mechanism that automatically corrects the inefficiencies of the market. One of the painful lessons of history is that government action often does not have the hoped-for and planned-

---

[7]Peter F. Drucker, "The Sickness of Government," *Public Interest* (Winter 1969), p. 5.

for results. Even well-designed programs based on humanitarian principles sometimes fail to meet their initial objectives. The quotation above, from Peter F. Drucker, reveals a cynicism that grew during the 1970s, replacing the optimism of the 1960s. The great hopes of many Americans during that decade for extensive social improvements through public sector action were to a large extent unfulfilled. The cynicism is to some degree a reaction to that disappointment.

We began this chapter by using economic analysis to assess the effectiveness of public sector action. Now we consider systematically some of the limitations of collective action as a vehicle for promoting economic efficiency.

Government Failure: Failure of government action to meet the criteria of ideal economic efficiency.

Government failure results when public policy promotes economic inefficiency. In the following sections, we analyze five specific types of government failure.

The Special Interest Effect

Many people think of government as the great equalizer, a tool to be used in controlling powerful economic interests. In reality, the relationship often seems to run the other way—strong interest groups seem to control the government. Can economic tools help to explain this phenomenon?

A special interest issue is one for which a small number of voters *individually* acquire large gains at the expense of a large number of citizens who *individually* suffer small losses. We cannot understand fully the political power of a special interest group without recognizing the widespread ignorance and unawareness of intelligent voters with regard to (a) the relevance of most issues to their personal welfare and (b) the position of their elected representatives on the issues. Voters are generally uninformed on most issues. This lack of information and concern is a function of the rational ignorance effect and its corollary, the cost of acquiring information. Typically, most of us decide to vote for or against a political candidate on the basis of the few issues that are of substantial importance to us. We ignore numerous other issues that *individually* exert (or seem to exert) little impact on our well-being.

Two additional factors enhance the power of special interest groups. First, special interest groups are an important source of funds for political campaigns. If a politician wants to win the support of voters who have little incentive to study the issues, free information must be provided to them. Newspaper ads, printed materials, television spots, and other advertising techniques are needed to create a positive image—and all of these cost money. Since special interest groups feel strongly about certain issues, they supply candidates who support their position with a ready source of campaign contributions.[8] Second, political entrepreneurs can often "package" issues so that most voters will be unaware of the cost that various positions on the issues will impose on them. The more complex the policy under question, the more difficult it is for the average voter to figure out how he or she would be affected. There is an incentive for politicians to make special interest issues very complex. The special interest group will most assuredly figure out that it stands to gain from a given proposal, but the typical voter will find it difficult to determine the seemingly complex proposal's actual impact.[9]

Clearly, political suppliers can often reap political gain by supporting special interest legislation, whether or not such legislation is economically inefficient. Since most voters will be uninformed on any given special interest issue, political entrepreneurs have a strong incentive to (a) support the views of a special interest group, (b) solicit from it both votes and money, (c) make the consequences of the special interest issue difficult for the average voter to understand (for example, by making the issue a part of a complex policy proposal), and (d) use funds obtained from the special interest group to promote their candidacy. In other words, political entrepreneurs have an incentive to solicit resources from special interests and use the resources obtained from them to, run not as a special interest candidate, but as the "candidate of the people." Politicians who refuse to follow this strategy run the risk of losing elections to those who accept such a course as a fact of political life.

Public policy in some areas appears to be motivated neither by economic efficiency nor by a desire for greater equality. For example, consider tariff trade

---

[8]Abundant evidence documents the importance of special interest campaign contributions. Senators, congresspeople, and presidents have long benefited from the financial assistance of businesses, unions, and other interest groups that are in a position to be rewarded by public sector decisions. Congressional committee chairpeople are, more often than not, well cared for by the industrial and labor interests that stand to benefit from the committee's actions. Analysis of state government reveals the existence of similar pressures. A study of political contributions in Florida indicated that the lion's share comes from special interest groups that are state regulated. A study in Illinois revealed a similar pattern.

[9]Gordon Tullock, in *Toward a Mathematics of Politics* (Ann Arbor: University of Michigan Press, 1966), emphasizes this point.

restrictions on such commodities as steel and automobiles. For years, economists have pointed out that tariff protection, particularly for an industry that possesses substantial monopoly power, leads to an inefficient allocation of resources. It would be difficult to find an issue on which there is more general agreement among economists. However, the benefits of the repeal of such legislation would be widely dispersed and difficult for consumers to perceive. The costs of the repeal imposed on automobile and steel manufacturers and employees would be highly concentrated. Despite the fact that political figures argue from time to time that automobile and steel prices do not respond to competition, political protection of the tariff legislation remains. Politicians obviously perceive that greater political gains are to be obtained from a continuation of the present high tariff policy on these commodities than from its repeal.

Why is it that politicians who support special interests are not removed from office by taxpayers? There is some incentive to do this, but it is greatly reduced because of the high cost of forming coalitions, particularly among a loosely knit group.[10] Each taxpayer has a strong incentive to "let the others do it"—that is, to act as a free rider. However, when everybody decides to ride free, nothing is accomplished.

Imprecise Reflection of Consumer Preferences

The collective process is likely to be imprecise in reflecting the wishes of "consumers" (voters) because they can usually express their wishes only through a broker (legislator) who represents a "bundle" of political goods and tax prices. The voter either gets the bundle of political goods offered by candidate A or the bundle offered by candidate B. Neither of these bundles of political goods necessarily represents what a specific consumer would like to have. The political consumer does not have the freedom to "shop around" on each issue, but must accept the bundle favored by the majority coalition.

In contrast to the market, the consumer's ability to make discriminating choices is very limited in the public sector. Circumstances change, new information becomes available, and relative prices change, but the political consumer has little opportunity to respond by making marginal adjustments. Approximately two-fifths of our economic resources are channeled through the public sector. Yet during a year, each of us makes approximately 1000 times as many market as public sector decisions.

Concealed Costs and Inefficient Public Policy

It is often difficult for voters to recognize the precise impact of public policy on their well-being. We have already noted that individual voters, recognizing that their views will not decide the issue, have little incentive to inform themselves on political matters. Because of imperfect voter information, the political process is biased against proposals with elusive benefits at the expense of easily identified costs. Anthony Downs believes that this factor often results in the rejection of beneficial public policy:

Benefits from many government actions are remote from those who receive them, either in time, space or comprehensibility. Economic aid to a distant nation may prevent a hostile

---

[10]Sometimes intense publicity will make the support of a specific piece of special interest legislation temporarily unpopular. In this case, entrepreneurs will take special care to modify or disguise their support of vested interest groups.

revolution there and save millions of dollars and even the lives of American troops, but because the solution is remote, the average citizen—living in rational ignorance—will not realize he is benefiting at all.[11]

Just as the failure to recognize personal benefits fully may cause voters (and legislators responsive to their constituents) to reject some economically efficient projects, the adoption of other proposals that are inefficient also results from imperfect voter information. Counterproductive proposals tend to be accepted when the benefits are clearly recognizable and the costs are partially concealed and difficult for voters to identify. Politicians will often seek to conceal the costs of a political proposal while fully promoting its benefits among voters who could gain from it. Vote-maximizing political entrepreneurs have a strong incentive to package public policy proposals precisely in this way. For example, taxes that are difficult for voters to identify are more popular with politicians than are direct tax levies. The splitting of payroll taxes between employer and employee, when the burden does not depend on who formally pays, suggests that legislators are interested in deceiving voters as to the personal cost of government. Similarly, the continued popularity of deficit spending and money creation is consistent with the theory. When this method of gaining control over private resources is substituted for direct taxation, voters are less likely to be fully aware of their individual tax burden. Thus, it is not surprising that political entrepreneurs continue to embrace inflationary policies even while denouncing rising prices and blaming them on unions, businesspeople, the Arabs, the wasteful consumption habits of consumers, or any other scapegoats.

The Shortsightedness Effect

The shortsightedness effect results because the complexity of an issue may make it extremely difficult for the voter to anticipate *future* benefits and costs accurately. Thus, voters tend to rely mainly on current conditions. Candidates and legislators seeking to win the current election have a strong incentive to stress public sector action that yields substantial current benefits relative to costs. Therefore, public sector action is biased in favor of legislation that offers immediate (and easily identified) current benefits at the expense of future costs that are complex and difficult to identify. Similarly, there is a bias against legislation that involves immediate and easily identifiable cost (for example, higher taxes) while yielding future benefits that are complex and difficult to identify. Government action on issues whose future consequences are unclear tends to be shortsighted.

Short-Term Costs and Government Inaction. It has been noted that public sector action is "crisis-oriented." In recent years, we have experienced a welfare crisis, a poverty crisis, an environmental crisis, an energy crisis, and an inflation crisis. One reason for this is that planning for the future tends to be unrewarding for those in government. Future costs and benefits are difficult for voters to identify. In addition, many of those to be affected in the future are not voting today. Given the public sector bias against proposals associated with current costs and difficult-to-identify future benefits, the government's crisis orientation is understandable. The vote-maximizing politician has an incentive to follow

---

[11]Anthony Downs, "Why the Government Budget Is Too Small in a Democracy," *World Politics* 12, no. 4 (1960), p. 551.

a policy of minimum current expenditures until the crisis point is reached, all the while paying lip service to the problem. Economics suggests that democratic decision-making is often inconsistent with sensible *long-range* planning.

Short-Term Benefits and Government Action.   Whereas proposals with future benefits that are difficult to perceive are usually delayed, proposals with immediate benefits, at the expense of complex future costs—costs that will accrue after the next election—are very attractive to political entrepreneurs. Both office-holders and candidates have a strong incentive to support such proposals and emphasize the immediate voter benefits.

Is there any evidence that the pursuit of short-term political gains has led to inappropriate public sector action? Consider the issue of macroeconomic instability. Only recently have politicians become completely convinced that the "tightness" of labor markets can be controlled by monetary and fiscal policy. Expansionary monetary and fiscal policy can be used to "heat up" the economy and reduce the rate of unemployment in the short run. However, an overheated economy leads to inflation. The shortsightedness effect predicts that the party in power will tend to follow an expansionary policy in the 12 to 24 months before an election, even if these policies will result in future inflation. The "stabilization" policies preceding the presidential elections of the last two decades suggest that incumbent political entrepreneurs made a substantial effort to give voters the impression that the economy was strong on election day. Yet there is little doubt that expansionary macropolicy overheated the economy in each case, causing a postelection increase in the rate of inflation.

The shortsightedness effect can be a source of conflict between good politics and sound economics. Policies that are efficient from the standpoint of social benefits and costs are not necessarily the policies that will enhance a politician's election prospects. Thus it is that grossly inefficient projects may be undertaken and potentially beneficial projects may be ignored.

Bureaucratic and Political Incentives for Internal Efficiency

Government has often been charged with inaction, duplication, delays, frivolous work, and general inefficiency. These charges are difficult to document or prove. How does government compare with the private sector? Certainly a great deal of seemingly meaningless activity goes on in the private sector as well, but private firms, even those with monopoly power, can gain from actions that improve operational efficiency. There is an incentive to produce efficiently because lower cost will mean higher profits. Although the stockholders of a private firm can seldom identify good and bad individual decisions, they can easily observe a "bottom line" index of efficiency—the firm's rate of profit. In the private sector, the possibility of bankruptcy, falling stock prices, and/or a takeover bid by the management of another firm are deterrents to economic inefficiency.

Public sector decision-makers confront an incentive structure that is less conducive to operational efficiency. Since there is no easily identified index of performance analogous to the profit rate, public sector managers can often gloss over economic inefficiency. Profits do not necessarily matter. If a public sector decision-maker spends money unwisely or uses resources primarily for personal benefit (for example, plush offices, extensive "business travel," three-martini lunches), the burden of this inefficiency will fall on the taxpayer. The public sector is also not subject to the test of bankruptcy, which tends to eliminate inefficient operations in the private sector. Political finesse, which leads to large budgets, is far more important to success in the public sector than is operational efficiency, which would lead to a lower cost of production.

Taxpayers would be the major beneficiaries of reduced costs and an improvement in public sector efficiency. However, since voter-taxpayers are rationally uninformed on most issues and largely unorganized, they are unable to police the situation effectively. There is no simple summary statistic comparable to the rate of profit in the private sector that provides low-cost information to taxpayers; proof of the operational efficiency (or inefficiency) of any given division of government is generally difficult and impractical to obtain or communicate. At election time, political candidates and parties must offer something more impressive than efficiency in government if they expect to win.

A public sector manager seldom reaps personal reward by saving the taxpayers money. In fact, if an agency fails to spend this year's allocation, its case for a larger budget next year is weakened. Agencies typically go on a spending spree at the end of a budget period if they discover that they have failed to spend all of this year's appropriation.

Insofar as political officials are interested in efficiency, they will tend to choose ways of improving efficiency that are visible and simple to communicate. A well-publicized campaign to save a few dollars by eliminating limousine service for high government officials can produce greater political benefits than a complex government reorganization plan that would save taxpayers millions of dollars. The latter idea is too complex and the outcome too difficult for voters to identify.

It is important to note that the argument of internal inefficiency is not based on the assumption that employees of a bureaucratic government are necessarily lazy or incapable. Rather, the emphasis is on the incentive structure under which managers and other workers toil. No individual or relatively small group of individuals has much incentive to ensure efficiency. There is no small group of persons whose personal wealth would be significantly increased or reduced by changes in the level of efficiency. Since public officials and bureau managers spend other people's money, they are likely to be less conscious of cost than they would be with their own resources. There is no test by which to define economic inefficiency clearly or measure it accurately, much less eliminate it. The perverse incentive structure of a bureaucracy is bound to have an impact on its internal efficiency.

THE ECONOMIC ANALYSIS OF THE PUBLIC SECTOR

Most economic texts make only brief reference to the major issues discussed in this chapter. Our purpose has been to analyze how we would *expect* the public sector to handle various classes of economic issues.

In the past, economists were usually content with a discussion of what the government *should* do, regardless of how unrealistic that solution might be. Without ignoring government's ideal activities, we have extended our analysis to what, in fact, government is *likely* to do and what the outcomes of its intervention are likely to be. The broad relevance of economic tools has helped us to explain the real-world influence of public sector action on an economy's efficiency.

Is the Economic Analysis Cynical?

We have stressed how economic factors influence the workings of the public sector. Our analysis may differ considerably from that presented in a typical political science course. Some of you may object that our approach is cynical, that not enough emphasis has been given to the dedicated public servants who devote all of their energy to the resolution of complex public sector issues. Our analysis does not deny the existence of such individuals. We merely emphasize that in a legislative democracy there are pressures at work that make it difficult for these individuals to survive without compromising.

One might also argue that voters are more public spirited than we have indicated. They may be willing to sacrifice their personal welfare for the public good. However, if voters are motivated primarily by what is in the public interest, how then does one account for the behavior of trade associations, business lobbyists, labor unions, public employee groups, lawyers, physicians, teachers, developers, and hundreds of other organized groups, all attempting to adapt the rules and regulations of the public sector to their own advantage?

The test of any theory is its consistency with events in the real world. Certainly, we have not outlined a complete theory of the public sector. However, casual observation of current events should give one sufficient cause to question the validity of theories that emphasize only the public interest, equal power, and the humanitarian nature of governmental action. Democratic governments are a creation of the interactions of imperfect human beings. Many economists believe that economic theory has a great deal to say about the types of public sector actions that will result from these interactions.

The Public Sector versus the Market: A Summary

Throughout, we have argued that theory can explain why both market forces and public sector action sometimes break down—that is, why they sometimes fail to meet criteria for ideal efficiency. The deficiencies of one or the other sector often will be more or less decisive depending upon the type of economic activity. Nobel laureate Paul Samuelson has stated, "There are no rules concerning the

---

Thumbnail Sketch

These factors weaken the case for market sector allocation:

1. External costs
2. External benefits
3. Public goods
4. Monopoly
5. Uninformed consumers

These factors weaken the case for public sector intervention:

1. Voter ignorance, inability to recognize costs and benefits fully, and cost concealment
2. The power of special interests
3. The shortsightedness effect
4. Little incentive for entrepreneurial efficiency
5. Imprecision in the reflection of consumer preferences

---

proper role of government that can be established by a priori reasoning."[12] This does not mean, however, that economics has nothing to say about the *strength* of the case for either the market or the public sector in terms of specific classes of activities. Nor does it mean that social scientists have nothing to say about institutional arrangements for conducting economic activity. It merely indicates that each issue and type of activity must be considered individually.

The case for government intervention is obviously stronger for some activities than for others. For example, if an activity involves substantial external effects, market arrangements often result in economic inefficiency, and public sector action may allow for greater efficiency. Similarly, when competitive pressures are weak or there is reason to expect consumers to be poorly informed, market failure may result, and again government action may be called for. (See the Thumbnail Sketch for a summary of factors that influence the case for market or for public sector action.)

The identical analysis holds for the public sector. When there is good reason to believe that special interest influence will be strong, the case for government action to correct market failures is weakened. Similarly, the lack of a means of identifying and weeding out public sector inefficiency weakens the case for government action. More often than not, the choice of proper institutions may be a choice among evils. For example, we might expect private sector monopoly if an activity is left to the market and perverse regulation due to the special interest effect if we turn to the public sector. Understanding the shortcomings of both the market and the public sectors is important if we are to improve and adapt our current economic institutions.

At one time, economists assumed that the private sector operated according to the perfectly competitive model. In the late twentieth century, we have sometimes assumed that government operates so as to fulfill the conditions of ideal efficiency established by economists. Both assumptions, of course, are simplistic. The application of economics to public choice helps us to understand why public policy sometimes goes astray and how public sector incentives might be altered to improve the efficiency of government action.

LOOKING AHEAD

Once we understand the sources of economic inefficiency, we are in a better position to suggest potential remedies. We close this section with a perspective that considers reforms for dealing with the political power of special interest issues.

CHAPTER LEARNING OBJECTIVES

1 It is fruitful to analyze the public sector in the same way in which we analyze the private sector. Collective action, through government, has the potential for correcting market failures and redistributing income. The public sector is an alternative to the market—it provides an alternative means of organizing production and/or distributing output.

2 Voters cast ballots, make political contributions, lobby, and adopt other political strategies to demand public sector action. Other things constant, voters have a strong incentive to support the candidate who offers them the greatest personal gain relative

---

[12]P. A. Samuelson, "The Economic Role of Private Activity," in *The Collected Scientific Papers of Paul A. Samuelson,* ed. J. E. Stiglitz, vol. 2 (Cambridge, Massachusetts: MIT Press, 1966), p. 1423.

PERSPECTIVES IN ECONOMICS
DEALING WITH SPECIAL INTERESTS

The special interest effect indicates that in the legislative process, a small group that is strongly interested in an issue may wield great influence. On that issue, the group may prevail over the interests of the majority of voters if most of those in the majority have only a small stake in the outcome. The majority voters are unlikely to be organized, to lobby effectively, or even to know how a politician voted on the issue. In addition, the bundle purchase problem reinforces the special interest effect. Only those with intense feelings about the issues are likely to let this single issue determine how they will cast the only vote they have.

Could political institutions be changed in a manner that would diminish the power of special interests? Although there are no easy solutions, we can suggest several steps that could be taken to help bring the personal interests of politicians into greater harmony with economic efficiency.

1. Force Legislators to Establish a Budget Constraint—a Maximum Level of Government Spending—as Their First Act during Each Legislative Session. The current system of appropriations for individual budget items permits legislators to cater to special interests without ever having to take a clear stand on economy in government. Essentially, the public treasury is treated as a common pool resource, available to anyone with political influence. Individuals in a household must make choices within the framework of a fixed budget constraint, in which more butter means less bread. In contrast, legislators are not so rigidly constrained. They can vote for more butter and pass the bill on to the unorganized taxpayers while maintaining the same level of spending on bread. In general, the system fails to force legislators to make careful choices within the framework of a fixed budget.

This defect, which favors special interest groups, could be corrected if a fixed budget were established at the beginning of each legislative session.[13] Then the issue of additional government spending versus lower taxes could be debated solely on the merits of each alternative. In contrast with the current system, a legislator's single vote on the size of the government's budget would provide voters with a reliable index of that legislator's support of taxpayer interests and governmental economic efficiency.

Once the size of the budget was determined, then and only then would appropriation decisions be made. Each special interest would then be pitted, not against the taxpayer, but against other special interests pursuing government moneys. The Department of Defense would have to convince legislators that additional Pentagon spending was more meritorious than additional spending on welfare, education, social security, college student loans, and/or subsidies to industrial interests. The Department of Education would have to argue that expanding appropriations would be more important than, for example, additional environmental spending. No longer could special interests so easily tap the public treasury when they sought additional funds.

2. Make More Use of Referenda in the Resolution of Special Interest Issues. When a decision is resolved by referendum, the special interest is much less likely to prevail, unless majority interests are also served. A referendum enables each member of the unorganized majority to register her or his opposition—albeit mild opposition—to a special interest issue *independent of other issues.* Voters need less information to determine and register their views, since alternative positions of political middlemen (legislators) on the issue are irrelevant. In contrast with legislative decision-making, a referendum virtually eliminates vote trading (so-called logrolling—"You support my special issue and I'll support yours") as a means to gain passage of legislation favored by interest groups. All of these factors make the referendum an attractive—if seldom used—means of undermining the power of special interests.[14]

3. Establish a Constitutional Budget Constraint Limiting the Size of Government as a Share of Total Income. Some believe that only a constitutional amendment limiting the amount of government expenditures would restore the balance between the interests of concentrated groups and unorganized taxpayers. Such a spending ceiling would limit the ability of legislators to grant the requests of powerful special interest groups. Special interest groups would be pitted against one another, rather than against the widely dispersed, unorganized taxpayers. Several states have adopted spending limitation amendments. A federal spending limitation is likely to be a hotly debated issue during the 1980s.

Discussion

1. Explain why you either favor or oppose each of the three suggestions outlined in this perspective. Do you think that any of these suggestions would prove effective?

2. How do you think that organized industrial interests, unions, professional associations, and bureaucrats would react to these proposals? Why?

---

[13]This procedure—establishing the size of the budget *before* funds are appropriated for specific programs—has been followed by the Wisconsin state legislature in recent years.

[14]See James D. Gwartney and Jonathan Silberman, "Distribution of Costs and Benefits and the Significance of Collective Decision Rules," *Social Science Quarterly,* (December 1973), pp. 568–578, for a more complete analysis of why referendum decision-making limits the power of special interest groups.

to personal costs. Obtaining information is costly. Since group decision-making breaks the link between the choice of the individual and the outcome of the issue, it is rational for voters to remain uninformed on many issues. Candidates are generally evaluated on the basis of a small subset of issues that are of the greatest personal importance to individual voters.

3   Market failure presents government with an opportunity to undertake action that will result in greater benefits/costs. Other things constant, the greater the social loss resulting from the market failure, the stronger is the incentive for public sector action.

4   A growing portion of public sector activity involves income redistribution. Economic analysis indicates two potential sources of pressure for income redistribution: (a) the public-good nature of antipoverty efforts and (b) self-interest. From the viewpoint of a vote-maximizing entrepreneur, there is incentive to support redistribution from unorganized to well-organized groups. Considerable income redistribution in the United States is of this type.

5   There is a strong incentive for political entrepreneurs to support special interest issues and to make the issues difficult for the unorganized, largely uninformed majority to understand. Special interest groups supply both financial and direct elective support to the politician.

6   Because of imperfect voter information, proposals whose benefits are elusive and whose costs are clear-cut tend to be rejected, even though they might promote the community's welfare. Counterproductive policies whose benefits are easily recognizable and whose costs are difficult to identify tend to be accepted. There is a strong incentive for politicians to package public policy in a manner that amplifies the benefits and conceals the costs imposed on voters.

7   The shortsightedness effect is another potential source of conflict between good politics and sound economics. Both voters and politicians tend to support projects that promise substantial current benefits at the expense of difficult-to-identify future costs. There is a bias against legislation that involves immediate and easily identifiable costs but complex future benefits.

8   The economic incentive for operational efficiency is small for public sector action. No individual or relatively small group of individuals can capture the gains derived from improved operational efficiency. There is no force analogous to the threat of bankruptcy in the private sector that will bring inefficient behavior to a halt. Since public sector resources, including tax funds, are communally owned, their users are less likely than private resource owners to be cost conscious.

9   Positive economics cannot tell us whether an action should be conducted in the public or in the market sector. However, analysis of how both sectors operate does help build the case for conducting any given activity in either sector. When market failure is prevalent, the case for public sector action is strengthened. On the other hand, expectation of government failure reduces the strength of the argument for government intervention.

THE ECONOMIC WAY OF THINKING — DISCUSSION QUESTIONS

1   Do you think that advertising exerts more influence on the type of car chosen by a consumer than on the type of politician chosen by the same person? Explain your answer.

2   Do you think that the political process works to the advantage of the poor? Explain. Are the poor well organized? Do they make substantial campaign contributions to candidates? Are they likely to be well informed? Is it surprising that a large amount of the approximately $300 billion of cash income transfer payments in the United States does not go to the poor? Explain.

3   Which of the following public sector actions are designed primarily to correct

"market failure": (a) laws against fraud, (b) truth-in-lending legislation, (c) rate regulation in the telephone industry, (d) legislation setting emission control standards, (e) subsidization of pure research, (f) operation of the Post Office? Explain your answer.

4 Do political entrepreneurs ever have an incentive to deceive voters about the cost of legislation? If so, when? Can you give any examples of cases in which this has happened?

5 The liquor industry contributes a large share of the political funds to political contests on the state level. Yet its contributions to candidates for national office are minimal. Why do you think this is true? (*Hint:* Who regulates the liquor industry?)

6 One explanation for the shortsightedness effect in the public sector is that future voters cannot vote now to represent their future interests. Are the interests of future generations represented in market decisions? For example, if the price of chromium were expected to rise rapidly over the next 30 years due to increased scarcity, how could speculators grow rich while providing the next generation with more chromium at the expense of current consumers?

7 What's Wrong with This Way of Thinking?

"Public policy is necessary to protect the average citizen from the power of vested interest groups. In the absence of government intervention, regulated industries, such as airlines, railroads, and trucking, would charge excessive prices, products would be unsafe, and the rich would oppress the poor. Government curbs the power of special interest groups."

PART FIVE

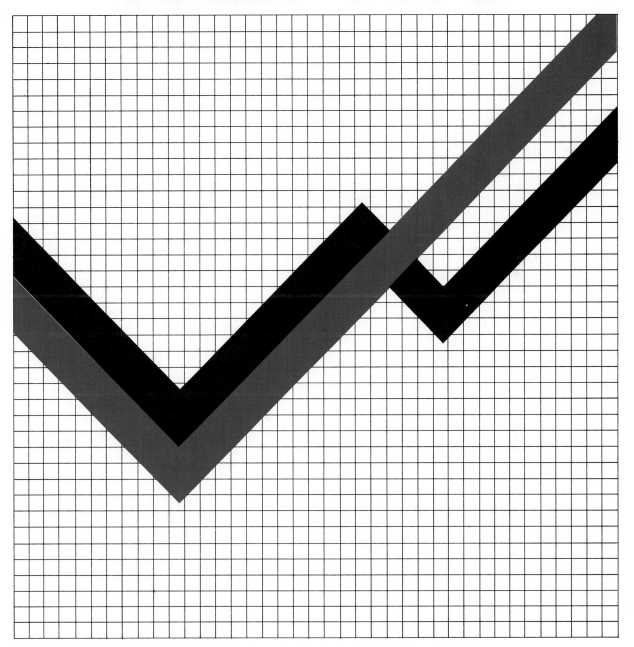

INTERNATIONAL ECONOMICS

21

GAINING FROM INTERNATIONAL TRADE

We live in a shrinking world. Wheat raised on the flatlands of western Kansas may be processed into bread in a Russian factory. The breakfast of many Americans might include bananas from Honduras, coffee from Brazil, or hot chocolate made from Nigerian cocoa beans. The volume of world trade, enhanced by improved transportation and communications, has grown rapidly in recent years. In 1979, the total trade among nations was approximately $3 trillion. Approximately 16 percent of the world's total output is now sold in a different country than that in which it was produced—double the figure of two decades ago.

In this chapter, we will analyze the impact of foreign trade on the price, consumption, and domestic production of goods. The effects of trade restrictions, such as tariffs and quotas, will also be considered. International trade is an area of economics where fallacies seem to abound. Indirect effects are often ignored. As we progress, we will discuss several examples of economic nonreasoning.

THE COMPOSITION OF THE INTERNATIONAL SECTOR

As Exhibit 1 shows, the size of the trade sector varies among nations. International trade comprises more than two-fifths of the GNP of the Netherlands and approximately one-quarter of the GNP in Sweden, Canada, West Germany, and the United Kingdom. The relative size of the trade sector is smaller for Japan, Australia, and the United States. Approximately 9 percent of the GNP in the United States results from trade.

However, the size of the international sector relative to GNP may actually understate the importance of trade. Many of the products we purchase from foreigners would be much more costly if we were dependent solely on our domestic production. We are dependent on foreign producers for several products, including almost all of our coffee and bananas, more than 90 percent of the bauxite we use to make aluminum, all of our chromium, diamonds,

---

[1]Adam Smith, *An Inquiry into the Nature and Causes of the Wealth of Nations* (1776; Cannan's ed., Chicago: University of Chicago Press, 1976), pp. 478–479.

EXHIBIT 1   The size of the trade sector for selected countries, 1980

Country	International Trade as Percentage of GNP
Netherlands	45
Sweden	28
Canada	24
West Germany	23
United Kingdom	23
France	19
Australia	13
Japan	13
United States	9

U.S. Department of Commerce.

and tin, and most of our cobalt, nickel, manganese, and asbestos. The life-style of Americans (as well as that of our trading partners) would be changed if international trade were halted.

Exhibits 2 and 3 summarize the leading products imported and exported by the United States. Petroleum comprised 31 percent of the dollar value of all

EXHIBIT 2   The major import products of the United States, 1980

Petroleum, machinery, and automobiles were the major products imported by the United States in 1980.

Statistical Abstract of the United States—1981.

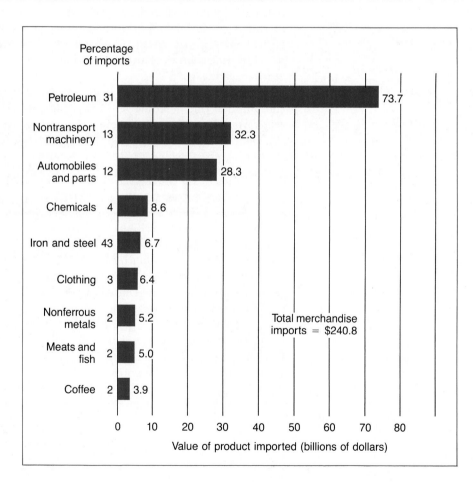

merchandise imports of Americans in 1980 (Exhibit 2). As recently as 1973, petroleum imports accounted for only 11 percent of our total imports. Needless to say, there has been a sharp increase in the dollar value of U.S. petroleum imports. In addition, automobiles, machinery (both electrical and nonelectrical), chemicals, and steel mill products are among the leading import items.

Exhibit 3 lists the major merchandise exports of the United States. Three items—chemicals, motor vehicles, and grains—comprise 24 percent of the total. Aircraft, metals, and mineral fuels (primarily coal) are also among the leading export products.

The structure of U.S. trade has changed during the last decade. Agricultural products (wheat, corn, and rice) and high-technology manufacturing products (for example, aircraft, computers, and machine tools) have comprised an increasing share of our total exports. Foreign producers have supplied more and more import products to our domestic markets in such established industries as steel, textiles, automobiles, and, of course, crude petroleum.

With which countries does the United States trade? As Exhibit 4 shows, Canada heads the list. In 1980, slightly less than one-fifth of the total U.S. volume of trade was with Canada. Japan, Mexico, and the nations of the European Economic Community (particularly West Germany, the United Kingdom, France, and Italy) are also among the leading trading partners of the

EXHIBIT 3 The major export products of the United States, 1980

Chemicals, motor vehicles, and grains were the major products exported by the United States in 1980.

Statistical Abstract of the United States—1981.

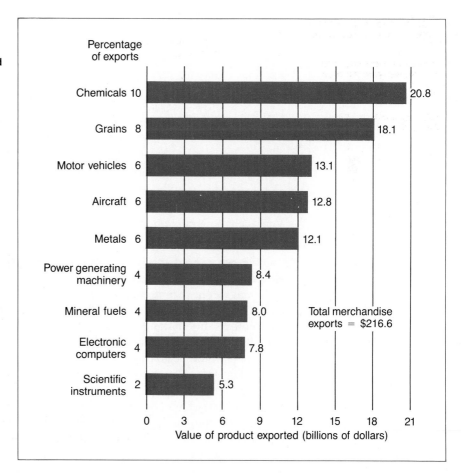

EXHIBIT 4 The leading trading partners of the United States, 1980

Canada, Japan, Mexico, and Western European countries are the leading trading partners of the United States. An increasing share of U.S. trade is with petroleum-producing countries, such as Saudi Arabia and Venezuela.

U.S. Department of Commerce.

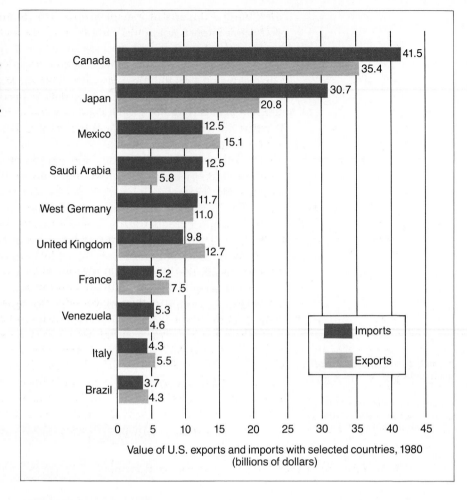

Value of U.S. exports and imports with selected countries, 1980
(billions of dollars)

United States. More than half of the U.S. trade in 1980 was with Canada, Japan, and the industrial nations of Western Europe. Beginning in the mid-1970s, U.S. trade with the petroleum-exporting countries grew rapidly. Saudi Arabia and Venezuela now rank among the leading trading partners of the United States.

COMPARATIVE ADVANTAGE AND TRADE BETWEEN NATIONS

Although we speak of international trade, for the most part the exchanges take place between individuals (or business firms) that happen to be located in different countries. International trade, like other voluntary exchange, results because both the buyer and the seller gain from it. If both parties did not expect to gain, there would be no trade.

The law of comparative advantage, which we discussed in detail in Chapter 2, explains why mutual gains arise from specialization and exchange. According to the law of comparative advantage, trading partners gain by specializing in the production of goods for which they are low opportunity cost producers and trading for those goods for which they are high opportunity cost producers. This specialization in the area of one's comparative advantage minimizes the cost of production and leads to a *maximum joint output* between trading partners.

Both international trading partners can gain if they specialize in those things that they do best. We know that the resource base varies among nations. Countries with warm, moist climates such as Brazil and Colombia specialize in the production of coffee. Land is abundant in sparsely populated nations such as Canada and Australia. These nations tend to specialize in land-intensive products, such as wheat, feed grains, and beef. In contrast, land is scarce in Japan, a nation with a highly skilled labor force. Therefore, the Japanese specialize in manufacturing, using their comparative advantage to produce cameras, automobiles, and steel products for export.

It is easy to see why trade and specialization expand joint output and lead to mutual gain when the resource bases of regions differ substantially. However, even when resource differences among nations are less dramatic, mutually advantageous trade is usually possible. Exhibit 5 illustrates this point. Here we consider the possibilities for the production of bicycles and wine in two countries, France and the United States. Initially, we analyze the situation in the absence of specialization and trade; then we consider the impact of trade. For simplicity's sake, we limit our analysis to just two countries and two goods.

Absolute Advantage: A situation in which a nation, as the result of its previous experience and/or natural endowments, can produce a product with fewer resources than another nation.

Suppose that France employs 2 million workers in these two industries, and the United States employs 4 million. The output per worker of both bicycles and wine is higher for France than for the United States. Perhaps due to its previous experience, France has an **absolute advantage** in the production of both commodities. French workers can make four bicycles per day, compared to only three per day for U.S. workers. Similarly, French workers are able to produce 20 bottles of wine per day, compared to only 10 bottles per day for U.S workers.

EXHIBIT 5 Comparative advantage and gains from international trade

Country	(1) Number of Workers (Millions)	(2) Output per Worker per Day[a]	(3) Total Output without Specialization[b]	(4) Total Output with Specialization	(5) Consumption after Trade[c]
France	2	4 bicycles *or* 20 bottles of wine	4 million bicycles *and* 20 million bottles of wine	0 bicycles *and* 40 million bottles of wine	5 million bicycles *and* 20 million bottles of wine
United States	4	3 bicycles *or* 10 bottles of wine	6 million bicycles *and* 20 million bottles of wine	12 million bicycles *and* 0 bottles of wine	7 million bicycles *and* 20 million bottles of wine
Combined	6	—	10 million bicycles *and* 40 million bottles of wine	12 million bicycles *and* 40 million bottles of wine	12 million bicycles *and* 40 million bottles of wine

[a]*For simplicity, we assume that the output per worker is constant for both products.*
[b]*Assuming that equal numbers of workers are employed in the bicycle and wine industries.*
[c]*Assuming that the international price of bicycles is 4 times the price of a bottle of wine.*

Exhibit 5, column 3, illustrates the total output of bicycles and wine in both France and the United States in the absence of trade. Assuming that the work force of each country is equally divided between the two industries, 2 million French workers produce 4 million bicycles and 20 million bottles of wine. In the United States, workers produce 6 million bicycles and 20 million bottles of wine. Prior to specialization and trade, the aggregate output of the two countries is 10 million bicycles and 40 million bottles of wine.

Given that French workers are more efficient at producing both bicycles and wine than their U.S. counterparts, are gains from trade possible? The answer is yes, because the opportunity costs of production in the two countries differ. For French workers, the opportunity cost of a bicycle is five bottles of wine. In the United States, the opportunity cost of a bicycle is only three and one-third bottles of wine. Therefore, U.S. workers are the low opportunity cost producers of bicycles, even though they cannot produce as many per day as the French workers. As column 4 illustrates, when the 4 million U.S. workers specialize in the production of bicycles, they can produce 12 million per day. Simultaneously, if the 2 million French workers specialize in the production of wine, they can produce 40 million bottles per day. Therefore, with specialization, the combined output will be 12 million bicycles and 40 million bottles of wine per day, an increase of 2 million bicycles compared to the no-trade situation. If the price of a bicycle is 4 bottles of wine (an "intermediate price"), France will be able to trade 20 million bottles of wine for 5 million U.S.-produced bicycles.

As Exhibit 5, column 5, shows, after specialization and trade, each country will be able to consume 1 million more bicycles per day compared to the no-trade situation. Both countries gain from the specialization in the production of the commodities for which they are low opportunity cost producers.

Thus far, we have ignored transportation costs. Of course, transportation costs reduce the potential gains from trade. Sometimes transportation costs, both real and artificially imposed, exceed the mutual gain. (See "Frédéric Bastiat on Obstacles to Gains from Trade.") When this is so, exchange does not occur. However, this does not negate the law of comparative advantage.

According to the law of comparative advantage, the joint output of two trading nations will be greatest when each nation specializes in the production of those products for which it is a low opportunity cost producer and trades them for those goods for which it is a high opportunity cost producer. Mutual gain to each trading nation will result from such specialization and exchange.

The Export–Import Link

Confusion about the merit of international trade often results because people do not consider all the consequences. Why are other nations willing to export their goods to the United States? So they can obtain dollars. Yes, but why do they want dollars? Would foreigners be willing to continue exporting oil, radios, watches, cameras, automobiles, and thousands of other valuable products to us in exchange for pieces of paper? If so, we could all be semiretired, spending only an occasional workday at the dollar printing press office! Of course, foreigners are not so naïve. They trade goods for dollars so they can use the dollars to import goods and purchase ownership rights to U.S. assets.

Exports provide the buying power that makes it possible for a nation to import other goods. Nations export goods so that they will be able to import foreign products. If a nation does not import goods from foreigners, foreigners will not have the purchasing power to buy that nation's export products. Thus, the exports and imports of a nation are closely linked.

Supply, Demand, and International Trade

How does international trade affect prices and output levels in domestic markets? Supply and demand analysis will help us answer this question. High transportation costs and the availability of cheaper alternatives elsewhere diminish the attractiveness of some U.S. products to foreigners. These factors may completely eliminate foreign purchases of some commodities. However, foreign consumers will find that many U.S. products are cheaper even when transportation costs are considered. When this is the case, the demand of foreigners will supplement that of domestic consumers.

In an open economy, the market demand curve for domestic products is the horizontal sum of the domestic and foreign demand. Exhibit 6 illustrates the impact of foreign demand on the domestic wheat market. When the demand of foreigners is added to the domestic demand, it yields the market demand curve D_{f+d} (where the subscripts f and d refer to foreign and domestic, respectively). Price P brings supply and demand into equilibrium. At the equilibrium market price, foreigners purchase OF units of wheat, and domestic consumers purchase FQ. The competition from foreign consumers results in both higher wheat prices and a higher output level.

At first glance, it appears that the entry of foreign consumers into the U.S. market has helped U.S. wheat producers at the expense of domestic consumers, who must now pay higher wheat prices (or else do without). That view is correct as far as it goes, but it ignores the secondary effects. How will foreigners obtain the purchasing power to import U.S. wheat? Primarily by exporting products for which they are low-cost producers to the U.S. market. The domestic supply of the products exported by foreigners to pay for the wheat will expand. The prices of those foreign products will be reduced (relative to the no-trade situation), actually benefiting the U.S. consumers who appeared at first to be harmed by the higher wheat prices.

Exhibit 7 uses the case of foreign banana imports to illustrate this point. The total supply of bananas to the U.S. market is the horizontal sum of (a) the

EXHIBIT 6 Exporting to foreigners

The demand of both foreign and domestic purchasers of U.S. wheat is shown here. The market demand (D_{f+d}) is the horizontal sum of these two components. Total domestic production of the product would be OQ, of which OF would be exported and FQ consumed domestically.

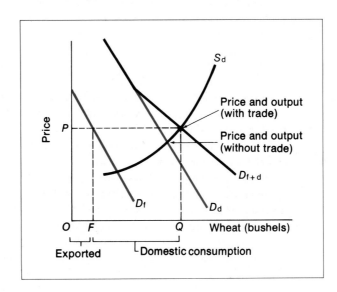

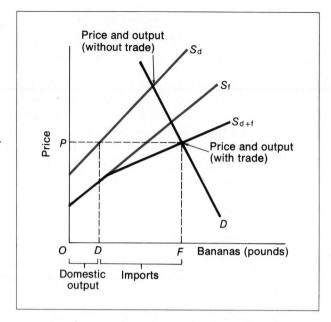

foreign supply to the domestic market plus (b) the supply of domestic producers. Since foreign countries, particularly Honduras, are low opportunity cost producers of bananas, they are able to supply this product to the U.S. market more cheaply than most domestic producers. The addition of the imported supply results in both lower prices and a higher consumption level than would exist in the absence of trade.

Relative to the no-trade alternative, international trade and specialization result in lower prices (and higher consumption levels) for imported products and higher prices (and lower consumption levels) for exported products. However, as the law of comparative advantage reveals, the net effect is an expansion in the consumption alternatives available to a nation.

RESTRICTIONS TO TRADE

Despite the potential benefits from free trade, almost all nations have erected trade barriers. What kinds of barriers are erected? Why are they used? Three factors contribute to the existence of trade barriers: sound arguments for the protection of specific industries under certain circumstances; economic illiteracy—ignorance as to who is helped and who is harmed by trade restrictions; and the special interest nature of trade restrictions.

Tariffs and Quotas

Tariff: A tax that is levied on goods imported into a country.

Tariffs and quotas are the two most commonly used trade-restricting devices. A **tariff** is nothing more than a tax on foreign imports. As Exhibit 8 shows, tariff barriers in the United States have fluctuated. Until the 1940s, tariffs of between 30 and 50 percent of product value were often levied. In recent years, the average tariff rate has been approximately 10 percent.

Exhibit 9 illustrates the impact of a tariff on sugar. In the absence of a tariff, the world market price of sugar is P_w. At that price, U.S. consumers

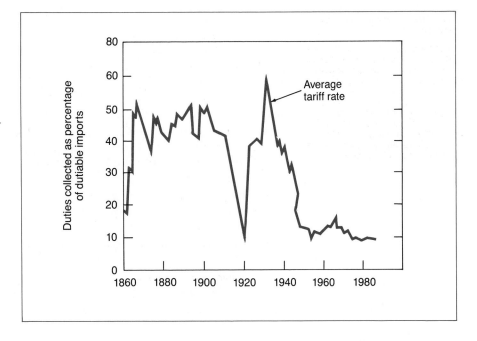

purchase Q_1 units. Domestic producers supply Q_{d1}, while foreigners supply Q_1 minus Q_{d1} units to the U.S. market. When the United States levies a tariff t on sugar, Americans can no longer buy sugar at the world price. U.S. consumers have to pay $P_w + t$ in order to purchase sugar from foreigners. Thus, the market price rises to $P_w + t$. At that price, domestic consumers demand Q_2 units (Q_{d2} supplied by domestic producers and $Q_2 - Q_{d2}$ supplied by foreigners).

Imports decline with the imposition of a tariff. In contrast, domestic producers, since they do not pay the tariff, actually expand their output in

EXHIBIT 9   Impact of a tariff

Here we illustrate the impact of a tariff on sugar. In the absence of the tariff, the world price of sugar is P_w: U.S. consumers purchase Q_1 units (Q_{d1} from domestic producers plus $Q_1 - Q_{d1}$ from foreign producers). The tariff makes it more costly for Americans to purchase sugar from foreigners. Imports decline with the imposition of the tariff. A higher domestic price ($P_w + t$) of sugar and a lower consumption level (Q_2) result.

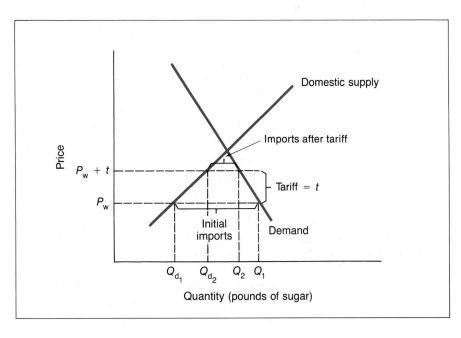

response to the higher market price. In effect, the tariff acts as a subsidy to domestic producers. It is financed by consumers, who as a result face higher prices.

The story does not end here. Since foreigners are unable to sell goods for which they are low-cost producers in the U.S. market, they acquire fewer dollars. Foreign demand for U.S. exports, products for which we are low-cost producers, declines because our trade restrictions have diminished the ability of foreigners to acquire the dollars necessary to buy our goods. Potential gains from specialization and trade go unrealized.

Import Quota: A specific quantity (or value) of a good that is permitted to be imported into a country during a given year.

An **import quota,** like a tariff, is designed to restrict foreign goods and protect domestic industries. A quota places a ceiling on the amount of a product that can be imported during a given period (typically a year). Many products, ranging from steel to brooms, are subject to import quotas.

Since quotas reduce the foreign supply to the domestic market, the price of quota-protected products is higher than that which would result from free trade. In many ways, quotas are more harmful than tariffs. With a quota, additional foreign supply is prohibited regardless of how low the prices of foreign products are. With a tariff, products are at least supplied to the domestic market if the cost advantage of foreign producers is sufficient to overcome the tariff.

Some Sound Arguments for Restrictions

There are three major, and at least partially valid, arguments for protecting certain domestic industries from foreign competitors.

1. National Defense Argument. Certain industries—aircraft, petroleum, and weapons, for example—are vital to national defense. A nation might want to protect such industries from foreign competitors so that a domestic supply of these materials would be available in case of an international conflict. Would we want to be entirely dependent on Arabian or Russian petroleum? Would complete dependence on French aircraft be wise? Most Americans would answer no, even if trade restrictions were required to preserve these domestic industries.

The national defense argument is sound; however, it can be abused. Relatively few industries are truly vital to our national defense. Partial reliance on foreign producers during peacetime may not weaken the capacity of certain domestic industries, particularly those that extract raw materials, to supply the nation's needs in case of war. When the merits of protecting a domestic industry are analyzed, the costs and benefits involved in the national defense argument must be weighed carefully.

2. The Industrial Diversity Argument. Economies that are largely dependent on the revenues from a few major export products or raw materials are characterized by instability. If a domestic economy specializes in the production of only one or two major goods, changes in world demand can exert a drastic influence on domestic economic conditions. Brazil's coffee-dominated economy is an example. Protection of domestic industries would encourage diversity. Clearly, this argument does not apply to the U.S. economy, which is already highly diversified.

3. The Infant-Industry Argument. The advocates of this view hold that new domestic industries should be protected from older, established foreign compet-

"Free trade with low-wage countries such as China and India would cause the wages of U.S. workers to fall."

Many Americans believe that trade restrictions are necessary to protect U.S. workers from imported goods produced by cheap foreign labor. How can U.S. labor compete with Indian and Chinese workers receiving 50 cents an hour? The fallacy of this argument stems from a misunderstanding of both the source of high wages and the law of comparative advantage.

High *hourly wages* do not necessarily mean high *per unit labor cost*. Labor productivity must also be considered. For example, suppose that a U.S. steel worker receives an hourly wage rate of $12. A steel worker in India receives only $1.20 per hour. Given the capital and production methods used in the two countries, however, the U.S. worker produces 20 times as many tons of steel per worker-hour as the Indian worker. Be-cause of the higher productivity per worker-hour, per unit labor cost is actually lower in the United States than in India!

Labor in the United States possesses a high skill level and works with large amounts of capital equipment. These factors contribute to the high productivity and the high hourly wages of American workers. Similarly, low productivity per worker-hour is the primary reason for low wages in such countries as India and China.

However, the availability of capital and the high productivity of the U.S. labor force do not mean that we can produce everything at a lower opportunity cost than foreigners. Low-wage countries are likely to have a comparative advantage in the production of labor-intensive products. When other countries can produce wigs, watches, textile goods, sugar, coffee, and miniature radios more cheaply than domestic producers, we can gain from specialization and trade. Importation of these products allows us to free labor (and capital) resources so we in turn can export more wheat, feed grains, airplanes, and electrical equipment, products for which we are low-cost producers. The net result is a reallocation of U.S. workers away from industries in which they are inefficient (relative to foreign producers) to industries in which they are highly efficient.

If foreigners, even low-wage foreigners, will sell us products that are cheaper than the products we our-selves could produce, we can gain by using our resources to produce other things. Perhaps an extreme example will illustrate the point. Suppose that a foreign producer, perhaps a Santa Claus who pays workers little or noth-ing, were willing to supply us with free winter coats. Would it make sense to enact a tariff barrier to keep out the free coats? Of course not. Resources that were previously used to produce coats could now be freed to produce other goods. Output and the availability of goods would expand. The real wages of U.S. workers would rise. National defense aside, it makes no more sense to erect trade barriers to keep out cheap foreign goods than to keep out the free coats of a friendly, foreign Santa Claus.

itors. As the new industry matures, it will be able to stand on its own feet and compete effectively with foreign producers. The infant-industry argument has a long and somewhat notorious history. Alexander Hamilton used it to argue for the protection of early U.S. manufacturing. While it is clearly an argument for *temporary* protection, the protection, once granted, is often difficult to remove. Nearly a century ago, this argument was used to gain tariff protection for the young steel industry in the United States. Today, not only is this industry mature, but many believe that competitive pressures are less than vigorous. Yet public policy has failed to remove the tariff.

Trade Barriers and Jobs   Part of the popularity of trade restrictions stems from their ability to protect or create *easily identifiable jobs*. Whenever foreign competitors begin to make inroads into markets that have traditionally been supplied by domestic producers, the outcry for "protection to save jobs" is sure to be raised. Political entrepreneurs recognize the potential gain from a protectionist policy and respond accordingly.

The recent history of the automobile industry in the United States illustrates this point. During the 1970s, imported automobiles gained a larger and larger share of the U.S. market. There were several reasons for these gains. High wages in the U.S. auto industry, improved efficiency of foreign producers, excessive government regulation of the domestic auto industry, and failure of U.S. producers to shift to small cars as gasoline prices soared were all contributing factors. The increased competition from imports caused both management and labor to seek trade restrictions.

The Reagan administration, firmly on record as favoring free trade, was reluctant to request either tariffs or quotas. Nonetheless, the administration bargained with the Japanese government, which eventually agreed to restrict "voluntarily" the number of Japanese automobiles sold in the U.S. market to 1.6 million. As is the case with quotas, these voluntary restrictions will result in higher consumer prices for automobiles. The maximum price that 1.6 million Japanese automobiles can command in the U.S. market will be the same whether they are subject to a quota or to restrictions imposed by the Japanese government. There is no reason to believe that Japanese firms and car dealers will charge less than a market equilibrium price for the 1.6 million cars. In addition, the import restrictions will lessen competition in the U.S. market, reducing the pressure on U.S. producers and workers to compete effectively.

The restrictions will also exert a secondary effect that usually goes unnoticed. Since the Japanese will be selling fewer automobiles in the U.S. market, they will earn fewer dollars with which to purchase grains, lumber, chemicals, and other U.S. export products. Workers in export industries will be hurt as the Japanese demand for their products declines. Jobs in these industries will be destroyed. Interestingly, the wage rates in most of these export industries are approximately half the wage rates of the automobile workers who will be helped by the restrictions.

In the long run, trade restrictions such as quotas, tariffs, and allegedly voluntary limitations can neither create nor destroy jobs. Jobs protected by import restrictions will be offset by jobs destroyed in export industries. The choice is not whether automobiles (or some other product) will be produced in the United States or Japan. The real question is (a) whether our resources will be used to produce automobiles and other products for which we are a high opportunity cost producer or (b) whether the resources will be used for agriculture, high-technology manufactured goods, and other products for which we are a low-cost producer.

What about industries that are long-time recipients of protection? Of course, sudden and complete removal of trade barriers would harm producers and workers. It would be costly to effect an immediate transfer of the protected resources to other areas and industries. Gradual removal of such barriers would minimize the costs of relocation and eliminate the shock effect. The government might also cushion the burden by subsidizing the retraining and relocation costs of displaced workers.

Protection of Special Interests

Even when trade restrictions promote inefficiency and harm economic welfare, political entrepreneurs may be able to reap political gain from their enactment. Those harmed by a protectionist policy for industry X will bear individually a small and difficult-to-identify cost. Consumers who will pay higher prices for the products of a protected industry are an unorganized group. Most of them will not associate the higher product prices with the protectionist policy. Similarly, numerous export producers (and their employees) will *individually* be harmed only slightly. The rational ignorance effect implies that those harmed by trade restrictions are likely to be uninformed and unconcerned about our trade policy.

In contrast, special interest groups—specific industries, unions, and regions—will be highly concerned with the protection of their industries. They will be ready to aid political entrepreneurs who support their views and penalize those who do not. Clearly, vote-seeking politicians will be sensitive to the special interest views.

Often, there will be a conflict between sound economics and good politics on trade restriction issues. Real-world public policy will, of course, reflect the politics of the situation.

Export Taxes, International Trade, and the OPEC Cartel

The law of comparative advantage explains why the *joint* output of nations is maximized by free trade. What about the economic welfare of a single nation? Can *one* of the trading partners gain if it imposes certain trade restrictions? Unilateral gain is possible if certain conditions are met. First, if an exporting nation is to gain from restrictions, it must be able to eliminate (or collude with) all other sources of substantial supply. An importing nation will simply buy from another seller if a small seller acts independently. Second, the demand of importers for the product must be inelastic, preferably highly inelastic. If the product demand is elastic, the bargaining position of the exporter will be substantially diminished. Third, the producers must be able to alter the quantity supplied at a low cost. This condition implies the supply curve of the exporter is elastic.

Exhibit 10 illustrates the mechanics of unilateral action when the demand of the importing country is inelastic and the supply of the exporting nation (or cartel of nations) is elastic. Under these circumstances, the exporting nation can gain by imposing an export tax on the product. The total revenue derived from the importing country will actually increase, even though a smaller *quantity* of the product is sold. The burden of the export tax falls on the importing nations. Note that the price of the product does not fall very much (from *AD* to *AP*), since the supply is elastic.[3] Like a monopolist, an exporting nation can gain by restricting output and raising prices if the demand of importers is inelastic.

This analysis helps us understand why OPEC nations were able to gain by substantially raising the price (or the export tax) on crude oil in the mid-1970s. Since the demand of the oil-importing nations was highly inelastic, at least in the short run, the primary burden of the high crude-oil prices (or export taxes) fell on the importers. The OPEC strategy would not have worked if all of the major oil-exporting nations had not cooperated. Suppose that a single country, Venezuela, for example, had imposed a heavy export tax on oil in 1970. Oil-importing nations would simply have purchased crude oil from other nations. Thus, it was necessary for the oil-exporting nations to form a cartel if their strategy was to work.

EXHIBIT 10   Gains from an export tax when demand is inelastic relative to supply

If the demand by foreigners for an export product of a nation is inelastic (and the foreign supply is elastic), a nation (or cartel of nations) can obtain unilateral gains if it imposes a tax on the export product. As illustrated here, after the imposition of tax *t*, the total revenue derived from the foreign consumers of the product increases from *ABCD* to *AB′C′D′*, *even though the number of units exported declines.* The primary burden of the tax falls on the foreign consumers, since the demand for the export product is inelastic relative to supply.

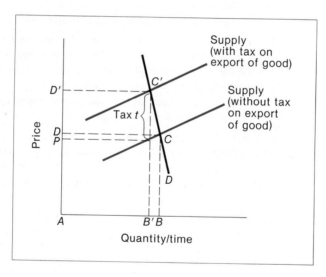

[3]On the other hand, if the demand of the importing country were elastic and the supply of the exporting country were inelastic, the burden of an export tax would fall on the producers of the exported product. The price (including the tax) of the product to foreign consumers would not rise substantially, whereas the price (less the tax) received by the producers of the exported product would decline sharply. When importing nations can produce the good domestically (or obtain it from another source) at a cost only slightly higher than the cost of importing, the demand for the exported product will be elastic. Under these circumstances, the burden of an export tax falls primarily on the producers of the exported product. As an exercise, construct a graph illustrating this case.

Many Americans have voiced support for the imposition by the United States of an export tax on wheat (or other steps that would raise the export price of wheat) as a means of retaliating against the oil price-fixing policies of OPEC. Since the demand of OPEC nations for U.S. wheat is likely to be elastic—there are many good substitutes for U.S. wheat—economic analysis suggests that such a strategy would be ineffective.

There are risks associated with this strategy of imposing an export tax (or forming a cartel of exporters). First, *new entrants* must be prevented from undercutting the cartel price if it is substantially higher than the competitive level. In the case of petroleum, Nature greatly reduced the difficulty of this task. Second, high prices induce importers to search for and use substitutes. With time, the importing nations develop substitutes and discover ways to reduce their consumption of the more expensive product. Eventually, as even OPEC discovered in the early 1980s, this process may significantly reduce the amount demanded from the cartel. Third, the theory of oligopoly indicates that there is an incentive for members of a cartel to cheat. As market conditions become less favorable to the cartel, the stability of the collusive arrangement tends to decline. Finally, there is the danger of retaliation by the importing nations. Eventually, they may impose taxes (or other restrictions) on goods exported to those nations that imposed the original export tax (or on member nations of an exporting cartel).

Although trade restrictions can sometimes lead to gain for one of the trading partners, the *joint* economic opportunities available to the participants are reduced. Artificial scarcity stemming from monopoly power always leads to economic waste. The consumers of the product—the importing nations—use valuable resources to search for substitutes and turn to alternatives that have a higher opportunity cost. An inefficient use of resources results, and the *joint* output of trading nations is diminished.

CHAPTER LEARNING OBJECTIVES

1 The volume of international trade has grown rapidly in recent decades. In the early 1980s, approximately 16 percent of the world's output was sold in a different country than that in which it was produced.

2 The trade sector comprises approximately 9 percent of the U.S. GNP. More than half of all U.S. trade is with developed countries, primarily Canada, Japan, and nations of the European Economic Community.

3 Trade between nations enables each to specialize in the production of those goods for which it has a comparative advantage. Through specialization and trade, aggregate output can be expanded. Mutual gain accrues to the trading partners.

4 Exports and imports are closely linked. The exports of a nation are the primary source of purchasing power used to import goods.

5 Relative to the no-trade alternative, international exchange and specialization result in lower prices for products that are imported and higher domestic prices for products that are exported. However, the net effect is an expansion in the consumption alternatives available to a nation.

6 The application of a tariff, quota, or other import restriction to a product reduces the amount of the product that foreigners supply to the domestic market. As a result of diminished supply, consumers face higher prices for the protected product. Essentially, import restrictions are subsidies to producers (and workers) in protected industries at the expense of (a) consumers and (b) producers (and workers) in export industries. Restrictions reduce the ability of domestic producers to specialize in those areas for which their comparative advantage is greatest.

7 High wages do not necessarily mean high labor cost. Productivity must also be considered. The law of comparative advantage explains why the United States can benefit from trade—even trade with low-wage countries.

8 National defense, industrial diversity, and the infant-industry arguments can be used to justify trade restrictions for specific industries under certain conditions. However,

it is clear that the power of special interest groups and ignorance about the harmful effects offer the major explanations for real-world protectionist public policy.

9   In the long run, trade restrictions do not create jobs. A decline in our imports from other nations leads to a reduction in those nations' purchasing power and thus a reduced demand for our export products. Jobs protected by import restrictions are offset by jobs destroyed in export industries. Since this result of restrictions often goes unnoticed, their political popularity is understandable. Nonetheless, the restrictions are inefficient, since they lead to the loss of potential gains from specialization and exchange.

10   An exporting nation (or group of nations) can gain by restricting output and raising the price of a product if the demand for its exports is inelastic and the supply is elastic. Under these circumstances, the burden of an export tax (or the price increases of an export cartel) falls on those importing the product. Trade restrictions of this variety, like other protectionist policies, result in a reduction in the *joint* output of the trading partners.

THE ECONOMIC WAY OF THINKING—DISCUSSION QUESTIONS

1   Suppose that at the time of the Civil War the United States had been divided into two countries and that through the years no trade existed between the two. How would the standard of living in the "divided" United States have been affected? Explain.

2   Do you think that the United States could benefit if all barriers to trade among North American nations were eliminated? Would Canada gain? Mexico? Why or why not?

3   Can both (a) and (b) be true? Explain.
(a) "Tariffs and import quotas promote economic inefficiency and reduce the real income of a nation. Economic analysis suggests that nations can gain by eliminating trade restrictions."
(b) "Economic analysis suggests that there is good reason to expect trade restrictions to exist in the real world."

4   "Tariffs and quotas are necessary to protect the high wages of the American worker." Do you agree or disagree? Why?

5   Suppose that the United States and other oil-importing nations levied a tariff on crude oil that was equal to the import price (approximately $34 per barrel in 1982) minus $20 per barrel. Thus, an increase in the import price (above $20 per barrel) would automatically raise the tariff by an equal amount. What impact would this policy have on (a) U.S. consumption of foreign oil, (b) the elasticity of demand for foreign oil as seen by foreign producers, and (c) the incentive of the international oil cartel (OPEC) to raise its price for oil?

6   What's Wrong with This Economic Experiment?

A researcher hypothesizes that higher tariffs on imported automobiles will cause total employment in the United States to increase. Automobile tariffs are raised and the following year employment in the U.S. auto industry increases by 100,000, compared to a three-year annual increase of 50,000 before the higher tariff legislation was passed. The researcher concludes that the higher tariffs on imported automobiles increased total domestic employment by creating approximately 50,000 jobs in the U.S. automobile industry.

CREDITS